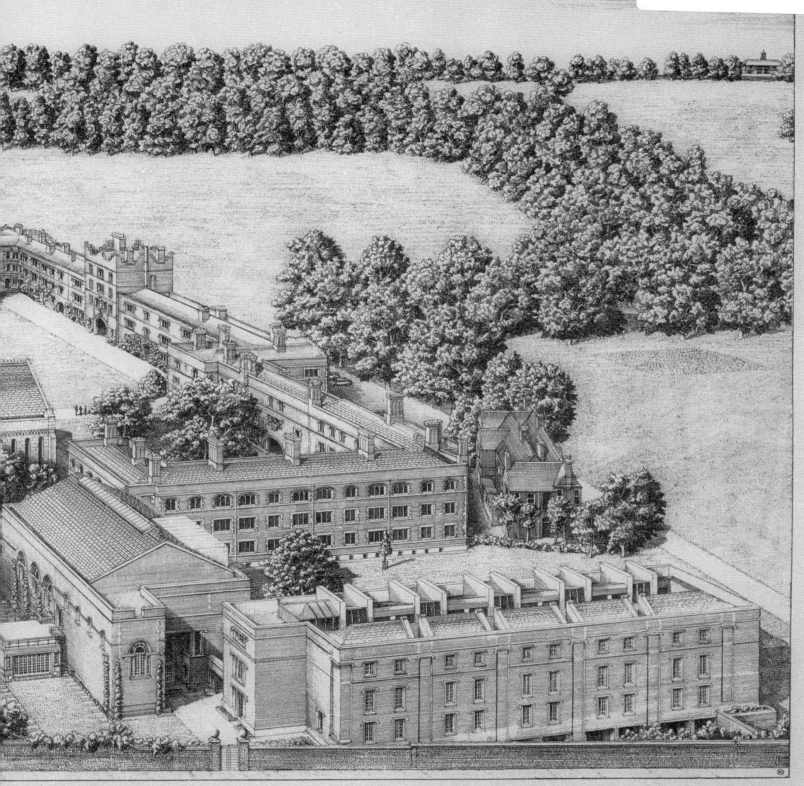

· CAMBRIDGE

of Ely, in the buildings of a former Benedictine nunnery which themselves date from about 1140. All the buildings around Cloister Court – the College Hall, the
nnery date from the last years of the 15th century. The north side of First Court was built between 1639 and 1642. *Alfred Waterhouse* designed Second Court,
he building called after him in 1930. North Court was designed by *David Wyn Roberts* in 1963, and Library Court by *Evans* and *Shalev* in 2000. The tree in the
in 1802.

Drawn by *Andrew Ingamells*, printed at *Hope (Sufferance) Press* in Camberwell and published by *Martin Village*, Islington, London in 2003

JESUS

THE LIFE OF A CAMBRIDGE COLLEGE

The Chimney Gate

Watercolour, artist unknown, *c.*1870.

JESUS

THE LIFE OF A CAMBRIDGE COLLEGE

Edited by Peter Glazebrook

GRANTA EDITIONS

© Jesus College, Cambridge 2007

Published by Granta Editions, 25–27 High Street, Chesterton, Cambridge
CB4 1ND, United Kingdom.
Granta Editions is a wholly owned subsidiary of Book Production Consultants Ltd.

ISBN 978 1 85757 087 8
A CIP catalogue record for this book is available from The British Library.

Designed by Peter Dolton
Design, editorial and production in association with
Book Production Consultants Ltd, 25–27 High Street, Chesterton, Cambridge
CB4 1ND, United Kingdom.
Repro services by MRM Graphics, Buckinghamshire, United Kingdom.
Printed and bound by Kyodo Printing Co. (Singapore) Pte Ltd.

Picture Acknowledgements

Most of the images reproduced in this book were provided by the College's
archives. The editor and publishers are also grateful to those listed below for
permission to reproduce other photographs and illustrations. Apologies are
offered to any copyright holder who is not credited. Despite much effort, it has
not been possible to locate the copyright owners of every image.

Front cover: Nigel Luckhurst (background); Andrew Houston (main image and
inset 4th from left); John Henwood (inset 1st, 2nd and 5th from left); Tim Soar
(inset 3rd from left).
Image of the Editor: Simon Tottman.
Endpapers: Engraving by Andrew Ingamells , 2003

John Adkins, pp. 91, 195–200; Pam Benstead, Worcester Branch, Richard III
Society, p.16 (top left); Julian Dowdeswell, pp. 1, 166, 294; Tina France, p. 16
(top right); The Fitzwilliam Museum, p. 9 (top); Dona Haycraft, pp. 218, 247,
258, 262, 266, 269, 291; John Henwood, pp. 10 (top), 11 (top left and top right),
12, 13, 17, 19–20, 27, 29 (top), 37, 43–4, 47 (top), 48–9, 79, 81, 83 (bottom
centre), 86 (bottom left), 169, 207 (top), 252; Andrew Houston, pp. 190 (top),
270; Derek Langley, p. 282; Nigel Luckhurst, pp. 24 (bottom), 41 (bottom), 42
(bottom), 50, 52, 56, 62–3, 66, 137, 172, 175, 226, 233, 239, 241; Jonathan
Miles, pp. 55 (bottom), 71 (top), 123, 154, 228, 235, 288, 290; The National
Portrait Gallery, p. 144; Eric North, pp. 18, 30 (top), 35, 88 (top), 90, 100, 193;
Bill Saslaw, p. 178 (top); Tim Soar, pp. 87; Paul Stearn, pp. 38, 42 (top); Stephen
Taylor, pp. 68 (left and centre); Simon Tottman, pp. ii, 4, 5, 11 (bottom), 23, 24
(top), 26 (bottom), 33 (left and centre), 34, 51, 53–4, 57, 60 (centre bottom and
top right), 64–5, 67, 68 (right), 73, 84–5, 89, 96–7, 108, 114, 125, 131, 138, 155,
160, 162, 186, 203, 217, 220–1, 246, 251, 261, 268, 274–8; Salima Virji, pp. 32,
45–6, 71 (bottom), 82, 126, 285–6, 293; Tim Wilkinson, pp. 58–9, 60 (left), 61.

Contents

THROUGH FIVE CENTURIES

SINCE 1945

Dates: *Unless the context indicates otherwise, a single date after a name is that of the person's admission to the College, coupled dates those of tenure of an office.*

The University comes to the College: Esquire Bedells lead the Chancellor (Prince Philip, Duke of Edinburgh), the Vice-Chancellor (Sir Alan Cottrell, Master of Jesus), University Officers and Honorary Graduands, June 1978.

Julian Dowdeswell

The College in the Twenty-First Century

ROBERT MAIR

In his book on Cambridge, Sir Hugh Casson remarks that Jesus is 'something of a joker in the college pack', and when one thinks of its long history, its setting within strikingly spacious grounds, and its distinctive atmosphere, one can understand why he should have seen it as unusual. It is also one of the four largest of Cambridge's thirty-one colleges, whose members are involved in every one of the University's activities and spheres of intellectual creativity and discovery, in its faculties and departments, laboratories, hospitals, libraries and museums.

Like all of the colleges, Jesus is an independent, self-governing entity, selecting its own members, senior and junior, caring for many of their needs, owning its own buildings and endowments, governed by its own statutes, running its own affairs. Yet it is an institution that is totally dependent on another, the University. Without the University, the College would have little point or purpose. Without the colleges, the University would be a very different, and vastly less attractive, place; without them it is most unlikely that world-famed scholars would be drawn from all points on the globe to this quite small East Anglian town, and be followed there by students as able, versatile and enthusiastic as those to be found anywhere. As the great international lawyer and judge Sir Robert Jennings said when looking back, at his ninetieth birthday celebrations in 2004, on his sixty-six years as a Fellow of Jesus: 'One of the most precious things in life is that of belonging to societies of people who have important interests in common. Such membership is a powerful aid to civilised living and is especially to be recommended at a time like the present which seems to be so good at cultivating loneliness.'

This book is a portrait of one distinctive part of a greater whole, telling something of the contribution the College and its members have made to Cambridge and, through Cambridge, to the world beyond it. Five hun-

dred years ago Jesus was a community of a couple of dozen people. Today it is one of over nine hundred engaged in teaching, research and study, and in supporting these activities. The Jesuans here in Cambridge in the first decade of the twenty-first century form a community that has its own complexities. To speak of the Master and Fellows (more than eighty of them) on the one hand, and of the students (seven hundred of them) on the other, or of senior and junior members, would again be to over-

St Radegund by Sir Edward Burne-Jones, stained glass window in the Chapel (1877).

simplify. The Fellowship extends from three or four research Fellows, elected in an annual competition open to young researchers in a wide range of disciplines, who are at the beginning of their academic careers, to the twenty or so Emeritus Fellows retired from regular teaching and administrative work, who continue to research and write, and to contribute to the life of the College in a variety of ways. In between there are close on sixty Fellows, most of whom hold appointments as professors, readers and lecturers in the University. Alongside the Fellows are ten Fellow Commoners, who have nothing in common except the high value of their work – as for instance Director of Chapel Music or Archivist – and support to the College, and a dozen or so Research Associates holding post-doctoral appointments in University departments and usually doing some supervision teaching of Jesus undergraduates.

The student body presents a comparably complex picture. Nearly five hundred are undergraduates studying for the Tripos examinations which will qualify them for the BA. Just over half come expecting to spend three years in Cambridge, a good many four, while some (notably those studying medicine) will usually be here for at least five, and yet others (the veterinary students) for six. And some – modern linguists and a few lawyers – will spend a year studying abroad before returning to Cambridge for their final year. There are currently around 270 graduate students, most of whom come from other universities, similarly pursuing courses of varying lengths. Many – those on Masters' courses – will be here for only a year, a few for two, while almost all those working for PhDs will spend four years in Cambridge as graduate students. With graduates now constituting almost 30 per cent of our student body, and with an annual rate of growth, University-wide, of 2 per cent for graduates, compared with 0.5 per cent for undergraduates, the question inevitably arises whether in Jesus – and throughout the University – graduate students may eventually become a majority, as they already have in many of the top research universities in the USA.

Anyone who contemplates the academic segments of the present-day Jesuan community, and especially anyone doing so who knew the College thirty or more years ago, will be struck not only by its size and by the way that the number of women is gradually approaching the number of men, but also by its remarkably cosmopolitan character – a reflection of Cambridge's standing as a world-class university. The admission of women to the College – of our first woman Fellow, Lisa Jardine, in 1976; of graduate students in 1978; and of undergraduates the following year – was one of the most important events in the history of Jesus. It would surely have pleased St Radegund, one of the College's three patron saints, who fourteen hundred years ago founded a monastery for both men and women and expected all its members to spend two hours a day in study.

The international character of the Fellowship is very striking and that of the graduate student body even more so. One in three of the Fellows under the retiring age first graduated from a university outside the UK: five in North America, two in Denmark and two in India; and others in Australia, Belgium, Germany, The Netherlands, New Zealand and Russia. And in recent years there have been Fellows from China, Italy, Malaysia and Sri Lanka. Of the graduate students there are currently thirty-eight countries represented among them; nearly half come from outside the UK, one in six are from the European Union, and one in three is from the rest of the world. These figures show how highly the postgraduate education and training that Cambridge can provide is valued around the world. The undergraduate body is understandably rather less cosmopolitan; currently only 11 per cent of them come from outside the UK. The undergraduates are divided almost equally between the arts and the sciences (for graduates the ratio is 10:17).

The College community is not limited to the eight hundred Jesuans, young and old, who are currently engaged in academic work in the University. There are also 130 staff. No members of our community are more loyal and devoted to serving it and furthering its role within Cambridge, or more proud of Jesuan successes and achievements. Many remain at Jesus for longer than many of the Fellows (and Masters), they are here all the year round, in term and vacation, and they know (what the rest of us recognise) that it is they – chefs and porters, gardeners and butlers, secretaries, bedders and janitors, and library, buildings, IT and accounts staff – who make everything possible.

Yet it is Jesus's graduates, more than seven thousand of them – often unflatteringly described as our Old Members – who are ultimately the College's justification. As I remind the graduands in the toast at their graduation dinner, once a Jesuan, always a Jesuan. The College succeeds in its avowed aims of furthering education, religion, learning and research only to the extent that it enables its members to develop their minds, acquire the specialist skills, and discover the interests and pursuits that will make their lives more fulfilling for themselves and useful to others. Certainly, Jesuans have received a due measure of recognition in the world beyond Cambridge. Our thirty Honorary Fellows illustrate the distinction that so many more Jesuans have achieved in every profession and walk of life – not only as scholars and writers, but as scientists, engineers, civil servants, parliamentarians, lawyers, bankers and businessmen, as musicians and diplomats, and in the churches, medicine and the media. One in seven Jesuans is pursuing a career in education: in universities, research institutes, colleges and schools.

In the last 140 years, and even more strikingly in the last 50, the College has grown immensely not only in number, but in buildings – in its 'plant'. Where there were once only three small courts – Cloister, First and Pump, set back behind high brick walls, there are now, with Chapel, North and Library courts, six. And (Westcott and Wesley apart) all the houses in Jesus Lane from the boundary of Sidney Sussex to Belmont Place, in Malcolm Street and Upper and Lower Park streets, together with an outpost on Maid's Causeway, are now owned and directly managed by the College as student accommodation. With over 670 residential rooms within a few hundred metres of Chapel, Hall, Library, Computer Centre and sports fields, we have what is, in effect, a Jesus village in this corner of Cambridge. It is one of the College's most distinctive features, shared by few others. It produces both a very strong sense of community and a beneficial integration between the different undergraduate

The shortest serving Master: Dr Humphrey Gower, July–December 1679 (when he returned to St John's as its Master).

Attr. James Fellowes

Dʀ GOWER

years that is fostered from a fresher's first day at Jesus, when he or she meets the 'College Parents' allotted to them by our Students' Union.

But the College has serious challenges to meet, and difficult problems to solve: challenges and problems that are primarily political and financial. The three areas of greatest concern are student access, centralising pressures within the University, and financial deficits that could become endemic. All stem, directly or indirectly, from the substantial reduction in government funding of university education – especially in student support – which has been accompanied by increasing governmental scrutiny of all levels of the nation's educational system, and the accompanying pressure on universities, as well as schools, to implement government policies, not all of them well judged.

On the critical issue of student access, we are committed unreservedly and without qualification to seeking out and admitting the best students, those with the capacity to take the fullest advantage of everything that Cambridge has to offer, and to ensuring that they are not discouraged from applying to us, or prevented from coming, by financial considerations. There is nothing high minded about this: all dons want the very best students they can get. There are widespread misconceptions about Cambridge's supposed social elitism, its actual admissions' standards, and the true level of student living costs here. In company with all the Cambridge and Oxford colleges, we are trying to dispel these myths: we now have an Access Liaison Officer responsible for maintaining contacts with LEA schools in a specific area (Newcastle upon Tyne and Tyne and Wear) and for arranging, with the help of Fellows and undergraduates, both local teach-ins and visits to Cambridge. We are also making increasing use in our admissions procedures, alongside A-level scores and interviews, of aptitude tests to help us in assessing the potential, as well as the achievements, of applicants. A great deal of time, thought and care is devoted to the selection of undergraduates. With an applications to admissions ratio in 2006 of 4.4:1 there are many extremely difficult decisions to be made. (Just over a hundred years ago, in 1905, there were fewer applicants than places; and only thirty years ago, in the years immediately prior to the admission of women, the ratio was 1.75:1). As I say when speaking to the parents of freshers on the day they bring their children to Jesus, any social barriers are broken down rapidly as friendships form between young people from all sorts of schools and social backgrounds. Within a very short time at Jesus undergraduates realise that what sort of school they were at could not matter less. That aspect of collegiate life is particularly striking at Jesus, which has a strong reputation for its exceptionally friendly social atmosphere.

The financial aspects of student access – at least for undergraduates – are, by comparison, simple. All the College requires are the funds to allow it to give bursaries and grants to those undergraduates whose needs cannot be met from either their families' resources or the student loan system, operating as it does on an income contingent basis (the loan does not have to be repaid until the graduate's income reaches a certain level). The financial difficulties facing graduate, and especially research, students, who will frequently have incurred a burden of debt after three or four years as undergraduates, are much harder to solve. The low number and the low level of grants available to UK research students lead a worryingly large number, especially in the sciences and engineering, to leave for the American universities which have much larger funds available to support them.

Centralising pressures within the University are twofold. There is great pressure on academic staff to devote ever more of their time and energy to research, writing and publication, which bring direct financial returns to University departments, at the expense of time-consuming undergraduate teaching, direction of studies and pastoral care. There is also some pressure for responsibility for the admission of undergraduates to be transferred from colleges to the University. It is claimed that this would eliminate any differences there may be between the standards applied by different colleges, and so be 'fairer'. But there is no reason to suppose that a University-wide admissions' system would be better able to balance one factor against another in each individual case and identify those applicants most likely to benefit from studying at Cambridge. It would certainly destroy that shared commitment and sense of responsibility that exists between the fellows of a college and the undergraduates that is such a marked feature of Cambridge. Pressures such as these can only be resisted if colleges have the resources needed to meet them.

There have been few times in the College's history when it has not faced financial problems, though the years between the early 1950s and the mid-1970s were probably one of them. Government support for both universities and university students was then at a peak from which there has since been a steady and, many would say, inevitable retreat. The colleges of Cambridge and Oxford have never received any direct government funding, but during that period they were substantially, if indirectly, helped in two ways. Government grants to the universities paid the major part of the salaries of most of their fellows, whom the colleges had therefore to remunerate only for their teaching and administrative work that was specifically college related. At the same time, the government also paid (through the LEAs) the fees and charges the colleges levied on each undergraduate, and often contributed to their living costs as well. Those maintenance grants for undergraduate students have long since been withdrawn, and undergraduates are now liable also for a portion of the cost of their tuition – in 2007 for £3,000 a year (much more for non-EU students), a figure likely to rise substantially in future years, for it amounts to little more than 20 per cent of the real cost of tuition in Cambridge averaged across all subjects. And while government grants still fund the salaries of fellows holding University appointments, and (through the University) some, but a declining proportion, of the costs incurred by colleges in providing services and facilities that would, in a non-collegiate university, have to be provided by the university, there is now a very substantial shortfall between the costs to the College of the educational services it provides for its students and what it receives through the University conduit. The College's endowment is, unsurprisingly, insufficient to meet both this shortfall and the costs of maintaining its buildings, old and new, for which it does not, and never has, received any government grant.

And the longest: Dr Charles Ashton, 1701–52. Like Gower, he is depicted wearing the Vice-Chancellor's cope.

Attr. Robert Pyle, *c.* 1720

Professor Robert Mair,
Master since 2001, in
conversation with
undergraduates, 2007.

It is crucial to the College to have the resources that will continue to enable it, first, to attract the best possible students – both undergraduate and graduate – regardless of their personal financial circumstances; secondly, to maintain a Fellowship of the highest calibre, reinforce the system of College teaching, and support the learning and research that underpin the intellectual life of Cambridge; and, thirdly, to care appropriately for its beautiful buildings and grounds, and all the other facilities we have.

At lunch and dinner, throughout the day and late into the night, on the staircases and in the common rooms, in the many activities of College life – sporting, artistic and simple leisure – students find themselves alongside men and women studying any of a wide range of subjects: from history to medicine, from architecture to modern and classical languages, from philosophy to mathematics, from engineering to biology. The College setting creates unparalleled opportunities for sharing knowledge and understanding. This diversity of learning and research within one community is deeply enriching, and a crucial dimension of a Cambridge education. We must at all costs maintain and protect this distinctive and very special environment at Jesus, but if we are to do so we shall need the continuing engagement and interest of our Old Members and our worldwide network of supporters, sharing our commitment to excellence in education, learning and research.

The setting

Aerial view from the north-west, 2007. The broad belt of trees on the left (once known as Jesus Grove) marks the boundary between the precincts of St Radegund's Nunnery and Midsummer Common (top) and Jesus Green (bottom left). Upper Park Street (bottom right) follows the course of the town – or King's – ditch.

St Radegund's Nunnery

PETER GLAZEBROOK

Jesus College would never have been called into existence had not three and a half centuries earlier – in the mid-1140s during King Stephen's troubled reign – a small group of women intent on leading together a life of prayer and contemplation secured the support of several prosperous and well-connected local people, enabling them to settle permanently on an area of dry land, surrounded on three sides by water, lying just east of Cambridge, beyond the town ditch and to the south of the river. They were one of more than a hundred such

A queen, probably St Radegund. Twelfth-century stone relief in the porch of the abbey church she founded at Poitiers.

communities of women formed in England in the century following the Norman Conquest, when there was a notable upsurge of enthusiasm for monastic life among both men and women and, as with many of the others, little is known about who the first nuns were or how precisely their convent began. It may well have developed gradually when one or two religious recluses – hermits or anchorites, men or women – who had withdrawn to this spot were joined by others seeking to follow the religious life. The site had the advantages not only of remaining dry even in winter, but also of being not too far from the town and within half a mile of Barnwell, to which it was linked by a causeway. At Barnwell there was a new and expanding community of priests following the Augustinian rule (so called because it derived from a letter of advice sent by St Augustine to a religious community of women), to whom they might look for spiritual guidance, advice on community living and, until they had a chaplain of their own, the celebration of mass and other sacraments.

There was no royal, noble or episcopal personage who could claim to have been the founder of St Radegund's Priory, as by the end of the 1150s when the community grew in number it came to be known. (St Radegund, 518–87, the founder of a famous double monastery at Poitiers, was a saint with an especial appeal to devout women who, like her, had found the idea – or the reality – of life with a husband picked for them by their fathers or brothers, unattractive.) A key figure in the community's early history appears to have been William Le Moyne, a goldsmith and financier, and probably a Cambridge burgher, who – like many, if not most, of their benefactors – was a relative of one of the first nuns (though we do not know her name). He owned land three miles away at Shelford, did business with Cambridge's Jewish community and had extensive financial dealings with Nigel, the second Bishop of Ely and Henry I's court treasurer, a prelate who, in the words of an eminent medievalist (David

Knowles), 'had devoted all his energies and abilities to matters purely secular; … his pride, wealth and military skill became the theme of chroniclers'. Significantly, when in the late 1140s William, who had been king's goldsmith to Henry I, gave the nuns part of his land at Shelford (which he may have received for his services in that office, and some of which the College still owns), he did so on condition that they prayed for the soul of that king who had died in 1135.

William's connections – local and national – would explain much of the support given to the nuns in these critical early years: their recognition by Bishop Nigel as a religious community, and of their property as having been given to God and therefore to be church property which the bishop and his successors would protect; the formal gift by the Ely monks (Nigel as bishop was also their abbot) to their sisters in religion of 4 acres of land – either that on which they had first settled or which adjoined it; and the underwriting of these gifts and guarantees by King Stephen in 1149 or 1150. William may also have acted as a banker to Malcolm IV of Scotland who, as Earl of Huntingdon and Cambridge, had certain fiscal rights over the town and the land surrounding it which the townspeople tilled and used for pasturing their animals, and would have needed a local agent to receive the revenues due to him. William may have had something to do with persuading the King/Earl to allocate – or consent to the allocation – to the nuns of a further 10 acres of this pasture to enable them to build a worthy church. It was a project of which his sainted great-grandmother, Queen Margaret, through whom he had acquired those rights, and his mother, who was a benefactor of the priory at Barnwell, would surely have approved.

Other local supporters of the nuns included William's neighbours at Shelford, Stephen de Scales and his wife Juliana, who in the 1150s gave them 80 acres on the Cambridgeshire–Suffolk border as a dowry for their daughter Sibilla (the earliest nun we know by name); several Cambridge burgesses who in that and the following decade left them their houses in the town and their strips in the common fields; and the brother of Lettice, the first prioress to appear in the records, one Sturm, who owned the nuns' parish church, All Saints'-in-the-Jewry. He gave it to them in or before 1180, thus enabling them to nominate as their parish priest someone also willing to serve as their chaplain, and to retain for themselves what remained of the income from tithes after his stipend had been paid. It is the elegant spire of the high Victorian successor of

(Above) Silver seal matrix of Prioress Helena (1284–99). Found at Bottisham, Cambridgeshire, 1978; acquired by the Fitzwilliam Museum from the finder, 2003.

(Left) Aerial view from the north-east, c.1985. The nuns' cloister was square: the present south walk is on the site of the north nave aisle of their church.

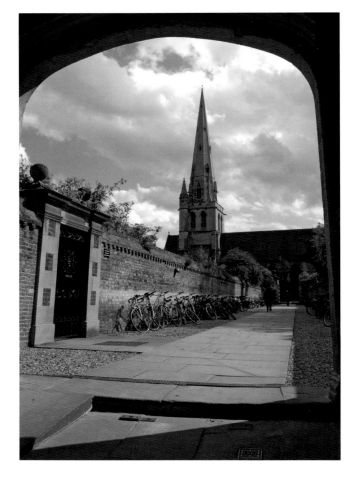

(Top right) All Saints'
Church and the Chimney
from the Gate Tower.

(Below) Thirteenth-century
coffin lid, probably that of
Bertha, wife of Walter de
Lindsey, a benefactress of
the nuns. Formerly near the
High Altar it is now in the
south transept.

with it; rather it was, as were many similar churches else-where, the manifestation of civic piety and pride. Each of Cambridge's twelve parishes had only its own modest church; the nuns' church was a project in which the parishioners of all them could combine. Shorn, as it was by the College's founders, of both aisles and of the chapels which opened to the east from its transepts and with more than half its nave absorbed in the Master's Lodge, its outlines and proportions are now best gauged from the air.

The nuns received almost all the endowments they ever possessed during this century: principally (though not solely) houses in the town and strips in the open fields to the east and west – by 1279 the nuns owned about 77 acres there – nearly all given by local people: as dowries when their daughters, sisters or widowed mothers became nuns, or for masses for the souls of dead family members; or to maintain votive lamps in the church. But these endowments, it seems, were never adequate both to maintain the community and to keep its buildings, and in particular its large church, in repair. In 1254 the Bishop of Norwich granted indulgences – a standard medieval device for raising funds for worthy causes – to those con-tributing to the support of the nuns, and diocesan collec-tions for them were ordered in 1268 (Lincoln) and 1277 (Norwich). By the end of the century the nuns were liv-ing off capital.

In 1313 disaster struck: all the convent buildings (almost certainly they were, like most buildings in Cambridge, thatched) and their contents were destroyed by fire. The community never recovered from this catastrophe though it managed, somehow, to limp on – and suffer more fires – for another 170 years. We know that in 1314, 1326, 1376, 1389, 1390 and 1457 bishops granted indulgences to those who responded to the nuns' appeals for financial help, and there may well have been other (unrecorded) occasions. More often than not the Priory was exempted from paying taxes levied on the clergy and religious houses (as well as from the legal fees due to diocesan officials) 'on account of their poverty'.

this church – the original one was sited a few hundred yards away, between Trinity Street and Sidney Street (hence All Saints Passage) – that now confronts everyone entering or leaving the College by way of the Chimney. And when, at the turn of the twelfth and thirteenth cen-turies, Bishop Eustace of Ely secured for the nuns anoth-er 5 acres of land between their precinct and Midsummer Common to enlarge their home farm, what is now the College Close – 26 acres of grass and trees in the heart of the modern city – was, to all intents, complete.

The century between 1160 and 1260 were certainly the Priory's best years. A huge church, an elegant chapter house, and a refectory and dormitories quite adequate for a community of forty or so nuns were built round a clois-ter from which the College's buildings have since spread in all directions. The church was built slowly and in stages and, since the earliest part is the north transept, it may well have replaced a smaller chapel on the site of the present choir – perhaps one no bigger than the Norman Leper Chapel that still survives a mile away on the edge of Stourbridge Common. The church was enormous, the largest in and around Cambridge until the building of King's College Chapel. About 200 feet long and 85 feet wide at the transepts (Great St Mary's is 150 feet long and 70 feet wide), it had a six-pillar, seven-bay, arcaded nave, and north and south aisles. No great name is associated

At St Radegund's things were going steadily downhill. In 1373 the Master of Peterhouse, inspecting the priory on behalf of the Archbishop of Canterbury, reported that the buildings were dilapidated, the refectory roof was leaking, and the prioress (who pleaded the convent's poverty) was failing to employ priests to celebrate masses for benefactors as her predecessors had undertaken to do. It would be hard to think of a better way of discouraging new benefactions. In 1390 the convent buildings were again badly damaged – this time by violent storms – and the Archbishop again offered indulgences to those who would help with repairs.

By the time John Alcock took his third step up the episcopal ladder – he had begun as Bishop of Rochester, then been moved to Worcester, and finally been transferred in 1486 to Ely, which was a much wealthier see, offering more adequate recompense for his long years of government service – St Radegund's was in a parlous state. There had been years in which the nuns had not been able to pay their bills; the buildings, including the church, were in a bad way; and now the prioress had died. There were only nine nuns, and none of them, the archdeacon thought, was fit to take her place. Ensuing events suggest that they may simply have been either too young or too old. In 1487 the decision was therefore taken to bring in a nun from another convent, in the hope, probably a desperate one, that she might be able to pull things round. The new prioress was Joan Fulbourn who, given her name, may well have been a nun at Swaffham Bulbeck or Ickleton (Fulbourn is four miles, Swaffham Bulbeck six, and Ickleton ten from Cambridge). But the task was too much for her. Within six or seven

(Above) The opening for the pantry turn, a device enabling food and drink to be supplied to visitors and workmen without face to face contact with nuns.

(Top left) Pillar and arches of nave now embedded in E staircase.

(Below) The chapter house uncovered, 1893.
Engraving by Celia Murray

Cambridge was badly hit by the Black Death of 1349, its population reduced, probably, by a third. While this made possible the development of its beautiful academic quarter – the Backs that now stretch from Queens' to St John's – where previously there had been lively warrens of lanes, houses, shops, warehouses, quays and even a parish church – it also meant that there were fewer local women wishing, or needing, to enter a convent. And just at this time (1339–51) the large and well-endowed Denny Abbey, a house of the new and fashionable Franciscan Order of Minoresses six miles to the north, was being refounded by Mary de St Pol, the widowed Countess of Pembroke (and founder, also, of the Cambridge college bearing her name), gaining for it aristocratic and, indeed, royal patronage. She and her ladies were often to be found living there. At her death in 1371 the community of forty-one nuns, many with Cambridge names, was flourishing. Denny possessed a spiritual and social cachet which St Radegund's had long lost, and it continued to attract gifts, bequests and new recruits on a scale which the older and impoverished Benedictine house no longer did. To the end – the abolition of all England's monasteries and convents – the religious life was lived at Denny with some fervour, the last abbess returning, with two of her nuns, to her family home in Warwickshire, where they established their own enclosure, wore their habits and observed their Rule, until they died.

years she found herself alone. The older nuns had, presumably, died. One – or perhaps two – of the younger ones had been given episcopal permission to move to another convent where community life was still viable (one of them was alive forty years later when her adoptive convent was dissolved). There was one nun who was, said the bishop's lawyers, *infamis*, which may have meant no more than that she, too, had left, but had done so without permission, so that (like the prioress who belonged to another house) she had no claim to be maintained out of St Radegund's properties. There is, it has to be said, no evidence in the diocesan or other legal records that survive to support the lurid tales about the nuns with which Jesuans and visitors to the College have long been regaled. And the huge church which had been in a bad state of repair when Joan Fulbourn arrived – much of it had been built of clunch, the least durable of building stones – was now described as 'ruined'. This we may well believe, for it is most unlikely that the drastic alterations made to church and chapter house in the early years of the College, which Nicholas Ray describes (page 27–37), would have been undertaken when money was so extremely short if these buildings had needed repair rather than rebuilding.

From its earliest and fervent days to its final collapse St Radegund's Priory was essentially a local institution. The nuns came to follow the rule of St Benedict but this did not make them members of a religious order of the sort with which we are now familiar: centralised, national, often international, bodies running schools, hospitals, old people's homes, or orphanages; whose members (and financial resources) can be directed wherever they are most needed. The nuns were from first to last nuns of St Radegund's – they were the nuns of Cambridge – and though, as happened in their final desperate days, their bishop might look for help to a nun from another convent, there was no organisation that linked together even the four Benedictine priories in Cambridgeshire.

As it was, by 1494 – if not before – it was apparent to the bishop and his diocesan officials that another use needed to be found for a redundant and dilapidated church, its associated buildings and the land surrounding them on the edge of Cambridge, to which was attached the ownership of certain other properties – what remained of the endowments of St Radegund's Priory – though precisely what these were, and how much they were worth, had still to be ascertained.

**Romanesque gallery,
north transept.**

Nunnery into College: the east side of Cloister Court, *c.*1500. In the Chapel a Perpendicular window replaces Romanesque ones, and staircases (marked by the two broad expanses of brick wall) with rooms for Fellows are built where chapter house and dormitory had been.

The College's Founders

PETER GLAZEBROOK

Founding a college is a process, not an event. In Jesus's case it was a process that extended over more than twenty years, was far from smooth, and involved four bishops of Ely, two popes, the King, the King's mother and three former members of her household who had become her son's trusted counsellors, the University's most forward-looking college head, and three former fellows of older colleges. Within fifty years the entire project had come within a hair's breadth of being abruptly terminated, and within seventy-five it had been so reshaped that its founders would scarcely have recognised it.

Traditionally, our College's foundation has been dated to 12 June 1496, when Henry VII issued Letters Patent to Bishop Alcock of Ely authorising him to suppress the derelict nunnery of St Radegund at Cambridge and to use

Henry VII's Letters Patent, 12 June 1496, authorising 'in so far as in Us lies' the Bishop of Ely to suppress St Radegund's Priory and use its property to establish a college.

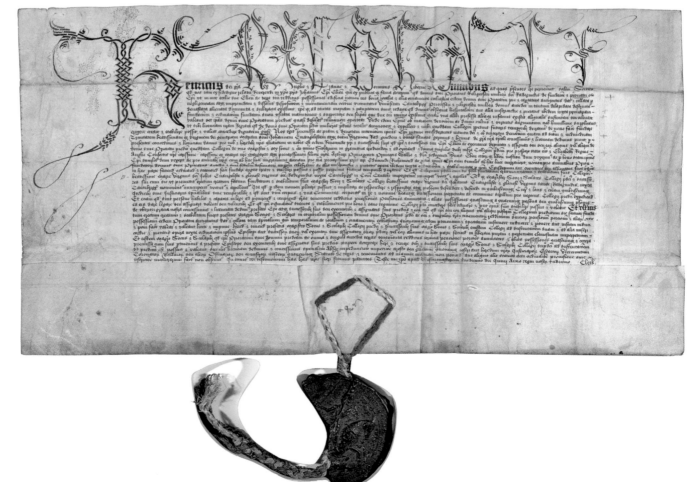

its property to found a college comprising a master, six fellows and an as yet unspecified number of grammar school boys – a college that was to be dedicated to the Blessed Virgin Mary, St John the Evangelist and the Glorious Virgin St Radegund. These Letters Patent constituted, however, no more than outline, and conditional, planning permission for its foundation. Not only do the royal registers contain at least nine cases of Letters Patent authorising the foundation of colleges that came to nothing, but those addressed to Alcock expressly said that the King authorised the nunnery's suppression and the application of its property to the new use only 'in so far as in Us lies'. For the King – or, at any rate, the lawyers who drafted the Letters, and certainly the Bishop – knew that although he might authorise the foundation within his kingdom of a college and confer on it certain legal privileges, the disposal of the property of a religious house required, so the Fourth Council of the Lateran of 1215 had decreed, the consent of the Pope. Alcock duly sought from Rome the permission he needed, and on 18 January 1497 Alexander VI gave it, conditionally upon the Bishop holding a formal inquiry into the facts alleged in his petition, and upon that inquiry confirming their truth. This was the customary procedure, one designed to protect vested interests, particularly those of any surviving members of a religious community that was no longer viable.

The royal Letters Patent and the papal Bull are not the only legal documents evidencing Alcock's plans for the derelict nunnery and its property. Someone of experience was needed to oversee the establishment of the new College, and Dr William Chubbes (or Stubbs), vicar of one of the two parishes at Swaffham Prior near Cambridge, had been chosen. He was a former fellow and treasurer of Pembroke who had studied in both Oxford and Paris, and he had been the first of that college's fellows to hold the office of president – it had had three absentee masters in succession (two of them archbishops), and so a deputy had been required.

Dr Chubbes now received a papal dispensation to hold up to three benefices at once and, *as long as he resided in a university*, to serve none of them in person. Such a dispensation was not as scandalous as at first sight it seems. Chubbes would have to pay curates to discharge all his parochial duties and, unless he was particularly fortunate in securing appointments to especially lucrative parishes, it would require the surplus revenues of several (he soon became rector of Stapleford, another village near Cambridge) to provide him with an income befitting his age, his new responsibilities, and his status as a doctor of divinity. For if he were to become, as he did, the College's first Master, he could not expect a stipend: endowments that had been insufficient for a convent of nuns could not possibly support a master as well as six

priests and a grammar school teacher. (His successor, Dr Ecclestone, obtained a similar dispensation in January 1512.) This arrangement, inherited from the medieval Church, was, as Stephen Taylor points out (page 94), to continue until H.A. Morgan became Master in 1885. Although a benefaction from Bishop Stanley had, from 1515 onwards, made it possible to pay Masters a stipend,

it was not large (only two thirds of that paid to the schoolmaster) and all Morgan's predecessors had, so as to maintain their dignity as Master, held some other church appointment as well and, being pluralists, many of them were often absent from Cambridge. Then, as again now, the Mastership was a part-time job.

Dr Chubbes needed help in claiming – or reclaiming – the property that had belonged to St Radegund's and in repairing – or rebuilding – its church and buildings, and he persuaded two other experienced men to join him. One, William Atkynson, had also been a fellow of

Bishop John Alcock. Painted in 1598 and costing 26s 8d, this picture was almost certainly based on an image in the Chapel's east window which was destroyed by William Dowsing's men on 18 December 1643.

(Top right) Two of the College's founders: Sir Reginald Bray and Richard Pigott, Serjeant at Law. Stained glass windows in the churches at, respectively, Great Malvern, Worcestershire, and Long Melford, Suffolk, of which they were also benefactors.

(Below) The Master's stall in Chapel, showing Bishop Alcock at prayer, c.1505.

From a drawing by Jeremy Gray (1972)

Pembroke, the other, William Plombe, a fellow of Gonville Hall: Plombe was exempted from his University duties so that he might be free to supervise the building works. In their first full year (1497), Dr Chubbes and his colleagues managed to levy rents totalling £70 6s from the tenants of nunnery properties. This was not, on any view, a large sum. In the 1490s a tailor might earn £7 a year, and the owner of a small business, such as a tannery, might have an annual income of £35. From 1499 onwards they were joined by a series of young priests who stayed for a few years until they obtained better jobs.

Bishop Alcock died on 1 October 1500 at the (then) advanced age of 70. He had not, as has often been noted, made any benefactions to the new College or made provision for it in his will. But this may be to misunderstand his relationship to it. For him the College was an official, a diocesan, not a personal project. He had, as bishop, been confronted (not for the first time) with the problem of a religious house in decay, and, given its location, a good solution had been found. It is unlikely that death took him by surprise. He had already founded both a grammar school in the parish in Hull where he had been born, and his own chantry, its chapel, seemingly designed for the ampler arcades of Worcester Cathedral, being squeezed (not very comfortably) into the north-east corner at Ely. He had, too, contributed to the rebuilding of Great St Mary's and been heavily engaged in building works at his palace in Ely and at his episcopal manors at Downham and Hatfield. So it would be wrong to see him – for he almost certainly did not see himself – as the founder of an Oxbridge college in the line of those great medieval prelates Wykeham, Chichele, Waynflete, Rotherham and Fox, or of those devout ladies the Countess of Pembroke and the Lady Margaret Beaufort, let alone of that saintly but unhappy King, Henry VI; and it would be a mistake to think of him as such a college founder *manqué*.

If, therefore, Dr Chubbes and his helpers were not surprised that nothing came to their College from their late Bishop, it was certainly an embarrassment for them to discover that, Alexander VI's Bull notwithstanding, Alcock had never got round to following the canonical procedures for the suppression of a religious house, which is what that Pope had stipulated, nor to doing what English law required to found a college, which is what the King, by his Letters Patent, had empowered him to do. The former Alcock may have considered, in the circumstances, an empty legal formality, the latter he probably thought premature: substantial additional endowments were needed if the College he envisaged, with its master, six fellows and its grammar school, and with its church and buildings repaired and adapted to their new uses, was to become a reality. It was not until 1513 or 1514 that his

successor but one at Ely, Bishop Stanley, reassured perhaps by another papal Bull, was to decide that the point had been reached at which the College could, at last, be formally constituted.

Meanwhile, the King had been induced to lend his name to a new petition to a new pope which, while regretting that the late Bishop of Ely had not actually done what canon law required to be done to suppress the nunnery and transfer its assets to a new college, stated that money had already been spent and asked the Pope to rectify matters – which Julius II may be assumed to have been ready to do. A draft Bull to this effect was copied into the papal registers in May 1504 and another copy was in Dr Ecclestone's possession when, ten years later, he was composing the College's first statutes. No formally issued Bull survives, but it may well have gone to Norfolk: the bishopric of Ely being vacant after the death of Alcock's immediate successor, Bishop Redman, the document was to be addressed to the bishops of Durham and of Coventry and Lichfield, and to the archdeacon of Norfolk, and it was, no doubt, the archdeacon who would be expected to do the necessary paperwork. There was, too, another reason for sending a draft back to England for its terms to be agreed before the Bull was issued. The King had had to admit to another embarrassment. Alcock's lawyers in Rome had been poorly briefed: they had thought that he wanted to suppress an abbey, presided over by a lady abbess with crosier and ring, a dignity to which even in St Radegund's heyday its prioresses had never aspired. It was therefore understandable that there should have been a wish to get everything right this time.

Happily, benefactors sufficient to set the College on its way were being found. They could all be assured, and were, that they would be prayed for in its chapel after their deaths as well as during their lives. The key figure was almost certainly Dr John Fisher. Like Alcock, he had spent his childhood at Beverley in the East Riding of Yorkshire; he had recently become Master of Michaelhouse (a college that was later to become part of Trinity), and was to go on to be President of Queens', Vice-Chancellor and, ultimately, Chancellor of the University – and the only head of a Cambridge college to be declared a saint. He had also, and significantly, in 1497 become the confessor and spiritual director of the King's devout mother, the Lady Margaret Beaufort, Countess of Richmond and Derby, who at his instigation was soon to found (or re-found) two other Cambridge colleges, Christ's and St John's. Nearly all the early benefactors of Jesus belonged to her circle, and it was Bishop Stanley, her stepson (it was almost his only qualification for the post) who, as we have already seen, finally took the formal legal steps needed to found the College. One of its first Fellows, William Atkynson, completed and in 1503 published the translation of Thomas à Kempis's *Imitation of Christ* that she had begun, thereby earning the accolade of being the first Fellow to appear in print (though Dr Chubbes had also written a book – a commentary on Duns Scotus – and Lady Margaret had paid a scribe to make a copy of it).

The most pressing need was money for building works: the creation of a chapel out of the nuns' church, and the conversion of their convent to accommodate a community of priests, ordinands, schoolboys, their teachers and domestic staff – works that were to take more than fifteen years to complete. Much of the funding came from Sir John Rysley and Sir Reginald Bray, both of whom had begun their careers in Lady Margaret's household. They had played key roles in the plotting, planning and conduct of Henry Tudor's successful rebellion against Richard III, which had culminated in victory at Bosworth in 1485; and were thereafter two of the new King's closest advisers. They were well rewarded for their services. Rysley's money went on the rebuilding of the Chapel and the construction of the enlarged cloisters, works described in pages 29–30. (Lady Margaret herself contributed £20 6s in 1503, and left another £2 in her will.) And when Rysley died in 1512 he bequeathed a further £160 (more than twice the total annual rental from the nunnery properties) to finish the work. Bray's gifts appear to have been spent on building the Hall and the staircases in the Cloister (he was a benefactor of Pembroke too), while after his death in 1503 his widow, Katherine, who had also been a member of Lady Margaret's household before moving to her daughter-in-law's, the Queen's, endowed the grammar school. Rysley also contributed to the creation of an additional fellowship, as did Lady Jane Hastings (wife of another courtier and widow of one of the King's lawyers), Bishop Stanley and Thomas Roberts,

a landowner at Over in Cambridgeshire, who was probably known to both Fisher and Chubbes. The first bequest of books the College received came, shortly after 1506, from one of Fisher's colleagues at Michaelhouse, Thomas Colier.

By 1513 the new College community was adequately housed and, it was hoped, financially viable, though it had become clear that the rents from the nuns' properties would support only five priest-fellows (rather than the six that Alcock had envisaged), four choirmen–ordinands, four choristers and five servants: a gate porter (the Master's servant), two cooks, a barber and a laundress. But those subsequent benefactions had enabled the creation of three additional fellowships and the endowment

The west walk of the Cloisters, looking towards the door to the Master's Lodge.

of the grammar school. So there was now a 'little flock' of twenty-three Jesuans who took in a few paying guests ('perindenants'). Their obligations to offer masses and say prayers for all their benefactors and their spouses, living and dead, as well as for the King and his family, were set out in great detail in the statutes Dr Ecclestone was drafting for Bishop Stanley to issue.

And they were soon to be joined by others: in 1518 Chief Justice Rede endowed a chantry supporting a priest-fellow who would pray for him and his family at an altar to be dedicated to St Catharine and St Margaret.

Chapel: interior of crossing tower, thirteenth century; restored by Pugin 1848–49 and (ceiling) G.F. Bodley and G.G. Scott, junior. 1869–70.

But why, and how, did this institution which so many benefactors had joined in endowing come to be called Jesus College? Alcock had, as we have seen, envisaged it being dedicated to St Mary (as the nuns' church had been), St John the Evangelist (his own name-saint) and St Radegund (the nunnery's patron). And precisely what sort of institution was this College of a Master, eight Fellows, four ordinands and a bunch of grammar school boys with their schoolmaster and his assistant, for which in 1517 Bishop West promulgated statutes, as his predecessor had planned to do?

The short answer to the question of how and why the College came to be 'commonly called' Jesus College is that the repair, reconstruction and adaptation of the nuns' church had been so extensive that it was felt that the building should be reconsecrated, that when this was done it was dedicated to the Name of Jesus; and it was decided that those – the members of the College – who worshipped in it should therefore be known as *Jesuani*. (Just twenty years later, at Dr Chubbes' former university of Paris, the group of student friends who had gathered around Ignatius Loyola were to adopt the same name.) But that is only to postpone the question: what motivated this change in the church's dedication from the Mother of God to her Son? Much of the explanation is to be found in the developments during the late fourteenth and the fifteenth centuries in religious devotion to the Holy Name of Jesus, a pious cult that stressed the tenderness and accessibility of the human Christ and was nowhere stronger than in England, where nearly every cathedral and monastic church, and many a parish church too, had its Jesus Chapel or Jesus Altar. A feast day (7 August), with its own special mass and other services, had been instituted in 1488/9; a prayer-book for lay people (*The Jesus Psalter*) and a devotional work (*The Imitation of Christ*) circulated widely; and – most significantly for us – Lady Margaret Beaufort had been designated patroness of the devotion to the Holy Name by the Pope in 1494, so that she might encourage it still further. Drs Chubbes, Atkynson and Ecclestone were strongly committed to it too. While still at Pembroke, Chubbes had given its chapel altar hangings or cloths with the name of Jesus woven into them, while in his will he asked to be buried at the foot of the statue of Our Lord which by then stood in the choir of Jesus's Chapel. Atkynson, as has been seen, had completed Lady Margaret's translation of the *Imitation*.

There may possibly have been a further and even more local reason for the new name. There is some evidence for thinking that the road running from the town to Barnwell, earlier known as Nuns' or Radegund's Lane, had by the later 1490s come to be referred to as Jesus Lane. If this was so, it could hardly have been on account of the new College that was still a building site. But it could have been because there had been, as was so often the case, a Jesus Chapel or Jesus Altar in the part of the nuns' church to which the laity had access – indeed it would have been mildly surprising if there had not been one there – a chapel or altar which had become, or been designed to become, a centre of devotion in Cambridge for the townspeople and an object of their alms. (Why, one wonders, was Prioress Elizabeth Walton using a seal with the Jesus monogram on it in 1473?) Yet it was this part of the nave that was being converted into staircases, and it would have been unthinkable for the College's founders, of all people, to do this without at the same time reaffirming and re-emphasising their devotion to the name of Jesus.

There remains the other question: what sort of institution was it that they were founding? Tutors and undergraduates whose families or patrons would pay for their education, their board and their lodging, were, of course, creatures as yet scarcely dreamt of. But colleges of priests serving cathedrals, parish churches (sometimes as curates) and the chantries endowed for the saying of masses and other prayers for the souls of their founders established in or near them, together with their associated grammar schools for the local boys, were familiar features of medieval towns.

Alcock himself had, as we have noted, founded such a chantry and school in Hull. But the emergence of universities at Oxford and Cambridge had led to a variation on the theme, dubbed by a historian of the medieval university (Christopher Brooke) 'the academic chantry'. The members of these chantry colleges – priests and ordinands – received, in return for their participation in the liturgical round of their chapels and, in the case of the priests, the masses they said in their chantries, and instead of the cash stipend they would otherwise have been paid, free bed and board and, most importantly, the opportunity to pursue the studies and obtain the university degrees which would fit them for senior church or government posts (often for both). It was an opportunity which Thomas Cranmer, who came to Cambridge in 1503, was to take with spectacular, and in the end tragic, consequences.

These 'academic chantries', along with all others, were threatened with extinction when in 1545 Parliament passed a statute authorising the suppression of all England's colleges, just as in the previous decade it had authorised the suppression of all England's monasteries and convents. It took some deft political footwork to persuade Henry VIII to reprieve, alongside the colleges that were of royal foundation, those in the two universities. Had Cambridge's colleges – there were then only fourteen of them, all small, and four of them less than fifty years old – shared the fate of the religious houses (Franciscan, Dominican, Augustinian, Carmelite and Benedictine) which had dominated both University and town for three hundred years and been their principal points of contact with European scholarship (and which had had their own 'academic chantries'), it is rather unlikely that Cambridge would have survived to become, in the twentieth century, one of the world's greatest universities. We might, instead,

Cloister Court looking north. The Hall windows were lengthened in 1801; those in the cloisters had been replaced by open arches in the 1760s. The windows on the second floor on the west light the Old Library.

Chapel stall end, *c*.1505.
A Doctor of Divinity in his
chair as if about to preside
over a disputation in the
School of his Faculty.

have been adding its name to the list of English towns –
Canterbury, Northampton, Stamford, Reading – to
which, during the Middle Ages, students had travelled to
sit at the feet of famed teachers.

But though the colleges in the two universities were
spared, the chantries within them survived for only a few
more years, chantries of every kind being abolished by
Parliament in the next, and avowedly protestant, reign.
When royal commissioners came to Cambridge in 1549,
they ordered the removal of six, now redundant, chantry
altars, and the nearby statuary, that were still in Jesus
Chapel; and, since priests to say masses at them were no
longer required, they decreed that henceforth only six of
the Fellows need be in Holy Orders. Revived during
Queen Mary's five-year rule, the chantries were to disap-

pear for good in 1559. The College's grammar school
that had formed so important a part of its founders'
scheme – the statutes that Dr Ecclestone drafted specified
that if ever there were not enough money for everything,
the grammar school should have priority over all but a
Master and two Fellows – was not to last much longer.
The schoolmaster was paid for the final time in 1567 and,
in accordance with government policy, the school was, its
separate endowment notwithstanding, formally abolished
by Elizabeth I's commissioners in 1571. It was not that
there was no need for such a school in Cambridge. In
1576 the town corporation formed a committee to explore
ways and means of meeting it, though it was not until
1615, when the town received Dr Stephen Perse's substantial bequest, that it had enough money to do so.
Desirable as it was that there should be an endowed – a
free – grammar school in Cambridge, the greater need, in
the government's view, after all the religious changes of
the last thirty years with their unsettling effects on clergy
recruitment, was for well-educated and godly ministers to
serve the Church. There was still much to be done if the
nation was to be converted to the protestant faith and, if
colleges in the two universities were unable to finance
both sorts of education, preference should be given to
educating clergy. Without a grammar school to run, the
new Queen's commissioners considered that Jesus had,
with the benefactions it had received in the last twenty-
five years, endowments sufficient for a Master, sixteen
Fellows and fifteen Scholars.

With no chantry duties to perform, with only the simpler and less time-consuming services prescribed by
Cranmer's Book of Common Prayer to attend, and with
the former school building now available for other uses,
it would not be long before there were Fellows who felt
they could supplement their incomes by taking private
pupils who could be accommodated there. The ground
was ready for the emergence of tutors and undergraduates, and of the idea, which would have surprised its
founders, that the College existed so that the former
might educate the latter.

Benefactors and Benefactions

FRANCES WILLMOTH and RICHARD DENNIS

ach year, towards the end of the Lent term, the service of Commemoration of Benefactors takes place in the Chapel, as it has ever since the College's foundation. During this service the Master, the Fellows and the Scholars, now with members of the Society of St Radegund (the College's most recent major donors), give thanks for the 'piety and liberality' of all those 'who have been our benefactors, and for all those who by their life and work have built up the living fabric of the College'.

Appropriately, for the College is, as those words of thanksgiving emphasise, a community of people, the first benefactors mentioned are those who have endowed fellowships and scholarships. The two terms were originally synonymous, only gradually coming to be distinguished: fellowships (usually) for graduates, scholarships (usually) for undergraduates. The College's first two decades, and those founding fellowships during them, have been described in pages 14–20. In the middle years of the sixteenth century, a clutch of fellowships and scholarships was created by legacies from three men. One of them, John Andrews, was a prebendary of St Paul's (d. *c.*1547), the other two, John Reston (d. 1551) and John Fuller (d. 1558), had both been Fellows and were subsequently Masters. In 1559 Elizabeth I's commissioners considered that with these bequests the College had resources sufficient for sixteen Fellows and fifteen Scholars. And as far as fellowships were concerned, at sixteen they remained until 1926, when fellowships without stipend or dividend were introduced.

Scholarships, however, continued to be created, though frequently subject to complex conditions. In 1579 William Marshall bequeathed 5 marks (£3 6s 8d) annually to each of three scholars, one of them at Jesus and two at other colleges, the beneficiaries to come from Lancashire, Cumberland, Hertfordshire, Essex or one of the schools (in Lancashire and Essex) founded under Marshall's will.

A similar benefaction came from Lady Price, wife of Sir James Price and widow of Dean Wood of Armagh, who gave money in 1620 for two Scholars to be nominated by her husband and herself during their lifetimes. The beneficiaries were to come from the parish of Fosters, where she was living; or St Peter's le Poer, London, where she was born; or Anglesey, where the Dean was born and buried; or Merioneth, where Sir James had lived. By 1850 there were fifty-one scholarships tenable at Jesus, but only fifteen were open to all comers. Many were for the pupils of named schools, including Sevenoaks (Lady Margaret Boswell, 1675), Loughborough (John Somervile, 1682), Tonbridge and Doncaster.

Tobias Rustat.

Kneller, *c.*1670

The restoration of the monarchy, and the revival of university life that followed, was marked by a spate of new scholarships. In 1671 a major benefaction came from Tobias Rustat, whose clergyman father, Robert, had been at the College. His life of service in aristocratic and royal households, and exile during the Commonwealth – he had been with the young King at the Battle of Worcester and was, in effect, his valet during all his subsequent wanderings – had culminated in his appointment as yeoman of the robes to Charles II and keeper of Hampton Court Palace. Of frugal disposition, unmarried and without offspring, he dispersed much of the wealth he accumulated in these offices in charitable gifts, finding, as his monu-

ment in the Chapel records, that 'the more he bestowed upon Churches, Hospital, Universities, and Colleges, and upon poor Widows and orphans of Orthodox Ministers, the more he had at the year's end'. His gift to Jesus funded eight scholarships of £15 each for orphans of clergymen of the Church of England and also provided 'for the relief of six poor Clergymen's Widows'. It was his own, small-scale, Cambridge version of the nationwide Corporation of the Sons of the Clergy, which only a few years earlier had been established with his royal master's support for exactly the same classes of beneficiary – they had been especially hard hit by the dismemberment of the Church and the confiscation of its property during the Interregnum. And, like the Corporation, Rustat's Trust still flourishes.

Rustat, like other early donors, was not ready to leave decisions about the administration of his trust entirely to the College: he drew up an elaborate set of statutes for it and wrote several letters to the Master, Dr Boldero, explaining his wishes. He recruited 'three knowing worthy persons' to help identify properties suitable as investments, and objected when the College appeared to be proceeding without consulting him or them sufficiently. Then he started putting forward names of potential Scholars. In April 1672 he mentioned one 'yonge Fuller' and 'young Edwards, who hath the report of hopefull youths wch. indeede was the cause why I deferred sendinge any others to you hopeing they might a proved cappable & to have filled up my full number before this tyme', and soon afterwards he wrote that 'young Edward will wayte upon you the latter end of the next weeke. I am mayd belive he is a hopefull youth when you have heard him examined by the signore fellows of Jesus Colledge I shall then I hope to heare from you and shall accordingly acte my part.' Rustat's formal nomination of Fuller and of a 'young Mr. Vicars' followed a few months later. In 1673 he expressed concern that the College was not following his statutes to the letter, especially the ninth (which lays down how the bursar of the foundation shall disburse funds, keep records and submit his accounts for audit). In the final surviving letter Rustat describes the distinctive gowns he wishes his Scholars to wear, 'of blacke cloth with wide sleves', which ought to cost 'but lettle more then the gownes they now ware'. A postscript asks for a list of names of all the Scholars of his foundation and which of the present Fellows had been amongst them. There would seem to have been rather more to Tobias Rustat than the 'very simple, ignorant, but honest and loyal creature' on whom the diarist John Evelyn passed judgement.

As befitted a courtier, Rustat also made provision for ceremony. An annual audit of the trust's accounts was to be combined with a public examination of the student

Monument to Tobias Rustat, probably by workshop of Grinling Gibbons, *c.*1694.

pension of twenty pounds for two Clergymen's Orphans from the Degree of Batchelors till they commenced Masters in Arts' (with funds for apprenticing the daughters of the same). In 1743 Archdeacon Robert Marsden founded a scholarship for the son of a living Anglican clergyman, with preference *ceteris paribus* to a native of Nottinghamshire or Lancashire; beneficiaries were to be governed by the same statutes as the Rustat Scholars, as were those of the similar, but orphan-oriented, scholarship founded by Edmund Tew (1757).

In the nineteenth century reforming legislation allowed colleges to remove local restrictions on eligibility for scholarships (and fellowships), and at Jesus the endowments of many such scholarships were, after 1882, merged into a general fund for scholarships and exhibitions (awards less valuable and less prestigious than scholarships). The endowments of the Rustat and related scholarships have, however, remained separate for the class of potential beneficiaries – the children of Anglican clergy – has continued to be sufficiently wide.

The creation of a general scholarship fund facilitated the introduction of open competitive examinations as part of the admissions' process. Entrance scholarships and exhibitions remained a key feature of student financing until the late 1960s, being given an added importance after the Second World War by the automatic grant of 'supplementary' State Scholarships to their holders. The College award and the State Scholarship together usually sufficed to meet an undergraduate's living expenses. Open entrance scholarships and exhibitions were soon

beneficiaries. Four Fellows were to conduct the examination; they were to be given 5 shillings each for their trouble, the auditors 10 shillings; and all were to enjoy a celebratory dinner costing not more than £3 out of the £12 allowed for general expenses. The Rustat Audit Feast continues and crown pieces are still distributed to the Fellows attending. As the trust's income expanded, the number of scholarships was increased, to eleven in 1769 and fourteen in 1848. The requirement that the Scholars should be orphans was dropped in 1861, and the scope of the trust has since been widened: any student of the College with a clergy parent is now eligible for a grant, as are clerical parents (widowed or not) who face higher-than-usual costs in educating their children. Since the trust's foundation in 1671 there have been more than 750 Rustat Scholars (some of them attracted from other colleges), among them Samuel Taylor Coleridge and Edward Daniel Clarke (pages 130–6); David Hartley, the philosopher; a Master (Lynford Caryl); many Fellows; and – the wheel happily turning full circle – several notable benefactors, including Thomas Man, Edmund Tew, Frederick Keller and Robert Tyrwhitt. For over 250 years Mr Rustat's Scholars maintained their own society within the College, with its own customs and rituals. Jesus would have been quite a different place without them.

For more than two centuries other donors followed Rustat's example in providing scholarships for sons (or orphan sons) of Anglican clergymen. In 1715 Dr Lionel Gatford 'sometime scholar here, and afterwards Archdeacon of St Albans and Treasurer of St Paul's, London', bequeathed not only his large library but also 'a yearly

(Top left) Frederick Keller (1732), **Rustat Scholar and Fellow.**
English school

(Left) **W.L.H. Duckworth (1889), Fellow and Master (1940–5).**
James Wood, 1946

followed by benefactions that reflected the growth of new Tripos courses. An exhibition for a student reading History was founded by a bequest from Mortimer E. Schiff in 1918, while the first to be offered for Natural Sciences was created by one from William Thomas Chapman in 1949. In 1957 another benevolent former Master, W.L.H. Duckworth (1940–5), established scholarships for medical students and/or (a backward glance this) pupils of Birkenhead School. Several benefactors since 1970 – including Sir Claude Elliot, Senior Tutor in the 1930s; John Curry Bane, a research student from Pittsburgh; and the eminent judge, Lord Reid – have established funds so that grants may be made 'to assist needy students', a welcome and flexible way of meeting financial difficulties that arise unexpectedly.

While scholarships and exhibitions were founded to enable students to come to the College and qualify themselves for a Cambridge degree, prizes have been established to encourage them to work hard and to reward those whose efforts met with notable success – a distinction which the abolition of entrance scholarships and exhibitions (page 169) has, however, now largely eroded. The first, and still the most prestigious, of the prizes was founded in 1784 by a bequest from Frederick Keller, a

(Top right) Richard Warren (1696), Fellow and Bursar.

Jon Verelst, 1706

(Below) Lord Chief Justice Bramston (1593).

Attr. Cornelius Johnson, *c.*1640

former Fellow (and Rustat Scholar), to reward the undergraduate whose performance in the University's examinations the Master and Fellows judged 'the most distinguished'. With the growth of the College, and in the (vain) hope of avoiding invidious choices, Keller prizes have proliferated and been subdivided into 'senior' and 'junior' prizes: the total of both categories is limited to 5, so there is little risk of the currency being depreciated. The first prize to be offered for a scientific subject (chemistry) was founded by the widow of Frank Allhusen in 1906. More recent benefactions – often made by or in memory of Fellows, Honorary Fellows and former students – have now ensured that there are prizes for distinguished performance in nearly all University examinations.

When, as the Commemoration Service does, we turn from benefactors who have founded fellowships, scholarships and prizes to those who have contributed towards the cost of constructing new buildings and renovating old ones (notable donors of books, paintings and silver are referred to in pages 44–61), it is immediately apparent that virtually all substantial building work during the College's first three centuries depended on them. The Chapel was (as pages 27 and 82 tell) a particular focus of attention. The first completely new building, begun in the later 1630s during Richard Sterne's mastership, was a new range on the north side of First Court (now C and D staircases) which cost £1,544. Of this £300 was provided from the College's accumulated reserves ('Dead College') and a loan; the rest came from individual donors. The former Master William Beale contributed, as did many former and current Fellows. But an appeal to old members was also launched. Sir Christopher Hatton (1619) responded by giving all the stone needed plus £100; Sir Anthony Cage gave '30 loads of timber valued at £50'; and others gave cash, in sums ranging from £50 (Lord Chief Justice Bramston (1593)) downwards.

In 1703 a bequest from another Master, William Saywell, and gifts from three Fellows and an old member, Lord Middleton, helped renovate the Hall and build the gate piers at the entrance to the Chimney. A few years later, in 1718, there were plans for adding an upper storey to the Master's Lodge and the range next to the Gate Tower (now A and B staircases). The effectiveness of the combined efforts of the Master, Charles Ashton, and the Bursar, Richard Warren, can be gauged from the documents illustrated here. Warren's letter to an old member, Lord St John of Bletsoe, is a model of its kind. It elicited

£50. The rest of the money came mostly from current Fellows, with Lord Middleton again contributing. One bill is annotated by Ashton: he had paid the workmen £100 from the College and another £166 16s 9d, which he 'paid out of my own money, chusing to have that for my share in the expense of a work so much for the use and ornament of the College'.

The nineteenth-century additions – K staircase and the Waterhouse and Carpenter buildings – were funded internally, principally from money paid by railway companies for land purchased from the College under statutory powers, but in the twentieth century gifts and bequests were once again all important. The construction of the Morley Horder building in 1929–30 was prompted by the bequest from a Fellow, John Campbell Watt, of his residuary estate, the balance coming from internal loans. In 1947 a modest appeal for a memorial to Jesuans who had fallen in the Second World War resulted in a new undergraduate library constructed on A and B staircases

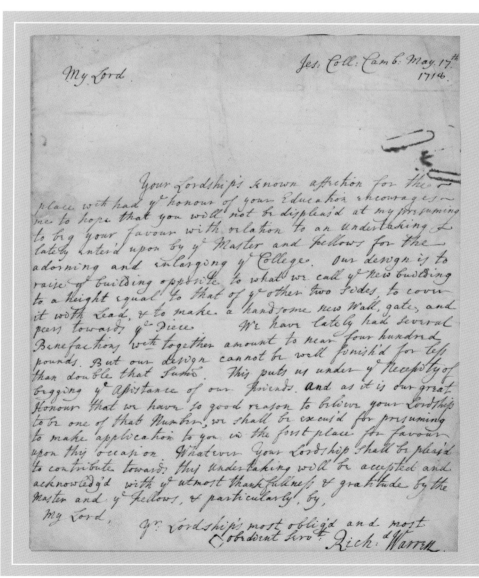

Jes: Coll: Camb: May 17th 1718

My Lord,

Your Lordship's known affection for this place which had the honour of your education encourages me to hope that you will not be displeas'd at my presuming to beg your favour with relation to an undertaking lately enter'd upon by the Master and Fellows for the adorning and enlarging the College.

Our design is to raise the building opposite to what we call the New Building to a height equal to that of the other two sides, to cover it with Lead, and to make a handsome new Wall, gates, and peers towards the piece. We have lately had several benefactions which together amount to near four hundred pounds. But our design cannot be well finish'd for less than double that Sum.

This puts me under the Necessity of begging the Assistance of our friends. And as it is our great Honour that we have so good reason to believe that your Lordship to be one of that Number, we shall be excus'd for presuming to make application to you in the first place for favour upon this occasion. Whatever your Lordship shall be pleas'd to contribute towards this undertaking will be accepted and acknowleg'd with the utmost thankfulness & gratitude by the Master and the Fellows, & particularly by

My Lord
Yr Lordship's most oblig'd and most obedient Servt:
Rich:^d Warren

[endorsed]
To The Right Honourable
The Lord St. John.

within the (recently fire-gutted) rooms that had been built in 1718. A more systematic appeal, for £90,000, was launched in 1963 to help fund a new accommodation building, North Court. Over 1,400 old members answered the call. Then, as the College approached its quincentenary in 1996, it launched an even more ambitious project. Funds were sought for two buildings: a library and a neighbouring one of five staircases which together now form Library Court. Over 1,800 members of the College subscribed, and their gifts – when added to notable bequests from L.A. Pars (1918), who had been a Fellow for sixty-three years, A.A. Overmass (1945) and N.W. Newcombe (1938) – met the entire cost of the Library and a substantial part of that of the other building.

The Chapel has continued to attract gifts from those wishing to support its spiritual and choral life and to help with the upkeep of the College's oldest building. Major benefactions have included, in 1971 the bequest of Mrs Zelie Timins (widow of Douglas Timins (1889)), in 1985 the bequest of £1.4 million by Frank Stammers (1931), in 1990 a fund to support Chapel music by Mr Charles Rawlinson (1952), and in 2007 a much needed new organ by Mr James Hudleston (a friend of the College).

In recent years the College has been especially fortunate in attracting support from well-wishers and friends

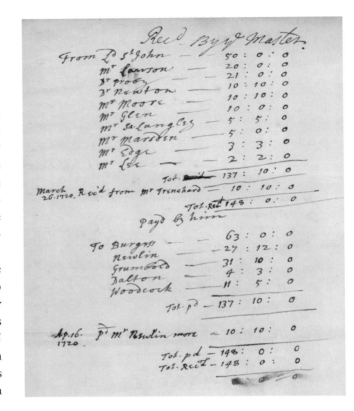

(Top right) The 1718 Appeal: Dr Ashton's accounts for 1720.

(Below) John Campbell Watt (1878). Fellow 1880–1931.

Sir William Nicholson, 1924

who (like Mr Hudleston) have come to know it only later in life. Particularly generous benefactors have included Mrs Yvonne Embiricos, the widow of the Greek shipping magnate, and the Embiricos Foundation, who in 1991 together endowed a research fellowship and graduate and undergraduate scholarships; and Mr Gurnee Hart, who in 2003 endowed the history fellowship carrying his name. These represent a most welcome return to a form of benefaction last seen at Jesus in the sixteenth century.

As the twenty-first century opened, sharply declining state support for university education and those pursuing it, together with the steeply rising costs of maintaining its elderly buildings, were being keenly felt in a college whose remarkable growth has not been sufficiently matched by increased endowments. A long-term development programme was therefore launched, and gifts for purposes that range across the full spectrum of the College's activities – from the endowment and funding of fellowships, bursaries and scholarships for graduates and undergraduates, to the maintenance and improvement of the buildings and grounds – are now being made. With the number of donors now exceeding one thousand every year, the College continues to be deeply grateful to each and every one of its benefactors, past and present.

Buildings: Present, Past and Planned

NICHOLAS RAY

Three characteristics distinguish the architecture of Jesus College from those of other ancient Oxford and Cambridge colleges. First, there is the remarkable openness of the site itself. John Sherman, a Fellow between 1653 and 1665 and the College's first historian, described the setting as 'a position most agreeable to the Muses, who delight in quiet and seclusion; a position, namely, as far removed as possible from the noise and confusion of the town'. Secondly, there is the way in which the pattern of the College is determined by its monastic predecessor. 'This college', wrote the nineteenth-century historians of Cambridge's buildings, Robert Willis and John Willis Clark, 'is a very curious and instructive architectural monument', noting that 'the distribution of the buildings differs entirely from that of every other college in the University, and is merely an adaptation of the structural arrangements of the nunnery'. As the Royal Commission on Historical Monuments points out, not only does Jesus retain more of the original buildings than any other comparable college, it is also the earliest example in Cambridge of the appropriation of monastic fabric for collegiate use. Finally there is a formal and architectural consistency, which makes for a quiet and unostentatious expression in all of its buildings.

The nuns were not the first occupants of the site. Archaeological investigations in connection with the recently (2005) constructed maintenance workshops and gardeners' compound to the north of North Court revealed not only flint implements from the Neolithic period and Bronze Age 'beaker-style' pottery, but also Roman pottery and coins. The College is sited in an area that was just outside the Roman settlement, and the second- to fourth-century pottery fragments that have been discovered were in ditches defining the suburban fields. More dramatically, numerous skeletons were discovered in 2001, when nos. 36 and 37 Jesus Lane were being renovated. As the archaeologists reported: 'there is something incongruous, and not a little surreal, in having the floor of what is otherwise a typical terrace house room – still complete with its fireplace and a student May Ball poster – tightly packed with the dead'. It seems clear that this was part of a substantial cemetery on the fringes of the Roman town. Evidence of Anglo-Saxon settlement is sparser, and the next artefacts chronologically tend to be medieval and associated with the twelfth-century nunnery.

Chapel: the north transept, the oldest surviving part of the building, *c.* 1170.

The nuns' buildings, set well to the north of the road to Barnwell (Jesus Lane), with ditches to the north, east and west, followed the common pattern of a cloister beside a convent church, with an upper-floor refectory (thought to have had a thatched roof) on the opposite side of the court, and a chapter house in the east range. But whereas the cloister usually lies on the south of the church, at St Radegund's it was on the north. There is no apparent reason why this unusual arrangement, which has obvious disadvantages, should have been adopted. It may, however, be worth noting – though there is only the most fragmentary evidence of the part played by priests in establishing the nunnery on a permanent footing (the gravestone of a priest described as the prior) – that it was customary, where a church was to serve a double community, as St Radegonde's at Poitiers did, to place the monks' (or canons') cloister on its south side, and the nuns' cloister on its north. The arched doorway and two windows to the chapter house are a prominent survival in the present Cloister Court – lower than the present cloister arches and lowered further by steps which would have increased the relative height of the chapter house beneath the uniform floor above. This housed the dorter, or dormitory, for the nuns. The west range contained the kitchens (to the north-west) and the lodgings of the prioress.

The survival of the central Cloister Court (even though the cloisters themselves were rebuilt in the eighteenth century) is, as Willis and Clark point out, a feature 'possessed by no other college in Oxford or Cambridge, although many have cloisters in their secondary courts'. But it is only by a close examination of the Chapel that the pre-collegiate fabric can really be studied. Construction of the conventual church was not begun until after 1159, when Malcolm IV of Scotland granted land for the purpose. It was cruciform, with a square tower at the crossing. The crossing piers, each of which differs slightly in profile, are casings to earlier fabric within. This was the largest church in Cambridge at the time, with seven-bayed north and south aisles to the nave and a substantial chapel to the south of the present chancel, which accounts for the large arch, now filled in, on the east wall of the south transept. The most ancient work that is visible internally is in the north transept – the three Norman round-headed arches, also filled in, and the arcaded passage on its east wall. The most admired features are probably the five slender lancet windows on the north wall of the chancel, and the four similar windows on the south side above the thirteenth-century piscina.

It is likely that the convent floor level was lower than the present level of the College (the steps down into the Chapel testify to this), but not quite as low as the chapter

Aerial view from the north-west. Butts Green, the triangular area surrounded by trees (top left), separated from Midsummer Common by the construction of Victoria Avenue, and now part of the football pitch, was yet to be acquired from the town. East and North (the Tutors') Houses, with outhouses and stables stand in their own gardens.

occupied by much of the north aisle was added to the cloister, thereby increasing it to its present dimensions. A large portion of the nave was converted to sets of rooms and, at its western end, to the Master's Lodge. Some of the embedded columns have been partially revealed in later restorations and are visible in the Cloister, and also internally from a recently inserted staircase, where the ruthless chopping of any mouldings that would have projected into the internal space can be seen. At the same time, the church was reroofed at a lower pitch and windows were inserted in the then current perpendicular style.

The Hall, with its splendid oak roof and finely detailed bay window, was placed in the same position as the nuns' refectory, above a buttery and cellars. Most importantly, the construction of three-storeyed ranges of rooms with low-pitched lead roofs behind parapets which established a pattern that has survived into the twenty-first century was initiated, on the east side of Cloister Court – the chapter house being demolished and used as hardcore and rubble infill for the new building. And what is now First Court was begun as a two-storeyed range with a steep pitched roof running up to the tower gateway. The range to the west of the gateway (A and B staircases), identical in style, was started in 1503, three years after Bishop Alcock's death, and contained the grammar school on the ground floor. Although much of this building campaign was completed in the sixteenth century, architectural historians have credited him with the plan. Rightly or wrongly, Alcock is commemorated in his ubiquitous rebus, a cockerel surmounting a globe, to be seen in the finely carved sixteenth-century bench end by the chancel screen door in the Chapel, as well as in stained glass, paintings and stonework throughout the College.

house. This structure, originally twelfth century, lay to the north of a vestry and was later replaced by the thirteenth-century chapter house, the western arcade of which, first rediscovered in 1893, forms such a prominent feature of the present Cloister Court. Further excavations in 1995 revealed the base of an octagonal central pier, and it is now possible to reconstruct with some confidence the form that the chapter house must have taken. For many years this area has been used for boilers, storage and lavatories, but plans exist for rooms which would be more worthy of their place in the heart of the College's ancient fabric, and eventually they will surely be realised.

After the fire of 1313 the fabric of both church and nunnery had remained in poor repair. Bishop Alcock, who had been the controller of the royal works and buildings, and so was well used to major projects, inaugurated an ambitious reconstruction scheme to accommodate the College. The work was expedient, casting aside without compunction any material that would not serve the new purpose, while reusing other parts of it quite pragmatically. In the church, the large south chapel was removed, and a sacristy to the north of the chancel, and the north and south aisles, were eliminated, leaving their fourteen columns embedded in new walls. The space previously

(Top left) The Chapel from the Cloisters.

(Below) The Chapel and Cloister Court from the east.

The first major extension to the College's buildings was begun in 1638, and is the range on the north side of First Court running east–west, C and D staircases. (An earlier plan to insert additional staircases into the nave of the Chapel was, fortunately, abandoned.) As Willis and Clark say, 'the architect of this range had the good fortune to build it in a style so nearly the same as the range on the opposite side of the court that there is no striking discrepancy between them'. But there is one contribution to the formal vocabulary of the College that was to have far-reaching consequences. At the rear are four dramatic paired chimneys set diagonally; Waterhouse's nineteenth-century range in Pump Court reflects this 45° angle, particularly in the bay window facing west, while the twentieth-century North Court was to be constructed entirely around a play between these orthogonal and oblique geometries.

By 1690, when David Loggan made his engravings of the Cambridge colleges (page 31), the central area of Jesus is easily recognisable – the Chapel dominates the ensemble of buildings which begin to radiate out from the central Cloister Court, the walled Chimney approaching the tower gateway is in place, gardens and fields surround the College as far as the ditch bordering Jesus Green. During subsequent decades and centuries it is detail that changes rather than the fundamental arrangement. The entrance to Cloister Court from First Court is moved, from the bay beside the Prioress's Room and underneath the Oratory in the Master's Lodge, to align with the northern range of the cloisters. These are refashioned with the open arches we know today, and the three-light perpendicular

windows are removed. The two-storeyed southern range of First Court is raised to three storeys with a leaded roof, thereby diminishing the effect of the gate tower, whose picturesque chimney shafts are also removed. Some alterations have been reversed, however, notably the insertion of sash windows, from 1791, in the upper floors of the south range, apparently so that visitors would be impressed by the modernity of the College's taste. (Their view of the ground-floor windows would have been obscured by the garden walls, which is why these windows were not altered.) The effect on the gateway, where the sash windows collided with the mouldings around the head, was particularly unfortunate. We must be grateful that in 1880 the windows were all returned to the earlier pattern.

The most significant reversal of taste was evident in the Chapel. In 1789 Robert Tyrwhitt, a former Fellow, gave £200 towards its refurbishment, and the College added more than £500. The result was a thorough Georgianisation: the oak roof in the choir was concealed by a flat plaster ceiling, the eastern arch of the tower was blocked up, a partition to the chancel with an entrance framed by Ionic pilasters was installed, and the gothic choir stalls were removed to the church at Landbeach. In 1815 the whole of the exterior was covered in Roman Cement by John and Peter Bernasconi. But by 1832 taste had changed and a restoration fund was started. Anthony

(Top right) Cloister Court staircase: behind the brick exterior, timber framing and lathe and plaster, c.1500.

(Below) View from the south (probably from the recently built tower of All Saints' Church) c.1871, showing the sash windows introduced in 1791 and the all-embracing ivy. To the north, the newly erected Waterhouse building (1869–70) stands alone.

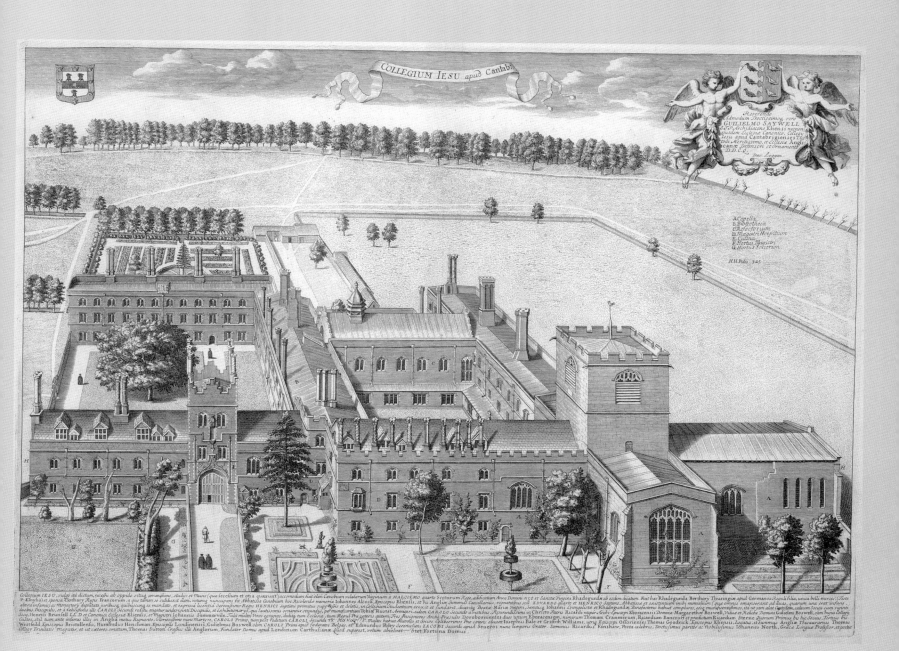

David Loggan's engraving for his *Cantabrigia Illustrata* (1690).

**The 'New Building' of
1638–41 (C and D staircases)
from the north.**

Salvin was hired as architect, and in 1846 he removed the partition and constructed a vestry and organ-chamber on foundations that had been discovered in the north-east angle between the chancel and transept. It was Salvin who had been responsible five years earlier for a complete rebuilding of the Round Church in Cambridge along the lines of the earlier Norman work, removing all the accretions of subsequent centuries. But Salvin fell ill and, his plans for the chancel and choir not finding favour, was superseded as architect by the end of the year by Augustus Welby Pugin, a Roman Catholic since 1834 and the author of two influential books which argued for the moral rightness of the gothic style, particularly of the Early English period – *Contrasts* of 1836, and *The True Principles of Pointed or Christian Architecture* of 1841. Pugin's first task was to strengthen the tower crossing, but he soon moved on to a thorough restoration of the chancel, removing not only the eighteenth-century plaster ceiling but also the low-pitched late fifteenth-century roof and perpendicular five-light east window (page 86). He installed a steep pitched roof and the three lancet windows we see now in the east end, inspired by those on the north and south transept walls but also based on fragments of the earlier thirteenth-century windows which remained

embedded in the fabric. Pugin designed the stained glass for these windows – supplying pieces of glass he had retrieved from the windows at Chartres while they were being reglazed to ensure that his glass maker (Hardman of Birmingham) matched the medieval colours – and also the screen and stalls, a pair of candlesticks and the magnificent lectern. The Chapel reopened for services in 1849, but it was not until 1878 that the College was able to buy back some of the original joinery that had been removed to Landbeach.

The present appearance of the Chapel owes as much to the work of G.F. Bodley, some twenty years later as it does to Pugin's (page 18). Bodley needed to strengthen the tower again by the addition of buttresses; he even contemplated removing its upper portion, following cracks which had appeared in 1862, but George Gilbert Scott Senior pronounced it fit for retention after an inspection by John Bacon, clerk to the works he was conducting at Ely Cathedral. That Bodley continued to be employed is partly due to his friendship with Gilbert Scott's son. George Gilbert Scott Junior had entered Jesus to read Moral Sciences at the mature age of 24 and graduated in 1866, coming first in his year. In 1869 he was offered a fellowship, though it had to be suspended for financial reasons, and when shortly afterwards Scott married he had to resign it, since the rule requiring celibacy was still in place. That same year, Bodley was suffering from blood poisoning, and there was renewed concern about the condition of the south-west pier of the tower. Scott decided that the pier could be repaired. His father visited the site with Mr Kett, of Rattee & Kett, and concurred; the corner was successfully underpinned and a new buttress constructed. The Master asked Scott if he would replace Bodley as the architect for the Chapel work, but to his credit he declined to usurp the position of his friend, who soon made a full recovery.

Bodley was already working on the new All Saints' Church in Jesus Lane, employing some of the very best artists of the time for painting, stencilling and stained-

Raphaelites, his reputation is again in the ascendant. Many of the charcoal cartoons for the figures survive, in the Victoria and Albert Museum, the City of Birmingham Art Gallery and the Tate Gallery. Jesus College possesses two: those for St Ambrose and for Bishop Alcock, appropriately enough; the latter also contains a little sketch of the tower gateway in the corner. After he had founded the Society for the Protection of Ancient Buildings in 1877, Morris decided it was improper for his firm to make new windows in ancient buildings because it smacked of the 'restoration' of old fabric that he so despised, though he continued to design stained-glass windows for new ones. He issued a circular to this effect, and sent a copy to the Dean at Jesus, noting 'Your chapel you see glazed but just in time.' During the re-lighting and decoration carried

(Left) Bishop Alcock (holding Henry VII's Letters Patent) and St Ambrose: Burne-Jones' crayon drawings for his great window (below) in the Chapel's south transept (*c.*1876).

glass design. It is thanks to Bodley that we have the three painted roofs and eleven stained-glass windows by William Morris's firm, executed between 1866 and 1878; he was a tireless advocate of Morris's work, even though from 1869 his partner, Thomas Garner, ran a rival organisation, Burlison & Grills, which Bodley also recommended. Working for William Morris at this time were the painter Ford Madox Brown, the architect Philip Webb – each of whom contributed to the decoration of the Chapel – and Edward Burne-Jones, whose figures occupy much of the magnificent windows in the south transept. The handling of colour is their principal glory, but Burne-Jones' draughtsmanship is equally notable, displaying his respect for Michelangelo. During his lifetime, Burne-Jones' work was widely admired, and his designs for Jesus were reproduced in numerous British churches; with the reappraisal of the work of the preout in 2004, a fragment of floral patterning was discovered on the north wall of the nave, and has been left exposed. Possibly this is by Morris, indicating a scheme for stencilling the whole interior, which, rightly or wrongly, the College rejected.

Unlike in the Chapel, eighteenth-century improvements to the Hall have not been reversed, but a significant nineteenth-century addition has been entirely eradicated. The deal panelling and screen, replacing an early seventeenth-century screen, dates from 1703, when Grumbold undertook repairs, and in the opinion of many was much enhanced by its redecoration in period 'baroque' style to celebrate the College's Quincentenary in 1996. The windows had been lowered in 1801, and the position of the screen was altered in 1875, when a wooden floor was inserted above the original flagstones. The screen was moved some 4 metres westwards and reversed so that what was the west face now addresses the Hall. The oriel window above is a survival from about 1500. The architect, Alfred Waterhouse, simultaneously under-

Pump Court with Waterhouse's Small Hall (built 1875, demolished 1962).

Engraving by Celia Murray, *c.*1895

took careful repairs to the roof and to the north-facing bay window, but it was also he who stripped the deal panelling of all traces of its previous decoration and painted it in the dark brown colours that survived until 1996. At the same time Waterhouse constructed a 'Little Hall', projecting northwards into Pump Court, containing a servants' hall below and a lecture room and muniment room above, replacing the awkward sixteenth-century stair with a new staircase between the two halls. But all this was swept away in the 1960s when David Roberts undertook a major refurbishment which restored Upper Hall and introduced both a lift to serve it and the stone

straight-flight stair that is the present approach to the Hall. This was a decision that would not have been sanctioned by conservation officers, nor perhaps by College taste, only some twenty years or so later, but it did have the virtue of returning the line of the wall on the north to that occupied by the convent building. When an escape stair from Upper Hall was required by the Fire Officer in the 1990s, this too was contained within the existing fabric.

To the east of the Hall, the Combination Room had been remodelled in 1762 by James Essex, who lowered the floor to the same level as the Hall's – thus creating a more Georgian proportion – introduced the panelling, and designed the fireplace. The tiling by William de Morgan in the surround is later and with its handsome brass fender is the only survivor of a comprehensive decorative scheme by Morris & Company from 1878.

The Master's Lodge was extended between 1718 and 1720, when the south range of First Court lost its steep roof and was made a full three storeys with parapets, and then refashioned in 1885–6 by Carpenter & Ingelow. Its most splendid room is the so-called 'Conference Chamber', above the Prioress's Room. This was probably the prioress's parlour, approached by an external stair from the cloister below. The panelling dates from around 1600, and the timber ceiling is coloured and stencilled. To the north, above the former entrance passage to the cloister, is the Oratory, with a similar ceiling and, attached to the south wall, fragments of the early sixteenth-century joinery from the Chapel, recovered from Landbeach in 1879.

The room above the Conference Chamber may have been the Master's Study. It connects to the Old Library and now houses its special collections. The east-facing windows in the Old Library have original early sixteenth-century glass. Bishop Alcock's rebus is everywhere visible; the cockerels have quotations from the Psalms and Fathers of the Church relevant to the subjects stated in the tags below each bird. The magnificent bookcases date from the 1660s, during the mastership of Edward Boldero, who funded their construction. His benefaction is recorded in a painted inscription over the north doorway.

The continuity of style we have noted is evident in the northward extension from Cloister Court (staircase L). This was entrusted to a Cambridge builder, James Webster, in 1822. The plan differs from Alcock's pattern, which alternates staircases and chimneys across the depth of the building, by having a central staircase with semicircular winders serving twelve sets, but the external expression is identical. In the early years of the twentieth century this range was extended northwards still further, to the same pattern externally. The northern range of

Pump Court was constructed in 1869–70 to the designs of Alfred Waterhouse. Work began in May 1869, and the first rooms were occupied eleven months later. Waterhouse ran a large practice, firstly in Manchester and later in London, and during the 1870s was to design substantial new buildings for Gonville and Caius and Pembroke, and the new building for Girton College. He favoured the use of hard red bricks which weather well but can create a mechanical effect to his façades. Then in 1884 Carpenter & Ingelow began on a complete new court to the east of Cloister Court. Only one range of what is now Chapel Court was completed, described by the great twentieth-century architectural historian Nikolaus Pevsner as 'a wholly dull design, red brick with a central gatehouse, as if it were some kind of training college'. The same architects were responsible for East House, designed as a family house for one of the Tutors and now used as the bursary, and the similar North House, demolished when North Court was constructed. Whereas Chapel Court is aligned with the Chapel itself and the ranges to its north, East House was set out orthogonally to Jesus Lane and to the track that led from it, a decision that has had repercussions for subsequent architects.

The completion of Chapel Court (page 40) was undertaken by Percy Morley Horder, an architect of some skill and subtlety, in 1927–30. His intention was to revert to the pattern of Alcock's ranges, using a pale brick and similar window pattern, but he needed to join on to Carpenter & Ingelow's building and weave round East House. This he achieved by facing the joining staircases (Chapel Court 6 and 7) with pinkish bricks (rescued from a ruined manor house in Suffolk), and adapting his plan to return to a regular three-sided court facing north. In the eastern range he placed a new gateway, directly on the axis of the Chapel, above which is a carving by Eric Gill, one of the most distinguished sculptors and typographers of the early twentieth century. Morley Horder was also responsible for the Fellows' staircase up to the Combination Room, for the thatched-roofed cricket pavilion (page 193), the new boathouse (page 185), and for the two-storey building (originally built as a bath house) connecting Waterhouse's range to the eastern extremity of Pump Court. Here, just as in Chapel Court, by welding his new buildings on to the Victorian addition he transformed discrete blocks so that they contributed to the creation of courtyards. As Arthur Gray's article in the *Cambridge Review* in 1931 puts it: 'The essential character of Mr Horder's work is its grave nobility contrasting with the florid artifices and cheap materials of Victorian builders. Towers, terricles and ineffective heraldic ornament have no part in it.'

Apart from the work to form Upper Hall already described, the conversion of the upper floors of A and B staircases and three major new buildings comprise the work of the second half of the twentieth century. But the archives also house some fascinating projects that were never realised. One is a scheme from 1946 by Geoffrey Jellico, perhaps the foremost British landscape architect of the twentieth century. He proposed the demolition of East House and North House, and the relocation of the cricket Pavilion to the western extremity of the grounds, overlooking a cricket pitch where the Orchard is now. The Morgan Avenue is removed (though the gates were to be kept), and a new access proposed with Porters' Lodge and cycle sheds at the eastern end of Jesus Lane, precisely where a new lodge was in fact placed some twenty years later. A water feature (or 'water hazard' as it is described on his plan) was to divide First Court from the cricket pitch to the west. Jellico also planned the perimeter path which now runs in the belt of trees all around the grounds. But his most adventurous suggestion was the placing of a new library across the centre of Chapel Court, joined to Cloister Court (which he intended to pave) by

Chapel: detail of nave ceiling by Leach to William Morris's designs, 1867.

an arcade. Jellico's plans were carefully considered, but the Council rejected his most radical suggestions.

After a fire in February 1950, the architect Marshall Sisson was commissioned to repair and convert the upper floors of the south range of First Court to form the War Memorial Library. Sisson was a modernist in the 1930s but had changed his position twenty years later and embraced a neo-Georgian style, so that the insertions were discreet and inoffensive (page 47). The first of the major new buildings was North Court (replacing the demolished North House), which was constructed in two phases from 1963 to 1966 by the local architect and fellow of Magdalene, David Roberts. It succeeded in being both 'modern', thus recognisably of its time, and also respectful to its context, by the manipulation of its geometry already referred to, its conformity to the established pattern of three-sided courts and its use of a hand-made buff facing brick, generally concealing the concrete of which its floors are constructed. The arrangement by which four rooms on each landing shared a gyp room and shower was praised at the time of its construction as a creative way of ensuring horizontal sociability whilst still maintaining the vertical society engendered by the staircase system – although this seems to have been a means of economising since Roberts had proposed individual bathrooms initially, which had been regarded as unnecessarily extravagant. These were eventually installed in 2004–5,

(Top right) North Court by David Roberts (1963–6).

(Below) Eric Gill at work on the arms of the College's Visitor (Bishop White-Thompson) over what is, unsurprisingly, now called Angel Gate, 1930.

when repairs and improvements were undertaken by John Allan of Avanti Architects, double-glazing the large window areas and reservicing the building entirely. The only alteration that is visible externally to the 1960s building is the lowering of semi-basement windows on to the court, where former store rooms have become kitchens.

In celebration of its quincentenary, the College decided that a new range of rooms, a purpose-built library and an auditorium should be constructed, and after some discussion voted to inaugurate a new court to the south of Chapel Court. Eldred Evans and David Shalev were appointed as architects, and the Library was completed in 1995 and formally opened by the Queen in 1996. It employs the same hand-made buff bricks as North Court, but with white cement pointing and stone surrounds and mouldings which follow the pattern of the College's other buildings closely. Indeed Morley Horder's Chapel Court building, which it abuts, seems in comparison more abstract, since he only employed projecting mouldings over the second-floor windows and brought his stonework elsewhere flush with the wall plane. Internally, the traditional collegiate library, whereby reading takes place within a perimeter defined by the arrangement of bookcases, is successfully reinterpreted. Evans and Shalev were even able to incorporate some of Marshall Sisson's bookcases in the ground-floor Law Library. A new accommodation building by the same architects followed in 2000, thus creating the third side of what has become

Library Court with
Quincentenary Library
(1996) (right) and Staircases
I–V (2000) (left): both by
Eldred Evans and David
Shalev. On the lawn is Philip
King's *Brake* (1996).

Library Court and following the familiar three-storeyed arrangement; internally four rooms open off each landing with south-facing kitchens set one floor lower to serve each staircase. It is a pattern Bishop Alcock would have recognised, even if enhanced bathing facilities are now provided, together with the wiring necessary for instant access to the internet. Here too, the external expression represents a deliberate retreat from Roberts' experiment of forty years earlier.

The College has contemplated the construction of an auditorium for many years. In 1979 the distinguished architect Sir Leslie Martin, who was a Fellow (page 256), prepared 'A College Social Building Scheme', which is illustrated in his *Buildings and Projects* of 1983, showing a multi-purpose theatre space between First Court and Pump Court. A working party in 1988 produced a comprehensive brief for a performing arts centre (then estimated to cost £2,300,000), and the brief for the architectural competition for Library Court included an auditorium as a major component. But rather than placing an auditorium along its fourth side, thus creating what would be the only other closed court apart from Cloister Court, the current intention is to construct an auditorium and related facilities as part of a new development at the far western edge of the College Close, adjacent to the Jesus Lane frontage formerly occupied by Marshall's garage.

Pevsner remarked that because of the size of the College's site, the Fellows of Jesus 'can, if they wish, go on for a long time building new ranges or courts. But one hopes that they will not need to. Everything so far has been spacious.' The challenge for the present generation, as for our predecessors, is how to make the most of the College's remarkable situation, and create new facilities to meet changing needs, whilst always acknowledging the strength and validity of the architectural context within which any new additions will find themselves.

Gardens and Close

PAUL STEARN and ANTHONY BOWEN

N o other old college in Cambridge has such large and immediate grounds. For the nuns who were first so blessed, it was land to be put to work, for growing food and grazing animals, and so it was used by the College too. Only in 1919 did the last tenant give up his lease to graze: interruptions from undergraduates playing cricket had become too frequent, and the compensation they had to pay (as noted in a lease of 1836) was simply not worth it. The animals had been kept from the courts by a ha-ha, shown in Loggan's print of 1690 (page 64), west of Second Court. The ha-ha lasted until the erection of the Waterhouse building in 1869,

surviving a suggestion in the 1820s that a fence or wall be built instead, so that 'all who live in that part of College may look upon something more interesting than mouldering cabbages and onions'. And into the 1930s the grass in the Orchard (the area immediately to the west of First Court) was still allowed to grow high every year until cut for hay, and was, as Freddy Brittain, who was later to be Steward, remembered, full of wild flowers – buttercups in May, big ox-eye daisies in June, masses of ragwort in July. Here in one paragraph are the three functions of the grounds: to nourish, to exercise and to delight.

The first function, of food, is now met almost entirely from outside, but herbs such as parsley, basil and coriander are still grown, and bay leaves are plucked from the garden of St Radegund close by the kitchens in Pump Court. This garden was a gift from the Graduate Society in 1996, to mark the College's quincentenary. Designed and planted by Paul Stearn, Head Gardener since 1989, with expert help from Jane Renfrew, the then Master's wife, it recalls the saint's own garden in Poitiers: there are two curving

Summer flowers: hanging basket in Cloister Court.

> **Visiting Jesus**
>
> [*Monday August 5, 1901*] Walked to Jesus with Walter Durnfold and went to Foakes Jackson, who took us all over the College: this was full of thrills. The tall dark Church; the beautiful ancient unvisited library – the dignified hall with its pictures. The beauty of all this is the *possible* union of dignity and comfort with great simplicity. The garden very sweet, with old verbenas and hollyhocks.
>
> *A.C. Benson*, Edwardian Excursions
> *(ed. David Newsome) (1981)*
> *pp. 23-4*

beds of apothecary's roses and wild violets, terminated by four bay trees, with a wild pear at the centre, underplanted with Madonna lilies; two crab-apple trees stand outside, underplanted with saffron crocus. There is another garden of herbs – scented ones – in the Master's Garden, featured in Jessica Houdret's book *Herb Gardening*, it, too, a joint work of Jane Renfrew and Paul Stearn. Another herb, with a long history in the Close, may be found against the east wall of the Fellows' Garden: birthwort (*Aristolochia clematitis*), which is known for its abortive powers.

If we except the potatoes grown during and immediately after the Second World War on what is now the football pitch, fruit is the most persistently recorded produce of the Close. In the Master's Garden there were raspberries, and a peach tree which gave a few choice fruits. Back in 1650 Dr Worthington wrote of 'storing the winter fruits', and in 1660 he wrote to his successor (and predecessor) in the Lodge, Dr Sterne, warning him of thefts of fruit by people coming over the mud wall. A brick wall had been put round the Fellows' Garden in 1609, but it was not until 1681 that the Master's Garden was similarly protected and the Chimney created. A mulberry tree in Library Garden still bears well, but the better-known mulberry is the one in the Fellows' Garden, planted in 1608 and still bearing a few berries on its prop-supported branches – too few now to produce the pot of jam per Fellow which it once did. Alan Sharpe recalls being given some in 1949 when he was a new research Fellow: 'That's very kind of you. Are you sure you can spare them?'

'Oh yes, sir', the Head Gardener replied, 'the real Fellows have all had theirs.'

Perhaps it should not be counted as a fruit tree. It was purchased for 18 shillings on the advice of M. François de Vernot, whom James I had instructed to get mulberry trees grown throughout the land, for the breeding of silkworms. Alas, here as elsewhere, *Morus nigra*, not *Morus alba*, was planted; as *Morus alba* comes from southern China, the climate might not have suited it anyway.

The great walnut tree (*Juglans regia*) which used to stand in First Court may also have fed the Fellows, but ornament was probably its chief business. It is first mentioned in 1589, and in Loggan's print it is a mature tree. It was felled early in the nineteenth century, having been commemorated in facetious verse by John Hall-Stevenson, a rich Fellow Commoner (page 142):

It overshadow'd ev'ry room,
And consequently, more or less,
Forced every brain, in such a gloom
To grope its way, and go by guess.

Whether in 'so wise a College' it was rightly designated 'a tree of Knowledge' may be open to question, but

with a span of 96 feet (as measured by a German visitor in 1720), it did rather fill the available space.

Even as it was felled, a successor was growing, to be of comparable stature. In 1802 Edward Daniel Clarke (page 134) brought back from Thermopylae seeds of the oriental plane and planted them in the College. Several took, and the mightiest survivor now dominates the Fellows' Garden; it is over 100 feet tall (page 137). On Midsummer Day in 2002 Fellows and staff with partners and children joined together to celebrate its two hundredth birthday. A jazz band played; Morris men danced; the Chapel choir sang Handel's *Largo*; David Hanke, Fellow in botany, spoke about oriental planes; Paul Stearn toasted the tree with verses of his own composition; and Anthony Bowen, Fellow and Orator, recited a Latin ode he had written. Meanwhile the children drew the tree. It should be good for at least another two hundred years. A sibling dominates the Master's Garden.

This all makes the point that the Jesus grounds are most obviously planted with trees, and the Close is big

enough for them to be seen to good advantage. There used to be a pair of Exeter elms at the Master's gate on Jesus Lane, but they fell victim to Dutch elm disease; fastigiate oaks have replaced them. Another pair at the Victoria Avenue gates succumbed too, and in their stead on the northern bank of Morgan Avenue three giant redwoods (*Sequoiadendron giganteum*) were planted in 1989. There are other notable individual trees in the Fellows' Garden: a large holm oak (*Quercus ilex*) planted in the early nineteenth century, a black walnut (*Juglans nigra*) planted in 1912, and a handkerchief (or ghost) tree (*Davidia involucrata*) planted in 2002. The holm oak partly died from a late frost almost at once, but survived to send up

View from the Carpenter building, *c*.1890.

four shoots the next spring which have become four thick trunks themselves. The black walnut bears a plaque saying: 'Henry Arthur Morgan's tree, whose wife and children planted me to keep green his memory'. And already the handkerchief tree's white leaf bracts are showing well.

In Pump Court, close by the bar, is a large and aged yew, its greater trunk propped by a two-legged crutch. More commented on by visitors are the eight trimmed yews set in four pairs on the Second Court grass nearby; several of them lean perilously, and twenty years ago they were reduced by 4 feet each to keep them stable. Once they were part of a formal garden, with a circular shrub bed surrounded by low box hedges together with a line of horse chestnuts and sycamore on its eastern boundary. The pairs of clipped yews straddled the north, south, east and west paths that led to the central circular path. This layout may have been based on Loggan's print. In their midst now grows a Persian ironwood (*Parrotia Persica*)

(Top) Second Court, *c.*1920.

(Bottom) Daffodils by the Morley Horder building, 2005.

JESUS COLLEGE. CAMBRIDGE.

planted in 2004, the gift of Christine McKie, widow of Duncan McKie who chaired the Gardens' Committee even longer than he was Steward and, like him, a considerable gardener. The tree will be a worthy memorial of his knowledge and care of our gardens. Further west still, in North Court, is another commemorative planting, of a yellow birch (*Betula lutea*), an American tree, planted in 2004 in the name of John Eliot, 'Apostle to the Indians', to celebrate the quatercentenary of his birth. A party came from the Latin school in Roxbury, Massachusetts, that he founded; the headmaster planted the tree and the school choir sang their anthem.

Chapel Court came into existence when the Carpenter building went up in the mid-1880s. It had till then been mostly the Master's paddock. A fine sycamore (*Acer pseudoplatanus*) stands at the south end; both it and the lime beside it were in their places well before the Morley Horder building completed Chapel Court in 1931. At the other end a cedar of Lebanon, planted in 1994, is beginning to make its mark where three predecessors had failed. The court was given at first a formal layout, as old postcards show, and a perimeter planting of pleached limes, but it was a considerable task to keep them in trim, and after neglect during the Second World War and some loss by death they were removed. It is the white horse chestnuts of Morgan Avenue – completed in 1931 when the three daughters of H.A. Morgan planted a tree in honour of their mother – which serve now as the College's example of an ordered group of one species.

The best massed grouping of trees is surely the Grove, which marks the College's northern perimeter at the Jesus ditch. Viewed from across the cricket field and the rugger pitch they stand easy to see in their full height, growing on land which may have come to the nunnery by gift of Henry VI. In 1590–1 ashes were planted over a considerable area, but Cromwell's men cut most of them down for firewood. The Grove revived and came to be much admired, and much used as a public walk; it is mentioned in *Cantabrigia Depicta*, published in 1763 and effectively the University's and City's first guide book. In the 1780s there was replanting with a variety of trees, horse chestnuts, oaks and beeches as well as more ash. Some from that planting still stand. Coleridge took the air among them, and wrote a poem called 'A Wish Written in Jesus Wood'. In the 1990s Paul Stearn and his colleagues began a further replanting, recreating as well the rambling path through the trees (as the landscape architect Geoffrey Jellico had first suggested in 1946) and adding hawthorn hedging to tempt back the nightingales which once graced the Grove with their song. Their project won the City Council's Biodiversity Challenge competition in 2003.

The west end of the Close, too, is heavily treed. Horse chestnuts spread their candles and later their conkers over

Jesus Lane from the Fellows' Garden, and the Orchard is a mini-arboretum with a great variety of trees. Most notable is a wingnut (*Pterocarya × Rehderana*). Tallest is a balsam poplar (*Populus balsamifera*), but coming up to it is a Californian redwood (*Sequoia sempervirens*). Among them are sculptures from the biennial exhibitions which have been held since 1988. Pieces from these exhibitions are now to be found in several parts of the Close, bringing many people in to share the College's pleasure in them and its gardens.

The bushes and flowers of the Close not only give variety and colour at a human level; they also provide the gradient between the great trees best seen from a distance and the more immediate neighbourhood of brick walls, paths and mown grass. Bushes and flowers are the underplanting of our trees and buildings; they bring into a manageable relationship two things that cannot be close together. The great wisteria on the 1638 building in First Court, planted soon after 1816, is a wonderful sight in all seasons, and spectacular when it blooms. Freddy Brittain's memoirs record a College that in 1919 was largely wreathed in ivy, and skirted with laurels. Both mostly went before the Second World War, in the case of the ivy to the benefit of the brickwork.

Shrubbery is perhaps less noted for its beauty and importance than the rest of the gardeners' work. Consider, however, both from far and from near, the long west border of Chapel Court and the various bushes which range north along the arm of buildings that springs from the north transept of the Chapel. The border, created by Head Gardener Graham Payne (1976–88), is a real bonus to the court. Or consider the work of shrubs in the Library Garden, between the Chapel's chancel and the Quincentenary Library. In Library Court itself the east wall of the Library is the setting for a wide border of shrubs, bushes and small trees. And how many know yet the sunken garden between the other Evans and Shalev building and the wall on Jesus Lane? There, ornamental ivies are planted, together with low-growing shrubs whose leaves change colour with the seasons; flowers would be starved of sunlight in so confined a space. There are also notable shrubberies against the north wall of the Hall, and along the Waterhouse building in Second Court. A border of trees and shrubs from New Zealand is planned for the south-facing wall of the Fellows' Garden.

The flowers of the Close mostly give embellishment in detail; the wallflowers that grow on the Chimney walls (as they should) are particularly delightful. There are, however, some significant continuous borders, most notably the long herbaceous border in the Master's Garden along the Chimney wall. It was extensively redesigned in 1999 by a trio of Johanna Crighton, the then Master's wife, Paul Stearn and Piet Oudolf, a Dutch expert. The last-named also helped to redesign an old shrub rose border on the other side of the driveway with a varied array of colours and scents. And in the Fellows' Garden – until the 1870s home of the peacocks for which the College was famous – there are two curved beds of flowers backed by a clipped yew hedge, giving a welcome touch of colour where in summer the green of the trees and the grass is dominant, for it was here that the Fellows had their bowling green. (Its elegant eighteenth-century summer house is still there.)

The show place for flowers is First Court. There are narrow borders on the three sides where the buildings

(Left) The Carpenter building, east front, *c*.1900, before the creation of the Morgan Avenue.

(Below) Clematis and wallflowers in First Court.

rise, and a broader fourth on the open side where a low wall draws a line without obstructing the view of the Orchard behind. Here a bright variety of annuals comes and goes, provided from the College's own greenhouses and potting sheds. The gardeners have licence to plant what they wish, year by year; the ever-changing displays bear witness to their range of knowledge and vigour of invention. Footnote is, perhaps, not quite the right word for hanging baskets, but their presence from June to October, in the difficult space of Cloister Court, where they were first introduced in 1951, must not go unnoted. More permanent there are decorative vines, such as Boston ivy and Virginia creeper; until 1951 common ivy had prevailed.

Most welcome of all the flowers in the Close are surely those that bloom in spring: snowdrops, crocuses, daffodils, narcissi, primroses. Both the Master's Garden and the Fellows' Garden have fine displays; that under the great plane tree is particularly spectacular. As the tree is late to come into leaf, the sunlight of April and May prolongs the display. There has been heavy planting of bulbs under the yew tree in Pump Court and under the sycamore in Chapel Court, and in 2004 hundreds of daffodils and narcissi were planted under the white chestnuts of Morgan Avenue.

A staff of 7 look after all these things, sustaining what thrives and replacing what fails, learning the past and present of the Close and preparing for the years to come. In addition to their buildings south of the Orchard, they now share with the maintenance staff a building behind

(Top right) First Court, looking towards the door to the Fellows' Garden.

(Below) In the Orchard.

(Facing page)
Looking towards North Court from the archway to Chapel Court, with (left) *Battersea III* by Geoffrey Clarke.

North Court designed by Nicholas Ray, put up in 2004, displaying through the trees of the Grove to people on Jesus Green a roof of sedum. Training of staff is *de rigueur*, and is not done only on the job. Long service seems to be almost the norm; on his retirement as Head Gardener in 1976, William Howard was presented with a bar to his long-service medal from the Royal Horticultural Society, and three of the present staff have over seventy years to their joint credit. The most knowledgeable Jesuan gardener of all, however, is almost certainly Edward Augustus Bowles (1865–1954), who graduated BA in 1887 and was the author of half a dozen standard books; he was awarded the Victoria Medal of Honour by the Royal Horticultural Society, which is the highest accolade possible in horticulture.

Gardeners plan from month to month with flowers, but they plan from century to century with trees. The trees are the College's greatest glory, but are they a fine context for the College or is the College a fine context for them? The great walnut tree of First Court is gone; the great plane tree thrives in the Fellows' Garden, in Chapel Court a cedar rises. The College sets the context, but maintaining the balance, both short term and long term, of trees, shrubs, flowers, grass, sculptures and buildings calls for continuing thought and attention. It is not something that can ever be taken for granted.

Libraries and Archives

PETER GLAZEBROOK and FRANCES WILLMOTH

nlike most of Cloister Court, the College's first library – now known as the Old Library – was a new, purpose-built room. On the second floor of the west side, it is structurally distinct from the Master's Lodge to which, on the traditional Cambridge pattern, it is connected. Long and low, with a handsome oak roof, it is lit by fourteen two-light windows, each with Bishop Alcock's rebus in painted glass, the cockerels crowing texts from the Bible and Church Fathers that allude to the subjects of the medieval university curriculum and of books kept nearby: Scripture, Canon Law and Civil Law, Physic (and so forth) – as small scrolls in lozenges below confirm for the benefit of the less learned.

Anthony Andreas, *Writings on Logic* (St Albans, 1483) in a contemporary Cambridge binding, and still in the Old Library though without the chain that once secured it (bottom edge).

The room has, since the 1660s, been furnished with robust bookcases (given by Edmund Boldero, Master 1663–79) which are also of oak, and are linked to the roof by characterful balusters, making this one of Cambridge's most memorable interiors. These bookcases, forming bays between the windows, almost certainly replaced reading desks of a type that were standard in the library rooms of the fifteenth and sixteenth centuries, with fixed seating, sloping tops and shelves below – on which lay, chained and in small piles, the College's exiguous collection of books. Some are still there: notably a copy of Anthony Andreas's *Writings on Logic* (a set-book in the University when the College was founded), which had been printed in the abbey gatehouse at St Alban's in 1483 by Wynkyn de Worde, Caxton's first apprentice. Bound in Cambridge, it bears the marks of the chain that secured it. Its chapter headings and the initial letters of each paragraph were left to be added by hand (usually in red) as they had been in manuscripts throughout the Middle Ages – a task that in this copy has never been completed. But those who planned the new College would not have envisaged the housing of the books they hoped it would acquire as the primary use of this large room; something very much smaller would have sufficed for that. Even fifty years later neither the University nor any college owned as many as two hundred books. Rather, the room was designed as the place in which the students, who would be living in shared chambers on the staircases round the cloisters, might study quietly. First and foremost a reading room, it was also the natural home for such books as the College acquired for the common use of its members.

Nearly all the references to its library in the College's early accounting records are to payments for repairs to the windows, and to blacksmiths for chains, nails and labour. For books it looked to the generosity of Fellows, former students and other benefactors. The very first bequest came, sometime after 1506, from Thomas Colier,

a scholarly resource as the common library of their college.

It was with Edmund Boldero's accession to the mastership in 1663, and as a consequence of his vigorous efforts to put the College in order again after the disruption of the Commonwealth, that the Library not only acquired its present appearance, but also rapidly expanded its collection of books, aided by the decision in 1680 to discontinue the feasts and entertainments customary when Fellow Commoners were admitted, and to require from them instead a payment of 40 shillings for the Library. (Since 1638 it had been receiving part of the sum paid by members of the College when they were presented for degrees.) One of the first acquisitions of the Boldero regime was the Library's most valuable book: the copy of John Eliot's translation of the entire Bible into Algonquian, the language of the natives of Massachusetts, printed in Cambridge, Mass. between 1661 and 1663, which the translator sent back across the Atlantic with an affectionate inscription (page 120).

The Old Library: (left) a window with Alcock's rebus and texts alluding to Medicine (*Physica*) c.1510. (below) Looking south to the entrance from the Master's Lodge.

a fellow of Michaelhouse, who left Jesus eleven books, stipulating that Fellows might borrow them for not more than three days, after which they were to be returned to the Library and immediately rechained. And one of the very largest legacies before the Interregnum came in 1603 from Lionel Ducket, who had been a Fellow since 1585 and had already made several important gifts. In addition to an eleven-volume edition of St Augustine's *Works* (Antwerp, 1576) he bequeathed 'soe many of the bookes for the Library as they can choose oute of all my bookes and whiche they have not already' – to librarians still quite the most welcome form of gift. The College chose twenty-nine. Shortly afterwards, the Bellasis brothers, Brian and Henry, who had been students at Jesus in the 1570s, gave forty law books that had belonged to their younger brother Charles and were in his study in Cambridge when he died, heavily in their debt. Fellows sometimes marked their election with the gift of a book. Thanks primarily to Lionel Gatford, who as Dean was responsible for the Library as well as the Chapel and in 1622 provided an extremely handsome Donors' Book, into which he transcribed their names, we know of about two hundred books that were given during the sixteenth century; and there were, no doubt, others. But we also know (from wills and probate inventories) of Fellows who owned as many books as any college, and sometimes more. Their private collections were shared with colleagues and pupils and must have been quite as important

To the seven medieval manuscripts, which were all that Thomas James, Sir Thomas Bodley's first librarian, found at Jesus in 1600 – among them a copy of Wycliffe's New Testament that had belonged to the puritan Archbishop Grindall when he was a fellow of Pembroke – Thomas Man, one of the earliest Rustat Scholars and a Fellow since 1676, added in January 1684/5 fifty more. Most of them had once been at Durham Cathedral Priory or some other religious house in northern England, and had been collected, it seems, either by his father (a Yorkshire man who had been curate at Helmsley and vicar of Northallerton) or himself. They include leaves from two tenth-century books; and the only surviving manuscript of Walter Daniel's life of St Aelred of Rievaulx, which was written soon after Aelred's death in 1167 and is not only one of the most moving of medieval biographies, but also a key text for the history of English monasticism. All these gifts were, however, dwarfed by that of the younger Lionel Gatford, who in 1715 as well as funding three scholarships gave over 1,600 books; they came from London in twenty-six bags. The son of the Fellow who had given the splendid Donors' Book, and now unquestionably earning his own place in it, he had been archdeacon of St Alban's and treasurer of St Paul's. His library included many continental books, not only editions of the classics, but also works of moral theology, casuistry and canon law – scholarly Anglicans would wish to keep abreast of contemporary Roman Catholic thinking and practice. Another significant bequest was of cash: £500 from Walter Gumbleton with which, in 1745, the College bought an estate at Tempsford, renaming it Library Farm and mystifying the visitor to rural Bedfordshire.

By the time Lynford Caryl became Master in 1758, Boldero's bookcases were overflowing. Caryl (page 73) was an able and energetic administrator. He had already brought some order into the affairs of the University

The opening page of the Library Donors' Book given by Lionel Gatford, Fellow and Dean, in 1622 and that recording his son's bequest of over 1,600 books in 1715.

Registry, the University Library, Addenbrooke's Hospital, and the estates and archives of Canterbury Cathedral, where he was a prebendary. The state of the College's Library concerned him and, since the College was too poor to contemplate a new building, he determined on a cull of the older editions and other books that he considered had lost their scholarly value. It was not until 1771 that he obtained the consent of the Fellows to the disposal of 708 volumes; and it was some years more before 48 incunables (books printed before 1500), over 250 sixteenth-century books and somewhat more seventeenth-century ones were actually sold. They were, of course, precisely the books that would now be most prized.

The nine-thousand-odd volumes that stand today on the shelves represent the Library as it was in the later years of the eighteenth century and early years of the nineteenth century, when Samuel Taylor Coleridge (page 130), Edward Daniel Clarke (page 134) and James Orchard Halliwell (bibliographer, lexicographer, antiquarian and Shakespearean scholar) supplemented their inadequate student incomes by serving as library clerks, making – as

When the Quincentenary Library – representing the larger part of the birthday present given to the College by its Old Members – was formally opened by the Queen in March 1996, the College at last had a working library of which it could be, and is, proud. With space (already well filled) for 50,000 books selected with the needs of undergraduates primarily in mind, and seats for over 125 readers (and a further 26 computer users in the Kwok Computer Room, which forms part of the building), books and reading areas are combined in the tradition of college libraries, rather than separated in the modern, functionalist, manner.

Gifts and bequests, of both single books and entire collections, have continued to enrich the College's two libraries. Impossible as it is to detail them all, mention must be made of one book and one collection. The book is Thomas Cranmer's copy of the 1527 edition of Erasmus's New Testament, with its parallel Greek and Latin texts, a seminal work of the Reformation, which had twice been forfeited to the Crown when its owners, first Cranmer, then Lord Lumley, were attainted of treason, only to be sold by the British Museum as a duplicate in 1812. Subsequently purchased by Arthur Gray, he bequeathed it to the College in 1940. The collection is the Malthus family library of over 2,000 books begun by (Thomas) Robert's father Daniel, and given to Jesus by one of his

(Top left) Three volumes with titles and shelf-marks on their fore-edges. Until the late seventeenth century books were commonly shelved in this way.

(Below) The War Memorial Library in the south range of First Court, 1952–95.

their subsequent careers showed – excellent use of the opportunities they had to browse freely along the shelves. Alongside substantial holdings in divinity, classics, philosophy, law and mathematics – the staple of every college library – they would have encountered a good many newer books of ancient and modern history; English topography and local history; some biography; a fair selection of works of travel and exploration; a little science; a few of the English poets, essayists and dramatists; and, perhaps a little surprisingly, a significant collection of books on the art of warfare made by John Clarke, governor of Senegambia, who had died of fever in 1778 within a few months of arriving there. These were given by his bereaved mother. The line that marked the boundary between a college library and a country-house library had begun to blur.

It was some while before the College recognised, and even longer before it began to meet, the library needs of undergraduates who were seeking Honours in the new Tripos examinations that were introduced after 1850. Eventually – prompted by a bequest from Hugh Shield KC, a Fellow who had for many years combined the roles of Bursar (the first not to be merely the Master's deputy), practising lawyer and Liberal MP for Cambridge – an undergraduate reading room (the Shield Library) was established in 1912 in a ground-floor room (believed to have been Coleridge's) on D staircase, entered from under the arch leading to Pump Court. It held only two or three thousand books, which in 1939 had to make way for the RAF and went to North House (the erstwhile Tutor's house that stood on the site of North Court). They remained there until the opening in 1952 of the War Memorial Library that had been constructed on the second (and fire-ravaged) floor of the range to the west of the Gate Tower. It was, as Nicholas Ray says (page 35), an attractive adaptation, but it soon became too small for a growing College with undergraduates confronting increasingly specialised Tripos syllabuses, and neighbouring rooms were colonised.

descendants in 1949. A good example of the kind of library that might, over the generations, be formed by the members of a cultured clerical family, it includes the copies Robert gave them of his own works – to the title page of the first, anonymous, edition of *The Essay on the Principle of Population* (1798) one of his sisters facetiously added 'Particularly addressed to Young Clergymen' – many of the books and pamphlets of his economist con-

The Quincentenary Library (1995): the second floor and (below) a bay on the first floor.

temporaries; and also two botany books, heavily annotated by J.-J. Rousseau, a gift from the annotator to Daniel Malthus, who had befriended him during his English exile. The College has, too, in recent years been given many modern finely printed books, most recently and notably, in 2006, a long run of Roxburghe Club volumes bequeathed by Philip Bradfer-Lawrence (1937).

Housed with the Malthus library, the medieval and oriental manuscripts, and these examples of fine printing, in the room adjoining the Old Library that must once have been the Master's Study, is the 'Jesuan Collection' of books (and now cassettes and CDs) by or about members of the College. It is an archive of the contributions made in print (or digital form) over the centuries by Jesuans not only to scholarship and science, but to literature, art and entertainment as well. Embedded within it are notable subcollections, such as that (almost complete) of the first printings of Coleridge's varied works, and nearly all of those of whom Stephen Heath writes in pages 138–45. It is a collection to which all members of the College are beseeched to add, and one to which it is hoped there will be no end!

Like the Archives of most colleges, Jesus's Archives house records of the College's business from the years of

Looking north from the first floor balcony. Antony Gormley's *Learning to See III* (1993) is at the head of the stairs.

its founding until the present time, though until 1618 these are solely financial accounts and documents relating to the properties it owned. A formal register was then begun:

> Because [as its first entry states] that many thinges have bene and are out of order for want of Registringe those thinges that are donne by consent in the Colledge, Bee it decreed from henceforth that there shalbe kept a contynuall Register booke, recordinge thinges with Care, and when they are donne, And hee that keepeth it, shall have such fees of such persons, as are appointed him hereunder.

There is, however, little material containing personal information about Fellows before the beginning of the nineteenth century, and until near its end almost nothing (except an admissions' register) about students, who were regarded as primarily the concern of the Tutors, not of the College itself. In the twentieth century this changed;

the Archives have become the depository for a wide variety of documents that illustrate the College's history, and many contributors to this book have drawn upon them. They include letters and diaries (notably those of Alan Pars, Percy Gardner-Smith and Freddy Brittain), albums of ephemera, the minute books of clubs and societies, and photographs. But what gives the Archives their special importance is the nine-centuries-long series of deeds relating to properties in Cambridge that belonged to the nunnery and then to the College. They are a key source for the history of the town over the last thousand years, and one which historians – following in the great F.W. Maitland's footsteps – continue to explore.

Treasures: Adventures with Art – Painting, Sculpture and other Media

ROD MENGHAM

Like many other Cambridge colleges, Jesus is well supplied with portraits of Masters, Fellows and distinguished former members, as well as with numerous watercolours and engravings of views of the College. But it is unique in the extent of its interest in modern art and especially in its commitment to contemporary sculpture. Since 1988 biennial exhibitions of sculpture have been held in the Close, and since that time the number of three-dimensional works in the permanent collection has grown steadily. It is impossible to visit the College without being made aware of its engagement with innovation and originality in the visual arts. The aesthetic experience offered by the Chapel is also an extremely rich one, ranging from the Romanesque architecture of the north transept to the pre-Raphaelite ceiling and stained glass. Its treasures are described in pages 27–37, so this one will concentrate on the secular legacy.

Probably the oldest work of art in the College is a fifteenth-century bronze sculpture from Benin, undoubtedly the most forceful of the many representations of cockerels to be found here. The earliest paintings are all portraits on wooden boards from the sixteenth century: of Bishop Alcock, of Henry VIII, of Thomas Cranmer and of Mary, Queen of Scots. Alcock (page 15) looks oddly diminutive when compared to Henry and Cranmer, although his painting is roughly twice the size of theirs; his recessed figure occupies a relatively small space at the centre of his 3 foot by 2 foot rectangle; while Henry's head and shoulders push straight out at the viewer, and the top half of Cranmer (page 95) is seen at a slightly oblique angle, the painter taking care to include both arms so that they can form a lectern for the all-important prayer-book. Alcock's portrait, painted for the College in 1598 at a cost of 26s 8d, was almost certainly copied from an image in the stained glass of the Chapel, which was still there in 1632. It might be wondered what Mary Stuart is doing in this company, and in a town that sup-

ported Parliament rather than the King during the Civil War. The implicit question is not easily answered. The painting is a copy of a lost original by François Clouet, and is one of a well-known series of *deuil blanc* (white mourning) images of the Queen. Until recently, the surface was disfigured with swathes of nineteenth-century overpainting that coarsened the portraiture. An interesting label on the back, affixed by the Fitzwilliam Museum in 1914 to replace an earlier inscription by E.D. Clarke (d. 1822; page 134), records the discovery of the painting

The bronze cockerel from Benin, given by G.W. Neville (the father of a Jesuan) who was a member of the British punitive expedition to the city in 1897 and a founder of the Bank of British West Africa.

by 'Mr. Kenrick … in an outhouse'. This is particularly intriguing; on Mary's death, her son James I commissioned a copy of the Clouet to hang over her first tomb in Peterborough Cathedral. It went missing when Cromwell's troops sacked the building. Perhaps an outhouse in Cambridgeshire would be the most likely place for it to resurface. Restoration has shed no light on this possibility, but it has revealed a much cleaner composition, with simple but decisive brushwork and a great deal of personality in the animated and curiously knowing expression in the subject's face.

More or less contemporary with these small formal portraits from northern Europe is our largest painting, the immensely dramatic *Last Supper*, usually attributed to the Bassano family (page 57). Keir Smith, an artist who has exhibited twice at the College, accounts for the dynamism in the following way: 'Christ has just told his disciples that one of them will betray him. This revelation is the cause of the violent gestures on the part of some of the protagonists. The subject is regarded as a dramatic prelude to the Passion rather than a reflection on the Mass.' The painting only really came to life after its recent restoration, which transformed an expanse of muddy varnish into a vivid array of Venetian colour. It also revealed details reminiscent of Tintoretto's versions of the same subject, but although the composition seems indebted to him, the style has been compared variously to that of the elder Bassano, of Bonifazio de' Pitati (Bassano's teacher), of Jacopo Palma il Giovane and several other minor painters from Venice and the Veneto.

Many of the most interesting paintings purchased, cleaned or retrieved from obscurity in the last few years have been anonymous or uncertain in attribution. A striking example is the seventeenth-century portrait of Sir John Bramston, Chief Justice of the King's Bench under Charles I, which may or may not be by Cornelius Johnson (page 24). The painting dwells on his copious robes of office, redolent of status and authority, but the chief interest lies in the sitter's probing and unquiet gaze. Another painting of a seventeenth-century subject, even finer than the complex representation of Bramston, is a portrait of Jacob Trip, the rich Dordrecht merchant portrayed by all the most important Dutch artists of his day. Our painting is a copy of the famous original executed in 1660 by Nicolas Maes. This is one of Maes's most Rembrandtesque works, both in technique and composition, with head and hands highlighted against a generally dark background. The seated Trip does not appear completely at rest, his attitude expressing alertness, energy and determination – as well as a freshness and openness unlooked for in one of his years.

With the turn of the eighteenth century, the College collection becomes much more diverse in genre. The bulk

of the paintings and engravings from these years are portraits, with an increasing number of views of the College buildings and grounds. But there is a masterly treatment in oils of *The Presentation in the Temple* by Jean-Baptiste Jouvenet (given in 1796 to serve as an altarpiece in the Chapel); several Dutch genre scenes, full of incident and cultural historical information; and a charming evocation by Francis Hayman of a performance of Milton's *Comus*. Relatively primitive in style but still very attractive is the earliest oil painting of a bird's-eye view of the College. This large canvas, based on an engraving by Johannes Kipp, seems to zoom in on the College from the south; the buildings are seen quite close up and from a fairly steep angle, as if from the spire of All Saints' Church (which had not yet been built). The background is especially

The Presentation in the Temple

J.-B. Jouvenet, c.1700

impressive – there is an imposing range of hills to the north-north-east, precisely where the Fens should be!

Among many eighteenth- and nineteenth-century portraits that dominate the public rooms in College, two of the most interesting subjects are the major literary figures Laurence Sterne and Samuel Taylor Coleridge. We possess several images of both. Perhaps the most appealing version of Coleridge is James Northcote's canvas of 1802 (page 131), showing a relatively youthful poet with a compassionate face that is decidedly abstracted, as if his imagination is held by some inner vision that dilates the pupils, even though these are looking away from the source of natural light. The most authoritative portrait of Sterne was Sir Joshua Reynolds's commission in 1760. This is now in the National Portrait Gallery, but we possess a good copy that reproduces the quizzical, transfixing gaze of Reynolds's sitter (page 141). Sterne is seen with a

sheaf of papers, the manuscript of his novel *Tristram Shandy*, under his right elbow, while his right hand supports his head. This is turned towards the viewer with the ghost of a smile that seems like a mixture of indulgence and contempt. But the most well-known image of Sterne – possibly the best-known image in the collection – is Thomas Patch's cartoon *Sterne and Death*, often used on the covers of paperback editions of *Tristram Shandy*. A cadaverous Sterne is seen bowing towards the Grim Reaper as if he were an accomplice in some practical joke; the gloomy wit of this little study in oils corresponds perfectly to Sterne's own acerbic regrets over the physical unreliability of human existence. There was to be a macabre echo of the painting's black humour after Sterne's own death, when his body was spirited away by grave robbers but saved from dissection by the author's great celebrity. He was recognised when already on the slab and secretly reburied.

The mordant humour of this small painting is a scarce commodity in the collection as a whole, although it is more or less contemporary with a watercolour sheet by Thomas Rowlandson showing mischievous caricatures of seven corpulent figures in varying degrees of indignity or insouciance. A light touch is conspicuous by its absence from the nineteenth-century canvases, and is not to be expected in the gallery of worthies they comprise. However, the twentieth-century holdings include a number of portraits that show *brio* and idiosyncrasy. Among the most distinguished are three works by William Nicholson: *Arthur Gray* (1937), *J.C. Watt* (1924) and *Sir Arthur Quiller-Couch* (1934) (pages 26, 108, 142). The first of these conveys an electric vitality, while the third, with its palette of pinks and ochres, is truly innovative. The portrait of Quiller-Couch, known as 'Q', has its whimsical side as well: 'Q' was a Rooster, a member of the debating society that commissioned the painting, and the infusion of redness may allude to this. Nicholson knew about the Roosters – he was elected a member himself, although not a Jesuan – and designed a gown covered in red herrings for the Grand Marshal of the Roost. 'Q' is depicted in his 'Q-bicle' on C staircase, with its wine-coloured walls, wearing distinctly non-academic, and even dandified, dress. Among recent portraits, the most arresting are Maggi Hambling's thickly textured study of Colin Renfrew and Louise Riley-Smith's contemplation of David Crighton. Although in repose, the figure of Lord Renfrew has been painted with a very active brush and a generous range of colours. The ripples of energy that seem to travel across the canvas portray brilliantly an ebullient and many-sided intelligence. Congeniality is the keynote in Louise Riley-Smith's presentation of David Crighton, who seems as much at home in his painting as he was in the company of members of the College.

Joie de Vivre
John Bellany, 1989

It is with the more contemporary of our works of art that a full range of subject matters and styles is reached, including several very ambitious paintings, in both figurative and abstract traditions. At the figurative end is John Bellany's *Joie de Vivre*, a still life whose title hints at its comprehensive subversion of the *nature morte* tradition; its cut flowers are alive and kicking, barely contained by the frame of the painting, let alone by the vessel in which they are placed. Its fulminating colours provide an effective contrast with the mostly unmixed palette of Albert Irvin's *Sandymount II*, perhaps the most dynamic abstract in the collection. This urgently layered work is like the snapshot of an irresistible process. Great horizontal flows of pigment are superimposed and transected by meteoric diagonals, improvised geometrical shapes and flying particles of colour that have escaped the design. The whole is a kind of painterly monument to sudden moves. Much closer to conceptual art, and incorporating both figurative and abstract elements, is Richard Long's *River Avon Mud Hand Circles*, a permanent wall-work created for the

The Sculpture Studio

Lithograph by Sir Eduardo Paolozzi,
1997

Quincentenary and which now dominates the Upper Hall. This circular arrangement of handprints not only recalls the prehistoric stone circles that Long's work often alludes to; it is also an amplified version of the earliest known form of self-expression, the 'signatures' of the Palaeolithic artists who stencilled the outlines of their hands directly on to their cave walls.

There is a powerfully archaic character also to Elisabeth Frink's *Blue Head*, *Grey Head* and *Red Head*, which hang suggestively on the wall opposite Long's great tattoo. These folkloric motifs belong with the iconography of the Green Man; the tendrils emerging from the three mouths echo the foliage carved into the beams of Upper Hall. The Frinks are part of a distinguished collection of screenprints that has grown in stages, decisively at three key moments: with the accession of thirty-two screenprints and lithographs by Eduardo Paolozzi, with the commissioning of the Quincentenary Portfolio in 1996, and with the donation of the Capital Prints collection in 2005. Paolozzi – whose sculptures *Daedalus on Wheels* and *Newton* are also here – first exhibited in 'Sculpture in the Close' in 1994, and enjoyed a close relationship with the College until his death in 2005. The Quincentenary Portfolio consisted of works commissioned from ten artists who had also had links with Jesus, mostly through 'Sculpture in the Close': John Bellany, John McLean, Albert Irvin, Eduardo Paolozzi, David Mach, Richard Long, Kim Lim, John Hoyland, Barry Flanagan and William Turnbull. This extraordinary canon of important contemporary artists was extended with the anonymous donation of almost the entire output of Capital Prints, the leading print-makers founded by old member Martin Village. An exhibition of this gift in Chapel in March 2006 included characteristic works by Peter Blake, Stephen Chambers, Eileen Cooper, Amanda Faulkner, Terry Frost, Richard Hamilton, Tom Hammick, John Hoyland, Jock McFadyen, Bruce McLean, Brendan Neiland and Marcus Vergette. It also featured the more traditionalist etchings of Andrew Ingamells, as well as the original ink drawing for his etching of the College, a clever updating of perhaps the most famous view of all, engraved by David Loggan, *c.*1690 (page 31).

But the most palpable evidence for the College's adventures with modern art is found in the rich diversity

statue of Marcus Aurelius on the Capitoline Hill – with the vital difference that Flanagan's horse has no rider, changing it from an expression of imperial control to a celebration of natural grace. Equally reticent is Antony Gormley's human figure in the Quincentenary Library (page 49), one of many sculptures by this artist using casts of his own body, in hieratic poses that recall the origins of monumental statuary in Egypt and Archaic Greece. The yardstick for this tradition, the Egyptian cubit, was derived from the proportions of the human body, referring specifically to the length of the forearm between the elbow and the tip of the middle finger. Gormley's work represents an important strand in British sculpture concerned to maintain the link with this perception of the body as point of origin for the scale of significance we are most comfortable with. The title, *Learning to See*, suggests the extent to which our visual appraisal of our surroundings is governed by an awareness of our own corporeality. Another work with seemingly deep historical roots is William Turnbull's *Head*, a convex lozenge with the least possible suggestion of human features, stylised in a way that pays homage to the prototypes of Cycladic art.

Most of the sculptures at Jesus are not figurative, and they date from 1963 to 2005. Among the earliest are three works by Geoffrey Clarke, *Battersea II*, *Battersea III* (page 43) and *Call It Hadrian's Wall*, which pioneered the development of an aluminium-casting process whose incidental benefit was the appearance it presented of a metal surface that had somehow been directly carved. Each work from the 'Battersea' group resembles a large artillery piece that has been abandoned and has mutated into a unique shape and function, the twentieth-century equivalent, perhaps, of a sword beaten into a ploughshare. Almost contemporary is Phillip King's 1996 work, *Brake* (page 37), a boldly minimalist construction that reflects a keen interest in 'primary structures'. With an extreme economy of means, King lays bare the most basic of artistic choices involved in joining and separating materials, reducing the creative process to a restricted number of fundamental decisions which he performs with absolute finality. The bold simplicity of this design is echoed in Diane Maclean's towering steel *Spine*, whose reserved intensity both complements and contrasts with the organic verticals of the trees that surround it, while the nearby glass sculpture *Empress*, by Danny Lane, has a curious solidity that seems to have been achieved as much in defiance of the properties of glass as in fulfilment of them. The unevenly finished edges and stratifications refract the light that often makes a vacancy of glass in public, transferring into visual form the instability that the physical tension of his sculptures keeps triumphantly at bay.

The Fellows' Garden is the setting for a group of three works that exemplify the genuine diversity of ways

of sculpture housed in the Quincentenary Library and throughout the Close. Apart from *Mortal Man* by Evelyn Herring, this range of works in bronze, steel, glass, concrete, aluminium and maple wood is the legacy of the series of exhibitions of sculpture inaugurated in 1988. Although these biennial events celebrating the scope of British carving, casting and fabricating have always involved collaboration on the part of all members of the Works of Art Committee, there is no doubt in anyone's mind that the inspirational chief mover has been Colin Renfrew; or that the exhibitions would simply not have happened without the unflappable Bill Stronge, curator for the first seven exhibitions, or the ever-resourceful Jim Roseblade, mastermind of all the openings. Such has been the success of this phase of the College's involvement with art that the iconic postcard shot of the place is now that of the bronze horse in First Court; this is a restrained work by Barry Flanagan's usual standards (also in College is his gigantically whimsical *Cricketing Hare*, a very generous gift by the artist himself) (page 194). The sculpture of the horse evokes comparisons with the most definitive works in the genre, especially the equestrian

(Left) Empress

Danny Lane, *c.*2001

(Below) Bronze head

William Turnbull, *c.*1990

San Marco Horse

Barry Flanagan, 1983

in which contemporary sculpture is conceived of and fashioned. Richard Bray's *Maple Three Piece* represents a tradition of carving that bends towards the highly specific demands of the material being worked as much as towards the artist's guiding intentions. Cornelia Parker's *Moon Landing* is a radically conceptual project, the visual evidence for which is a small plaque that refers to the landing of a meteorite in the Fellows' Garden: 'here in this garden / on the night of the full moon / a lunar meteorite fell / and was lost'. The inscription we read is like a museum label informing us that the object we seek has been removed. Generic similarity between this plaque and others we have encountered (shape, design and lettering recall the inscriptions of the National Trust) provoke questions about the extent to which these deploy a house-style of interpretation that displaces the object of scrutiny instead of retrieving it. What Parker is doing is illuminating the way we attempt to fix the meaning and control the approaches to a work of art. Alison Wilding's *Melancholia*, the gift of an anonymous donor, is the most site-specific work in College, having been designed for the location where it remains, in the penumbra of the great plane tree and its cycles of growth and decay. In the Middle Ages and the Renaissance, melancholy was often

associated with scholarship, although as one of the four 'humours' it was also an essential component of the human character. The ashen hues of this concrete and terracotta assemblage also suggest the problematic link between the unresolved state of melancholia and the closure of mourning. Just as the circular and foliate shapes of the sculpture seem to suspend it between the figurative and the abstract, so its replacement of colour with whites and greys suggest its incomplete detachment from a set of naturally occurring conditions whose loss it cannot finally come to terms with.

At any one time, the College is well stocked with sculpture, although many of the works on view are here on long-term loan and may depart. Their presence reflects the extraordinary generosity of the many artists whose support we continue to enjoy. They have helped to ensure that the College is now well known for its collection and for its loyalty towards the visual arts. Literally hundreds of sculptural objects by over forty artists have been installed here during successive exhibitions. The works come and go, and the rhythm of their arrivals and departures reflects one of the best qualities of Jesus, its openness to new ideas, to different sensibilities, to the challenges of the life of the mind and the adventures of the imagination.

self were in danger. Word was sent to H.A. Morgan, the Jesus Tutor. He hurried to the scene, confronted the crowd from the steps of the house, and told them they should be ashamed of themselves, frightening women and children. Then he pulled out his watch and said that for three minutes he would be blind, after which time he would recover his sight. Morgan was immensely popular and the crowd broke into cheers for the Tutor of Jesus. They dispersed peaceably and, to judge by the epergnes, to the Mayor's immense relief.

Not all the stories end so happily. It was recently discovered that Joseph Raphson, originator of the Newton–Raphson algebraic theorem known to all mathematicians (and others), who was admitted as Fellow Commoner in 1692 when he received his degree by royal mandate, had given the College a substantial silver monteith (a large ornate bowl or vessel for cooling wine) in that year, which, alas, we no longer have. It may well have been lost in the burgling of the silver room described by Rachel Wroth (page 175).

There are just a few sixteenth- and seventeenth-century items remaining today, among them a pair of large flagons and a chalice with tazza, all given for the Chapel by Edmund Boldero in 1676 with the help, it seems, of another great benefactor of the College, Tobias Rustat (page 22). These particular items are relatively common and functional, whereas the two items shown here are a combination of the rare and the beautiful.

The beaker is an unrecorded donation and a remark-

(Top) Argyle, London, 1779.

(Below) Porringer, London, 1682.

(Below left) Beaker, London, 1692.

able example of seventeenth-century workmanship (London, 1692, maker's mark TC with fish) in terms of its size, shape and – more difficult to quantify – the way it feels when held. The pieces in the College's collection are used as much as possible, so if you lunch at High Table there is a chance of being served your chilled ale in this beaker. The second item is a very unusual porringer (London, 1682, maker unknown: IA+star) with acorn finial that was given by Lord Justice Luxmoore in 1942. This design has been featured in many different silver books, however no other piece bears the very ornate and unusual

chasing of birds and leaves which appears on this one. The decoration is definitely of the period of the piece – there seems to be a Middle Eastern styling in the artwork. It is a unique item and a very stylish way to serve one's porridge.

Most of the collection consists, as might be expected, of pieces from the eighteenth and nineteenth centuries, many hailing from the very prolific period in English silverware, 1750–1800. Significant London makers, such as Paul Storr (a pair of side dishes), John Le Café (twelve resplendent candlesticks), Hester Bateman and George Adams, are well represented.

Many different styles and functions are present: sugar casters, soup tureens and candlesticks as well as another very desirable epergne. Most of these items are fairly utilitarian in nature. One of the more unusual is the argyle (London, 1779, possibly John Rowe), donated by Richard Tylden, intended for pouring single cups of tea or coffee.

(Above) Telescopic Candlestick, Sheffield, 1805.

(Top right and right) Ewer and Rosewater Bowl, London, 1977 (with reflections of the Combination Room).

Jackson (1948) and Emma Thomson (1969). Illustrated are two remarkable twentieth-century pieces. The ewer and rose water bowl is a Jubilee piece from 1977, created specially for the College and funded from the bequests of five old members: C.C. Garbett (1900), T.E. Morell (1912), C.E. Newham (1912), J.S. Sedgwick (1895) and T.H.C. Ottley (1909), with a further donation from the then Master, Sir Alan Cottrell. The ewer has been designed to fit snugly into the rose water bowl to give the illusion of a single piece. The hallmarks bear the Queen's head as 1977 was her Silver Jubilee year and the maker's mark of Mrs G.E.P. How (contained within a lozenge, denoting the work of a widow). The second piece is a sugar bowl given in 2000 by the Jesus College Cambridge Society (JCCS). It bears a cockerel motif and was made by Sarah Jones. It is accompanied by an unusual blue-green glass bowl and is a good example of the skill of the modern silversmith.

Its handle has been placed on the side so that it can be left in front of a fire to keep warm. The candlestick on the far left (one of a pair, Sheffield, 1805, Thomas Law) had seemed an unremarkable object until the plate audit of 2003, when the valuer pointed out that it was in fact a very early and very rare telescopic candlestick (here shown newly extended).

There is a modest quantity of twentieth-century plate in the collection, most of it donated by Clara Foakes

The full collection set out for the 2006 plate audit is shown below. For some pieces the audit is their only outing for the year, so it has become a regular part of the College's calendar, with Fellows viewing it before, during and after lunching. The splendour of the display seen here, along with the security, upkeep and maintenance of the more functional items used on a daily basis on the High Table, is testimony to the tireless efforts of the Butler, David Cockram. His enthusiasm and dedication to the plate collection follows a long tradition; no one could be doing more to ensure that it survives another five hundred years.

(Top left) Sugar bowl, London, 2000.

(Left) The plate audit, 2006.

Images of the College: Prints

STEPHEN TAYLOR

Between the end of the Second World War and the mid-1980s it was common for a certain sort of undergraduate to buy prints of the College as presents for friends and mementoes for themselves. Depending on pocket and preference, they would purchase, often from Jean Pain's bookshop and gallery in Trinity Street, copperplate prints by Le Keux and Harraden, though Ackermann's delicate aquatints were the preference of the more discerning who could afford them. Loggan's view of the College was perhaps too austere and too uncommon, as well as too expensive, to be a frequent purchase.

The prints of Ackermann, Harraden and Le Keux, which all date from the early nineteenth century, must now decorate the walls of hundreds of alumni. But what

do they tell us about the history of Jesus? Most obviously, they provide valuable information about the development of the College's buildings, though that is not what this chapter is about. Nor is it a contribution to the history of print-making. Rather it is an attempt to sketch what we might call a social history of the prints of the College. The history of English topographical prints is largely unwritten: it is often forgotten that they are themselves artefacts, that there is a story to be told about why and for whom they were created, and how they were used and displayed.

The earliest print of Jesus is also one of the most exceptional, whether judged in terms of quality, accuracy or perspective: David Loggan's engraving of 1690 (page 31), which appeared as one of twenty-eight engraved views of Cambridge and its colleges in his *Cantabrigia Illustrata* (1690). Like most of his engravings of Oxford and Cambridge colleges, it provides a bird's-eye view of the College, a perspective that was common in many early prints of country houses and the buildings of London, but was not to be repeated for Jesus until Andrew Ingamells issued his engraving in 2003. The reasons for the production of Loggan's two series of views of Oxford and Cambridge are unclear. *Cantabrigia Illustrata*, which was fifteen years in the making, almost certainly had its origins in a desire on the part of the University to emulate its rival – or, at least, from Loggan's belief that he could persuade its members that they wanted to do so. The support for the earlier project – *Oxonia Illustrata* was published in 1675 – probably stemmed from a desire to celebrate the antiquity and significance of the universities, both as institutions of education and nurseries for the Church of England, in the context of the restoration of both Church and monarchy following the years of civil war and republic. At Oxford, certainly, Loggan's work was frequently presented to distinguished visitors to the University, often

'Le College de Jesus'

Engraving after Loggan for *Les delices de La Grande Bretagne*, P. van der Aa, Amsterdam, 1707

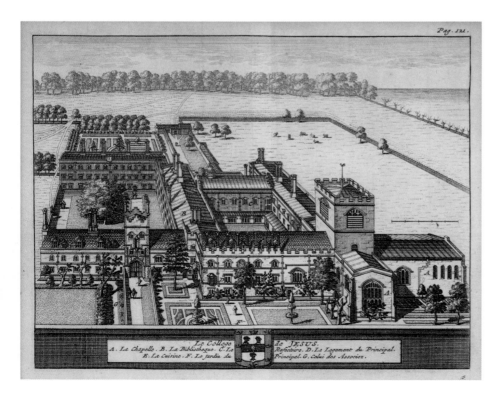

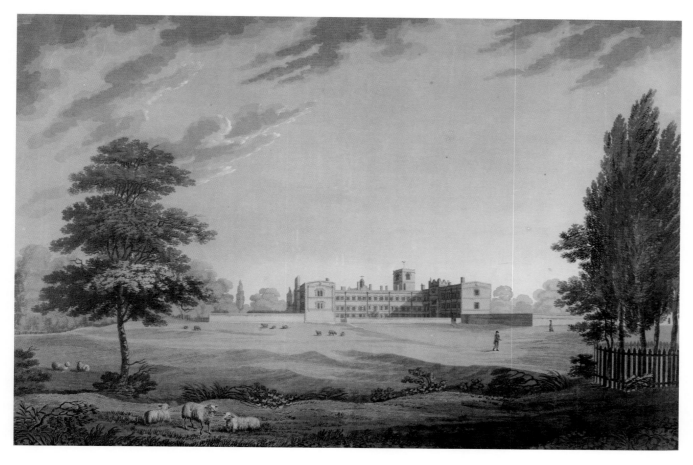

together with Anthony à Wood's *Historia et Antiquitates Universitatis Oxoniensis.*

Loggan's prints had an interesting afterlife. A new edition of *Cantabrigia Illustrata* was published in 1716 but, before that, in 1707 there appeared under the imprint of the Dutch publisher Pieter van der Aa *Les delices de la Grande Bretagne.* Even by the standards of the vibrant Dutch print trade of this period, van der Aa was a remarkable figure, producing dozens of illustrated works containing literally thousands of maps and plates. *Les delices,* in nine volumes with a text by James Beeverell, was typical of a genre that was popular at the beginning of the eighteenth century – lavishly illustrated accounts of the countries of Europe. Van der Aa himself published another set about Spain and Portugal but, while he was highly productive, he made little claim to originality as most of his prints and maps were copied from others. The illustrations for Oxford and Cambridge in *Les delices* were, predictably, copied without acknowledgement from Loggan, though they are much smaller, measuring barely 6 inches by 5. Van der Aa's purpose, however, was very different from Loggan's. In effect, he was producing a guide book in which text and pictures were equally important. It was not quite the eighteenth-century precursor of Baedeker; while it was small enough to be portable, it is hardly conceivable that there were enough continental travellers to Britain to make publication com-

mercially viable. Van der Aa should be taken at his word when he claims that his aim was to please 'les personnes curieuses', the ever-increasing community of educated Europeans anxious to inform themselves about the architecture, manners and character of other countries. Thus, through these pirated images, Loggan's views of Jesus and other Oxbridge colleges determined how they were seen throughout Europe in the eighteenth century.

Remarkably, however, after the publications of Loggan and van der Aa, no prints of Jesus appeared for almost a century. Then, over a period of fifty years beginning in the last decade of the eighteenth century, a group of prints was produced which, collectively, established the image of the College that most readily comes to mind when we imagine what it looked like before the twentieth century. It is, in fact, possible to identify two rather different developments, occurring simultaneously, though both may be said to have their roots in the work of Loggan.

First, picking up on the tradition represented by van der Aa, Richard Harraden – a London print-maker who had just moved to Cambridge – published a series of prints of the town in 1798. He produced thirty-one aquatints in two groups: one of seven folio views, including one of Jesus from the Close; and a second of twenty-four octavo views, among which Jesus does not appear. The collection as a whole was aimed explicitly at the tourist market. Accompanying the prints, but sold separately

**From the road to Barnwell,
Cambridge Almanack, 1805.**

From Jesus Green

Aquatint by W. Westall and J. Stadler

for R. Ackermann's *History of the*

University of Cambridge (1815)

JESUS COLLEGE.
THE ENTRANCE GATEWAY
1842.

The Gate Tower

Engraved by J. Le Keux after

F. Mackenzie, 1842

under various titles, was a text which provided a guide for the visitor to Cambridge. The seven large views corresponded to the seven stages of a 'cursory Tour' for the traveller who had only a short time to spare; the twenty-four views, together with the text, provided a description for 'those who are desirous of taking a narrow and close survey of the University'. It is easy to imagine the large views being framed and hung together, perhaps on a staircase, and the smaller ones being kept in a portfolio or perhaps pasted on to a screen or wall. They were priced to suit a variety of pockets, starting at 2 shillings for a single octavo view, a small sum for any of the middle and upper classes who could afford to take tours around the country, and rising to 2 guineas (£2 2s) for a complete set of either the small or the large views.

Other prints were produced for tourists seeking mementoes of their time in Cambridge, and perhaps also for college residents who wanted to add interest to the walls of their rooms. By the 1830s a wide variety was available. At the top end of the market were the folio engravings produced for the *Cambridge Almanack*. Two featured Jesus: in 1805 a view from the unusual perspective of the

road to Barnwell was published, followed in 1850 by one of the interior of the newly restored Chapel. Copies of these prints were also struck off separately, presumably for sale. The cheaper end of the market is illustrated by a small volume, about the dimensions of a postcard, preserved in the University Library and published in Cambridge by W.P. Grant, probably in the 1830s. It contains a series of thirty-two small plates, many of them copies of engravings by R.B. Harraden. The view of Jesus – as so often, there is only one – is from Jesus Lane, looking at the east end of the Chapel. Of particular interest in this context, therefore, is the work of James and Henry Sargant Storer, who published some ninety engravings of Cambridge in four series between 1827 and 1837, including five views of Jesus.

Secondly, prints were also produced to illustrate histories of Cambridge and its colleges. These works owed something to Loggan's original conception, but much more, perhaps, to the tradition of antiquarian scholarship which had generated many lavish county histories in the second half of the eighteenth century. They were prestigious and expensive works, including detailed accounts of the

colleges – their foundation, their endowments, their alumni and their paintings. The prints were intended to illustrate the text rather than to be cut out and displayed separately – the disembowelment of these volumes was the work of twentieth-century print-sellers, not of contemporaries.

The first of these late-Georgian 'coffee-table' books, *Cantabrigia Depicta*, was published by Richard Harraden in 1809 and illustrated with engravings from drawings by his son Richard Bankes Harraden. It contained the first view of Jesus from the Chimney entrance, described as 'a grand gate'. It was followed six years later by Rudolph Ackermann's *History of the University of Cambridge*, dedicated, like Harraden's work, to the Chancellor, the Duke of Gloucester. This was an opulent work, a testimony to the high quality of British printing: Ackermann's coloured aquatints skilfully create the impression of watercolours, the then-favoured medium for much landscape painting. But it was also a serious work, offering one of the fullest accounts of the University then available – the description of Jesus alone extends to forty-four pages and is illustrated with three plates: a view from the north-west, the ante-chapel (page 84) and a portrait of John Alcock. Of almost equal importance for its text was John Le Keux's *Memorials of Cambridge*. Publication began in parts in 1837, and then the whole work appeared in two volumes in 1841–2, containing well over a hundred illustrations in

a combination of engravings and woodcuts. The prints are smaller than those of Harraden and Ackermann, but the two copperplates of Jesus – the Chimney entrance and a general view from the meadows – are among the most iconic images of the College in the nineteenth century, if only because they were reprinted so frequently. Both Cooper's *Memorials of Cambridge* (1860) and Atkinson and Clark's *Cambridge Described and Illustrated* (1897) are illustrated with Le Keux's engravings.

One puzzle remains: why were no views of Cambridge produced for most of the eighteenth century? Why, indeed, are so few produced of anywhere in Cambridge?

Loggan was, without doubt, exceptional, not only for the quality of his work but also as an English print-maker (although he was, in fact, a native of Danzig). Many of the best English prints of the late seventeenth and early eighteenth centuries were imported, from Holland in particular. But by the 1740s the domestic print trade was well established and the market for topographical prints was taking off rapidly. Many views were produced of country houses, of the villas, gardens and sites of the Thames Valley, and of the pleasure gardens, churches and royal palaces and parks of London. So why was Cambridge neglected?

Part of the explanation is that there was little demand for prints of Cambridge. Many prints of country houses were paid for by the owners, anxious to demonstrate their wealth and status. But the market was also created by

JESUS COLLEGE.

Drawn by R.B. Harraden Junr.

Etched by Elizabeth Byrne.

(Left) The Gate Tower and Master's Lodge and (below) First Court

R.B. Harraden, junior, engraved by Elizabeth Byrne, *c.*1850

domestic tourism: visitors to country houses and other sites wanted souvenirs of their trips. There are more prints of eighteenth-century Oxford than of Cambridge because Oxford was on the Thames Valley tourist route, which extended as far as Blenheim Palace. Relatively few travellers, by contrast, ventured into East Anglia.

By the end of the eighteenth century, however, this situation was beginning to change. Travelling became easier as roads were improved. But we can also detect signs of a shifting aesthetic. The predominantly medieval buildings of Cambridge were coming to be regarded as 'picturesque', a point made explicitly by the Harradens in the titles of their works. The emphasis in all the publications of the first half of the nineteenth century is as much on 'views' or, in the words of Harraden senior, on 'the many pleasing Scenes with which Cambridge abounds', as on architectural detail. Jesus was singled out for comment in a way which highlights this new sensibility: 'The scenery of this College … is marked by an air of calm retirement to many minds far more interesting, than the proud display of studied avenues and splendid structures.'

The period between the 1790s and the 1840s represents the high point of the print in Cambridge. Thereafter, it was replaced by the photograph both in the illustration of books and in the tourist market. The coming of the

JESUS COLLEGE.
THE FIRST COURT.

railway was accompanied by the beginning of the mass production of photographic images which could be sold to the new tour groups. The popular *cartes de visite*, small images only 4 by 2½ inches, were sold in large numbers in the 1860s and 1870s, allowing new views of the College to be collected, as the illustration of the Waterhouse building, produced by Stearn of Bridge Street, reveals. By the early twentieth century postcards provided cheap souvenirs for the ever-increasing number of tourists. And photographs also emerged as the preferred format for illustrating books about Cambridge, whether glossy volumes for visitors or accounts of college architecture.

Prints have, nonetheless, continued to play a part in creating the image of the College through the twentieth century. Reproductions of W.G. Blackall's drawings, for example, including the gate at Jesus, illustrate *The Charm of Cambridge* (1927). Revealingly, S.C. Roberts candidly admits in his preface that the justification for the volume

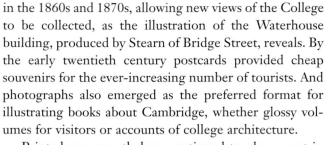

(Top right) The Gate Tower
Lithograph by John Fuller, 1960

(Right) Waterhouse building
carte de visite c.1875.

(Facing page)
Chapel: nave ceiling designed by William Morris, painted by Leach, 1867. The angels display the verses of the hymn, *Vexilla regis prodeunt*, written for St Radegund by Venantius Fortunatus.

lies in the drawings rather than in his own derivative text. The same point can be made of other books. But the twentieth century also witnessed the revival of the print as a work of art, intended for collection and display. The etchings of Arthur L. Cherry or Sydney Jones and John Fuller's lithographs, for example, were produced for galleries and collectors, among whom alumni are doubtless prominent. Most are within a tradition of English landscape painting that is intrinsically conservative – it is rare to detect even the modern topographical style of John Piper. In the late nineteenth century Robert Willis

commented on the enormous significance of the printmakers from Loggan to Le Keux for the architectural historian. That, however, is only part of the story. In an era when literally hundreds of images of the College are easily available, no print – not even Ingamells' remarkable architectural depiction of the modern College (reproduced on this book's endpapers) – can hope to rival the iconic power of those early images. For many people it is the prints of Loggan, Harraden and Le Keux that define what the College *was*.

College Heraldry

COLIN MUMFORD and PETER GLAZEBROOK

As a former Master, Arthur Gray, observed: 'In an ancient seat of learning heraldic emblems should be historic and accurate.' He regretted that many of those adorning the College's buildings (and, he might have added, much of its stationery and crockery) are neither. Nor are the arms granted the College in 1575 – let alone their irregular variants – those it had originally adopted. These had shown the Five Wounds of Jesus displayed in the customary medieval way. They are to be found at the foot of the College's ancient, and still used, seal, which is dominated by the figures of Christ,

the Virgin Mary and St John. The mitre and cocks' heads of Bishop Alcock are conspicuously absent.

By 1575, however, when the College, in common with others, applied to the College of Arms for a formal grant of arms, puritan winds were blowing through Cambridge and symbols of medieval Catholic piety were something of an embarrassment. So what Robert Cooke, Clarenceux King of Arms, provided for the College was a shield with Alcock's personal arms (minus the mitre on the cross-band, since it was not the College that was a bishop) bordered by ten (no more and no less) crowns, symbols of the see of Ely whose cathedral church had been founded by the saintly Queen Etheldreda. These new College arms were topped by Cooke with a crest showing a full-bodied black cock with red comb and wattles (not just a head) emerging from a golden crown, the latter a reference, perhaps, to Henry VII and his Letters Patent. This whole ensemble is now best seen at the Morgan gate, erected during Gray's mastership, at the College's Victoria Avenue entrance.

Gray also ensured that the Five Wounds of Jesus were again to be seen in the College – over the archway from Chapel into Pump Court (his own arms are on the other side) – and that the arms that are displayed of his predecessor, H.A. Morgan, and of the Visitor (Bishop White-Thompson) carved by Eric Gill (page 36) which have given the Angel Gate its name, were heraldically impeccable. Also impeccable, of course, are the striking arms and crest of a later Master, Lord Renfrew (page 154), with their references to his career as a prehistoric archaeologist; they are to be seen in a window lighting the screens' passage into Hall. But the attractive late nineteenth-century glass in the beautiful oriel window at the north end of High Table and the magnificent ceiling over the nave of the Chapel (both designed by William Morris) are to be admired for their artistic rather than their historic or heraldic merit.

Grant of Arms, 1575.

(Left) The Brittainic
Cockerel Collection.

(Below) The College seal,
c.1520.

Mottoes are, strictly speaking, not part of a heraldic coat of arms and may be adopted and varied at will, while heraldic arms must be distinguished from heraldic badges which may be, and often have been, freely used as proprietary symbols to indicate the ownership of moveable property and the builders of buildings. The motto *Prosperum iter facias* (May your journey be successful), derived from a verse in Psalm 68, which appears on a scroll across the cock above the archway from First Court into the Cloisters, and on the Victoria Avenue gates (and elsewhere), is to be read as a simple expression of good wishes to those entering and leaving the College. And the verse from Psalm 133, *Ecce quam bonum et quam jucundum fratres habitare in unum* (Behold how good and joyful a thing it is, brethren, to dwell together in unity), inscribed in 1935 on the panel under Queen Anne's 1702 arms over the High Table (and the source of Lord Renfrew's motto *Quam iucundum*) is equally appropriate to its position.

Bishop Alcock's heraldic badge, a good example of the pictorial puns widely indulged in during the late fifteenth and early sixteenth centuries, of a cock perched on an orb, the cock of all – Alcock – is for most Jesuans their College's most enduring symbol. It makes appearances innumerable: on the Gate Tower, at the entrance to the Kitchens, in the windows of the Old Library (page 45) and the Hall, and in the Chapel, culminating in that most extraordinary of roosts, the Brittainic Collection of Cockerels – hundreds of them, of all sizes, materials and provenances – a sight for many sore Jesuan eyes.

College Finance – Estates, Investments and Earned Income

STEPHEN BARTON

THE SOURCES OF THE COLLEGE'S INCOME

Nowadays, the College's income has three main sources. First, the charges it levies for the services it provides – fees payable by students, room rents, catering and conference charges – commonly referred to as 'corporate internal income', since it arises inside the College from the uses to which its buildings and facilities are put. Secondly, the investments representing its other endowments (other, that is, than the College buildings themselves and those used for operational purposes, in particular student accommodation) – commonly referred to as 'corporate external income' – to which the money received from 'annual giving', a recent and important development, is now added. (Benefactions and bequests, unless given for specific purposes, have traditionally been added to endowment capital, so that they have had a significant impact on the College's income only in the longer term.) And, thirdly, the investments held on trust for specific purposes, such as providing scholarships and bursaries, and supporting the libraries and music making.

Without these last two income sources – the corporate external and the trust incomes – the College could not survive. 'Education, religion, learning and research', which are what the College exists to further, are not activities that pay for themselves, and in the nature of things those pursuing them are rarely, if ever, able to meet all the costs of doing so. This, of course, is why these activities have for centuries been regarded as charitable, and continue to attract certain legal and fiscal advantages. Indeed, until the third quarter of the nineteenth century, and the beginning of the College's great expansion, its internal income played only a very minor part in determining its fortunes.

COLLEGE ESTATES

The principal source of the College's investment income has always been its interests in land. It began, in 1497–8, with a total annual net income of £70 6s; about two-thirds of this came from agricultural land in Cambridgeshire and the Isle of Ely, and one-third from houses in Cambridge and strips in the town's common fields. All this property had belonged to the nunnery. It was added to over the years by gifts and purchases of land both in and around Cambridge and elsewhere – the College's revenues more than doubled in the first half of the sixteenth century – though in such a way that the financial history of the College has, thanks largely to the nuns' benefactors, been inextricably linked to that of the town.

The management of this landed estate was, for more than three hundred years, constrained and complicated by two factors. The first was a series of Acts of Parliament, dating from Elizabeth I's reign, which originally applied to all corporate bodies in the Church – cathedrals as well as colleges – and were generally known as 'the disabling statutes' because they restricted the powers which these corporations would otherwise have had to deal with their property as freely as any individual. Their combined effect was that a college could neither

- dispose of its land, save with the authority of an Act of Parliament; nor
- grant a lease of agricultural land for longer than twenty-one years or three lives, or of a house in any city, borough or market town for longer than forty years; nor
- raise money on the security of its landed estate.

These restrictions (which were originally coupled with limits on rent levels) were designed to prevent one generation exploiting the corporate property for their own benefit at the expense of their successors, and remained in force until they were gradually amended and dismantled by a series of Universities and College Estates Acts, starting in 1858, though it was not until 1964 that the last traces of them were finally removed.

The second complication arose from the College's own statutes which (like those of many others) remained unchanged from 1591 to 1841, there being much legal uncertainty as to by whom, or how, they could be altered. Under these statutes each Fellow, in addition to free board and lodging, received, despite all subsequent changes in the value of money, a fixed yearly stipend of £2.

Ways of circumventing both sorts of constraint – those of the 'disabling' Acts of Parliament, and those of the College's own statutes – had therefore to be found.

Beneficial leases and fines

The College did not farm its land itself. Its income came principally from rents or from 'fines'; other income came from manorial court fees and the sale of timber and coal. Throughout the sixteenth century rents generally remained the same as they had been in nunnery days, in a few cases even being reduced, despite the fact that there was a rapid rise in prices of commodities, for the disabling statutes had required that land be let at the old 'customary' rent. An Act of 1576 ameliorated this by providing for one-third of the rent to be paid in wheat or malt – in practice the tenant paid in cash at the rate at which the best wheat or malt was sold in Cambridge market immediately before the rent fell due. As the price of corn rose, all agricultural rents (at least to the extent of one-third of the old rent) rose also, so that in time the third part was in practice worth more than the whole. Corn rents continued until the Estates Acts.

Fines were sums payable on the grant or renewal of a lease or tenancy. Changes in the value of money had made a lease for a term of years at a fixed money rent a valuable property; tenants were therefore ready to offer a 'fine' (at the beginning of the sixteenth century generally a sum equal to one year's rent) for the renewal of their lease at the old rent some years before the original term had run out. These were known as 'beneficial leases', and blunted the disabling statutes' prohibition on colleges mortgaging their land to raise ready money, for the fines were treated as income though they really amounted to a realisation of part of the land's capital value. It became common for tenants of town houses to renew their leases every fourteen years, and of agricultural land every seven years. So only a small part of the annual value of the property leased was paid in the form of yearly rents; the remainder was paid in the form of a fine at these fixed intervals. The fine for renewing a 21-year lease after seven years, at the then current rate of interest of 10 per cent, would have been approximately the traditional one year's rent. Throughout the seventeenth century the College was asking only the same amount, one year's rent, for the renewal of a forty-year lease of which fourteen years had elapsed. From about 1660 onwards the fine was calculated on the 'extended' rent – that is the rack-rent as far as could be estimated, less the reserved rent – but the multiplier remained one year's rent (despite changes in interest rates that should have justified higher multiples) until about 1770. Between then and 1800 the multiple became $1^1/_2$, being raised thereafter to $1^3/_4$, rising during the course of the nineteenth century to 2. Dr Caryl, Bursar and subsequently Master (1758–81), who had attempted to wean the College from beneficial leases – a process which would have involved a drop in income in the shorter term – was ahead of his time.

Dr Lynford Caryl (1723),
Fellow, Bursar and Master
(1758–81).
Joseph Wright of Derby, *c.*1770.

Rack-rents for agricultural lands eventually started in 1816, and gradually became more common thereafter. Rack-rents for houses in Jesus Lane and New Square began to appear after 1819, and from the early 1830s Cambridge house rents became an increasing proportion of College income. But, despite their many disadvantages from the College's point of view, some beneficial leases continued to be granted until the early years of the twentieth century.

'Dead College' and the Dividend Book

The College is an eleemosynary corporation, namely one 'established for the perpetual distribution of the free alms or bounty of the founder'. The beneficiaries of the foundation are the Master, the Fellows and the Scholars. In the past everyone else admitted to the College were regarded as mere paying guests – 'pensioners' as they were traditionally called. This perhaps explains what to modern eyes look like confusions of interest between the College on the one hand and the Master and Fellows on the other in the management of its assets and the distribution of its income, for it is now assumed that the College exists for the benefit of all who have been admitted to study and research in it, and, furthermore, that in deciding whom to admit it is those judged best able to benefit from coming to the University who should be chosen.

As far as the Fellows were concerned, the fiction that their stipend was £2 a year was maintained in the Bursar's accounts until 1841. The corn rents were by the Act of 1576 to be 'expended to the use of the relief of the commons and diet of the colleges'. Before long, the funds available for commons exceeded the cost. The practice therefore grew up of carrying this surplus income, after all the payments specified in the statutes had been made, to another account, 'the Dividend Paper', adding the fines payable on the renewal of leases, and then distributing the balances to the Master and Fellows. The dividend thus naturally became a matter of far greater consequence to the Fellows than their statutory stipend.

In 1634, the new Master, Richard Sterne, agreed with the Fellows that the proceeds of fines should be divided into twenty parts, two to go to the College, two to the Master, and the balance to the sixteen Fellows. This settlement encouraged non-residence, as Fellows who were absent with permission continued to receive their dividend as well as their statutory stipend. Fellowships thus became financial prizes, rather than the sources of duties, giving a Fellow (so long as he remained unmarried) simply an opportunity which he might (but often did not) take to remain in Cambridge to study and to teach. The fees paid to those Fellows who did remain in residence and were acting as Tutors were a matter between them

and their pupils' parents, with which the College was not directly concerned. This remained the position until late in the nineteenth century.

The principle of the payment of dividend was formally recognised when the College statutes were revised in 1841, with one twentieth of the divisible income reserved to 'Dead College' – that is, for general College purposes. (The term later came to mean the capital derived from the surplus of income over corporate expenditure.) But after 1883 non-resident Fellows could continue to draw dividends only for so long as they remained unmarried and their other income was below a specified amount. (Dividends only finally disappeared in 1968.)

NINETEENTH-CENTURY DEVELOPMENTS

By the end of the eighteenth century the College held many separate strips and tithe interests in the common fields around Cambridge. Under two Enclosure Acts, of 1801 and 1807, the College received allotments of over 225 acres. Some idea of the effect of this can be seen from the illustration which shows the approximate boundaries of the land awarded to Jesus, overlaid on a modern map of Cambridge.

These awards, which were followed by many developments on the land, were a key factor enabling Jesus, which had formerly been among the poorer Cambridge colleges, to become, in the course of the next eighty years, one of the wealthiest half dozen. Initially the developments took the form of housing in the areas around the College, in Jesus Lane, Malcolm Street, New Square and in the 1830s in Park Terrace and then beyond. In 1846 the College sold the land for the new railway station. A condition of the sale was the construction of Station Road, and building leases were subsequently granted there and in Hills Road. There were further sales of land in this area to railway companies in the 1850s and the 1870s. The College also had to sell land for railways elsewhere, including, in 1862, properties in Ludgate Hill, London. All the proceeds were held by the Court of Chancery and invested in trustee stocks on which the College received the interest. In 1883 the College withdrew all the Cambridge Station and Ludgate Hill moneys to enable the construction of the Carpenter building (to accommodate students) and North House and East House (for the newly married Tutors and their families).

The agricultural depression which began in the 1880s and rapidly worsened greatly affected the College's finances, though not as badly as those of colleges with little land suitable for building. Fellows of all colleges being now permitted to marry, most of them did so, creating a new demand for substantial houses from dons who

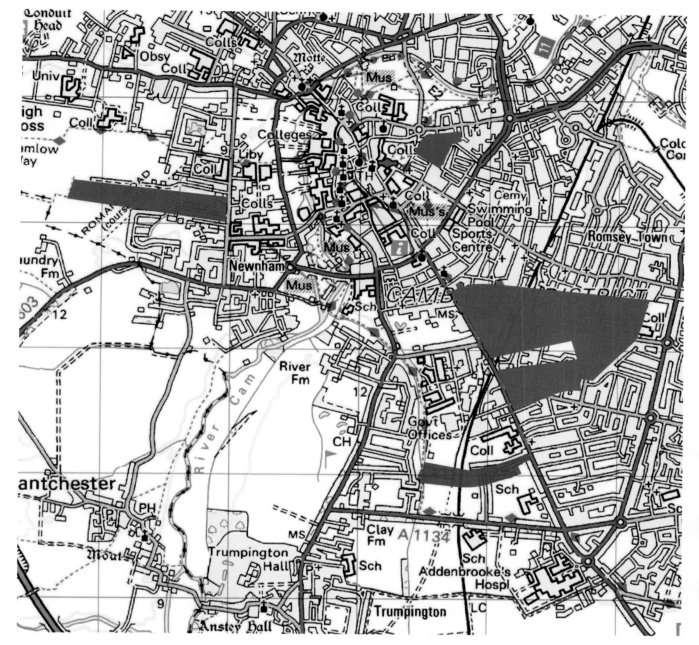

**Map showing property
allotted to Jesus College
under:**

**Cambridge St Giles (West
Fields) Enclosure Award, 1805**

**Trumpington Enclosure
Award, 1808**

**Barnwell Enclosure Award,
1811 (two pieces)**

wished to buy for their own occupation and preferred a longer term than the traditional forty years. Colleges had been allowed to grant building leases for ninety-nine years since 1858, the first such leases by Jesus were of sites in Tenison Road and Tenison Avenue. In 1895 the College planned Cranmer Road and made up the first section of it, development continuing until the outbreak of war in 1914.

ROYAL COMMISSIONS AND NEW STATUTES

The affairs of the University and its colleges were investigated by Royal Commissions, first in the 1850s, then in the 1870s, and again in 1922, with a view to seeing what changes in their statutes would be needed if they were to

be brought into the (then) modern world, and devising procedures for varying the purposes to which trust funds might be put when, with the passage of time, their original objects could no longer be fulfilled.

The evidence given to the 1872 Royal Commission included details of the financial position of the colleges at the beginning of that year:

> The landed estates of [Jesus] College comprise 3,168 acres, of which 2,352 are held for the corporate use, and 655 subject to trusts. [Most of this land was in Cambridgeshire, but there were also holdings in Surrey, Essex, Suffolk, Bedfordshire, Yorkshire and Leicestershire.] Of the land let for the corporate use, 1,919 are let at rack-rent at an average rental of £1 8s 10d per acre. The lands held for trust purposes are all let at rack-rent; and the average rent

per acre is about £1. The lands let on beneficial leases comprise 613 acres, of which when in hand the net annual value may be estimated at £1,012; while the actual income received therefor, and which consisted of corn rents, amounted in 1871 to £122 16s 5d. Since 1858 the College has only in one instance renewed any of these beneficial leases, and with that exception they will all run out in a few years. The College owns house property in London, and also a large amount in Cambridge. By far the greater part of this property is let on beneficial leases of 40 years, which it has been the custom of the College in most cases to renew after 14 years on the payment of a fine.

Despite what the Commission had been told, Jesus (like most colleges) was not in fact refusing to renew the old forty-year leases. It was only after the Finance Act 1910–11, under which a college would, where a lease for forty years was renewable by custom every fourteen years, on each renewal have to pay tax on a sum which it had never received, that Jesus finally decided that existing forty-year leases must be allowed to run out, and fines ceased to be a source of income.

The College's external corporate income in 1871 was £6,782, while its internal income (at this date primarily room rents) was £2,817, a total corporate income of £9,599. In addition it received £3,043 trust income. Its corporate expenditure had been £9,275, and £2,639 of the trust income had been spent. So the books balanced. The Tuition Fund received £1,939, but tuition was still regarded as a private affair, the Tutor retaining the balance of the tuition money after paying the four lecturers and incidental expenses, so this income did not appear in the College's accounts. This balance amounted to about £850 in 1871. The annual value of a fellowship was £283. In 1871 £1 was worth about £62 in 2005 money.

By 1922, as the third of these Commissioners reported, Jesus's total gross income from its estates had risen to £15,105, its internal income was £12,853 (including tuition fees), and the net receipts from trusts amounted to £2,509. Total income was thus £30,467. College expenditure amounted to £27,326, plus £581 repayment of loans. In 1922 £1 was worth about £36.37 in 2005 money. External income, total corporate income and total income had thus all improved in real terms since 1871.

The 1922 Royal Commission had been prompted by the need of both Oxford and Cambridge universities for financial support from the State. The Commission recommended increased grants for the universities from the Exchequer – but not, directly, for the colleges. Rather, it endorsed, and widened, the provisions of statutes made in 1882 (following the recommendation of the 1872 Commission) which for the first time required each college to pay a proportion of its income to the University (a requirement that still continues, in modified form – the University now redistributes this money to the poorer colleges). At the same time, a large number of changes to the governance and organisation of both the universities and the colleges were recommended; these were put into effect by new statutes for all the colleges in 1926. One of the longer term results was that after the Second World War the University became the primary employer of most of the teaching staff.

The 1922 Commission was critical of the fact that some colleges paid from their endowments substantial subsidies indirectly to the general body of students by

(a) contributing to, or meeting losses on, their kitchens; and/or
(b) levying fees and other charges which were insufficient to cover the relevant expenses; and/or
(c) not charging the full economic rent for college rooms.

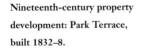

Nineteenth-century property development: Park Terrace, built 1832–8.

It felt that subsidies from endowments might mask the need for more economical management, but that even where this was not the case they were open to the objection that they benefited all resident members of a college, and not just its needy students. It believed that if charges were raised to economic levels, the needy students could be assisted without any additional cost to the colleges. It accordingly made various recommendations designed to ensure that charges to students for rooms and services covered their economic cost, and that the costs of teaching (and so of dons' stipends) should not be subsidised from a college's endowment income.

These recommendations were supplemented by the introduction of a new, obscure, form of accounts applying to all colleges, which were designed not to reveal their overall financial position, but rather to show the allocation of resources between different internal funds, the uses to which they could be put being statutorily defined. Accounts in this form continued until 2004.

But neither the proposals nor the new form of accounts achieved their desired effect. Even had they so wished, it would have been impossible for most colleges to offer substantial numbers of 'free' places to students. And, as the century wore on, it became more and more difficult to follow the recommendations, the value of the local education authority maintenance grants (to which all UK students were entitled) being seen as limiting what could be charged. Room rents fell behind their full economic value (although there was a determined effort in the late 1990s to correct this), catering accounts were frequently in deficit, and in 2006 (and for some time before) all colleges had to subsidise teaching from their endowments as college fees (which colleges had lost the ability to fix independently) were (and are) insufficient to meet the true cost.

LOCAL PROPERTY DEVELOPMENTS

The College continued in the twentieth century the policy adopted in the nineteenth of developing its Cambridge land. Station Farm was gradually redeveloped and sold off. Cherry Hinton Road began to be built up from about 1900, but building was still going on in the 1930s. The Jesus connection can be traced in the names of the roads: Coleridge, Davy, Flamsteed, Greville, Radegund, Rustat. The freeholds have however now all been sold off, sometimes as a matter of College policy, but more frequently as a result of the enfranchisement (or, as college bursars categorised it, 'confiscation') provisions in the Leasehold Reform Act 1967.

In 1955–6 the College entered into arrangements for the development, on Bradwell's Yard, St Andrew's Street and adjoining land owned by Christ's College, of a shopping precinct known as Bradwell's Court. It was demolished with few regrets in 2006. Also in 1956 the College sold the last of various properties in London left to it by Dr Reston, Master from 1546 to 1551 (most of the rest having, as already noted, been compulsorily purchased by railway companies earlier). The cash raised was used for the development of a new block of shops named Reston House in Fitzroy Street. This building, too, was to be demolished and the site again redeveloped in 2004–5. On both occasions the College itself carried out the development. The Highsett site in Hills Road was let out on long leases and developed (in a strikingly attractive way) for houses and flats between 1959 and 1962. Most of the leasehold houses were gradually to be enfranchised under the 1967 Act, while the freehold of the flats realised some £730,000 when it too was enfranchised in 2005.

Three other developments that were to occupy the College for many years were those on land north of Fitzroy Street, on the north side of King Street, and on the south side of Station Road. Planning for the Fitzroy Street area, where the College owned many scattered properties, began in 1959, but it was to be 1981 before it was able to sell most of them to the City Council to enable the development of what became the Grafton Centre. The College had worked to promote the development of this area for shopping – initially in opposition to the proposals for Lion Yard (although this too was to be built to a small extent on College land), but after that development was approved as a complementary shopping centre. It commissioned proposals from a young architect called Richard (now Lord) Rogers (whose designs were not, in the event, used), protracted negotiations with the City Council and potential developers were undertaken, and there was then a lengthy planning process. The whole experience was controversial and frustrating, and expensive to the College in terms of both fees and rents; for many years the College's property in Fitzroy Street was the least financially rewarding of any major part of its estate, even including its residential property. In the event, the development was successful, but there were times when it seemed that it would never come to fruition.

The King Street redevelopment took almost as long. It was for a mixed commercial and residential development in conjunction with the King Street Housing Society, which was founded by the College and was to be granted long leases of the residential elements. Planning started in 1961 in response to the City's scheme for a car park there, and site assembly began (the College had to buy freeholds it did not already own in order to make the project viable). The first phase (Malcolm Place) was finished in 1970, but it was to be 1977–8 before the second

(Manor Place) was completed. The residential element of the scheme was not particularly profitable for the College but it retains the freehold, and the commercial properties still make a useful contribution to income.

The redevelopment of the south side of Station Road started in 1959–60 with the grant of a long lease of the site on the corner with Hills Road to enable the building of an office block, Kett House (the freehold of which was to be sold at a handsome profit in 1980–1). Planning for the development of the remainder began in 1962, but again progressed slowly. In 1965 Lord Esher was asked to prepare a comprehensive scheme for the redevelopment of most of the south side of Station Road. Over the next nine years much of the Esher plan was put into effect, with the building of three office blocks: Jupiter, Leda and Demeter Houses. A fourth, Daedalus, was to follow in 1984, but some elements (particularly a road from Brooklands Avenue to the station) were eventually abandoned. The developments were profitable in producing for the College both capital sums and a share in the income generated from the buildings. They, together with a fifth office block in Regent Street, Janus House, remain important parts of the College's commercial property portfolio.

The most recent major redevelopment on College land, apart from those of Fitzroy Street and Bradwell's Court, is the Grand Arcade in the city centre. The College owned some 80 per cent of the land underlying the Robert Sayle store; it was sold in 2001 to enable the store to be demolished. The Arcade was built in 2005–7.

ASSET ALLOCATION

In 1954 the College was, with some difficulty, persuaded to make its first investment in equities (all its financial investments having previously been in stocks and bonds): £2,000 in each of six companies. Investment in equities remained a tentative process, but there was a gradual change; by September 1960, for example, of a total £335,000 invested in financial securities, £105,000 was held in equities. For many years, every purchase or sale was authorised in advance by the Bursarial Committee; only gradually was authority given to the Bursar, initially in consultation with a subcommittee of Fellows, to act on the brokers' advice. In 1987 Cazenove's, who had been the College's brokers since 1963, were at last given a discretionary mandate to manage the financial investments, but for another ten years the Bursar was in practice consulted before each transaction and allowed to vary or veto it.

But by far the major part of the College's endowment was still invested in land. In 1961 the Bursar reported that, while the gross annual yield from marketable securities was about £15,000, that from land was about

£86,500. There were twelve medium to small farms totalling some 3,600 acres, yielding about £13,300 a year; and residential and commercial properties in Cambridge yielding about £73,300 a year. According to the Bursar, the residential properties included a small proportion of good-quality property, but 'the greater part of it is of indifferent quality or frankly slummy'.

In Cazenove's first report in October 1963 there is a tentative suggestion that the College had too much invested in property. This point was made more forcefully by others as time went on, and the College responded by gradually selling the freehold reversions of houses in various parts of Cambridge. Such sales, together with the forced sales resulting from the 1967 Act, continued for many years. In 1974 a new Bursar was to complain:

> For a good many years we have regarded the residential part of our estate as of greater importance and value in providing a social service to the College and the City, than as a lucrative investment. The rents we have charged have been remarkably static, and even now only about 20 per cent of our houses have had Fair Rents fixed by the Rent Officer. Many of these are several years out of date … We have been very slow to reap any financial benefit from the vast sums of money we have poured into the College's houses – on which we have spent in maintenance and improvements some £350,000 during the last 12 years – and the current economic climate suggests that we should not put off a thorough overhaul of our residential rental much longer.

Much of the money received from sales and developments was ploughed back into property (the capital costs of the King Street development, and repairs and maintenance of and improvements to retained houses, such as those in Eden Street). By 1976, when the subject was again discussed in detail, property (excluding operational property) still formed 90 per cent of the College's endowment capital, producing a net income of 4.24 per cent. A quarter of it was rented houses, which on average yielded a net income of only 1 per cent – this at a time when inflation was significantly higher than that. As a result the College Council agreed that:

- the College should sell any house outside Claremont, Park Terrace and the main blocks near the College that became vacant;
- an endowment portfolio containing not more than 80 per cent in property should be aimed at;
- eventually the College should restrict its housing property other than operational property to New Square, Malcolm Street and Park Terrace; for the time being, Claremont too should be retained.

While the policy on sales of houses was followed, so that in 2007 relatively few non-operational houses are still owned by the College, there was little immediate impact on the proportion held in property. By 1980 indeed it was up to 91.25 per cent. This was at least partly because agricultural property seems to have been regarded as exempt from the policy; the response in 1980 was to decide that any opportunity to sell second-class shop property at reasonable values should be taken, and to accelerate the sale of residential property, while agricultural properties continued to be purchased until 1982. The College also seemed rather ambivalent about the policy itself. When, after contentious internal discussions, Park Terrace was sold in 1982 to Emmanuel College, it was agreed to invest the proceeds in first-class property outside Cambridge and, later the same year, to apply the same policy to the residue of the proceeds of the land sold to the developers of the Grafton Centre. In fact, however, only one further significant property purchase was made: a shop in Wood Green, London, in March 1983. This turned out to be a rather unsatisfactory investment and was sold in 1988.

The proportion of the portfolio held in property did subsequently decline to 75 per cent in June 1985, and to 70 per cent the following year. Despite this, the College's commercial property agents, appointed in 1984, regularly advised that too much was invested in property, and made specific proposals for disposals of both commercial and agricultural properties. Most of these were not accepted. For example, a strong recommendation in early 1987 to sell a farm that the College had inherited from the nuns was rejected. It was sold for the same price five years later, when a general review of agricultural property finally resulted in a number of sales.

In the 1990s a combination of factors – continued disposals of (particularly residential) properties, investment of surplus cash in financial securities, and changes in the relative values of property and equities – led to a more substantial decline in the percentage of the endowment held in property: to 68 per cent in 1991, and to 46 per cent by 1996 (although by then there was no specific target). More recently, there have been further changes both ways. Following a further strategic review of agricultural property, a number of farms were sold between 2004 and 2006, those retained being those judged to have long-term development potential. On the other hand, in 2004–5 the College invested some £10 million (of which £8 million was borrowed) in industrial property in various locations outside Cambridge in order to obtain diversity in type and location. The net effect was that by 2005 the proportion held in property had gone back up again to 60 per cent. Despite this, the College will continue to diversify away from property; the current target is 37 per cent.

The Carpenter building, 1885 – paid for with money received from railway companies which had acquired land from the College under statutory powers.

Steps have also been taken in recent years to increase the diversity of the College's financial investments. In 2002 separate managers of its equities on the one hand and bonds on the other were appointed, replacing Cazenove's, and in 2004 the College's statutes were changed to allow it to adopt a total return investment strategy. This was followed after much discussion by a first tentative investment in hedge funds in December 2004, and a more whole-hearted move into both hedge funds and private equity funds in 2006 (the cautious nature of the process being reminiscent of the move into equities in the 1950s).

THE COLLEGE'S FINANCIAL POSITION IN 2006

The College's efforts to improve the performance of its investment portfolio over the last few decades have been successful. In the year to 30 June 2005 actual income from the College's investment portfolio (excluding interest on cash) was £3,409,000, and would have been higher if one of its major commercial properties had not been undergoing redevelopment. In 1922 the College's gross income from its estates had been £15,105, which is about £550,000 in 2005 money. But overall, the financial pressures have increased. The per capita fee income (which remains subject to government controls) has been reduced in real terms, while costs have increased dramatically. Greater numbers of students have meant more Fellows to teach them, and more accommodation needed to house them (between 1930 and 2000 three major residential blocks and a new library were built, former lodging houses were converted to 'external staircases', and tenanted houses in Park Street and Lower Park Street were converted into accommodation for graduate students), resulting in higher maintenance and other running costs. The College was also faced during those years with very high bills to renovate both its housing stock and the College buildings themselves.

So there have been regular calls by successive bursars for economies. These have been made (e.g. in the arrangements for cleaning of student rooms, and periodic reductions in the costs of social functions), and the College has invested in IT, which has enabled its affairs to be managed more efficiently. But significant cost reductions have never been easy to achieve, and some that were made seem with hindsight to have been short sighted (e.g. cutting back on planned maintenance and repairs). Economies have been coupled with efforts to increase income. As well as ensuring that the investments are managed as efficiently as possible, the College has been increasing charges to its students (particularly for room rents) to more economic levels, expanding its conference trade, and seeking donations from its alumni and others.

In 2004 most of the Cambridge colleges, including Jesus, adopted a more typical and (relatively) comprehensible form of accounts. (The latest accounts are available on the College website.) Comparisons with those for 1872 and 1922 supplied to the Royal Commissions are, therefore, very difficult. But what can be said is that in the income and expenditure account for the year ended 30 June 2006, income was £9,322,000, and operating expenditure was £7,999,000, giving a surplus before depreciation of £1,323,000. After a depreciation charge of £2,451,000, however, there was an operating deficit of £1,693,000. This is a gap that will have to be closed if the College is to continue to maintain the range of activities and amenities – academic, cultural, sporting and social – from which in recent decades an enlarged student community has benefited.

Reliable comparative figures for the other colleges are similarly impossible, for a wide variety of accounting principles have been adopted. We may, however, note that in 1872, of the seventeen colleges, thirteen had a higher external income and ten had a higher total corporate income than Jesus. But Jesus had comparatively high trust income, and only six colleges had a higher total income. By 1922 there were only seven colleges with higher gross income from estates, six with higher total corporate income, and five with higher total income. In 2006 the position was not very different. Five of the (now thirty-one) colleges had higher income recorded as 'endowment income and donations' (broadly equivalent to the old 'external corporate income'), while six had a higher total income than Jesus. A Bursar must leave to his readers the conclusions to be drawn from this.

Through five centuries

The Chimney and Gate Tower (*c.*1500). The ground and first floors of the building to the left of the Tower were occupied by the Grammar School 1507–67; its second floor, and that of the Master's Lodge (to the right of the Tower), was added in 1718–20, replacing the earlier attics. The Fellows' Garden lies behind the wall on the left (built 1608), the Master's behind that on the right (built 1682).

The Chapel and English Religion

JONATHAN COLLIS

The College has a Chapel whose complex building both reflects some of the many changes in English religious life over eight and a half centuries, and provides an insight into the place of the Christian religion in the life and development of the College. In tracing the rhythm of quickening and quietening that has left marks upon the building, we need a sense of what the College inherited from the convent. In terms of the physical legacy, the north transept with its Romanesque arches and the chancel with the finely carved double piscina are complemented by the tower gallery. The only fitting that can be dated to the nuns' time is a wax paschal candle holder that was discovered during the Victorian restoration by Pugin, which now may be seen in the Fitzwilliam Museum.

But in terms of the religious life of Bishop Alcock's new College, the monastic style of regular offices; masses for the repose of the souls of the king and members of the royal family, of Alcock himself, and those of other benefactors; and the continued maintenance of the (cut-down) nave for parochial use were strong lines of continuity with the past. The College had a small school, four of whose boys were to lead the singing at the offices, assisted by an organ and four older youths. The Chapel itself had much pictorial stained glass – of which, after a visit by Puritan iconoclasts in 1643, only a few fragments now remain – and side altars for particular saints or for masses for the dead. It was within this tradition that Thomas Cranmer, the College's most famous son, was brought up after he entered it in (as tradition has it) 1503 at the age of 14. There he became familiar not only with the highly developed and complex rituals of late medieval English religion, but also with the first stirrings of the movement of change within Church and state that resulted in the Reformation. The New Learning of those who wished to breathe life into the sterilities of theological debate by reference to the original Greek and Hebrew scriptural texts combined with the zeal of those who

wished to reform the Church of abuses and corruptions. When allied to powerful forces at Court, enormous energy was released that swept away much of what Alcock had known, in changes notable for their speed. Cranmer himself came to prominence from his donnish obscurity by offering a way for Henry VIII to extricate himself from his marriage to Catherine of Aragon, and rose quickly to become Archbishop of Canterbury in 1533.

The changes he facilitated and encouraged – the simplification of the services of the Church, the stripping away of images and relics, and the move away from the musical elaborations of the Middle Ages – had their effect

Double piscina in the chancel, early thirteenth century, rediscovered in 1815.

at Cranmer's College as elsewhere, though less rapidly. While one or two Fellows were sympathetic to the theological views of their erstwhile colleague, the day-to-day practice of the Chapel seems to have been little affected. When the Commissioners of Edward VI came in 1549 to ensure that the progress of the reforms was up to speed, they found much to amend. They directed that six altars in the nave and transepts were to be pulled down, and several Fellows were deprived of their fellowships. One of them, Robert Harrison, left Cambridge for the staunchly Catholic University of Louvain; another, arraigned for a misdemeanour of what one must assume to be a theological kind (after two days the penalty was lifted), was John Badcock, the last of the priors of Barnwell, who lived in the College and who not improbably was wedded to the old ways.

But the changes that were set in train under Edward VI were reversed under Mary, who in her turn sent Commissioners in 1557 to ensure that the medieval rites and ceremonies had been revived. While his predecessor had apparently already reversed many of the Edwardian reforms, John Fuller, the Master appointed in 1557, set to this work with an even greater will, and the accounts reveal a commitment to resuscitating the old ways second to none in Cambridge. Candles, singing, ceremonial and images were all restored. But Fuller outlived Mary by only four months, and the next swing of the ecclesiastical pendulum on the accession of Mary's Protestant sister Elizabeth in 1558 took effect with an extraordinary degree of smoothness. The revival of the old ways was halted, and the Elizabethan settlement brought violent shifts in religious life within the College to an end for nearly another century. (Harrison, who had returned under Mary to be the vicar of a Cambridgeshire parish, Linton, felt able to accommodate himself to the new regime in a new parish in Huntingdonshire, Great Stukeley.)

The Marian furnishings were removed from the Chapel, and a simple Communion table was installed. Holy Communion was thenceforward celebrated only three times a year, and with the disappearance of the grammar school the musical life of the Chapel fell away. The organ was sold by 1570: the new Elizabethan statutes expected Fellows and scholars to take singing lessons before their election – Genevan metrical psalms now enlivened the worship. Fellows were required to attend services on Sundays and saints' days, while for students there was a daily service made up of a recitation of the Apostles' Creed, the Ten Commandments and the Lord's Prayer in either Latin or English, with a sung Litany on Fridays. Austerely Protestant as this might sound, in Cambridge terms Jesus was definitely within the Anglican rather than the Puritan party – the surplice was still used, and this without the wranglings that were to be found in colleges such as St John's and Trinity. The stained-glass windows portraying saints were repaired. Only one Fellow, John Dod, is known to have been a convinced Puritan. His spiritual awakening was occasioned by a dispute with the Bursar, who had falsely accused him of fraud.

In the 1630s, under Archbishop William Laud, this dryly orthodox attachment to the Elizabethan settlement

(Above) Medieval paschal candle holder discovered in 1848 during the restoration of the Chapel.

(Far left) Wooden pulpit, *c*.1505, originally in the Chapel and now in Landbeach Church, Cambridgeshire.

(Left) Holy water stoup at north door, *c*.1505.

was modified by a strain within the Church which sought to restore to it something of what had been lost in the Reformation in the previous century. Its leading proponents found favour with Charles I, enabling them to effect significant changes in English religious life and in doing so to stir up sufficient anger to fuel a civil war. In Jesus Laud's views found a keen supporter in Richard Sterne, who had been appointed Master in 1634, though some – such as John Eliot, student of the College and 'Apostle to the Indians' – disagreed strongly enough to migrate in 1631 across the Atlantic to a purer New England. A couple of years before Sterne's arrival Latin versions of the Book of Common Prayer had been bought – Parliament having allowed the two universities the privilege of continuing, if they so wished, to pray in Latin – and Sterne saw to it that a new organ was purchased, the organist being paid for by a tax on all – save for the poorest sizars, who were to blow the instrument. Laud's visitation of the

University in 1635 remarked favourably on Jesus's adherence to order and devotion, which were further enhanced by the purchase in 1636 of a litany desk and new plate, candlesticks for the Communion table and an altar rail, and also by the raising of the altar on a dais with a frieze and hangings around it.

These enrichments of the religious life of the College were not to last long, for in 1641 the House of Commons, in an attempt to stamp out the Laudian developments and generally to bring to a more radical conclusion the changes begun in the sixteenth century, ordered the heads of all Cambridge colleges to move Communion tables from the east end of chapels, to take away altar rails and candles and to level chancels. In 1643, after Sterne's arrest, William Dowsing, the man deputed by Parliament to put its wishes into effect, smashed more than 120 images in the stained-glass windows – an appalling amount of broken glass – and had the altar dais removed. Happily, the Fellows had previously dismantled and concealed the organ together with the plate. In the turmoil of the Commonwealth the College came off lightly, fortunate to have two Masters who were not extreme in their religious views. Indeed, John Worthington, who occupied the Lodge throughout the 1650s, was a man of distinctly moderate opinion; during his tenure the organ was reconstructed (though not replaced in the Chapel) and a bell hung in the belfry.

The restoration of Charles II and the consequent re-establishment of the Church of England saw another oscillation in the College's religious life. The organ was replaced and in 1688 rebuilt, twice-daily services were restored, and the ornaments and furnishings that had been hidden were set once again in their place. The College appealed to old members for help in restoring the Chapel 'to its former comeliness', and the chancel was paved in black and white (paid for by a bequest of £100 from John Sherman, the College's first historian) and the east end wainscoted. The strongly Anglican and clerical tone of the College's life, supported by Tobias Rustat's benefaction (page 22) manifested itself in the very high proportion of its graduates going on to ordination. Two of them, Matthew Hutton and Thomas Herring, both matriculating in 1710, became Archbishops of Canterbury, bringing, with Cranmer and the Elizabethan Richard Bancroft, the number of Jesuan Primates of All England to four. (Another future Bishop attracted to the College by the prospect of a Rustat Scholarship was the saintly non-juror Nathaniel Spinckes.) A corollary was that those reluctant to conform to religious orthodoxy had a hard time of it. In 1699 an undergraduate was disciplined for attending a Quaker meeting house, and then expelled for continuing to do so. The energy released in the Church of England by the Restoration gradually

The ante-chapel with the wall enclosing the Chancel erected in 1789.

Aquatint by F. Mackenzie and J. Black for R. Ackermann's *History of the University of Cambridge* (1815)

declined over the course of the next hundred years. The old traditions of church music signified by the organ which had been replaced in the Chapel came to an undignified end when in 1764 it was decided to discontinue the salary to the organist.

Neither the nascent Methodist movement, nor the stirrings of revived Evangelicalism, was matched by any noticeable signs of Jesuan religious activity during the half-century Mastership of Dr Ashton, a High Church Tory of the old school, but after his death in 1752 some of the disputes that had been stirring elsewhere in the English Church and within the University entered into the College. As the easy-going attitude of the prevailing latitudinarians, who were content to allow a broad measure of difference in opinion on doctrinal issues, moved into departure from orthodox Christian belief – as encapsulated in the Thirty-Nine Articles of the Church of England, which everyone had to subscribe on graduating in the University and again on being ordained, as nearly all the Fellows were – so at Cambridge the divisions between those who held increasingly heterodox views of the divinity of Christ and the academic establishment widened. This was exemplified by two Fellows, Robert Tyrwhitt and William Frend. The controversies that Frend engendered are described elsewhere (pages 96 and 122); he greatly influenced Samuel Taylor Coleridge, whose own early Unitarianism did, however, later evolve back into a Trinitarian variety of Christianity. Robert Tyrwhitt, who had been an undergraduate in the College and for twenty years a Fellow, resigned his fellowship in 1777, having embraced a Unitarian doctrine of God. He continued, nonetheless, to live in the College and in 1788 made a generous gift of £200 towards beautifying the Chapel, which, save for the work on the floor and the removal of the organ, had scarcely changed since 1660, and which still had a strongly medieval feel. Alcock's woodwork was removed, a flat false ceiling erected over the chancel, and the chancel itself walled off from the nave, with a gallery for the Master's family on the wall. The effect, as far as can be gleaned from contemporary prints, was one of unexciting and comfortable elegance, suitable, indeed, for a nobleman's chapel. Although it came to be deplored for its style and for what it destroyed, it nonetheless reflects a continuing commitment on the part of the College to maintain its religious character. It was no one-off action, for a new altarpiece – J-B. Jouvenet's *Presentation in the Temple* (page 51) – was given by the Master, Dr Pearce, in 1796 and the east window was newly glazed in 1800.

A revival of quite a different kind happened in the 1840s, under the impetus of what became known, however misleadingly, as the Oxford Movement. This complex phenomenon within the life of the Anglican Church had emerged out of the desire to assert the authority of the Church of England on grounds more secure than that of the sanction of the state, in the wake of such events as Catholic Emancipation and the removal of religious tests for public office. Such grounds were to be found, in the view of a number of influential Oxford clerics such as John Henry Newman and John Keble, in the ancient and continuous history of the Church from apostolic times as a divine institution. This rapidly became linked with the Romantic movement's rediscovery of medieval precedents and exemplars in music, literature, architecture and religion. In Cambridge there was a particularly distinctive factor in that two undergraduates – inspired by revulsion at the alteration of ancient buildings and at the sort of Gothic to be seen at, say, Sidney Sussex or New Court, St John's – founded the Cambridge Camden Society, which was dedicated to 'breathing new life into England's musty mediaeval churches, transforming them

The inner chapel before Pugin's restoration.
Engraving by J.N. Ince, 1838

(Right) Preliminary ink
sketch (1846) by A.W.N.
Pugin, drawn before he had
seen the Chapel, indicating
how he thought it might be
restored; and (below) the
lectern (1849), inspired by
that at King's, which he
designed.

(Facing page)
The Chapel: work of the
thirteenth, sixteenth and
nineteenth centuries.

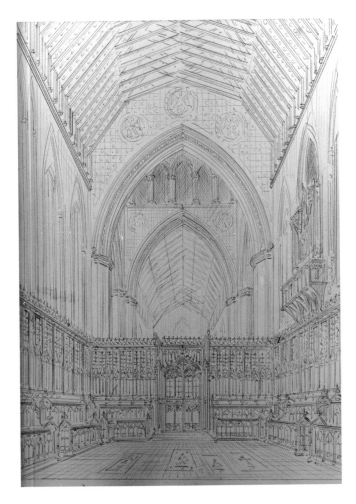

striking move on the College's part to employ Salvin to restore its Chapel. He built an organ chamber on the north side of the newly uncovered chancel arches, removed the gallery and partition and stripped the plaster from the walls.

The designs Salvin proposed for the chancel itself did not, however, meet with the College's approval, and when he fell ill he was sacked. After Gibson and other Fellows had overseen the work themselves for a while, they employed an even more controversial figure to undertake the rest of it. Augustus Welby Pugin, a convert to Roman Catholicism, had been a pungent critic of three recently built Cambridge churches, and was well known for his commitment to the restoration not only of medieval buildings but also of the worship that went on within them. The comprehensive restoration he undertook is dealt with elsewhere (page 30), but the approval of the Camden Society was warm: 'It will be acknowledged that, whether ritually or architecturally, few restorations are more complete or correct than Jesus College.' Even while the Chapel was out of commission during the building work, chanted services had begun in the Hall, with a small choir of boys. A new era was about to begin.

This renewal in the Anglican religious life of the College was accompanied by changes in the religious make-up of the student body. A Roman Catholic had been admitted as an undergraduate as early as 1803, and in the 1840s so was a nonconformist, though neither was permitted by the University's statutes to take a degree. Through the nineteenth century and until the First World War undergraduate attendance at services remained compulsory, once on weekdays (at 7.30 a.m. or 4.30 p.m.) and twice on Sundays. As the College expanded in numbers in the 1870s it became necessary to transfer services to the nave, which was fitted out with seating and, in the 1880s, with an organ on a gallery at the west end.

Although Jesus came to be reputed a High Church place verging on the Anglo-Catholic (as its two Cambridge parishes – All Saints' and St Clement's – certainly were), and the closest Cambridge had to an Oxford Movement establishment, after 1849 it had in Dr Corrie a Master who was antipathetic to both Romanism and nonconformity, and a Tory of the highest kind. Although in 1856 religious tests for the BA degree were abolished by Parliament, soon afterwards Jesus removed from its books a man who had converted to Roman Catholicism, and then in 1861 it revised its statutes to require both the removal of the Master should he cease to be an Anglican and also that Fellows took an oath to ensure their Anglican allegiance at election. An Act of Parliament in 1871, however, abolished religious tests altogether for virtually all college and university offices, and for all lay fellowships. Compulsory chapel attendance for non-Anglicans was

into blazing signs of faith; icons, even, of piety and high purpose'.

Two Fellows of Jesus, Osmond Fisher and John Gibson, were members of the Camden Society and so well placed to seize the opportunity that came their way in the early 1840s. Firstly, they were instrumental in ensuring that the newly revised College statutes (in the first changes for 270 years) made official provision for twice-daily services, and for at least termly celebrations of Holy Communion as well as at the three great festivals of Christmas, Easter and Whitsun. Secondly, the accumulated legacies for the restoration of the Chapel spurred them to encourage the fellowship to begin reversing the changes made in 1790, which were now increasingly unfashionable. While the work in 1790 had not had an explicitly ethical purpose, the nature of the Cambridge world fifty years later meant that whatever was done was charged with significance. There had recently been a great row at Holy Sepulchre (the 'Round') Church, where the architect, Anthony Salvin, had made changes in the fabric to bring it back to what he and the Camden Society considered original and medieval. The non-resident vicar, after much legal wrangling, reversed these changes, not least because he and others regarded them as tending towards Roman Catholic practice. Accordingly, it was a

also abolished, though at Jesus they were expected to satisfy the Dean that they would instead attend the services of the religious body to which their parents belonged. The College continued to produce many clergymen – perhaps a third of mid-Victorian alumni took holy orders – and a higher than usual proportion seems to have been of a High Church persuasion.

Elsewhere in Cambridge the latter part of the nineteenth century, and the earlier part of the twentieth, manifested something of a crisis of confidence in the continuance of the privileged place of the Established Church within the colleges. In Jesus the transition from the Victorian world was smoothed, perhaps, by a certain conservatism of temperament within the fellowship, and especially by the personal piety of Arthur Gray, Senior Tutor from 1895 and Master 1912–40. Moreover, the long-serving Dean, Frederick Foakes Jackson (page 111), a keen supporter of rowing and sport, was a much loved figure for the undergraduate body as well as being a considerable ecclesiastical historian. He had become firstly Chaplain in 1882, then Dean in 1895, succeeding the (as J.A. Mangan relates on pages 161–163) very different 'Red' Morgan, and remained in post until he went to the United States in 1916. He raised the intellectual standard of theology within the College, and was an inspirational if quirky teacher.

Alexander Nairne, Foakes Jackson's successor, was a distinguished Hebraist. He instituted altar servers and a choral eucharist on Sundays, and abolished compulsory Chapel attendance, though for some time after its abolition the then Chapel Clerk continued out of habit to take a register of those present. Although Nairne was Dean for only some five years (he remained at Jesus as Lady Margaret Professor of Divinity), his successor, Percival Gardner-Smith (page 269), held the office for thirty-four

(Above) Stall end: copy by James Rattee, 1849, of a sixteenth century one, originally in the Chapel, but then in the Cambridgeshire church of Landbeach from which it was (with others) bought back in 1878.

(Below) The Chapel *c.*1900 with Laudian prayer desk of 1636, and organ at the west end (removed 1927).

years from 1922 (the longest tenure in the College's history), having been himself a pupil of Foakes Jackson. The organist-cum-schoolmaster, a post dating from 1849, was replaced by an organ scholar in 1919, and the choral tradition revived after the vicissitudes of the war years. After the Great War the religious base of the fellowship broadened, including such scholars as the ecumenically minded Congregationalists Bernard Manning and C.H. Dodd (the latter, the first nonconformist to be appointed to a divinity professorship in Cambridge, and the greatest biblical scholar of his generation, was to be the general director of the New English Bible). This broadening was reflected in the publication in 1963 of *The Roads Converge: A Contribution to the Question of Church Reunion by [10] members of Jesus College Cambridge.* Under Gardner-Smith the Chapel's tradition itself remained within the high but orthodox style which had become characteristic of Cambridge, and which carried on into the 1950s, when Sunday choral evensong was attended by some hundred students, fifty of whom would have been at communion in the morning.

It becomes harder to discern patterns and movements the closer in time the events under examination are, and the religious life of the College is no exception. But the Church of England, in common with other Churches, was to find the 1960s a difficult period and it was a Jesuan, John Robinson, who in *Honest to God* expressed some of the doubts and anxieties that many Christians felt about

Jesus College Chapel, Cambridge.

traditional means of talking about and responding to God. In Jesus, as elsewhere, this developed into a series of experiments with established ways and practices. This can be discerned in the records of the Chapel in the abandonment of sung matins, the movement of the altar away from the east wall to permit the celebrant to face the congregation, the introduction of folk music into the liturgy, and, perhaps, the moving of Sunday Holy Communion from 8 to 8.30 a.m. A sense, nonetheless, persisted that despite (or maybe because of) these changes to accommodate contemporary circumstances, attendance was disappointing and that it was a period of decline.

But this period of radical experimentation was replaced by the end of the 1980s by a more settled one, with a renewed sense that the worship in Chapel could serve the College not only in its traditional choral form – and since the Second World War there had been a number of outstanding organ scholars – but also in more informal ways, such as corporate Communions for all Christians in College, the hosting of the Christian Union and late night compline services. What is also clear is that there was a growing sense through the twentieth century of the value of the pastoral office of the Dean and Chaplain, not least as the teaching and other loads on Fellows became more intense. The innovative appointment of, firstly, a female pastoral assistant (Jane Tillier) and then a female chaplain (Rosalind Hunt), together with the introduction of a mixed choir of men and women, reflects the broadening of the College's life with the admission of women. This has gone hand in hand with the much higher academic profile of the Deans. Peter Baelz (1960–72) and Christopher Rowland (1979–91) left for chairs at Oxford, Barnabas Lindars (1976–8) for one at Manchester; while Edward Hardy (1972–6) came with a legendary reputation as a scholar from his chair at New York's Union Theological Seminary.

As the Chapel enters the twenty-first century, it is arguably in good condition. The fabric has recently been restored to splendid effect, there is a new organ and there is once more a Director of Music as well as a Dean and a Chaplain. There is less of a sense of a formal establishment – paid officials such as the Chapel Clerk have been replaced by students, and there is a much greater degree of student input into the worshipping life of the College. A majority of the student body attends worship during

The first nonconformist to be a Cambridge professor of divinity: C.H. Dodd CH (Fellow and Honorary Fellow).

Edmund H. Nelson, *c*.1960

the course of the year, even if it is only one of the ever-popular Christmas services, and the College produces a steady trickle of ordinands and candidates for baptism and confirmation. Firmly within the Anglican tradition, and hospitable to all, choral services according to the Book of Common Prayer sit alongside informal services within that pattern of twice-daily divine service which has been followed almost continuously since the sixteenth century.

College Prayer

O everlasting God, who through many generations has blessed the college which bears the name of Jesus, grant that we, its latest sons and daughters, may be fortified and clad in his raiment, and may by grace keep Jesus in our hearts, through him who lived and died for us, the same Jesus Christ our Lord.

Chapel Music

DANIEL HYDE

Music has been a part of Chapel life in some shape or form since the College was founded. The statutes drafted in 1514–15 required that at least one of the four choirmen 'shall have skill in organ-playing, and serve the choir and the organ when occasion needs'. Located at the physical heart of the College, the Chapel and its music have enhanced the spiritual, cultural and educational development of Jesuans throughout the College's history. Whether they attend as regular members of the congregation or occasional visitors at matriculation, at Christmas or upon graduation, the Chapel and its music touch almost all students at some point.

As in so many other chapels of Oxford and Cambridge, the pipe organ has played a pivotal role in enhancing the choral liturgy. At Jesus we have had our fair share of organs since the Reformation. In 1582 puritan aversion to the use of organs in worship led to the College selling an instrument, and it was not until 1634 that the Master, William Beale, entered into a contract with the renowned builder Robert Dallam, paying just £200 for one of a number of instruments that the Dallam family constructed within the University in the late 1620s and 1630s. This instrument was short lived and was dismantled in 1643, the year in which Cromwell converted Cambridge into

The 'Sutton' organ in
A.W.N. Pugin's case, 1849.

an armed camp. A curious entry in the College accounts of 1652 reads, 'For discovery of the Organs £1.00.00'. Most of the Fellows left in November 1643, but before going they hit upon an ingenious plan to hide the College's plate and organ from the eyes of any visiting Parliamentarians; legend has it that the remaining Fellows forgot where it was that they had hidden the treasure, and a chance discovery revealed the organ and plate buried in the Master's garden. If the instrument believed to have been resurrected, and tuned from 1669, was that which had been exhumed some years earlier, one can only guess at what it would have sounded like.

In 1693 the College commissioned an instrument from Renatus Harris; its case may now be seen in the parish church of Little Bardfield in Essex. The Chapel fell into a state of some disrepair during the early eighteenth century, and the organ's maintenance was felt to be beyond the resources of the College. In 1776 an agreement was made to lay off the Organist, seeing the instrument as a 'useless Piece of Lumber and Expence'. Whether it was due to the unsavoury singing of 'dubious' songs as an entertainment before dinner or just the changing views of the fellowship, a College Order of January 1790 'agreed to make a present of the remains of our Organ to the Parish of All Saints in Cambridge'. Sadly, a musical vacuum was to follow for some sixty years, before a new enthusiasm for ecclesiastical and musical pursuits was spearheaded by the arrival of John Sutton as a pensioner in 1840.

Sutton's arrival was a watershed moment in the life of the Chapel in general, and music in particular. Widely travelled, well connected and wealthy, Sutton breathed new vision and enthusiasm into the place, supporting and encouraging two young and like-minded Fellows, John Gibson and Osmond Fisher, in overseeing the restoration of the Chapel to the heart of College life, working alongside his friend Augustus Welby Pugin. Sutton was particularly interested in the development of a choral tradition centred around a first-class organ. As well as instituting a choir school within the College, teaching local boys himself in both music and general subjects, he spent much of his time at Jesus writing *A Short Account of Organs built in England from the Reign of King Charles II to the Present Time*. As C.H. Davidson says in his exhaustive study of the man, 'The organ is an instrument that gets into people's bones; those who love it can always talk about it, sometimes to the boredom to despair of their friends, and because no one is exactly like another there are endless possibilities of design of cases, variation of stops and position in buildings.' Installed in 1849 and built by Bishop, Sutton's instrument epitomised his involvement in the philosophy of the Ecclesiological Movement. Placed in the chancel directly above the singers and with the primary function of accompanying the choral service, it

enabled Sutton to initiate the choral liturgy that we know today. The *Guardian* newspaper, reporting the restoration of the Chapel in November 1849, commented:

> The organ, which is placed in the north aisle, is a fine instrument of most beautiful tone, built on the old models of Messrs. Bishop of London, containing however two stops of Father Smith's, one of which, a Flute, is from the old organ in Durham Cathedral. It has two rows of keys. The case is extremely elegant, and has doors folding over the front, painted on the outside with a presentation of a choir of angels. It is a unique specimen, harmonizing with the other beauties of this richly-decorated chapel.

Following Pugin's extensive restoration, the Chapel was reopened with choral Matins and Holy Communion on All Saints' Day, 1849. 'A full choral service, said and sung, in the manner of our cathedral churches, as was the case originally in all college chapels in the University', was how a contemporary described the celebrations: words equally applicable to our services today. The involvement of the then Professor of Music, T.A. Walmisley, gave the ceremony great significance; Walmisley had written his anthem 'Ponder my Words' specifically for the occasion. The manuscript survives in the College Archives, the front cover bearing the names of the four choristers who sang it. Whether by design or not, this is the same number of choristers as prescribed by the statutes of 1514–15.

Detail of Pugin's organ case.

Later in the nineteenth century a second organ was installed on a gallery on the west wall of the nave, covering two of the recently installed Burne-Jones windows and, in Freddy Brittain's view, 'spoiling the appearance of the Chapel'. It is not entirely clear whether it was the huge increase in the number of undergraduates, coupled with the expectation that all would be present at Sunday services, leading to services being held in the ante-chapel; or whether it was the prevailing contemporary tastes for sheer power and wide dynamic levels that led to the installation of a large three-manual organ in 1887. This organ was, however, allowed to fall into disrepair, and was sold in 1927: the Bodley case went to St Matthew's Church in Portsmouth, where it was destroyed by bombing during the Second World War; the pipework was incorporated in the organ of the City Temple, Holborn Viaduct; and the gallery on which the instrument stood is now across the road in the chapel of Westcott House.

In order that the daily liturgy might be restored to the chancel, and the ante-chapel cleared, the Sutton organ was augmented by the firm of Harrison & Harrison in 1927. This work was in turn reversed in 1971, when Noel Mander installed a new three-manual organ alongside the newly refurbished Sutton organ. Both schemes were very much a product of their times, times from which we now shy away. Having proved very unreliable and ineffectual at meeting the Chapel's choral needs, the Mander organ was removed in March 2007 to make way for a new state-of-the-art instrument from Orgelbau Kuhn of Switzerland. Despite distinct limitations of space and position, it is hoped that the unapologetically Romantic style of the Kuhn organ will fulfil the many different needs of the Chapel music programme, not only by accompanying the

choir, but also as a world-class instrument on which to train the organists of the future. It is with great pride that the College delights in the number of distinguished organists who were once its Organ Scholars; among them are the world-renowned Bach interpreter and former organist at St Alban's Abbey, Peter Hurford (1949); Richard Lloyd (1952), formerly organist of Hereford and Durham Cathedrals; Malcolm Archer (1972), formerly organist of Bristol, Wells and St Paul's Cathedrals; and James O'Donnell (1979), organist and master of the choristers first at Westminster Cathedral and now at Westminster Abbey. It is, as has been said, 'an astonishing record for a College that has not its own choir school'.

The celebration of the choir's 150th anniversary in 1999 gave many of its former members the opportunity to come back and renew old acquaintances. After exhaustive research, including advertising in the local newspaper, 350 invitations were issued and 118 accepted. John Cook (1924), the oldest former chorister at the reunion, shed some light on the life of a chorister in the 1920s: 'There was no pension, but a wonderful life for a boy who enjoyed singing.' The boys wore Eton suits and 'squares' on Sundays, attending Sunday School for an hour before the service, to be read to from Foxe's *Book of Martyrs* amongst others. In addition to the daily evening services and the Sunday morning service, there were annual summer camps and cricket and football matches, at which undergraduates acted as leaders. During the war the Chapel windows were boarded up and rehearsals and services took place around a spinet under the tower.

From the time of Peter Hurford's tenure as Organ Scholar one can trace the development of the choir through the medium of recorded sound. With somewhat patchy contemporary accounts prior to the first wax recordings and radio broadcasts, the surviving recordings offer a glimpse of just how the choral sound has changed over the years, reflecting both social and domestic developments. Hurford's early radio broadcasts prompted glowing praise in *Chanticlere*; successive Organ Scholars have left their mark with imaginative LP compilations and, more recently, cassettes and CDs. With the advent of the internet, it is hoped that some of these recordings, and the services currently held in Chapel, may be available online.

With the consistent maintenance of a cathedral-style liturgy from the early twentieth century onwards, choral singing has thrived as part of the wide cultural life of the College. Initially the preserve of the men and boys that form the Chapel choir, Chapel music was greatly enhanced following the admission of women to the College in 1979: the choir of men and women has continually held its high ranking amongst the choirs of Oxford and Cambridge. With each choir singing twice a week during

T.A. Walmesley's anthem 'Ponder my Words' written for the reopening of the Chapel, 1 November 1849; the opening lines of the composer's manuscript.

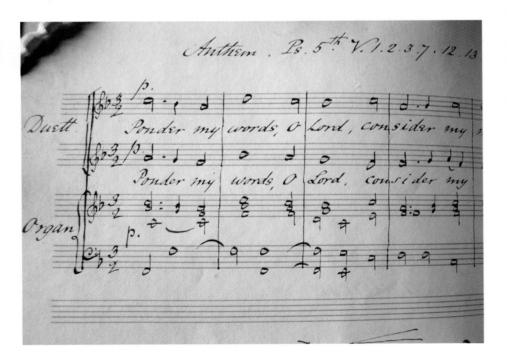

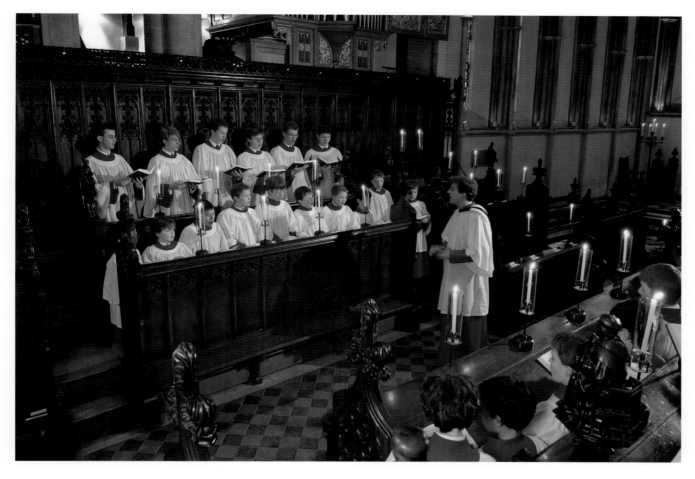

Choirmen and choristers
rehearse before Evensong.

term; regular tours as far afield as Copenhagen, Paris, Estonia and Germany; broadcasts for BBC radio and television; and recordings and performances with professional orchestras such as the Britten Sinfonia and the Saraband Consort, both choirs enjoy a varied and exciting schedule.

David Crighton's election as Master in 1997 quickly led to the appointment of Timothy Byram-Wigfield as the College's first Director of College Music in 1999. Now organist and master of the choristers at St George's Chapel, Windsor, Timothy oversaw the first stage in the transformation of the College's choirs from student-run groups to fully professional enterprises. As his successor, I have been working hard to develop outreach links with local schools, ensuring not only the current standards of musical excellence, but also laying the foundations for the future support and development of Chapel music.

As one walks through the Cloister in the late afternoon, the tolling Chapel bell reminds those nearby that one of the fundamental experiences of Anglican worship is about to take place. Choral Evensong, said and sung according to the Book of Common Prayer of 1662, envelops that perfect mixture of psalmody, canticles, prayers and anthems, affording a moment for reflection upon the rich tapestry of College life. It is the combination of language, music and cultural awareness that has kept the Chapel and its music thriving over five centuries. A healthy College cannot fail to be enhanced by a lively and active Chapel, which in turn benefits from a flourishing music programme. With the commissioning of new music for the choirs and opportunities to perform outside the College, it would be easy to forget the real reasons for the choirs' existence, as an educational enterprise whose *raison d'être* is the singing of services within the daily liturgy of the Chapel. Future generations will continue to enjoy the great benefits to be had from the maintenance of this, whilst also finding new and innovative ways of keeping the Chapel and its rituals relevant to contemporary everyday life.

Masters and Bishops: Dr Chubbes to Dr Corrie

STEPHEN TAYLOR

The public rooms of Jesus, like those of most Oxbridge colleges, are hung with portraits. These often attract little attention, even from those who regularly eat and drink beneath their gaze. To the undiscerning observer they are dull objects, both literally, as they are often covered in layers of old varnish, and metaphorically. But these paintings provide one of the most tangible reminders of the fact that the College is more than those who currently live and work within its walls, more indeed than its alumni stretched across the globe. It is an historic community whose experiences and memories now stretch back for more than five centuries.

Among the portraits we find the occasional benefactor, like Tobias Rustat (page 21), and a few famous old members, like Laurence Sterne and Samuel Taylor Coleridge. But the dominant, recurring image from the origins of the College well into the second half of the nineteenth century is of men in clerical dress, in drab black and white, occasionally relieved by a touch of academic scarlet. This should not surprise us. At the time that these portraits were commissioned, the College's most successful alumni were predominantly those who went on to climb the ladder of preferment in the Church to the bench of bishops. The single largest category of portraits, however, is those of former Masters. A few were both Masters and bishops. The fine portrait of Philip Yonge, which is traditionally, though probably erroneously, attributed to Sir Joshua Reynolds and now hangs in the Combination Room, portrays one of the four Masters who subsequently attained episcopal rank. Even the most striking portrait that currently hangs in Hall, the copy of Reynolds's penetrating full-length study of Laurence Sterne, implicitly highlights the same link (page 141). Sterne, who was himself a clergyman by profession, was the fourth generation of his family to attend Jesus. His uncle, Jacques, admitted in 1711, was an archdeacon in the diocese of York; his grandfather,

Simon, had been a Fellow Commoner in 1669; and his great-grandfather, Richard (page 114), is the only person to have served two terms as Master, before being elevated to the bishopric of Carlisle and thence to the archbishopric of York.

What do these Masters and bishops tell us about the life of the College? The succession of Masters can, of course, be used to provide the structure through which we can tell the history of the College as a community, as a place of education, as part of the wider University, and in its relations with the world beyond Cambridge. This task, however, has already been accomplished in Arthur Gray and Frederick Brittain's *History*. So I shall focus on some of the characteristics shared by this group of men to illuminate a few key aspects of the history of Jesus. But, before doing that, I want to pick out a few episodes in the lives of just a handful of them to illuminate some of the interactions between the life of the College and the life of the nation.

The Masters of Jesus before Sterne are not well documented, and we know, if anything, even less about what went on in College in its early years. We are, therefore, remarkably ignorant about the education and early career of Thomas Cranmer, who came to Cambridge in 1503 to pursue a course of studies leading to the BA. His early relations with the College were good: having resigned his fellowship to marry, he was promptly re-elected when his wife died in childbirth. Later, however, a coolness and distance opened up between Henry VIII's reform-minded Archbishop and a College which became a bastion of religious conservatism under the long mastership of William Capon (1516–46). As Diarmaid MacCulloch pithily noted in his magisterial biography, 'Cranmer was not a good College man.' Even so, few, surely, can lay a better claim than Cranmer to being the College's most distinguished alumnus. Certainly none has had such a great impact either on the character of the Church in England or, through his authorship of the Book of Common Prayer, on the development of the English language and culture.

By the time that Capon resigned as Master in 1546, he was doubtless a disillusioned man. But his College was, as yet, relatively untouched by the deep ideological divisions engendered by the Reformation. This was not to remain the case for long. John Fuller, appointed to the mastership in 1557, achieved notoriety in Foxe's *Book of Martyrs* as the hammer of Protestants in East Anglia. As chancellor of the diocese of Ely he played a leading part in the imposition of the Marian counter-reformation in the University, and passed sentence on, among others, John Hullier, who was burned on Jesus Green in 1556. Under Elizabeth divisions among Protestants came to the fore as different factions competed to secure the triumph of their vision of the doctrine and government of the Church of England. In 1595 John Duport (1590–1618), as Vice-Chancellor, secured the condemnation of William Barrett, whose attack on Calvinist doctrines of sin and faith scandalised the moderate puritan party that was in the ascendant in the University.

Religious intolerance also appears to mark the history of the College at the restoration of Charles II, when John Worthington, who had been serving as Master since 1650, was forced to vacate the office in favour of Richard Sterne. Sterne's claim to the mastership was difficult to deny – he had, after all, been ejected from it sixteen years earlier because of his royalism – but he was already destined for better things, and Worthington's friends canvased support for him in London. Unfortunately, the choice of Sterne's successor lay neither with the Fellows nor with the King, but rather with the Bishop of Ely, Matthew Wren, an unreconstructed Laudian who had spent the years of civil war and interregnum incarcerated in the Tower of London. Wren was determined that the leadership of the restored Church would be placed in the hands of men who shared his vision. Someone who had taken the Engagement and accommodated himself to the Republic was hardly likely to be an apostle for a revived Caroline Anglicanism, and the mastership went instead to John Pearson, who had spent the previous decade eking out a living as a chaplain in royalist families.

Even in Jesus in 1660, however, there were signs that the climate of religious opinion had begun to shift. Relations between Worthington and Sterne were cordial. Sterne left his predecessor in possession of the Lodge for some months during the late summer and autumn, and Worthington repaid the favour by organising a dinner and concert in Sterne's honour. More significantly, perhaps, Worthington was not a zealous puritan. He had no problem accommodating himself to the new regime, retiring from College to his living of Fen Ditton and then subscribing to the Act of Uniformity in 1662.

Many clergymen, of course, survived the religious turmoil of the sixteenth and seventeenth centuries by giving quiet allegiance to the powers that be, whoever they were. But Worthington was no vicar of Bray. He had been a pupil of Benjamin Whichcote and was a friend of the Cambridge Platonists Henry More and Ralph Cudworth. He responded to the conflicts which had torn Protestantism apart over the previous century with a reluctance, both private and public, to enter into doctrinal controversy. Instead, as he reflected in 1660, 'My spirit & behaviour

has been for peace & charity … It was my perpetual song to persuade men to moderation, & an obliging fairness to those persons, that were lately depresst.' Worthington was one of the precursors of that spirit of anti-dogmatism and moderation, sometimes described as latitudinarianism, which was to come to dominate the Church of England during the next century.

In contrast to the English revolution of the mid-seventeenth century, which had deeply divided the clergy,

Thomas Cranmer (?1503),
Archbishop of Canterbury.
English school, *c.*1590

**Two more archbishops of
Canterbury:**
(Left) Richard Bancroft
(1569)
Circle of Marcus Gheraerdts the
younger
(Right) Matthew Hutton
(1710)
Thomas Hudson, 1753

the French revolution prompted a virtually unanimous response. To most of the clergy of the established Church and, indeed, to most of the British elite, the revolution represented anarchy, republicanism and atheism; opposition to its principles became a matter of Christian duty. Inevitably, the reverberations of these attitudes were felt in Cambridge, and nowhere more than at Jesus, which, under the long mastership of the Whig Lynford Caryl (1758–81) (page 73), had attracted some of the more liberal minds in the University. Even before the outbreak of revolution in France, however, William Frend (page 123) had already pushed the boundaries of orthodoxy beyond what was acceptable. In 1788, following his conversion to, and public advocacy of, Unitarianism, he was removed from the office of Tutor. Frend's appeal from the decision of the Master, Richard Beadon, to the Bishop of Ely was a predictable failure – a role so intimately concerned with the education of aspiring clergymen could hardly be left with a man who had publicly repudiated one of the Church's central doctrines. It says much about the character of Jesus at this time that Frend retained his fellowship and remained on friendly terms with his colleagues. Even William Pearce, Beadon's successor as Master, was, as Coleridge recorded, 'very intimate with him'. Frend can hardly have believed, however, that he would be immune to the changing political climate as the revolution gathered pace in France. By the end of 1792, when Tom Paine was burned in effigy on Market Hill, a loyalist reaction was sweeping Britain. Frend's publication in

February 1793 of *Peace and Union Recommended*, urging sweeping political reform and making irreverent attacks on the Church of England, was a rash and provocative act. He may have been hurt, but he can hardly have been surprised when the Master and Fellows voted to remove him from College. It says much for the eighteenth century's respect for property rights that he nonetheless continued to enjoy the emoluments of his fellowship until he had to resign it on his marriage in 1808.

Following the appointment of G.E. Corrie to the mastership in 1849, Jesus developed into a bastion of conservatism. D.A. Winstanley's memorable description of the new Master, 'the last ditch was his spiritual home', possesses the kernel of truth essential in all good caricature. As Norrisian Professor of Divinity he had already opposed the institution of a voluntary examination for students studying theology with a view to ordination, a course which was, at this time, distinct from the studies leading to the BA. Within months of becoming Master he refused to answer any of the questions proposed to him as Vice-Chancellor and a head of house by the Royal Commission on the University, arguing that it was 'unconstitutional' and, in a clear reference to the assaults launched on the University by the Roman Catholic James II, 'of a kind that was never issued except in the worst of times'. In the following year he dispatched an angry letter to the directors of the Eastern Counties Railway, complaining about their plans to run trains to Cambridge 'on *Sundays* at such fares as may be likely to tempt persons who, having no regard for Sundays themselves, would inflict their presence on this University on that day of rest'. Corrie's views do, of course, benefit from contextualisation. Virulent anti-popery and mild sabbatarianism were entirely consonant with the spirit of Cambridge conservatism in the middle of the nineteenth century, as was his characterisation of visitors to the town as 'foreigners'. The railway company was provocatively attempting to evade the terms of the parliamentary statute which had established it, prohibiting trains from picking up and setting down passengers at Cambridge (or within three miles thereof) between 10 a.m. and 5 p.m. on Sundays. Even so, by the time of his death at the age of 92 in 1885, following the mid-Victorian reforms of the universities, Corrie's attitudes were redolent of a distant world. Three years earlier, when new statutes finally allowed Fellows to marry, he (a life-long bachelor) is supposed to have expressed the hope that none at Jesus would take advantage of their new freedom. Within a year, however, all the resident Fellows except one had done so.

Let us now turn to consider the Masters of Jesus from Chubbes to Corrie as a group. Is it possible to identify any common characteristics? If so, what do they tell us about the history of the College?

First, and most obviously, all were clergymen ordained, after the Reformation, according to the rites of the Church of England. They presided over a society that was unequivocally clerical in character. Until 1841 all but four of the Fellows were obliged to take orders, and many went on from Cambridge to benefices in the Church, as did most of the junior members. At the time that admissions to Jesus fell to their nadir in the mid-eighteenth century, it became almost exclusively a clerical seminary and it was rare for someone who had graduated BA not then to seek ordination. Between 1760 and 1764, for example, only twenty-three undergraduates were admitted, sixteen men took the degree of BA, and eighteen were given testimonials certifying their suitability to become clergymen. Jesus, indeed, like most Oxbridge colleges, resembled a monastic institution in a manner that may now appear remarkable in a Protestant country: a celibate, male community, enclosed behind high walls and dedicated to learning and prayer. In this community the Master alone was allowed to marry, though neither of the College's longest serving Masters, Ashton and Corrie, did so.

Secondly, by modern standards Masters were remarkably young at the time of their appointment. A significant number – including Sterne, Saywell and Ashton – were in their thirties; John Worthington was a mere 32. Corrie's long tenure of the mastership is the more remarkable in that, at 56, he was one of the oldest men to be appointed. Their youth was reflected in the College as a whole. Before the late nineteenth century Cambridge was a

much more youthful environment than it is today. Very few Fellows remained in College until death; most had removed long before to a country parish, often waiting only long enough to secure one of the better livings in the College's gift. The career of many Masters followed a similar path. Half of them served fewer than ten years; nine for fewer than five. For most the Mastership was not the culmination of a distinguished career in academia or public service; it was, rather, a step on the ladder of preferment, a point made effectively and vividly in Gillray's 1788 print, *Questions and Commands; or, the mistaken road to He–r–f–rd; a Sunday evenings amusement*, satirising Richard Beadon's grovelling efforts to take advantage of the fact that Prince William of Gloucester was his pupil. Four Masters – Sterne, Pearson, Yonge and Beadon – went on to bishoprics, a well-established career trajectory. The abilities of others took them elsewhere. In 1662 Bishop Wren moved Joseph Beaumont to the Mastership of the rather more troublesome society at Peterhouse, where, combining his duties with those of the Regius Professor

Dr Philip Yonge, Master 1752–8 and subsequently bishop of Bristol and of Norwich.

After Reynolds, 1769

QUESTIONS & COMMANDS; or The ROAD to HE_R_F_RD; a Sunday Evenings Amusement.

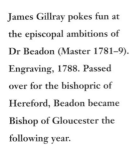

James Gillray pokes fun at the episcopal ambitions of Dr Beadon (Master 1781–9). Engraving, 1788. Passed over for the bishopric of Hereford, Beadon became Bishop of Gloucester the following year.

of Divinity, he developed into one of the most powerful figures in late seventeenth-century Cambridge. John Pearson went on to be master of Trinity after sixteen months at Jesus and Humphrey Gower (page 4) stayed for only five before becoming master of St John's. But then, as now, academic distinction was not an essential qualification for a head of house. Beaumont's theological lectures were renowned and Pearson can lay claim to being one of the most significant theologians in the history of the Church of England – his *Exposition of the Creed*, first published in 1659, remained continuously in print for more than two hundred years – but in many cases administrative ability was at least as important. In 1752 Philip Yonge's main claim to preferment was that he was a pair of safe Whig hands, who could be trusted to rule a solidly Tory College following the long mastership of Charles Ashton. It was the same qualities that brought him promotion to the bishoprics of Bristol (1758) and Norwich (1761). Yonge had few pretensions to scholarship. Throughout his career he published only two slim volumes, both after he had left College: a routine episcopal charge and a jejune charity sermon. But, as Parson Woodforde wrote in his *Diary*, he was 'a Man much beloved by his Clergy'.

Thirdly, all Masters were pluralists. Few, indeed, engaged in the practice on the scale of Roger Andrewes,

who prevailed on his brother Lancelot Andrewes to appoint him to the richest benefices in his gift to an extent that scandalised even contemporaries. A dispute with the Fellows in 1628 suggests that he was every bit as grasping in his management of the College. All Masters, however, found it necessary to supplement their income with at least one other appointment. Most were canons of Ely, if they did not already hold some more desirable dignity. This was hardly surprising in view of the proximity of the cathedral city and the fact that the bishops of Ely appointed both the cathedral canons and the College's Masters. Occasionally, as in the case of Corrie, the Master was appointed to one of the richer parochial livings in the diocese of Ely. The reasons for this practice are clear: masterships were rarely places of great profit, and that of Jesus was one of the poorest in Cambridge. Even in 1849 it was worth only £400 per annum, less than a modestly comfortable Victorian country rectory. What is less clear is the effects. The fact that the Masters held other positions in the Church reinforced their clerical identity, and it may also have added to their authority. The status of William Pearce was certainly enhanced by the fact that he was also Dean of Ely. On the other hand, Masters were already separate from the College in many ways, resident in the Lodge and, if married, enjoying the comforts of domesticity. Thus, while the statutes of the College facil-

itated the non-residence of its Masters, the duties required of a chancellor of the diocese of Ely, such as John
Fuller, or a rector of Newton near Wisbech, such as G.E.
Corrie, or even of a canon of Ely, must have increased the
distance between the Master and the Fellows.

Finally, as has already been noted, the Masters of Jesus
were appointed by the bishops of Ely. One consequence
was that very few Jesuans were elevated to the headship of
their own College. Duport, who was an undergraduate,
and Beale and Ashton, who were Fellows, are exceptions;
of these, only Ashton was a Fellow at the time of his elevation. Appointment by the bishop of Ely also gave the
mastership and, through it, the College as a whole some
of their character. The bishopric of Ely may no longer
have enjoyed the prestige that it had through much of the
middle ages, but it was still one of the most distinguished
ecclesiastical preferments in the gift of the Crown.
Successive bishops were senior, establishment figures,
and their appointees tended to be made in their own
image: radical puritans, doctrinaire liberals, mavericks of
any kind are conspicuous by their absence.

Nonetheless, in the appointments of Masters it is possible to see a reflection of the shifts in ecclesiastical policy
through the three centuries after the Reformation. In the
1630s Matthew Wren selected William Beale and Richard
Sterne, men whom he was confident would work to advance
the Laudian programme of the 'beauty of holiness' and
Arminian theology in Cambridge. Following the Restoration he turned to John Pearson and Joseph Beaumont,
both men who had suffered under the Republic and who
were committed, like Wren, to a vision of the religious
settlement that was exclusively and intolerantly Anglican.
In the mid-eighteenth century the College felt the influence of the Whig establishment. Thomas Gooch, the
Bishop of Ely, despite an early flirtation with toryism as
Master of Gonville and Caius, had risen in the Church as
a close ally of the Duke of Newcastle, who was one of
George II's leading ministers and the foremost Whig
grandee of the period. The Masters appointed by Gooch
– Philip Yonge and Lynford Caryl – reflected the views of
the Duke: court Whigs in politics and moderate latitudinarians in religion. And gradually the College followed
suit, transforming itself, as we have seen, from a bastion
of toryism under Ashton to a moderately liberal society
on the eve of the French revolution.

But the patronage of the bishops of Ely and the access

Dr George Elwes Corrie
(Master 1849–85).
Photograph by Thomas Stearne,
Cambridge, *c.*1870

that gave to the establishment in Church and State brought
risks as well as opportunities. For Sterne and Yonge the
mastership was but one rung on the ladder of preferment;
for Charles Ashton (page 5), by contrast, it was a dead
end. A former chaplain of Simon Patrick, Bishop of Ely,
he appeared destined for a glittering career in the Church,
holding the rectory of Rattenden, the chaplainship of
Chelsea Hospital and a canonry of Ely before being
appointed to the mastership of Jesus in 1701 at the age of
only 36. But, with the death of William III in the following year, Patrick lost his influence at court, and on the
death of Patrick himself in 1707 Ashton lost his patron. A
moderate but convinced Tory, Ashton found himself
increasingly out of sympathy first with his new diocesan,
the resolutely Whig William Fleetwood, and then with the
succession of Whig ministries that ruled Britain for half a
century after the Hanoverian succession of 1714. His
retreat into scholarly seclusion was, thus, as much as anything the product of disappointed ambition. There is a
certain irony in the fact the College's longest serving
Master almost certainly viewed his own career as a failure.

Tutors and Undergraduates

Ralph Josselin (1632)

Ralph Josselin, a farmer's son from Steeple Bumpstead on the Essex and Cambridgeshire border, matriculated as a pensioner in 1632, took his BA in 1636, and then worked as a schoolmaster until in 1641 he became vicar of Earls Colne in Essex. Living there for the rest of his life, he kept a detailed diary of his activities as parson, farmer and book collector; of his health, physical and spiritual; and of his friendship with the family of Thomas Harlakenden, the Lord of the Manor, who died in Cambridge in September 1652 while on a visit to his undergraduate son.

1632. March

My fathers love was such towards mee that when I was neare 16 yeares old I went to Cambridge to Jesus Colledge entred pentioner under Mr Tho: Lane, my loving and I hope godly and honest tutor he dealt lovingly with mee, but I was forced to come from Cambridge many times for want of meanes and loose my time in the contry yett would I endeavour to get it up and I thank god notwithstanding all hindrances I was not behind many of my time and standing: …

In Cambridge in my studies I was close and diligent: my fault was to omitt too many mornings by reason of my tenderness, either in bed or by the fire: the supersticons of the Church were a perplexity then unto mee: god gave mee mercy in blessing me with love, and prospering in the Colledge, few fallings out, but one to speake by or rashnes, which wee lamented as being upon a Sabbath day when wee should have beene at publique ordinances; there god kept from infection strangely:

For my health god was good unto mee: preserving mee from the small poxe when I have oftentimes beene neare and in danger.

1636

While I was in this way compassed with mercyes: being newly come up to Cambridge on Tuesday night Oct: 25: came up my brother Hodson about 10 a Clocke at night and brought mee word my father was sicke, speechlesse,

senseles, and like to dye: I rid home that night, but had not the comfort to have one word from him that he knew mee, so as on Friday: Octob: 28: my Father gave up the ghost, and is now in rest, in joy and glory: he was about 53. yeares old or very nigh and I wanted one quarter to 20: Now was my condicion sad: young, and friendles and pennylesse: my father making no will. October. 30: wee buryed him in Bumpsted Churchyard: with greife of heart I layd him into the grave, but my god lives for evermore: My mother in law [step-mother] tooke not as I conceived a course to doe us Justice, wee could not agree I departed from her; tooke my degree at Cambridge: Batchelor of art with money I had from her, and putt my selfe into apparell, so that of 20ˡⁱ my share in my fathers estate. I spent 10ˡⁱ before Feb: 1: 1636:

But now what course should I take, sometimes I thought upon my fathers farme: then upon the Law, but god and the perswasions of Mr Borradale [vicar of Steeple Bumpstead] and Mr Thornbecke settled mee againe upon Cambridge, well I tooke my degree and in Feb: ult: … a letter sent to him from Mr Neale in Bedfordshire to helpe him to an usher, he sent over kindly … to mee … I lookt upon it as a gratious providence, returned to Bumpstead, payd thee messenger, and resolved into a Country and among persons that I never heard of before: all my things at Cambridge I sold to my sister Anna and in conclusion I gave her them: I made even with all the world, provided mee my horse, one suite of clothes, and

(Facing page)

First Court from the Gate Tower. The right-hand ground floor room facing the gate was occupied by S.T. Coleridge (1791).

Coate which I borrowed at 1ˡⁱ.12ˢ.4ᵈ. upon my uncle Miles his credit, when I had fitted all, disposed my bookes and some linen in my trunke, I left it with a carrier to bring after mee: I tooke horse and rid towards Huntington, ...

June: 18: 1649:
Rid with Mr Harlakenden to Stortford, ... *19.* wee and Mr. H: son rid to Cambridge where I viewed with delight my old colledge, the Master and fellows, very good men hope of their good: *20:* Mr R.H. admitted fellow commoner of Jesus, wee returned to Stortford, and I to Colne:

Jan: 9: 1649/50
Mr Harlakenden troubled at the greatnes of his sons expences at Cambridge, I writt to Mr Richard, to be frugall of his fathers purse, and to improve his time for learning and pietie, god blesse my advice to him

Sept: 26:
a messenger with mee from Cambridge to acquainte mee with the sicknesse of Mr Richard Harlakenden, I went downe to his father, he was very much composed in spirit, for which I rejoice, he sent to Cambridge

Sept: 29:
good hopes of Mr Ri: Harlakenden at Cambridge the lord spare him for his goodnesse sake.

Oct: 2:
a very comfortable day, wee heard also good newes from Mr Richard from Cambridge, of his recovery the lords name bee praised for it.

from *The Diary of Ralph Josselin,*
ed. Alan Macfarlane, London 1976

Roger North (1667)

North entered the College on 20 October 1667 as a nobleman Fellow Commoner (he was the fifth surviving son of the fourth Baron North), following in the steps of his brother John, who had matriculated in 1661 and been made a Fellow by royal mandate in 1664. (John moved to Trinity in 1672 on becoming Regius Professor of Greek, and was later, and unhappily, Master of that college.) Roger, a Member of Parliament and a successful lawyer, was a book collector and a polymath, the author of important works on architecture, music, accountancy, fish-farming, history, legal study, and the theory of biography, as well as of the lives of three of his brothers and an autobiography, Notes of Me, written in the 1690s, which contains in addition to the passage printed here a lengthy description of his mathematical instruments (given by his son to the College) and of the uses he made of them.

At Cambridg I livd a year, in which time nothing extraordinary happned to me, unless it were, that I was forct to live in the quality of a nobleman, with a very strait allowance. I was not capable to conduct my self, but had a brother who was in the place of tutor, and provided all things for me. Besides the first cost of a gowne which was not over rich few of ordinary quality spent less, then I did, and it chiefly lay in not going in company for I had not confidence, nor mony, and very seldome on my owne account made or received a visit.

This way of living with a brother, for I had the same chamber, engaged me to spend my time in reading, as he did, who was a most strict student. But I am sensible, that if I had not bin under such restraint, tho it was not of force, but a sort of grave silent authority, with which I could not for shame contend, I should have bin very idle. I did most extreamly envy the common scollers for the joy they had at foot ball, and lament my owne condition, that was tyed up by quality from mixing with them, and enjoying the freedomes of rambling which they had. And not having either mony or assurance to mix with my equalls, who were wild and extravagant enough, was oblidged to walk with grave seniors, and to know no other divertion. This infelicity as I then thought it was in truth the greatest felicity I could have. For by the common liberty I was inclined to follow, I should have bin in great danger of being hardned in some sort of vice, idleness, for certein, and carryed it to London with me, and there improved it to very ill porposes. So that I must owne much of my preservation to the strait fortunes of my family, which put such a bridle on my propensitys of youth which are at best to idleness and liberty; that I could not make any dangerous excursions.

As to study there, I followed my owne appetite, which was to naturall philosophy which they call phisicks, and particularly D[es]Cartes, whose works, I dare say I read over 3 times before I understood him; the 3d time my braines were inlightened, and I gained the notions of his

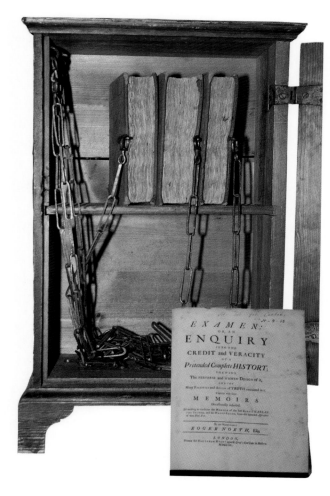

is here to prove that one line is equall to another, to what end is it? And troubling my brother often with such talk, he used constantly to say, that it was a rule I might depend on in the study of the mathematicks, that if I were not pleased, I did not understand. This at last set me on work againe, and when I once got hold on the thredd, and found it come, that is, perceivd the drift of the many, (seeming,) useless propositions, tending to prove others of consequence, I devoured the science with great greedyness. And this illumination, I had upon consideration of the 47[th] proposition which is that in all ∇^s the square of the greater [side], is equall to those of the 2 others. This entered me alive as I may say, and I digested it with great satisfaction, and having gott, Barrow, which is much the best, I la[u]ncht farther, and made my self master of so much as served to comon practicall geometry; but the more abstruse secrets tending to algebra, I was not a match for.

I had books of ethicks and metaphisicks, also to peruse, but my delight was in philosophy, and mathematicks, which my brother did not interupt, being glad that I was imployd, and so long did not disturb him, with prat[t]le and idle questions. Logick I did not touch upon there, having had enough at home, but improved that , by seeing the practise of disputation, in the publik scools, and colledg. And never thought of performing any exercises in publik. Logick is a very dull science, especially that which relates to disputation, and must be driven by a tutor, well verst in it, as a smith hammers iron out of a lump in to a barr. And to say truth an age more advanct, then ordinary youths fresh in the university, is most proper for the study of logick. But in regard that is a time when somewhat must be learnt, and the rules of logick regulates the mind, and makes it more just to weigh other learning, and altho the person neither is delighted, nor

vortixes, vapours, and striatas. I had this labour, for want of a tutor, for my brother, was but so in name for protection, and answering the colledg, but never read any lectures to me, nor cared to answer my impertinent silly questions, which came upon him so thick, that I perceived his temper disturbed at it; for he was a most thoughtfull indefatigable man. Therefore I forbore; and at that time New Philisofy was a sort of heresie, and my brother cared not to encourage me much in it. I had the old phisicks, as Magirus, and Senertus but could not thresh so at them. I read most of the latter, but without content. … I had a book of atomicall philisofy, after Demoncritus, which enterteined me better. But I found such a stirr about Descartes, some railing at him, and forbidding the reading him as if he had impugned the very gospell, and yet there was a generall inclination, especially of the brisk part of the university, to use him, which made me conclude there was somewhat extraordinary in him, which I was resolved to find out, and at length did so, wherein the nititur in vetitum, had no small share; I had not bin so furiously fond, if the author had bin obtruded, but shewne, and then withdrawne, made us more deviously prosecute him … I joyned with this study some mathematicks, to which also I had an inclination. And having read Fournier on Euclid, I wondered at the emptyness of that study; and used to say what a stir

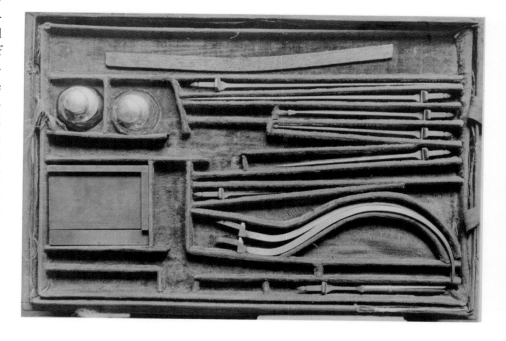

throly understands the drift, nor perhaps the force of what he reads, yet it is fitt to be learnt early, for when the mind is more advanced and comes to work critically upon points of other learning and hath need, memory brings into use the former dull rules, and they are a great help, which els would not at such pinch be at hand.

My brother used to recommend to me translating, and accordingly I englisht Salust's Cataline, with some essay of paraphrase, intending to season the style, which is in bare translation dull, with somewhat of English quickness, but this was farr from being considerable enough to preserve, however it is a most usefull exercise, and fitt to

be recomended to all students. This is a mixture of language and invention; exercises which are onely of invention, torment yong minds too much, and after all are not usefull, as the exercise of language, the readyness and neatness of which, prevailes more than deep sence.

At the last I was sent home with a fen-ague such as will be buisy thereabouts, and returned no more, but stayd at home untill the Parliment called my father to London in the year [1669].

Notes of Me: The Autobiography of Roger North,
ed. Peter Millard, Toronto 2000 (pp. 92–4)

William Reneu (1705)

William Reneu, who was to remain at Jesus until 1721, having been elected a Fellow in 1710, kept in touch with his old schoolmaster, the church historian John Strype, who had himself matriculated at Jesus in 1662.

[Endorsed] Wm Reneu's first letter to me [John Strype] from Jesus Coll: Cambridge

Cambridge 8ber 9 1705

Honoured Sir: …
I Like the college very well and I find my Commons with the addition of an half pennyworth of Cheese or butter full enough for the most part. The Lads are very civil and kind to me, and now and then they ask me to come to their Chambers and I do the same to them again. But among themselves they are up to the ears in divisions about high Church and Low Church, Whig and Tory. But for my part I strive to leave them when they are going to that sport – Mr Trencher my Chamber fellow is very good natured young gentleman and very civil to me, and I don't doubt but he and I shall agree very well together. For the present I do nothing but a Chapter of the Epistle to the Romans every morning in greek to Mr Grig. But I shall do something else in a little while … I understand I am to make some petty speeches and disputations in Hall next term. I wish they well over, but I believe I am more afraid than I shall be hurt when I come to it. …

I am
Hon^d Sir Your most obliged friend and humble Servant
W Reneu

I did not write you in Latin Because I was afraid the Post would be gone before I could finish it and some other letters I had to write.

To his next letter, on 14 December, which was in Latin and accompanied transcriptions of the epitaphs in the Chapel of Tobias Rustat and Dr Boldero (Master 1663–78), he added a note to Mrs Strype.

Hon'd Madam

I am glad that you are got pretty well again of your fever which you had when I was with you last. And am much obliged to you for your kind offer of sending me Cake, which you may be sure when ever it comes will be very welcome for though we have pretty good Commons yet we have not such a vast deall but we can make shift with a bit of Cake after them …

I remain
Hon'd Madam,
Yours at Command
W Reneu

May 6, 1707

My year is so very large that though I have been half a year Junior Soph I have not gotten a Scholarship nor can't expect one these 6 months; its largeness has brought another inconvenience upon me, viz. that I neither have nor shall keep much exercise in Colledge, which would have helpt to wear off that faulty Bashfulness which I have. I don't know whether I may expect a fellowship for there are severall to be served before me, if they stay.

My Tutor went to London about a month ago and from there to Bath. I received a letter from him on Sunday night last dated the 28th April wherein he wrote he intended to leave Bath in about three weeks.

Honoured Sr

Last Fryday I got over all the troublesome business attending my Degree and was capped by the Vicechancellor; news I fancy that won't be very ungratefull to you who have always shown such a kind concern for my welfare and happiness ... I intend to be at London (if weather alters and mends the Roads) within ten dayes. In the meantime I fancy my Father would be glad if you'd dine with him one day, and you'd particularly oblige me if

you'd tell him, he must expect pretty large Bills this Degree-time. I have this day sent him a very large one which I don't know how he'll like. But intend he shall have no more such; for now I be Bachelour I know I can find severall ways to retrench my Expences; I live for three score pds perAn: very handsomely, that he's willing to allow me.

Your aff.ate humble servt
W Reneu

Jes: coll: Jan 25
No 8/9

University Library, Baumgartner MSS, vol. iii, nos. 88, 140, 146.
(Add MS.4)

Gilbert Wakefield (1772)

After a distinguished undergraduate career Gilbert Wakefield was elected a Fellow in 1776 and by the time of his death in 1801 at the age of 45 his fame as a classical scholar rivalled Richard Porson's. His conscientious scruples at subscribing the Thirty-Nine Articles had, however, prevented his taking either his MA or holy orders. He became, in effect, a Unitarian; he questioned the need for any form of public worship, and engaged in political controversy, with the unhappy consequences described on page 122.

As Mr Wooddeson was on the eve of giving up his school, and my father, though I was not yet *sixteen years* old, had judiciously determined to place me under no other master, a situation at college became now the object of attention.

Dr. Jeffries, since a residentiary of St. Pauls, but then a canon of Christ-church, kindly offered his assistance in procuring for me a studency in that house. I never reflect but with profound gratitude to the Almighty Superintendant of my existence, on that predilection of my father for his own college in *Cambridge*, which rescued me from a place of education, where no such studies are the objects of academical emulation, as are calculated to give full exercise to the reasoning and investigating faculties of the mind; or rather, I believe, if we may credit her own sons, no established studies of any kind whatever. Their powers of invention are unexerted, their ambition is at rest. ...

At that time a scholarship, in Jesus College, Cambridge, became vacant. It was founded not many years before by Mr. Marsden, archdeacon of Nottingham, for the son of a living clergyman born in that town: both which conditions were united in me. *Dr. Caryl* too, the master of the college, had long been an intimate acquaintance of my father, and was a Nottinghamshire man, his father being

rector of Cotgrave. These inducements contributed to establish me in that college; where I was admitted in April 1772; and my transport and enthusiasm, at going thither, are still alive. ...

The *College Tutors*, at my admission, were Messrs. *Milner* and *Derby*; both respectable for their abilities, but, in my opinion, deficient in that activity and zeal absolutely requisite for such a momentous office. ... As soon as I was settled in college, I resumed my *classical* studies, which had suffered a long suspension by a most severe sore throat and fever, fatal to multitudes at that time, and by a vacation of several months.

Our college lectures in *Algebra* and *Logic*, were odious to me beyond conception; and I am persuaded by experience, that *Logic* and *Metaphysics* are by no means calculated for those early years. ... As to the *Elements of Geometry* and *Algebra*, these are in themselves so extremely plain, so accessible to every capacity, and carry with them such beautiful and engaging evidence – Truth in her very essence! – that I can scarcely account for an indisposition to such theories, but from a defect of judgment, or dexterity, in the teacher.

So enamoured, however, was I with the beauties of *classic ground*, that no considerations could for some months prevail upon me to step out of this flowery path into the regions of *Science* and *Philosophy*, intricate as they *then* appeared. I endeavoured, but in vain, to prevail upon myself to open *Euclid*, the OLD CARPENTER! As one of our year, like myself, a mathematician by *compulsion*, was wont to call him in derision. At last, *emulation* effected, what *reason* and *inclination* were unable to accomplish. Upon hearing that several of my contemporaries had already made a considerable proficiency in Geometry, I resolutely sat down to encounter this formidable adversary, with all the assiduity that I could bear, and all the faculties that I could summon. ...

During the two first years of my residence at college, I pursued my *mathematical* and *philosophical* studies with a stated mixture of *classical* reading, except when a strange fastidiousness, for which I could never account, occasionally took a bewildering possession of my faculties. This impediment commonly recurred in the spring of the year, when I was so enamoured of rambling in the open air, through solitary fields, or by a river's side – of the amusements of cricket and fishing, that no self-expostulations, no prospect of future vexation, nor even emulation itself,

could chain me to my books. Sometimes for a month together, and even for a longer period, though tormented all the while with the reflection, have I been disabled from reading a single page without extreme restlessness and impatience.

As a counterpoise to this constitutional inconvenience, I made the best use of time when my inclinations were compliant; but seldom to the neglect of plentiful recreation and stated exercise, to which I religiously attended. During a *five years* continuance at college, I rose, almost without exception, by *five o'clock*, winter and summer; but never breakfasted, drank tea, or supt *alone*, half a dozen times during all that space; enjoying society, from the first, beyond measure, as a most delightful and rational relief from study. Nevertheless, abundance of time and exertion was misapplied by me in this career of laborious ambition, for want of a *private* tutor to direct and superintend my studies.

Memoirs of the Life of Gilbert Wakefield, BA
(1804), vol. 1 (pp. 59–87)

Samuel Taylor Coleridge (1791)

John Cornwell describes Coleridge's Cambridge career on pages 130-134. The passages printed here come from Coleridge's two letters written during his first term to his eldest brother, George.

[Early November]
As I am now settled in my rooms, and as college Business is commenced, I shall be able to give you some little account of matters. We go to Chapel twice a day – every time we miss, we pay twopence, and fourpence on Surplice days – id est, Sundays, Saints' days, and the eves of Saints' Days. I am remarkably religious upon an economical plan.

We have Mathematical Lectures, once a day – Euclid and Algebra alternately. I read Mathematics three hours a day – by which means I am always considerably before the Lectures, which are very good ones. Classical Lectures we have had none yet – nor shall I be often *bored* with them. They are seldom given, and when given, very thinly attended.

After Tea – (N.b / Sugar is very dear) I read Classics till I go to bed – viz – eleven o'clock. If I were to read on as I do now – there is not the least doubt, that I should be Classical Medallist, and a very high Wrangler – but *Freshmen* always *begin* very *furiously*. I am reading Pindar, and composing Greek verse, like a mad dog. I am very fond of Greek verse, and shall try hard for the Brown's

Prize ode. At my Leisure hours I translate Anacreon – I *have* translated the first, the second, the 28th, the 32nd, the 43rd, and the 46th – Middleton thinks I have translated the 32nd (Άγε, ζωγραφων αριστε) very well – I think between us both, we might translate him entirely – You *have* translated 6 or 7, have you not?

Dr Pierce is not come up to College – The Rustat Scholarship will be worth to me 27 pound a year – There is a new regulation at our College, they tell me – that without any exception the man, who takes the highest honour in his year of the candidates, is to be elected Fellow – This will be a bit of a stimulus to my exertions.

There is no such thing as *discipline* at our college – There was once, they say – but so long ago, that no one remembers it. Dr Pierce, if I am not very much misinformed, will introduce it with a vengeance this year. We have had so very large an admittance, that it will be absolutely necessary.

We do one declamation every term – two are spoken in a week, one English, one Latin. Consequently when the college was very thin, the men were pestered with two or three in a term. Themes and verses are in disuse at our College – whether the doctor intends to [restore] them [or] no, I cannot tell.

I have a most vio[lent] cold in my head – a favour, which I owe to the dampness of my rooms.

The Rustat Scholarship depends in some measure upon residence – otherwise it would be worth 30£ a year to me. But I should lose by this gain – while in the country, I can be at no expence: but unnecessary residence is a very *costly* thing …

[28 November]

… I was very unwell, when I wrote last to you; but the day after I grew so much worse, that I was obliged to take to my bed. Cambridge is a damp place – the very palace of winds: so without very great care one is sure to have a violent cold. I am not however certain, that I do not owe my Rheumatism to the dampness of my rooms. Opium never used to have any disagreeable effects on me – but it has upon many …

My dear Brother, I assure you, I am an ŒEconomist. I keep no company – that is, I neither give or receive invitations to wine parties; because in our college there are no end to them. I eat no suppers. Middleton acts to me with great friendship. While I was confined to my bed, though he was reading for an act, and could ill spare his time, he yet came, and sat with me often. After he has taken his degree, he has promised to read Mathematics with me, which will be of infinite service to me. As I had *got* before my lectures, my illness has not thrown me behind them. We have not had a classical lecture yet. Dr Pierce is not come to College yet …

The Letters of Samuel Taylor Coleridge, ed. E.L. Griggs, vol. 1 (Oxford 1956)

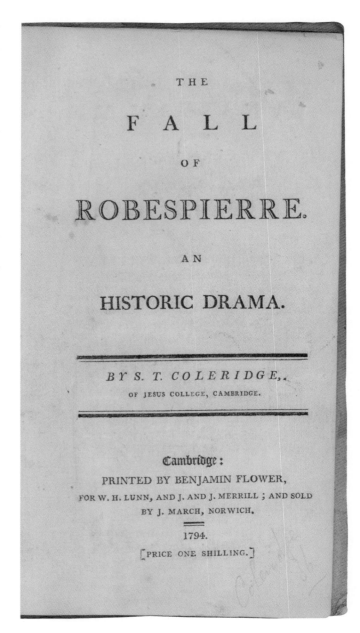

E. Sharwood Smith (1883)

Edward Sharwood Smith came, aged 18, from King Edward's School, Birmingham, as a classical Scholar. He became a schoolmaster and was successively headmaster of Whitchurch Grammar School, Shropshire, and Newbury Grammar School, Berkshire.

My own tutor and accredited guide and director of studies was Arthur Gray. That slim, stooping figure with the deep-set eyes, framed in glass, the pine-and-white cheeks, honey-coloured moustache and Punch-like chin concealed, as was proved afterwards, a personality not lacking in vision and power. But in my undergraduate days he had not found himself. He had not long been a tutor, and his shy, stiff manner and pedantic ways repelled rather than attracted his pupils. His lectures were dull, detailed and uninspiring. Though he had taken a high degree in classics he showed little enthusiasm for classical literature. The great Hellenic originals for him, as for many other classical teachers, merited a close and careful study not for what they said but for the way they said it. It was surely a mistake for him to direct a study which, conceived and carried out in a narrow, critical, almost fault-finding, spirit, is of all others most distasteful to the keen, healthy appetite of the young. It must be remembered that this was the day of compulsory Greek, obligatory on all who wished to graduate and expounded both at the school and the university by too many dry-as-dust who focussed their attention on the linguistic eccentricities of the great writers of Greece and Rome.

It came as a shock to me soon after I went up to learn that if I desired to attain high honours in my Tripos I must go to a private tutor. This meant a considerable expense, so much so that for the poorer student it was an all but impossible luxury. The tutorial system in vogue at Oxford, whereby each student had to present himself with an essay and other work once a week at least to a special supervisor and receive his criticism and advice was unknown at Jesus. It is true that Gray gave me half-an-hour a week to run through my compositions and 'unseens', supposed to be dropped in his private letter-box a day previously, but he never enquired about the work I was engaged on by myself, nor offered me any advice on my private reading. I listened but hardly profited by three lectures from him a week, given on alternate days, and on the other three days to another lecturer from another college, hired (I presume) to supplement our deficiencies, who discoursed learnedly but tepidly on some classical author. One had the privilege moreover on payment of a guinea a term to attend certain lectures at other colleges. In my earlier terms I eagerly availed myself of this opportunity, expecting much, but gaining little, from the weight of erudition carried in the frail bodies of those whom I had looked upon as intellectual giants. I had not realised then the futility of most lectures. They could and sometimes did inspire and stimulate, but the only knowledge that is of real service must be acquired by one's own exertions and one's own thinking … There was no discussion, no questioning and answering, nothing of what Plato calls dialectic, whereby one mind catches fire from another, and together ideas are struck out which glow and sparkle and illuminate one's whole experience.

I was only able to afford the help of a private tutor for three terms, two of them Long Vacation terms, in my three years, and in each case I went, for reasons which I cannot recall, to a different tutor. Two of them no doubt helped me to a certain extent: there was one from whom I learnt what outweighed all that I got from all my other instructors put together. In James Adam, insignificant of person but great of soul, product of the patient, plodding, considering peasantry of Aberdeenshire, and lately appointed Fellow and Tutor of Emmanuel College, I found the man whom unconsciously I had been seeking all the time. He infected me with the virus of Platonism from which, I am happy to state, I have not completely recovered after seventy years. Before I went to him Plato meant

Arthur Gray (1870), Master 1912–40.

Sir William Nicholson, 1937

merely difficult Greek and mystical and mysterious subject-matter. Adam's enthusiasm opened for me the gate into a world of ineffable beauty strange to the great majority of classical tutors and professors. Arthur Gray told me many years after that he had read only one or two dialogues of Plato. And Gray won a first class in the Tripos.

But besides being a classical teacher to a few scholars he had many under his charge who had no love for any study; and the manner, upright and conscientious if lacking in finesse, in which he carried out his duties, made him at that time obnoxious to the 'blues' and 'bloods' and those who had come up to have (as they put it) 'a good time', and who formed too large a proportion of the number. They openly derided his authority and indeed, on more than one occasion, wrought havoc in his private garden, which adjoined the College courts, and actually when he was Proctor used physical violence toward his person. He was thought to be unsportsmanlike when, accompanied by his 'bulldogs', he drew the coverts of a certain outlying quarter to the town – a minor Alsatia long since no doubt cleaned up, a haunt of those unfortunates whom the poet in a beautiful meiosis calls 'daughters of desire' and even entered their penetralia to search their mantelpieces and albums for portraits of familiar faces. I once saw him during the turmoil of a general election, returning from a proctorial round, badly bruised and battered, his 'colleger' shapeless, his gown in ribbons and evidence on his whole person of having been rolled in the dust.

In saying this I do not wish to suggest that there were many undergraduates who were violent and loose-living.

On the contrary the gross were good-natured and amiable young gentlemen, unendowed with much brain and unappreciative of aesthetic or scientific values, who were content to pass their three years pleasantly and aimlessly, and with a minimum of mental exertion … But for this Gray was not to blame. He could not stand up against it then; but, when his time came and the chief direction of College affairs was securely in his hands, he showed the real greatness that had been suppressed so long. That was a good few years after my time, and I only mention it here because I might leave an altogether wrong impression of a great benefactor to the College. Though I learned little or nothing from him, I always felt there was much that was likeable in his personality.

In the after-years I got to know him well. I greatly enjoyed his friendship and appreciated his humour, his anecdotes and his modest depreciation of his own services to the College. He was, as I have said, no classical scholar, but he was an antiquary not far off the highest rank, and his researches into the story of the College and the town, and above all his discovery and revelation of some beautiful features in the architecture long hidden under the plaster and stucco of a Vandal past – for he knew and loved every stone in the buildings – give him a high place on the roll of College worthies. I do not know if during his mastership he interested the undergraduates in the architecture and the story of the genesis and development of the College. I know that I myself regret greatly that there was no one in my time to instruct and improve our taste and our appreciation of the skill of the craftsmen of a bygone age and the beauty of their handiwork.

Chanticlere, Easter term 1953

Percival Gardner-Smith (1906)

Percival Gardner-Smith came from Wakefield Grammar School to read Theology and, after being in the first class in both Parts of the Tripos, he was ordained priest in 1912. He was Vicar of Comberton, Cambridgeshire, from 1916 until 1922, when he returned to the College to be Dean. He remained a Fellow until his death in 1985 at the age of 97. This extract is from the tape-recording of the wide-ranging speech he made in 1968 at a lunch marking his eightieth birthday.

In 1906 when I came up we were still a small place. I think the year before I was a freshman there were only thirty-six or even fewer entries. We were going up a bit and in my year there were about fifty. But it was a small place and I'm afraid it must be admitted that our reputation was not very good. I remember when I told my form master at school that my father was going to send me to Jesus, he pulled a rather a long face and said, 'I don't think you'll be happy there.' He'd been up at Cambridge in the early nineties and he remembered the days when it was a common saying that you never saw a sober man come out of Jesus. Things had improved since then, but drunkenness was a very serious matter, and there was a great deal of senseless and rather brutal rowdyism. In fact the College was sort of an ill-disciplined public school. Some of the rowdyism didn't amount to much, but some things were regrettable. For instance, the custom of ragging the rooms of an unpopular man. If some harmless freshman was deemed to have put a foot wrong, six or eight senior toughs would visit his room, turn all his furniture upside down, smash his crockery and in extreme cases throw it all out of the window. That was a brutal business, but it wasn't new. I remember hearing how in the days of E.H. Morgan, who died in 1895, one perfectly harmless young man had had his rooms ragged, everything was destroyed. So E.H. Morgan, who was Dean and Tutor and everything else, sent for the victim next morning and said, 'Mr so and so, I've heard that your rooms were ragged last night. I've sent for you to tell you that if there is any more ragging this term I shall know that it is you retaliating. You'll be sent down.' These ragging expeditions didn't always come off. Some years earlier Tyndale-Biscoe was up here, a sturdy little man who afterwards became cox of the University boat, a friend of Steve Fairbairn's, and also a man of great piety. He organised a Bible class to meet in his rooms. This was considered an insult to the College by the upper members and he was visited one night by about eight of them. Well primed, they burst into his rooms and there they saw Tyndale Biscoe sitting by the fire with Steve Fairbairn and nearly all the first boat roundabout and they retired with more haste than dignity. Yet I shouldn't like to create the impression that there were not many good men in those days. There certainly were. Not a few of them became Honorary Fellows of the College. Still more are commemorated on our war memorial as having laid their bones in France.

As for the Fellows of those days, never more than sixteen by statute, and we undergraduates didn't know a great deal about them. The Master was H.A. Morgan, Black Morgan (not to be confused with Red Morgan, the defunct Dean), who was enormously popular, although few of us had spoken to him. Masters didn't mix with undergraduates much in those days. Yet we knew of the great services he had rendered to the College in the past and we appreciated his huge enthusiasm for rowing. He was a very human person, but he was also almost impenetrably deaf throughout all of his later years and that was a very great handicap to him. He carried with him always a hearing aid which consisted of a cup, made of black vulcanite, about the size of a tea plate, and a flexible tube and an earpiece, and anyone who spoke to him was presented with this cup. It was undoubtedly embarrassing. One of his daughters told me that on one occasion he went to a feast at Trinity and the waiter came round and asked him

in a gentle voice whether he would take port or burgundy. Of course he couldn't hear what was said, but he knew someone was speaking to him and he held the cup up like this, whereupon the waiter poured in half a pint of burgundy. In my fourth year I was asked to lunch at the Lodge and I was put to sit next to the Master, and rather to my horror I was given the speaking end of this tube. I thought this was going to be a terrible luncheon, but amongst his other qualities H.A. Morgan was the world's greatest raconteur. And no sooner did we sit down he began to tell me funny stories, mostly about his time at Shrewsbury where he'd been under the headmastership of the great Kennedy, and he went on telling stories until we got up at the end of the lunch. All I had to do was to say a 'Ha Ha' at intervals. But he was a great man.

The Senior Tutor in my time was Arthur Gray, to whom the College owes a very great debt because he pulled it together. He made the rowing toughs understand that they were not here simply to row but they must occasionally do a little work. In the words of one of his sons, who wrote a poem in *Chanticlere*, 'he ever smote or wasted', and so he did and made himself very unpopular in doing it. He was not the most tactful of men. If some outrage had occurred he guessed who it was who'd done it, sent for the man, berated him soundly and gated him for the rest of the term; and it wasn't any good at all for the man to say that he'd had nothing whatever to do with it, and wasn't there at the time, gated he was. Although the older Fellows, or at least the undergraduates and those who'd gone down, deplored Arthur Gray for having destroyed the College, as a matter of fact he built it up again. And I think I ought to mention that we were not altogether decadent in my time – a generation which could put the Lent boat head and in 1909 restore the headship to the first May boat for the first time since 1885 was not altogether to be despised.

Of the other Fellows there were the two friends, Abbot and Welsh. Abbot from Caius, a very quiet, gentle man, and, I believe, a really great classical scholar in the old Cambridge tradition. He knew every word, so it was said, that was mentioned in any classical dictionary and could tell you where it was to be found. But that the classical writers had anything to say, I don't think ever occurred to him. He was probably not a very inspiring classical teacher. Welsh was a mathematician, Senior Wrangler and generally regarded as one of the greatest mathematicians of his time. He was greatly revered and much liked by his pupils, who profited greatly by his instruction. But the curious thing about Welsh was that he was entirely lacking in ambition. He never did anything except teach with admirable results, but as for writing anything, no. And as in mathematics so in golf. Welsh was regarded as the best golfer in Scotland, but there

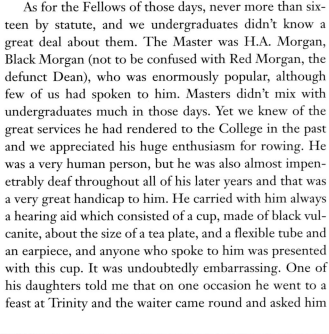

Dr H.A. Morgan (1849), Master 1885–1912, with his daughter, Iris, using his speaking tube.

Photograph *c.*1910

were no amateur championships for him or anything of that sort. His favourite occupation was to play golf against Sir Robert Ball, the astronomer, to whom at a moderate estimate he could concede four strokes a hole. He married late and in his later years he enjoyed playing golf with his wife. I think Foakes Jackson really summed it up in a letter to me when he died on the golf course in 1924. 'His was the brightest talent ever buried in a napkin.' Then there was Watt, another Scotsman who came to us from Trinity. John Campbell Watt, universally known as Tommy. He didn't like being called Tommy. If you wanted to make him angry you'd refer to him as Tommy. The reason I believe was that when he first came to this College, it was pretty well known that he came because he thought he'd get a fellowship which he would never do at Trinity. That was rather resented and he was called Tommy rather as a term of contempt, but it remained as a term of affection. Academically he was negligible. He may have taught a little very elementary mathematics, but most of his life was spent in teaching Paley's *Evidences* for candidates for the ordinary degree. But by the undergraduates he was adored. He was the kind of don which is now becoming almost extinct. He was the perfect link between the High Table and the rest of the College. The undergraduates thronged to his rooms every night and he discoursed to them and gave them tea and biscuits, not sherry in those days, and they came again. Not that he ever cultivated popularity, there was nothing of that about him. He was extremely outspoken and he told the undergraduates what he thought of them. If a man had got drunk or if he'd missed a pass on the football field or failed to score a goal he heard all about it the next time he met Tommy. He was outspoken, not only to undergraduates but to everybody else. But he was a great asset to the College even although he never pursued his mathematical studies.

There were others, but I must say something about Foakes Jackson, the Dean, perhaps at my time the best-known man in Cambridge. I wish I could convey to you who didn't know him some idea of his extraordinary character. If you read the *Dictionary of National Biography* you will see that he was described as the 'last eighteenth-century wit'. I think that's a fair description. I wrote the article. He was extraordinarily amusing. The pearls of wit which fell from his lips during supervision, I only wish I'd recorded more of them, but they often crop up in my mind. 'My boy, whatever job you have in life make a mess of it, and they'll promote you to get rid of you.' He wasn't simply a wag, still less a buffoon. But there's a certain wicked understanding of life behind most of his amusing remarks. I can remember another: 'Clark has

just been telling me that there are different kinds of socialists. I said to him "Clark, tell me this, do they all want my money? If so they're all the same to me."' Or, more seriously, 'The bishops of the eighteenth century had good incomes and thankful hearts and they did far less harm than the present hungry lot.'

Foakes Jackson was tremendously proud of the number of first classes obtained by his pupils. It certainly wasn't spoon feeding. I can't remember that he ever taught us anything very much, except that it was all great fun, and if we wanted to do any good we must work and the results were quite sensational. There was a time when nearly all the deans and theological lecturers in Cambridge were pupils of Foakes Jackson and he didn't

F.J. Foakes Jackson, Chaplain (1882), later Fellow, Tutor and (1895–1916) Dean.

Photograph, *c*.1890

forget to remind us. In Chapel he was a little unpredictable. He used to come in generally five minutes late, probably half-dressed. If it was a morning service he read the collects for the evening and vice versa and he constantly lost his place. We used to have long pauses while he was looking to see where he'd got to. Wynne, who was afterwards Bishop of Ely and was Chaplain here with Foakes Jackson, said that the real reason was that he brought his morning letters in with him to Chapel and read the service and his letters at the same time. He could be apparently devotional. At the end of the service he would kneel most reverently before the altar and one thought he was saying his prayers, but Wynne said that he'd generally got the collecting plate in his hand and was counting the collection.

Revolutionary Reverberations

Civil War and Commonwealth

ARTHUR GRAY

Had it been possible for the Master and fellows, as they sat at their 'audit chear' in the founder's chamber on 12 January 1641–2, to exclude from their thoughts the troubles brewing in the political world, they must have regarded their position and prospects with considerable complacency. They had that day closed the New Building account; the college had acquired on the north side of First Court a range of chambers fairer to outward view and more commodious than the old cloister buildings; it was free from debt; the number of its students was at least as large as it had ever been within living memory; the fellows were at harmony among themselves, and shared the satisfaction of their Master – Richard Sterne, a former chaplain of Archbishop Laud, who had presided over the College since 1634 – in the restoration to the chapel services of that beauty and reverence which had been wanting since the changes of 1558. But it is not hazardous to guess that their talk was of other and less cheerful matters. Eight days before their Audit meeting the King had made his abortive attempt to arrest the five Members; the final rupture with Parliament and the King's departure for York was the latest piece of intelligence that had reached them from London. The national question was already involved in one personal to themselves. The committee which the House of Commons, in its last session, had empowered to consider abuses in religion and civil government at the universities had singled out Jesus as the first object of its inquiries at Cambridge, and the Master and fellows had been compelled to bring up their statutes and account-books to be examined by the committee, sitting in London. And, though trouble on that account was perhaps for the moment over-past, a deeper anxiety must have occupied their thoughts in connexion with the recent order of the Commons requiring heads of colleges to displace the Communion table from the east end of their chapels, to take away the rails and level the chancel, to remove crucifixes, tapers, and basons from the Communion table – to undo, in fact, all that the society of Jesus had been at such pains to effect in the improvement of the chapel services.

Trouble deepened as the year 1642 advanced. There was plague in the town in the summer, and the College contributed to the relief of the 'visited'. On 29 June the King addressed a letter to the Vice-Chancellor, requesting the University and colleges to contribute money for his defence. On 24 July he followed it up with a request that the colleges would send him their plate. To both applications Jesus College gave a prompt and favourable answer. On 29 July it passed an order that 1,201 ounces of plate – the pieces being specified in a list – should be delivered to Mr John Poley for the King's use, and on 29 August it obtained a loan from a friend of the Master's, at Newstead in Nottingham, with the same object. The plate with that contributed by other colleges, was safely conveyed to the King at Nottingham in spite of the vigilance of Cromwell, who lay in wait for it with a disorderly band of peasants on the road between Cambridge and Huntingdon.

Retribution was swift to overtake the heads who were chiefly responsible for sending the plate. The story of Dr Sterne's treatment is told in Walker's *Sufferings of the Clergy*:

Together with Dr *Beale* Master of St *John's*, and Dr *Martin*, Master of *Queens*, he was seized by Cromwell (who had with some Parties of Soldiers surrounded the several

Chapels, whilst the Scholars were at Prayers) and carried in Triumph to *London* … In the Villages, as they passed from *Cambridge* to *London*, the People were called by some of their Agents to come and Abuse and Revile them: They were also led leisurely through the midst of Bartholomew Fair; as they passed along they were entertained with Exclamations, Reproaches, Scorns and Curses; and it was a great Providence, considering the Prejudice which the People had to them, that they found no worse Usage. After their Confinement (in the Tower), tho' they often Petitioned to be heard, yet they could never obtain either a Trial, or their Liberty. They had been a full Year under Restraint in other Prisons, when they were at length, *Friday August* 11, 1643, by order of the Parliament, sent on board the Ship; the name of which was the *Prosperous Saylor*, then lying at *Wapping* … Being come on Shipboard, they were instantly put under Hatches, where the Decks were so Low, that they could not stand upright; and yet were denied *Stools to sit on*, or so much as a *Burthen of Straw to ly on*. Into the *Little Ease*, in a small Ship, they crowd no less than 80 *Prisoners of Quality*; and that they might stifle one another, having no more Breath than what they suck'd from one another's Mouth, most maliciously and (Certainly) to a *Murtherous Intent*, they stop up all the *small Augur-Holes*, and all other inlets which might relieve them with Fresh Air.

In December 1642, the fellows of the three colleges joined in a petition to the House of Commons for the release of the imprisoned Masters, but the House took no further notice of it than to order the latter to be transferred from the Tower to the custody of the 'Keeper of Lord Peters's House in Aldersgate Street, to be there kept until the pleasure of this House be further known'. Dr Sterne was allowed to perform the last offices of piety to his old friend, Archbishop Laud, on the scaffold at Tower Hill, and soon afterwards regained his liberty. He seems to have been in trouble again in 1650–1, the year of Worcester fight, for the Audit accounts of that year have an enigmatical item: 'To Bailies for apprehending Dr Sterne, £1'. In the following year there is a charge for 'the Butler's journey to Dr Sterne', who was then, possibly, at Stevenage, where, until the Restoration, he maintained himself by keeping a school. Dr Beale, less happy than his successor in the Lodge at Jesus, did not live to see the triumph of the cause for which he suffered. He died at Madrid in 1651.

Sterne was not at once deprived of the Mastership when he was arrested, and the fellows continued to pay his dues to Mrs Sterne until they were themselves dispossessed. On 23 February 1642–3 they agreed, because of 'dangers and difficulties', to grant all fellows leave of absence until Michaelmas. On 7 November 1643 it was agreed by the President and nine fellows to extend this leave until Michaelmas 1644.

It was a bitter constraint that rendered these resolutions necessary. During the year 1643 Cambridge was converted by Cromwell into an armed camp, and no scholar was allowed to pass outside the town unless a townsman vouched that he was a 'confider'. A breastwork was raised at the eastern end of Jesus Lane, and Jesus Grove – 'no idolatrous one', says Fuller – was cut down.

Multitudes of soldiers [says the *Querela Cantabrigiensis*], were quarter'd in those Glorious and Ancient Structures which the Devout and Royal Founders design;d for *Sanctuaries of Learning and Piety:* but were made by them mere *Spittals* and *Bawdy Houses* for sick and debauch'd Soldiers. To this must be added that they Tore and Defac'd the Buildings, Pull'd down and Burn'd the Wainscote of the Chambers, the Bedsteds, Chairs, Stools, and Shelves for Books.

The 'New Building' of 1638–41: two staircases on the north side of First Court with six pairs of chambers for tutors and their pupils.

The following entries in the Bursars' book suggest conditions of life which must have been intolerable to the quiet scholar:

1643–44 – To soldiers y^t came to be billeted, Oct. 20, 1643,   2^s 6^d.
       For mending windows, locks, bedsteads, etc., broken by ye soldiers billeted in ye College,   18^s.
1644–45 – To three troopers out three days in Bedfordshire,   6^s.

After the resolution passed in November 1643, the majority of the Fellows quitted the College. But before they went they took down and concealed the organ, and buried the College plate – such of it as had not gone to the King – in the Master's orchard. Throughout the year following nothing but formal business was transacted. The register only notices two admissions, and only three undergraduates had licence *ad respondendum quaestioni*, and so qualify themselves for a degree.

Dr Richard Sterne, Master 1634–44, 1660, subsequently Bishop of Carlisle and Archbishop of York.

Oil, English school, *c*.1660

In the last days of the same year the notorious William Dowsing came to Cambridge armed with power to put into execution the ordinance of Parliament for the reformation of churches and chapels. The curious diary kept by this ignorant enthusiast informs us of the extent of his depredations. He visited Jesus on 28 December, and, in the presence of one of the fellows, Mr Boyleston, 'digg'd up the Steps there and brake downe Superstitions of Saints and Angels, 120 at least'. Mr Boyleston may have been an unwilling witness of the desecration, but the fact that he was one of the two fellows who were not 'outed' by the Earl of Manchester in the following year raises a presumption that he was an assenting party. The 'superstitions' which were broken down were evidently in the windows. The Audit Book this year mentions payments amounting in all to £10. 16s. 0d. for mending windows in the chapel, and there is another item of £3 6s 6d 'for levelling ye chapel, tiles, lime, sand, and labourers' wages'.

On 22 January 1643–4, the Houses of Parliament passed an Ordinance for Regulating the University of Cambridge which empowered the Earl of Manchester to endeavour the reformation of the University, and to eject such masters or fellows of colleges as were scandalous in their lives or doctrines, or opposed the proceedings of Parliament. The Earl came to Cambridge in February, and notified the masters and scholars of each college to be in residence on 10 March next ensuing, then to answer such things as should be demanded by him. Stephen Hall, the President of Jesus, seems to have ignored the summons. The Audit Book disappeared, and was not produced for inspection. The Sequestrators were obliged to force the locks of the Treasury, and of the College plate three pieces only were discoverable. For this contumacy – though the assigned reasons was his refusal to take the Covenant – the President was ejected on 14 March. This was the first ejection by parliamentary order at Cambridge. Hall was also imprisoned for more than three years in the Compter in Southwark. On 12 April the Earl came in person to the chapel, and in presence of all the fellows then resident declared Thomas Young to be Master of the College in the room of Dr Sterne, put him in the Master's stall, and delivered to him the statutes of the College. The new Master signed a declaration in the register that he would promote piety and learning in the College agreeably to the late Solemn National League and Covenant. Probably only two fellows were present at the induction, for the remainder, fourteen in number, were all ejected before the year was ended. The two who made their peace and apparently accepted the Covenant were John Boyleston and Thomas Allen. Of these renegades Sherman, the College's first historian who was a furious Royalist, somewhat obscurely remarks: 'The one [i.e. Boyleston] stood behind a curtain to witness the evils which others endured with firmness and courage; the other, afflicted to behold the exequies of his Alma Mater, made his own life a filial offering at her grave and, to escape the hands of wicked rebels, laid violent hands upon himself'. Neither of them retained his fellowship after Michaelmas 1645. Boyleston retired to a living in Derbyshire, overlived the Restoration, and died a Canon of Lichfield. Seven of the vacant fellowships were filled up by the Earl of Manchester between 3 October 1644 and 5 May 1645, and a few more in succeeding years. But until the Restoration the number of Fellows was never greater than twelve.

Thomas Young had been approved for the mastership by the Assembly of Divines at Westminster, of which he was himself a member. He had been Milton's tutor before the poet went to St Paul's School, and a friendly correspondence had been kept up between them in later years. He had won credit by his book, *Dies Dominica* (1639), on the observance of the Sabbath, but it was his activity in controversial theology which commended him to the Assembly. 'Presbyterianorum Smectymnianorum Primipilus' is Sherman's contemptuous description of him, referring to the leading part which he took in the work published under the assumed name, Smectymnuus, a name made up of the initials of the five contributing divines, T and Y standing for Thomas Young. The book is best remembered now because Milton championed the cause of his former teacher in the *Apology for Smectymnuus*. Young was a Scotchman, and had not graduated at either of the English universities. Such a man might seem to the divines eminently calculated to carry out that reformation, 'as well of the statutes as of the members of the College', of which the Earl of Manchester gave warning in the mandate for his admission. Singularly little is to be gathered of his career as Master; he did not attempt any very striking changes. In spite of his anti-episcopalian bias, he was a King's man, and even when Charles was a prisoner in the hands of the Parliament there were sanctioned bonfires in Cloister Court on his coronation day. His reputation as a minister in the eastern counties, where he held the living of Stowmarket, attracted to the College considerable numbers of the sons of Puritan families in that quarter. In spite of the disturbance of the Civil War the College rapidly regained its numbers. In the five years ending 1649 ninety-two admissions were accounted for.

In October 1649 the Parliament ordered the Committee for Reforming the Universities to call upon all heads and fellows of colleges to subscribe the Engagement whereby they pledged themselves to be faithful to the Commonwealth of England, as established, without a King or House of Lords. Thomas Young fell under the general suspicion with which the Government looked upon the Presby-

terian ministers after the Battle of Dunbar and, as he took no notice of the summons to subscribe, he was ejected from the mastership on 14 November 1650, and in his place the committee appointed Mr John Worthington, a fellow of Emmanuel. Four of the fellows, were dispossessed for the same reason and about the same time.

It was in a happy hour that the Commissioners, looking around them for a successor to the ejected Young, made choice of John Worthington. At this distance of time his chief title to remembrance is that he was one of the group of Cambridge Platonists, and the editor of the works of 'the incomparable' Joseph Mede and of John Smith's *Select Discourses*. To his contemporaries he was endeared by the lovable qualities of his character, qualities discernible by us in his letters and diary. Archbishop Tillotson, preaching his funeral sermon, said that:

> His whole Demeanour was Pious and Grave; and yet not blemish'd with any Moroseness or fond Affectation. And as his Knowledge was great, so was his Humility. He was a zealous and sincere Friend where he profess'd Kindness … He was universally inoffensive, kind and obliging, even to those that differ'd from him: And, to set off these Virtues, there was added to them, in a very eminent degree, *the Ornament of a meek and quiet spirit, which in the sight of God is of great Price.* Especially in Debates and Controversies of Religion he was not apt to be passionate and contentious … But that which was most singularly Eminent in him was the Publickness of his Spirit, and his great Zeal and Industry to be profitable and useful to the world, especially in those things which tended to the promoting of Learning and Piety.

The new Master, indeed, had none of the intractability of his Presbyterian predecessor and, as he had received episcopal orders, his appointment was regarded with some degree of favour by the exiled churchmen. Though his predecessor had been 'outed' for declining the Engagement, it seems that Worthington was not asked to accept it, nor had he taken the Covenant. He had been moved to deep sorrow by the death of King Charles and, preaching on the occasion, he chose for his texts, 'The beauty of Israel is slain. How are the mighty fallen!' and 'Behold and see if there be any sorrow like unto our sorrow.' Of his appointment at Jesus Worthington writes: 'When I came hither first it was not my seeking, and I could have left it as willingly for Dr Sterne, if he could have brought himself in. He desired of me to accept of it, and procured the Fellows to desire me.' Sundry symptoms show that old grudges presently died away under the Master's gentle influence. In 1651 'widow Welsh', inspired, no doubt, by some of the old society, became the means of restoring the lost Audit Book. Next year, through the agency of a certain Mr Buck, one of the Esquire Bedels, the buried plate was brought to light. In the same year the organ was discovered; the time had not yet come when it could be replaced in the chapel, but the 'discovery' looks as though it had a delicate reference to Worthington's devotion to music.

The year 1660, of course, brought the restoration of the old society, or rather the remnant of it spared by death or matrimony. Of the fourteen ejected fellows three only were reinstated, the President, Stephen Hall, being one of them. Two of the three died, and the third resigned his place within two years from their restoration. Had the number of the restored been greater it might have gone hard with some of the intruded fellows; but as there were only twelve of the latter, the statutable number of fellowships would not be exceeded by the inclusion of them all. But institution by the Visitor must, of course, be a condition of the retention of their places, for during the interregnum the College had been empowered by order of the House of Commons (7 November 1645) to elect and admit fellows without presenting any names to the bishop of Ely, who was then a prisoner in the Tower. 'It was suspected that there would have been a refusal of some.' But Matthew Wren, the restored bishop, 'was very fair and civill towards them, and dispatched them without the usuall height of the fees, and persuaded them to studiousness and peace, against all animosities, etc.' The unanimity with which the intruded fellows submitted themselves, and the readiness of the bishop to accept their submission, show that they had not committed themselves to any opinions hostile to episcopacy. Some of them (like Sherman) were perfervid churchmen and royalists, and made no secret of their attitude in the interval between Cromwell's death and the proclamation of Charles. At the Commencement in July 1660, before Worthington had left the lodge, a Johnian prevaricator, in his speech, styled the 'Jesuits' papists, with double reference to their name and religious leanings.

Justice could not be complete without the restoration of the mastership to Sterne; but before he returned to the College it was well understood that he was destined for the bishopric of Carlisle. Worthington's friends hoped that after a formal cession of his office he might be reappointed to it by the Visitor. But Bishop Wren had already decided on giving it to Dr Pearson, whose *Exposition of the Creed*, published the previous year, was for two hundred years to remain the classic statement of Anglican beliefs. With unruffled serenity Worthington withdrew with his young wife to his poor vicarage at Fen Ditton, 'standing bleek and alone, and therefore obnoxious to the cold weather and the violence of disbanded soldiers, of which there have been some late proofs'. At Ditton he hoped that he might still be able to do service to the University, though his disposition was inclined rather to devotional retirement, 'about which I did love to talk with worthy Mr Thristcross, who knew Mr Ferrar and Little Gedding'. There is a charming interchange of courtesies in the letters which passed between him and Dr Sterne on the subject of the return of the latter to the lodge, and when Dr and Mrs Sterne arrived there they were entertained by the out-going Master with an elaborate musical performance in their honour.

Worthington died in 1671 at Hackney, where he was at the time lecturer in the parish church. Sterne became archbishop of York in 1664 and died in 1683. In 1671 he gave to the College an annual rent-charge of £40, to make provision for four scholars, two of them born in that part of Yorkshire which is in the diocese of York, the other two born in Nottinghamshire, and of them one in Sterne's native town, Mansfield. The archbishop's great-grandson, Laurence Sterne, was a scholar on this foundation.

From Chapter V of *A History of Jesus College,
Cambridge*, 1902

Early American Connections

MICHAEL O'BRIEN

The links between Jesus College and the British colonies in North America were not extensive. This was typical of most Cambridge colleges, except, famously, Emmanuel which supplied so many pulpits in New England and helped to create Harvard College. For its part, Jesus sent the occasional minister, received the stray sons of planters, and looked upon those far parts with much indifference. In the seventeenth and early eighteenth centuries little or no distinction would have been made between those colonies which subsequently became the United States, Canada and various West Indian countries, for all belonged to a zone of

British power, unstably holding its own against imperial competition from France, The Netherlands, Spain and the Native Americans who tried to resist conquest and avoid extinction. So the College would have regarded as 'American' undergraduates like Thomas Fultun and Samuel Alpress, who came from Jamaica as pensioners in 1713 and 1756; and Butler Fenton and Joseph Webbe, who came likewise in 1732 and 1733 from the 'West Indies', about which the College records are thus vague.

It is probable, though difficult to prove – we have only scraps of information – that familial connections with Cambridge were often of moment. This was certainly the case with Maryland's Peter Dent (b.1667), the eldest of nine children of an affluent and turbulent planter, Captain John Dent (c.1645–1712), who came from St Mary's County on the western shore of Chesapeake Bay to the College in November 1700 at the unusually advanced age of 23. The Dents, originally a Yorkshire family from Gisborough in the North Riding, had migrated in substantial numbers to the Americas. Of those that remained in England, another Peter Dent (c.1628/9–89), of Ormsby in Yorkshire, went to Trinity, became an apothecary and surgeon in the town and belonged to the circle of botanists who gathered around John Ray, to whose *Historia Plantarum* (1686–1704) he contributed useful observations. His cousin, a third Peter Dent (1637/8–1717), also lived in Cambridge and seems to have furnished food to the colleges.

In Maryland Captain John Dent was involved in the insurrection of 1681 which tried to overthrow, and that of 1689 which succeeded in ending, the proprietary rule of Charles Calvert, the third Lord Baltimore. (Calvert was Roman Catholic, the Dents Protestant.) The captain prospered and lived well, owning and then selling Cool Spring, whose waters were said – mostly by him – to possess healing powers. But all may not have been well between father and son. That Peter came to Cambridge as a sizar, that is, an undergraduate who paid his way by serving in Hall, would suggest that he came without his father's blessing and money. And when, in September 1711, the father made his will, he seems to have been very uncertain about his son's fate. Land was left him, but only 'if my son Peter Comes to Maryland to settle', which he evidently never did and so never obtained, among other things, 'all that tract of Land Called Horserange 200 acres', which by default went to his sister Christian. Peter never obtained a Cambridge degree, either, and it seems likely that he stayed in England, in a manner and place now lost to memory.

Less obscure is East Apthorp (1733–1816), who sounds like a village but was in fact a worldly Anglican minister from Boston, where his father was a merchant. The younger Apthorp was educated at the Boston Latin School, then matriculated at Jesus in 1751, received his BA in 1755, his MA in 1758, won the Chancellor's Medal in 1755 and was a Fellow from 1758 to 1761. Then he became a missionary for the Society for Propagating the Gospel in Foreign Parts, the particular foreign part being Cambridge, Massachusetts. There Apthorp established the first Anglican congregation, Christ Church, amid that sea of Congregationalists and set himself up with a munificence which much troubled the locals, inclined to stern minimalism. From his inheritance Apthorp built what John Adams was later to speak of as 'a great house, at that time thought to be a splendid palace', set in many acres, extending down to the Charles River. The house still survives, is still called Apthorp House and now serves as the master's residence for Adams House of Harvard College. In the early 1760s, however, it came to be called the 'Bishop's Palace', to denote the inhabitant's pretensions and ambitions. In 1764 Apthorp, much bruised by Congregationalist abuse (especially from Jonathan Mayhew), returned to England and rose with unspectacular regularity through the hierarchy: he was vicar of Croydon (1765–93) and rector of St Mary-le-Bow, Cheapside (1778–92). In about 1790 he became blind, was briefly chancellor of St Paul's Cathedral (1791–2), and in 1796 he received the prebend of Finsbury, a lucrative sinecure at that cathedral. In his last years he returned to Cambridge, which is how he came to rest in the north transept of the Chapel, where he lies beneath a black marble slab. It is said that when conducting tours Frederick Foakes Jackson, Dean (1895–1916), used to pause there and remark, 'Here you have the grave of the last great canon of St Paul's. By the manipulation of the cathedral funds he made for himself a profit of £85,000.' If true – and there is no accessible evidence beyond this anecdote – Apthorp's mind was more financially agile than scholarly, for he was a dutiful and orthodox author who delivered worthy and unnoted discourses on prophecy, missionary work, the happy effects produced by the Plague and the Great Fire of London for Christianity, and national progress, such as 'The Felicity of the Times' and 'Character and Example of a Christian Woman', as well as sacred music and poetry. He thought well of the fine arts, which 'under the conduct of a good imagination, have so much influence in polishing and humanizing the mind' – but he was fleetingly and best known for contributing to those 'vollies of ... Ecclesiastical ordnance', which tried to pepper Edward Gibbon. Apthorp's *Letters on the Prevalence of Christianity, Before its Civil Establishment: With Observations on a Late History of the Decline of the Roman Empire* (1778) is said to have earned him St Mary-le-Bow. The historian was less than amused, even a little startled, but did note that Apthorp said little or nothing of substance in the mere three pages devoted to refuting him, though promising a future volume, which was never to appear. In his *Memoirs*, Gibbon recovered his amusement and observed that, by his useful scepticism, he had 'enjoyed the pleasure of … collating Dʳ Apthorpe to an Archiepiscopal living'. So Apthorp is best known, as many eighteenth-century clerics are, for being the object of Gibbon's wit. The fact is unrecorded on the tombstone, which instead speaks of Apthorp's expectation of Christ's mercy in life eternal, which is a different sort of immortality. But Apthorp, who liked music in sacred places, might be pleased to know that today the Chapel's grand piano often sits above his grave.

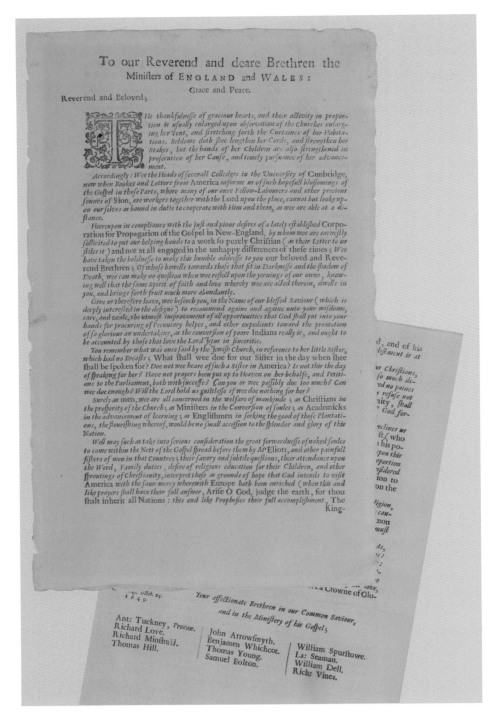

Of the Jesuans who went from east to west, the most famous now is John Eliot (1604–90), the so-called 'Apostle to the Indians'. He came from a yeoman family in Widford, Hertfordshire, but grew up mostly in Nazeing, Essex. 'Yeoman' sounds misleadingly humble to the modern ear; his father, in fact, had extensive lands. Eliot was admitted, aged 14, at an undocumented moment in 1618, matriculated as a pensioner in March 1619, and graduated in 1622. His father died in 1621 and left a will that included – in the words of a dying man who described himself as 'crasie and weak in body (yeat blessed be god) of perfitt memory' – a bequest 'unto my sonne John Elliott the somme of Eaight pownds a year of lawfull mony of Englond for and toward his maintenance, in the University of Cambridg where he is now scoller'. So we may infer that he lived comfortably in College. Little is known of his life in the 1620s, the decade in which he was perhaps ordained as an Anglican priest, except that he became by 1629 an 'usher' at Thomas Hooker's small school in Little Baddow (near Chelmsford) and lived with Hooker's 'blessed family' in a house known as 'Cuckoos'. Hooker was a Puritan, educated at Emmanuel, someone whose stringent Independency and hostility to gaudy ritual had led to his being officially 'silenced' by Bishop Lancelot Andrewes, brother of the then Master of Jesus, 'on the complaint of King James'. But this silence came to be regarded as too noisy, for the Archbishop of Canterbury, William Laud, moved in 1629 to try Hooker before the ecclesiastical Court of High Commission, a prospect which induced the worried minister in 1630 to jump bail and flee to Holland. This left Eliot exposed, and in 1631 he opted to move to New England, which, as Hooker was to put it, had been planned by God to be 'a refuge for his Noahs and his Lots, a rock and shelter for his righteous ones to run unto'. Eliot travelled on the *Lyon*, with John Winthrop's wife and children, and – perhaps more consequentially for Eliot and even Massachusetts – 'twenty-three barrels of books'. Within a year he was attached to a Congregationalist church two miles from Boston in Roxbury or, in Eliot's usage, 'Rocksborough', the town of rocks. He quickly became a husband (to Ann or Hannah Mumford, also from Essex), the local minister for the rest of his long life, and a middling landowner possessed by 1640 of 39 acres. There he continued his interest in teaching by co-founding the Roxbury Latin School, 'that little nursery', as Cotton Mather was to call it, intended to create 'godly citizenship' through the 'succeeding ages'.

As a minister, Eliot was remarkable at first for an unforgiving orthodoxy in matters small, such that men should not have long hair; in matters great, such as the banishment from the colony of Roger Williams and Anne Hutchinson for their theological liberalism, which spread 'such lies'; and in matters very great, such as whether the world ought to be ruled by a theocracy, since the Scriptures regarded legislatures, secular courts and temporal kings as inessential to God's purposes. On the last score, in *The Christian Commonwealth*, written in 1649 but not printed until 1659, he wrote:

> I am bold to present this Scripture–Platform of Government … because I do believe it to be a Divine Institution of a Civil Government; and seemeth to me to be such, as will well suit the present condition of England, Scotland, and Ireland, or any other religious people in the world, who fear the command of God, and tremble at his word: and being persuaded in my heart, that it is the minde of the Lord, that Nations should be governed by Scripture-Institutions, the time being come that the Lord is about to shake all the Earth, and throw down that great Idol of humane wisdom in Governments, and set up Scripture-Government in the room thereof.

Even the General Court of Massachusetts thought this an unwise vision, considering the recent and likely pressure of Charles II, ordered all copies of the book to be destroyed, and demanded a recantation, which Eliot sheepishly gave.

Later he softened somewhat, indeed became a reformer by advocating the Half-Way Covenant, which allowed the semi-ungodly a partial church membership: without the right to vote or partake of Holy Communion. But by then the world of New England was beginning to drift away from earlier ecstatic and stern hopes and expectations, and the issue had come to seem survival over the long haul, not the imminent shaking of the earth and the Millennium. The year 1631 had been very different, for then it had seemed that the migrants in their wilderness had entered the presence of God, that the fate of the universe would turn on the stringency of their piety.

They had also entered a world peopled by those to whom Sexagesima, Limited Atonement, and the raising of Lazarus were unintelligible gibberish. There is little evidence that, at first, Eliot was greatly interested in the Narrangansetts, Wampanoags, Pequots, Niantics, Massachusetts and Mahicans, even though the charter of the Massachusetts Bay Colony had proclaimed that its chief purpose was 'to wynn and incite the natives of the country, to the knowledge and obedience of the onlie true God and Saviour of mankinde'. But the Pequot War of 1636–7, which saw the defeat of a once-powerful people, then sold into slavery, changed matters. It led many Indians by the mid-1640s to think it prudent to seek English protection and made them more available for conversion, a task now urged by the colony's officials and undertaken by Eliot – himself the owner of a Pequot bond servant, known as Cockenoe, who had begun to teach him

the Algonquin language. Soon this servant was succeeded by another, Job Nesutan, who long acted as an adjutant missionary and deepened Eliot's knowledge of this intricate tongue. It was highly inflected and possessed of compound nouns whose enormous length might amaze even a German, nouns which were distinguished not by what was masculine and feminine – as Latin and English alike agreed was proper – but between what was animate and inanimate.

By 1646 Eliot was ready to venture to an Indian village, Neponset, and try out a sermon in English with the aid of an interpreter, but it was a failure. The natives 'regarded it not, gave no heed unto it, but were weary and despised what I said'. A month later he tried again at Nonantum on the banks of the Charles River, and did better, especially with the children, though it is hard now to imagine what they made of his discourse on Ezekiel 37:9, 'Then said he unto me, Prophesy unto the wind, prophesy, son of man, and say to the wind, Thus saith the Lord God; Come from the four winds, O breath, and breathe upon these slain, that they may live.' But they were interested enough to ask puzzled questions. Encouraged, he moved towards learning the language more thoroughly and acquiring a commission, which grew to £20 a year, as a missionary. (Later this money became an issue, for he was thought, improbably, to be dishonest in his financial dealings, whereas he was just careless in bookkeeping, if punctilious in demands for his due.) Unusually, he decided that proselytising would work best if he could convert Algonquin from an unwritten to a written language, translate Christian texts into it, and then educate Indians who might read these texts. Others thought it simpler to teach Indians to read English, but Eliot charismatically argued for the necessity of this plan, coupled with the creation of what became known as 'praying towns': the villages of 'praying Indians' who would do more than believe in the God of Abraham and Isaac, Peter and Paul, but would dress like Englishmen, observe English morality, become farmers with thatched cottages, learn the complicated pleasures and duties of English family life, and set up schools and churches. Eliot himself created the first of these towns, at Natick, about eighteen miles from Roxbury. There a village was laid out on opposite sides of the Charles River, a footbridge was made to connect the two, and a palisade was made, within which carpenters built a meeting house and, as Samuel Eliot Morison was to mention in 1930, 'a prophet's chamber for the Apostle when he came to preach, as he did fortnightly'. By 1674, it was claimed, there were 1,100 Indians in such towns, mentored since 1656 by a 'Superintendant of the Praying Indians', all of which seemed close to a fulfilment of Eliot's prediction in 1647 that 'in forty years more, some Indians would be all one English, and in a hundred years, all Indians here about, would be so'.

This conviction required an immense endeavour, expensive in money and labour, for there were many texts in need of printing. He developed between 1654 and 1688 an Algonquin library of sermons, tracts, catechisms, psalms, grammars and confessions of faith. Its centrepiece was his translation of the Bible, whose New Testament he published in 1661, followed by a complete version of both Testaments in 1663, which was not only the first such translation into an Indian language but the first Bible of any description to be published in British North America. Indeed it understates Eliot's range and accomplishment to write of it as a translation from English into Algonquin, since he took care to consult original Greek and Hebrew

Title page for the complete edition of John Eliot's translation of the Bible into Algonquin, Cambridge, Mass. 1663.

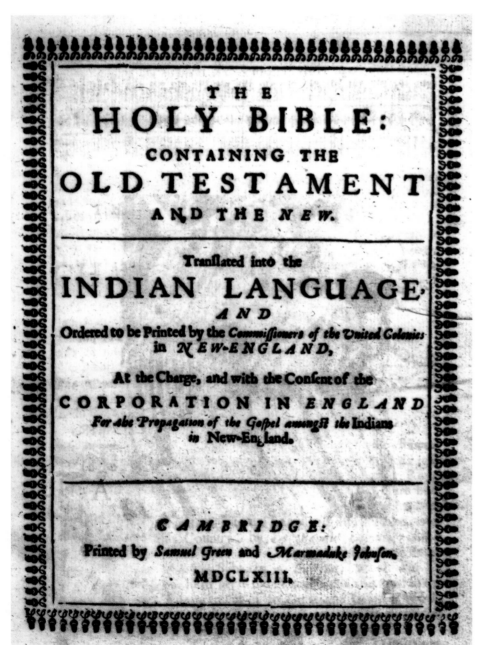

texts and, in that sense, his was also a reconsideration of what even an English version ought to say. He sent a copy back to his old College, perhaps with a pride which the book's inscription denies:

> *Pro Collegio Jesu:*
> *Accipias mater quod alumnus humillimus*
> *filius, oro preces semper habere tuas offert:*
> *Johannes Eliot.*

That is,

> *For Jesus College:*
> *Please accept, Mother, what a most humble student offers.*
> *As a son, I beg to be always in your prayers.*
> *John Eliot.*

His life was once unambiguously celebrated as great and worthy. In 1854 Convers Francis's biography said that Eliot's name 'must always stand in distinguished brightness on that roll of the servants of the Most High, whom New England delights, and ever will delight, to honor in the records of her moral history'. In that eternity of honour, Eliot permanently inhabits a float in a Macy's Thanksgiving parade, on which he and the praying Indians are carried amicably along. But, in truth, eternity has ended for the moment, since modern scholarship (and even modern Christian ethics) is unconvinced that extinguishing a way of life is to be admired. As it turned out, Eliot's achievement proved ephemeral, for within a few generations no one survived who could speak or read Algonquin, now an adjective best known for being attached to a hotel bar in New York where in the twentieth century gathered wits like Dorothy Parker. John Eliot would be appalled, for though he was known sometimes to be affable, he was better known for his gravity of manner.

Among the Jesuans who went westward, less famous in modern times than Eliot but more notable in the seventeenth and eighteenth centuries, was Francis Higginson (1586–1630). Even in 1891, a little eccentrically, a New York publisher thought it worthwhile to include him as one of the 'Makers of America' in a series which also memorialised John Winthrop, Thomas Jefferson and Charles Sumner. Earlier, Cotton Mather, the most indefatigable of Puritan historians and, infamously, the chief agitator of the Salem witch trials, in the *Magnalia Christi Americana* (1702) – that majestic and wayward jeremiad celebrating the founding of New England and chastising its subsequent degeneracy – thought it right to place Francis Higginson as the first of Puritan divines. Subsequent histories, notably the canonical work of Perry Miller on the Puritan mind, have not endorsed that judgement, but Boston in 1702 thought otherwise.

Francis Higginson's father John was a Trinity man – MA 1568 – who became the vicar of Claybrooke in Leicestershire, and had several sons, one of whom, John, was later described as 'a gentleman that kept high company'. This can scarcely be said of Francis, who after moving to Jesus from St John's came to haunt evangelical circles, which tended to the middling and stern. In the nineteenth century, his descendant and biographer Thomas Wentworth Higginson – himself famous for being an abolitionist, an advocate of women's rights, and an officer during the Civil War in the Massachusetts 54th, an experience he documented in the classic *Army Life in a Black Regiment* (1869) – was to speak of 'the somewhat isolated and stately air of Jesus College; its sombre brick walls and ancient gateway; its heavy tower surmounting a chapel of the twelfth century; and the meadows, extending to the river, and still making the situation beautiful', which was thought somehow to explain Francis's proclivities. (It did not, of course.) Upon graduation, Higginson became first his father's curate and then in 1615 his successor. A reputation as a preacher grew, but one inclining more and more to nonconformity, a man fussy about excluding 'ignorant and scandalous *persons*' from communion, someone given to fasts and often consulted by the anxious about – as Mather was to put it – 'their *interiour state*', people who like Higginson were worried by the 'hour and power of darkness' emanating from William Laud, then Bishop of London. It was unsurprising, therefore, that Higginson, having been deprived of his lectureship at a church in Leicester for nonconformity, should have responded to a call from the Massachusetts Bay Company, who were planning to send five ships to their barren plantation in 1629 and needed ministers to tend souls and enlist God's help for their purpose. He probably gave a sermon – there is some dispute over its authorship – outlining the cogency of migration. His reasons were many and apocalyptic: among them, to spread the Gospel and 'raise a bulwarke against the kingdom of Antichrist which the Jesuits labour to rear up in all places of the world', to find a refuge against the 'general destruction' threatening Europe, and to ease the strain on an England whose 'land grows weary of her inhabitants'. In what might have been a commentary on his old College, whose Master in 1629 was the overbearing, quarrelsome, and unscrupulous Roger Andrewes, Higginson also lamented that 'schools of learning and religion are so corrupted, as … most children (even the wisest, wittiest, and of fayerest hopes) are perverted, corrupted and utterly over powered by the multitude of evill examples and licentious governors of those seminaries'. His wife Ann was unconvinced and 'fell a weeping' at the prospect of leaving Leicestershire, but to no avail. In theory, Higginson got a good bargain: £30 to prepare for the voyage, £10 for books, an annual salary of £30 for three years and, during that time, provision of 'family necessaryes of diuett, housing and firewood', which extended to a house, land, cattle, and care for his widow (which turned out to be necessary). He was even promised 'a man servant to take care and look to his things, and to catch him fish and foule and provide other things needful and also two maid servants to look to his family'.

Two documents give greatest insight into Higginson: the journal he kept on board the *Talbot*, which sailed in company with the *Lion's Whelpe* from London on 25 April 1629 and reached New England on 27 June; and his propaganda pamphlet, *New-Englands Plantation, or, A Short and True Description of the Commodities and Discommodities of That Countrey, Written by a Reverend Divine Now There Resident* (1630), published in London by Michael Sparke, 'dwelling at the Signe of the Blew Bible in Greene Arbor in the little Old Bailey'.

The former is one of the best extant accounts of such a voyage: its delays ('staying for a wind'), storms ('sore and terrible'), quarrels ('a notorious wicked fellow that was given to swering and boasting of his former wickednes … mocked at our daies of fast, railing and jesting against puritans'), progress ('a fayre gale of winde'), sporting aquatic life ('an abundance of grampus fishes, 2 or 3 yards long, and a body as bigg as an oxe'), sights ('a mountayne of ice shining as white as snow like to a great rocke or clift on shoare'), illness ('some of our men fell sicke of the scurvie and others of the small pockes'), and death. The Higginsons lost a 4-year-old daughter, whose loss was 'a griefe to us her parents and a terrour to all the rest'.

The latter is a document of artful sensuality, full of intoxicating lists intended to encourage more migrants and written when Higginson was newly (and quickly) established as the schismatic minister at Salem. It gives an extended account of what was blessed and cursed in New England, whose qualities were quaintly classified by reference to earth, air, fire and water. All God's plenty is said to be in Massachusetts: 'good Clay to make Bricke and Tyles', rich grasses which fatten 'Kine and Goats, Horses and Hogges', new plants and old ones 'bigger and sweeter then is ordinarily to be found in *England*', 'Penyroyall, Wintersaverie, Sorrell, Brookelime, Liverwort, Carvell and Watercresses', 'plenty of single Damaske Roses', 'Wolves, Foxes, Beavers, Otters, Martins, great wild Cats'. The rivers and ocean furnish richness (lobsters, bass, salmon, whales, 'Herring, Turbot, Sturgion, Cuskes, Hadocks, Mullets, Eeles, Crabs, Muskles, and Oysters'). The air is clean and agreeable, with the happy effect of driving away 'Cold, Melancholy, Flegmatick, Reumaticke temper of Body'. Birds crowd the sky and the earth. Of 'discommodities', on the other hand, Higginson speaks with evasive brevity. Indeed he mentions but four difficulties.

There are mosquitoes in the summers, which he admits are hot. In winter there is snow and 'Frosts, something more sharpe then is in old *England*'. The woods abound in 'Snakes and Serpents of strange colours and huge greatnesse', not least the alarming rattlesnake, which will 'flye upon' a man 'and sting him so mortally, that he will dye within a quarter of an houre after'. The population is scanty. But these are the only problems. Even the Indians, who are curious people with strange ways, are manageable: 'We use them kindly, they will come into our Houses sometimes by halfe a douzen or halfe a score at a time when we are at victuals, but will aske or take nothing but what we give them.' Still, it was pertinent to note that 'we have great Ordnance, wherewith we doubt not but we shall fortifie our selves in a short time to keepe out a potent Adversarie'. And God was on their side.

Higginson quickly carried many with him away from the Church of England, for he was as skilful a preacher as he was an artful writer. Local tradition spoke of him as not tall, but 'slender and erect', with a manner said to have been 'courteous and obliging', a man 'well cultivated in the fields of literature and divinity' and 'able to convince gainsayers'. But he had little chance to exercise these charms and skills, for he was dead scarcely more than a year after his arrival. All the benign gifts of New England did not prevent consumption and a 'hectic fever', as Mather has it. He was only 43. He left a widow, who moved to New Haven and lived another ten years, but the couple had had nine children, of whom one (Neophytus) was born in Salem; eight survived their parents. Not all stayed in New England. Francis (b.1617) went back to England and became a minister in Westmoreland. Three became mariners, who captained East-Indiamen and plied the Jamaica trade. Most of the numerous Higginsons of New England are descendants of the eldest son, John, who became a minister and eventually took over his father's congregation at Salem, where he became notable for standing against the frenzy of the Salem witch trials.

Francophilia: Fellows on Trial

PETER GLAZEBROOK

Within the space of five years, 1793 to 1798, two Jesuans, one a Fellow, the other a former Fellow, published pamphlets sympathetic to republican France which brought down on them the wrath of the academic and political establishments, and led to their being put on trial and punished for their temerity. The two men, William Frend and Gilbert Wakefield, were of an age (Frend had been born in 1757, Wakefield in 1756); were friends; had been much influenced by Robert Tyrwhitt, the noted Hebraist who had also been a Fellow; and, like him, they had abandoned the Church of England, making no secret of their Unitarian and pacifist convictions. But there the similarities end. Frend's trial – which lasted for eight days in May 1793 in the Vice-Chancellor's Court sitting in the Senate House in Cambridge – though it resulted (after he had refused to recant) in his expulsion from the University for having 'impugned religion, as established by public authority within this realm, and also all ecclesiastical ranks and dignities' (contrary to the University's Elizabethan statutes), was sheer comic farce, providing considerable entertainment to the undergraduates who filled the galleries. Wakefield's, in February 1799 in the Court of King's Bench sitting in Westminster Hall, for having written and published a seditious libel, though over in an afternoon, was a deep tragedy. Having spent more than two years in prison, he died, aged 45, only fourteen weeks after his release, succumbing in his overwrought and exhausted mental and physical state to typhus.

Wakefield, widely regarded as an outstanding scholar, forfeited his Fellowship on his marriage in 1779. For many years he made a living teaching at the academies established for dissenters, first at Warrington and then at Hackney, while writing profusely on both scriptural and classical subjects. After ordination as a deacon in the Church of England his conscientious scruples at being required to subscribe the Thirty-Nine Articles – which he would have had to do again if he were to be ordained priest or take his MA – had hardened, and were advertised on the title-pages of the more than forty books he published, which announced that they were the work of 'Gilbert Wakefield, B.A. Formerly Fellow of Jesus College, Cambridge'.

Frend's separation from the Church took longer – perhaps because he had, while an undergraduate at Christ's, been a pupil of that pillar of Anglican orthodoxy

William Paley. Placed Second Wrangler in 1780 (as Wakefield had been in 1777), Frend was elected a Fellow of Jesus, and for some years energetically combined his duties as Tutor – T.R. Malthus and E.D. Clarke were among his pupils – with those of the Vicar of Madingley and Longstanton (where he began a Sunday school). But by 1787 he had decided that he could no longer officiate as an Anglican minister and resigned his livings, making his religious position clear in *An Address to the Inhabitants of Cambridge* the following year. Though he claimed that he was, he cannot really have been surprised that the Master thereupon dismissed him from his Tutorship for, as Stephen Taylor has said (page 96), no college could entrust the education and moral guidance of its undergraduates to someone who blatantly rejected the Church's creeds. The doctrine of the Trinity, Frend had declared, was 'rank nonsense'.

Freed from both parochial and tutorial responsibilities, Frend was introduced into radical circles in London where the French Revolution was, at least at first, widely welcomed – the French, it was thought, were at last to enjoy the constitutional and political benefits brought to England a century earlier by its own Glorious Revolution – and where a large number of legal and constitutional reforms were being canvassed. It was these reforms – in, notably, parliamentary representation and the suffrage, the criminal law, the poor laws, the game laws, legal education, and the established Church (including, of course, the repeal of the Test Acts, those bastions of Anglican privilege) – that Frend outlined in the pamphlet he published in February 1793 which brought him into the Vice-Chancellor's Court. Its title, *Peace and Union Recommended to the Associated Bodies of Republicans and Anti-Republicans*, fairly indicates its main theme: that the precise form of government, monarchical or republican, mattered little. What was crucial if social harmony were to be achieved and the violent excesses then being seen in France avoided, was for all parties to unite in implementing the reforms needed to remove the causes of widespread popular grievance and discontent, reforms that had, in fact, to wait for more than thirty years – till the decade 1829 to 1838 – to be brought about.

Frend then went on, in language of crystal clarity, to 'impugn religion established by public authority within this realm, and also all ecclesiastical ranks and dignities' – they were 'all repugnant to the spirit of Christianity' – though he thought that dissenting ministers were almost as bad as churchmen in bringing 'the great truths of religion' into disrepute among the laity:

> The same passions will everywhere produce on certain minds the same effect: and the priest in every age, whether he celebrates the orgies of Bacchus or solemnises the rites

of the Eucharist, will, should either his victims or his allowance fail, oppose in either case every truth which threatens to undermine his altars or weaken his sacerdotal authority.

So the appeals he brought from the Vice-Chancellor's Court to the Court of Delegates and then to the King's Bench inevitably failed, riddled with irregularities though the proceedings in the Senate House (like those of so many academic tribunals) undoubtedly were.

Few people, however, thought that it was Frend's blatant attack on the established Church, its doctrines and its ministers, that led five Fellows of Jesus to delate him to both the Vice-Chancellor and the College's Visitor; and then the Vice-Chancellor to encourage a clique of die-hard dons to mount the Senate House prosecution alleging the breach of an obsolescent University Statute, and, in the end, to his exclusion from the College – though not from his Fellowship and its dividend, for there was no College statute that he could be said to have broken. No one had previously been prosecuted in the University's court solely for publishing unorthodox views. In matters of religious belief late eighteenth-century Cambridge was quite a tolerant place. Once admitted to his fellowship and to all the degrees he sought, a don

William Frend, Fellow 1781–1808. This bust, formerly in his London house in Tavistock Square, was given to the College by a great-great-granddaughter.

would not, unless and until he was offered some other appointment in the Church, have to subscribe the Thirty-Nine Articles again, and unless he was, or hoped to be, a Tutor, he could write as well as think what he liked. His professed Unitarianism notwithstanding, Wakefield's many-volumed *Silva Critica*, was, until he came out in support of Frend, being published by the University Press at the Syndics' expense.

It was widely believed that what had really caused offence in Frend's pamphlet, and what had made him an intolerable embarrassment to the authorities in the University and his College, anxious as they were to be well thought of in government circles – the source of so much ecclesiastical preferment – was not its main text, but its two appendices. In the first, 'On the Execution of Louis Capet', he claimed that 'no Englishman need be alarmed at the execution of an individual at Paris' – not even if that individual were an anointed king – and in the second, 'The Effect of War on the Poor', he argued that it was they, and they alone, who would suffer, and suffer unjustifiably, solely for the sake of their betters, if, as then seemed all too likely and soon happened, Britain declared war on republican France. But these were not sentiments for which he could be punished by either the University or the College.

Frend, supported in the Senate House by Tyrwhitt, appears to have relished his forensic contests, and for him neither expulsion from the University nor exclusion from his College, in both of which he had long since forfeited the chance of filling any remunerative office, was the end of the world. He was to live happily to the ripe age of 84, seeing most of the reforms for which he had argued implemented, and enjoying the income from his Fellowship until 1808 when, despite all his strictures on 'ecclesiastical ranks and dignitaries', he married the daughter of a parson and granddaughter of an archdeacon. Two years earlier he had been appointed the first actuary of the new Rock Insurance Company and for twenty years he enjoyed a salary vastly larger than any he would have received in Cambridge.

Wakefield's pamphlet, bearing the mind-numbing title, *A Reply to Some Parts of the Bishop of Llandaff's Address to the People of Great Britain*, was written in anger and in haste and, though more extreme, is less readable than Frend's. Published first in February 1798 shortly after Pitt's government had rejected French overtures for a peace that would have ended the war whose outbreak Frend had feared, and at a time when it had become hypersensitive to its critics and shown itself ready to resort to the criminal courts to silence them, the pamphlet had been provoked by one Richard Watson, the Bishop of Llandaff (who combined his episcopal duties with those of the Regius Professorship of Divinity at

Cambridge – he had previously been Professor of Chemistry). The Bishop had been supportive of the government's policies, of its decision to continue the war, and in particular of its plans to finance it by taxation rather than borrowing, though he would have preferred a tax on capital to one on income. Wakefield's response expanded at some length on Frend's theme of the suffering the war inflicted on the poor, who had, he said, nothing to fear from, and so no reason to join in resisting, a French invasion, for they could not be worse off under French rule than they already were – though given the strength of the British navy he did not believe that any attempt at invasion could possibly succeed. He accused the government of bad faith in rejecting the French overtures for peace – its members were concerned only to keep themselves in power; questioned the Bishop's motives in writing his pamphlet; and for good measure threw in scathing attacks on the corruption of the parliamentary system, the venality of government ministers, their and their lawyers' cruelty in prosecuting their critics for treason or sedition – between them the Prime Minister and the Attorney-General had made this 'the Age of Peerages and Prosecutions' – the absurdity of the hereditary principle manifested in the House of Lords, the hypocrisy and time-serving behaviour of the higher clergy, and (for Wakefield an oft-repeated complaint) the religious and political intolerance enshrined in the Test Acts.

A jittery government was certainly not going to tolerate such a biting attack on the system on which its power was based. Its usual tactic was, however, to strike not at the author of an offending publication who might seek to justify what he had written in open court – it had earlier considered, but then decided against, prosecuting Wakefield for his *Letter to William Wilberforce* (1797) – but at the publisher and some of the booksellers who were distributing it. They would have no interest in arguing that it was not in truth seditious and would (like every other bookseller who learnt of the pending prosecutions) at once withdraw it from sale hopeful that they would be rewarded with more lenient sentences. The government would thus have suppressed the objectionable publication with the minimum of both trouble and counter-productive publicity.

The printer of Wakefield's pamphlet and two booksellers were accordingly selected for prosecution, its seditious character, which these defendants were not expected to question, being said to lie pre-eminently in his contention that the working classes – 'the poorer sort' – could not be worse off under French republican rule than they already were, and that this amounted to 'most unlawfully maliciously and seditiously devising and intending to dissuade and discourage the liege subjects … from resisting' any French forces making 'a hostile invasion into this

Kingdom'. It was a far-fetched interpretation to place on Wakefield's words, but more than one judge and more than one jury readily accepted it.

Incensed by the Attorney-General's tactics, Wakefield confirmed that he was the pamphlet's author and that responsibility for its publication and sale was his alone – the printer and the booksellers had not the slightest reason to suppose that anything in it would be regarded as seditious – and he offered to take their places in the dock, an offer which was ignored. This was too much for Wakefield who, angrier now than ever, not only had his pamphlet reprinted but added to it *A Letter to Sir John Scott, His Majesty's Attorney-General on the Subject of a Late Trial in Guildhall*. It was an unsparingly bitter attack on the moral and political integrity and the intellectual and professional competence of the addressee – Scott had led the University's legal team resisting Frend's appeal to the King's Bench, and was soon to become the notoriously indecisive and dilatory Lord Chancellor Eldon. 'As a polemical and political writer [Wakefield] indulged in an asperity of language which he had learnt from his favourite philologists', was Robert Southey's comment. Both pamphlets stated that they were 'Sold by the Author at Hackney'. With the gauntlet so publicly thrown down, the Attorney-General could no longer avoid prosecuting Wakefield himself. But he took the precaution of adopting two exceptional procedures: an *ex-officio* information rather than a routine indictment, and a special jury (that is, one handpicked by the Crown) rather than an ordinary one for the trial. In this way he avoided the risks that a grand jury might be unwilling to send for trial, and an ordinary jury to convict, a rather eccentric and extremely irritable, but famous, scholar whose sincerity no one could doubt, for an offence punishable with imprisonment when what he had done, though it might have upset the government, had in truth caused no harm at all to anyone.

Thomas Erskine, the greatest advocate of the day, offered to appear for Wakefield at his trial, as he had at those of his printer and the booksellers, but his offer was declined. Wakefield was determined to make the most of his day in court, unconstrained by barristers' conventional courtesies. Erskine must have had a shrewd idea of what was to come but he did his best for Wakefield when defending, before the same judge and jury as would try him, the second of the two booksellers (whose trial had been postponed from an earlier day), presenting the pamphlet and its author as quite innocuous. When his own turn came, Wakefield, not content with seeking to demonstrate, in three separate ways, the logical absurdity of claiming that his pamphlet revealed a 'malicious and seditious' intent – had he not presented a copy of his three-volume edition of Lucretius to the King, and twice gone into print to attack Thomas Paine's *The Age of Reason?* – repeated in even more abusive terms the personal attack he had made on the Attorney-General in his *Letter*. A former fellow and tutor of an Oxford college (as Scott was) might have been expected to understand the wickedness, the inhumanity and the irrationality of using the force of the law to suppress the free expression of honestly held opinions: if their roles were reversed what objection would Scott be able to raise against Wakefield prosecuting him for expressing his? He also questioned the impartiality of the judge – Lord Chief Justice Kenyon – and told the jury that no man of sense could convict him, which they thereupon did without even retiring to read the pamphlet. They had been kept in court all day and had missed their dinner. They had heard, too, the Chief Justice go to the Attorney-General's defence, reproving Wakefield for failing to practise the Christian forbearance that he preached, and making it as clear as he could that he had no answer to the charge.

Remanded to the King's Bench prison to await sentence, Wakefield was overwhelmed by visits from admirers and

Gilbert Wakefield (1772), Fellow 1776–9.

Mezzotint by R. Dunkerton after the painting by W. Artaud, 1802

sympathisers – among them Charles James Fox, Lord Holland and the Duke of Bedford. Returning to the court to be sentenced, he preached the judges a sermon which can have lasted little less than two hours, replete with biblical quotations and classical allusions, on the absurdity, the inhumanity and the irreligiousness of punishing a man for his opinions, a sermon that seemed designed to aggravate rather than mitigate his offence. Sentence was again postponed, and when it eventually came it was two years' imprisonment to be served in Dorchester gaol – sufficiently far from London to discourage excessive prison visiting by his many admirers – to run from his arrival there.

Wakefield had unquestionably brought his martyrdom upon himself, but his conviction and sentence were nonetheless bizarre travesties of justice. The professorial bishop, however, comes out of the story rather well, though the then Master of Jesus and his predecessor do so poorly. Bishop Watson remained on friendly terms with his critic, and did what he could to dissuade the government from prosecuting him. Drs Beadon and Pearce, on the other hand, coldly declined to provide the Court of King's Bench, either in person or in writing, with the character references that the most scholarly eminent of living Jesuans sought from them.

In passing sentence Mr Justice Grose had said that Wakefield was an artful hypocrite and worse, and hoped that his imprisonment would produce 'contrition and sincere repentance'. It did not, of course. But it did produce from friends and sympathisers a fund totalling £5,000, which would have made him, and did make his widow, financially independent for the rest of their lives. It was, as he wryly observed, something for which he was indebted to the Attorney-General.

The offending pamphlets.

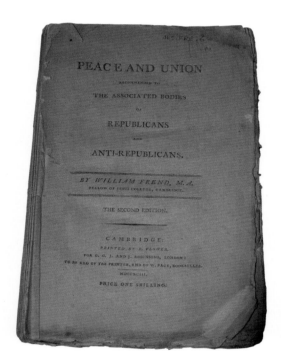

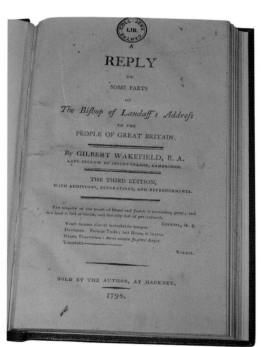

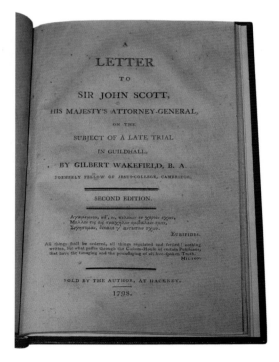

A Golden Age

Thomas Robert Malthus: Jesus's first 'dismal scientist'

GEOFF HARCOURT

According to Maynard Keynes, 'Malthus' is an adaptation of 'malthouse' and should therefore be pronounced 'Maultus' (just as Keynes is pronounced 'Kaynes', Milton Ke[e]ynes not withstanding). Thomas Robert Malthus (known to family and friends as Robert) was born on 13 February 1766, the second son of Daniel Malthus. '[W]hen the babe was three weeks old … two fairy godmothers, Jean-Jacques Rousseau and David Hume [both friends of his father], called together at The Rookery [Daniel's elegant small mansion near Dorking], and may be presumed to have assigned to the infant with a kiss diverse intellectual gifts.'

Daniel, who had 'allowed diffidence to overmaster ambition', also had unorthodox views on education. Young Robert was privately tutored by his father and others before he came up to Jesus in 1784, aged 18. One of these others was a former fellow, Gilbert Wakefield, whose wild opinions were, as the previous chapter relates, in 1799 to land him in gaol. The University was just emerging from deep intellectual slumbers, and of the colleges, Jesus, though 'amongst the sleepiest, was becoming a centre of intellectual ferment'. Malthus found stimulating and highly agreeable friends, both intellectual and sporting. (I am glad to say he was fond of cricket.) Chief among them was the future Bishop Otter, his first biographer; and Edward Daniel Clarke (about whom Michael O'Brien writes on page 134). Though noted for his shyness, diffidence and great modesty and being 'impassive to unmerited abuse', at Cambridge he was 'a gay companion'.

Malthus was a competent mathematician – he was ninth Wrangler in 1788 – but also took a lively, intelligent interest in classics, philosophy and history. He was much influenced by William Paley's *Principles of Morality and Politics* (1785), as well as by his tutor, William Frend who had been a pupil of Paley. Frend was a mathematician, an algebraist and second Wrangler in 1780. He was a kind and helpful tutor, a patient and clear supervisor and a brave critic who took on the heavies, academic and political. Sir Isaac Newton's writings on algebra, he considered, left much to be desired.

Malthus took holy orders in 1788, having consulted the Master about whether his speech defect – he had a hare-lip and cleft palate, inherited from a great-great-grandfather – would be an insurmountable obstacle; evidently not in a quiet rural living. (Nor did it prove to be a bar to his great friendship with Harriet Martineau, who was deaf and worried when they first met that 'his hare-lip [would] prevent [her] offering him [her] tube … [she] was delightfully wrong … His worst letter was "L" and when [she] had no difficulty with his question, – "would not you like to have a look at the lakes of Killarney?", [she] had nothing more to fear.') He was elected a Fellow on 10 June 1793 – a few months after Frend's vocal pacifism had provoked the denunciation which led to his being expelled from the University – and remained a Fellow until he married one of his pretty cousins in 1804. (The Malthus family specialised in marrying cousins.) He was also a curate and then vicar of a couple of parishes before he was appointed in 1805 at 39 years of age to the first professorship of political economy in England at the newly founded East India College, soon to be located at Haileybury, which became the training ground for recruits to the East India Company before they went, as the agents of British (private) imperialism, to India.

William Godwin had published his *Political Justice* in 1793, in which – while damning the present – he looked forward to a distant future with (in Robert Heilbroner's words) 'no war, no crime, no administration of justice, no government … no disease, anguish, melancholy or resentment'. Daniel Malthus become interested in these doctrines of the possibility of human perfection, and his conversations with Robert stimulated our hero to write his famous essay on *The Principle of Population as it Affects the Future Improvement of Society*, the first edition of which was published in 1798. The rest, as they say, is history.

In the preface, Malthus says, 'The following essay owes its origin to a conversation with a friend, on the subject of Mr. Godwin's Essay' (for friend, read Daniel). Like Keynes, I much prefer the first edition to the second. It is a wonderful read, a splendid example of deductive reasoning written in an ironic, often witty manner, with a grace and style he was rarely, if ever, to show again – certainly not in the second edition of 1803, which is too cautious, too overlaid with empirical examples, and with too many qualifications and ifs and buts. Many of the examples were gathered on his travels with Jesuan friends, notably with Clarke.

In the first edition, Malthus erects his arguments on the base of 'two postulata', which he thought he 'may fairly make':

> First, that food is necessary to the existence of man.
> Secondly, that the passion between the sexes is
> necessary, and will remain nearly in its present state …
> These two laws ever since we have any knowledge of
> mankind, appear to have been firm laws of our nature;
> and, as we have not hitherto seen any alteration in them,
> we have no right to conclude that they will ever cease to
> be what they are now.

Malthus refers to Godwin's 'deviation in the land of conjecture' that passion between the sexes may in time be extinguished, adding that he sees no progress towards this. He admits of 'individual exceptions' that do not, however, increase in number over time. Therefore, 'it would surely be a very unphilosophical mode of arguing to infer merely from the existence of an exception, that [it] would, in time, become the rule, and the rule the exception. Assuming then, my postulata to be granted, I say, that the power of population is indefinitely greater than the power in the earth to produce subsistence for man.'

He then proceeds to develop his arguments that, because of finite quantities of plots of land of given fertility at both the extensive and intensive margins (as we economists call them), the expansion of food output is at a lower rate (Malthus uses an arithmetical progression as

his example) than population (Malthus suggests expansion at a geometrical rate), so that by the application of the second postulate (once couples are married) there will always be pressure of population such as to reduce the workers' standard of living to bare subsistence. If momentarily the wages of labour rise above subsistence, the extra energy so entailed will induce such a burst in population growth as soon to return wages to subsistence level. Similarly, if wages fall below this level, perhaps through war and pestilence, population will fall off until the subsistence wage is restored. No wonder political economy was later called by Carlyle 'the dismal science'. For even if population grows, subsistence is so miserable an existence that this growth serves but to maximise the sum of human misery.

Malthus's first edition burst upon the reading public like a bombshell, releasing strong emotions both for and against its author and his arguments. A biographer, James Bonar, called him 'the best abused man of his age … a man who defended smallpox, slavery, and child-murder … who denounced soup-kitchens, early marriages and parish allowances … who "had the impudence to marry after preaching against the evils of a family".'

One of those who railed against Malthus was his fellow Jesuan, Samuel Taylor Coleridge: 'Finally, behold this mighty nation, its rulers and its wise men listening – to Paley and – to Malthus! It is mournful, mournful.' Coleridge 'solemnly [declared] … that all the heresies and

Thomas Robert Malthus
(1784), Fellow 1793–1804.

After Linnell

sects and factions, which the ignorance and the weakness and the wickedness of man has ever given birth to, were [not] altogether so disgraceful to a man as a Christian, a philosopher, a statesman, or citizen, as this abominable tenet.' Shelley (Godwin's son-in-law) was not too impressed either: 'Metaphysics … moral and political science, have become little more than vain attempts to revive exploded superstitions, or sophisms like those of Mr. Malthus, calculated to call the oppressors of mankind into a security of everlasting triumph.'

Malthus was seen as being very hard on the poor and the working class generally. But it was not hardness of heart but the implications of his own arguments that made him argue against parish houses for the poor and the provisions of the Poor Law generally. He was searching in vain for sensible limits to population growth (having ruled out birth control as inconsistent with his Christian beliefs). Marx, of course, thought Malthus's views were a libel on the human race committed by a plagiarist (the latter, a most unfair charge).

Though Keynes admired his first essay, the reason why he called Malthus 'the first of the Cambridge economists' was not so much because of his views on population but because of his arguments with his great friend, David Ricardo, about the possibility of general gluts, prompted by the great and sustained unemployment they witnessed after the end of the Napoleonic Wars (Keynes, who never considered modesty a virtue, thought Malthus was the first person to think like Keynes). Ricardo was a remarkable man, the son of a Jewish merchant banker immigrant from Holland, he became a Unitarian in order to marry a handsome Quaker woman, was elected to the House of Commons, and made a fortune on the stock exchange. (He followed a very simple but wise rule of thumb, based on observing that people in general exaggerated the importance of events, of buying early in order to realise early on a rise, and selling early on a fall.) Ricardo sometimes gave Malthus tips and traded on his behalf. He made a killing over Waterloo by keeping his nerve on British bonds. Malthus did not, however, keep *his*, asking Ricardo to sell his holdings for a modest profit, and was rather discomforted by Ricardo's response: 'This is as great an advantage as ever I expect or wish to make by a rise.' He had, he said, 'been a considerable gainer by the loan', adding 'Now for a little of our old subject.'

Making a fortune allowed Ricardo to retire at an early age to become a landed gentleman (he bought Gatcombe Park, now owned by the Princess Royal). He was listened to with great respect, if not comfort (he evidently had a high pitched voice), by all sides of the House. Though a landowner, he argued for the repeal of the Corn Laws, which would have greatly and adversely affected rents. Malthus, in contrast, was a defender of landlords and

their large expenditures, taking a differing view of the impossibility of general gluts.

Malthus and Ricardo never, in fact, agreed on anything in political economy and they argued incessantly, usually because they were arguing at cross-purposes. Malthus could never put his finger on the key point of his argument on gluts. He concentrated on immediate effects and outcomes, while Ricardo ignored them and spelt out what he felt to be the permanent consequences when the system had settled down in its new situation following an initial disturbance. Yet as Ricardo wrote in his last letter to Malthus – he died soon after, unexpectedly and far too young, aged 51 – 'And now, my dear Malthus, I have done. Like other disputants, after much discussion, we each retain our own opinions. These discussions, however, never influence our friendship; I should not like you more than I do if you agreed in opinion with me.' As Keynes tells us, they conversed 'together in peace and amity all their days'. (And now the copies of Ricardo's books and pamphlets that he sent to Malthus stand alongside his friend's in the library that had belonged to the Malthus family which was given to the College in 1949.)

'Let us,' said Keynes in his centenary allocution:

think of Malthus … as a great pioneer of the application of a frame of formal thinking to the complex confusion of the world of daily events. Malthus approached the central problems of economic theory by the best of all routes. He began … as a philosopher and moral scientist … applying the *a priori* method of the political philosopher. He then immersed himself … in the facts of economic history and of the contemporary world, applying the methods of historical induction and filling his mind with a mass of the material of experience. And then finally he returned to *a priori* thought, but this time to the pure theory of the economist proper, and sought … to impose the methods of formal thought on the material presented by events, so as to penetrate [them] with understanding by a mixture of intuitive selection and formal principle and thus to interpret the problem and propose the remedy … from being a caterpillar of a moral scientist and a chrysalis of an historian, he could at last spread the wings of his thought and survey the world as an economist!

Malthus was a very happily married man. There were three children of the marriage, of whom there are, however, now no direct descendants. (Daniel and his wife had so many children that there are still plenty of their descendants around, many in New Zealand.) His colleagues and pupils adored him, his pupils calling him 'Pop' – behind his back, of course. Ricardo had died in 1823; Malthus lived for another eleven years. Maria Edgeworth recalls what it was like at Haileybury, drawing on her last visit there a year before Malthus died. She was:

> pleased with the well-planted country of Herts. Almost daily we went forth when work was done – a pleasant riding party of five or six, and explored all the green lanes, and enjoyed all the fine views … The families of the other professors made up a very pleasant society – to say nothing of the interest of seeing in the students the future administrators of India. The subdued jests and external homage and occasional insurrections of the young men; the archery of the young ladies; the curious politeness of the Persian professor; the fine learning and eager scholarship of Principal le Bas, and the somewhat old-fashioned courtesies of the summer evening parties are all over now.

I can never read this passage without being deeply moved. For as Sir James Mackintosh wrote: 'I have known Adam Smith slightly, Ricardo well, and Malthus intimately. Is it not something to say for a science that its three greatest masters were about the three best men I ever knew?' 'There is', Keynes added, 'something about these three figures to evoke more than ordinary sentiments from us their children in the spirit'. Would that I could find three modern economists of which this could be said of them and their subject!

SACRED TO THE MEMORY
OF THE REV. THOMAS ROBERT MALTHUS
LONG KNOWN TO THE LETTERED WORLD
BY HIS ADMIRABLE WRITING ON THE SOCIAL BRANCHES OF
POLITICAL ECONOMY
PARTICULARLY BY HIS ESSAY ON POPULATION
ONE OF THE BEST MEN AND TRUEST PHILOSOPHERS
OF ANY AGE OR COUNTRY
RAISED BY NATIVE DIGNITY OF MIND
ABOVE THE MISREPRESENTATIONS OF THE IGNORANT
AND THE NEGLECT OF THE GREAT
HE LIVED A SERENE AND HAPPY LIFE
DEVOTED TO THE PURSUIT AND COMMUNICATION
OF TRUTH
SUPPORTED BY A FIRM CONVICTION OF THE
USEFULNESS OF HIS LABOURS
CONTENT WITH THE APPROPRIATION OF THE WISE AND GOOD
HIS WRITINGS WILL BE A LASTING MONUMENT
OF THE EXTENT AND CORRECTNESS OF HIS UNDERSTANDING
THE SPOTLESS INTEGRITY OF HIS PRINCIPLES
THE EQUITY AND CANDOUR OF HIS NATURE
HIS SWEETNESS OF TEMPER URBANITY OF MANNERS
AND TENDERNESS OF HEART
HIS BENEVOLENCE AND HIS PIETY
ARE THE STILL DEARER RECOLLECTIONS OF HIS FAMILY
AND FRIENDS
BORN FEB: 14·1766   DIED 29·DEC: 1834

Monument to T.R. Malthus in Bath Abbey

Samuel Taylor Coleridge

JOHN CORNWELL

On a blazing June morning in 1794, Samuel Taylor Coleridge, 21 years old and in his third year at Jesus College, marched west out of Cambridge. That summer, a year into war with revolutionary France, the population was expecting an invasion any day from across the Channel. The zeal of the English political radicals, seen as revolutionaries in the French style, had resulted in a fierce Church-and-King reaction. Spies abounded, the Habeas Corpus Act had been suspended. Coleridge did not then realise it, but despite the fact that he had not taken a degree, his university career was effectively over. He had embarked not only on a walking tour but on a life's journey of poetic and intellectual adventure.

Three days and ninety miles later Coleridge entered Oxford, where in his view the University had slumbered peacefully on, 'plus royaliste que le Roi'. Yet here, at Balliol College, he found a kindred spirit in one Robert Southey – a radical capable, said Coleridge, of making 'the adamantine gate of Democracy turn on its hinges to the most sweet music'. There were excited discussions in Southey's rooms as the new friends formed a scheme to put their radicalism into practice. They would found a new society called a Pantisocracy, a commune in which personal property would be banned. They would start with twelve men and their wives, although they would hold an open mind about the dissolubility of marriage and free love. They would emigrate to America, buy land and live in a Utopia, free of personal possessions, sharing an equal burden of manual labour (which, pinning their confidence on an assertion of Adam Smith's, they were convinced would absorb no more than two hours of the day). 'When

Coleridge and I are sawing down a tree we shall discuss metaphysics', enthused Southey, 'criticise poetry when hunting buffalo, and write sonnets whilst following the plough.' Isolated from the depravities of civilised society, they would shape their children's minds and hearts according to a master-plan that would ensure a perfect society.

What had brought Coleridge to this point of optimism on the perfectibility of human nature, providing an impetus, as we now know in retrospect, for a boost of poetic energy over the next five years? Was it the predicament of his extraordinary intellect – poetic, enquiring, restless? Or the inner psychology of a troubled youngest child with nine siblings, whose parson father had died when he was only 9? Whatever the shaping inner and outward influences, Jesus College, Cambridge, had exerted a decisive effect on this young man.

Coleridge, the Jesus undergraduate, had been subjected to two distinct and opposing intellectual attractions before he arrived in Cambridge in the autumn of 1791. Born on 21 October 1772, the last of a large family, he had become oversensitive, a prey to passionate feelings, 'fretful and timorous', living within his own imagination. Solitude at Christ's Hospital in the city of London, where he had boarded for ten years, had turned him into a 'library cormorant'. In addition to plundering the classics, he explored the works of mystics such as Plotinus and the German theosophist Jacob Boheme. At the same time he found himself drawn to the scientific, the physiological, the empirical and rational. He had gutted Voltaire's *Philosophical Dictionary* – a work written for the entertainment and confirmation of atheists. He had a passion for medical works, which he read avidly for pleasure. His older brother Luke was a surgeon at the London Hospital in Whitechapel, where Sam would spend time on the wards and dissecting rooms on Saturday mornings. The young Coleridge who began his residence at Jesus on 16 October 1791, having been admitted as a sizar in his absence on 5 February, found himself strongly drawn in two directions – towards a strictly scientific and empirical tendency, on the one hand, and in a metaphysical and spiritual direction, on the other.

He arrived at the College with high hopes of distinguishing himself academically and in search of stimulating tutorial guidance. Initially he was crestfallen. Dr Pearce, the Master, was away and not expected to return until the summer: 'what is still more extraordinary – (and rather shameful),' wrote Coleridge, 'neither of the tutors are here. … Neither lectures, or Chapel, or anything, is begun.' He sat down to dinner in Hall on his first night in silence, 'except the noise of suction, which accompanies my eating'. The College eventually swung into action in early November and he could report to his elder brother George, a schoolmaster in Hackney, 'I read Mathematics three hours a day … After Tea I read Classics till I go to bed – viz – eleven o'clock.'

Brought up in the established Church, Coleridge nevertheless made early contact with reforming groups who were attempting to overturn the Test Acts, which denied degrees to those who could not assent to the Church of England's Thirty-Nine Articles. A Fellow of Jesus, William Frend, was a crucial dissenting figure in Cambridge. He had resigned his Church ministry and gone over to the Unitarians, a group that denied the divinity of Christ, the theology of the Trinity and the existence of original sin. Frend further provoked his colleagues by braving the Jesus Combination Room in a blue coat with brass buttons (today it would be like a Fellow dining at High Table in a T-shirt).

Coleridge joined Frend's circle with its contacts among notable radicals – including Joseph Priestley, Horne Took, George Dyer and William Godwin – and he led a campaign to chalk up graffiti around Cambridge, including the slogan 'Frend for Ever'. One night he and his

Samuel Taylor Coleridge
(1791)
James Northcote, 1804

friends traced and burnt in gunpowder the legends *Liberty* and *Equality* into the lawn of Trinity College.

It was through Frend and Priestley that Coleridge came to be influenced by a book entitled *Observations on Man, His Frame, His Duty and His Expectations* by the psychologist David Hartley, who from 1727 to 1730 had been a Fellow of Jesus. First published in 1749, and republished in 1791, a copy of the *Observations* is to be found today in the College's Old Library, where Coleridge supplemented his income by working as Library Clerk. The book arguably constitutes the first detailed attempt at a non-dualist, determinist, mind–brain body theory in the modern period, grounding consciousness in neurophysiology. The central concept is association of ideas, widely discussed by British philosophers and psychologists at the time, and paying tribute to key notions in Newton's *Optics*. Hartley's *Observations* was a recipe for the perfectibility of society, abolishing original sin without entirely abolishing the deity: the radicals of the early 1790s placed it on the same level as the Bible. Several years on, Coleridge would name his first child after Hartley. For Coleridge, as for Priestley, Hartley's attractions and repulsions and vibrations amounted to a theory of man in nature and of course his final destiny: a theory indeed of everything, including, in Coleridge's case, an explanation of the growth of language, a theory of the imagination, and a decidedly pantheistic notion of God's presence and action in the world. Hartley's influence can be detected in Coleridge's poem 'The Æolian Harp', written in August 1795:

> And what if all of animated nature
> Be but organic Harps diversely framed
> That tremble into thought, as o'er them sweeps
> Plastic and vast one intellectual breeze,
> At once the Soul of each, and God of all?

Coleridge's rooms in Jesus, 'on the right hand ground floor of the staircase facing the gate', wrote a contemporary, 'were a centre of conversation, largely on politics'. At these parties, 'Aeschylus and Plato and Thucydides were pushed aside with a pile of lexicons to discus the pamphlets of the day' – some written by Frend, who was being attacked around the town by a series of counter-graffiti: 'Frend of Jesus, Friend of the Devil.'

By his second year (1792–93), Coleridge was neglecting his studies, spending more and more time away from Cambridge, making trips to Manchester for Unitarian get-togethers, where it was noticed by Robert Owen that 'Mr Coleridge had a great fluency of words.'

He began to be plagued by personal difficulties. He was in debt to a tradesman who had furnished his College rooms, expense no object; and ran up debts to his Tutor too. Then his favourite sister, Anne, died, and shortly

afterwards he fell in love with a Cambridge girl called Mary Evans. All the same he won the coveted Browne Medal for a Greek Sapphic ode on the slave trade, but he was bitterly disappointed at narrowly failing to win the Craven Scholarship, which would have enabled him to remain in Cambridge after graduating. He became depressed on hearing news of the death of his soldier brother Frank, killed in the fall of Seringapatam. 'I became a proverb to the university for idleness,' he wrote, 'the time which I should have bestowed on my academic studies, I employed in dreaming out wild schemes of impossible extrication.' His brothers clubbed together to pay off his debts, but all in vain. He went to London on a spending spree, returning to the College and a 'multitude of petty embarrassments which buzzed round me like a nest of hornets'. He considered doing away with himself, but instead enlisted as a trooper in the Light Dragoons under the pseudonym Silas Tomkyn Comberbache. He was not a good soldier; his musket was always rusty. He was put in charge of a ward of troopers suffering from small-pox.

Again his brothers bailed him out. He was discharged from his regiment on the pretext that he was insane in April 1794 and returned to Jesus, where he was gated and given the task of translating Demetrius Phalereus. Once again his debts were fully paid by his brothers and he

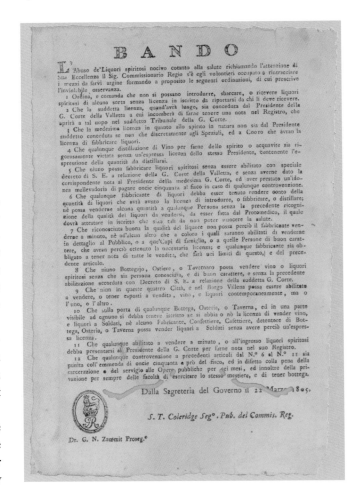

Proclamation regulating the supply of *Liquori spiritosi* issued under Coleridge's name when he was Secretary to the Governor of Malta, 22 March 1805.

addressed himself to a life of self-discipline. 'Every enjoyment, except of necessary comforts, I look upon as criminal', he solemnly wrote. But the hectic experiences of the past year had unsettled him for the life of an undergraduate, and he had in any case already taken the best the College and Cambridge could offer him. He was looking further afield.

As Southey and Coleridge planned their commune in June 1794, Southey told his new friend of his love for Edith Fricker, one of five daughters of a manufacturer of sugar pans whose business had gone under with the cessation of trade between England and the United States. Coleridge, in a fit of what he later called the 'ebulliance' of schematism, offered to marry another of the Fricker girls, Sara, in expectation of the departure for America. The decision was complicated from the start since he was still in love with Mary Evans. A third Fricker girl then became engaged to a third Pantisocrat, Robert Lovell. Coleridge returned briefly to Jesus in the Michaelmas term of 1794, but he disappeared for the last time from the College on 16 December. A place was kept for him until 6 April 1795. The final entry on him in the College records reads:

> Whereas Coleridge is still in arrears with his Tutors, and has been absent for some time from the College (where we know not), it is ordered by the Master and Fellows that his name be taken off the boards on the 14 day of June next, unless cause be shown to the contrary, or some one of the Fellows declares himself willing to be his Tutor before that time, and that his present Tutors do endeavour to inform him of this order.

In the meantime the entire Pantisocracy scheme, which had taken Coleridge away from Cambridge, collapsed when Southey's aunt, who had promised to underpin its finances, withdrew her support. Coleridge, however, now engaged to Sara Fricker, went ahead and married her on October 1795, more out of duty than love. They settled in a cottage at Nether Stowey, Somerset. At first they seemed content. Their first child, Hartley, was born in 1796. There would be three further children – Berkeley (who died in infancy), Derwent and Sara. Within two years of Hartley's birth, however, Coleridge became disillusioned with his first-born's namesake, realising that the boy was by no means learning to speak according to the Hartleian deterministic theory. As a poet, moreover, he realised that authentic poetic metaphor is dynamic, breaking free of the rules of association of ideas.

In 1797 William Wordsworth, whom Coleridge judged 'the best poet of the age', and his sister Dorothy became neighbours. Wordsworth gained much from the relationship, especially in philosophical insight, foreshadowing

Coleridge's role of quiet influence on many of his contemporaries. He was, said the philosopher and essayist John Stuart Mill, one of the greatest 'seminal influences' of the nineteenth century in his combative challenge to the utilitarian ideas of philosophers like Jeremy Bentham. After the Wordsworths came into his life, there followed a period of productive collaboration resulting in the joint publication in 1798 of a volume of verse, *Lyrical Ballads*. But Coleridge was often in ill-health, even in these early years, largely due to his increasing consumption of opium.

Coleridge and the Wordsworths travelled together to Germany in 1799. While Wordsworth went in search of landscapes, Coleridge learned the language and spent time at the University of Göttingen, embarking on a study of Kant and contemporary German philosophers who would shape his future thinking, especially in the realms of literary criticism, religion and aesthetics. Returning to England in 1800, he settled with his family close to the Wordsworths and Robert Southey in the Lake District. By now his marriage had begun to fail and he was in love with Sara Hutchinson, whose sister Mary would later marry Wordsworth. Coleridge was never to consummate his love for Hutchinson and his idolisation of her contributed to marital tensions. Domestic strife and illness were made worse by opium. His poem 'Dejection: an Ode', published in 1802, reveals the depths of his melancholy.

In an attempt to convalesce and rediscover his creative impetus, Coleridge travelled out to Malta in 1804 to become secretary to the island's governor. Later he went to Sicily and Italy, spending time in Naples and Rome. He returned to England in 1806, sick and addicted, determined at last to separate formally from his wife. The era of great poetry was over, but he was to find intellectual fulfilment in a prodigious output of lectures, essays, letters, notebook entries, journalism and conversation. He became the publisher, editor and the sole contributor of a periodical, *The Friend*. It survived for only fourteen months, but its issues are a source of many valuable Coleridgean insights. Among his prose works were the *Biographia Literaria*, a remarkable account of his poetic and philosophical development, *Aids to Reflection* and the *Statesman's Manual*.

In 1816 he went to live in Highgate in north London as a lodger in the house of a doctor, James Gillman, who helped him control his opium consumption. The remainder of his life was spent in quiet study. Many eminent figures visited him at the Gillmans' home, anxious to hear his remarkable disquisitions on literary and philosophical topics. He died in 1834.

After his death Wordsworth said that he was 'the most wonderful man that I have ever known'. Charles Lamb said, 'Never saw I his likeness, nor probably the world can see again.' Coleridge had opposed the materialistic and determinist philosophies of his era with the promotion of the imagination as a free, dynamic and creative force. His influence, which spread throughout the English-speaking world, had far-reaching consequences for literary criticism, politics and the study of the philosophy of religion and theology. He is justly praised as a great poet of the late eighteenth century for his major work, *The Ancient Mariner.* Equally impressive, although different in genre, are his Conversation Poems: 'Lime Tree Bower', 'Æolian Harp', 'Frost at Midnight' and the 'Dejection' ode. Throughout his life he had dreamed of writing an epic or an all-embracing philosophical system. The great works never appeared; the materials out of which he had striven to realise a total vision of things lay scattered in a huge circuit of published and unpublished work. In the past

half-century, however, Coleridgean scholars have produced critical editions of his complete writings.

He regretted all his life the manner in which he had parted from his College. 'In an inauspicious hour,' he wrote in *Biographia Literaria*, 'I left the friendly cloysters and the happy grove of quiet, ever honored Jesus College, Cambridge'. In 1818 he wrote a note to his sons in the fly-leaf of a book: 'O with what bitter regret, and in the conscience of such glorious opportunities … at Jesus College, Cambridge, under an excellent Mathematical Tutor, Newton, all neglected.' He returned to Cambridge only once, in 1833, nearly forty years after he left, for a meeting of the British Association: 'My emotions at revisiting the University,' he told a friend 'were at first overwhelming. I could not speak for an hour; yet my feelings on the whole were very pleasurable.'

Edward Daniel Clarke

MICHAEL O'BRIEN

He began as a traveller to the world's wonders and ended as a modest phenomenon whom strangers came to see, a living curiosity of the University. Oddly for so domestic and virtuous a clergyman, his fame threatened briefly to be Byronic, for he had seen the Hellespont and more. All this came as a surprise, especially to his contemporaries. Bishop William Otter, his friend and later his sceptical biographer, was very puzzled, for Clarke had been a lazy undergraduate, known chiefly for sending a kitten aloft in a balloon, launched from Cloister Court and chased by delighted horsemen through the countryside. He had been only the fourth Junior Optime, a mediocre achievement in the Senate House Examination, and it was thought his election to a fellowship owed more to patronage than rigour. But Clarke had gifts inaccessible to bishops. He was handsome and had charm, he was indefatigable and enthusiastic, he had a remarkable memory, he was a good Tutor if a vexed and short-lived Senior Tutor, and he collected things on a heroic scale, such that ships were to come from the Levant stuffed with his seventy-six packing cases of plants, coins, maps, statues, vases, jewellery and ancient bric-à-brac.

All this endeared him to a magpie age. But, unlike the seed which he brought back from Greece and planted in the Fellows' Garden, where now an immense plane tree competes in height with the Chapel tower, Clarke's reputation did not grow. No one has troubled to write his biography since 1824, two years after his early death,

though his name fleetingly appears in histories of his various endeavours (the classics, archaeology, travel literature, natural science). Indeed the only sustained modern study, a Cambridge doctoral thesis, examines him upon the defensible rationale that, though Clarke is more than an 'eccentric', he was 'a minor figure' who best serves to furnish 'new and productive angles from which to approach the history of collecting and archaeology'. Perhaps so, when seen from the Faculty of Classics on Sidgwick Avenue. His College is obliged to be more indulgent and think him more than, as a contemporary put it, 'sometimes learned'.

Edward Daniel Clarke was the descendant of many scribbling antiquarians, one of whom in his time failed to finish a digest of the laws of Hoel Dha, a tenth-century Welsh king you may be forgiven for not knowing. He was born in 1769 in Willingdon in Sussex. There his father was the local vicar, quietly and impecuniously settled after having been chaplain to the British ambassador to Madrid and the lieutenant-governor of Minorca. Out of this experience had come *Letters Concerning the Spanish Nation* (1763) and *A Defence of the Conduct of the Lieutenant-Governor of the Island of Minorca, in Reply to a Printed Libel, Secretly Dispersed, Without a Name* (1768). These ancestral and itinerant works seem to have diffidently inspired the son, though only eventually. At Tonbridge Grammar School he was thought 'deficient in application' and short of 'classical attainments'. In 1786, when 16, he came up, surprisingly, to Jesus College, for St John's was the family's usual destination. But Clarke needed money, Dr Richard Beadon, the Master, was a family friend, he could be paid as a Chapel Clerk and, after his father promptly died, a Rustat Scholar. As was then observed from the lofty munificence of Trinity College, Jesus was 'a good college for clergymen's orphans', though in all Clarke received only £90 a year, half the usual expenses of a commoner. But indigence did not occasion alienation, only debts. If anything, Clarke suffered from being too popular as 'a very delightful fellow', making only 'languid and capricious efforts in the regular studies of the place'. Nonetheless, as even Otter had to admit, he was 'scrupulously and conscientiously correct', especially in attending Chapel, and was inexplicably averse to getting drunk, 'the prevailing vice of the place'.

He left in 1790, to do what young graduates often did, become tutor to recalcitrant aristocrats and gentlemen. Throughout the 1790s, with the Honourable This and the Lord That, Clarke lived well on country estates, travelled the British Isles, went to Paris, ascended the Rhine, traversed the Alps and scowled at Roman Catholics. Thereby, as he himself put it, he strengthened 'an unbounded love of travel' which he felt he had possessed even as a child. His election to a Jesus fellowship in 1795 – he became Bursar briefly in 1798 – scarcely interrupted this passion, but subvented it. A fellowship was first a piece of property, which paid a dividend, and only secondarily a responsibility, and there is little evidence that he ever developed a conscience about College affairs, though he did take an interest in the University. As Arthur Gray was later to put it, for Clarke 'the routine of College life was supremely distasteful'. Later, he seems to have looked on the College as a good gentleman's club, where 'if a man has no other engagement, he is sure of finding a comfortable rubber, and a party of friends; and if he does not like cards, there are newspapers and reviews for his amusement'. At first, though, the College was of most use for furnishing travelling companions: the young William Otter and Thomas Malthus briefly, and, for years at a time, his tutorial charge John Marten Cripps, a man usefully 'possessed of a larger fortune than he could spend'.

Clarke's reputation was made by a great and unusual journey, conducted between May 1799 and October 1802 and recorded in his *Travels in Various Countries of Europe, Asia, and Africa*. There were many editions, but the posthumous one of 1824 runs to eleven volumes, amply illustrated with maps and sketches. In many ways, Clarke travelled as the standard English gentleman, for whom travel evidenced English superiority over benighted foreigners, tyrannical governments, ignorant peasants, obtuse priests and thieving postillions. Regarding the classical past with respect, the alien present with condescension, Clarke saw travel as an opportunity for acquiring relics. Such acquisitions, occasionally scrupulous, not infrequent-

ly passed into plunder. Famously then, notoriously now, by bribing the Turkish governor of Athens with 'an English Telescope', Clarke wrenched from the 'idle and mercenary' villagers of Eleusis a giant statue much venerated by them, in the mistaken belief that it was of Ceres and carved by Phidias. He later gave it to the University, which placed it with honour (to the puzzlement of many, including Maria Edgeworth the novelist, who saw only a mutilated lump) in the vestibule of the old University Library; today it is in the Fitzwilliam Museum, which labels it a caryatid and only an 'architectual element', carved by no one in particular.

In other ways, however, Clarke was peculiar. He went the wrong way, to places scarcely on the cultured European's map. He first set out for Denmark and Scandinavia (as far north as Lapland), went to St Petersburg and Moscow, then south-east through Russia and the domain of the 'Don Cossacks' to Taganrog and the Crimea, and crossed the Black Sea via Odessa to Istanbul. He thereafter sailed down the western coast of Turkey and crossed from Rhodes to Alexandria, from whence he made expeditions deeper into Egypt (a little south of Cairo), and to Palestine and Cyprus. From Egypt he sailed to Athens and went into the Peloponnese, where at Thermopylae he discovered a *Platanus Orientialis* said to be 1,300 years old and from it took 'many of the seed-vessels in a mature state, hanging from the branches: and being desirous of bearing away a living memorial from a spot so celebrated … gathered many of them'. He then returned north, passed through Thessalonica to Istanbul, then launched

Edward Daniel Clarke (1786), Fellow 1795–1806.

John Opie, *c.*1805

Apparatus for using the Gas blow-pipe, and for securing the safety of the Operator.

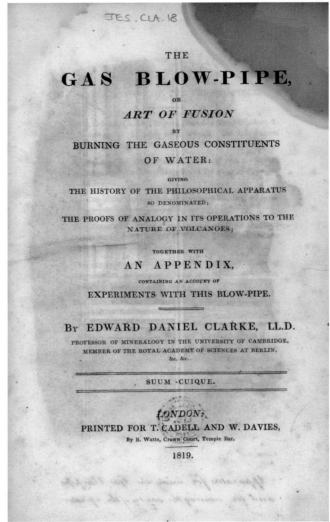

THE
GAS BLOW-PIPE,
OR
ART OF FUSION
BY
BURNING THE GASEOUS CONSTITUENTS
OF WATER:

GIVING

THE HISTORY OF THE PHILOSOPHICAL APPARATUS
SO DENOMINATED;

THE PROOFS OF ANALOGY IN ITS OPERATIONS TO THE
NATURE OF VOLCANOES;

TOGETHER WITH

AN APPENDIX,
CONTAINING AN ACCOUNT OF
EXPERIMENTS WITH THIS BLOW-PIPE.

BY EDWARD DANIEL CLARKE, LL.D.
PROFESSOR OF MINERALOGY IN THE UNIVERSITY OF CAMBRIDGE,
MEMBER OF THE ROYAL ACADEMY OF SCIENCES AT BERLIN,
&c. &c.

SUUM ·CUIQUE.

LONDON:
PRINTED FOR T. CADELL AND W. DAVIES,
By R. Watts, Crown Court, Temple Bar.
1819.

(Facing page)

The oriental plane in the Fellows' Garden. Planted in 1802, Edward Daniel Clarke had brought it as a seedling from Thermopylae.

himself through Bulgaria, Transylvania, and Hungary to Vienna, from whence via Paris he made his return to England. Along these ways, he showed a remarkably various curiosity, far beyond the traveller's usual polite interest in manners and morals, and a great intrepidity. Unlike most eighteenth-century gentlemen, he did not mind discomfort and he infectiously revelled in oddities, especially of landscape.

The rest of his life proceeded evenly. Back in Cambridge, he returned to the College briefly, before marrying, being ordained and acquiring College benefices in Harlton and Yeldham, moving to a 'splendid château at Trumpington', and having seven children. The University was dazzled by his accomplishments in the world that lay beyond Royston and gave him an honorary degree for donating innumerable antiquities, invented the Professorship of Mineralogy for him (he knew little of the subject but came to understand gas blow-pipes and was an exceptionally popular lecturer), and eventually bestowed the University Librarianship on him, for no evident reason – other than that he liked books and emoluments. Amid this comfort he did not lack for critics, who questioned his scholar-

ship, thought his curiosity merely undiscriminating, and wondered about the veracity of his imaginative and meticulous descriptions. The Russians, especially, took inexplicable offence at his insults. He was vexed by this, but found comfort in the patronage he received and bestowed, in very large royalties, in tidy profits made from selling his collections, and in many affidavits from the likes of the Regius Professor of Greek. He died, aged only 53, of a fever that puzzled the doctors and defied the twenty-four leeches applied to his back. He was buried in the Chapel and, near him, was placed a memorial tablet upon which was carved a bust by Francis Chantrey and an elegant Latin epitaph. He was regretted by many, for he was a likeable man, liked even by those, like Bishop Otter, who could never understand how so ordinary a man – prone to 'rash and erroneous conclusions', with achievements 'disproportioned to the means with which he was endowed' – had done what the times denoted extraordinary and were reluctant to concede that, perhaps, Clarke was extraordinary. Byron, a better critic, could see what Clarke was for. 'You have awakened all the gypsy in me', he wrote to the vicar of Harlton in 1812, and that was worth much.

Literary Jesus

STEPHEN HEATH

In his weekly paper *The Friend*, Coleridge (1791) spoke of 'the many illustrious nurselings of the College to which I deem it no small honour to have belonged – Jesus, Cambridge'. He had particularly in mind John Jortin (1715), a Fellow (1724), a Church historian

Samuel Taylor Coleridge

Attr. Henry Wyatt, *c.*1840

and the author of a much praised life of Erasmus. A piece of Jortin's Latin verse was rendered into English by Coleridge in his undergraduate poem 'A Wish Written in Jesus Wood, 10 February 1792', thanks to which something of Jortin is remembered today (naturally, Freddy Brittain found a place for Jortin's piece in his 1962 *Penguin Book of Latin Verse*, an anthology not short of affectionate nods in the College's direction). Coleridge – poet, philosopher, dramatist, critic, writer on religion and society – is, of course, one of the College's supremely illustrious nurselings and without doubt the most famous of its literary figures, meriting an essay to himself (page 130). There are many other writers, however, who have produced works of distinction and played significant roles in English literary life; too many indeed for all to be considered here, in what is regrettably but necessarily a selective account of the contributions made by Jesuans to literature.

In the wider historical sense of the term, that of the learning and practice of letters, the College and its members have always been involved in literature. Studying, translating, annotating and composing texts were from the start an engagement in literary practice, and Thomas Cranmer's (1503) Book of Common Prayer (1549) can be rightly seen as the major contribution to literature made by a member of the College. It powerfully shaped the language and culture of the English-speaking peoples over the following centuries, with the words and rhythms of its marriage, funeral and other services everywhere to be heard in our literature. As too are heard those of the King James Authorized Version of the Bible (1611), in the production of which two Masters – John Duport (1590–1618) and Roger Andrewes (1618–32) – played an important part; both serving on one of the six committees of scholarly divines commissioned by the King to make the new translation. That a Jesuan, C.H. Dodd (1936), was three centuries later to be the director of the panels of translators responsible for the New English Bible was an appropriate renewal of this particular form of Jesuan contribution to the English language and its literary resources.

A College contemporary and friend of Cranmer was John Bale (1515?), in his College days a fierce defender of orthodoxy but later a convert to Protestantism and an even fiercer champion of that cause. Rhetorically strident propaganda is the dominant characteristic of most of his nigh-on ninety works (not for nothing was he known as 'Bilious Bale'), including his plays of which five are extant and which make him the first of the College's more specifically literary figures; one in fact who participated innovatively in the development of several genres. Of the plays that remain, the most interesting is undoubtedly *King Johan* (c.1538), a positive Protestant rewriting of John as a heroic opponent of the tyranny of the Roman Church that is often regarded as the first English history play. To Bale too we owe a pioneering, and still valuable, bibliography of English writings and writers, *Illustrium maioris Britanniae scriptorum summarium* (1548–9) based on the examination of numerous manuscripts. Common to all Bale's work is an apocalyptic conception of the imminent end of the world and the salvation of the true faithful; the accompanying vision of the ravages of ecclesiastical conflict on a cosmic scale that Bale everywhere urgently and forcefully promoted was to be central for such later writers as Spenser and Milton. In his *Vocacyon of Johan Bale to the Bishoprick of Ossorie in Irelande* (1553), Bale also produced one of the earliest autobiographical works written in English.

The period from the accession of Elizabeth to the Restoration saw a flourishing of Jesuan authors. Chief amongst them is Fulke Greville (1568), almost all of whose works were published in the years following his death in 1628. After Shrewsbury School, where he began his close friendship with Sir Philip Sidney, Greville entered Jesus as a Fellow Commoner under the tutorship of Thomas Legge, the latter noted for his humanist interest in the promotion of literature and himself the author of a Latin Senecan tragedy *Richardus Tertius* (c.1579), which anticipated Shakespeare's treatment of that monarch. Legge may well have encouraged the literary talent of the young Greville, who would later turn to the same Senecan dramatic form in his own plays, *Mustapha* (published in 1609) and *Alaham* (1633), in order to express political and religious ideas. It is as a poet, however, that Greville is known and read today. The 109 poems published in the collection *Caelica* (1633; written c.1580–c.1600) move from kinds characteristic of Elizabethan love poetry, increasingly filled with frustration and despair, to sterner, sombre poems concerned with matters of state and religion and the reality of the fallenness of our earthly existence; a movement which Greville expressed as the exchange of 'images of wit' for 'images of life' and as reflecting the emergence of his desire 'to study to sail a right course', in full acknowledgement of 'the depth of [his] iniquity'. The rigour of a Calvinistic conviction of human wretchedness and degeneration often receives startling poetic expression: imprisoned in flesh, elect 'angel-souls' are:

Fulke Greville writes to the Master offering to pay for the conversion of the Chapel's nave into staircases, 27 May 1617.

Like strangers living in mortality,
Still more, and more, themselves inspirited,
Refining Nature to eternity,
By being maids in earth's adulterous bed.

The paradoxes and difficulties of the experience of this 'wearisome condition of humanity' give an intense poetry that earned Greville his place in Helen Gardner's defining 1957 anthology *The Metaphysical Poets*, which acknowledged his 'close, mysterious and sententious ways of writing'. Yet Greville's public life was not 'close' but full – a favourite of Elizabeth's, an MP, the holder of many government offices, he was created a peer by James I and died one of the richest men in the kingdom, murdered by a disgruntled servant.

Greville was not the only Jesuan to figure in Gardner's anthology. Sir Richard Fanshawe, a Fellow Commoner some fifty years later (1623) and, like Greville, a public figure, served Charles I during the Civil War, was captured at the Battle of Worcester, went into exile with Charles II, was appointed Secretary of the Latin Tongue to the King and after the Restoration fulfilled important diplomatic duties in Spain and Portugal, as well as being MP for the University (he shared exile with his former tutor William Beale, whom he described as 'a most excellent Latinist' and who in the early 1630s was briefly Master). Fanshawe was the author of a number of poems in his own right, but his great works were translations: *The Faithful Shepherd* (1647), a rendering of the late sixteenth-century pastoral tragi-comedy by Battista Guarini *Il Pastor Fido*, the inspiration for operas by Handel and Salieri (regrettably, the former did not use Fanshawe's translation for his libretto); and *The Lusiad* (1655), a version done in the original's ottavia rima of the Portuguese national epic *Os Lusiádas* by Luis de Camões. Q, of whom

more below, included Fanshawe's sonnet 'The Rose' in his *Oxford Book of English Verse* (1919), making it his best-known poem today ('Blown in the morning, thou shalt fade ere noon, / What boots a life which in such haste forsakes thee?').

Translation, it needs stressing, was a major literary practice, contributing importantly in the Renaissance to the development and exercise of English as a literary language. There is no finer an example of this than Arthur Golding's rendering of Ovid's *Metamorphoses* (1565–7). Golding (1552) published a great many translations from Latin and French, including *A Tragedie of Abraham's Sacrifice* (1577) from the French of the Calvinist Theodore Beza, which in Golding's English has been argued to have significant echoes in Shakespeare. It is his Ovid, however, that was decisively important, known and used by Shakespeare and other Elizabethan writers and still read today as a major Renaissance work (it is in print as a Penguin Classic). Ezra Pound declared it 'the most beautiful book in the language' and a book 'from which Shakespeare learned so much of his trade'.

The eighteenth century too saw translation or *imitation*, the casting of the Ancients into contemporary verse, as a significant literary endeavour, and it was one in which a number of students and Fellows of the College excelled. Thus Thomas Nevile (1735) published *Imitations of Horace* (1758) and *Imitations of Juvenal and Persius* (1769). Nevile was also reputed to be the author of *The Capitade* (1750), an irreverent attack on Cambridge Heads of House in which, diplomatically enough, the Master of Jesus came off lightly. Undoubtedly, however, it is Elijah Fenton (1700) who is the most interesting and important of Jesus's eighteenth-century literary translators, and one of our most interesting and important literary figures across the centuries.

Fenton is remembered now as 'Mr Pope's Friend' (the title of a piece on him in Charles Dickens's magazine *Household Words*). Pope indeed wrote his epitaph, praising him as 'A poet blessed beyond the poet's fate', blessed inasmuch as Fenton had kept modestly retired from the patronage of the proud and borne his life on earth with great serenity. He left Jesus in 1704 but was prevented by religious and political scruples – what Dr Johnson who devoted one of his *Lives of the Poets* to him called his 'nervousness of integrity' – from taking the oaths that would have qualified him for public employment and the Church. He eked out an uncertain living as a private secretary and tutor (for a while he was a master at Sevenoaks School) and was, in Johnson's words, 'never named but with praise and fondness, as a man in the highest degree amiable and excellent'. He was one of Pope's two collaborators in the translation of the *Odyssey* (1725–6) and the four books for which he

This modest stone, what few vain marbles can,
May truly say, here lies an honest man.
A poet blest beyond the poet's fate,
Whom heav'n kept sacred from the proud and great:
Foe to loud praise, and friend to learned ease,
Content with science in the vale of peace.
Calmly he look'd on either life, and here
Saw nothing to regret, or there to fear;
From nature's temp'rate feast rose satisfy'd,
Thank'd heav'n that he had liv'd, and that he dy'd.

Alexander Pope's epitaph for Elijah Fenton on his memorial in St Michael's and St Mary Madgalene's Church, Easthampstead, Berkshire.

was responsible are indistinguishable from Pope's own (quotations in the *OED* attributed to Pope are very often Fenton's). His principal book of poetry was *Poems on Several Occasions* (1717), but his most publicly successful work was *Marianne* (1723), a tragedy set in Jerusalem in the reign of Herod and treating of the latter's jealous passion for his young queen, the Marianne of the title. While the source material was bloody and violent, Fenton's play, in keeping with the literary manners and stage propriety of his time, offered, not without some difficulty, a Herod of 'milder mien', 'soften'd with the deep distress of love'. Contemporaries praised his verse for its 'smoothness and delicacy' and indeed the softening of the fevers of love was often a theme; as in the poem 'Kisses', which celebrates the power of kisses to 'remove / Our cares and cool the calenture of love' (the delightful 'calenture'!). Making what money he could from writing, Fenton was also biographer (a *Life of Milton*, 1725), editor (an edition of the poems of Edmund Waller, 1729), and anthologist (*Oxford and Cambridge Miscellany Poems*, 1708).

It is, of course, Laurence Sterne (1735) who is the most tremendous of Jesus's eighteenth-century literary figures. 'I well remember', says the narrator of *The Life and Adventures of Tristram Shandy, Gentleman* (1760–7), 'when [my father] went up along with me to enter my name at Jesus College in ****'; and Sterne remembers too, though he himself was enrolled as a poor sizar *in absentia* in 1733 and his father had died by then. Appropriately enough, given the importance attached to names by Mr Shandy and his comic despair at the mistake made at Tristram's christening, Sterne was registered by the College not as Laurence but as Henry. He left in 1737, by then returned to 'Laurence', having taken his degree and been ordained; his life thereafter to be in principle, but not quite in practice, that of a modest Yorkshire parish priest.

Often invoked as a precursor of twentieth-century literary experiments for its playful concern with the movement of images and ideas in the mind, *Tristram Shandy* marries its representation of mental processes with an intellectual satire and humour whose precursors are Rabelais, Montaigne and Robert Burton's *Anatomy of Melancholy*. 'Shandy', indeed, is a word of obscure origin meaning 'wild', 'crack-brained', 'half-crazy', and Sterne's novel is proposed as 'a careless kind of a civil, nonsensical, good-humoured *Shandean* book'. Though it starts with his parents in the act of conceiving the narrator, the Tristram of the title, he is not born for many pages and then disappears in the course of the novel. With no linear sense of direction – everything proceeds by associations of ideas and whimsical digressions ('Digressions, incontestably, are the sunshine; – they are the life and soul of

reading! – take them out of this book, for instance – you might as well take the book along with them') – the book continually defies conventions, and not least those of the new form of the novel as it was being established in Sterne's time. Typographical waywardness – blank or black or marbled pages, wiggly lines, missing chapters and various other eccentricities – is just one (highly visible) means by which Sterne seeks playfully to involve the reader in the 'making up' of his novel. However much, Sterne wrote of himself, he tried 'to think strait on, and clever', he inevitably struck out 'into the beautiful oblique'. No wonder he chose peristalsis and the corkscrew to characterise his practice:

> Therefore, I have no one notion,
> That is not form'd, like the designing
> Of the peristaltick motion;
> Vermicular; twisting and turning;
> Going to work
> Just like a bottle-skrew upon a cork

Laurence Sterne (1735)

After Sir Joshua Reynolds, *c.*1770

The success of the first volumes of the novel (there were nine all told) brought Sterne a fame and a reputation not wholly in keeping with his priestly position. It also encouraged spurious imitations and would-be continuations; in response he began the practice of signing and thereby authenticating copies of subsequent volumes as they appeared in pairs (he signed volumes V, VII and IX). In 1768 *A Sentimental Journey through France and Italy by Mr Yorick* appeared, Yorick being a figure from *Tristram Shandy*, a jester-parson and a man of feeling serving as a persona for Sterne, who often referred to himself by that name in letters. The journey described is not a matter of places and sights but rather of small intimate encounters with people in which comedy and sentiment and a certain eroticism combine in the exhibition of a particular sensibility – and enjoyment – of moral feeling.

Of Sterne's life at Jesus we know little, though as we have seen the College is invoked in *Tristram Shandy*, which also indulges in some bawdy Jesuan play regarding 'the pricks which entered the flesh of St Radagunda in the desert'. Most important in his time here was the lifelong friendship he struck up with one of the College's wealthy Fellow Commoners, John Hall, a Yorkshire man like

Sterne (hoping – mistakenly as it turned out – to increase his chances of an inheritance, Hall later took his wife's name and became Hall-Stevenson). He shared with Sterne a liking for the pleasures of wit and sociability, and remembered the College in verses recalling the great walnut tree that dominated First Court somewhat as, on a lesser scale, the Barry Flanagan horse now does. Jesus had sunk from the eminence attained during the mastership of Sterne's great-grandfather, Richard Sterne (1634–44) and Hall-Stevenson facetiously takes what ought to have been 'the Tree of Knowledge' as a symbol of the College's present obscurity:

> It overshadow'd ev'ry room,
> And consequently, more of less,
> Forced every brain, in such a gloom,
> To grope its way, and go by guess.

The verses appeared in Hall-Stevenson's *Crazy Castle* (1762), a collection of typically ribald stories told by a group of his friends (one was assigned to Sterne). 'Crazy Castle' was Skelton Hall, the North Riding family home that he had inherited while still a boy and where in adult life he gathered a group of like-minded cronies, Sterne included, for convivial excess and field sports (reportedly and a little surprisingly, Sterne was rather a good shot). Calling themselves the 'Demoniacs', they looked to Rabelais for their device and design: *Fay ce que tu voudras* (Do what thou wilt). Gay and gregarious, Hall-Stevenson was also eccentric and hypochondriac, refusing to get out of bed should the Castle's weathercock indicate a wind blowing from the north-east. Sterne is said to have fooled him once by having the weathercock tied to show a westerly wind, whereupon Hall-Stevenson got up, only to hasten back to bed immediately when the string broke and a dreaded north-easter was revealed.

Hall-Stevenson and the Demoniacs were not the most obvious society for a country parson and *Tristram Shandy* raised clerical eyebrows. That was nothing, however, compared to the reprobation incurred by Hall-Stevenson's *Two Lyrick Epistles* (1760), issued by Sterne's publisher a few weeks after the first volumes of *Tristram Shandy*. One epistle was addressed to 'My Cousin Shandy' as a welcome to Sterne on his coming to London; the other to 'the Missess of ****' was simply a piece of obscenity in the form of a mock warning of the dangers awaiting provincial ladies in the capital. They were, the great William Warburton, Bishop of Gloucester, cautioned Sterne, the work of 'a monster of impiety and lewdness' and association with their author was imprudent folly (some people, Warburton cautioned, were even attributing the *Epistles* to Sterne himself). The Bishop had every reason for his censure: Hall-Stevenson moved in rakish

Sir Arthur Quiller-Couch,
Fellow 1912–44.

Sir William Nicholson, 1934

circles, was probably a member of the infamous Hell-Fire Club and certainly kept company with the notorious radical John Wilkes, author of the egregiously lewd *Essay on Women* (1763), who was expelled from Parliament for obscene libel. Sterne knew Wilkes and there was promise of a collaborative Hall-Stevenson and Wilkes biography of him after his death but, alas, nothing came of it.

Something at least of the Shandean spirit of Sterne's writing lives on today in the work of Wesley Stace (1984), a devoted admirer of his Jesuan predecessor, as well as a highly successful folk and pop singer–songwriter under the name John Wesley Harding. Stace's novel *Misfortune* (2005), set in the early nineteenth century, deploys wit and learning – invented or not – in the telling of the trials and tribulations of its central character, Rosa, abandoned as a male baby and adopted as daughter and heir to the family name and fortune of Lord Loveall of Love Hall. The novel's attention to the Hall's library, filled with rare and arcane books and manuscripts, pays homage to the author's own bibliophilia and his collection of Sterne editions.

With the magnificent exception of Coleridge, the nineteenth century was a relatively lean period for literary Jesus, though Arthur Quiller-Couch (who became a Fellow in 1912), writing as 'Q', had established his reputation in the late 1880s and 1890s following the popular success of his novel *The Astonishing History of Troy Town* (1888). A prolific writer of novels and stories, he is perhaps now best known for his completion of Robert Louis Stevenson's unfinished novel *St Ives* (1898), which has been adapted several times for film and television. There is, however, the striking instance from the nineteenth century of a Jesuan who, while not a literary author, played a significant part in the lives and work of writers. This is John Elliotson (1810), who was for many years the Dickens family doctor and whose patients also included Thackeray, Wilkie Collins and other famous authors. With his reputation quickly established through posts held in London hospitals and with a promising professional career already under way, Elliotson in the late 1830s became a convert to mesmerism, which he introduced into his wards at University College Hospital, where he was Senior Physician. Mesmerism was respectable neither medically nor socially and Elliotson's semi-public demonstrations endeared him not at all to the medical establishment. Scandal was feared – 'What father of a family would admit even the shadow of a mesmeriser within his threshold?', thundered *The Lancet* – and he was forced to resign his post (Dickens, who had attended Elliotson's demonstrations and was possessed of unbounded confidence in his own mesmeric powers, naturally had him to dinner on the evening of the resignation). From then on, Elliotson devoted himself to the

cause of mesmerism and played a leading part in its propagation, not least amongst writers, for whom it offered a way of exploring and representing psychical processes at a time when conventional forms of understanding were seen as lagging behind actual experience. Wilkie Collins's *The Moonstone* and Dickens's *The Mystery of Edwin Drood*, to take two well-known examples, are shaped by Elliotson's work and quote directly from his massive and oft-revised *Human Physiology* (1840), which, contentiously, came to include a chapter on mesmerism. That textbook, a very significant contribution to the medical teaching of the day, has long been forgotten, but Elliotson, one of the most controversial of Jesuans, must be remembered still for his very real influence on Victorian literary works and their authors.

Wesley Stace is only one of the numerous twentieth-century writers, novelists especially, whom the College has nurtured, far more than can be mentioned here. Gerald Bullett (1919) will doubtless remain the only undergraduate ever to have gained entry to the College on the strength of a published novel. He sent *The Progress of Kay* (1916) to Q, requesting his help; Q thought well of it and a place at Jesus was duly found. Bullett went on to publish over fifty books – among them novels, children's books, supernatural fiction, poems, anthologies and essays. After his death the then Master, E.M.W. Tillyard (1945–59) gathered together and published his *Collected Poems* (1959).

Bullett's children's books are among many written by Jesuans. James Reeves (the pen-name is of John Morris, 1928) began his writing career as a poet with a volume entitled *The Natural Need* (1936), but his major achievement was as a writer of children's literature. Indeed, he can lay good claim to being the twentieth century's finest English children's poet and was much concerned throughout his life with the way in which young people should be introduced to poetry in schools and elsewhere. Dennis Hamley (1956) is another leading example of the College's children's writers. The author from 1976 on of a great many novels and stories, as well as plays and anthologies, Hamley is perhaps best known for such works as the *Joslin de Lay Mysteries* (1998–2001), a series recounting the adventures of a young minstrel in medieval England as he seeks to discover the reasons for the murder of his father; or the *Hare Trilogy* (1989–93), three books in which schoolchildren tell stories prompted by their imagination of a hare, a badger and a hawk. More recently, Clare Sambrook (1982), with her well-received debut novel *Hide and Seek* (2005), in which a young boy recounts the year his little brother disappeared, has offered further proof of the contribution Jesuans have and are making to writing for and about children – fittingly enough for a college that had as a student D.W. Winnicott

(1916) (page 149), internationally renowned as a child psychiatrist and a pioneer in his psychoanalytic work with children.

Sambrook is one of many Jesuans in the post-war years who have established or begun to establish themselves as novelists. A playwright and writer for film and television as well as a novelist, Carey Harrison (1962) offers in his *Liskeard Quartet* (1990–) a series of engagingly subtle novels in which different narrators chronicle their progress towards reunion in the Cornish town. Claire Messud (1987) has published three critically acclaimed and stylishly accomplished novels, the last of which, *The Emperor's Children* (2006), deals with the lives of three friends and those around them in New York in the months immediately preceding 9/11; precisely observed and felt, it has established her reputation as one of today's most significant novelists. *The Stone Boat* (1994) by Andrew Solomon (1985) is a movingly elegiac novel concerning the relationship between its concert-pianist narrator and his mother who is dying of cancer; but mention must be made too of Solomon's *Noonday Demon* (2001), 'an atlas of depression' in which autobiography, erudition, digression and fieldwork conjoin in a work that bears comparison with Robert Burton's seventeenth-

century *Anatomy of Melancholy*. John Cornwell (1990), in addition to a study of Coleridge and many writings on science and religion, has published novels, starting with *The Spoiled Priest* (1969), and most recently a memoir, *Seminary Boy* (2006), in which he powerfully and movingly tells the story of his troubled education for the priesthood. Tash Aw (1995) wrote an impressive first novel, *The Harmony Silk Factory* (2005), which brings together three differing accounts of the life of its central character at a critical moment in Malaysian history. Michael Arditti (1972), author of five novels to date, caused controversy with *Easter* (2000), about the Anglican Church and hypocrisy over homosexuality and has most recently published *Unity* (2005), an exploration of Unity Mitford's friendship with Adolf Hitler. Stephanie Theobald (1985) has so far published three novels, the last of which, *Trix* (2004), a vivid and funny account of a road trip across the United States taken by an English waitress and a Californian dominatrix, was praised by the *Guardian* as 'an ode to food, foreigners and lesbian sex'.

One Jesuan novelist must be singled out for the wide appeal his work has had and its impact on contemporary culture. This is Nick Hornby (1976), one of today's best-known British writers. *Fever Pitch* (1992), Hornby's memoir of measuring out life in Arsenal fixtures and the intertwining of life as a football fan with the events and crises of childhood, adolescence and adulthood, gave a new style to autobiographical writing at the same time that it offered insight into what it is to be a fan and made an interest in football newly attractive and fashionable. *Fever Pitch* was followed by a series of novels exploring male passions, problems and crises: *High Fidelity* (1995) has as its narrator an obsessional record collector, owner of a shop called Championship Vinyl and with a propensity for failed relationships; *About a Boy* (1998) brings together an awkward adolescent from a single-parent family and a self-centred 30-something man intent on getting off with women and avoiding all commitment; *How to Be Good* (2001), however, switched to a female protagonist and charted her exploration of morals, marriage and parenthood. The most recent novel, *A Long Way Down* (2005), involves four strangers bent on suicide who find themselves together on New Year's Eve on a north London rooftop and begin to talk through the night.

All show Hornby's characteristic skill at observing and showing the details and feelings and concerns of modern life, and his ability to render the ups and downs, the ironies and emotions of relationships, in a writing that mixes sharp comedy and unemphatic pathos to create a distinct fictional truth. Best-sellers all, most of the books have been made into successful films. Hornby himself wrote the screenplay for the British adaptation of *Fever*

Sir David Hare (1965),
Honorary Fellow.
Paula Rego, 2005

Pitch (there was an American version which changed London's Arsenal into Boston's Red Sox!) and was also executive producer; he pops up briefly in the film as – what else? – an Arsenal fan.

Where Hornby is widely read, J.H. Prynne (1957) remains known only to a limited circle of readers willing to face the difficulties his work presents – though media attention following the claim in the recent *Oxford English Literary History 1960–2000* that he had been the significant poet of the late twentieth century pushed him momentarily into public view. Since *Force of Circumstance and Other Poems* (1962), there have been some thirty or so volumes of poetry, mostly in the form of small pamphlets brought out by specialist presses. The poetry does indeed make severe demands on the reader; it is not easy immediately to know what to do with a poem such as 'Unanswering Rational Shore' that begins:

> Profuse reclaim from a scrape or belt, funnel do
> axial parenthood block the mustard dots briefly
> act forward, their age layer for layer in this
> tied-off accession.

Disturbance of conventions of syntax goes along with a complex vocabulary of unequalled breadth and richness, ranging across specialised areas of interest (finance, genetics, agriculture, microbiology and many others) and locking into historical layers of meaning (words are reactivated by philological and etymological incursions). Multiple contexts and the absence of any unity of point of view other than that of the poems themselves makes reading a continually unsettling experience. Prynne has talked of his aspiration, 'to establish relations not personally with the reader, but with the world and its layers of shifted but recognisable usage; and thereby with the reader's own position in the world'. This certainly is achieved and, for all their difficulty, the poems offer an experience that is vitally engaging and not without a lyricism of its own.

If at the very beginning of the College's literary history we find Bale's use of dramatic form to express views regarding political history, it is more than apt that today the College should have as one of its Honorary Fellows David Hare (1965), internationally recognised as one of the most significant playwrights of the last decades. After graduation, Hare co-founded with Tony Bicât (1964) the experimental travelling theatre company Portable Theatre and began his career as a dramatist when, the company suddenly finding itself without a play to put on, he had to come up with a replacement and quickly turned out 'a primitive satire on the unlikelihood

of revolution in Britain'. His first major play, *Slag*, dramatising issues in feminism through the debates and difficulties of three women who set up an all-female boarding school, was produced in London in 1970 and has been followed by over thirty plays that have won numerous awards. Hare's theatre is fully contemporary, one in which the political and the personal are brought together in plays that confront the audience with intensely felt, dramatically effective representations of the matter of today's politics and society. From *Plenty* (1974) with its portrayal of disillusionment in post-war Britain to the recent *Stuff Happens* (2004) dealing with the events leading up to the decision to begin the war in Iraq, they offer a dramatic record of the crises and debates of the last half-century. Hare has also written for television – *Saigon: The Year of the Cat* (1983) juxtaposes historical events with personal lives in the context of the Vietnam War – as well as film (his screenplay for *The Hours* won an Oscar nomination). He has also successfully directed feature films from his own original screenplays: the first of these, *Wetherby* (1985), shared the first-prize Golden Bear Award at that year's Berlin Film Festival. As well as directing while at Cambridge (including a memorable *Oh What a Lovely War!* with Germaine Greer), Hare also acted (his performance in *The Comedy of Errors* has stayed in the mind) and he returned to the stage more recently with performances on Broadway and in the West End of *Via Dolorosa* (1998) – his meditation on a visit to Israel and the Palestinian territory, giving dramatic voice to the confrontation of beliefs and value systems, his own included, that he witnessed and experienced there. It would, finally, hardly be right not to remember here the play *Teeth 'n' Smiles* (1975), set during a May Ball and close to the playwright's time in College (the depiction of the Head Porter may bring back memories to those who were students then).

Coleridge wrote in his *Biographia Literaria* of 'the inauspicious hour' in which he left 'the friendly cloysters and the happy grove of quiet, ever honored Jesus College'. The Cloisters are today not always so quiet and the feelings of our literary figures over the centuries on leaving the happy grove have been various and sometimes mitigated; for Nick Hornby, for instance, Arsenal came long before Cambridge and Cambridge United figured as much as, if not more than, Jesus College during his student years. Yet whatever their feelings, the College itself can take pride in the literary achievement of its students and Fellows past and present, and look with pleasure on the contribution they have made. All the signs are that the future will see achievement and contribution continued.

Between the Heavens and the Earth: Eight Scientists

Three Astronomers Royal

FRANCES WILLMOTH and WILLIAM SASLAW

There have been fourteen holders of the office of Astronomer Royal since its institution in 1675, and three have been Jesuans: the first, John Flamsteed (1675–1719); the tenth, Sir Harold Spencer Jones (1933–55); and the thirteenth, Sir Martin Rees, now Lord Rees of Ludlow (1995–2005). The work of each has reflected astronomy's changing concerns and needs. Flamsteed established the Royal Observatory at Greenwich; two and a half centuries later it was Spencer Jones who moved it out of the increasingly polluted environment of London to Herstmonceux in Sussex. Rees has been a leading figure in the development of the 'New Astronomy' that began in the 1960s.

In all of John Flamsteed's (1646–1719) voluminous surviving correspondence, there is just one letter written from the College: on 20 June 1674, when he was in Cambridge to take his MA. Addressed to Flamsteed's patron Sir Jonas Moore, Surveyor-General of the Royal Ordnance 'at his house in the Tower', it begins:

> Sir
> That you may see how little Idle I have beene of late how propense to the old amidst the avocations and resolves I had made of new studies and how glad of any opportunity of writing to you, I here send you a short account of a day or two's converse with your Ricciolus [that is Giovanni Battista Riccioli's *Astronomia Reformata*, Bologna, 1665] in which the observations of Cassini invited mee to make a triall of the goodnesse of my solar tables, and whether it were needful to admit of any sensible refractions in heights above 30 degrees from the horizon …

After much discussion and tabulation of astronomical details, the letter concludes:

> I shall be glad to see you at the commencement that I may have your advice how to dispose of my selfe: for I shall soon be aweary of Cambridge tho all my expence is over, and I live now at a moderate charge: this night I hope to mount my longer tube of 14 foot and to begin my observations if the heavens be cleare: which will be my best diversion whilest I stay here. I intend sometime this weeke to visit Mr Newton to confer with him about refractions of which I heare hee has made severall experiments with various spirits and liquors. I have the company of a very dextrous Anatomist here with whom I am resolved to learne a little of that knowledge and the manner of dissecting, his company makes my being here onely not intollerable to
>
> Your much obliged servant
> John Flamsteed

Flamsteed had been formally admitted to the College in 1670 when he was already 24. While remaining in touch with his notional tutor, Dr Nathaniel Wroe, he had never come into residence and so had not qualified himself for even the BA. Now, when he was 28, his MA was being conferred by royal mandate, a privilege granted because he was already well known as an astronomer and 'hath made already such usefull observacions as have been well esteemed by persons eminently learned in that science' (University Archives Lett. XIII, 170). But he had still to pay the fee for the degree: this was the principal 'expence' that was now 'over'. (The algebraist Joseph

Raphson (*fl.*1689–1712), originator of the Newton–Raphson method of solving complicated equations, was similarly to receive his MA by royal mandate through the College in 1692, three years after his election as a Fellow of the Royal Society.)

The problem of how Flamsteed was 'to dispose of' himself was resolved less than a year after the date of this letter, when Moore and other Fellows of the Royal Society secured his appointment as Charles II's 'royal observatory'. He is thus recognised as the first Astronomer Royal and, though that title was not much used in his own lifetime, he styled himself 'Astronomicus Regius' in his inscription in a book he presented to the College Library (a copy of Kepler's *Rudolphine Tables*). After helping to supervise the building of the new Royal Observatory on the top of Greenwich Hill, he was to live there, retaining his royal post, until his death in the reign of George I. For at least a quarter of a century he carried on an extensive and systematic observing programme, first with a large sextant paid for by Sir Jonas Moore and later with a mural arc constructed at his own expense. These highly advanced instruments allowed Flamsteed to aspire to an unprecedented level of accuracy.

His chief task as 'observatory' was 'to apply himselfe with the most exact care and diligence to the rectifeing the Tables of the motions of the heavens, and the places of the fixed stars, so as to find out the so much desired Longitude of places for the perfecteing the Art of navigation'. He never lost sight of the ultimate aim of producing a star catalogue, with tables of the sun, moon and planets, but took a wide view of the kind of investigations that might assist the process and of the responsibilities of his role as England's leading practical astronomer. Thus he used the Observatory's great clocks to establish the constancy of the earth's rotation (a matter fundamental to the reliability of all other observations), studied atmospheric refractions (almost as fundamental), analysed the orbital patterns of Jupiter's satellites in the hope that they would provide an alternative longitude method, and corresponded with foreign astronomers about eclipses and other observations. But he became embroiled in conflicts – with a young rival, Edmond Halley (later of comet fame), and eventually also with Sir Isaac Newton. In the early 1700s both were involved in a dispute with him that culminated in the 'unauthorised' publication of Flamsteed's star catalogue, in a form edited by Halley (*Historia Coelestis*, 1712). This episode affected Flamsteed's subsequent reputation, especially in the nineteenth century, when it seemed shocking for anyone to have been an adversary of the famous Sir Isaac. But this was not the whole story. Flamsteed and Newton had corresponded civilly for a number of years (first through the good offices of James Crompton, a Fellow of Jesus) and Flamsteed had supplied numerous observations to assist Newton's work on his *Principia*. They only fell out badly in 1695, when Newton was working on lunar theory for a second edition and Flamsteed failed to supply data in the form he demanded. Flamsteed's observations were eventually published in a form closer to what he had originally planned, in a three-volume edition of the *Historia Coelestis* produced in 1725 (by his widow, Margaret, and his former assistant, James Hodgson), and then in the 1729 *Atlas Coelestis*.

By the time Harold Spencer Jones (1890–1960) became the second of the Jesuan Astronomers Royal in 1933, the focus of astronomy was no longer, as it had been for Flamsteed and his contemporaries, the charting of the positions of the stars and the orbits of the moon and planets. The emphasis was now on the application of physical theory to the understanding of the nature of the sun and stars, the formation of planets, the role of the galaxies, and the expansion of our universe. His years at Jesus (1908–16), reading first Mathematics and then Physics, followed by three years as a research Fellow (Honorary Fellow in 1933, and only narrowly escaping being elected Master in 1945), coincided with one of the most revolutionary decades of physics. It began the modern era with Einstein's theories of special and general relativity, Rutherford's experiments on atomic nuclei, Planck's mysterious quantum hypothesis, and Bohr's quantum theory of the atom. All these and other developments would have profound implications for astronomy.

Spencer Jones realised that their exploration would require much more accurate fundamental astronomical data than was yet available. After several years as an astronomer at the Royal Greenwich Observatory, the

Lord Rees of Ludlow (1967),
Honorary Fellow.

for determining distances to other planets, distant stars, galaxies and ultimately the size of the universe itself. It was while carrying out this research (in which systematic errors were later shown to have made the result slightly inaccurate), Spencer Jones began the move of the Greenwich observatory to Herstmonceux.

The third of the Jesuan Astronomers Royal (1995–2005) – now largely an honorific office that makes its occupant the senior spokesperson for British astronomy – is Martin Rees (1942–), Master of Trinity and, since 2005, President of the Royal Society. An undergraduate and research student at Trinity, he was a research Fellow at Jesus from 1967 to 1969, and since 1996 has been an Honorary Fellow. The 'New Astronomy' began with the rapid discoveries of extended double-lobed radio galaxies, quasars (now known to be extremely energetic nuclei of galaxies visible at great distances and probably containing massive black holes), the cosmic background radiation (a remnant of the big bang in the very early universe), pulsars (rapidly rotating magnetic neutron stars) and a host of other objects such as complex molecules in interstellar space, binary x-ray stars and powerful infra-red newly forming stars. Other very important discoveries followed. Many of the questions and problems associated with them have been gradually understood, and others have arisen in their place.

Throughout this process, Martin Rees has been in the forefront of astrophysical research, the discussions of new solutions and the raising of new questions. With others, he recognised that the often symmetric lobes of radio emission on both sides of some giant galaxies were created by huge beams of particles and radiation, anchored by supermassive black holes in the galaxy's nucleus and colliding with clouds of intergalactic gas. He used the distribution of quasars in space to provide convincing evidence against the steady-state cosmology and in favour of the big bang. Then he went on to predict how properties of the cosmic background radiation, such as its polarisation, could provide insight into the big bang's very early stages. More recently, he has worked on the sources of powerful gamma ray radiation which may come from the collapse of massive stars or the collision of neutron stars.

More speculatively, in books addressed to a wider readership, he has advocated the idea of the 'multiverse' in which our universe is just one of many. We cannot communicate with the others, but ours must belong to a subset – of uncertain size – which has properties consistent with life as we know it. *Our Final Century: A Scientist's Warning* (2003) examines the likelihood that externally caused catastrophes such as a collision with a large asteroid, or internally caused catastrophes such as pollution and global warming, will make this humanity's last century on earth.

leading centre of observational astronomy in Britain, followed by a decade (1923–33) at the Royal Observatory at the Cape of Good Hope in South Africa, he was well placed on returning as Astronomer Royal, a position then held concurrently with the directorship of the Greenwich observatory, to continue and promote his programmes of measuring fundamental astronomical data.

The first major results, announced in 1939, were a detailed analysis of changes in the rotation of the earth and their effects on the apparent motions of the moon, sun and planets. Tidal interaction between the earth's rotation and the moon's changing orbit have been lengthening the day over the last two thousand years by about one thousandth of a second per century. On top of this, there are large irregular variations caused by earthquakes and other shifts of the earth's mass (current measurements are so precise that they can detect the effect of the flow of oil out of the Middle East on the planet's rotation) and these may amount to one second over a year. This led Spencer Jones and his colleagues to more precise astronomical definitions and measurements of time, which were used for several decades until the even more exact atomic clocks displaced them. In recent years, there has been renewed interest in the difference between atomic time and earth's rotation time as an indicator of changes in the earth's local and astronomical environment.

The second major project, published in 1941, which earned him several prizes, was a decade-long international study to determine an accurate value for the average distance between the earth and the sun, a fundamental basis

A Child Psychiatrist

JULIET MITCHELL

owards the end of his life, Donald Woods Winnicott started an unfinished autobiography in which he jotted down a prayer: 'Oh God! May I be alive when I die.' He had come up, one of only twenty-eight freshmen, to Jesus from the Leys School, Cambridge, in October 1914. Planning to become a doctor, Winnicott was exempt from service but did in fact work in the military hospitals into which a number of colleges had been converted, and in 1917 he left the University for the navy, to be stationed as medical officer on a destroyer. Of his slaughtered contemporaries, he reflected that he had subsequently experienced his own life as part of a universal 'whole', the rest of which was composed of their deaths. The wish to be alive when he died on the surface indicated that, suffering as he was from coronary disease, he did not want to die old, ill and incapable; but beneath this we can speculate that he had to die, like the men of his generation, when he was still young – at least in spirit – and very much alive. He died aged 76 in 1971, treating his deathday playfully.

This paradoxical experience of living till old age the life of the dead young men of the 1914–18 war seems to be the motivating thrust of Winnicott's enormous success and originality both as one of the world's greatest paediatricians and as a renowned and idiosyncratic psychoanalyst, clinician and theorist of a particular kind. Feeling *their* death to be the meaning of *his* life, Winnicott memorialised child's play as what life can offer to its survivors. At Cambridge Winnicott had continued to party, sing and dance as in his happy home and school-life, but the context had changed. He was embedded in a generation who died before or on the edge of adulthood. Their trauma on the killing-field of France was to be echoed for Winnicott in the beleaguered child of all times. Studies of his work single out his famous ideas or dicta – 'there is no such thing as a baby without a mother', the new mother is in a state of 'primary maternal preoccupation', the infant will start to separate from its mother by using a 'transitional object' – a favoured rag fragment of a teddy-bear for instance. Each idea of Winnicott's conceptual construction is like a toy, something to be played with, form a pattern, build a tower. As commentator after commentator notes, it was not just that Winnicott had a remarkable gift for understanding children but that children understood him: they picked up the toys he offered as objects or ideas, and played.

When I first read in the *Oxford Dictionary of National Biography* that Winnicott had a third-class degree in biology at Jesus, I burst out laughing: it was characteristic of him both not to be academically brilliant and also to feel free to do spectacularly badly. He was, as his successor at Paddington Green, the NHS paediatric clinic which he founded, said, quite simply 'a genius' in his work, both theoretical and clinical, with babies, small children and mothers. None of the biographies with which I am familiar mentions his degree or gives more than a cursory nod towards his university education. Though prosperous middle class, Winnicott's father had not been to university; Jesus was probably selected because his housemaster at the Leys was a member of the College. He admitted to being restless in Cambridge and much more settled when he joined a destroyer. With the commons, parks and 'pieces' of Cambridge robed in military tents, the feeling of a need-to-be-elsewhere-than-at-university was common: from immensely happy home and schooldays, what Winnicott brought to his profound pain at the tragedy of war was, paradoxically, his joyfulness both as a playful person and as what he was to become – the theorist of play.

In his Second World War work with evacuees and then in the National Health Service, Winnicott encountered the anti-social psychopathological and psychotic child more regularly than the neurotic. He considered that it was the environment that had failed these children, but that while the environment could be improved for the future, its past failure could only be treated in the illness of the child. Play (and humour) was therapeutic because it was the child's natural way of coping with abuse, neglect, lack of protection or too much frustration. Instead of having to deny what had gone wrong and develop a false, compliant personality, the child who can be helped to play can transform untenable reality into some everyday creative act and perception, and through this make use of positive elements in his experience to come to terms with the traumatic experience.

One of the loveliest houses in Cambridge, Kettle's Yard, belonged to the family of Winnicott's close school and life-long friend, another survivor of the First World War, Jim Ede. There is an elective affinity between Ede's beautiful, imaginative cottage decor, his art collection, the playful arrangement of beach stones and other objects and Winnicott's theoretical, clinical and personal emphasis on play. Nearly a quarter of their classmates are known to have been killed in action. They had been playing schoolboy sports and pranks as they left for death.

Two Nobel Prize Winners – The Biochemist

STEPHEN HLADKY and MICHAEL WARING

In December 1978 Peter Mitchell received the Nobel Prize for Chemistry – a gold medal and a cheque for 725,000 crowns – from the King of Sweden in Stockholm. He was the sole recipient of the prize at a time when joint awards to two or three scientists involved in a critical discovery were becoming commonplace. His contribution to our understanding of the fundamental processes underlying energy generation and utilisation in biological systems – the science of bioenergetics – was hailed as one of the most important developments in biology during the twentieth century. All living things need a supply of energy, a basal amount just to stay alive plus more to engage in any of the activities regarded as characteristic of life such as growth, motility or reproduction. Part of that energy demand relates to the maintenance of an electrical potential across the bounding membrane of living cells, and that turned out to provide a crucial clue to solving the mystery of how the energy content of food is transferred to the synthesis of a high-energy molecule, adenosine triphosphate (ATP), which serves to deliver the energy to all the machinery of living organisms.

Mitchell, elected an Honorary Fellow in 1979, was not a remarkable student when, forty years earlier, he came up to Jesus from Queen's College, Taunton, to read Natural Sciences. He got off to a poor start and had considerable difficulty in expressing himself clearly, which resulted in his being placed only in the third class in Part I in 1941. He did better in Part II Biochemistry the following year with a 2:1, though even this was disappointing given that his fellow students considered him the brightest member of the class. His PhD, delayed partly because of the war, was similarly marked by difficulties with examiners who required resubmission. And, as E.C. Slater, his Royal Society memoirist and one of his major competitors, observed, 'Mitchell's apparent inability to get his thinking across to others, especially those in established positions, continued into his later career. He was by no means indifferent to this; indeed it may have been a contributing factor to periods of deep depression.'

By the early 1950s it was already known that the components of food like starch and fat are broken down to a few standard intermediary metabolites (products of metabolism) which are delivered to the mitochondria within cells. There the energy content is released by a chain of chemical reactions called oxidations and the energy is used to phosphorylate low-energy adenosine diphosphate to make high-energy ATP. Mitochondria are intracellular organelles containing two small volumes of aqueous solution, one inside the other, separated from each other and from the rest of the cell by membranes (like a room within a room, separated from each other and the rest of the house by walls). Many researchers were pursuing the idea advanced by Slater in 1953 that the oxidation was coupled to the phosphorylation by forming special high-energy intermediates within the inner membrane (i.e. part of the wall), and a great deal of unrewarded effort was devoted to finding these coupling factors. In 1961 Mitchell formulated a clear counter-proposal, the chemiosmotic hypothesis. In his hypothesis the intermediate was not a new chemical but rather the creation of an electrochemical gradient of hydrogen ions across the inner membrane of the mitochondrion so that the inner compartment would contain fewer hydrogen ions (positively charged, hydrated protons) and thereby become electrically negative. The oxidation of metabolites would pump hydrogen ions from the inner to the outer spaces within the mitochondrion; their flow back across the membrane down their electrochemical gradient would then be used to drive the production of ATP.

Peter Mitchell (1940),
Honorary Fellow.

Not surprisingly, the scientific community was reluctant to accept this revolutionary idea, and scepticism (not to say outright antagonism) was the common attitude among those who made the considerable effort needed to understand and evaluate the hypothesis. And a considerable effort it was, too, in the early days – partly because Peter Mitchell adopted his own system of nomenclature rather than using standard terms from physiology and physical chemistry. For instance the new term 'proton motive force' he coined to describe the combined effect of the concentration and electrical gradients may have misled many into thinking this was a new concept, whereas in fact it is identical to the concept of a hydrogen ion electrochemical gradient that was already well established in physical chemistry. Similarly, it might have helped others understand his case had he drawn attention at an early stage to the close parallels between the role of the combined hydrogen ion and potential gradients in mitochondria and that of the combined sodium ion and potential gradients already shown by physiologists to be critical for coupling reactions in the bounding membranes of cells.

For whatever reasons, opposition to Mitchell's hypothesis was widespread. Controversy and debate continued for many years – a sure testament to the intellectual calibre of the arguments and the fundamental importance of the questions. Nevertheless, he stuck to his guns (a phrase which he disliked, preferring 'courage of his convictions') and used his best powers of gentle persuasion through dialogue to convince others, while modestly acknowledging that he might well be wrong – at least

from their point of view. However, evidence gradually accumulated, both before and after the award of the prize, to support the essential predictions of his theory, much of it coming from his own work with Dr Jennifer Moyle in the independent laboratory that they established on Bodmin Moor in Cornwall.

The chemiosmotic hypothesis, is, however, now firmly established, as is the distinction which attaches to its author and indefatigable champion. Its concepts are indispensable components of biochemistry teaching, and they have found a lasting place in biology at large. Few would now doubt the relevance of chemiosmotic ion gradients to every aspect of energy metabolism in the living world, be it plant photosynthesis, bacterial bioenergetics, active transport of small molecules across cell membranes, or oxidative phosphorylation. As two obituarists (Hinkle and Garlid) wrote:

> Mitchell's achievements inspire, not only because they were correct, but also because of the philosophical purity of his approach. The idea came before the experiment, and refutable hypotheses were prerequisites for experimental design. Few scientists have demonstrated so fully the utility and proper application of the scientific method. Peter Mitchell was also a lovely man. Hours spent in his company were enriched by his *joie de vivre* and gentle good humour, which tempered the most spirited scientific arguments. This elan sustained him to the end. As cancer overtook him, he was simply thankful for his full and happy life.

– The Physicist

S.S. SAXENA

In 2006 Philip Warren Anderson was named by a Spanish scientist 'the world's most creative physicist', though many would say that neither this, nor even his Nobel Prize in Physics twenty-nine years earlier, does full justice to the myriad contributions he has made to science and humanity. He was a Fellow of Jesus from 1969 till 1975, and has been an Honorary Fellow since 1978.

The idea, which Anderson propounded with Sir Sam Edwards in Cambridge, that ordinary glass, which does not have a regular arrangement of atoms like a crystal and so might be mistaken for a very viscous liquid, nevertheless has persistent order: a configuration of atoms is remembered for *ever*, and there is a distinction – a

phase transition – between liquid and glass, has had applications far beyond physics, into engineering, neuroscience and computing. And his insight that electrons may not be able to pass through a disordered metal, not because of absorption but, with all the multiple diffracting paths cancelling, because the incident energy of the electron wave is completely reflected – for which he was awarded the Nobel Prize – has impact on fields ranging from the electrical conductivity of semiconductors to the propagation of radio waves in cities. The two theories have revealed the elusive nature of order in disordered quantum and classical systems that we might otherwise naturally, but mistakenly, have thought uninteresting and random.

Phil Anderson was born in Indiana in 1923, attended Harvard and took his doctorate in physics in 1949. His academic career had been interrupted by the Second World War: 'in those wartime years (1940–3) we were urged to concentrate in the immediately applicable subject of "Electronic Physics" and I was then bundled off to the Naval Research Laboratory to build antennas (1943–5). It may be remembered that such war work was advisable for those of us who wore glasses, the "services" at that time being convinced that otherwise we would be best utilised as infantry.' Living through the excesses, in the name of 'security' and 'loyalty', of the McCarthy years strengthened his political interests. He never accepted classified government work and joined in the campaign against the Vietnam War.

His Cambridge links were forged in 1953, in Kyoto, Japan, where Sir Neville Mott, the doyen of Cambridge and international physics, was presiding over a meeting of the International Union of Pure and Applied Physics which the 28-year-old Fulbright Scholar Phil Anderson attended. A year at the Cavendish Laboratory in 1961, where Mott, Sir Brian Pippard and another young Nobel laureate-to-be, Brian Josephson, were all active, followed. Anderson's impact on the Cambridge scene was so strong that Neville Mott lobbied for and succeeded in 1967 in establishing for him a permanent visiting professorship – for two terms out of three each year – a joint appointment with Bell Telephone Laboratories of New Jersey, which brought him back to the Cavendish and, at John Adkins's suggestion, to a fellowship at Jesus. Certain 'medieval customs' notwithstanding, he and his wife Joyce enjoyed Cambridge and felt that a genuine attempt was then being made to bring women into the life of the College. 'Our most excruciating memory is of working up our courage into having Sir Denys and Lady Page (then Master, a time when Sirs were much thinner on the ground) to dinner, only to encounter one of the coal-strike blackouts,

and willy nilly to have a "candlelit supper" cooked on the spot on a kerosene stove. They were of course marvellous sports about it, but it was not what they were used to.'

Phil Anderson returned, full-time, to the United States in 1975 to a joint position at Bell Telephone Laboratories and Princeton University, retaining, however, a cottage in Cornwall as a connection with England. But for the rest of us it is the 1977 Nobel Prize in Physics that he shared with Neville Mott and John van Vleck for their fundamental theoretical investigations of the electronic structure of magnetic and disordered systems that is the lasting monument to the years he spent in Cambridge.

Towards the end of his stay he formulated, with Sir Sam Edwards, the 'replica' theory of the phenomenon he had earlier named 'spin-glass':

> This concept typifies a deeper matter of principle: the idea of studying randomness and dirt as qualitatively different from regularity, rather than trying to average them out. It is interesting that one of our spin-glass papers is the basis of the most widely used algorithm today in complex optimisation – my old student tells me there are thirteen different names for it now, one of which is 'belief propagation'.

The impact of such conceptual development is not generally appreciated for it is too wide ranging to be summarised. Yet it is this 'spin-glass' concept that has led to the popular wireless internet (wi-fi) becoming available in the dense concrete jungle of the modern urban space through the optimisation of wave propagation strength.

The concept dearest to his heart – certainly one of the deepest insights into the nature of the universe gained at any time in history – is that of broken symmetry and its universality. Anderson explains: 'what else is the "landscape" but the fact that the actual universe is a broken symmetry, emergent from something simpler, and is unpredictable?' It is the amazing abstractness and originality of Anderson's ideas that has often helped understanding of more tangible phenomena that mankind continues to confront.

In 1987 a new manifestation of a broken symmetry state – the high-temperature superconductor – brought about a new paradigm in physics. Researchers in Switzerland had found that a compound of lanthanum, strontium, copper and oxygen went superconducting at the unprecedentedly high temperature of –243 Celsius. Superconductivity is the phenomenon where electricity flows without resistance, and it is resistance, or the loss of power, as electrons travel through a material (wire), that effectively constitutes the major component of our electricity bills. Raising superconducting temperatures brings, therefore, the promise of cheaper electricity.

Phenomena have, however, to be understood before they can be applied to practical situations, and conceptual difficulties, combined with the complex chemistry of these materials, has made the study of such superconductors one of the 'richest' problems in physics today. From that moment of discovery Phil has remained one of the most lucid interpreters of these phenomena: he characteristically describes the field as an epistemological train wreck. Since 1986 he has also been the co-vice-chairman of the well-known Santa Fe Institute, dedicated to emerging scientific syntheses, especially those involving the sciences of complexity, co-chairing the workshops that have founded the interdisciplinary study of the bases of economic theory.

The Nobel Prize has given him, as he says, the opportunity to take public stands: 'I happened to be in a position to be caught up in the campaign against "Star Wars" very early (summer '83) and wrote, spoke and testified repeatedly, with my finest moment a debate with Secretary George Schultz in the *Princeton Alumni Weekly*, reprinted in *Le Monde* in 1987. I have also testified repeatedly and published some articles in favour of Small Science.' Interventions like these have had profound effects on how science is conducted internationally today. That individual creativity which leads to ground-breaking insights and the opening of new ideas, which are essential in addressing complex and correlated problems of society, environment and science, has another and subtle facet: it allows many younger scientists to reflect on the wider implications of their work and the impact it can on have issues well beyond their current field of expertise.

A Materials Scientist

KEN JOHNSON

Sir Alan Cottrell, who has been acclaimed as 'the very father of modern materials science', was the College's Master from 1974 to his retirement in 1986, the first physical scientist ever to be elected. He presided over the most notable changes in the College's history: the admission of women at all levels of the society and the inclusion of students in the governing body. To those of us with long enough memories, his mastership separates what we think of as the 'old College' from the contemporary one. He supported the admission of women with enthusiasm and successfully opposed a proposal by the University to restrict the rate at which colleges became mixed.

Elected Vice-Chancellor for 1977 to 1979, he was the first Jesuan V.-C. since Corrie in 1851. At the same time HRH Prince Philip, Duke of Edinburgh, was elected University Chancellor; there was a good rapport between them and this, no doubt, paved the way for Prince Edward choosing Jesus. Prince Philip dined in Hall on his sixtieth birthday, which occasioned free wine for all and an impromptu 'Happy birthday to you'. Together with his wife Jean, Alan continued the tradition of making the Lodge a social centre of the College.

Cottrell's scientific distinction was well established before he ever set foot in the Chimney. With a sound northern grammar-school grounding in physics and mathematics, he graduated in metallurgy from the University of Birmingham. After war work on the practical problem of welding tank armour, he returned to Birmingham with the assignment of revising undergraduate teaching in light of modern atomic theories of metals. His *Theoretical Structural Metallurgy* (1948) transformed the teaching of

Sir Alan Cottrell (Master 1974–86), 1974.

the subject throughout the country, from a descriptive course in 'heating and beating' into a respectable scientific discipline. His teaching book, *The Mechanical Properties of Matter* (1964), is one which, as an engineer, I frequently consult. At the early age of 30 he was appointed Professor of Physical Metallurgy.

Cottrell realised more than anyone else at the time the crucial role of microscopic defects (point defects, dislocations and cracks) on the mechanical behaviour of crystalline materials. These researches produced new concepts which subsequent generations have used extensively. *Dislocations and Plastic Flow in Crystals* (1953) is a classic which predicted with uncanny accuracy observations subsequently made by transmission electron microscopy. The international pre-eminence of his research into the nature and strength of metallic materials led to his election as an FRS in 1955 and earned him sixteen honorary degrees and over twenty medals and awards.

In 1955 he was appointed deputy head of the Metallurgy Division, Atomic Energy Research Establishment, and became involved in the choice of power-generating nuclear reactors. The integrity of the pressure vessel was the crucial issue. His research into crack stability played a critical role in the acceptance of the Pressurised Water Reactor for use in the UK. He came to be regarded as a source of balanced judgement on the future of nuclear power. His book, *How Safe is Nuclear Power?* (1981), was written for the general public, with a view to presenting a factual account of all the aspects involved: scientific, engineering, statistical and psychological. He remains convinced that nuclear power provides a safe, sustainable and carbon-free large-scale resource in a power-hungry world.

Cottrell was elected Goldsmith's Professor of Metallurgy at Cambridge in 1958. Teaching was revitalised, and new research teams were set up, establishing the scientific legitimacy of the Department in the natural sciences community. In 1968 he left to become Deputy Scientific Adviser to the Ministry of Defence and then Chief Scientific Adviser to the government, appointments based, no doubt, on his reputation for explaining complex scientific and engineering concepts in nontechnical language. However, he still ran up against C.P. Snow's *Two Cultures*. Afterwards he recounted that there were only two ministers in Heath's cabinet who understood what he was saying: Heath himself and Margaret Thatcher! He was also frustrated by politicians' lack of interest in events beyond the next election. Perhaps it was with some relief that he returned to Cambridge to be Master of Jesus.

Neither the duties of the mastership nor retirement curbed his devotion to scholarly work. The books, *Modern Theory of Metals* (1988), *Chemical Bonding of Transition Metal Carbides* (1995) and *The Electron Theory of Metals* (1998) are tributes to a remarkable scientific career. His advice to me on retirement was: 'Give up teaching; give up administration; but never give up science.'

An Archaeologist

MARIE LOUISE STIG SØRENSEN

No clear line separates the humanities from the sciences, as Colin Renfrew's life and fame as a prehistoric archaeologist demonstrates. Master from 1986 to 1997, and Fellow and Honorary Fellow since then, in 2004 he received in Rome one of the Balzan prizes – now widely seen as the equivalent in the humanities and social sciences of the Nobel Prizes in science and medicine – the citation proclaiming him as 'among the promoters of outstanding innovations in processual archaeology, and the author of a series of brilliant works on central themes in European and world prehistory which are marked by great interpretative acumen and have had a revolutionary impact'. For what, perhaps more than anything else, underlines this great international reputation is his continuing insistence on the importance of the debate as to what constitutes the archaeological project. In the '60s and '70s he played a major part in bringing about the paradigm shift to the 'New Archaeology', campaigning for systematic and transparent research methods and the formulation of testable hypotheses (*Explanation of Cultural Change*, 1973, a volume he edited, is the key text). And throughout succeeding decades he has unrelentingly contended for scientific clarity about how the development of all facets of human endeavour, including such intangible aspects as religion and art, can be meaningfully explored and analysed.

If the child is the father to the man, the undergraduate and research student may often be the father to the professor. Renfrew came to Cambridge in 1959 to read Natural Sciences at St John's, changing to Archaeology and Anthropology only in his second year, and he has often said that the discussions in the philosophy of science which were taking place while he was working on his PhD inspired much of his thinking. And no one who

engaged cannot be briefly summarised, but all his work has been marked by a deep curiosity about how and why societies change and about how we investigate the human past, giving to his writings a resonance far beyond archaeology. His work on Aegean prehistory, which he still continues in the field as well as at his desk, began in the 1960s when he focused on social and economic changes in the Cycladic Islands during the third millennium BC. *The Emergence of Civilisation* (1972) was remarkable in introducing a systematic social framework for the explanation of change in material cultures and became a model of how social change, in any area, may be investigated.

Archaeology and Language: The Puzzle of Indo-European Origins (1987), his study of the origin and spread of the Indo-European language, attracted much international attention and debate: it has been translated into eight languages. Invoking a wealth of detailed archaeological evidence, he proposed that language dispersal could be related to the origins of farming and consequential population changes, and so dated much earlier than had been assumed previously. He has followed this with cross-disciplinary work on human history that utilises the tools of modern genetics, notably mtDNA, and aims to integrate archaeology, the history of climate change and genetics into a chronological framework through which human evolution and dispersal can be understood. It is yet another of his projects that defies traditional academic categories. But that is not all. His ability to use the newest developments in science to answer questions about the past co-exists with, and is enriched by, a great sensitivity to the aesthetic dimension of things. In *Figuring it Out* (2000) he used many of the pieces in the College's art collection to reflect in an extraordinarily challenging way on the differences as well as the links between archaeology and art.

Lord Renfrew of Kaimsthorn,
Master 1986–97.

Maggi Hambling, 1995

has heard him debate, whether in lecture hall or on television, Carbon-14 dating, the spread of the Indo-European languages or the significance of Cycladic art – or almost anything else – in his ever-amusing, articulate, erudite and very sharp way will be surprised to learn that he was active in Conservative student politics and the Union Society (of which he was president), that while a young lecturer he had fought a parliamentary election, or that in 1991 Mrs Thatcher appointed him a life peer. From his seat in the House of Lords he has fought hard both for the universities and against the illicit traffic in antiquities.

The range of topics with which Colin Renfrew has

'Oars and the Man': Victorian Expansion

J.A. MANGAN

In the year of Queen Victoria's Diamond Jubilee, the journalist and author Hadley Peek opined in the *Fortnightly Review* that the past fifteen years had witnessed one of the most remarkable revolutions in popular taste in Great Britain and Ireland. Sport of various kinds had become 'not only the ruling passion of the people, but well nigh the chief topic of conversation'. What he had witnessed was, in fact, not merely a recreational but an educational revolution. It was not only social inclination that had changed, but educational fashion. This change was neither casual nor spontaneous. The 'mania' of 'athleticism' – an obsession with physical activities, especially team games, that later came to be deplored – had been introduced deliberately into the upper-class educational system. By 1897 it was a feature of life in both the public schools and their 'finishing schools', the universities of Oxford and Cambridge. The same forces of hedonism, casuistry, pragmatism and idealism were at work in both, and the relationship was cyclical: the mania was mutually sustained and reinforced.

There were, in fact, three Cambridges: one predominantly of the mind, another predominantly of the body, and a third of both mind and body. There were reading men, rowing men and men who attempted both. If King's saw itself as an Athenian shrine of high culture – 'civilised and proud of its civilisation', as E.M. Forster claimed – Jesus was seen as a haven of hearties and a home to muscular addition that subscribed to the ideology of athleticism as completely as Harrow, Lancing, Loretto, Marlborough and Uppingham.

Few things depict better the similarity between the Victorian and Edwardian public school and Jesus than the College magazine, *Chanticlere*. In the main it is hearty, philistine, taken up with athletics and preoccupied with the issues which so greatly concerned the English public schoolboy of the period – athletic heroes, successes and regalia. In 1889 the editors, with a certain perspicacity and some irony, amused themselves by speculating on the eventual fate of the volume which they had produced: 'We can picture the joy of some learned professor of English on finding this priceless treasure, a relic of the remote past. Aided by this work he will prove that the Universities of the ancient English were really devoted to athletic pursuits.' Whatever the learned professor's conclusions regarding the universities, he would not have been too awry in coming to such conclusions about Jesus. As the magazine reveals, the undergraduates gave much thought, effort and time to athletics. The first number devoted eighteen of the twenty-eight pages to boating, cricket, rugby, soccer, athletics and lawn tennis. In the second the news that yet another attempt was to be made to resusci-

First VIII, May 1890. The figure in the bowler hat in the back row is a future Master: W.L.H. Duckworth (1889) (page 23).

tate the College Debating Society provoked the clearly rhetorical question, 'Is the slander true that we care for nothing and excel in nothing but athletics?' A little later it was disclosed that the *Sporting Times* 'is generally torn in two one hour after it has arrived, so eagerly do men dispute the proud privilege of reading that high class paper'. In contrast, *The Nineteenth Century*, *Saturday Review* and *Spectator* lay untouched between their covers!

In October 1886 the lament of a discontented intellectual with a taste for epigrams was published: 'once a small college of tasteful students, now a large body of rowing athletes'. The statement was a little harsh. The editors for the Easter term 1887 were correct: '"the older order changes, giving place to new". We are no longer Head of the River and we have a College debating society.' There was also a society to discuss political, social and economic matters – the Cranmer Society, established in 1897 – and within two years there was a literary and philosophical society, the Coleridge Society. These cultural endeavours gave the editors confidence a little later to remark of a Fellow of the early part of the century, that 'in a sterner age when athletics were then unknown as a serious pursuit', he was a typical Jesus man possessed of 'the spirit of athleticism tempered with learning, which has since been characteristic of so many distinguished members of our College'. Content contradicted compliment. While the Debating Society found difficulty attracting support, a meeting held to debate the desirability of a blazer for members of the College Athletic Club 'was a large one and many men spoke'. The proposition was carried by a substantial majority.

As in the magazines of the public schools, former alumni in the Empire wrote of their staunch attempts to maintain the essential aspects of an English heritage despite tropical downpours flooding the wicket; they tempted the adventurous: 'a swift bowler of the type so well known of Jesus of late is badly wanted here'. Letters requesting improved facilities of the right sort: 'racquets and five courts, a cinder path, a gymnasium … and everything else which would help to render happy the life of the athletic scholar'; and 'athletic scholars' received fitting prominence in death. H.E. Rhodes, whose gallantry in abandoning a cricket match and, quite untrained, taking the place of a sick colleague in the winning boat of 1876, was 'so intimately associated with the athletic history, and particularly the rowing history of the college, that his death could not be passed over in silence'. Again, as in the public school magazines of the period, the plaintive demands of editors desperate for print and the disenchanted comments of the disgruntled occasionally surfaced. In 1894 one long-suffering editor wondered

dejectedly 'when a literary contribution had last been sent in for the delight of the overworked staff', and shortly before the Great War, a brave if anonymous voice was raised in protest against the tone of the place which one long-lived Jesus don (Percival Gardner-Smith) was to recall as, at that time, 'a place of senseless and brutal rowdyism' and not unlike 'an ill-disciplined public school'. 'Mother of Seven' complained of the callous imposition of a way of life modelled on the 'perfect' undergraduate who 'will swear – but not too often, … will keep chapel – but not too many, … will work – but not too much [and] the more games he plays, the nearer will he approach perfection [attaining] the apotheosis by representing the

University and gaining his "Blue"'. Sporting doggerel of a cheery moralistic nature so familiar to the reader of the *Harrovian*, *Lorettonian*, *Uppingham Magazine* and similar products, also appeared in *Chanticlere*:

The Cranmer Debating Society, 1887.

O batsman play the game, or a 'duck' will blot your fame;
    Don't shiver when the umpire sings out 'PLAY!'
But be wary, wise, and ready; play 'em straight and true
    and steady.
And watch the ball and gently feel your way.

Perhaps the clearest evidence of institutional priorities is its meticulous listing of the athletic talents of newcomers to the College:

FRESHMEN 1895

Beck, A.C.T.	Exton, C.G., Oundle[1]
Breakey, H.L., Eliock[1]	Ford, E.B., Hastings
Bower, G.F., private	Harries, O.W. Bury St Edmunds
Brydone, P., Lancing[2]	Harvey, Winchester
Busby, G.H., Repton[2,3]	Lucas, R., Cheltenham
Chapman, W.T.,	Maclaren, W.V. St C.,
Loughborough[2,3]	Merchiston Castle
Coode, A.T., Fauconberge,	Maddison, J.R.S., Durham
Beccles[2,3]	Marriott, H.S., Bradfield
Dickson, A.C., Rossall	Sedgwick, J.S., Lancaster[1]
Sadler, H., Durham[4]	Thorburn, K.D.S.M.,
Siddons, A.W., K. Edward's	Wellington[1,3]
Birmingham[1,3]	Turner, W.G., Chatham House
Skrimshire, H.F., Gresham[3]	Walton, H.G., Newcastle
Stevens, H., Beaumont[2]	Whitty, R.F.L., Felsted[2,3]
Swanson, A.W., Loretto[1]	Wigram, G.E., Bradfield
Thompson, W., Ripon[1,3]	Woolston, Wellingboro[2,3]

(1) denotes 1st XV Rugby colours; (2) 1st XI Association;
(3) 1st XI Cricket; (4) first boat.

It seems reasonable, therefore, to suppose that the typical Jesus undergraduate of the late nineteenth century would have had much in common with B.H. Stewart, who matriculated in 1893 and graduated in 1896. Stewart opened his short book of *Reminiscences* (1945) with this categorical statement: 'To anyone who should pick up this little booklet … I feel under an obligation to state that it is concerned mainly with sport – touching lightly on cricket, football, running, swimming, rowing, gymnastics, golf, tennis and boxing with chess, billiards and cards thrown in.' He added unnecessarily, 'all my life sport has been and still is – a passion with me'. He measured his degree of contentment at the University exclusively in terms of his athletic accomplishments and activities. He underwent the obligatory period of 'compulsory rowing' as a freshman, became an enthusiastic but indifferent cricketer, won a worthy Blue at soccer and became an efficient president of the Jesus College Athletic Club. He took full advantage of the opportunities available 'in the most sporting College in Cambridge' and ended his brief and breezy memoirs with a sententious homily for the young reader, on games as a training for life which set three years of hedonism in proper moral perspective:

And if you're beaten – well, what of that?
Come up with a smiling face.
'Tis no disgrace to be knocked down flat,
But to lie there, that's disgrace.

The harder you're knocked, the higher you bounce,
Be proud of the blackened eye.
It isn't the fact that you're licked that counts,
But *how* did you fight – and why?

Stewart's typicality is underlined by the contrasting nature and experiences of Mark Sykes, who resided at Jesus at about the same time. Sykes was worthy, serious 'and held firmly to high principles'. It is hardly surprising, therefore, to discover from his biographer, Shane Leslie, that, having little in common with his own College, he had no liking for the river: 'He was one of those of whom it might be said that they neither toiled nor did they spin up and down the green and scented courses of the Cam.' He devoted himself to his eastern travels, theatricals and journalism and inevitably gravitated away from Jesus toward King's, the undisputed centre of intellectual affairs. To King's men he was a curious acquisition. 'Jesus men', remarked Leslie, 'were seldom called into King's circles unless to improve the style of a racing crew.' However, he quickly won the respect of, and was at ease with, an Olympian academic of the stature of Montagu James. He was not missed at Jesus. The College grandees were the athletes. For the most part they defined reality, set the tone, determined the values, coerced the unwilling and disciplined the recalcitrant.

The ethos of Victorian and Edwardian Jesus was not, however, just the product of hearty public schoolboys with hearty period enthusiasms, who danced to their own tunes despite the feeble piping of despairing dons. In the universities, as in the public schools, the games cult was supported by those in authority, who legitimised, encouraged and sustained it. It was the product of a curious amalgam of self-interest and altruism. By the 1850s the dons, irritated by the dominance of the coaching system, were imitating the 'beaks', but Thring (of Uppingham) rather than Arnold (of Rugby). The collegiate ideal was redefined to lay emphasis on personal influence and character formation. This ensured legitimacy, promoted self-respect and improved professional image. Of course, this is not the whole story. Some casuistic dons, like some 'beaks', were little more than perpetual public schoolboys. Others were calculating realists to whom institutional athletic repute meant institutional prosperity. Yet others were commonsense pragmatists who followed the expedient practices of mid-century public school headmasters. They promoted the river and the playing fields as necessary mechanisms of control. As undergraduates increased in number as a consequence of the growing wealth of Victorian Britain, the associated expansion of the public school system and the university reforms of the mid- and late nineteenth century, the colleges faced a classic public school problem – sizeable numbers of students in the grip of boredom born of restriction – which traditional procedures: college lectures, college examinations, compulsory chapel and dinners in hall; and punishments: admonitions, rustication, expulsion, prohibitions and literary impositions, did not always resolve.

Throughout the later part of Victoria's reign Jesus was in the charge of two (unrelated) men, H.A. and E.H. Morgan, who strongly encouraged the rise of athleticism. Known, respectively, as 'Black' and 'Red' Morgan, they were typical athletic pedagogues of the period and 'Red's' experience as an assistant minister at Lancing College was to be valuable to him as a College Fellow. Both had been undergraduates in the College during Dr Corrie's first decade as Master. Both were able, enthusiastic and committed athletes – H.A. was captain of the College Boat Club in 1851, E.H. in 1860 – and only moderate academics. Both acquired awesome, if rather different, reputations. They ushered in 'high and balmy days' in which 'the Master', 'the Tutor' and 'the Dean' formed a great triumvirate, powerfully influencing the ethos of the College and transforming its standing. This was just as well. By the 1850s it had fallen on hard times.

Customarily portrayed as an 'Evangelical High Churchman equally opposed to Dissent and Popery', with pronounced conservative inclinations in political, social and educational matters, Corrie had become Master in 1849. His virtues, summarised on his memorial tablet in the Chapel – *Votis, Studiis, Moribus, Christo Devotissimus* – do not seem to have had much appeal. His early years as Master witnessed a disastrous drop in admissions: in 1849 there had been fifty-nine undergraduates (as many as the College could house), by 1859 there were only thirty-two, of whom just five were freshmen. This continued until shortly before the appointment of H.A. Morgan as Tutor in 1863. The immediate rise in numbers – by 1869 there were 104 undergraduates – was attributable, at least in part, to Morgan's interests and efforts. The cause of its continuation was obvious to the College's historian, Arthur Gray, writing in 1902: 'It was in the decade of the "seventies" that the College sprang into … athletic prominence … it was, not unnaturally, accompanied by a great rise in the number of undergraduates.' It was, in fact, in 1875 that Morgan's efforts came to fruition and the College boat 'attained the proud position of Head of the River'. The College moved quickly from sixth in 1869 to, in 1879, third largest in Cambridge after Trinity and St John's, with 216 undergraduates. Growth, of course, was due in part to a general expansion of the University after the Act of Parliament in 1871 abolishing religious tests for all degrees except Divinity, but the fame of Jesus oarsmen was the main reason. Jesus retained the Headship of the River for eleven years. The College now enjoyed an athletic pre-eminence which

Gray (perhaps ironically) observed comprised 'its greatest glory in modern times'.

Towards the end of the 1870s the 'inflow of freshmen became phenomenal'. Additions to the College buildings made (to Waterhouse's designs) in 1869–70 had to be extended. The Hall was enlarged in 1875 and the Small Hall built next to it. Further extensive additions (the Carpenter building) resulted in 1885; there were tangible returns to be gained from sporting prowess. A similar expansion occurred after the legendary Steve Fairbairn returned to coach the Jesus boats in 1904. He was informed by the then Tutor, F.J. Foakes Jackson, that 'the position of the College boat on the river was an index of the prosperity of the College'. As successes on the river mounted, Foakes Jackson said he was refusing two men a day as there was no room for them. Yet condoning athletic excess had not always guaranteed College prosperity. Despite continued victories on the river, by the time the new buildings were completed in the later 1880s numbers had fallen by one third from 216 in 1880 to 147 in 1884. Athletic dominance brought both popularity and, when coupled with the rowdiness and idleness of many of the rowing men, unpopularity. In view of what was acceptable, the licence must have been considerable; some recorded behaviour savours of mob rule. The ringleaders came from the first and the pre-eminent of the social clubs, the Rhadegund Society for the leading athletes, established in 1874. Even H.A. Morgan felt obliged to remark that 'The College is becoming nothing but a boat club, and it will do it much good if the boat comes down.'

Jesus Blues, 1890.

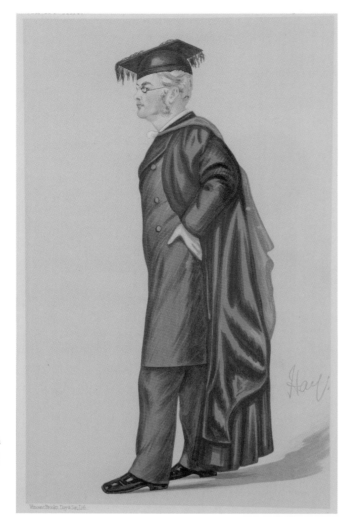

'Black Morgan': H.A. Morgan
(1849), Fellow 1860, [Senior]
Tutor 1863–85, Master
1885–1912.

Vanity Fair, 1889

advice. When the College became Head of the River in 1875 he remarked that 'this could not have been done without courage and self-denial and he trusted that they would carry their qualities into after life'. Later the same day, a chance meeting with a group of excited undergraduates gave him the opportunity for a further brief homily: 'I am very glad that you have done so well on the river. I hope you do as well with your books as you have done with your oars.'

But if Corrie helped in laying the foundations, it was the two Morgans who ensured the College's image as one for athletic toughs. At the time of his death in 1912, H.A. Morgan, who had succeeded Corrie as Master in 1885, was described by Charles Whibley in *Blackwood's Magazine* as 'a don of the old school – a sportsman and a gentleman'. The College in which he had resided for over half a century was peculiarly his own creation:

> He filled it with undergraduates, and then endowed it with a soul – a soul of energy and patriotism. He gave to one and all a just cause of pride in their College, and warmed their courage at the fire of his own enthusiasm. In all sports … he took the keen and intimate interest of one who had practised them … For half a century he encouraged the College boat by his voice and presence; he watched its rise and fall upon the river with the stern enthusiasm of a general watching his army in the field, and his enthusiasm was rewarded by so long a list of victories as has never been claimed by any other College in the world.

The Jesuan 'general' chose his 'army' with care: his students were selected in his own image. Charles Hose, for example, on seeking entrance to the College in 1882 was closely interrogated by Morgan about his athletic record.

While 'Black' Morgan wholly lacked the intellectual ability of his close friend Leslie Stephen, he almost matched him in his enthusiasm for physical exercise. Walking was a great passion and strenuous walks of anything up to thirty miles in the Cambridgeshire countryside were undertaken with colleagues during term-time, while in the vacations the Alps frequently beckoned. In the summer of 1862, with a casualness of purpose typical of the amateur gentleman of the period, having nothing better to do, he went with Stephen on an expedition to Switzerland and unostentatiously achieved the first crossing of the Jungfrau-Joch – as late as 1925 still considered a hazardous undertaking. When mountains were not available to tire them and cultural interests drew them to Vienna, Prague, Dresden and Berlin, Stephen and Morgan would get exercise by racing back to their hotel by different routes; 'great judgement and discrimination were required', Stephen wrote, 'to decide whether or not

Corrie's and the two Morgans' accord on matters of educational principle was closer than Gray and Brittain suggest. The impression given of Corrie is of a crusty, anchoritic 'student of many of the bye-paths of theological research', who loathed rowing men. Yet, H.A. Morgan himself acknowledged that Corrie approved 'vigorous, manly recreations' and frequently watched his boys playing cricket and football. He also supported the athletes. Percy M. Thornton, writing of the origins of Jesus athletics in the early 1860s, desired 'to place on record how generously and enthusiastically the late venerable and beloved Master of Jesus, Dr. Corrie, supported the athletics, frequently coming to see the sports on Jesus Close.' In fact, Corrie saw the same ethical qualities in sport as did thousands of his contemporaries. He might have had mysogynic objections to the camp followers who, he alleged, followed the boats along the banks of the Cam, but he had mellowed since his days as a fellow of St Catharine's, where while countenancing 'boating for recreation and exercise independently of the racing', he had deplored the boat club's influence on his pupils. He now saw moral worth in the efforts of the oarsmen. He was judicious in his praise and opportunistic with his

it would be advantageous to dash down some narrow street or not'. Stephen was long reputed to be the creator of the inter-varsity athletic sports, but there were also a number of Jesus Fellows, including H.A. Morgan, who helped win over the hostile University authorities to the idea of 'fresh inter-University competitions of a non-intellectual nature' and made it possible for Thornton, the Jesus undergraduate, and C.B. Lawes, an undergraduate from Trinity, to visit Oxford early in 1864 to make arrangements for the first inter-university athletics meeting, which took place later that year on Christ Church cricket ground.

But it was rowing that was Morgan's great love – seemingly for moral as well as sensual reasons: 'athletics were too much for self-glorification, another pot for this or that, and so on, till [a man] has a row of silver pots or cups. Boating was the ideal, no pots or personal rewards, all for the honour of the College and the University.' Morgan's own rowing feats were impressive. He rowed in the Jesus College boat for ten years and coached the College boats for many years after that, becoming a well-known figure riding on his white horse Gehazi along the tow-path shouting instructions to 'the boat with the red and black oars'. He held the record for the number of 'eight-oared' races on the Cam – over a hundred – and his daughter in an untypically boastful attempt to place this considerable feat in proper perspective, wrote 'in endeavouring to surpass this record another oarsman rowed sixty-eight races and died'. Morgan himself was to be buried within sight and sound of his beloved river in the churchyard at Fen Ditton.

He was acutely conscious that from 1861 to 1869 Oxford had won the Boat Race nine years in succession and it occurred to him 'that Cambridge might possibly be labouring under a disadvantage of having to undergo constant practice on a shallow river, whereas Oxford had the advantage of deeper water'. He incessantly worried all those interested in University rowing until in 1868 a meeting was held in his rooms at Jesus and funds were promised for improving the river. Eventually a subscription list was opened in London and Morgan had the pleasure of placing Queen Victoria herself at its head. The Queen donated £100, 'believing that she was only carrying into effect the wishes of the Prince Consort, the late Chancellor', and the Prince of Wales £50. The work of deepening and widening the Cam was completed in 1870. Cambridge won the next five races in succession!

Even in the most extreme of circumstances his support for the Jesus boat was assured. Apparently at death's door with fever in 1875, when Jesus went Head of the River for the first time, the whole College stood silently under his window. It slowly opened and a stick on which was suspended his straw hat with the Jesus ribbon was waved slowly up and down. Perceptive students, we are told, dated his recovery from that moment. In his passion for the boats he was as prone to rationalisation as any other zealot. He 'encouraged men to take up rowing,' observed one of his pupils, 'not merely because he knew it promoted their bodily and moral health but because it interfered less than anything else with their work'. He clearly chose to disbelieve the well-known university axiom of the time: 'He who runs may read but he who rows simply cannot.' First as Tutor and later as Master, Morgan was more like a glorified public school headmaster than a distinguished university scholar. He was ideally suited to the Jesus undergraduates of his time.

Edward Henry ('Red') Morgan, elected a Fellow in 1864, Dean in 1866, a Tutor in 1882, and Senior Tutor in 1885, was a more controversial figure than his namesake. He aroused strong passions. He was described by one undergraduate, who took a very pronounced dislike to him, as 'an enormous man, over six feet in height, with a stomach and feet to match, a closely trimmed red beard, and a voice like a bull – one of Nature's bullies'. Elsewhere he was compared to those massive warriors 'who from their northern homes sallied out to harry and destroy feebler men'. He was an ardent devotee of sport. *Granta* reported in May 1890: 'he fostered *esprit de corps* in every pursuit; he encouraged the genuine athlete; ... Such a man at the head of affairs soon effected a change in a College that had grown somewhat sluggish, and the

The Rhadegunds, 1889.

'Red Morgan': E.H. Morgan
(1858), Fellow 1864, Dean
1866, Tutor 1882, Senior
Tutor 1885–95.

Vanity Fair, 1889

for example, is filled with telegrams dispatched to him from scenes of Jesuan sporting success – Lords, Henley and elsewhere – reporting famous victories on the Thames or informing him of the doings of men in the university cricket match. It includes records of work done for the University cricket, boat and athletic clubs and of meetings of the famous Isthmian, Queen's and Leander sports clubs, of which he was a proud member. For many years treasurer of the leading University athletic clubs, in addition he played a major role in organising the subscription fund for the purchase of Fenner's cricket ground from Caius College. Perhaps the clearest indication of his excessive zeal is an item entitled 'Muscular Education' in *Punch*, the merciless recorder of the extravagance of the English gentleman. He appears under the not very opaque pseudonym of R.E.D. Horgan of Jesurum College, Cambs., as a referee for an exciting new preparatory school where boys are trained 'to the real requirements of modern life (rowing, cricket, football, swimming, racquets, boxing, hockey, billiards, poker, nurr and spell)', in preparation for the great public schools and universities. Extras at this utilitarian establishment (for which there was an additional charge) included reading, writing and arithmetic.

'Red' Morgan was a man to be feared rather than loved. He found few lions in his path and those he quickly tamed. One of the Fellows, however, summoned up enough courage to compose this disrespectful verse:

Red Morgan: I am the tutor, bursar, butler, dean:
I rule the college with imperial sway
The very Master owneth me supreme,
The Fellows tremble and my rule obey.
Chorus: The Czar of Russia and our gracious Queen
Are not so potent as our noble Dean.

H.A. Morgan's daughter, in her book about her father, recounted with delicate malice several of his stories about 'the noble Dean'. She herself wrote euphemistically that he possessed 'a vigorous and resolute personality combined with a masterful will'. Clearly she shared her father's antipathy towards him. His motives appear to have been more hedonistic than moralistic. There is no record of his advancing any moral arguments for sport. Yet 'the Dean' was considered by many of his contemporaries to have been 'an admirable type of muscular Christian'. His personality and predilections dominated Jesus for much of the last quarter of the nineteenth century; it was his values that prevailed in the College. If H.A. Morgan was a glorified headmaster with a taste for sport, E.H. Morgan was a glorified games master with an obsession for it.

consequence is that at the present day Jesus men have increased in numbers to such an extent as to require and possess new College buildings and … [are] to be found in the front rank of every branch of athletics.' Others were less convinced of his merit, seeing his rise to prominence as malign. Morgan's propensity to turn a blind eye when it suited him is revealed in Stewart's *Reminiscences*. He recalled that S.M.J. Woods, a double Blue in his first year and 'too priceless to lose' always got his way with Morgan. In his autobiography *It's a Don's Life*, Brittain attributed both the restless reforms and the reckless iconoclasm of Arthur Gray, who on E.H. Morgan's death in 1895 succeeded him as Senior Tutor and was Master from 1912 to 1940, to the need 'to administer an antidote … [and] smash the idol of Red Morganism … To the end of his life he could always be roused to wrath by any mention of the repugnant name. Anyone who did not know might have thought that Red Morgan's enormities had been perpetrated a few weeks previously, whereas he had been dead for forty years.'

Despite the systematic removal of Morgan memorabilia under Gray, clues to the extent of his absorption in sport remain in the College archives. His scrapbook,

In their schoolmasterly efforts to nurture the bodies and to a lesser extent the minds of their charges, the Morgans received steady support from dons of far less athletic ability but just as much enthusiasm. The most quietly persistent was J.C. Watt (page 26), who in 1927, when Jesus yet again went Head of the River, brought a long life of involvement in Jesus athletics to a contented close, remarking that he could now sing his 'Nunc Dimittis'.

The essence of Victorian and Edwardian upper-class educational purpose, character training through athletic endeavour, was well captured by R.C. Lehmann. The University and college oarsman, he wrote:

> will have suffered much, he will have rowed many weary miles, have learnt the misery of aching limbs and blistered hands, … he will have laboured under broiling suns, or with snow storms and bitter winds beating against him, he will have voluntarily cut himself off from many pleasant indulgences. But on the other hand his triumphs will have been sweet, he will have trained himself to submit to discipline, to accept discomfort cheerfully, to keep a brave face in adverse circumstances; he will have learnt the necessity of unselfishness and patriotism …

Boating was pre-eminently 'a means of university education … a high moral lesson', wrote a contributor to the *Fortnightly Review* in 1887, quoting as authority an Anglican bishop. He himself believed that 'one of the highest objectives of a university career should be the formation of character', and expressed disgust at the youth without this objective who remained indoors 'addling his brains in the investigation of obscure historical and philological problems'. It was this muscular morality above all else that the British product of public school and ancient university took to every corner of the Empire. It served school teachers, missionaries and colonial administrators well in their efforts to train the child at home in Britain and the 'child-like' native in the colonies.

A mere handful of Jesuan men must suffice to illustrate what was typical of many more, and to demonstrate how deeply the games ethic became embedded in professional action. James Robertson (1854), headmaster of Haileybury from 1884 to 1890, made substantial contributions to the school fabric, its intellectual life and athletic organisation. Like so many of the Victorian sporting pedagogues, he showed himself to be possessed of a persistent youthfulness, a firm commitment to athletics as a moral instrument and a determination to ensure they had a central role in educational theory and practice. 'Our progress under six years of wise and liberal government has been immense', wrote the authors of his *Valete* in the *Haileyburian* of 1890 'all the older games [are] better organised and more vigorously pursued than before'.

While Robertson trained embryonic imperial administrators on the Haileybury playing fields, one Jesuan imperialist, Charles Hose, was making excellent use of his College experience as Government Resident in Sarawak, Borneo. Hose left Jesus prematurely in 1884 without a degree, for a post under the legendary Charles Brooke:

> With my love of outdoor life, of Nature, and of Romance, an opportunity of realizing my ambitions by work in the Adventurous East was one that was sure to prove an irresistible temptation. Thus it happened that when my uncle, Bishop Hose, wrote to my family offering to get me, if possible, a Cadetship on Sarawak, of all places, … my delighted acceptance was conveyed in the single word … Rather.

Rugby XV, 1881.

Soon after he found himself in charge of the Baram district: 'Raiding and head-hunting were rife, and constant local feuds prevailed. Interference by an intrusive government was not welcomed and was opposed with vigour.' Hose was patient. After ten years, having played himself in as Resident, he felt the time was ripe to call a conference of the tribes. The purpose of the meeting was to bring *Pax Britannica* to Baram. He wrote later in *Natural Man: A Record of Borneo*:

> In calling the conference, I felt that in order to suppress fighting and head-hunting, the normal young Bornean's natural outlet, it would be well to replace them by some equally violent, but less boisterous, activity; and I suggested to the tribes a sort of local Henley, the chief feature of which would be an annual race between the war canoes of all the villages. The proposal was taken up eagerly by the people.

The great boat race duly came about. In his own words:

At daybreak the racing-boats set off for the starting-post four miles up-river. Strict orders had been given that no spears or other weapons were to be carried … but as they started the boats were inspected in turn, and in one or two cases were relieved of contraband … It was a grand neck-and-neck race all through between the two leading boats, and every man rowed it out to the end.

THE SCHOOL FLEET OUTSIDE THE BOATHOUSE ON THE DAL LAKE

'May week in Kashmir': the Srinagar Mission School's racing shikaras, *c.*1925.

The undertaking was not without its difficulties. Athletic competition had its dangers for tribesmen unfamiliar with the obligations to lose well. Victory on this auspicious occasion presented a considerable problem since the winners were a pacific coastal people who were more skilful at making boats than war. Design, not aggression, had brought triumph. Fortunately, good humour prevailed, and on the following morning the various parties dispersed to their distant villages, taking with them the news 'of the great boat race … how they swore peace and goodwill to all men, and how there now should be peace and prosperity through all the land'. Imperial policy and Jesuan practice had combined to good purpose.

The efforts of Robertson and Hose, however, are dwarfed by those of Cecil Earle Tyndale-Biscoe (1881) who, from 1890 to 1947 – with extraordinary strength of purpose, honest Christian zeal and incredible personal stamina – took the athletic activities of English public school and ancient university to the Hindu Brahmins of Kashmir, where he sought, as he said, to strengthen sinew and develop muscle on the river and the playing field in the interests of knight-errantry.

These three men represented a clear-cut attitude to individual, social and political behaviour which, in their simple but certain view, games in part both determined and reflected. For them games encapsulated a great deal more than personal pleasure, private recreation, disciplinary expedience and egocentric aggrandisement. They were part of an ethical endeavour disseminated from the colleges of both Oxford and Cambridge to places as varied as the squalid slums of London's East End, the spacious acres of Harrow 'footer' fields, the hot and humid hillsides of Ceylon, the high savannah of the South African veld, the tropical rain forests of Equatorial Africa, and the elegant Chieftains' Colleges scattered throughout the Indian subcontinent.

Jesus contributed enthusiastically to this ethical effort. It was at the centre of a concentric world; close to the centre stood the English public schools, halfway to the centre stood the English grammar schools, while at the circumference itself stood Australian, African, Indian and other imperial emulators. The College provided the wider society with moral exemplars, ideologues and diffusionists who preached and practised athleticism in Cambridge, Britain and Empire. Jesus played its full part in a movement which transformed exercise into ethical endeavour, influenced the educational practices of Empire and Commonwealth and inspired the future recreational habits of the world.

This is an edited version of '"Oars and the Man": Pleasure and Purpose in Victorian and Edwardian Cambridge', which appeared in the British Journal of Sports History *vol. i (1984), pp. 245–71, and is printed by kind permission of Routledge Journals, Taylor and Francis Ltd.*

Getting into Jesus: 1790–2006

ADAM TOOZE, JONATHAN COOK, ANN MURRAY, LIAM RICHARDSON, ANTHONY BAGSHAW

As a matter of general public interest, the question of 'Oxbridge admissions' would seem to date to 1963, when a discussion erupted concerning the structure of the Cambridge and Oxford admissions system and its harmonisation with that in use in the other English universities. Even then, the Vice-Chancellor was clearly aware of the PR problem facing Cambridge and the need to present the University and its colleges as co-operative members of the national educational system. Ever since, the argument has ebbed and flowed.

Spectacular individual cases make the headlines. But, in its serious form, the admissions debate is a numbers game. Annual reports are anxiously scanned by University and colleges to check for obvious signs of bias between male and female applicants and applicants from different types of school. The numbers tell us that though Jesus has a fellowship that is highly committed to the 'access issue', the percentage of students applying to it from the state-maintained sector has in the recent past been consistently below the University average, 54 per cent for Jesus in 2005 as opposed to 62 per cent for the University as a whole. On the other hand, the numbers also confirm that those that do apply to the College, from whatever type of school, are treated with scrupulous even-handedness. The number of offers of admission is in close proportion to the numbers applying from each type of school and not far off the figure for the University as a whole. Of offers made by Jesus in 2005, 52 per cent were to applicants from state-maintained schools as against 56 per cent for the University as a whole.

In this increasingly ritualised debate, memories are remarkably short. A great fuss is made of variations of a few percentage points over a matter of only a few years. However, there is no doubt that underpinning the annual commotion there is a more or less hazy historical narrative, which divides the modern history of Oxbridge into three periods. There were the days of 'public school Oxbridge' – the world of the early 1920s fixed in the popular imagination by re-runs of Granada Television's 1981 adaptation of *Brideshead Revisited*. Then there is the Oxbridge of the 1950s and 1960s, the Oxbridge of the grammar school boys, whose media face is the evergreen cast of Footlights, *c*.1957–66. Finally, there is the present era, marked by polarised attitudes towards the fraught experiment with comprehensive education, an era spanned in media terms by Phil Redmond's long-running school soap *Grange Hill* (1978 to the present).

But how much substance is there to this narrative? Can one add any historical precision to the approximate datings of anecdote and dinner-table argument?

To cast some light on these questions, 'we' – a band of undergraduates and the Gurnee Hart Fellow in History, Adam Tooze, with the expert assistance of College archivists – have set about exploring the College records. In a few months of occasional work we have managed to sample only a small fraction of the College's copious archive. However, some interesting historical patterns do emerge.

Lured by the thrill of digitising the matriculation record of 'Coleridge, Sam. Taylor' *in Schola Xti Hosp [Christ's Hospital] educatus*, we started our investigations in the academic year 1790–1. Thereafter, up to 1850 we took samples of the student records every ten years.

Admissions to the College in the early nineteenth century fluctuated quite considerably: eighteen in 1790–1, only nine during the second phase of the Napoleonic Wars in 1800–1, eleven in 1810–11, thirteen in 1830–1. Then from the 1840s onwards there begins a significant surge. Twenty-three were admitted in 1840–1 and twenty-six in 1850–1. Altogether, our first sample between 1791 and 1851 includes 105 students.

Record-keeping at this point in the College's history was far from complete. However, for the vast majority of students we do have some indication of their schooling prior to admission. The long-established public schools, those that were later to be included amongst the so-called 'Clarendon group', provided 14 per cent of the early nineteenth-century undergraduates. At the other end of the social scale, grammar schools provided 20 per cent. And some of them were very important indeed. In the early nineteenth century the venerable Louth Grammar School (royal charter from King Edward VI, 1551) sent as many boys to Jesus as did Eton or Rugby. Unfortunately for the College, Alfred (later Lord) Tennyson, who was schooled at Louth between 1816 and 1820, chose Trinity, not Jesus. The real boom in public school education was still some decades in the future. However a sign of things to come was King's College School, London, which, founded in 1829, sent no fewer than four young men to Jesus in 1850–1. Alongside these 'school boys' in the conventional sense, the records also include a significant number of men identified as having been educated by private tutors, 20 per cent in our early nineteenth-century sample.

The student population of the College was clearly on the rise already in the 1840s. However, the College's modern history may properly be said to begin in 1864 with the appointment of H.A. Morgan, 'Black' Morgan, as (Senior) Tutor. Unlike George John Elwes Corrie, who had been elected Master in 1849, Morgan was an enthusiastic exponent of the Victorian cult of muscular Christianity. And it was, as J.A. Mangan has written (page 159), as an athletic powerhouse that the College underwent its dramatic expansion in the late nineteenth century. During Corrie's long tenure as Master between 1850 and 1885, the College admitted no fewer than 1,242 men

The Waterhouse building, 1870.

Julian Dowdeswell

and boys – more than 80 per cent of them after 1864 (when H.A. Morgan became Tutor), doubling its number of undergraduates within a decade, from 100 in 1870 to 200 in 1880. And thanks to the tireless energy of Arthur Gray, we are remarkably well informed about this group. Of 1,242 students, 217 came from grammar schools. Proprietary schools or tutors provided 207. But the overwhelming majority came from schools belonging to the Headmasters' Conference group of public schools. The Clarendon elite contributed 20 per cent, with Harrow and Eton leading the way. Behind them came the expanding ranks of newly founded Victorian public schools. In total no fewer than 62 per cent of Corrie's (Morgan's) undergraduates were drawn from recognised public schools.

At this point, therefore, Jesus certainly conformed to the stereotype of 'public school Oxbridge' and in this respect it was like every other college for which we have reliable information. The differences between the colleges, and they were no doubt significant, were differences of culture – vastly more muscular at Jesus than at King's, for instance – and differences in the precise composition of the public school intake. Trinity was the most exclusive by far, recruiting 68 per cent of its students from the twenty-two most prestigious public schools. King's followed with 54 per cent. Legend tells of one provost of King's who liked to eat breakfast with old Etonians, deigned to say good morning to Wykehamists and simply ignored the rest. Late nineteenth-century Jesus was clearly not in this class. It resembled colleges like Caius, where 30 per cent of the undergraduates came from the top twenty-two public schools.

To go beyond school background to generalise about the precise social composition of the student body is not possible, given the lack of adequate records. However, relative to Britain's adult population as a whole, of which as late as the 1930s roughly 80 per cent earned their living through various forms of manual labour, it is safe to assume that Jesus undergraduates were a homogenously upper middle-class group. As the Clarendon Commission had revealed, in 1861 the number of scholarship boys at even the most well-endowed public schools was small. At Harrow and Eton, from which the College recruited most heavily, the ratio was roughly ten fee-paying students for every foundationer. As Gray and Brittain put it with commendable frankness, 'the talk of the continuous stream of poor boys who are alleged to have entered the older universities before the twentieth century is humbug, if "poor" is taken to mean working-class. … The working-class boy at Cambridge before the twentieth century is as rare as a needle in a haystack.' 'The so-called "poor boys" were poor only by contrast with the wealthy Fellow Commoners. They were middle-class boys, whose parents were able to support them partly during term and wholly during vacations.'

What mattered with regard to the social composition of the Oxbridge intake were the nuanced gradations within the 5 per cent of the population who constituted Britain's middle and upper class. And one of these groups in particular demands close attention – the Anglican clergy.

Mid-Victorian Cambridge was still overwhelmingly an Anglican institution. Indeed, educating the sons of the clergy and producing future clergymen was arguably the University's only clearly defined educational role. And though these ties were loosened by the reforms of 1856, which abolished the religious test for all undergraduates not studying theology, the link between Cambridge and Anglicanism remained profound. This was nowhere more true than at Jesus. The College's Anglican enthusiasm manifested itself in the glory and expense of Pugin's restoration of the Chapel. It revealed its darker side in the decision of the College in 1856 to strike a former student from the list of MAs 'in consequence of his having joined the Romish mission in this country'. Of 1,242 young men admitted between 1850 and 1885, no fewer than 391, or almost 30 per cent, were the sons of clergymen. And no fewer than 448 of those who left Jesus in those years went on to careers in the Church, more than one third.

By the beginning of the twentieth century this clerical preponderance was already in sharp decline. Of the new students admitted to Jesus in 1911 only 18 per cent had clergymen as fathers. And by 1931 the share had fallen to 12 per cent. The rapid secularisation of secondary education in the early twentieth century can also be indexed through the names of those providing references for new admissions to the College. In 1911 over a third of the intake came to the College with a reference from a teacher-clergyman. By 1921 the number had fallen to a quarter. By 1931 the records show only 'Housemasters' or 'Headmasters', some of whom may of course have been clergymen, but this was no longer considered worthy of special note. The process further accelerated after the Second World War. Of the 3,681 students matriculated between 1945 and 1979, fewer than 70 studied theology at any point during their time at the College. As for subsequent employment, of the 2,700 students for whom we have information, only 3 per cent are identified as clergymen, a spectacular reversal of the nineteenth-century pattern.

When Corrie died in office in 1885, the College's links to the new establishment of Victorian public schools were very solidly entrenched. According to our data, this was not yet the absolute high point of public school dominance. This came, true to the stereotype, in the early decades of the twentieth century, with the extinction of private tutors as an important category and their replacement by a near exclusive reliance by the British upper middle class on public schools.

The College's annual intake of students increased by a factor of 4 between 1901 and 1931 – eighty new admissions in 1931 versus only twenty-two in 1901, in the depths of the agricultural depression. The vast majority of this increase was accounted for by recruitment from the second-tier public schools. The number of grammar school boys admitted to Jesus increased as well, but only from seven in 1901 to fifteen in 1931. In other words, as the College expanded, the share coming from state-maintained schools actually fell, to 9 per cent in the 1911 and 1921 cohorts. For the inter-war period as a whole the average was something like 15 per cent, lower than for most of the

Freshmen, 1897.

nineteenth century. A similar decline is also visible in the Caius data, which is all the more striking because it stands in stark contrast to national trends. In the history of British education, the period between 1900 and 1939 stands out as the period of most rapid growth in state-funded secondary schools, with the number of pupils in grant-aided secondary schools in England almost quadrupling.

Amongst the near uniformity of ex-public school boys, the only element of variety in the inter-war period was the influx of students from schools in the dominions and colonies. These accounted for between 7 and 9 per cent of the annual intake in the first half of the twentieth century, with Australia and Geelong Grammar School in particular being the main provider. By the 1960s the share of students from the Commonwealth had risen to a remarkable 14 per cent, with students being drawn in roughly equal measure from Africa and Australia, and a small but steady stream coming from India. But in the early 1930s a gathering of the student population of the College would have yielded the following homogeneous picture: 150 public school men, of whom 35 came from the most prestigious Clarendon schools, 30 grammar school boys and perhaps 15 'colonials', all of them from fee-paying schools.

The event that finally broke the social pattern established in the mid-Victorian period was the Second World War. If we focus our attention only on the balance between state-funded and fee-paying education, then the quarter-century between 1950 and 1975 is the period of most dramatic change in the College's entire history. It was in those years that the College's social complexion was fundamentally changed by an influx of upwardly mobile young men, including amongst them the father of the first-named author of this article, the son of what would now be termed a 'routine non-manual worker', who entered the College in 1958 with a scholarship – the product of the 11 plus (retaken), Handsworth Grammar School and National Service.

Again, this change in the social make-up of the College was in large part a product of expansion. In the aftermath of the war the annual intake of students increased. But this time the additional students were drawn from the state-funded grammar schools, which were now consolidated on a nationwide basis by the Butler Education Act (1944). The 1950–1 cohort of eighty-two admissions included no fewer than twenty-six grammar school boys. Products of famous establishments such as Manchester Grammar and the Royal Grammar School, High Wycombe, were prominent amongst them. But that year the College took boys from a total of twenty different grammar schools dotted across England.

There can be no doubt therefore that the Second World War marked a break with the Victorian model. However, the 1950s were hardly a period of social revolution. By the early 1960s the percentage of public school boys in the Jesus intake was up again. And the portrait of Oxbridge provided by the Robbins Committee on Higher Education in 1963 was anything but meritocratic. Long-established patterns of recruitment were still leaving their imprint on the student body. Perhaps the most striking fact was that as late as the early 1960s almost 50 per cent of public school boys attending any university in England and Wales were admitted to either Oxford and Cambridge, and this despite distinctly inferior performance both in A-levels and Tripos exams. After the initial break marked by the Second World War, it was therefore in the 1960s that the real modernisation of Oxbridge admissions began. And this was powerfully reinforced by the introduction in 1962 of compulsory local education authority grants, which made university education in

Britain, for the minority who could gain access to it, more affordable than virtually anywhere else in the developed world. By 1970 out of an intake of 107 students to Jesus, only 9 came from the elite Clarendon group, as compared to 54 from the grammar school system.

School background of course did not translate simply into class background. For the University as a whole it was estimated that, in the early 1970s, roughly one sixth of the male undergraduates could be classified as sons of manual working-class fathers. This was before the era of deindustrialisation. The census of the late 1960s had recorded no fewer than 64 per cent of men of the relevant age group, between the ages of 45 and 59, as manual working class. Across Britain's universities as a whole in the early 1970s, 29 per cent of the student population was drawn from a manual working-class background. Clearly, the state-maintained schools from which Cambridge recruited were themselves highly socially selective. The social complexion of the University and the colleges remained resolutely middle class. However, in the long history of the University, there can be little doubt that the early 1970s were the moment at which the range of class backgrounds represented amongst the undergraduates was at its widest. For a select few and for a space of roughly twenty years, the glittering prize of truly long-range social mobility was genuinely on offer.

In the 1960s the near monopoly that the boys' public schools had established over Oxbridge in the early twentieth century was broken. In the 1970s this was compounded by the rapidly expanding admission of women, who were drawn disproportionately from grammar schools and comprehensives. As a result, across the whole University in 1980 a remarkable 65.8 per cent of new admissions were drawn from the state-maintained sector, a figure that remains out of reach today and, if it were attained, would immediately raise questions about 'political correctness' and declining admissions standards. No such worries were in evidence in the 1970s and with good reason. In academic terms, by the late 1960s fee-paying private schools appeared to be losing the battle with highly selective, state-funded grammar schools. Though the independent schools were still coaching their students to disproportionate numbers of scholarships and exhibitions awarded by means of the seventh-term entrance examinations, this was not matched by equivalent success either at A-levels, or, more importantly, in Triposes. Throughout the 1970s the discrepancy that had caught Robbins's attention in the early 1960s persisted. Grammar school boys performed consistently better than their independent school counterparts, both at A-level and in the Triposes.

Somewhat surprisingly, therefore, it was the 1970s that marked the real heyday of the grammar school boy at Cambridge. But this was not to last. In the early 1980s funding cuts forced a sudden 10 per cent reduction in admissions across the University. At the same time, the University in the early 1980s began finally to feel the full effect of the broader shift in state educational priorities. Rather than aiming to cater to the academic needs of a select few, state secondary schools were from the late 1960s onwards increasingly directed towards delivering a comprehensive education for the entire teenaged population. Though an unintended side effect, the impact on the quality of schooling for the highest performing students was undoubtedly adverse, especially when reorganisation was combined with the severe funding cuts of the early 1980s. As the grammar schools, which had achieved such remarkable success in the Cambridge entrance system, were amalgamated into comprehensives, the number of male applicants from the state-maintained sector, excluding the elite direct grant grammar schools, fell by 28 per cent between 1978 and 1986. After the abolition of their special funding regime in the early 1980s, the direct grant schools, from which Cambridge by the late 1970s was recruiting roughly six hundred men and women per year, defected *en masse* to the independent sector. Meanwhile, after years of decline, the independent sector underwent a minor revolution. The Victorian public schools dramatically raised their academic standards and loosened the social rituals that had encrusted school life for the previous hundred years. The combined effect of these changes

was most evident in the expanding stream of female undergraduates. In 1979 out of 810 women admitted to Cambridge from English and Welsh schools, 640 had been from the state-maintained sector. Ten years later the number of women admitted had risen to 1,063 but the number coming from the state-maintained sector had fallen to 539. Overall, in the space of only five years between 1980 and 1984, the share of students admitted to the University from state-maintained schools fell from 66 to 43 per cent. After two decades of apparently relentless advance, the egalitarian trend of the 1960s and 1970s had been broken. It is barely an exaggeration to say that, twenty years on, we are still coming to terms with the consequences.

It is safe to assume that no Cambridge college was more dramatically affected by this abrupt reversal than was Jesus. By the 1970s the College was behind the University average for state-school admissions, with a share of somewhere between 50 and 55 per cent coming from the state-maintained sector. However, as a result of decades of effort by Admissions Tutors, the College had well-established and mutually beneficial connections with many of the major grammar schools. And these were reflected in a remarkable surge in entrance scholarships and exhibitions gained by Jesus applicants in the 1970s and early 1980s. When women were admitted in 1979, out of thirty-four female students twenty-three came from state-maintained schools. In the early 1980s this

Chapel Court from the
Close, 2006.

network of contacts suddenly collapsed. By 1986, 78 per cent of male students admitted to the College came from independent schools, a figure not seen since the Brideshead era. By contrast, the new comprehensives provided a derisory 13 per cent of the intake. And even allowing for the 'old grammar schools' whose position in the state sector was far from secure, only 26 per cent of the intake could be counted as coming from state-maintained schools.

It was this sudden shock in the early 1980s that turned the admissions question into such a burning issue for the College and indeed for the rest of the University. The tone of the papers produced by the College's Admissions Tutors in the early 1980s may politely be described as angry. A system of state-funded secondary education, which in the post-war decades had for the first time given the College a genuine claim to be providing education on the basis of intellectual merit, was being dismantled. The very identity of the College was at stake. It is no surprise in light of this that by the late 1980s both the student body and the Fellows were riven by painful debates about College 'culture', anxieties which focused in particular on the activities of long-established drinking clubs, whose riotous revival was blamed, rightly or wrongly, on the enormously increased public school intake.

The tensions of the Thatcher era have subsided. However, in retrospect it seems that much of the present-day institutional structure of the College may be traced back to this conflict-ridden period. The system of College discipline was revamped: a 'Dean of College' was appointed and provided with more far-reaching preventative checks on disorderly behaviour, conduct that was likely to prejudice the College's efforts to recruit from the widest possible array of schools. The old tutorial system was dismantled. And the now familiar paraphernalia of admissions procedures was born. The first College open day for potential applicants was held in 1985. The century-old system of entrance scholarships was abolished in pursuit of equity. The entire admissions system was overhauled. Thousands of prospectuses were dispatched to schools across the country. The Target Schools Scheme began its tireless efforts at outreach.

The result of two decades of argument and effort is the College we inhabit today. The figures for admissions from the state sector, though no better than the University average, are back to the highest levels achieved in the College's history. The student body, though it certainly does not mirror the UK population as a whole, or even the population of school students with suitable A-level grades, is drawn from a fairly wide range of family backgrounds. The opening of the College to female applicants has transformed the composition of the student population at least in that respect. Most importantly, perhaps, although the school-leavers applying to the College still come from too narrow a range of backgrounds, there is no doubt that students today are selected on the basis of academic potential alone. In that respect at least, the last two hundred years in the College's history, and the years since 1945 in particular, can be written as a story of progress.

College Servants: The Nineteenth Century

RACHEL WROTH

In the days before electricity, telephone or computer, colleges nevertheless functioned well, thanks to generations of loyal and hard-working servants. Fellows and undergraduates had their meals prepared by the cook and his staff; their bread, butter and beer provided by the Butler; their rooms cleaned by the bed-makers; and other chores done by the gyps, personal servants performing functions today's undergraduates might not recognise, like brushing their clothes and delivering messages. The posts of organ blower (paid £1 a year in 1848), lamp lighter, coal porter, shoeblack and laundress, too, have long since disappeared, but indicate some of the services needed. The Porter was responsible for security and the gardener kept the lawns in good shape. A room called the College Office and secretaries came much later.

At the beginning of the nineteenth century, there were about ten full-time servants at Jesus (excluding those the cook employed in the kitchen) and an unknown number of part-time waiters, bed-makers and laundresses. In the year of Queen Victoria's Golden Jubilee (1887) sixty-eight servants enjoyed a celebration dinner. There followed a 25-year period of substantial fluctuation in the size of the College, but servant numbers remained virtually static. In 1902, when almost all the servants were vaccinated, there were twenty-nine men (including a 'bicycle boy') and thirty-nine women. Vacancies rarely needed to be advertised and were often offered to other family members: a practice which had probably resulted in some overstaffing.

As the tables show, several generations of the Jiggins and Diver families were servants at Jesus. John Thomas

---

Four generations of the Jiggins family

Mary [Mrs] (bed-maker at Jesus, 1812) had family

1 **John** (*c.*1787–1859; bed-maker's help, then gyp at Jesus) had sons

   i **Thomas** (*c.*1825 – after 1851; college servant) and wife Isabella (bed-maker at Trinity) had sons

      I **John Thomas** ['Tom'] (1848–1931; clerk at Trinity, Butler at Jesus)

      II **R. Herbert** (*c.*1850 – after 1895; college servant at Trinity)

   ii **John** (*c.*1830 – after 1861; College servant at Jesus)

2 **Ann** [Miss] (*c.*1790–1857; bed-maker's help, then bed-maker at Jesus)

Probably related were

Anne [Mrs] (*c.*1744–1824; bed-maker and Chapel cleaner at Jesus) and

William Whyman (*c.*1778–1831; gyp at Jesus) and wife Maria (college servant) had son

   i **Thomas Whyman** (*c.*1812–83; shoeblack at Jesus) and wife Louisa (college servant)

Jiggins (1848–1931), Butler for fifty-five years, was the last of a family which had been employed in the College since the eighteenth century.

Opportunities for employment in Cambridge were limited, and anyone who was offered a position in a college counted themselves lucky. Loyal service meant a job for life (critical in the days before retirement pensions), as the tables show, and many senior servants gained considerable status and respect within the town as well as in their college community. Porter Charles Calver was respected as a parish constable, and Butler Richard Rowe (1797–1878) was involved in many charitable works and was an alderman on the borough council, eventually becoming deputy mayor of Cambridge in 1877.

Most Victorian domestic servants lived in their employer's house. College servants had, however, the 'luxury' of having their own homes to which they could return in their hours off duty. Before 1860 over 95 per cent of the Jesus servants lived within half a mile, and the rest had no more than one mile to walk to work. In the period 1861–1920 about two thirds still lived within half a mile. Not all colleges had a room set aside for the servants, but Jesus had a servants' hall as early as 1823.

One of the attractions for young men of working in a college was the offer of sporting facilities. They were allowed to use the cricket ground and there were annual matches between them and the undergraduates who were in residence in the summer. There were football teams and some had a chance to try rowing, under the auspices of the University Servants' Sports Club. The annual cricket matches and rowing races against Oxford college servants were popular events, when a train was chartered

**First Court, Cloisters'
entrance, with a gyp on his
way to the Buttery.**
From a drawing by P. Skelton for
Whymper's *Picturesque Europe, c.*1880

to carry teams and supporters to Oxford and everyone stayed overnight, some dancing late into the evening.

These were the days of oil lamps and candles and the servants were often working in dark and potentially dangerous conditions, especially during the winter months.

The Diver family

Joseph (1775–1859; college servant at St John's, later waterman) had seven sons

  1 **Matthew** (*c.*1801 – after 1845; college porter) had son

    i **Alfred James Day** (*c.*1823–?; cook at Jesus)

  2 **John** (*c.*1802–56; College cook at Jesus) had son

    i **Joseph** (*c.*1831 – after 1881: College cook at Jesus)

  3 **Benjamin** (*c.*1805–54; College porter at Jesus)

  4 **James** (*c.*1808–84; musician and gardener) had son

    i **James** (*c.*1835–1909; college porter, then college butler) had sons

      I **Charles J.** (*c.*1863 – after 1891; clerk – in a college buttery?)
      II **Arthur Bertie** (*c.*1866 – after 1901; college head porter)

  5 **William** (*c.*1810–77; college coal porter)

  6 **Charles** (*c.*1818–1910; cook at Jesus)

  7 **Robert** (*c.*1821 – after 1851; coal porter, waiter and gardener at Jesus)

We get a glimpse of working conditions in 1797 when the College allowed Butler Pearson Styles (*c*.1761–1806) £3 a year for coal in the buttery, 'he not being expected to keep fires there' between 1 May and 1 November. The Hall and the kitchen may have been the first places to have gas installed, and in 1854 all the staircases were fitted with gas lighting. Each room (excluding the bedrooms) had an open fire and there was a bunker for coal or peat on most landings. The coal porters carried sacks upstairs and the bed-makers had to clean out dirty grates and carry the ashes away to the back yard. There was no internal sanitation or piped water: chamber pots were in all bedrooms, a large 'saucer' bath was stored under each bed, and there was a washstand with jug and basin. Kitchen servants and bed-makers spent many hours filling water containers and carrying them up and down stairs.

The working lives of the shoeblacks must have been particularly monotonous, but promotions occurred – Henry Stearn(e) (*c*.1851–1938), who started as a shoeblack, served as a porter from 1884 to 1922; and Herbert Austin Wheaton (*c*.1866–1909; known as 'Bottles'), after a few years as a boy chorister at Jesus, worked successively as buttery assistant, under porter, gyp and waiter in Hall. He later became Chapel Clerk, earning an annual wage of £38. Some individuals had a variety of tasks. One of the under gardeners had to wind up the clock in the Chapel tower each week. Access was by the roof and up a ladder about 25 feet high to a window, which must have been precarious in windy or icy weather. Selected porters were appointed University 'Bulldogs', accompanying the Proctors on their nocturnal perambulations around the town, apprehending not only undergraduates who were misbehaving but also 'street walkers'. As well as sharing gate duties, the under porters had to sweep the courts, keep oil lamps cleaned and filled, and wait in Hall, where some would act as carvers (roast joints were generally served every day). Each summer they beat the carpets and cleaned windows, and one was paid annually from 1851 until 1855 for 'filling the cisterns'. For almost fifty years William Henry Meek (*c*.1856–1933) was employed as a gyp, Chapel Clerk and assistant Fellows' Butler, receiving occasional cash payments of a few shillings for extra duties like serving at Boat Club dinners.

For most of the nineteenth century there were no fixed wages, and servants were paid through a variety of charges and from fees. For example, if pensioners used College knives in their own rooms, the Porter could charge 2d per dozen for cleaning them and the Butler made a similar charge for cleaning silver forks and spoons. In 1815 Anne Jiggins received only £6 a year as a bed-maker but supplemented this by 10s 6d a quarter for cleaning the Chapel and 10s for washing surplices. A century later, in 1911, bed-makers were being paid about £30 a year and it became popular for them to spend the summer vacation,

when there were few residents in College, working in one of the many guest houses on the east coast. In 1846 the Porter was paid 10s 'for destroying rats', and in 1855 his accounts show that his income included separate payments from the Tutor, the Steward, the Bursar and Fellows (private bills) totalling £215, and 'remnants' (jobs like delivering letters, window cleaning and certain fines from undergraduates) totalling £108. Out of this, the Porter paid the wages of the under porter, the coal porter, the hall waiters, the chimney sweep, and 'men for cleaning Hall and Cloysters'. He was also reimbursed for postage stamps and parcels, sedge (and freight and cartage thereof), oil for the Hall and staircase lamps, newspapers (*The Times* and the *Cambridge Chronicle*, for the Fellows), brushes, black lead, soap, cleaning cloths, and so on giving him an income of £156 for the year. In 1871 the wage structure was rationalised, and the Porter received £111 and the under porter £89. In 1901 the Head Porter's wages were only £100 a year, but additional payments were reintroduced 'for cyclostyle work, fellows news, etc'.

To take another name from this list: William Bell (*c*.1879 – after 1946), who started working in College as a boy of only 15, stayed for fifty-two years, apart from his period of military service. As a buttery boy, he had tasks like cutting the butter into pieces for commons, making toast, cleaning silver, laying the High Table, and lighting the fire in the Combination Room. A year later he was accused of 'purloining meat' and was 'solemnly warned' by the Master. As a gyp and waiter in Hall, he got to know the undergraduates on his staircase well, and keenly followed their subsequent careers. He was eventually trusted sufficiently to be put in charge of the Combination Room and served there for thirty-seven years.

Undergraduate's keeping room, Carpenter building, *c*.1895.

Cooks

The college cook was not a servant like the others. He was an 'independent contractor', running his own business in the College kitchens, so few records have survived about the staff he employed. Handsome profits could be made: few Fellows ever shopped for food items, they accepted the prices he set for the meals he provided. Some cooks built up small fortunes and rose to become property owners and members of the 'gentleman' class in Cambridge society. John Willis (c.1783–1830) left the impressive sum of £4,000; his will mentions property in All Saints' parish and four houses in Jesus Lane. John Diver (c.1802–56) left £3,000, while in 1899 Samuel Kettle's estate was valued at almost £8,000 (he had certainly benefited from the great increase in the number of undergraduates under the two Morgans and might well have been the wealthiest man in the College).

College bill, Michaelmas term 1852, with details of sums due to College servants.

In 1824, following complaints about his bills, John Willis agreed to deliver a weekly account to each gentleman, according to a form 'printed and fairly filled up', and to pay a fine of one guinea to the Addenbrooke's Hospital fund for every omission in delivery or inaccuracy found. He was paid £1 a quarter for furnishing plates and dishes for the pensioners' table (it was common for college cooks to own these items and to charge the colleges for using them). When Willis died, all the cooking utensils and serving dishes belonged to him and not to the College, and had been left to his widow Mary who, as one of the Fellows wrote, 'for a considerable time past she has had the chief management of the kitchen … has worked very hard and has given satisfaction … she is very careful and industrious in addition to being skilful as a cook'. He recommended that she be appointed for a year, with help in money matters and in 'applying to the young men for settlement of their accounts'. She was not the first widow of a cook to succeed her husband, though she may have been the first at Jesus, and she stayed in charge for about eight years. She was followed by John Diver (c.1802–56), who had probably been taken on by John Willis. He would have been involved in boiling twelve joints of meat and roasting thirty-two joints for the College's contribution to the feast for 15,000 poor people on Parker's Piece celebrating Queen Victoria's coronation in 1838. In 1844 he sued James Orchard Halliwell, a Scholar who had hosted frequent breakfast and dinner parties in his rooms and then left after only five terms (he soon married an heiress), for non-payment of his account (£53 was owing, equivalent to about half the annual income of a college porter).

Joseph Diver became cook on his father's death. A bachelor and in his early thirties, he began the tradition of annual parties for College staff. In the summer of 1871 he prepared a dinner for them, cooking 56 lb of meat (roast beef and boiled mutton), Yorkshire puddings and vegetables, followed by fruit tarts, plum puddings and sauce. By the age of 49 he was 'Retired Chef de Cuisine' living in Lancashire. His successor, Samuel H. Kettle (c.1833–99), was the last of the cooks who ran the kitchens as their own business. In June 1881 he prepared a picnic, hired a boat and a band of musicians for a servants' 'water party'. This was a day trip, probably to Clayhithe, and was the fashionable annual treat which several colleges organised, until the end of the century. When his reign ended in 1897 the system changed. With impressive testimonials from the Provost of King's, William Charles Vinsen (c.1864–1940) took Kettle's place as an employee on a fixed wage and later became the first Kitchen Manager, a post he held until 1933.

Butlers

The Butler looked after the buttery, the wine cellar, and the College silver. For the Commencement Dinner in 1815 Butler Richard Brett was paid £7 9s 6d for supplying bread, cheese, butter, ale, porter (a dark, bitterish beer), small (a weak beer), port wine, sherry, tea and coffee (and for the servants, ale, bread and cheese). The Butler paid the laundress 3s (for tablecloths and napkins) and the scullion 2s 6d (for washing up and boiling kettles). In 1828 he was paid 1s a quarter for snuff (for the Fellows, presumably) and £1 a quarter for cleaning the silver, not only items used on High Table, but also those used by the pensioners.

Some of the butlers, like the cooks, were able to profit from their buttery businesses. In 1813, when William Brett died suddenly leaving a widow and seven children, his estate was valued at £600. Richard Brett (*c.*1784 – after 1851), who was probably his nephew, succeeded him, and the College, sympathetic to the plight of William's widow, required him 'From his profits … [to] make an allowance to Mrs Brett, widow of the late William Brett, butler, £30 p.a. for the first ten years … after that of £20 p.a. for the remainder of Mrs Brett's life, to be paid quarterly, to cease should she again marry.'

Jesse Batchelor (*c.*1818–80) received a stipend of £70 but his income was believed to be greater than £450 a year, mostly derived from buttery profits. Arthur Gray remembered him as 'a prosperous tradesman, penurious and exacting. In my freshman term he informed me that he was not allowed to provide me with other buttery commodities unless I took the ordinary commons from his shop – an interpretation of the law which, I think, was not in the articles of his agreement with the authorities'. He left £3,000, as had Butler Richard Rowe in 1879.

Rowe was the most remarkable of college servants. His mother died when he was young and his father was imprisoned for debt. To raise money to get his father out of prison, he sold vegetables from his grandfather's garden, but realised that he could exploit his handwriting skills to earn more by writing out five hundred lines of Ovid for a Fellow Commoner at Jesus. He was taken on as private secretary to the Tutor, William Hustler, who polished up his Latin, and he became expert at proof reading. As secretary to Romilly, the University Registrary, he transcribed the University's Grace Books in his neat and regular copperplate. He then worked for a time at the University Library, but it was unheated in winter and his health was permanently injured by bronchitis. From this unlikely background he was appointed Butler at Jesus in 1840 and served until 1859 when, his health having further deteriorated, he resigned in favour of his son.

In August 1843, while he was away from Cambridge, his wife discovered there had been a burglary in the buttery. An extensive amount of plate had been taken from unlocked cupboards: silver valued at £250 of which £25 worth belonged to the Butler – some of the spoons were marked with his predecessor's name (Brett). 'Young Rowe', his son, must have worked often with his father, because he was able from memory to furnish the police with a list of the missing articles. It seemed that a duplicate key to the buttery door had been made, and the thieves had locked the door after them. Naturally, an inside job was suspected. Robert Diver, coal porter and waiter, was charged, but no evidence was produced and he was discharged. This event must have hit Rowe hard, and by 1847 he had become a member of the Association for the Prosecution of Felons and Thieves, a group of tradesmen, college butlers and others who shared information about security matters.

By 1873 the practice of independent tradesmen operating inside the colleges had been stopped and John Thomas

The Hall

Engraving by Celia Murray, *c.*1895

Jiggins (1848–1931), known as Tom, butler's clerk at Trinity, was appointed to succeed Batchelor, and 'as he was an excellent book-keeper the business became a source of considerable profit in College finance'. In 1897 he was suspended for several weeks because of 'certain indiscretions in his relations with the other college servants', and the rather pathetically small sum of 4s 6d from his petty cash was paid to Mrs Newman, a bed-maker's help, who was obliged to retire. He was reinstated and remained for many more years.

Porters

The Porter was responsible for security, for discipline in Hall and for extinguishing unattended fires in College rooms. He was also responsible (in the days before the invention of stainless steel) for the knives for the pensioners, and he had to show them, properly cleaned, to the Steward every quarter day.

In several colleges the porter and his family actually lived in the Porters' Lodge, but not at Jesus: Benjamin Diver (*c.*1805–54) and his family lived in Jesus Lane. In 1839 he was accused of stealing from the buttery, but – thanks to his brother John, the cook, and the College's solicitor – he was found innocent and received damages of 10s.

In 1855 the Porter and one under porter shared the gate duties: the Porter had shifts totalling 65¼ hours and three overnight periods each week, and the under porter covered the rest. It was important for undergraduates to keep on good terms with the Porter. Arthur Gray recalled Edmund Adson (*c.*1814–83): 'He ruled in the porter's lodge – an austere man of few words and those comminatory. His professional high hat was a halo of authority and awe. Well I remember his pained and painful address to me when, returning late from the river, I had the audacity to present myself at 5.30 dinner instead of the 4.30 meal legally appointed for me.' In 1871:

the great man's career came to an abrupt end in the Long Vacation. Summoned to the presence of one of the two resident Fellows on some question of dereliction of duty he took the opportunity of imparting to him a confidential

statement regarding the general estimate of that gentleman's character. 'The Fellows 'ate yer, the undergradjats detest yer, and the servants loathe yer.' The injured Fellow summoned the other to an immediate meeting in the Fellows' Garden, and by their unanimous verdict Adson was dismissed.

James Hoppett (*c.*1860–1929), who was Head Porter from 1895 to 1928, was the son of Charles, the well-known 'Gentleman Hoppett' whose tall figure and gracious manners were familiar to generations of Trinity men when he was head porter there, and James would have known well what the job entailed. His disciplinary duties included reporting to the Tutor those students who disturbed the quiet of the College during the night, and any who had come in after 10 p.m. Anyone who brought a dog within the precincts, or smoked in the courts, was also reported. And the Head Porter was 'to be always present when the Undergraduates are dining in Hall: when there, to exercise a general supervision of the waiters, and to report at once … any neglect of decorum which may occur'. He was one of the College Servants' best batsmen.

Gardeners, messengers, bed-makers, laundresses and scullions
In 1875 there was one gardener responsible mainly for the Fellows' Garden, 'the remainder keeping in order the courts and other gardens'. There were stables where the

Lives of College service

Mrs Elizabeth Gray (*c.*1865–1947)	Bed-maker	56 years
John Thomas Jiggins (1848–1931)	Butler	55 years
William Bell (*c.*1879 – after 1946)	Gyp and Combination Room man	52 years
Frederick Gatward (*c.*1869–1936)	Kitchen porter, gardener and Chapel Clerk	50 years
William Henry Meek (*c.*1856–1933)	Gyp, waiter and Chapel Clerk	almost 50 years
John Jiggins (*c.*1787–1859)	Gyp	45 years
Miss Ann Jiggins (*c.*1790–1857)	Bed-maker	over 40 years
Thomas Whyman Jiggins (*c.*1812–83)	Shoeblack	over 40 years
Alfred George Parsons (1855–1924)	Boatman	over 40 years
Moses Waters (*c.*1820–97)	Groundsman/gardener	over 40 years
Mrs Mary Langton (before 1790–1849)	Scullion	40 years
Thomas Hones (*c.*1863–1938)	Messenger and porter	38 years
Sidney Horspool (*c.*1868–1927)	Chief clerk	37 years
Charles Calver (*c.*1838–1908)	Porter and Head Porter	over 36 years
Henry Stearn(e) (*c.*1851–1938)	Shoeblack and porter	36 years
William Charles Vinsen (*c.*1864–1940)	Head cook and Kitchen Manager	36 years
Elijah Frisby (*c.*1815–84)	Gyp and Chapel Clerk	35 years
John Foster (*c.*1827–78)	Buttery assistant, gyp, porter and Head Porter	34 years
James Hoppett (*c.*1860–1929)	Head Porter	32 years
George Unwin (*c.*1865–1940)	Under gardener	over 30 years

College staff, 1987. The tall figure in the second row is Erik Friman who continued in charge of the College's wine cellar until shortly before his death, aged 90, in 2001.

gardener kept a horse (used to pull heavy rollers and lawn mowers). Special boots were put on to the horse's feet so that the lawns were not churned up; most animals resented having those put on and were inclined to kick! Moses Waters (*c*.1820–97) was a groom before he joined Jesus as a gardener and groundsman and that previous experience would have been invaluable. According to Gray, it was not only horses he could deal with: 'he controlled the Dean's unruly pack of collie dogs'. Gray remembered:

[his] mild, patient, lovable … soft smile, slow speech and faithful duty … bulky frame treading down the new laid turf. He began life as a stable lad at Newmarket, 'fust thing I recklets is strokin' the orses' legs', was coachman to the Bishop of Peterborough and used to drive him to the House of Lords … Where is his tombstone … with perchance some note of his long service in Jesus? He would have loved to lie under the cricket pitch, with no mound above to mar the beautiful level of the sward that was his creation, and to tend which was the happiness of his simple life.

Both Moses's sons, James (*c*.1844 – after 1871; known as 'Aaron') and Charles (*c*.1845–89) ('Little Aaron') were employed in the College, Charles as a waiter and messenger: 'The College had its own post office in the porter's lodge, and distributed letters in the town. There was a College postal stamp – it must be a rarity now.' Little Aaron had to deliver the letters, 'but as he could not read, it was the porter's business to inform him of the address on each letter'.

It is often said rather unkindly that bed-makers were always old, married and ugly. Of the twenty-two bed-makers identified as working at Jesus during the nineteenth century, only two were unmarried and both were already known in the College, having worked as 'bed-maker's helps' with their mothers, a common practice. By and large, the bed-makers were aged over 40, though Mrs Elizabeth Gray (nee Peck; *c*.1865–1947) was only 24 when she started as a 'help' on staircase 5 in Chapel Court (she stayed for almost sixty years), and Mrs Naomi Large (*c*.1862–1922) was only 25, with three young children to look after. It would have been easy to pop home during the day to attend to their children, and in the vacations only those working for the Fellows went into College. Susannah Hutt (*c*.1814–96) was widowed at the age of 35 with three small children and three nieces and nephews to care for. She worked, first probably as a bed-maker, and then moved from Park Street to Jesus Lane where for over twenty years she was a lodging-house keeper and looked after Jesus undergraduates. Another young widow with six children was bed-maker Esther Purkis (nee Duce; *c.*1828–1908). She eventually retired in 1898 with a pension of 6s a week. When she died, her daughter Agnes Purkis (*c.*1859 – after 1911) inherited not only £400 but also her place as bed-maker. Her wages in 1911 were £9 a term.

A bed-maker must have relied heavily on perks. No bed-maker was allowed to carry out of College any coals or cinders, under pain of dismissal (the Porter had to enforce this regulation), but she could take home left-over commons – the bread, butter and milk she had brought from the buttery every morning for the undergraduates on her staircase – and other uneaten food from students' rooms, and expected a generous tip from each of 'her men' at the end of each term.

There was a 'hall sempstress' who in 1868 was paid £26 7s 2d for tablecloths, and a 'hall laundress' who washed and ironed them. In 1824 she received £7 a quarter; this had risen by 1871 to £56 a year. As College sempstress in 1815, Mary Manser was paid a total of £3 7s 6d

from sixteen undergraduates for such items as bed linen, counterpane, sofa cover, curtains, surplice, dressing gown and shooting jacket. Jane Townsend (nee Thorp; *c.*1748–1832) was another laundress and in 1815 she was paid £2 8s 6d for one term's washing for fourteen undergraduates (an average of 3s 6d per undergraduate).

> The duties of the scullion in 1849 were listed as:
> To light the fires and get the kitchen clean by 8 a.m.
> To keep all the plates, dishes, stewpans, kettles, etc. clean and take them to their proper places. To attend all the fires. To pluck all wild fowl, game, etc. for which they receive the feathers. To dress the vegetables and dish them up, and to peel potatoes. To attend Hall. To clean the water plates for dinner, fill and empty them, likewise the tin and copper ware.

The position was not always filled by a woman, but the only named scullion found mentioned in the archives was Mrs Langton (before 1790 to 1849). In 1830 she was paid an extra 2d per week for cleaning and taking care of the water plates. These were placed in the Hall empty and with the covers off, at least fifteen minutes before the time of dinner, and were then filled with boiling water. The serving plates could then be put onto these to keep the food warm. We can only speculate on what she would have thought of the equipment in the College's new cafeteria.

(Top right) 'Happy Henries':
bedmakers' Numatic
sweepers marshalled in
Chapel Court for their
annual maintenance check.
Bill Saslaw, 2001

(Below) 'Caff': Hall cafeteria,
2006.

Food and Drink

MARY LAVEN

*E*cce quam bonum et quam iucundum fratres habitare in *unum* (Behold how good and how joyful it is for brothers to live together in unity). These words from Psalm 133 are incised in gold letters in the Hall, emphasising the fact that living together has always meant eating together. The earliest statutes of the College (1515–16) provided for the employment of a 'cook, honest and provident', paid 26s 8d annually, with a scullion to assist him, paid 13s 4d. In addition, one Fellow was to act as Senescal, with 'knowledge and supervision in the purchase, preparation and laying out of all victuals'. Food for Master and Fellows was not to cost more than 14d a week, for 'boys and other Scholars' 8d; but things improved on 'festival days' and at Christmas everyone got to feast on boar. Dining in Hall was obligatory for all – a quasi-monastic occasion with grace and Bible readings, followed by modest conversation (during which nobody was to be 'noisy, wordy, quarrelsome or abusive'). Anyone who dared to speak in any language other than Latin was to be rebuked 'with moderation', and that rebuke was to be received by the offender 'with patience and mutual charity'. College members were also warned to 'abstain from tippling and drunkenness'.

But living together has never been without its tensions, and by the early seventeenth century it appears that the Master, Roger Andrewes, had not dined in Hall for seven years. The enthusiasm of Fellows for the commensal ideal also seems to have waned, and in 1632 the Visitor, Dr White, had to use his powers to coerce them into eating together again. The difficulty of appointing satisfactory cooks was the burden of an entry in the diary of Dr John Worthington for 1651, shortly after he had been appointed Master. Following the death of Reuben Fitches, the Fellows of Jesus had to choose between the under cook, John Cole ('slovenly, no creditable person, & ... observed to fuddle'), Robert Bates of Emmanuel (Worthington's former college), 'a sottish fellow &

slovenly, as devoid of honesty, as skill' and 'One Jordan', who 'had been a cook in London, & served under a lady, but for the present did cut tobacco for Mr. Lawrence'. Worthington, secretly worried 'lest one that deals in tobacco, coming to the College, might not be some temptation to the scholars, to that vanity', went on a mission to rescue Bates's reputation from unjust scandal, and eventually got him appointed.

Soon after the Restoration there was a new danger on the horizon. As a young man at Jesus, the Greek scholar, arachnophile and later master of Trinity, John North, became in the 1660s a frequenter of Cambridge's only coffee-house, with its single news-sheet. Some years later, his younger brother reported that 'the case is [now] much altered, for it is become a custom after chapel to repair to one or other of the coffee-houses (for there are divers), where hours are spent in talking, and less profitable reading of newspapers, of which swarms are continually supplied from London'. The scholars, Roger North complained, were 'so entête with news ... that they neglect all for it'. And this was disastrous, 'for who can apply close to a subject with his head full of the din of a coffee-house?'

It was drink, rather than caffeine and news, that was intoxicating the students of the mid-nineteenth century. Undergraduates were drinking beer at breakfast, lunch and dinner, downing some more 'with the evening pipe'. Colleges had their own brew houses which provided Strong Ale, Bitter, and Small Beer or 'Swipes'. After dinner (held at 4.30), your tutor might command you to come to a 'Wine', in which decanters of port, sherry, claret and burgundy did the rounds. These delights must have taken students' minds off the food, which in this period was generating horrified protests at a number of colleges. A student at Trinity complained to *The Times* in 1863, having been served 'a dinner (?) I should have been ashamed to have given my servant ... Why should gross injustice be done to 500 undergraduates, for the sake of one cook?' At Sidney Sussex in 1868 the undergraduates heard the grace and then 'left the hall in a body and dined together at an hotel'. Arthur Gray, remembering his undergraduate years at Jesus in the 1870s, claimed that Hall was 'deadly cold', that 'bleeding bullocks' hearts' were served twice weekly, and that 'frozen gravy and caterpillars supplied with the vegetables were principal constituents in our diet'. He was a signatory to a petition of 1871 complaining to the Steward about the inferiority and cost of meals, and hoping that the 'irresponsible cook' to whom the College had contracted out the catering could be replaced by a College servant (like that envisaged in the original statutes). The petition was apparently quelled by instituting the 'entrée' (an extra course between the fish and the roast) – such things as 'beefsteak pie and haricot mutton'.

The College kitchen, 2003. It is in the same place as the Nunnery's.

In 1897 the College finally listened to the Jamie Olivers among its undergraduate body and put an end to contract catering. At the same time, it overhauled the kitchens – which had not moved since the days of the nunnery – and replaced the enormous fireplaces and 10-foot spits with 'ignoble gas ovens'. No one, recalled a nostalgist of 1934, 'could fail to regret the passing of the spitted joints and turkeys, revolving solemnly to the sound of gravy hissing as it filled the trays below, though one might readily dispense with the pervasive smell, and

above all the (literally grilling) heat'. But a number of new developments were on the horizon. In 1929 a committee packed with colourfully named undergraduates like Pistol Byron and Boulay Lance was celebrating its 'greatest triumph ... the introduction of a cheap and good lunch in Hall, which has been a crying need for a long time'. Breakfast in Hall would have to wait until the Second World War, although it was already served to members of the Boat Club. The modern world of College dining was taking shape.

Despite these improvements, complaints about Hall were perennial. In 1934, for example, a long letter to *Chanticlere* from 'A Jesus Man' complained of cold vegetables and insufficiently ceremonious service. 'I suggest that the waiters be instructed to behave with more dignity; that they should not whisk our plates from beneath our noses almost before we have finished with them; that they should not, above all, pointedly remove our glasses from us when we have finished eating as if to say, "Go on; get out."' The staff was clearly serving up the veg long in advance of dinner so as to get it onto the tables the second that grace was read. 'I am told by my sisters', continued our indignant Jesus Man, 'that vegetables are difficult to keep hot under the most favourable conditions'; covers for the dishes might help in this respect. One last moan: 'the tables are covered with a thick sludge of bees-wax which adheres to one's bread'. Yet 'for all our protests and grumblings there are not more than two or three Halls in Cambridge which are consistently better than our Hall at Jesus'.

The next major revolution in Jesus dining came in 1977 in the wake of the 'Glazebrook Report', an investigation of kitchen finances conducted by three Fellows and one undergraduate. The result was the invention of 'Caff', serving breakfast, lunch and dinner daily. Students paid cost price for the food, and labour was financed through the Kitchen Fixed Charge. 'Formal Hall' became the optional affair that it remains today, and early reports commented with pleasure on the popularity of the changes.

Alongside the communal dining in Hall ran the more select gatherings of the dining clubs, societies and sports teams. The Natives, comprising expatriates from the big-name public schools, was founded in 1877 and specialised in the consumption of oysters. Their menu cards, in the shape of flagrantly pink oysters, trailing coloured ribbons, were fantastic exercises in high camp. The menu in 1926 proposed nine courses, beginning with *huîtres au naturel* and ending with *huîtres à la Colbert*. The Rugby Club has always attracted some of the most refined and delicate spirits of the College. Some 1929 menus surviving in the Archives preserve their drunken banter in the form of extensive marginal annotation. 'I'm pissed as a

Fellows' and Graduate Students' Dinner, 2005.

fart but cheerio', 'In out! in out! till you come old boy', 'Work it up your dirt box old boy', 'Balls, old chap, are useful', 'Tiger, my darling, poker is the game'. (Other entries are unquotable.) The menus of the Roosters and the Boat Club are also festooned with raucous annotations, but without the obscenities.

If behaviour at dinner could be rowdy, the contents of the menus aspired to be genteel. The early twentieth century was the heyday of the fabricated French dish; Edwardian menu cards for successive Audit Feasts advertise *Croûte à la Bengal*, *Croûte à la Braunschweig* and *Croûte à la Burlington*. Dishes were highly subject to the vagaries of fashion. The Audit Feast of 1908 offered *Bombe à la Massey Stanley*, named after a family of minor aristocrats, but things had hotted up by 1913, when Fellows at the Rustat Dinner enjoyed *Fraises Sarah Bernhardt* – with the vanilla ice-cream, Grand Marnier and pineapple purée favoured by the celebrated actress. By 1926 these had given way to *Poires Melba*, named after the Australian opera singer Dame Nellie Melba. Two weeks before the assassination of the Archduke Franz Ferdinand, diners at June 1914's May Ball were partaking of *Filets de Sole en Aspic à la Venitienne*, *Galantine de Dindon à la Financière* and *Gelée à la Prince de Galles*.

It was the Second World War, however, that would put such Frenchified delicacies on ice. The Natives continued to produce their oyster-shaped menu cards, but they found themselves sorely lacking in crustacea. In a far cry from their earlier nine-course glories, they were reduced in 1943 to *Pôtage Windsor*, *Perdreau Rôti* (roast partridge) and *Pouding de Noël*. The rest of the population, clutching their ration-books, might not have been moved to pity by this spectacle of decline. Meanwhile at High Table the Fellows were (according to Freddie Brittain's diary entries) shaking their heads:

At dinner Q [Sir Arthur Quiller-Couch] cursed the carrots in the soup and said, 'Everything we get is infected with carrots.' … The Dean said: 'Why do they call this stuff strawberry fool? There isn't a drop of cream in it.'… Jam roly-poly in Hall at which Raby, Alan Percival and I expressed pleasure. The Dean said, 'It would be better if it wasn't made with mouldy flour.'

By 1941 the English dons were hallucinating about food: 'Tillyard said he had a curious dream last night. He went into a church and was surprised to see Q pushing faggots under the font in which he was making a big stew.' Worse was to come. In 1942 the bursarial committee proposed rationing the supply of wine to Fellows; they were not to be allowed more than eighteen bottles each per term, and the weekly issue was not to exceed three bottles. The following year the Fellows' termly allowance was restricted to six bottles, and it was agreed that 'Port, not exceeding in amount one dozen each term', could be 'supplied to undergraduates for use on special occasions at the discretion of the Senior Tutor'. Such largesse would have been undreamt of outside College walls.

Today, eating and drinking continue to define the structure of social life in College, articulating the nuances of status and moulding time into distinctive and highly coloured units. For all the changes that have taken place over the years, College dining is a thoroughly conservative affair, geared up to preserve traditions and to foster the illusion of a deep continuity with the past. Yet, despite the litany of complaint and dissatisfaction that inevitably attends them, occasions for eating and drinking can also be occasions for the exchange of ideas and the fostering of intellectual community. A college (like an army, but in contrast with most corporate institutions of the twenty-first century) still marches on its stomach.

The College Grace

Before dinner: Oculi omnium in te aspiciunt et in te spirant, Deus. Tu das illis escam tempore opportuno, Aperis tu manus, et imples omne animal benedictione tua. Benedic nobis, Domine, et omnibus tuis donis, quae ex larga liberalitate tua sumpturi sumus, per Jesum Christum Dominum nostrum. Deus est caritas. Qui manet in caritate manet in Deo et Deus in illo. Sit Deus in nobis, et nos maneamus in illo.

The eyes of all look towards you and trust in you, O God. You give them food in due season. You open your hands and fill every living thing with your blessing. Bless us, O Lord, and all your gifts, which through your great generosity we are about to receive, through Jesus Christ our Lord. God is love. He who abides in love abides in God and God in him. May God be in us and may we abide in him.

After dinner: Laus Deo *Praise be to God*; Deo gratias *Thanks be to God.*

The Boat Club

CHRISTOPHER McDOUALL and DAVID WOOTTON

The Jesus College Boat Club is a unique part of a unique College. The College's uniqueness is in part attributable to its location, geographically slightly off the beaten track: it has been said that 'Americans with a complete week in Europe had been known to miss it'. And the Jesus Boat Club may be unique amongst Cambridge boat clubs in part because Jesus is the only college which is within sight of its own boathouse. Members of the Boat Club certainly find themselves in a unique culture within the College.

The club's history down the generations has been recorded in three volumes, published in 1928, in 1962 and in 1994 (details in Further Reading, page 309). They are labours of love which combine the best facets of institutional history, both telling a story and being works of reference, providing detailed almanacs of College crews and individual Jesuans. Elsewhere in this book (page 156), J.A. Mangan has traced the relationship between the College's great expansion in the last thirty years of the nineteenth century and the fortunes of its Boat Club and other sportsmen. We offer here something different: a portrait of what has made the Jesus Boat Club distinctive, both from other sports and societies and from other college boat clubs, with an impression of the part it has played in the life of the College. We try to convey what it is like to be a member (which both your authors do know) and what it is like looked at from outside (which they do not). When one of them first arrived at Jesus and was collecting his key from the Porters' Lodge, he was greeted with 'I gather you are going to be a boatman, Sir?' This was Mr West, then Head Porter; it was obvious what the right answer was.

But first, inevitably, a little history

The club was founded in 1827. Jesus was in the first group of colleges to take up organised rowing. The first races between colleges rowed that year and following the

bumping model, allegedly borrowed from Oxford, involved Trinity and St John's, as well as Jesus, with Caius being the next college to take part. Jesus was still very small, and its annual record on the river was for long undistinguished; in fact nothing was won until 1872. In one year the first boat was as low as twenty-ninth on the river and in 1847 the College could put out no May Boat at all.

From the first winning of a University event in 1872, however, a more successful period followed, culminating in the eleven consecutive years' headship of the May races from 1875 to 1885 inclusive, during which the Grand Challenge Cup at Henley was won twice and the Ladies' Plate five times. The JCBC produced seventeen Blues, four in the Boat Race crew in four of those years and five in one year. This ten-year headship, as it is referred to despite having lasted for eleven, gave rise to one of those

Head of the River for the eighth successive year: the First VIII, May 1882.

unwritten conventions which appear to come from nowhere but then are applied absolutely: a college which is Head of the Mays for five consecutive years is entitled to install a weather vane on the roof of its boat-house, while a ten-year consecutive headship earns a clock tower. Other colleges may have a weather vane but only Jesus has a clock tower – with the preceding weather vane, of course, on top.

The years following 1872 were an age of brothers: Steve Fairbairn, to whom we shall return, rowed in six of those head crews, being one of five Fairbairn brothers and one of twelve members of the Fairbairn family to row in the Jesus first boat, while there were three Armytage brothers who did so and, like the Fairbairns, were Australian. It was also an age when one could row for the College for

Jesus First Lent Boat

The first boat house by W.M. Fawcett (1868) (built 1883, destroyed by fire 1932) with the First VIII, Lent 1891.

as long as one liked, so long, it appears, as one had at some stage been connected with it. While H.A. Morgan was Tutor, for example, he rowed in the May Boat for ten consecutive years. He became Master in 1886, just – as it happened – at the start of the decline in the club's fortunes. The Master throughout the eleven-year headship, G.E. Corrie, had not been so enthusiastic: 'you must not ask me for support to rowing, an occupation to which I can give no countenance, owing to the bedizened women on the bank'.

The club was in the doldrums until 1904, when Steve Fairbairn returned to Cambridge, where he spent much of his time coaching Jesus until his death at the age of 75 in 1938. The club was most successful in the years just before the First World War, in the late 1920s and

throughout the 1930s. The last period produced a great number of the characters with whom later generations have come to associate the Boat Club.

The club again did well in the late 1940s and throughout the 1950s. Success, however, became more intermittent during the '60s and early '70s, and tough competition from other colleges, and time pressures on students, have taken their toll in ensuing years. The Jesus men were Head of the Mays in 1972 and of the Lents in 1974. The women have fared better: since they arrived in 1979 they have been Head of the Mays five times and of the Lents three times. They won thirty-five sets of oars in their first fifteen years. And the club is now in very good heart and moving very much in the right direction. More people now row than ever before.

A few statistics

The bare statistics of the club's achievements are indeed remarkable. Head of the Mays thirty-five times. Head of the Lents forty-three times. More than 380 Jesus crews have 'won their oars' for making four bumps or more in Lents or Mays or winning other University events. The Fairbairn Cup has been won 37 times, as have been 117 other University events. The Head of the River Race on the Tideway in London has been won three times. At Henley twenty-seven trophies have been won, including the top event, the Grand, three times. And there has been the kind of occurrence beloved of sports statisticians and quiz-setters: one Jesuan winning two events at Henley in the same year, one on bow side and one on stroke side. Collectors of matters in the 'not many people know that' category may wish to note that the record time by a Jesus crew at Henley – 6 minutes 38 seconds – involved a crew which lost its race. Strength in depth has been a strong feature of the club. The second boat was in the first division in the Mays for fifty years until the mid-1960s and, when it was third on the river, the University felt it necessary to change the rules to levy a penalty should one boat bump another from the same college, for fear that the Jesus second boat would go second and enable Jesus to retain the headship permanently by simply allowing the first and second boats to bump each other into eternity. In both Lents and Mays at some time in the past the Jesus second boat has bumped the first boat of all other colleges.

At University level the JCBC has more than made its contribution: 174 Blues, 38 Goldie and Blondie and 20 lightweights. Twenty-one CUBC and CUWBC presidents – including uniquely, in 2002, both men's and women's presidents – though as it happens they both lost their respective races. In 1993 nine Jesus students rowed for University crews and Cambridge won all six races against Oxford: a great achievement celebrated by a dinner given by the Master for those involved. Internationally, Jesus has made its mark: twenty Jesuans have rowed for Great Britain: two World Champions, one Empire Games gold medal, four Olympic silver medals, four silver and three bronze world or European championship medals, one Commonwealth Games bronze medal.

People and personalities

Statistics, however magnificent, do not convey an impression of what the club is like. The most dominant individual has been Steve Fairbairn, who coached the Jesus boats from 1904 to 1938. Once, when asked why he had come to Jesus, he replied that until he arrived in Cambridge as an undergraduate he did not know that there were any other colleges. A large man both physically and in personality, he was a prolific writer on rowing, and from his writings a strong sense of self-belief clearly emanates. His coaching methods, which resulted in what was erroneously known as the Fairbairn style, were pioneering and highly controversial. He rebelled against what he called orthodoxy, which stressed the importance of going through particular motions with the body regardless of the effect on the boat's speed. Steve espoused the natural and easy way to move the boat. He saw the rowing stroke as an endless chain movement and sought to express his views in short, if ungrammatical, sentiments: 'spring and draw, loose and easy, lazy and long'; 'if you can't do it easy [*sic.*], you can't do it at all'; 'sit back until the cows come home'; 'One can never really row; one can never become a perfect example of an oarsman; one can only illustrate in a boat what one thinks rowing is.' He wrote an 'Oarsman's Song' of five verses but with no accompanying music, which begins:

> *The willowy sway of the hands away*
> *And the water boiling aft,*
> *The elastic spring, the steely fling*
> *That drives the flying craft.*

Like many such compositions, it is magic to disciples and utterly incomprehensible, and even risible, to everyone else. His motto was 'mileage makes champions', which meant long outings covering lots of miles of river. The result was Jesus crews who were both fitter and technically better than their opponents. It was to encourage this approach nationally that in 1926 Steve founded the Tideway head race, rowed over the Boat Race course in the reverse direction.

Steve's powerful personality – 'charisma' is the modern word – his endless willingness to talk about rowing, his enthusiasm and his ability to convey that enthusiasm to his followers, all created not only success on the river but also generations of Jesuans who enjoyed their rowing at

Jesus and have done well. They keep in touch with the club throughout the rest of their lives and spend a great deal of time doing what is now fashionably referred to as 'putting something back in': providing a pool of coaching resource and constant influence and support to successive generations of students. The impact of that body of support has been profound. Names such as Mays-Smith, Carpmael, Stammers, Savill, Coulton (both of them), Bell, Langton (all three of them), Hewitt, Burrough and Fraser spring instantly to mind; and, in later years, Peter Blaker, Ewan Pearson, Charlie Francis, Pete Convey and John Beveridge, the last a Jesus CUBC president and past secretary of Leander Club.

This strong and continuing influence of past members, advising, supporting, setting standards and expecta-

New boat house, by P. Morley Horder, 1933.

tions, as well as just being there, has been a key reason for the unique character of the Jesus Boat Club. Other colleges have their supportive past members – known collectively as 'Heavies' – but the Jesus network has probably been the strongest. In this sense, the Boat Club has been not a student club at all: the rowing members are, of course, students, as are a number of coaches, particularly of the lower boats. But the majority of coaches have been past members who had 'done it before', usually to a higher standard than the then current crews. And beyond the body of active coaches lies a much larger group of supportive past members. News that one or more of them was coming down to the river to watch an outing has almost always produced that extra bit of effort. The clan was always on parade in force at Henley, with black and red braiding on blazers and boaters and College ties much in evidence.

It is this continuity of the support of past generations of members that has immediately impressed new members of the club. On the first outing on the river, in his first week at Jesus, of one of this chapter's authors, there were more people than places in the boat and he spent part of the time cycling alongside the crew. With him was a distinguished gentleman who, as they cycled, gave a very eloquent overview of the history and current state of Cambridge college rowing, from which the author gathered that Jesus was, in the gentleman's words, 'one of the great Boat Clubs'. The gentleman, who did not introduce himself, turned out to be Derek Mays-Smith, a colossal influence on and supporter of the club over many years. It was 'Uncle Derek' (as he was affectionately known) who for years after Steve Fairbairn's death organised the coaching teams and programme and, at a time when professional and working commitments still permitted this, informed coaches when their services were required, and the coaches duly complied. In many instances the same coach took the same crew at the same time in the rowing

calendar each year for many consecutive years: Derek himself coached the men's first boat at Henley for about twenty years; John Savill 'finished' the men's first May boat for seven years; Patrick Delafield, a Jesus CUBC president and current president of Leander Club, for eight; and Christopher Rodrigues, likewise a Jesus CUBC president and past chairman of Leander, for fifteen. This continuity has also given rise to family occasions, including Patrick Delafield coaching his daughter Anita to the women's headship of the Mays. Patrick's father-in-law and, accordingly, Anita's grandfather, was another distinguished Jesus oarsman: Jimmy Fraser, who was the father of Joe Fraser, yet another Jesus CUBC president, who was also chairman of the Boat Club Trust (to be mentioned later) for some sixteen years.

Very few coaches lived in Cambridge. Another source of continuity and influence, however, did: the College boatmen, few in number but long in commitment, inspiration and support. Alf Parsons, the first Jesus boatman, for forty years to 1924, was followed by Percy Bullock, who served for forty-seven years and will always be remembered as an excellent coach and wise counsellor, both at the boat-house and in the invariably hospitable welcome to his home in New Square. As John Savill recalled, 'nobody could fail to be warmed by the enthusiasm of his welcome when he opened his front door to see who was on the doorstep. "Oh, how lovely to see you. Do come in." He would sit his visitor down in the corner of his sitting room, press a glass of refreshment into his hand and then would follow a long discussion on the art of rowing.' Percy was especially helpful to captains who had become stuck on a particular problem to which they could not see the answer: talking it through with Percy invariably clarified the issue. He was also remarkably subtle in dealing with people, never aggressive or confrontational, just tactful and astute. On one evening when he was visited by a crew at his home, one member was dominating the conversation. None of the others felt able to tackle this. Percy however suggested that, as the conversation was so good, he should record it so that everyone could listen again. He put on his tape-recorder and the conversation continued as before. On the replay, the presence of one particular dominating voice was at once obvious even to the dominator, who thanked Percy for making the point so kindly but effectively.

Percy himself was supported by his wife, Dorothy, similarly known to generations of Jesuans. She listened to all those discussions but said very little at the time. She was, however, a person of great intuition. Percy's verdict would be delivered immediately; Dorothy's would be delivered by Percy at the boat-house the following day. The steady stream of past members returning to visit Percy at his house or at the boat-house – usually before

Steve Fairbairn (1881)

James Quinn, 1926

visiting the College itself – often many years after they had left Jesus, and sometimes after many years abroad, was sure evidence of his influence on the club. Percy was succeeded by Tony Willson, who served from 1971 till his untimely death in 1997. Tony was not a conventional Fairbairn coach, but just as enthusiastic: 'slowly forward', a notable Fairbairn phrase, was not in his repertoire. With a more direct approach than Percy, Tony generated huge enthusiasm and affection in those many he coached, particularly women's crews. The relationship between Tony and the students was, unsurprisingly, more that of equals than in Percy's day. By nature a supporter of the underdog, Tony masterminded the first women's Lent headship in 1985 and enabled the women to carve out a tradition of their own, to add to the rich heritage of the men. He was a huge influence on almost thirty years of club membership and his death was a grievous loss.

Since then there have been three boatmen. The third, Don McLachlan, has been both boatman and coach, greatly aided in the latter by his wife Mary, who is also a skilled rowing coach. Under Don, coach first and boatman second, the club has made the transition to a modern, professional boat club: fully stocked and equipped boat-house, fully equipped gym in College – provided by the Boat Club Trust but available for use by all members of College – and a state-of-the-art training programme. We have just learned with a mixture of pride and sadness that Don has been recruited to coach at GB national level. His departure is however marked by heart-warming achievements. At the end of the Michaelmas term 2006, the Jesus men's and women's first crews each won their division of the Fairbairn Cup race, a historical first; and in the Mays in 2007 the women went Head.

The Boat Club Trust

Much, but by no means all, of the continuing support from past members is now – when everyone has so much more to do – channelled through the Boat Club Trust and organised by the trustees (drawn from every generation from the 1950s to the current decade) who manage it and work with the boatman and the captains. The trust was launched in 1971 when Percy Bullock retired. John Savill's invitation to an initial meeting provides a good cameo of Boat Club culture. He proposed an agenda of three items: the safeguarding of Percy's future, the safeguarding of the club's future, and 'to enjoy ourselves'.

Having confined itself for its first twenty-five or so years to the original declared purpose of providing new equipment, meaning boats and oars, the trust has more recently widened the range of its support. Fewer undergraduates now arrive at Jesus having rowed at school, or indeed having done any significant amount of sport. A lower level of athletic fitness necessitates more concen-

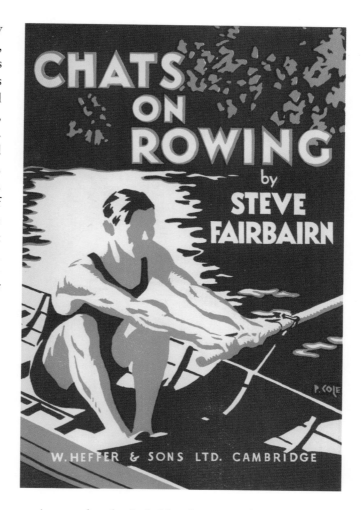

tration on the physical side of training: hence the trust-funded gym and collection of ergometer rowing machines; and on the teaching of basic rowing technique: hence trust-funded training camps away from Cambridge and the restoration of a bank tub at the boat-house.

A final piece of history

On their arrival in the College in 1979 women quickly became an integral part of the Boat Club. The club's history records the date in capital letters: '16 OCT 1979 INAUGURATION OF THE J.C.W.B.C.' There was a women's eight in the Fairbairn Cup that term and 'ladies were present at the Fairbairn Dinner for the first time'. Formal structures took a little longer: the following year there was a JCWBC secretary but not until 1982 was there a women's captain, Elizabeth Dann (now McMeikan). As we have noted, since 1979 the women have been more successful on the river than the men. Here, in the Boat Club, as throughout the College, and across Cambridge, women have joined existing organisations and structures, which have adapted and changed for the better as a result. Now, on the river, every event incorporates women's crews in separate races but on the same terms. There are separate officers for men's and women's crews but they do not have to be men and women respectively. Women can and

The Lawns at Fen Ditton,
May Week *c*.1925.

do coach and cox men, and vice versa. It really is one club with a common purpose.

Common purpose

The way in which this common purpose has for so long transcended the generations, and now transcends the sexes, is probably the Boat Club's most distinctive characteristic, not, perhaps, readily to be found among the College's other sports' clubs. Another distinctive feature has been the club's strong sense of identity – something which, though repelling some members of the College, has attracted others to it. For many years the Boat Club sat together in Hall at their own end of the undergraduate tables – top left, with the captain sitting in his own spacious armchair across the top end of that table; the rest of the College sat somewhere else. Ahead of important races, crews went into 'full training', which involved early morning exercises followed by huge breakfasts, and extra rations at dinner followed by early nights. Members spent much time in each other's company. This must at times have led to, and been seen by others in the College as, isolation, even a college within a College. And there have been members of the Boat Club who have had no interest at all in anyone else in Jesus. But equally, a non-member's identification of a new acquaintance as a Boatie may have been instantly determined – by the non-member – to be fatal to whatever relationship there might otherwise have been.

Reality has, of course, been more complex. One of the authors read Classics and Law, the other Engineering.

They were not undergraduates at the same time and it is unlikely that, but for the Boat Club, they would have had much to do with one another. In the classicist/lawyer author's first year, the top end of the club consisted of three classicists, one medic, one mathematician and one economist, and all the rest were engineers. The common purpose of the Boat Club made it a social ice-breaker, though engineers who joined the Boat Club were different from other engineers … The Boat Club has always welcomed practitioners of other sports – a rugby VIII has been a regular feature – and, as John Hudson relates (page 242), the compliment has sometimes been (painfully) returned. One member of a rugby VIII recalls being a last-second substitute – the one-minute gun had gone! – for an 'unregistered female in a male crew': the crew was bumped in eight strokes.

Externally the Jesus Boat Club identity took a different form. The Fairbairn approach, or style, was not adopted widely in the University – their loss, Jesus would say – and particularly not by the University Boat Club itself. The two boat-houses are next door to one another and, as time passed following Steve's death, a mutual scepticism developed which was not good for either. As new equipment – spade blades – and new training methods were introduced in the 1960s, Jesus appeared to reject both and to wish to bolster its identity by positively not 'moving forward' – or that was how it was seen elsewhere. Still, the last Jesus men's eight to row Head of the Mays did so with 'pencil' blades against opposition universally using 'spades'.

A final word of advice from
the towpath at Baits Bite,
May Races, 2005.

These things are now happily in the past. An identity based, even unintentionally, on being seen to be different – whether through rowing in a way different from other crews or through sitting together in Hall – is no longer viable. Particularly with the technological advance in boats and oars, the original 'Fairbairn style' has lost its attraction, while the exigencies of modern student life do not permit everyone to have dinner at the same time and place every day. Those same exigencies have also done for the other regular meeting point: historically, crews went out every day in the afternoon between 1 and 5 and they would pass or coincide daily. The academic regime no longer permits this, and many crews go out early in the morning so as to be back in time for lectures, the river now being at its most crowded before 8 a.m. Much training is done by individuals on their own and is increasingly done by rowing away from the Cam. It is hard for those steeped in tradition to comprehend the extent of this change or the difficulty crews have in finding a time they can all make. Indeed, if rowing in the early morning had been the only option, many past stalwarts of the club might have reconsidered their decision to row.

These factors, and the emollient influence of women, have given the club a different identity, but one still based on the entirely proper common purpose of wanting to row and wanting to win – for the College as much as for one's self or for one's crew – and of enjoying each other's company while doing so. The women have not, it should be said, reduced the enthusiasm with which bump suppers are enjoyed and which are quite as vigorous as they ever were.

Two other Jesus Boat Club traditions have gone. One is that of not naming boats. New boats are now named, invariably after someone who has been a supporter of the club. The new women's eight is very happily named *Muriel Brittain*, and the latest four *Brian Coulton*. The other is that of only inviting the Master to a bump supper when there was a headship to be celebrated. Now the Master and his wife are always invited and, to the delight and honour of the club, they always come. But one tradition in particular remains: that of not sporting willow branches after a bump, on the premise that Jesus boats always make a bump.

What does the College think of all this?

It is reassuring to find that the issues which appear to cause most discussion between the College and the Boat Club have done so repeatedly down the generations: whether the Boat Club receives too much money (from the Amalgamated Clubs, JCR or JCSU, depending on the era), whether a room or rooms in College should be allocated to the Boat Club captain or president, and whether rowing interferes with academic achievement. In your authors' day, members of the Boat Club used to earn a fairly high proportion of lower classes in the Triposes, but whether this was in fact due to rowing is very much in doubt. What can now be said, if only because such facts suit the cause, is that in 2005 more than half the two first boats earned firsts or 2:1s and each of the last two men's captains have achieved firsts. Caius and Downing are colleges which, at different times, but within recent memory, have, it has been rumoured, changed their admissions policy to benefit their boat clubs. While it would undoubtedly be nice if Jesus were to do the same, and bring success more quickly, the diplomatic view is that this is entirely a matter for the College. As one would expect, some members of the Senior Combination Room have been extremely keen and active supporters – Alan Percival and Michael Waring are notable examples – but the majority have not been so active, and there is no reason why they should be. Masters in recent times – unlike G.E. Corrie – have been much in evidence on race day. The present Master and his wife are very keen supporters, and have breathed new life into an old tradition of watching the May Bumps from the Paddock – land owned by Jesus on Ditton Corner with the best view of the course. There is now a wall of Jesus support there for our crews on the way down to the start and during the race, all gathered together 'enjoying ourselves'.

Personal memories

In a book like this there is, we are assured, room for some personal reminiscences. One author recalls with nightmare-like regularity the last day of his bumping career, rowing at six and seeing the bows of Trinity, who had been bumped by Jesus the day before, coming up very quickly and ever closer on the inside as the crews rounded Grassy Corner. Trinity had a huge overlap but tried to take the Jesus crew on the corner and missed. He can still see it now. His aunt was sitting on Grassy Corner at the time

and wrote to him afterwards, thanking him for providing such good entertainment – which shows that things are all a matter of perception. He remembers, too, staying for two weeks each Henley in wisteria-clad cottages at the top of Remenham Hill owned by three delightful Miss Marple-esque spinsters: dining each evening, formally dressed, down by the river at Phyllis Court; and being entertained with amazing generosity at their nearby homes by 'Uncle Derek', John Savill and Bunjie Langton, occasions which, for young people, were both very enjoyable and very educational. Those were the days …

But perhaps the most appropriate event on which to end this chapter is the experience of the sixth May boat in 1964. Coxed by the then College Chaplain, James Owen, on one day they scored a triple over-bump: one bump for each Commandment.

(Top right) Getting ready for an outing.

(Below) Inside the boat house, 2004.

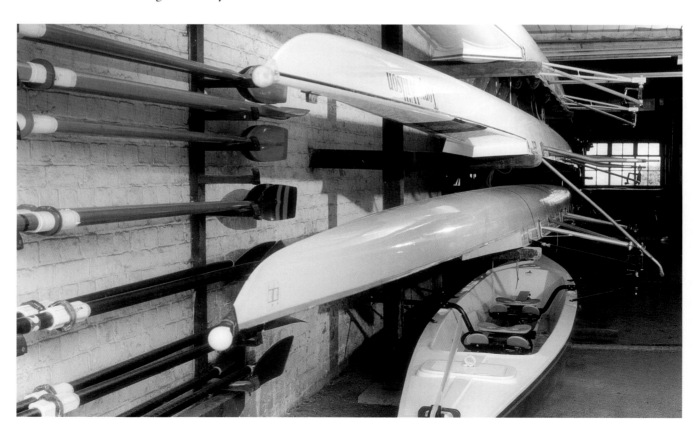

Cricket – A Greatest Ever Jesuan XI

GEOFF PARKS

Being blessed with what is widely regarded as the most picturesque cricket ground in Cambridge, it is no surprise that Jesus cricket has a long and distinguished history. The earliest record of cricket at Jesus is in the memoirs of Gilbert Wakefield, the famed – and seditious – classical scholar (see page 105), who mentions fishing and cricket among the amusements of his undergraduate days (1772–6). The College's first cricket Blue was one Henry Grazebrook, who in 1829 batted at number 3 in the second Varsity match. Since then a further seventy Jesuans have represented Cambridge against Oxford, eight of them captaining the University. Eleven members of the College have played Test cricket, with four having the honour to captain their country.

With eleven Test cricketers to call on, one might think that picking a greatest ever Jesuan XI – a favourite pastime of the cricket afficionado – would be a pretty straightforward task. However, as three of the eleven were wicketkeepers and in such exercises it is *de rigueur* to select a balanced team, some further research has been required! In the somewhat fragmentary accounts of College cricket in *Chanticlere* and the *Annual Report* a consistent lament of those correspondents who did report on the season has been the difficulty of fielding a full-strength XI. In the early days this was most often due to the number of Jesuans whose services were required by the University; in the more recent past the academic pressures of the examination term are cited ever more frequently.

The performance of the 1890 Jesus side casts a long shadow. As Arthur Gray noted, 'The season 1890 was phenomenal; of fourteen matches played thirteen were won, and the remaining one drawn; Trinity was defeated by eight wickets. In county cricket Jesus names are almost as plentiful as blackberries. It is sufficient to record that at the time of writing [1902] no less than four first-class counties are captained by Jesus men, viz. – Middlesex by G. MacGregor, Somerset by S.M.J. Woods, Notts by

A.O. Jones, and Hampshire by A.J.L. Hill.' All bar Jones were regulars in the 1890 side, when not representing the University, and there was such strength in depth at the College then that when wicketkeeper MacGregor was absent his replacement was a future Middlesex player, Henry Menzies.

The strength of that team was clearly formidable, but home field advantage also played its part. The game against the Magpies, then the most important fixture, seemed destined to be drawn as time ran short, but, as *Chanticlere* reports: 'Hossack and Hill were bowling magnificently, and aided by the sun, which was shining straight behind Hill's arm, sent batsman after batsman back. Naturally everyone became very excited as each wicket fell, and when the last man was out half a minute before time the enthusiasm was tremendous.' The 6 o'clock sun, when the sun deigns to shine, continues to be an important tactical consideration on The Close and has helped to prolong the career of many a veteran spinner, the real secret of success being to make the ball pass through the sun twice, once on the way up and again on the way down!

So, the 1890 side provides a good starting-point for our XI. Sammy Woods had already made his Test debut for his native Australia in 1888. He bowled fast right arm with a deadly yorker and a fine slower ball. Woods also played Test cricket and international rugby for England, and enjoyed a long and distinguished career at Somerset County Cricket Club. His obituary in *Wisden* stated: 'Unquestionably he reached a measure of excellence which entitled him to a place among the great fast bowlers of all time.' He was also a fine fielder and a useful bat. Arthur Hill was described by *Wisden* as 'a splendid batsman with a free natural approach to the game'. He was also a useful fast–medium bowler who later in his career took to bowling lobs. After Cambridge he balanced a career as a banker with playing for Hampshire. He was selected for Lord Hawke's England team that toured South Africa in

1895–6, where he played three Tests. Statistically Hill can claim to be England's greatest all-rounder with a Test batting average of 62.75 (unaided by not outs) and a bowling average of just 2.0, having taken four wickets for eight runs on the one occasion he was asked to turn his arm over.

If we were picking a side for a limited overs game, the claims of Martin Scott would need serious consideration. He never got his Blue, despite being twelfth man for the Varsity match twice, but was described in *Chanticlere* as 'a first-class cricketer with brilliant hitting powers; his scoring on several occasions was sensational. … We remember the match against Emmanuel when at the end of ten minutes the board read 71, 1, 66 and he was out; it was with quite a new reverence that we exclaimed "Great Scott"!' One can deduce that the over rates in 1892 must have been somewhat faster than today, and that the boundary on the Jesus Green side of The Close was not then surrounded by an award-winning wildlife habitat, the retrieval of a well-struck ball from which can prove challenging! The same 1892 side, captained by Hill, featured Arthur Jones, who went on to win his Blue the following year and then to a career with Nottinghamshire that last-

ed until his untimely death in 1914. Throughout his career Jones was renowned for his brilliant fielding, particularly close to the wicket, and his batting developed to such an extent that he was eventually picked for England a dozen times.

As a freshman in 1909 Bruce Lockhart took 100 wickets for the College in May alone with his leg-breaks and googlies. He went on to win his Blue that year, taking nine wickets in the Varsity match. The correspondent for *Fifty Years of Sport* reported: 'No more peculiar bowler has been seen in the University match. Bowling round the wicket he tossed the ball very high in the air with a leg-break action … the ball, if allowed to pitch, generally turned from leg … he relied mainly on the mistake of the batsman.' In a first-class career that lasted twenty-four matches, 121 batsmen made mistakes against Lockhart's bowling. He took five wickets in an innings ten times, ten wickets in a match thrice, and his wickets cost under twenty runs each. In admittedly a not overly strong field these figures are good enough to win 'Lockie' a place in our side as a specialist spinner.

The first Jesuan to captain England was the Hon. Frederick Calthorpe. In all he won four Blues either side

Cricket in the Close, 1889.

of the First World War. His *Wisden* obituary mentions rather mysteriously that he 'would have captained Cambridge in 1919 had not the letter of invitation miscarried'. A useful all-rounder, Calthorpe was a stylish bat and swung the ball well at medium pace. He captained Warwickshire for nine years from 1920, and in the twilight of his career led England in the first Test series in the Caribbean. Unfortunately the series was only drawn after Calthorpe made the decision, described as 'extraordinary' by that doyen of cricket writers, E.W. Swanton, not to enforce the follow-on in the final Test after the West Indies had made a mere 286 in reply to England's 849.

Jack MacBryan started his first-class career with Somerset in 1911, but did not come up to Cambridge until after the Great War. His choice of college may have been influenced by his mentor, Sammy Woods. Despite suffering a serious wound during the war to his right arm that rendered him unable to throw the ball any distance, MacBryan won his Blue in 1920, and returning to Somerset his batting continued to develop to the extent that in 1924 he forced his way into the England team. His debut has gone into cricket folklore for unfortunate reasons. In a rain-affected game he neither bowled nor took a catch in South Africa's only innings and never had a chance to bat. Somewhat unfairly, MacBryan was never capped again. At the time England had a plethora of fine opening batsman to choose from, including the legendary Jack Hobbs, the son of the College groundsman. Sadly, the strict rules of this game prevent Hobbs counting as a Jesuan, thus allowing MacBryan another, and long overdue, chance to open the batting.

The year 1924 also saw a major advance at The Close with the building of the fine pavilion. Previously a tent had provided shelter for the teams. However, the new facilities were not beyond criticism. In 1927 *Chanticlere*'s correspondent noted:

As regards last season, one or two suggestions come into my mind. The first concerns the Pavilion and the lack of shelter or protection for those gentleman who after tea, and just before they go in to bat or field, may be seen wandering nonchalantly towards the back of the Pavilion (some do this quite blatantly), and returning a few minutes later hitching up the belt and giving the customary flick to each trouser leg. People do pass on the other side of the stream, and might be curious.

This deficiency was not addressed until the pavilion was extended in 2005. One of the earliest Jesuan cricket Blues to enjoy the new building wins the other opening berth in our side. Tom Killick played in three consecutive Varsity matches from 1928, and in 1929 was picked for England in two tests against South Africa. His subsequent first-class career with Middlesex was curtailed by his calling to the priesthood, but he continued to play on and off until 1939, retiring with a career batting average of 40.35.

Number 3 in the batting order is a selectorial nobrainer. Ted Dexter was one of the finest and most exciting Cambridge players to represent England since the Second World War. An amazing natural sportsman, he captained the University at cricket and played for the Sixty Club (the University second team) at rugby. It was said that the University Golf Club made him captain at an early stage so as to persuade him to concentrate on golf rather than rugby. His involvement with University sport meant that he was not much seen around the College and, in his third year, his Tutor became more and more irritated with his desire to go with the University cricket team rather than with his studies; finally he was gated. ... So, as *Chanticlere* records, on 21 May 1958 Dexter turned out for the College and beat West Norfolk (a good Club side) by nine wickets, taking 9 for 20 with the ball and then scoring 30 not out in the run chase. He

Cricket pavilion, by P. Morley Horder, 1924.

The Cricketer

Barry Flanagan, 1989

(Below) A fearsome spin-
bowler: J.H.B. Lockhart
(1908).

Chanticlere (1910)

returned to England in 1927 and 1931 with the first two New Zealand touring sides, captaining the latter. *Wisden* rated him 'a fine attacking bat, always at his best in a crisis' but only 'a competent wicket-keeper'. Our third wicketkeeper, Murray, won Blues in 1965 and, as captain, in 1966. His Test career spanned no fewer than seventeen years, coinciding with many of the greatest years of West Indian cricket. His neat, understated keeping was mostly done standing back to a succession of legendary fast bowlers – just eight of his 189 Test dismissals were stumpings. Murray's batting was not of the highest calibre, but a first-class average of 28.34 is not to be sneezed at, and in a very close-run thing he dons the gauntlets in our side.

A contemporary of Dexter in the 1957 and 1958 Blues' sides was Ian McLachlan. An accomplished right-hand bat, McLachlan went on to play for South Australia, helping the state to win the 1963–4 Sheffield Shield. He was named as twelfth man in the 1962–3 Ashes series, but was never capped by Australia. McLachlan has gone on to a distinguished career in politics and then cricket administration, and at the time of writing is president of the South Australian Cricket Association and a director on the board of Cricket Australia.

We now have ten of our XI, and for a balanced side we need an opening bowler to partner Woods. The candidates are Philip Wright, a Blue from 1922 to 1924, who went on to play with some success for Northamptonshire, ending his career with 343 first-class wickets at an average of 23.55; and Tony Pearson, a Blue from 1961 to 1963 and one of that select band of cricketers to have taken ten first-class wickets in an innings, a feat he achieved playing for the University against Leicestershire in 1961. Wright gets the nod on the basis of his greater first-class experience.

So, in batting order, our final XI is:

1. E.T. Killick
2. J.C.W. MacBryan
3. E.R. Dexter
4. I.M. McLachlan
5. A.O. Jones
6. A.J.L. Hill
7. F.S.G. Calthorpe
8. S.M.J. Woods
9. D.L. Murray
10. P.A. Wright
11. J.H.B. Lockhart

Woods and Wright would open the bowling, backed up by Dexter, Hill and Calthorpe, with Lockhart providing the spin. There are several candidates for the captaincy, but it is hard to look past a captain of England and Dexter must get the honour over Calthorpe, if only to keep Jim Swanton happy!

went on to captain Sussex and England, winning sixty-two Test caps. His ability to raise his game for the big occasion is evidenced by his Test batting average: at 47.89 it was seven runs higher than his first-class average. Dexter's most famous innings was the 70 he scored from just 73 balls against Wes Hall and Charlie Griffith in the Lord's Test of 1963. Keeping wicket for the West Indies that day was Deryck Murray, who would later that decade grace The Close and Fenners – which brings us onto the dilemma of choosing a wicketkeeper for our side. The candidates are Murray, MacGregor and Tom Lowry.

MacGregor, the captain of the great 1890 Jesus side, was in his day rated by *Wisden* as 'the best wicket-keeper that Cambridge had ever possessed'. His fearless skill in standing up to Woods, then the fastest amateur bowler in England, was acknowledged to play no small part in Woods's success. *Wisden* notes that: 'To see the two in the University match was something never to be forgotten.' MacGregor was capped eight times by England and played for Middlesex until 1907. Like Woods, he was also a rugby international, albeit for his native Scotland. But if we were following the current obsession of picking wicketkeepers on their batting ability, then the New Zealander Tom Lowry would be our choice. He won Blues in 1923 and 1924, and toured Australia and New Zealand with England in 1922–3 without winning a cap. After Cambridge he went back to New Zealand, but

The Music Society

JOHN ADKINS

The Music Society is one of the most active and high profile in the College. Each year it puts on three major orchestral concerts, runs weekly evening recitals, organises other occasional musical events and provides support for those wishing to make music in small informal groups.

It was founded in 1929, but there had been earlier incarnations. The first seems to have been in 1879. Cambridge University Music Society (CUMS) had been

Jesus College Smoking Concert.

1 PIANOFORTE SOLO..Selection from "H.M.S. Pinafore"
 W. D. COPLESTONE.
2 SONG........"The Longshoreman"..............
 A. T ISAAC.
3 'CELLO SOLO..."Salut d'Amour"...............
 T. R. H. BLAKE.
4 SONG....."The Golden Dustman"...........
 G. D. BURNABY.
5 SONG....."A Song of Thanksgiving;"........ ...
 O. B. BULL.
6 SONG........ ..."Archie"...............
 E. K. FORDHAM.

1 PIANOFORTE DUET."Mozkowski's Spanish Dances"
 W. D. COPLESTONE AND F. H. SHERA.
2 SONG............"Anchored"..............
 A. M. BASHFORD.
3 SONG......"Whether you like it or not".........
 J. HEARD.
4 WHISTLING SOLO..From "Florodora"...........
 J. B. W. JONES.
5 SONG..............."Class"..................
 E. K. FORDHAM.

Nov. 13, 1901.

formed some thirty years earlier – a moving spirit was the physicist William Thompson, later Lord Kelvin – but Cambridge's musical life had subsequently declined until the appointment of C.V. Stanford as organist at Trinity in 1875. It may have been the renewal he inspired that led to the founding of the Jesus society, but its concerts were largely taken up with old-time music-hall items: comic or sentimental songs and glee-club numbers with only a few weightier works. The College provided several of the Saturday evening Penny Popular Concerts in the Guildhall. The *Cambridge Chronicle* review of one of ours on 12 March 1881, noted:

> this concert was greatly appreciated by the townspeople who filled the body of the hall and the gallery in every part … Mr A.W. Ivatt's song and the duet 'Love and War' were most enthusiastically received. Mr A.J. Foster gave a novelty in the shape of 'Fairy Bells', which he was obliged to repeat. He also gave a pretty imitation of church bells.

Of another of our Penny Popular Concerts, four years later, the future Master Arthur Gray wrote, 'considering it was attended by 1269 persons, and that four shillings and six pence more was taken at the door that night than at any other concert of the season, we may conclude this to have been a decided success'.

Within the College there were many 'smoking concerts' (the amount of smoke sometimes making it difficult for performers to read their music, we are told). These too were generally collections of short items, most of light weight. A critic in *Chanticlere* opined:

> The familiar common-place one-and-sixpenny songs are pretty, and not too much trouble to get up, but are too mixed up with antiquated ideas. The music which depicts a young lady in thrilling expectations in the first verse, in wild despair in the second, eventually wafted away by

The College Orchestra
rehearses, May Week 2006.

angels in the third, may perhaps contain the germs of the philosophy of life; but let it be understood that these are only the germs, and if sometimes they tread near the sublime, they come within a very measurable distance of the ridiculous.

However, things did improve. Concerts in May Week gradually became the norm and little by little more substantial items were included. The May Week concert of 1898 even included a cantata with orchestral accompaniment. Afterwards, there was a reception for guests, who were entertained in the Fellows' Garden by a band playing under the plane tree, foreshadowing by some hundred years our present custom of having the College's swing Band provide entertainment in the same venue during the interval for refreshments at May Week concerts.

While informal music-making clearly continued, organised societies came and went. After the privations of the First World War, *Chanticlere* remarked that the Music Society seemed to have pined away despite there being much talent in the College. For a time there was a music club which gave occasional concerts and sometimes ran weekly meetings to study specific works like *The Mikado*. But it was not until the present JCMS was founded in 1929 that real continuity was achieved. By 1930 the Master (Gray) was its president and this set a pattern fol-

lowed ever since: JCMS is the only student society which has always had a senior member as president.

In the early 1930s the society was giving several concerts a term with works by major composers. For example, concerts during the Lent term of 1931 included works by Stravinsky, Poulenc, Walton, Dohnanyi, Palestrina, Loeillet and Couperin. For one of them, Professor Dent lent his harpsichord – an instrument then rarely heard. Many took place in the Master's Lodge and this regular hospitality for small chamber concerts continued through various Masterships, initially in the Old Hall of the Lodge, but after this became the Prioress' Room (1946) in the present drawing room.

The society organised concerts of gramophone records. Many were held in the rooms of W.H. Thorpe, who became a Fellow in 1932 and was later for many years the society's president. Bill Thorpe had a large record collection and a wind-up gramophone with an enormous horn, a model which must have been at the peak of hi-fi of the day, and similar to that shown on the famous HMV record labels which pictured a dog listening intently to His Master's Voice issuing from it. The discs were played with thorn needles that had to be recut after each side of a record. The quality of sound was amazingly good. It could also be remarkably loud: students in neighbouring rooms claimed to have been disturbed.

Both the number and quality of concerts increased markedly during the 1930s. Full orchestras began to feature and major works were performed: symphonies, concertos, cantatas and large choral works like Brahms's *Requiem*. A driving force was Charles Wilson, who was an accomplished violin and viola player and was to become a director of the Carl Rosa Opera Company. An undergraduate in the early 1930s, he became a Fellow (modern history) in 1938. He was a vice-president and, for a time, when Thorpe was away, took over the presidency. The years of the Second World War were necessarily lean for music, with the numbers of students and Fellows depleted by military service, but gramophone recitals continued to be popular and there were still concerts in the Master's Lodge.

The person who most contributed to the development of the Music Society as we now know it was, without doubt, Laurence Picken, about whom Roger Scruton, Sumantra Nag and Michael Black also write in this book. A Trinity man, his contact with music in Jesus pre-dates his election as a Fellow in 1944: he gave a clavichord recital here the previous year. On his return from China in 1946, he threw himself into the College's cultural life through the Music Society and the Literary Society. He was an outstandingly able musician and himself took part in many of the society's concerts. He also contributed lecture/recitals on topics such as 'Music of the Far East' and

'18th Century Harpsichord Music', and he devised a symposium on Restoration music and literature. Initially he joined the Music Society committee as a vice-president, later becoming president, an office he held until 1972. Throughout this time he worked tirelessly with the College musicians. There was a notable series of May Week concerts involving joint productions between the Literary and Music Societies – *Comus* with music by Lowes and Arne in a joint programme with Purcell's *Dido and Aeneas* (1948), *King Arthur* by Dryden with music by Purcell (1949), *Le Bourgeois Gentilhomme* by Molière with incidental music by Lully (1950) – and there were more light-hearted productions like *Toad of Toad Hall* with music composed and played on two pianos by Richard Lloyd and David Newbold, who were then music students of the College (1954).

These May Week productions took place in Cloister Court, which provided a delightful outdoor setting. A particularly memorable occasion was in May Week 1959 when Alfred Deller and Desmond Dupré offered their services for a serenade, which they gave sitting on the grass on a beautiful summer evening. But there were difficulties with presenting performances in the Cloisters. The space was limited, and there was an ever-present danger of interruptions from inebriated junior members drowning their examination sorrows, celebrating the end of Bumps or simply partying at the end of an academic

Programme of medieval music with a mystery play, Michaelmas term 1954.

" Gaudete fratres, Christus nobis natus est; Deus homo factus est "
Fleury Play-book

A Sumerian Hymn on the Creation of Man (*pars*)   *c. 1600 B.C.*

DEUS CREATOR   *Towneley Cycle, c. 1475*
(*from the Barkers' and Playsterers' Plays*)
In saeculum (Instrumental Motet)   *School of Notre Dame, XIIIth Cent.*

VERSUS SIBILLE DE DIE IUDICII   *Cordova, c. 950*
(The Sibyl foretells the coming of Christ as Judge)
Fanfare (Instrumental Motet)   *Guillaume de Machaut, XIVth Cent.*

THE PAGEANT OF THE COMPANY OF SHEARMEN
AND TAILORS (*pars*)   *Coventry Cycle, XVth Cent.*

THE PROPHETS
Nowell, Nowell (Carol)   *English, mid-XVth Cent.*

THE ANNUNCIATION
Lullay: I saw (Carol)   *English, early XVth Cent.*
Clausula: Benedicamus Domino   *School of Notre Dame, c. 1200*

THE SHEPHERDS IN THE FIELDS
Gloria in excelsis (Mass Movement)   *Worcester, XIVth Cent.*
As I rode out (Shepherds' Carol)   *Coventry Cycle*
Gloria (reprise)

THE ADORATION OF THE SHEPHERDS
Dominator – Ecce – Domino (Motet)   *School of Notre Dame, c. 1225*
Down from Heav'n (Shepherds' Carol)

OFFICIUM STELLAE (Plainsong)   *Fleury Play-book: Orleans Bibl. de la Ville MS. 201, XIIIth Cent.*
MAGI   SYMISTIS
HEROD   SCRIBE
HEROD'S SON   MIDWIVES
KNIGHT   ANGEL
INTERPRETER

Lully, lulla, thou little tiny child (Carol)   *Coventry Cycle*
The Return of the Christ Child   *Coventry Cycle*
Domino fidelium—Domino (Motet)   *School of Notre Dame, c. 1225*

'A Sumerian Hymn on the Creation of Man' is arranged from the transcription by Canon F. W. Galpin.

The carols 'Nowell, Nowell' and 'Lullay: I saw' are edited by Dr. John Stevens.

The performance of the Fleury 'Officium Stellae' has been made possible through the generosity of Dr. W. L. Smoldon, who kindly placed his unique transcription of the MS. at the disposal of the producers.

A Silver Collection will be taken

year. The simple stratagem of recruiting likely culprits as extras in the plays significantly reduced such problems, but the vagaries of the weather were less easy to deal with. And as May Week productions came to include items with larger orchestras, the events gradually migrated into Chapel, still their normal venue while the society (and others) waits impatiently for the College to build its much-needed auditorium.

Another outstanding series of events for which Laurence Picken was largely responsible were the cycles of miracle and nativity plays that he organised at the end of Michaelmas terms, again combining the College's musical and dramatic talents. He hunted out manuscripts of the plays and researched, arranged and usually took part in the music that accompanied them. These started in 1948 and continued for some ten years. Such plays were little known at the time and the productions aroused wide interest. Typically, we had a dress rehearsal on a Monday evening and then continued with performances on subsequent evenings through to the end of the week, packing the nave and transepts each night. (The programme of

Daniel Hyde (2005)
conducting a College choir.

the 1954 production, *Christus Nobis Natus Est*, is reproduced on page 197.) Quite apart from the excitement of their content, these productions were great fun: a papier-mâché dove complete with a sprig of olive in its beak descending jerkily down an all-too-visible string from the top of the tower, or choruses climbing up to sing from the gallery there, with particularly vertiginous sopranos sheltering in terror behind the stone columns. Features of the Chapel were used in other productions too: the little pickled boys in Britten's *St Nicholas* were restored to life in the Norman arches of the north transept. That production of *St Nicholas* in 1958 was a very moving experience.

In the early 1960s Laurence Picken oversaw the conversion of the former bath-house into a properly equipped Music Room, large enough for rehearsals or recitals by smaller groups. Acoustic tiling on the ceiling and suitable soft furnishings were chosen to produce good acoustics and there was provision for storage of music and books. At the same time, he presented the College with a valuable collection of music, a copy of *Musica Britannica* and various historic books, all to be available in the Music Room. Recently, the room has been restored to music after some twenty years' use as a party room (*sic.*), and renamed the Picken Music Room in recognition both of Laurence's singular contribution to the musical and cultural life of the College, and also of his pioneering work in his (second) academic field of ethnomusicology.

Meanwhile, the round of concerts and recitals in Chapel, the Master's Lodge and Hall continued with a steadily rising standard of performance, this largely the result of the stream of talented musicians choosing to come to the College. There were, of course, leaner years, but the general trend has been upwards as Jesus became known as a good college for those who like music. We can now assemble a full symphony orchestra in which more than two thirds of the players are Jesuans.

Putting on large orchestral concerts is an expensive business. Hiring parts for a single piece of modern music still in copyright can cost several hundred pounds, and there are the costs of instrumental hire, of advertising, and, if we need a more spacious venue than the Chapel, of renting the Music Faculty's Concert Hall in West Road. Although a central student fund, the Amalgamated Clubs, financed by a uniform levy on all undergraduates, had been set up in 1884, this was used exclusively to support the various sports clubs. Nothing was made available to bodies like the Music and Literary Societies until the late 1940s. Previously, they had had to be supported by members' subscriptions. In 1930 that for the Music Society was 2s 6d (13p) per term (for a time, during the war, this fell to 1s 6d (7.5p – which probably explains the restricted nature of the society's programmes, despite the presence of considerable musical talent within the College). Nowadays, budgets are prepared each year and the society receives grants from the Jesus College Student Union that are sufficient to provide a basic working capital for its activities and which, with takings at concerts, enable us to present ambitious programmes. And trust funds have been established to support a wide range of musical activities.

The first of these was a Music Society Trust Fund, set up in 1985 with generous donations from both old and current members of the College. Then, in 2001, the David Crighton Music Fund was established. David Crighton

modest annual cash sum, similar to that received by exhibitioners, together with generous funding for professional lessons. Mention of them in the admissions prospectus, along with other information about musical activities in the College, has encouraged yet more talented musicians to apply to Jesus. There are also two College music prizes: the Renfrew Music Prize awarded each year to the junior member who has made the most significant contribution to the College's musical life, and the David Crighton Music Prize given annually to a first- or second-year undergraduate who is distinguished as a performer or conductor.

Jesus is an outstandingly musical college in an exceptionally musical university. But there are downsides to this. Good players have such a choice of opportunities to play that they skip rehearsals, spoiling sessions for others and making it difficult to decide how many rehearsals will be needed to optimise performances at the concerts. Student concerts, and ours are no exception, too often show the ragged edges that result from lack of disciplined preparation. We have had a session preparing for a per-

(Top left) Belinda Sherlock (2005) at a rehearsal.

(Below) Professor David Crighton (Master 1997–2000) after conducting the College Orchestra at its Lent Term concert, 2000.

had been Master from 1997 until his untimely death in 2000, had loved music and throughout his life had pursued this passion with boundless energy and delight. He enthusiastically supported the Music Society, conducted pieces in two of its concerts, and, at the time of his death, was learning the trumpet so that he could play alongside the students. His widow made very generous personal donations to the fund which the College had created in his memory, and also worked hard to bring in money from other sources, particularly from friends and colleagues of her husband. The object of the fund being the same as that of the Music Society itself – the promotion of music-making by members of the College – the two were amalgamated and have grown into one of the largest of the trust funds held by the College for the benefit of its students. The society also received a generous donation from Hitachi in recognition of David Crighton's scientific collaboration in their research programmes, specifically to fund a series of annual David Crighton Concerts – events that have built up a wide following in Cambridge.

With these resources, we are now able to hire professional tutors to train our instrumentalist: both in intensive weekend courses at the start of Lent terms, and ahead of specific concerts. There are usually two tutors, one for the strings and the other for the wind sections of the orchestra. The society is also acquiring instruments, which previously we had to hire for concerts – notably a set of pedal timpani and various other percussion instruments. These we can hire to other colleges, thus adding to our own income stream. Grants can also be made in exceptional circumstances to individual students.

The College itself has an Instrumental Awards scheme, set up in 1983 to reward outstanding musicians. Four awards are made annually to first-year students on the basis of a competition, which normally involves performing in the Freshers' Concert. These can continue throughout their undergraduate careers, providing a

formance of *Carmina Burana* for which only two violas appeared – to find that their parts required them to play *divisi a 6*! And there was an important performance of Mozart's *Requiem* for which we had to import a bassoonist at the last minute. The work opens with a prominent solo line for the bassoon into which he confidently launched at double speed. Disasters like this are fortunately rare, and the talent of our musicians is such that their playing often reaches its best at the actual concerts. Recently, a College practice orchestra has been meeting once a week through most of the academic year, breaking the mould of under-rehearsal. Coupled with the professional tuition, this has improved the standard of performance in our concerts remarkably.

The hard work of making it all happen falls, of course, to the committee. Junior members fill the posts of secretary, treasurer, orchestral managers ('fixers' for arranging players), librarian (responsible for music hire), recitals manager, and social secretary (dealing particularly with freshers and special events), with other members responsible for publicity and 'front-of-house' (arranging seating,

'Settling the score' before a concert.

ushering and so on at the concerts themselves). The Senior Organ Scholar is on the committee *ex officio*. Senior members are the president of the Music Society, the Director of Studies in Music, the Director of Chapel

Music and, from time to time, others (vice-presidents) willing to help.

Some of the committee's most protracted and tortuous discussions concern the choice of items for concerts. Having sought the suggestions of members, it is a continual battle to avoid an arbitrary assembly of various peoples' favourite pieces with no regard to the overall structure of a programme. The criteria evoked can be diverting too. The minutes of the meeting of 28 February 1994 record one such discussion:

> The Secretary had prepared an extensive list of possible pieces for the May Week concert. Dr Ian Cross came into his own here in offering or withdrawing his considered approval. The choices were rapidly cut down, either because some were technically demanding, bad or the wrong length, or because of the political persuasion of the composer. It was remarked that Enescu was a fascist. [This is not true, but the comment was enough to prevent him from being considered further.] The Doctors weren't keen on Delius either, but not for being a fascist. They just found him tedious. In the end, it was the President's desire for a cosmopolitan programme, or 'topographical complementarity' if you like, that proved most influential. The menu contained French, German and Russian servings. Debussy was rejected for appetiser since it was felt that his fluffy textures might emerge from the JCMS furnace more like charred meringue. On a culinary note, the Secretary pointed out that Smetana in Czech meant 'sour cream' so he was immediately out of the running.

Finally the programme emerged: Offenbach, Beethoven and Tschaikovsky.

Making music brings together people from all cultural, academic and social backgrounds in a way that only it can. The society's activities give tremendous pleasure and satisfaction to its members and, we hope, some pleasure to our audiences too. We are fortunate to have the resources and support that we now enjoy, but little would be possible without the extraordinary talent and enthusiasm of the gifted musicians who choose to come to the College.

Jesus English

STEPHEN HEATH

nglish came late to Cambridge, emerging as an independent subject for study only after the First World War. An account of the creation of the new Tripos can be found in *The Muse Unchained* (1958) by E.M.W. Tillyard, who as a young Fellow of the College had an important role in what he rightly saw as 'the revolution in English Studies at Cambridge'. That Jesus should have been and thereafter continued to be at the forefront of those studies was only right for a college with a rich literary history and which had nurtured one of the finest of literary critics, Samuel Coleridge, whose *Biographia Literaria* (1817) with its discussion of poetic language and the imagination is a major text in the history of English criticism. Just as 'Cambridge English' carries more than the simple reference to the possibility of studying English in the University, so 'Jesus English' has often been used to acknowledge the nature of the exceptional contribution made by the College.

The new university foundations had led the way in recognising English as a fit subject for university education. As might be expected, Oxford and Cambridge were slow in following suit, and it was not until 1885 that Oxford's Merton professorship was established for 'the history and criticism of English language and literature'. The first professor, however, was a conventional philologist and the Oxford English School was taken in a linguistic direction that determined its subsequent emphasis on Anglo-Saxon and Middle English. English in Cambridge meanwhile was merely an optional language in the new – 1884 – Medieval and Modern Languages Tripos, with the focus again primarily linguistic and philological. Proposals in 1909 to shift the balance more towards literature were rejected, but the following year the University accepted press magnate Sir Harold Harmsworth's offer to endow a professorship in memory of the late King for the study of English literature from Chaucer onwards 'on literary and critical rather than on

philological and linguistic lines'. The first King Edward VII Professor, Arthur Verrall, a classical scholar, died shortly after delivering his inaugural lecture, a tragedy that turned out to be Cambridge English's good fortune since the Crown next appointed Sir Arthur Quiller-Couch, whose sympathies lay very much with the freeing of English from Anglo-Saxon in favour of literary studies.

Professor Sir Arthur Quiller-Couch in the Fellows' Garden, *c.*1930.

Quiller-Couch (1912), or 'Q' as he was known as a writer, had taught classics for a year at his old Oxford college but was no academic. A successful novelist, short-story writer and literary journalist, he was also an active supporter of the Liberal Party, which rewarded him with a knighthood and the Cambridge chair (Asquith and Lloyd George agreed that the appointment should be a party one). He chose Jesus as his college and for over thirty years lived here during term (his wife stayed in Fowey where Q, a staunch Cornishman, had his family home and where he officiated as Commodore of the Royal Yacht Club). His conduct and manner were those of a traditional gentleman (though the master of Magdalene cattily declared him to have the air of 'a racing tout'). Q's was a world in which one dressed for dinner, lectured in morning dress, and tackled leisure occasions – cheering on the Jesus first boat – in suits of the most emphatic checks, gaiters and a brown bowler hat (the suits found their way into undergraduate verse: 'Q is for "Q" in the late Verrall's boots / His bedder plays draughts on his cast away suits'). He entertained with robust generosity. When his fellow Cornishman A.L. Rowse visited him there was dinner in Hall with wine from Q's cellar, whisky galore in the Combination Room, breakfast with beer next morning in Q's rooms, rounded off by lunch with oysters and stout at the Pitt Club.

Tillyard described Q as counting as more 'for a college man than as a University Professor'. Perhaps, but, as *The Muse Unchained* also makes clear, Q's support was vital in the move towards an English Tripos. He gave

---

A FRAGMENT FOUND IN A LECTURE-ROOM (April 1792)

Where deep in mud Cam rolls his slumbrous stream,
And bog and desolation reign supreme;
Where all Boeotia clouds the misty brain,
The owl Mathesis pipes her loathsome strain.
Far, far aloof the frighted Muses fly,
Indignant Genius scowls and passes by:
The frolic Pleasures start amid their dance,
And Wit congeal'd stands fix'd in wintry trance.
But to the sounds with duteous haste repair
Cold Industry, and wary-footed Care;
And Dulness, dosing on a couch of lead,
Pleas'd with the song uplifts her heavy head,
The sympathetic numbers lists awhile,
Then yawns propitiously a frosty smile. ...
[Caetera desunt.]

S.T. Coleridge

---

much thought to it and wrote of his concern 'weakly or not, to be remembered for a hand in [its] making'. He left as his particular mark a paper dear to his heart, 'The English Moralists', which has been the intellectual delight of many Jesuans. Asked what he meant by 'the English Moralists', he would, Tillyard records, launch into 'a roll-call of the great names: "Hooker – Hobbes – Locke – Berkeley – Hume", which he ended with an exhausted "my God", as emotion got the better of him'. His lectures were crowded and delivered, as the *Cambridge Review* reported, 'with every sentence carefully weighed and fashioned as though for publication'. As indeed they were, quickly collected in volumes by the University Press for an eager public; the American Helene Hanff, of *84 Charing Cross Road* book and film fame, paid tribute in *Q's Legacy* (1985) to the first of them, *On the Art of Writing* (1920), as having inspired her to become a writer. Q also held informal classes in his rooms, where coffee and cigarettes were plentiful and he would pace up and down responding to undergraduate contributions. Though one of the editors of the *New Cambridge Shakespeare*, he was no scholar and left the textual editing to his co-editor. His interest lay rather in the plays as theatre, and he was active in setting up a local branch of the British Empire Shakespeare Society, with himself as president, the then Master as treasurer, readings in the Lodge, and a play performed each summer in the Master's garden. Q's most influential publication, the *Oxford Book of English Verse, 1250–1900* (1900), which had a wide readership and shaped popular poetic taste, preceded his Cambridge years. Its influence was much decried by F.R. Leavis, for whom Q's style of literary appreciation represented everything that was wrong with English culture. Ironically, Leavis had been supervised by Q for his PhD and, despite his critical animosity, always had praise for what he regarded as Q's 'natural manly decency' and his avoidance of the moral failings of the aestheticism to which, as Leavis saw it, his ideal of writing exposed him.

Q's presence in Jesus ensured English a valued place in the College's academic life and a series of outstanding Fellows made Jesus English a force in the University and beyond. The first of them, Tillyard, had read Classics and been awarded a fellowship in 1913 for his research on Greek ceramics. Back from the Great War, he agreed to lecture on the history of criticism for English students and thereafter made the new Tripos his academic home. A Shakespeare and Milton scholar, he is now mostly remembered for *The Elizabethan World Picture* (1942), an account of the medieval and Renaissance conception of a divinely ordained hierarchical universe – 'the Chain of Being' – showing how it everywhere informs the literature of the time. The book was much used in schools and universities, contributing to the perception of Jesus as a college for English.

When Tillyard became Master in 1945, the College elected a new Fellow, A.P. Rossiter. He had read Natural Sciences at Selwyn but took English Part II after completing his BA and taught English in Japan and then Durham. He published little, but a posthumous collection of lectures on Shakespeare, *Angel with Horns* (1961), evidences his fine critical intelligence. A novel, *Poor Scholars* (1932), written soon after taking Part II and with the central character reading English, remains of interest for its representation of student literary – and sexual – discussions of the time (its Jesuan attraction lies in a thinly disguised portrayal of Steve Fairbairn, 'who had made more oarsmen than anyone but God', and the description of a boat-burning in the Close). It was as a teacher that Rossiter stood out: charismatic, rigorous, passionate about his subject, dedicated to his students' education. An experienced rock-climber, he contributed to climbing guide books to his beloved Lake District, where he was killed in a motor-cycle accident in 1957. For some – golden – years Rossiter was seconded by Philip Brockbank, who was appointed a College Lecturer in 1955 and was later to be a distinguished editor of Shakespeare. Tony Tanner (1955) often spoke warmly of the excitement of his time in College under these two men, imbibing from Brockbank above all a 'fine, complex, ironic humanism'.

Rossiter was succeeded by David Daiches, who came from Cornell to a University Lectureship in 1951, leaving in the early sixties to become dean of English studies at the new University of Sussex. He published many books on many subjects, including in his Jesus years a valuable *Critical History of English Literature* (1960). The Sunderland-born son of an immigrant Lithuanian rabbi, he was raised in Edinburgh and devoted numerous works to Scottish literature and culture; not least an appreciative volume *Scotch Whisky – Its Past and Present* (1969) and a memoir, *Two Worlds: A Jewish Childhood in Edinburgh* (1956), which describes growing up in both 'the secular world outside' and 'the internal closed Jewish world'. 'A Cambridge Dialogue' (collected in *Literary Essays*, 1956), written just before he became a Fellow, presents a clutch of dons gathered postprandially in the Combination Room entertaining themselves over port in learned debate as to what might be the earthly equivalent of the 'celestial liquor' of the gods – opinions range from Montrachet to Montilla and, inevitably, a Highland malt. Daiches had already dined and combined on a number of occasions in College and it would be nice to think that the 'Dialogue' was of directly Jesuan inspiration.

Daiches's successor was Raymond Williams, who had been a supervision pupil of Tillyard's while an undergraduate at Trinity. Though there was disquiet during an informal interview over the appearance of 'society' in the title of one of his books, he was nevertheless elected to a fellowship. (He is one of the dons in the 'Group Portrait' on page 258.) He eventually moved into Coleridge's rooms in First Court (D2), a fitting link to a writer important in the line of thinking about culture that Williams had analysed in *Culture and Society* (1958). Politically engaged, Williams was a leading figure of the New Left and it was in D2 that the *May Day Manifesto* (1967), proposing a strategy for socialism in the face of the failure of the Labour government of Harold Wilson, was elaborated. Unsparing in the support he gave students in the late sixties and early seventies (giving supervisions in prison, for example, to one convicted after the so-called 'Garden House Riot'), Williams was a source of inspiration and hope for the student Left.

It was at Williams's instigation that the only-just-graduated Terry Eagleton arrived from Trinity in 1964 to share the teaching. Eagleton had become intellectually and politically close to Williams during his undergraduate years and, like him, saw the academic study of English

Dr E.M.W. Tillyard (1908), Fellow 1913–45, Master 1945–59.

Eric Kennington, 1951

as having a significance that went beyond its limitation to some sphere of the 'academic' or any assumption of some purity of 'the literary'. The impact – the brilliance – of Eagleton's teaching for the College was huge; sharply illuminating, it raised issues that challenged our given responses and asked us to think about literature in ways that most Faculty teaching simply refused to do. Failing to obtain a University post (his radical stance had greatly upset the Faculty), Eagleton left for Oxford in 1969, thereafter to become the most widely read contemporary literary critic and theorist in the English-speaking world, his *Literary Theory: An Introduction* (1983) alone selling over a million copies. Like Williams again, Eagleton has been novelist and dramatist as well as critic; and as for Williams, so for Eagleton the English Tripos remained ever present in his work: the Part II Tragedy paper, for example, taken by both, leads later to Williams's *Modern Tragedy* (1966) and later again to Eagleton's *Sweet Violence: The Idea of the Tragic* (1988).

The decades after Eagleton's departure saw the Faculty increasingly divided over the future of Cambridge English. The division was expressed dramatically at the beginning of the 1980s in the 'MacCabe affair' which attracted national and international media attention. The terms in which the affair – sparked off by the refusal to provide a lectureship for an assistant lecturer at the end

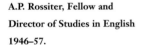

A.P. Rossiter, Fellow and Director of Studies in English 1946–57.

of his tenure – was reported were confused and misleading, with 'Marxists and Structuralists versus Traditionalists' being the commonplace view. The reality was simply that of resistance to the need to rethink Cambridge English studies, take stock of current debates and approaches, and recapture the modern sense of the subject that had been so vital at its beginnings. A special relationship had developed between Jesus and King's, and the two colleges together, guided by Williams and Frank Kermode, were at the forefront of the rethinking and the call for change. Important here too was the College's first woman Fellow, Lisa Jardine (1976), who played an essential role in the Faculty, where she was instrumental in bringing feminist and gender issues into the Tripos. Concerned with developing historical readings of literature (witness her *Reading Shakespeare Historically*, 1996), she has done much innovative work on the intellectual and scientific history of the sixteenth and seventeenth centuries, with studies of Bacon, Wren and Robert Hooke ('the man who measured London'). Since taking up a chair at Queen Mary London, she has also gained a strong public presence, appearing regularly on radio and television.

In this, as in her Jesus fellowships – she became an Honorary Fellow in 2005 – and her focus on literature and science, she followed in the footsteps of her father, Jacob Bronowski (1927), also an Honorary Fellow (1967), who must have a place in any account of Jesus and English. A mathematician and scientist of distinction, Bronowski was profoundly concerned with literature and the arts, publishing *inter alia* an important study of William Blake. Creativity and the imagination were, as they had been for Coleridge, matters of fundamental importance and 'the relation between the truth of science and that of poetry' was to be acknowledged and explored. While a student Bronowski was a founder editor of *Experiment* (1928–31), a magazine of poems – including Bronowski's own – and articles by such Cambridge contemporaries as William Empson of Magdalene, Malcolm Lowry of St Catharine's and fellow-Jesuan James Reeves (1928), with whom Bronowski wrote and published in *Experiment* notes 'Towards a Theory of Poetry'. The publication of an extract from James Joyce's *Work in Progress* was sufficient in itself to vindicate the magazine's title and indicates the contribution it and Bronowski were making to the vitality of English in Cambridge – and Jesus – in that initial exhilarating moment of the subject's existence when literary experiment indeed was its living context.

Jesus English has been its students as much as its Fellows, all those who for the last eighty years have made it so successful and who have gone on to make contributions in so many fields, including as themselves authors of literary works. A substantial number too have gone on to achievements as academics and critics: Eric Robinson

(1942), who revived interest in the poet John Clare and produced the scholarly nine-volume edition of his works; Robin Wood (1950), who while he has written on Henry James is known especially as one of the most significant writers on film of the last half-century; the distinguished medievalist Tony Spearing (1954) and his contemporary Tony Tanner, Cambridge's first Professor of American Literature; Anthony Julius (1974), whose successful law career (representing Diana, Princess of Wales, and Heather Mills McCartney in their divorce actions) has not prevented him doing important academic work, as in his controversial *T.S. Eliot, Anti-Semitism, and Literary Form* (1995); Suzanne Raitt (1980), whose studies of such twentieth-century women writers as Virginia Woolf, Vita Sackville-West and May Sinclair have been much praised for their scholarship and critical acumen; and too many more than can be remembered here.

Particular mention must, however, be made of James Wood (1985), one of today's finest literary critics. After a distinguished undergraduate career, Wood decided to go into literary journalism rather than pursue the university career that could easily have been his, convinced that current academic criticism was damagingly impairing literary criticism, flattening it into an increasingly abstract discourse that fails to engage with the specific experience of literature. What for Wood are necessary concerns with feeling and value have come to be treated with suspicion in the wake of the success of 'theory', the recourse to quasi-sociological explanations, and the imperatives of externally imposed research targets in university departments, which leave neither time nor space for response to literature and the literary. As senior editor of the *New Republic* and contributor to other influential journals, Wood regularly offers pieces that, unfashionably, approach past as well as contemporary works with regard to their aesthetic achievement, asking 'Is this good?', 'Why is this moving me?' – questions Coleridge would have understood. *The Broken Estate: Essays on Literature and Belief* (1999) and *The Irresponsible Self on Laughter and*

the Novel (2004) collect some of Wood's major pieces, and a sensitively thoughtful novel, *The Book against God* (2003), differently explores the matter of belief so important to him.

Wood has an earlier Jesuan namesake, James Wood (1908), who was also concerned with the aesthetic. While this Wood did not read English (he could not then have done so), he made a small contribution in the years leading to the Tripos. Described by his friend I.A. Richards, to whom Cambridge English owes practical criticism, as possessed of 'a queer shaped head', permanently erupting with ideas but with no capacity to develop them, he co-authored with Richards and C.K. Ogden *The Foundations of Aesthetics* (1922). Written in a room on King's Parade to the energising accompaniment of an ozone machine, the book was a programmatic statement of the concern to understand how literature and art affect us that preoccupied Richards in those early years. Wood also produced a short experimental fiction, *Mayvale* (1915), which won acclaim from revolutionary Vorticist Wyndham Lewis, who extolled its 'little crazy shells of action … rigidly exteriorised in vision'. Vision indeed was central for Wood, who instructed Richards in pictorial aesthetics and was himself an accomplished painter – to him we owe the portrait of W.H.L. Duckworth (Master 1940–5) that hangs in College (page 23).

The development of Cambridge English between the two wars, shaped by Richards and Leavis, gave the subject a powerfully influential definition, in which close reading and the evaluation of literary texts went with a critical engagement with culture and society. Jesus English has been marked by the same engagement, never taking for granted accepted conventions of teaching and studying English – not least those deriving from Richards and Leavis which were hardened into an accepted 'Cambridge English' – and never losing sight of the critical nature of English studies. Jesus English has been and remains a constantly questioning academic and more than academic pursuit.

In the Master's Lodge

MARGARET MAIR

If Queen Elizabeth I had had her way, there would not have been a Master's Lodge. A royal order of 1561 expressly forbade the residence of the wives and families of Masters in colleges, but by the end of her reign this prohibition was a dead letter. Masters, like bishops and cathedral deans, but unlike Fellows, had secured, and retained, the right to marry, and they expected to have their families with them when college statutes required them to be in residence. The houses occupied by the Heads and their families, frequently an integral part of the college buildings, are now one of the most distinctive features of Cambridge and Oxford colleges.

The Jesus Lodge forms the south-west corner of the Cloisters and the south-east corner of First Court, and adjoins the Gate Tower with which it was originally interconnected; the Master's servant doubled up as gate porter. Unlike the lodges at Trinity, St John's and Queens', with their imposing staircases and long galleries, that at Jesus was not a grand house, the College having for long been one of Cambridge's poorest. It centred on a nucleus of four or five rooms and over the centuries expanded and contracted in all directions, east, north and west. Before the creation of a Combination Room in the eighteenth century it was the only place, apart from the Hall and the Chapel, where the Master and Fellows could meet, whether for business or socially, and until well into the twentieth century nearly all College meetings were held there.

The earliest reference to the entertainment of undergraduates in the Lodge is a charming description of a St Valentine's Day occasion in 1608. William Boswell (Fellow 1606–20) wrote to Sir William Waldegrave, whose grandson, a young Mr Clopton, was his pupil, to deny reports that Clopton had become romantically involved with a daughter of the then Master, Dr Duport. After begging Waldegrave 'not to lend credit to flyinge reports' and protesting against 'any such underhande dishonest dealings or any such marriage or love matter', he continued:

> From whom such a report should arise I know not. About a quarter of a year since, Mr Clopton was, amongst other fellows and gentlemen of our colledge, drawne by paper lots to be Valentine to one of Dr Duport's daughters: which being tould unto Mr Clopton, he came presently and asked me what he should doe; I resolved him as the other company did; which afterward giving gloves unto their Valentine, wee also bought a paire costing 2s.6d., and bestowed them upon her, which (God is my witness) was done without any such intent, as the report falsely carieth. Neyther did the gentleman or myself ever speake twice unto those daughters in our lives.

The picture of one of Dr Beadon's parties in Gillray's cartoon *Questions and Commands; or the mistaken road to*

The Conference Chamber, panelling *c.*1600. The room is so called because most College meetings were long held in it.

He–r–f–rd; a Sunday evenings amusement (1788) (page 98) is, no doubt, as unreliable as it is malicious, but from Dr Corrie's long bachelor mastership (1849–85) – an old friend's two daughters kept house for him – come stories of dinner parties. His successor, H.A. Morgan, recalled how in his own early days as the Tutor (he was appointed in 1863):

Heads of Houses lived in a little magic circle of their own. To be Master of a College was to occupy a position of the highest social glory, beside which everyone else was of no account. My dear old predecessor used sometimes to say to me: 'You know, my friend, Heads of Colleges never dine with anyone except Heads but they might sometimes ask their Tutors to dinner. One day I received an invitation to dine at the Lodge and forthwith I was raised into this magic circle.

In recalling this party I do not wish to say one word against the dear master who invited me. He always treated me with kindness and in asking me, the Tutor, to this dinner he ignored my social inferiority and raised me temporarily to the position of a 'Head.' Not so his guests. They were all 'Heads' or worse still in those days, Heads' *wives*, and they could hardly believe their eyes when they

realised that the College Tutor had been invited to meet them at dinner. Unmitigated disgust was written on every face. From the time they arrived to the time they left, they never once addressed one single word to me. Never in my life had I been made to feel so utterly out of it … I might just as well not have existed. Sometimes between courses a 'Head' would raise his eye-glass and look me up and down, as if to satisfy himself there had not been some mistake, and every now and then the four Heads and their four wives would look at me as much as to say, 'What dirt is that?'

There were, however, occasions on which Dr Corrie invited even undergraduates to dinner. They remembered him, frail and silver haired, picking up a candlestick from the table at the end of the meal and holding it up before portrait after portrait of College worthies as he told them of their places in its history.

Times change and styles change. H.A. Morgan (1885–1912) interviewed each freshman in his study, and he and his wife 'would receive them all at luncheon in the Lodge in the October Term. He enjoyed talking to the undergraduates on Sunday afternoons when it was always the custom for them to assemble in considerable numbers for tea, many of them being the sons of his own old pupils.' In his later years he was extremely deaf but, as Percival Gardner-Smith, who came up in 1906, recalled:

His wife and daughters made up for it. We used to call and we sat in a circle and the poor Miss Morgans hopped about between us and asked us questions, 'Are you rowing this term?' 'Will the boat go up?' 'Is Mr Fairbairn here?' and so on. When you'd answered all these questions, in a sort of general post, another daughter came and sat next to you and asked you all the same questions again.

Arthur Gray (1912–40), by all accounts a splendid raconteur, continued this pattern. These gatherings took place in what is now the Prioress's Room, but was then

(Top left) **Master's Lodge, porch built *c*.1885. The stone plinth of the wall on the right formed part of the west front of the nunnery church.**

(Below) **The Dining Room prepared for a supper party, 2007.**

part (the Old Hall) of the Lodge, where it was easy for undergraduates to come and go. There was, anyway, not a great deal for them to do on Sunday afternoons: no boat went out on the river, and no sports were permitted in the Close.

The early years of Eustace Tillyard's Mastership (1945–9) were the post-war ones of some austerity, and he was a modest and rather shy man. John Hudson remembers being invited with the other Maths freshmen to take sherry in the Lodge.

> It turned out to be a rather embarrassing occasion. Tillyard had very little small talk, and we were new and nervous and, in my case at least, somewhat socially inadequate. The day was saved by Mrs Tillyard, a small, charming, rather bent lady, who kept the conversation going. Eventually the Master offered to take us on a tour of the Old Library. We moved through a succession of ancient looking doors with strange door furniture until we found ourselves in the undergraduate library and the Master was closing the door behind us. Sherry time was over.

The arrival of Denys and Katie Page in 1959 must have been a welcome change. Page was evidently an entertaining and provocative conversationalist. He and his wife enjoyed parties and they entertained extensively, both formally and informally. Together with their three daughters, they made the Lodge a hub of the College's

An impromptu performance of *Trial by Jury* in the Drawing Room, 2007.

social life. Their regular Tuesday evening dinner parties, at which Fellows and their wives joined guests from other colleges (Masters included), were formal affairs which harked back to the thirties: the gentlemen were black-tied, and were left to their port after the ladies had retired to the drawing room. Sir Alan Cottrell's vice-chancellorship, supported by his wife Jean who was an engaging and lively hostess, brought a stream of distinguished visitors to the Lodge: the Duke of Edinburgh, the University's Chancellor, came regularly. And in Lord Renfrew's time it was not unusual to find prominent government ministers helping him and Jane entertain students.

Incoming Masters and their wives inherit their predecessor's traditions, and naturally add their own, which makes for a busy diary. We continue many of these traditions, including Colin Renfrew's breakfast for the first eights during May Week and David Crighton's parties for the musicians after their concerts. All freshers come to drinks in their first term, usually in groups of about thirty, and we have introduced informal suppers with literary games and a quiz for all second-year undergraduates. As well as two or three formal dinner parties each term, at which we like to ensure a mix of Fellows of the college, other Heads of House, members of the University and visitors from outside the academic world, we also hold dessert evenings or Sunday lunches for smaller groups such as the choir or the Student Union's committee. And there are also parties for alumni and the parties for college staff: a coffee morning for the bedders, a twenty-fifth anniversary party for the Head Chef, and various small parties for the porters, gardeners and maintenance staff.

There is nowadays an openness to the Master's Lodge which earlier generations might not recognise, borne perhaps of the sense that a place of such history and beauty should be used to the full and enjoyed, particularly of course by the College, but also by the wider Cambridge community. It is a house that lends itself ideally to a range of occasions. The garden might be used for a charity coffee morning, with stalls set up all round it and a hundred visitors, while in the dining room later in the same day there might be a formal dinner for sixteen or a supper party for thirty. There might be an atmosphere of quiet dignity at a reception for over two hundred following a memorial service for a student, or informal frivolity as when the Chaplain directed the choir in *Trial by Jury* in the drawing room. The Lodge is part private home, and as such the natural venue for many family gatherings at Christmas and during vacations, but it is primarily a centre for the social life of the College, to which each Master and his family bring their individual tastes and talents, and contribute during their tenure to its collective memories.

In Three Wars

The Boer War

CHANTICLERE

The magazine's first references to the Boer War occur in its issue for the Michaelmas term 1899:

> At a general meeting of the University held at the Union it was resolved that a collection should be made for the Transvaal War Fund, and R.W. Bell was appointed the Jesus Representative, and he has already, we believe, collected no mean sum.
>
> In connection with the Transvaal affair we are sorry to hear that F.E.W. Fichardt, an old Jesus man, but by birth a citizen of the Orange Free State, has returned to the Cape to fight if possible in the Free State forces; but on the other hand the College in the present crisis is reassured by the knowledge that it has furnished so redoubtable a Militia officer as J.A. Joicey, who has left us to join his regiment, the 3rd Batt. Northumberland Fusiliers.

The following term (Lent 1900) its readers were informed that there had been

> a large and most gratifying increase in the numbers of the Jesus Contingent of the Cambridge University Rifle Volunteers, which now totals nearly 50. This is due to the loyal enthusiasm evoked by the present war, and to the great efforts of the Master [H.A. Morgan] who at a meeting presided over by the Dean [F.J. Foakes Jackson] urged upon all the duty of becoming volunteers, and expressed a hope that a college prominent in athletics would be among the first to realise this duty. He pointed out that England's isolation made it imperative that every man capable of bearing arms should receive the military training which alone would render him of use for the defence of the country. That this argument appealed to the hearers was evidenced by the number of those who immediately enrolled themselves in the corps. Mr Jackson, who on this occasion as on all others has taken the very greatest interest in recruiting Jesus men, must have felt the liveliest satisfaction at swearing in so many new members.
>
> It is necessary that a tradition should be established in the college that all freshmen ought to join in the corps, and the large proportion of prominent athletic men now enrolled should go far to ensure this result. Formerly there was a popular delusion that work and athletics left no time for volunteering, but this like many other fallacies has now been exploded, and we hope that as the college increases in size, we shall gradually attain to a company of our own …

The Easter term issue printed verbatim the text of the Master's recruiting speech. He began by recalling a similar occasion:

> More than forty years have elapsed since I addressed a meeting in this College on the subject of the Volunteers. It was at the time when the French Colonels appealed to their Emperor to permit them to invade our shores. I well remember how crowded was the room where we met, and how well our men responded to the call for National Defence. Both our Tutors joined the movement as well as other Fellows. Doubtless their examples will be followed on the present occasion! Mr Goodwin has already become a recruit.

He reminded his hearers:

that the country at the present time is almost entirely denuded of regular troops, nearly all our regiments being either in South Africa or India. Even Militia are being sent to the Front. All these battalions require, from time to time, to be supplied with fresh men, most of them – owing to the losses which occur in time of war – to a very large extent. As our reserve forces become thus weakened, where are we to look for men to fill their places and above all to ensure adequate defence for our mighty Empire in case an attack should be made on one of its vulnerable points? It seems to me that if this war be of long duration, and no man can tell how long it may last, our Volunteers will constitute our principal Reserve, and it is on them, much increased in numbers and advanced in proficiency, that the safety of our Empire will chiefly rest.

He considered it:

the most gigantic crime on our part to run the slightest risk of invasion of our shores, or of imperilling, in the least degree, the safety of our glorious Empire which has been passed down to us by our fathers, after many a hard fought battle, and which it is our duty and privilege to guard and maintain

The Master (Dr H.A. Morgan) with the Jesuan section of the Cambridge University Rifle Volunteers, 1901.

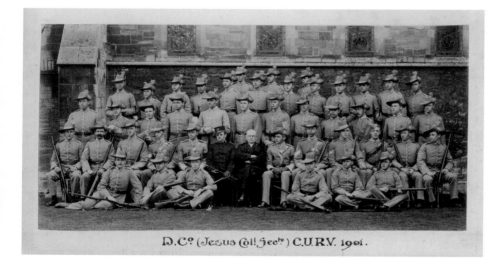

D. Cº (Jesus Coll Jecᵗ) C.U.R.V. 1901.

and thought it 'surprising that the Government are not, at the present moment, straining every effort to render our defensive forces as effective as possible'. He believed that the nation would do as well to rely on 'five distinguished bishops', or even 'five distinguished heads of colleges' as on the five members of the Cabinet's 'Committee of National Defence'. In due course, came his peroration:

I trust I have now shewn you that all Englishmen, whose circumstances justify their doing so, should rise for the defence of their country, and for this purpose there is no better course at the present time than to join the Volunteers. Further it behoves you – members of this University – to swell, as far as you are able, the ranks of these forces, for do you not justly pride yourselves on being mentally and physically superior to average young Britons? You ought, I think, on all grounds, to prove highly efficient Volunteers from amongst whom intelligent, capable and thoroughly competent officers may be chosen to lead others as occasion requires.

And now in conclusion I have only a few words to add, and these I address to those of you who are about to proceed to the Front. I need not tell you how much our thoughts will be with you, how heartily we wish you a safe return, and how confident we are that the honour of the College and of the British soldier may be entrusted to your keeping. Rely upon it that when you return to the old College, and the Red and Black takes the place of the Union Jack, having covered yourselves with glory and, if it be permissible to add, your enemies with wounds! you will receive a welcome the warmth of which will in some degree repay you for the dangers and hardships through which you may have passed.

J.A. Joicey may have been disappointed not to get further than Malta, but not, perhaps, to learn that J.O. Haldane of the 1st Suffolk Regiment, who had reached Cape Colony, was able to report that 'Our Sergeant Major had a talk with Fichardt, late of Jesus, who curiously enough passed through here [Beaufort West] as one of our prisoners!'

Six members of the College died in the fighting.

First World War

ARTHUR GRAY

It was the second week in August 1914. The few men who were up for the 'Long' were preparing for flight to lake or sea or mountain, and Cambridge was settling down to the two months of torpor, when college courts are silent, porters sleep, and tradesmen offer their wares to townsmen at prices which they deny to undergraduates. War had been declared a week before. We were all in tremulous excitement. Nothing was certainly known. Was it three, four, or five divisions of British troops which were crossing the sea – to France, Belgium or whither? The only ascertained fact was that Russians, landed at Wick and Thurso, were being rolled through Cambridge station in countless myriads! But they travelled by night in darkened carriages, and the station was strictly closed when they passed. So it seemed that Cambridge was to be altogether outside the trail of war, and somehow we felt that our immunity was a slight to our patriotism. But night and day the Board of Military Studies and the staff of the C.U.O.T.C. sat in Corpus Hall, receiving and forwarding applications for commissions. Most of us helped. At night some snatched moments of repose on the floor. Elderly tutors and professors enrolled themselves in the O.T.C. and drilled on Jesus Close. Mr Abbott in khaki looked fiercer than we had known him. Dons yet more elderly patrolled the streets as 'specials.' Everybody else – except Hun spies who were everywhere – slaved for Red Cross in the new lecture rooms.

One day in that second week of August, coming in from a walk, I found a crumpled pencil note awaiting me. It was from General Benson, since killed. He asked permission to put up tents and marquees on the college close for the staff officers of the 18th Infantry Brigade and officers of the 2nd Durham Light Infantry. I went out to Midsummer Common, and to my amazement found the whole of it covered with tents. Men were lighting fires: food was being cooked: some men were kicking footballs about. I found the General, and he told me this was the 6th Division. They arrived mostly from Scotland that morning. Not only Midsummer Common was occupied. Stourbridge Common, Parker's Piece, and every open space about the town was similarly populated. Horses were tethered along the eastern wall of our close, on Christ's Piece, along the Grange road, and elsewhere.

On the night of their arrival the officers of the Durhams messed in Hall with the Fellows – the beginning of much good fellowship. Presently wives followed their husbands to Cambridge, and lodgings filled. Despite the tension of the time, the ill news of the Mons retreat,

and rumoured Hun barbarities, it was a happy time – at least for us who were outside the penumbra of war. On four Sundays of glorious August sunshine there were great parade services on our close – sights and sounds unforgettable – and addresses by the Bishop of Ely, the Dean of Durham, and others.

One day, early in September, Brigadier-General Congreve called on me and asked me for the loan of a Latin dictionary – an odd request at such a time, but the General was an Oxford man, and it might be conjectured that he was cramming Vegetius *De Re Militari*. A few days later came a letter from the General accompanied by a splendid silver gilt cock and globe – the College emblem – with a Latin inscription beneath it, stating that it was a gift of the officers quartered on the Close, 'as a token of gratitude we feel to you for all your kindness, which none of us will ever forget'.

And we shall not forget our gallant guests. Almost within twenty-four hours they came to tell us that they had their marching orders. They had been heart-sick at the delay, and great was their relief to find that they were not to be left in England. To us the parting was inexpressibly sad. True, friendly, gentle men, they most of them met the end that they had steadily faced within a month of their departure in the battles on the Aisne.

In October 1914 the College re-assembled about seventy strong. We suffered a greater proportionate diminution in numbers than any college, except perhaps King's and Clare. During the term our ranks were rapidly thinned by further enlistments, and in December we barely totalled forty. And the Roll of Honour began – how our hearts were stricken for the first glorious few – Myddleton, Payne, 'Willoughby' Shields, and David Wilson. Little we foresaw that four years would not see the close of the list, and that many a recent freshman's year was to be far more than decimated.

From hour to hour the scene shifted like the pictures on a cinema film. For a time the cloisters of Nevile's Court at Trinity were used as a hospital for the wounded, and some officers were tended in the Research Hospital on the Hills Road. Belgian refugees flocked into the town – many of them University professors and students – and were hastily housed under any hospitable roof that offered. There was a big reception for them at Jesus Lodge on New Year's Day. In gratitude for the hospitable entertainment of the Jesus crew at Ghent in 1911 a Fund for Belgian Relief was started by Jesus men, and brought in nearly £800. Alas! M. Lippeus, who as President of the

Belgian Club should have received and administered the find, was deported on account of his patriotic energy by the Huns, and only after four years of internment in Germany was able to render thanks to his Jesus friends. The great city known as the first Eastern General hospital was begun in 1914, and gradually ate up the whole of the King's and Clare cricket ground. The first walking cases among the blue-coats had the time of their lives. They were motored about the country, and entertained in private houses and cafés, until the authorities thought it wise to impose some limits on Cambridge hospitality. Shall I ever forget the dinner which I shared with the 'Contemptibles' in hospital in August 1916?

In January 1915 came a division of Welsh Territorials, and many of them were billeted in colleges. Wild Wales wreaked on the town the vengeance which it had smothered since the days of Hengist. The Master's courts at Trinity were as Louvain, and Green Street out-did Ypres. Some who were quartered in our boat-house lighted fires on the floor, but failed to burn the place down. The officers of the Cheshire Field Artillery were our guests in Jesus. And good fellows we found them. From this time military services in chapel on Sundays became usual. On Easter Day three hundred attended. Our own services diminished at first to three on week-days, and later on week-day services were given up altogether. The bell and clock of course were silenced: we groped in darkness about the courts, and blue curtains were put up to obscure the lighted windows of the Hall.

Gradually our numbers melted. In June 1918 our complement was a round dozen – most of us 'crocks'. Games of course had long since vanished. The last effort was in Lent 1915, when a Jesus clinker four defeated Trinity Hall by inches. The grass grew high at the boat-houses and on the towpath. Alf Parsons went sorrowfully away to build aeroplanes. Stubbens was drawn into the tide of war. The cricket pitch was woefully neglected, and Mr Watt lost his occupation and his spirits.

Things became more cheerful with the arrival of the first batch of the cadets. A company of the G.O.C.B. was established in the Chapel Court, and overflowed into K and L staircases. Colonel Cradock and his family occu-pied North House, as other colonels had done before him. The officers were quartered over the way in Westcott House. How shall I describe the geniality and kindness of officers and men? They gave us concerts and recitations in the Hall, theatricals at the A.D.C., revues at the Guildhall, dances at Westcott House. As each batch left us we were invited to share their parting dinners, and heartily we bade them god speed. They were of all sorts – Oxford and a tailor's cutter, Eton and a North Sea fisherman, and their ages ranged from 18 to 55: among them an actor, a pressman, several barristers and clergymen. There was generally a professional organist to train the choir and 'preside' on Sundays, and never a deficiency to supply the Dean's place after Dr Foakes Jackson took wing to America. The cadets rolled and mowed the cricket field. Football and cricket revived. Mr Watt became gay, and though Mr Duke's Board unfavourably controlled his hospitalities, he never lacked cheerful company – nor they. The river was alive again with racing eights, and the Headship was contested, I think, eleven times in two years and a half, and – as is recorded on a challenge 'pot' which the cadets kindly bequeathed to the College – the Jesus cadets won the place not less than six times, which, with other things, made these Jesus men – who could deny them the name? – extraordinarily proud and boastful of their college; and wonderful tales of their Jesus days they will have to tell the generation that comes after them.

Then Armistice Day – so recent that a few veterans among us can remember how we silenced St Mary's bells, and broke the windows of the *Cambridge Magazine* – happy editors who so cheaply earned the reward of their ardent patriotism and prudent pacifism. Was it all very foolish, or was it Wisdom that cried in our streets for joy that one old wickedness was dead, and that the Dayspring had visited England from on high? And along with the clanging of the bells and the roaring of the crowd, there were memories, more tender than sad, of faces and voices from a happy past, and some present visions of rude crosses in other lands – France, Mesopotamia, Gallipoli … where not?

Reprinted from the Michaelmas term 1919 number of Chanticlere

There are 152 names on the College's memorial to its members killed in the First World War.

Second World War

FREDERICK BRITTAIN

The censorship has hitherto prevented us from telling our readers that half or more of the College was occupied by the Royal Air Force from the beginning of the war until the spring of this year [1945].

On 6 September 1939 an advance party of four officers arrived to set up the headquarters of the 1st (soon afterwards styled the 2nd) Initial Training Wing in the College. In order to provide their Wing with an office they commandeered the ground floor of D Staircase, which at the time was occupied by the College Office and Shield Library. The College, before the war began, had arranged to move the Office and Library to North House, but the new premises were not ready. Consequently, the office files and library books had to be moved hurriedly on a barrow. The office found a temporary home in the undergraduates' Common Room, the books in heaps on the floor of North House.

About 250 members of the Wing – officers and others – arrived next day. We can still see them sitting on the grass in the brilliant sunshine in First Court, waiting for orders shouted from time to time from their new office, out of which barrow-loads of books were still being trundled. No one who was present is likely to forget the scene in Hall after dinner that night, when our guests lined the walls and our venerable Master, Mr Arthur Gray, who had been at the College ever since 1870, welcomed them all with a charming speech, just as he had welcomed the men of 1914.

At first the officers, so long as they were few, dined with the Fellows at high table. When they increased in number they dined at the middle table in the body of the Hall, at the same time as the members of the College. Before many weeks their hours of duty made it essential for them to take their meals in the Hall Lecture Room, which they used until the end of their stay.

The other ranks always had their meals in Hall, at a different time from the members of the College. There were difficulties about service in the middle of the day, and as a result our Hall lunch, from the last day of October 1939, was served in the premises of the Pitt Club, of which the College obtained a lease when the war caused the Club to suspend its activities. Towards the end of February 1942 the Pitt Club premises were taken from us and converted into a British Restaurant; but a re-arrangement of times by the Air Force enabled us to take our lunch in Hall again.

In the following month the Training Wing was reinforced by a detachment of the Women's Auxiliary Air Force. The R.A.F. had publicly advertised their presence in the College almost from the first by erecting a pole on the Close and flying their pennant from it, but we were not allowed to mention their presence in writing, or even the presence of the new arrivals. We managed, however, to hint at the latter in our *Report* for 1942, in which we remarked that 'in one respect, part of the College had reverted to conditions which prevailed before 1496'. To our surprise, a number of old members failed to understand the allusion.

We made many friends among our guests. They played many games on the Close, against the College and against other opponents. Some of them were elected to the Roosters and other social clubs. One of the officers, who already had a degree from another university, became a keen and valued member of the College and valiantly qualified for an honours degree in his spare time. Another of our guests, serving in the ranks at the time, was already a member of the College, and indeed a Fellow of it, before he was billeted on us. Once, in the darkest days of the blackout, he was put on guard outside the Porter's Lodge with fixed bayonet; but we did not know that he was in Cambridge and Fellows of his own college passed him without recognising him.

On 18 May 1944 the 2nd Initial Training Wing was replaced by the 54th Maintenance Unit. These and the W.A.A.F. moved out of the College in March 1945. The W.A.A.F. had occupied Staircases A, B, O and P. The R.A.F. had occupied the rest of Second Court with the exception

Jesuan members of the University's OTC, 1941.

Pass to permit Dr W.H.
Thorpe (1921), Fellow 1932–
86, to enter the College.
He was, as a Quaker, a
conscientious objector,
working during the war
on ways of eradicating
invertebrate pests, one
aspect of the drive to make
the UK self-sufficient in
food.

of one staircase (originally K, afterwards J), Staircases 1 to 6 in Chapel Court, the whole of East House and, as we have already said, the ground floor of D Staircase. Their meals were cooked at first by the College, afterwards by their own cooks in our kitchen.

There were 424 air-raid alerts at Cambridge during the war, during which the enemy dropped 118 high-explosive bombs, 3 oil bombs and about 1000 incendiaries, and 29 people were killed. The Round Church, the Union Society and houses in Jesus Lane were hit in July 1942, but the College buildings came through the war unscathed.

Labour and materials are not yet available to redecorate all the rooms recently vacated by the Air Force, but the work has begun. The tall ventilation shafts of the underground shelters have been removed, as have the water tanks at the foot of each staircase and nearly all the sandbags, and most of the Chapel windows have already been brought back from the country.

Our difficulties in carrying on throughout the war have been considerable, but the loyalty and persistence of our staff have been beyond praise. We wish that those Jesus men who have not been at the College since the outbreak of war could have seen them at work. Whether permanent or temporary employees of the College, they have carried on through all difficulties – in the kitchen, the buttery, the porter's lodge, the gardens, the Close, and elsewhere. Without their persistence, we should have had a break in the continuity of the College for the first time since its foundation, and we are grateful to them.

Over a hundred and twenty members of the College have fallen in the war. They included some of our youngest and some of our best. We can commemorate them but we can never replace them nor can we ever be adequately grateful to them.

Majorem hac dilectionem nemo habet, ut animam suam ponat quis pro amicis suis.

Reprinted from 'College Notes' in the Jesus College Cambridge Society Report *for 1945*

There are 124 names on the College's memorial to its members killed in the Second World War.

Since 1945

North Court by David Roberts 1963–6, with (right) P staircase on Waterhouse's building, 1869–70.

An Ever-changing College: 1940–2005

ALAN SHARPE and KEN JOHNSON in conversation with PETER GLAZEBROOK

P.G.: Let's begin at the beginning and ask you, Alan, how it was that you came to Jesus in 1940.

A.S.: Almost chance. I had a headmaster at the City School, Lincoln – not Lincoln School, an inferior one – who was a good man, ambitious for his pupils. He'd been here himself, post First World War, with a grant at Fitzwilliam and he had some contacts in Cambridge and he advised me to try for Trinity. I had no objection to Trinity, indeed, I rather liked the look of it! But I took the scholarship examination as it was called then and put in a performance which was not very distinguished. My chemistry was quite good and I think the phrase used by whoever reported on me was that my mathematics was weak and my physics was not much better, so that in the pooling system which operated then I must have been very near the bottom of the list. In those days Trinity took the cream, particularly on the sciences side, and so I was pooled at what was then called 'the auction' and picked up by Bernard Manning, a Lincolnshire man rather like myself, and I was offered and immediately accepted an exhibition here. I'd never been into the College and knew nothing about it. It was in fact, my bottom but one choice. Then I needed some money. I was hoping, what subsequently turned out to be the case, to get a State Scholarship, but as a safety- net I applied to the Education Department which was a way then of getting about £150 a year, provided you promised to be a teacher. Since I wanted to be a teacher at the time and, indeed, perhaps missed my vocation really, I came up for a session at the Department and was briefly interviewed there. My interviewer said, 'Have you been and met the Admissions Tutor at Jesus?', and when I said 'No', he said, 'Well, I'll ring up for you. You might like to go and see him.' So I went and Manning – in the middle of the afternoon – was kindness itself and made me sit down and offered me a drink and a cigarette. I was treated like a young adult. That was the way he treated everybody. I was very impressed by him. And then I came up in the following October, in 1940.

P.G.: The war's on.

A.S.: Yes, the war. The College was occupied mainly by the No. 2 Initial Training Wing of the RAF and some WAAFs. They had nearly all of the College. Most of the dons had gone away. Many of the undergraduates went away quickly and it was quite a small party of us. I suppose the total strength – I'm guessing now – would probably be thirty or more. But we didn't all last very long because the policy at the time was to allow scientists, engineers, medics and anyone who might be useful or was medically unfit to stay on for a couple of years and perhaps qualify for a degree. The others were allowed to have, I think it was one year, but sometimes it was two terms because they took to coming up after Christmas after the examination in the preceding year and this served as a bit of pre-training for the services. It was a condition that we joined the OTC, the Air Squadron or the Home Guard or something similar, and then most people disappeared. As scientists, we were virtually all allowed two years, and very clever ones – like Denys Wilkinson, for example – were allowed three, and of course stayed on afterwards. I departed after two. I'd been summoned by the Joint Recruiting Board and they told me that there was some sort of choice and I don't remember what they were, but anything that they suggested was something that they were short of. They had exhausted the supply of chemists. So they sent me into chemistry.

P.G.: But then you already wanted to be in chemistry and you concentrated on this.

A.S.: I wasn't so sure at the time as it was a natural sciences system here. I thought I did want to be in chemistry until I'd been here for a little bit, and then I watched all these very clever people. They were not chemists on the whole. Wilkinson was obviously going to be a physicist. My life in the College in fact has been dominated, first as an undergraduate and then as a Fellow, by meeting among my contemporaries someone whom I instantly recognised as a person infinitely more talented than myself. It was Wilkinson when I was an undergraduate, who came up on the same day, and when I became a Fellow it was Lloyd-Jones, who was admitted to a Fellowship on the same day. And I at once saw that was the genuine article. I was going to be a worthy, but I was never going to be in the same class.

P.G.: Anyway, you had the two years from '40 to '42. Who else besides Manning struck you? You've said Denys Wilkinson, of course, but anyone else among the teachers or your fellow students?
A.S.: I don't remember many of my fellow students very well; among the Fellows, most of them had gone away, of course, but there remained Pars who was too old; Thorpe, a Quaker, conscientious objector; Freddy Brittain; Alan Percival, who was an engineer and therefore in a reserved occupation for producing other engineers, who was required to stay. There were two or three people who came along sometimes; Robbie Jennings, for example, I remember meeting briefly during that period.

P.G.: Did you feel life very intense during that period? Were you trying to get more in?
A.S.: Not particularly. This you might think was rather curious, but Part I of the Natural Sciences Tripos course remained the same except that virtually everybody was directed to do a new subject called electronics. For some reason I escaped that. Lots of scientists found it extremely useful afterwards because they learned the sort of things about switches, valves, currents and so on that they wouldn't otherwise have done. One other name I'm omitting – he was the only Fellow who actually supervised me. This was W.H. Mills, who was famous.

P.G.: Tell us a bit more about Mills.
A.S.: He was a very clever man and what impressed me about him afterwards (I didn't know at the time whether it was put on or not) was that he said he didn't do experiments unless they were necessary. He didn't have a large group; he tackled a series of problems in stereo-chemistry (the shapes of molecules) by a method which is now obsolete of finding out whether they did things to the plane of polarised light or not. It doesn't matter very much what that is. He was very good at yes/no tests. If the molecule was planar around the middle atom it would have one effect; if it was tetrahedral around the middle atom, it would do something else. And he was the best man in the world in this field at that time. He never became a professor; he was somewhat in the shadow of Sir William Pope, who was the Head of the Department and a public figure. Mills was never really a public figure, though he was a great survivor; he'd actually retired about 1938 but

W.H. Mills (1892), Fellow 1899–1905, 1912–59.

Pencil drawing by Randolphe Schwabe, 1945

he was still around and he still did some teaching, though not in the laboratory. I'd never seen him at a class there.

P.G.: Didn't he become an FRS?
A.S.: Yes. I'm not sure when, probably the 1920s [1923]. He was for one year, it might have been two, actually President of the Chemical Society. He was perfectly suited to this. The great thing about him was he was retired by this time, 1942; he was available and I think he was quite pleased to do some teaching. He was good but fundamentally he was a rather retiring type. He was very interested in blackberries. He was one of the world's experts on the varieties of blackberries. He used to go on holidays looking for new blackberries. And he had a nice line in obituary notices.

P.G.: So you were away then from '42 to '45; what were you doing while you were away?
A.S.: It was to do with explosives. I was nominally in the Chemical Inspection Department. A lot of it was merely doing routine analysis, for which I was rather over qualified, but some of it was research work.

P.G.: To make sure that the explosives exploded?
A.S.: That was the purpose of the whole set-up. I was in quality control effectively, but, when new compositions were suggested, methods had to be devised for analysing them as a routine. I got involved in that a bit as well.

Alan Sharpe (1940), Fellow
1948– , Senior Tutor
1964–70, 1984–5.

Dona Haycraft, 1970

A.S.: Yes, I came back in a hurry. Because when the war ended there were systems of release if one had been called up, and it was obvious of course there wasn't going to be much future in explosives. I was offered in fact a permanent job in the Scientific Civil Service in that department to go to Woolwich. But I thought I don't want to do this. So I noticed other people were disappearing and, since it didn't seem possible to get much sense out of anyone I could get in touch with, I said to the boss, 'I would like to take tomorrow off, if you don't mind. I'm going to London, to the Ministry of Labour', and without an appointment I sat on the doorstep outside and was let in to see somebody or other and I explained my predicament. I said, 'I'm ready to go back now. I've already done two years and I've got another year to come.' And then I played my trump card. I said I realised there are all sorts of people

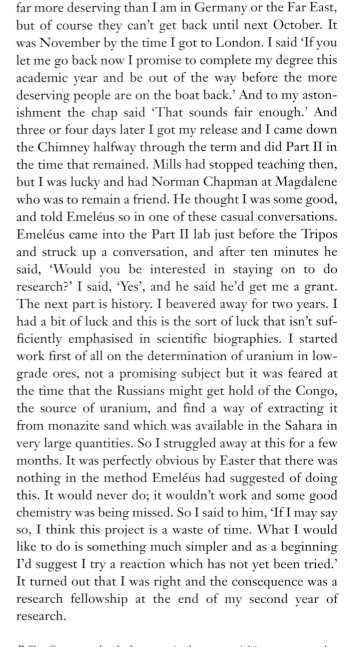

far more deserving than I am in Germany or the Far East, but of course they can't get back until next October. It was November by the time I got to London. I said 'If you let me go back now I promise to complete my degree this academic year and be out of the way before the more deserving people are on the boat back.' And to my astonishment the chap said 'That sounds fair enough.' And three or four days later I got my release and I came down the Chimney halfway through the term and did Part II in the time that remained. Mills had stopped teaching then, but I was lucky and had Norman Chapman at Magdalene who was to remain a friend. He thought I was some good, and told Eméleus so in one of these casual conversations. Eméleus came into the Part II lab just before the Tripos and struck up a conversation, and after ten minutes he said, 'Would you be interested in staying on to do research?' I said, 'Yes', and he said he'd get me a grant. The next part is history. I beavered away for two years. I had a bit of luck and this is the sort of luck that isn't sufficiently emphasised in scientific biographies. I started work first of all on the determination of uranium in low-grade ores, not a promising subject but it was feared at the time that the Russians might get hold of the Congo, the source of uranium, and find a way of extracting it from monazite sand which was available in the Sahara in very large quantities. So I struggled away at this for a few months. It was perfectly obvious by Easter that there was nothing in the method Eméleus had suggested of doing this. It would never do; it wouldn't work and some good chemistry was being missed. So I said to him, 'If I may say so, I think this project is a waste of time. What I would like to do is something much simpler and as a beginning I'd suggest I try a reaction which has not yet been tried.' It turned out that I was right and the consequence was a research fellowship at the end of my second year of research.

P.G.: So you solved that particular one within a year and a half.

A.S.: No credit really is to be attached to it. It was not particularly clever, it was just shockingly obvious. There it was. Now it involved, as with all these things, another element of luck. The reagent which Eméleus wanted to use on monazite sand to get the uranium out involved a very powerful fluorinating agent which sets fire to asbestos. This, of course, makes a splendid lecture demonstration. That must have been shown to goodness knows how many people: Mills came to have a look and, sure enough, when I poured it on the asbestos the asbestos caught fire. To set things in true perspective, I believe there may have been as many as six candidates for the research fellowship. It was open to Jesus people only, but for the first time open to people in all subjects.

P.G.: And how long were you a research Fellow before you were asked to do College jobs or to teach?
A.S.: As soon as I became a research Fellow (we were elected in May/June at that time) – I started doing some teaching in the October term.

P.G.: And then you got a University job.
A.S.: I was offered a University job, for which I had not applied, in the following spring. All normal systems were in abeyance. There was nobody else in inorganic chemistry younger, active and thought to have any promise. Eméleus just said, 'Leave it to me.' And Todd came into the lab one day and said, 'I hear you're interested in the University Demonstratorship?' And I said, 'Yes'. 'Then you'll be glad to know we've appointed you.' And of course he liked really to show how powerful he was, and indeed he was. And so that was that. After two years of research, one year in a research fellowship, I found myself firmly on the academic ladder with no obvious rival in the inorganic field. That's very different from now.

P.G.: Ken, you reached the College by a different route; you did your Higher School Certificate just after the war had broken out and you were immediately offered the place at Manchester University to which you went.
K.J.: On the C.P. Snow scheme. It was a take it or leave it thing. So it was this tricky choice. We took the bird in the hand as there was no guarantee that I would get an Oxbridge scholarship after the war. It's done me proud. No regrets.

P.G.: You went there, you graduated, you were engaged in war work, and you went back to Manchester University to teach.
K.J.: Yes; I was an assistant lecturer, and I set out to do a PhD, which you could do at the same time in Manchester in those days.

P.G.: So how exactly was it that you came to Cambridge?
K.J.: The first trip was a conference on teaching mechanics which Alan Percival was involved with. In fact I think he was perhaps the moving spirit in the Department. I was involved with a bulletin about engineering education and had written some articles about how best to run teaching laboratories, and on the strength of that I was invited to come and talk about it here. So that was one connection. The second was that David Tabor was my PhD examiner, but I'd had some sort of contact with him before and he'd taken an interest in what I was doing and invited me to come here to go to the Cavendish and see what was going on there in friction. And I am sure it must have been he who put some right words in the right place when there was an advertisement for a demonstratorship in the press which I put in for and he was mentioned as someone who might write on my behalf.

P.G.: And you were appointed to the Cambridge demonstratorship and you've been here ever since?
K.J.: Ever since.

P.G.: But when you came to Cambridge in 1954 as a demonstrator you didn't immediately become a member of any College.
K.J.: It was pretty immediately, although I didn't immediately become a Fellow. Alan Percival had just been appointed Bursar and he had a side-kick called Dick Bishop who had just been offered a fellowship at Pembroke which he accepted. So immediately my appointment in the Department was announced Alan wrote a letter and said we will make you a member of High Table and probably a College Lecturer in return for six hours' teaching a week. Really taking Dick Bishop's place, which I of course gratefully accepted. I came for a weekend's vetting too. You weren't signed up without being looked at. Alan Percival was on the interviewing committee too and we'd met at that conference before. So I was interviewed, taken into dinner, met some people, went out and played bowls with the then Senior Tutor, Robbie Jennings, and Alan Percival. And then I was offered membership of the College and achieved that status by that devious back-door route.

P.G.: How long was it before the question of your becoming a Fellow arose?
K.J.: That was quite interesting in itself. Magdalene were looking for an Engineering fellow, and of course Magdalene had mixed reputations at that time, and I was interviewed there and offered the fellowship, but Alan rather put me off Magdalene and I turned it down. Shortly after that I was approached by Clare. That seemed quite good, but they wanted me immediately to be an assistant tutor with quite a lot of administrative responsibility and I was still finding my feet. So I told Alan that if Jesus will match the offer of a fellowship I'd prefer to stay, but if they didn't I felt I couldn't pass the other up.

P.G.: What was your impression of this place that you had joined?
K.J.: A bit overawed, of course, but I had come from a fairly scholarly background, so I had a good feel about what Oxford/Cambridge was like from my father who was a schoolteacher.

P.G.: All colleges are different, as we know; what would you say about the atmosphere and ethos of Jesus in the mid-'50s?
K.J.: It's a beautiful old College. You really felt you were in the Oxbridge system. You weren't perched on the outskirts in any sort of way and that in a sense was pleasurable and rewarding. One didn't get the impression that it was an overly scholarly College. Bill Thorpe was significant

at the time, the only FRS besides Mills, and slightly eccentric in the Cambridge way. Rowing was certainly a big thing at that time. At the interview Alan Percival said, 'Did you ever row?' 'No'. Robbie Jennings said, 'Are you a cricketer?' 'No, I'm not.' But there were a number of Fellows with young children who went out of their way to be particularly welcoming before I was a Fellow. Actually Freddy Brittain was extremely welcoming and so was Alan Pars. I used to get invited to their things. I introduced my new wife to Freddy straight from our honeymoon. He said, 'I must explain, I'm married to the College.' Robbie had just married too, we were both expecting children at the same time. They went out of their way – I wasn't even a Fellow, just a newcomer from Manchester – to include both of us in things that were going on. A family thing.

P.G.: Not an overly scholarly place?
K.J.: When one comes to Cambridge, particularly as a scientist, you are told that this is where Newton trod and one of the chaps who was a hero of mine – G.I. Taylor – was still going strong at Trinity. I have family connections with the Cockcrofts, too, and of course there were all

those pre-war years with high-energy physics going on at that time with Rutherford, so you really felt that you had moved into the leading scientific base in this country. But I didn't get the impression that Jesus was at the cutting edge of that. That wasn't necessarily a disappointment but this is what I observed.

P.G.: Was there any sense then that the scientists – the few of you there were – were second-class citizens, or had that gone?
K.J.: No, I don't think I ever felt a second-class citizen – but the engineers were, in comparison with pure science. In my early years' teaching, there was a general feeling that it was easier to get into Engineering than it was to get into Natural Science. And of course schools had quite a lot to do with that. Most of the bright boys were taught by pure scientists or mathematicians. That was what was the right and proper thing to do, and there was this aura of glamour about Cambridge science at the time. But if you weren't quite up to it you tried for Engineering. And, of course, it wasn't just scholarship entry then: it was principally common entry so public schools put their also-rans in for Engineering. So I did have to cope with quite a few people who weren't particularly interested in the subject but felt it was right and proper to go out into the world with a Cambridge degree whatever they did. So that's a big change.

P.G.: And when do you think that change really began to be felt?
K.J.: At what point did anyone qualifying for Cambridge, or any other university, get automatic local government support? When was the Cambridge colleges' scholarship system not necessary?

P.G.: It must have been in the late '50s that everybody who gained admission to university was automatically given an award that was administered by the local authorities though it was centrally funded, and the old State Scholarships disappeared.
K.J.: In a sense, the old scholarships system gave kudos, of course, both to the chap and school, and had the advantage of spreading talent around the colleges rather than putting it all into Trinity – but in a way the need for it had gone and we gradually eased it out: it seemed to be a fairly slow process – what the old system did provide is what in some ways is missing now, something in addition to A-levels to pick entrants from. But I think it wasn't a clear-cut event which produced the change, but certainly at some stage – I suppose in the '70s to '80s – having a father a Jesuan wouldn't get you in.

P.G.: Whereas in the immediate pre-war period there'd been a club in College called the Younger Brothers, the qualification

Ken Johnson (1954), Fellow 1957– , President 1986–8, 1989–90.

Pencil drawing by Richard Sell, 1997

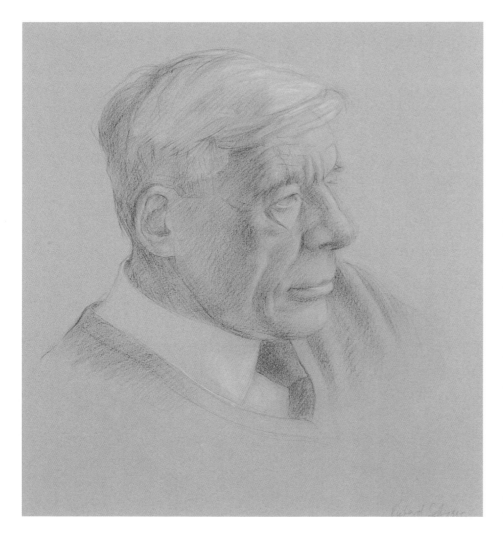

for membership being that there were members of your family that were already members of College – in 1937–8 more than fifty undergraduates qualified – and over it, Manning, the Senior Tutor, presided!

K.J.: A bit before the '70s: at a graduation dinner – the Master must have been away – Gardner-Smith spoke. It was the dinner where it was just the graduands themselves – 'When you go down some of you will write books. We will welcome a presentation of your books to the College library. Also some of you might produce sons. That's a bit more difficult.'

P.G.: *Once you were, as you put it, Alan, firmly on the academic ladder, you were committed to teaching, but I remember you telling me that your first College job was as Junior Bursar.*
A.S.: Yes. Charles Wilson had come back and was the Senior Bursar, Freddy was the Steward. Charles was busy because the planning world was coming in then; farms were being bought, sold, whatever. The Bursary was really a big job so I looked after the petty sort of undergraduate stuff. The rooms, for example. It was rather uninspiring. It was a job where someone was needed who could keep his temper, although I never felt much like losing mine. It wasn't important enough to get too worked up about. My fundamental job as defined by Vivian Fisher was to keep the peace between Charles and Freddy, who didn't get on. And if it cost a few hundred a year to have a Junior Bursar, Vivian said that was worth it. I did all sorts of things. I was responsible for having all the coal fires replaced throughout the College by gas fires. The Carpenter building was transformed from two-room sets into bed-sitting rooms. But I was only technically the person in charge of it. I didn't know very much about it. I did learn a bit about the accounts, and I did learn what was very valuable: the ability to say 'No'.

P.G.: *In the post-war period freshmen went into lodgings and moved into College in their second year and then there was a change, sudden or gradual, in which the freshmen were put into College? When did that happen, and why?*
A.S.: I think it must have been one of the consequences of the war, after which very large numbers of people returned; everything that happened then – where the returned warriors were put – for many years determined what happened afterwards. We probably went over gradually. One reason would have been the amount of accommodation in College – the switch here into bed-sitting rooms was beginning; it seems an unimportant factor, but when forty rooms suddenly become eighty bed-sits instead of two-room sets; and there was the building of North Court. That was opened when – '64? That would have made it possible without thinking too much about higher policy. It would in fact have been really rather difficult not to do it. I don't remember a great debate about it. It just happened.

P.G.: *Within five years of your coming here, Ken, Tillyard retired as Master and Denys Page was elected. Did that election seem to be of any particular significance at the time it was made?*
K.J.: It was an event for me as it was my first mastership election. We were all involved; everybody felt that they wanted a change of scene – everybody wanted a change of scene from Tillyard who was so retiring and had no charisma, whether that matters or not. It was taken really quite seriously. I think Robbie was an internal candidate and Charles Wilson too; I was a Robbie admirer. So it was a serious business and there were lots of small dinners to which the candidates were invited. Denys Page was invited. It was a significant event.

A.S.: Oh! Yes. No doubt whatever about that. Unless you go back to appointments by the Visitor, Page was the first non-Jesus man to be Master. When Tillyard announced his intention to retire, of course, names were put forward.

Professor Sir Denys Page, Master 1959–73.
Sir William Coldstream, 1962

Robbie, Charles, Bill Thorpe, Leslie Martin were suggested. That was probably all of them. We had a series of meetings and a series of votes in which no one secured the necessary majority. So that on 1 October that year we had no Master. We went into the Chapel one last time. Many of us had switched our allegiances. I had, for example. Robbie was the leading candidate, of course. Meeting Denys and seeing the general reactions, I wrote to Vivian Fisher, who was co-ordinating, and said, I have to say I have changed my mind.

P.G.: Looking back, first of all perhaps if one can place oneself towards the end of Denys Page's mastership, in retrospect what was your feeling about it by the end? He'd been Master for about fourteen years.
K.J.: At the beginning, of course, it was splendid. There'd been a real change. You felt there was a heavyweight in the Lodge and we were all slightly afraid of him in a way. You didn't happily produce his displeasure. And he had strong views about a lot of things. The College had a leader and significant Master in their Lodge and it made a difference – and those four daughters! He did a lot of entertaining and knew all the right people and so on. So the early years, and as Alan will tell you, and I remember Vivian Fisher saying, were just so marvellous. It was just such a change for the College from before. And then through the difficult years of student revolt and agitations about admission of women and undergraduates on Council he took a completely uncompromising attitude – as you know – and was then embittered by being vilified by the left because of his unwillingness to actively protest against the regime in Greece which had become a bit of a political issue at the time. Although, as he said, he was almost a socialist when he was a young man, he acquired the reputation as one of the most reactionary masters in Cambridge, which was unfair in some ways. I think the thing about Greece was that it was about putting on labels: in the political situation at the time people wanted labels which divided us into goodies and baddies. He became increasingly irrational about it all. Then, of course, there was this consultative committee / staff student committee, which he chaired and a number of quite clever undergraduates were members from the student side who rather liked taunting him and it became an embarrassment to us. Really not meeting the comments in a rational way. He just said, 'I'm not having women residents while I'm Master of this College.' He just felt he couldn't cope with the pressures that that would put on him in the mores of the time in the relationship between young men and young women.

P.G.: My recollection is of the questions both of student representation on Council and of women having been postponed because of Denys's opposition, and that by the time Alan Cottrell became Master they proceeded easily and smoothly within the College.
K.J.: I think they did. I think it's fair to say that Alan's views were canvased beforehand. If he'd not been prepared to go along with it he wouldn't have been elected.
P.G.: Concentrating on the period, Alan, before you became Senior Tutor, first of all during the Tillyard mastership. I take it you were a Tutor and Director of Studies in Natural Sciences.
A.S.: I was. I was Director of Studies in all Natural Sciences, briefly, after Denys Wilkinson had complained about the inefficiency of the then system.

P.G.: How important were Tutors in the late 1950s?
A.S.: They were much more important academically because they were the undergraduate's real point of contact with the College. More so than Directors of Studies.

P.G.: Why was that?
A.S.: Often it hinged on the personalities of the two. The Tutors on the whole knew what they were doing. Some Directors of Studies were pretty ropey, to put it bluntly. We still had cases then of undergraduates not seeing their Director of Studies. But in some areas, the Director of Studies did control what went on: Natural Sciences pretty well; and, for example, History. English – I don't think I could summarise what went on there.

P.G.: By the time I came here in 1967 there seemed to be a lot of emphasis on the disciplinary functions, which were of course by then being questioned. How important were the disciplinary functions of the Tutors when you were first appointed?
A.S.: I wouldn't say they were particularly important. Of course, they were enshrined really in common law; the age of majority was 21, so that nearly all undergraduates were minors for nearly all of their time and this meant of course that their rights were considerably circumscribed – not least by the wishes of their parents, who resented the idea that they were handing over their children to somebody else who'd just give them a cup of tea occasionally and pat them on the head. There were College regulations and some of them were really quite strict. No ladies after whatever time it was. A rigid system for absences and exeats because of the emphasis on residence. But people didn't worry very much about it – discipline didn't seem to play a large part in it. Indeed I remember there was a book, a gating book, because this was one of the standard punishments. You could fine people, not very profitably, but you could gate them. They had to be in College by 10 o'clock at night for a fortnight or something like this. This was the sort of thing, the orthodox penalty for riotous behaviour, when there was riotous behaviour. I inherited Robbie's book – I don't know why, but it was a pity to waste a good book. Robbie hadn't used

much of it and when I retired after several years, I hadn't used it much more. One didn't in fact. One had the threat of being able to do things. For my part I didn't do them. The nastiest thing I was inclined to do was to say this was so serious a matter that it required further consideration involving, say, the Master, or the other Tutors, or something of this sort and sentence would be passed in a week's time. On the whole one didn't do anything except just say 'You're lucky, so go your way and sin no more.' The general mood of 'Why should it be that senior members of the College control our way of life?' – the resentment that was building up, built up progressively during the '60s.

K.J.: I think Vivian Fisher summarised it to me – the merits of the old tutorial system – because of the talk about changing it. He said you only see them for a minute or two, but you do see them and can ask an odd question even though they've only come for your signature. And that's invaluable when they really need you. If you just have what the Americans call office hours, the first time you see them is when something serious has happened that needs your assistance or intervention. And I think that summarises a lot of the advantages of some sort of system whereby one is somehow involved on an almost – well it isn't quite an informal basis, is it? If you do away with the need to get any sort of permission to do anything other than putting on a May Ball, it's hard to see how you can go back to a system that I think worked quite well. And in cases that I was involved with with students, accidents, committing suicide, serious breaches or illnesses, the old system worked particularly well and one was certainly glad it was in place. I suppose it would have fallen much more on myself as Director of Studies otherwise.

P.G.: And it was intended when the change was made – I'm not sure if it's worked out that way – that the Directors of Studies, of whom most, or almost all, were by then Fellows of the College, which had not been the case earlier, would do the Tutor's work, so that they could concentrate their attention on their own pupils both directorially and tutorially. You mentioned, Alan, contact between Tutors and parents, was there much of it in fact?
A.S.: Under normal conditions, no, but I used to find often if an undergraduate was in trouble academically or something else, it was well worth while – of course a lot of the parents were old Jesus men. I remember once after, I forget who it was, didn't pay his bill, I wrote him a letter, a good tutorial letter, and his father came to see me. He said, 'There's something wrong with my son. If I had had that letter I should have fainted.' One was independent in my earlier time, rather like holding a commission. The welfare of one's pupils was a large part of one's interest in them. One had more control over them, but particularly, what does strike me now as I remember, and I

remember this with pride and pleasure, one took a good deal of interest – at least I did – in their academic careers and I don't mean how they did in their examinations because that was public record, but they used to come and talk to me about whether they were doing the right subject, or if they ought to change. You must have met a few people whom I encouraged to think of giving up Natural Sciences. They said, 'I've got a scholarship in it and I work hard and so on but I'm not really interested.'

P.G.: One of my earliest experiences after I came here when you were Senior Tutor: you sent a natural scientist over who then got firsts in Law, has remained devoted to the College, and all four of his children have come here to read Law, and done so rather well!
A.S.: There were a few people like that. In fact, I felt rather proud of this. The advantage of it, as I saw it, and it was a big advantage, was that the Tutor was never, except under rare circumstances, also the Director of Studies, and so undergraduates could complain, if complaint was what was needed, or Directors of Studies could have their views, if they were right, reinforced by somebody who was obviously slightly aside from the subject. English was a bit different. English never wanted to be part of any system really. Starting with Rossiter, they all wanted to be in a little world of their own.

P.G.: I suppose before we leave the subject of being a Tutor in the mid-'50s to early '60s, I ought to ask you about the Head Porter. This would still have been Captain Austin?
A.S.: It was, yes. He was really rather lovely. He really belonged to the pre-war generation, but he knew the world was changing and I think he regretted it. He worked the other porters pretty hard. He had a system of shifts which he imposed and they didn't like it very much. He was really very efficient and he carried immense respect among the parents, the ones who'd known Austin in pre-war days.

P.G.: My understanding is that in the First World War he'd been non-commissioned and in the Second he'd been commissioned in the Royal Marines.
A.S.: He was a captain, something quite substantial.

P.G.: Talking about Austin being well thought of by College parents who were often Jesus people, and these references to so many of the undergraduates having been the children of Jesus people, can we talk for a moment about the student body of the 1950s, early '60s, academically, intellectually and socially? What do you think were the characteristics of them? Was it a different student body from that around the place now?
A.S.: It was in a way, of course. By and large they were well satisfied to be here. They did grumble, but they didn't

grumble very much. On the whole I think the College officers to whom they did grumble were reasonable and often they had a point, one met them partway. I didn't think of the student body as being anything very much until after I'd been Senior Tutor for two or three years, and I became aware then that there was a student body and the President of the JCR was a figure of considerable importance in the College who was, in a way, representative of them. And to whom it was prudent to listen. With Steve Hockman … an occasional glass of sherry. I took him to see *Don Giovanni* when he was President of the JCR. Roger Toulson was a rather tougher character, but still by and large they seemed reasonably satisfied with things. I don't remember him crusading for anything very much, maybe because I've forgotten, maybe because it wasn't very important.

P.G.: That's a significant point, that the JCR President emerges as a representative figure in the mid-1960s.
A.S.: Slightly later, I would have said. I would have said '68, if I had to put a date on it. I remember this only because it was '64 when I became Senior Tutor and I remember the general mood of sweetness and light, and occasionally undergraduates said 'How lucky we are here – we haven't any great cause to grumble about', whereas by the time I retired in '70, well, of course, then the student revolutions were taking place, the troubles at the Garden House Hotel and all the rest of it. They didn't affect Jesus very much. This you may think was surprising in view of the fact that Denys Page, of course, in many of these things was a real autocrat, but he was nevertheless widely liked as a person. He supported things that went on in the College and Katie was similarly widely liked as a person. And I think they thought I was fundamentally a reasonable chap. Bruce Sparks summed it up in a way which applied even more when he became Senior Tutor, 'We had a relatively easy time of it here because the fact of it was we were to the left of them politically.' In many respects we didn't represent tradition or standing on our rights. I wonder now if I deceived myself. There was local discontent with some things. English was one of them. It was impossible to deal with that one. Anything that was dealt with by Raymond – they thought the world of Raymond Williams's reputation, although they hardly saw him.

P.G.: But they'd come here because of him.
A.S.: Yes.

P.G.: Ken, you spoke of the way Denys handled the students badly; what longer-term impact did you think those student discontents had on this College?
K.J.: They were not serious. One got over them. I think there was one occupation or slightly riotous behaviour with some sort of damage done but not too much, but in

the main the College came through rather well, even though Denys didn't handle it too well over some of the substantive issues. Somehow the College didn't become riotous as a result of it. The President of the JCR at the time was Steve Young. And Steve Young had a dazzling academic career in Cambridge. But he got on the wrong side of Denys, probably because he was held responsible for some of his minions' actions, and when it came to the Keller Prize the obvious candidate was Steve Young and you could see Denys gritting his teeth. But of course, Steve's winning all sorts of awards around the world at the moment as Professor in the Engineering Department.

P.G.: Alan, I just want to get you back into the late '50s, early '60s, before you became Senior Tutor. One question to ask is what was the proportion of undergraduates then who you thought were working hard, were ambitious and wanted to do well? And what were the proportion that were here just taking Cambridge as a matter of course and enjoying it?
A.S.: I find it difficult to put a figure on that. Most of them I thought were working fairly hard. There weren't many purely social, although there were some who were purely athletic. I had the misfortune, or good fortune I suppose in one way, to have some *causes célèbres* to deal with. Herb Elliot, I was his Director of Studies. He was

worshipped by the athletics group because he'd been good. The next one, Murray, I had to deal with that one. I think I dealt with it firmly without any real trouble despite the newspapers taking an interest in it. He'd been admitted to read Estate Management. After he'd been promised admission, the University changed its system and abolished the ordinary degree in Estate Management. Murray had a year off to represent the West Indies at cricket, and he came back to find he had to read for an honours degree. And the nearest thing would have been Economics. He managed to fail it. He was given another chance, exceptionally; well, he failed again. Of course he appealed, as he'd been pre-elected captain of cricket for the University. Denys Page was firm on this. He'd been a cricketer himself and he was really rather relieved that a tougher line was being taken. He said that frankly it was a mistake of admissions and its policy to take people on the sporting ticket. The word got round quickly and indeed most of the parents seemed to think the same.

P.G.: When did we stop considering admitting a person to read for an ordinary rather than an honours degree then?
A.S.: At that time you couldn't read for it deliberately. The ordinary degrees were abolished. You could be allowed an ordinary degree if you failed to get an honours degree but it became impossible by design to get an ordinary degree.

P.G.: And that was as a result of a change by the University in the regulations?
A.S.: Yes. That had undoubtedly had a stiffening effect in the academic world in general. 'Cambridge abolishes the ordinary degree' sent out a message which was Nelsonian in clarity. We still had people who didn't really work.

P.G.: The interesting thing then is you thought most people were working pretty well.
A.S.: Pretty well, maybe. It's a subjective term really. The ones I taught I thought were working reasonably well. Or more. Very few of the people I actually taught got by without doing a fair amount. I think that became general.

P.G.: Ken, you became the second of the College's Graduate Tutors. Had you been an undergraduate Tutor?
K.J.: It had been suggested, but somehow it didn't actually happen. Whether that was my dragging my feet, I'm not sure. There was a bit of a movement – it was about 1962 – there was quite a concern in Cambridge generally about the raw deal that graduate students got in return for their College fees. There was a report and some discussion about things that ought to be done, otherwise it was going to put the University into a tricky position, with the colleges insisting on college membership for

which the graduates didn't get anything. So most colleges moved to do something. Some did a lot. We did a lot. Corpus put up that building on Grange Road. And there were others. So we formed this Graduate Society and the Graduate Hall on Thursday evenings in Upper Hall, and Bob Dart was appointed Graduate Tutor, which he only did for one academic year; then he was elected Professor of Music and had to give College office up. So I took it over and got a number of additional things done. Pushed for the accommodation – got Little Trinity sorted out – and we did quite a lot of entertaining.

P.G.: And how many graduate students were there when you started? And how many when you finished?
K.J.: The figure of 70 comes to mind in total. It's a lot more now [270]. So it wasn't all that big a side, but they had their problems and it was a job I enjoyed.

P.G.: It was a job I enjoyed doing, too. The proportion, roughly speaking, of people doing PhDs to those doing taught or shorter courses out of that seventy would have been roughly how many?
K.J.: Certainly more doing PhDs than other things. Included in my flock were people doing the education certificate. That was a group. In the main, it was principally research PhDs. I would think 60 per cent.

P.G.: The figures are the other way round now.
A.S.: It was in your time, presumably, Peter, the vast expansion began. It seemed to me, and this may be libellous, in the end it has been driven more by financial considerations than anything else. Limitations on the numbers of graduate students would have deprived us of a vital source of income. Graduates, we don't have to teach them as long as we can house them, and if we house them we're doing really rather well by the standards of the Cambridge colleges in general.

P.G.: I think we have almost from the start. Little Trinity, then the conversion of all the Lower Park Street cottages.
A.S.: Yes, there's nothing to be ashamed of, but nevertheless I think it's probably financially driven and with all the new Masters' courses that there are, the graduate is no longer necessarily a PhD student writing his thesis. That's probably the biggest change of all.

P.G.: And more than a third of the total student body are now graduate students.
A.S.: We have behaved very well in an operation where it's a pity it had to happen.

P.G.: Why do you say it's a pity it had to happen?
A.S.: I'm not much in favour in principle of large numbers of people staying on in universities writing something or

other which nobody wants to read in order to acquire another professional qualification. Learning, what is it the composer says in *Ariadne of Naxos*? *Die Musik ist eine heilige Kunst* (Music is a holy art), and it seems to me that learning is the same.

P.G.: After you'd ceased to be Graduate Tutor Ken, you were a key figure in your Department of Engineering but you were still Director of Studies in Jesus until you yourself got a chair. What did you think about the students during that latter period as a teaching Fellow?

K.J.: One of the things that struck me then was that the quality of Engineering applicants and people we admitted was steadily increasing and did eventually push Natural Science into second place. We got increasingly better exam results, increasingly better candidates – those that came just to get a Cambridge degree were fewer – and that was a major thing in my contribution at that time and to try and get a good team of supervisors. There are now three professors of engineering in Cambridge

Little Trinity

Linocut by Rosemary Myers, *c.1970*

who were pupils of mine – Steve Young, Norman Fleck and Ian White. Norman Fleck we allowed to escape. We don't normally elect research Fellows after only one or two years of research. 'He'll be on the list next year'– but he wasn't. Pembroke took him. He was quite a mark in my life, we've collaborated and we had a good working relationship and he is very clever. When he graduated he went off on a holiday in Greece and Crete and sent me a postcard of a Grecian urn with boxers on it. 'I thought you might like this; it reminds us of our supervisions.'

P.G.: So this leads us, I suppose, to admissions policies and procedures at the time you, Alan, were taking over as Senior Tutor, when the Senior Tutor was the key figure in admissions to the College. Where were most of the candidates for admission to the College coming from by then?

A.S.: Well, I suppose more were coming from the independent sector, the significance of the state sector has been systematically underestimated ever since records began. Whenever the question came up, one had only to say, 'Look at the fellowship.' Where did they come from? The Master? Well, of course, Tillyard was a local boy; Denys Page from Newbury Grammar School; Bruce Sparks, who succeeded me as Senior Tutor, from Chislehurst Grammar School; Derek Taunt was from the City of London School, having been at Enfield Grammar School on the way; I came from a third-rate, more or less technical, place.

P.G.: Robbie Jennings came from Bellevue Modern School, Bradford.

A.S.: Vivian Fisher, I think, was from somewhere in the Shenfield area. I never actually worked out what the percentage was as one wasn't particularly interested in that. We had a good system in those days when applicants took the entrance and scholarship examination first; then they were summoned for interview if their performance suggested they were reasonably likely to get a place. Not surprisingly, the ones who'd been better taught got more of the places. My memory, and of course it's subjective here, because the position was a bit different in the science subjects, they'd always have more non-public school people anyway. Now and again I did look at the distribution and I remember noticing that nearly all the medics had fathers who were medics and something similar would have been true of Classics as well. There weren't any social sciences in those happy days. Subjects like History and English had a wide range of people. The reason I can't answer this in a way is because we didn't bother to present the percentages with great satisfaction: whether the percentage of women had gone up or down, or independent schools had got fewer places. We didn't worry

because Pars was a distinguished mathematician. There was a certain amount of ill-feeling and I think that was carried on. I was never very involved in The Club. Like other clubs and societies such as Friends of Kettles Yard, I pay my subscriptions but never go. That kind of thing.

P.G.: Looking back, Ken, over fifty years – with this longer perspective than almost anybody except Alan has got – what strikes you most? I suppose from the fellowship point of view, the most striking thing about the College over the time you've been here has been the enlargement of the fellowship.
K.J.: Twenty-three when I was elected.

P.G.: And now over sixty if you don't include the Emeritus Fellows, eighty if you do. What do you think about that? What have been the gains, and what have been the losses?
K.J.: They're fairly obvious. It was a very small community, we knew each other very well, we dined very regularly and there was a matiness about it all, which of course is difficult to replace when you can't remember their names. In the context of Cambridge as a whole, it was far too small and selective. Most of the science subjects then were recruiting rather heavily and expanding, getting people from away – I was one of the first, at least in this College, but the Department discovered that there was quite a bit of talent around the world. And I think that a lot of the Cambridge talent, if they hadn't already been snapped up, found that there were more profitable ways of employing themselves than being assistant lecturers. So the newcomers needed to be absorbed. You were either a Fellow and you were in, or you weren't and you were out. There wasn't even a University Centre then. It was partly this pressure and the business about graduate student fees that got the University Centre built, which in a sense has been a success. So it was very necessary and I think you had to be pretty reactionary at the time of the Bridges's Report [1962] not to welcome it. Vivian said, 'Well if we're going to go along with it, let's make sure we get in quick and get people who can be useful to the College, not just decorative.'

P.G.: And in fact that happened. I believe that the Bridges's Fellows were Bruce Sparks, Ilya Gershevitch.
K.J.: And Denis Whitehead and Austin Gresham. And then we took Ewing, the philosopher.

P.G.: So, as you say, before that appallingly restricted. Have we now gone too far the other way, do you think? Do you like the College the way you now see it?
K.J.: Well, I'm not really involved. In a sense quite rightly, people in my position shouldn't be making these decisions, even if they can express a view. Fellows seem to come and go pretty rapidly. I don't get to know the younger end, but then that's my fault. I don't blame them.

It does seem a bit unwieldy, but then no more than St John's was when I was first a Fellow. I don't have strong views about this. It's very easy to talk nostalgically about the past when you did know everybody, when you felt to be part of an organised team, and of course it's grown with Emeritus Fellows, too.

P.G.: Alan, what do you think about this enlargement of the Fellowship from sixteen in 1940 to sixty plus all the emeriti? What are the gains, what are the drawbacks, reflecting on it and observing it?
A.S.: Well, I have a third question. And what is the cost? That, of course, you may say is the drawback. It means now really that almost anyone who has a University office, a teaching office or not, becomes a Fellow of College, partly so that colleges can have say, reasonable numbers of women fellows. And that in a way is a political necessity: as I'd said long before that, if we have lots of women undergraduates it will not do if the only person to whom they can confess that they are pregnant is a man. This is not on. Various things like that. You must have a kind of welfare side, but it is not really part of an academic, it's a social need.

P.G.: Presumably even among the men Fellows in the past there were Fellows who weren't forwarding their subject very much? They were acting as social workers and general guides and pastors in the College.
A.S.: Yes, I suppose they were. And, of course, we're protected now, if 'protected' is the right word, by the consequences of the frequent research assessment exercises which make sure that at least if people don't do anything else they write pages at any rate. It's not all part of any grand plan, it's just happened. But it's not the same any longer. We now have Fellows who hardly ever appear except perhaps at a dinner, or something of that sort. I think this is a loss.

P.G.: It is a question of the priorities of the individual, isn't it?
A.S.: It is, but of course some people have more time, energy, sense of duty, to distribute among their different priorities than others.

P.G.: Taking 1950, 1970, 1990: which of those years do you think were those that were most pleasant to be a Fellow at Jesus?
A.S.: Out of the limited choice, 1970, but even more 1965.

P.G.: Why 1965?
A.S.: Well, 1970 was when I gave up being Senior Tutor. It wasn't that reason. By this time Denys had lost his popularity, he hadn't become Vice-Chancellor. He became a bit soured by things. I remember that awful degree-day lunch, by a dreadful phrase. He was sort of regretting that

things were not as they were: 'And the cradle has now been replaced by abortion. And the grave by euthanasia.' It struck me that this epitomised his view. It had recently changed – very great change from the first half of his reign. You would never have expected that at all.

P.G.: But that's a very significant answer to my question, if I may say so: '65, and I can see why you say that. Where do you think the place will go from now?

A.S.: I don't know. Who can tell?

P.G.: Ken, what changes that you have seen happening during fifty years in Cambridge, if any, do you regret, and in a middling way or strongly?

K.J.: I certainly don't have any strong regrets. I'm not a complainer about the set-up. What other regrets might I have had?

P.G.: In what way was life better in 1960 than in 2006?

K.J.: I think it's commonplace, and I agree, the situation for a University Lecturer has changed in a whole lot of ways: economic ways to some extent, mainly I suppose as a fall out from the higher education system in the country as a whole. The expansion of the universities, the pressure on government money, it has had an effect on the College. It's hard to do it the same sort of way that we were used to, and all the research assessment exercises and these sorts of things I think put young staff under pressures that we didn't have. Maybe we should have had them, but we didn't. I thought I worked quite hard but it was more relaxed from day to day. And this was beyond our control. It wasn't the College who'd taken any decision it shouldn't have taken that's made a change in the whole business.

P.G.: What would you say you have got out of being a Fellow of Jes: Coll: for half a century?

K.J.: How to put this into words when you're not good with words? I got an awful lot out of being a member of Cambridge University. Let's say that first. I wouldn't have wished for anything more and Jesus College is within the fold. It's not the centre of the University but it's an integral part of it and part of the ethos of the University. It would have been hard to be here just as a researcher. Being here and being involved in the teaching and being on the College Council for a long, long time on and off was part of being a member of this great institution and therefore a matter for satisfaction. A friend who'd been a research student in applied mathematics here – eventually he went as a professor in New Zealand – and he invited Dorothy and me for a sabbatical there and to teach a course for a term. We got on very well and they were very hospitable. At weekends he had a car which we didn't have and we'd go off and do things. He certainly got the correct impression that the mountains, the sea, the scenery and the general space of New Zealand we'd enjoy, which we certainly did. I remember walking along a beach with our shoes in our hands with the tide on the sand just lapping over our feet, and the sun shining and not another soul in sight. It was really idyllic, just like the pictures in the travel magazines. Ian said 'If you'd got a completely free choice of where you'd like to live and work, where would it have been?' Dorothy waited, although she must have known the answer. Cambridge University Engineering Department, Jesus College, Park Terrace and New Square, and that's it. So that's what I got out of it. I think I went on to say things about stimulating colleagues and bright if sometimes difficult students and so on, filling it out just a little bit in those sorts of ways.

Cambridge in 1945

MICHAEL BLACK

Then and now, how different ... At the beginning of each Michaelmas term I watch the family estate cars delivering the next generation, and unloading all the necessary equipment. Clothes, books, sports gear – that's all familiar. But then, what were at first the surprises: the computers, the TV, DVD and audio equipment, the micro-wave. You really need a car for all that. I came up by train, having sent on ahead a trunk full of books and clothes – such as I had, for clothes were rationed, and so was food and petrol. I observe the clothes too. We all wear some sort of uniform without knowing it. The current student uniform is a bit drab, but practical: you can pop it into the washing-machine and put it back on when dry. My uniform could only be dry cleaned, at very long intervals. We wore sports jackets – usually tweed – flannel or corduroy trousers, heavy leather shoes which had to be polished, buttoned-up shirts, and ties. Come to think of it, I still do; it marks me out as of my generation. We were proud of the college affiliation: wore blazers in summer with the college arms on the breast pocket, college or club ties, long college scarves in winter. A bit naïve perhaps. If the jacket had leather patches on the elbows, this was not an affectation: it was because the cloth had worn through and we needed to go on wearing the jacket. We had a suit for formal wear: I remember paying £5 15s 6d (five and a half guineas) at Montague Burton for a ready-made one (a bit common looking).

I came up from a little country grammar school in Cornwall. My headmaster had been at Jesus, and wanted, now that the war was ending, to start a tradition of sending boys (we were in the age of separate schools and colleges) to Cambridge. So he entered me for the scholarship exam in spring 1945.

It was in March, and the war had not yet ended. Railway journeys were long, tortuous and slow, and I seem to remember that, approaching London, the train stopped to allow one of the last of the flying bombs to pass overhead. When I finally got to Cambridge I had to rush straight in to my interview with E.M.W. Tillyard, then Senior Tutor, and gave him a stumbling excuse for my up-all-night appearance. 'Oh, you POOR THING!' he hooted, and I had my first experience of the Cambridge–Bloomsbury intonation pattern.

Jesus formed a group with Pembroke for scholarship and entry, so we did the exams in the Old Library in Pembroke: three days of long hard papers, but I had got the habit and almost found it soothing, given what had been going on in the world outside. I was awarded a £40 exhibition, increased to a £60 minor scholarship after my first year. It sounds negligible today; but £40 then was worth more than £800 now, and apart from the remission of fees you got rooms in College for all three years (pensioners got only one year). I won a State Scholarship on my Higher School Certificate results that summer, but my parents' income meant that I had no money from that until my fourth year in 1950, after National Service, when I was over 21. I had a County Scholarship, and my school did have a fund bequeathed by a benefactor that gave me a quite useful sum; the rest had to come from my parents. (I go into all that because we are entering another fee-paying age, where students will have to try to make up some such financial package to see them through with not too big a debt in the end. We old people have been there.)

The war ended in Europe in May, in Asia a few months later. So when I came up in October people were having to think: were we going to go back to the old days, or was everything going to be made new? Making Cambridge new was never a light matter, and the instinct was to go back to the old days because they were the only way of life that was known; but the country as a whole was determined to change.

Immediately, however, the war still dominated everyday life. I look at the freshman photograph. There are eighty-two men in it. Of these, nine are in uniform. On the left of the front row Geoff Bartlett has visibly lost one leg; actually he had lost both in the landing at Anzio, but was wearing one of his prostheses. Harry Johnson, later a distinguished economist, is wearing Canadian Army uniform, next to a GI in US Army uniform. Geoff was my neighbour in the Old Q Staircase, in North House, removed to make way for the new building. It was the only staircase which a severely disabled man could manage. It was still difficult, and I had to help him at times, for instance getting in and out of bed and washing. I once dropped him, very painfully – I still wince at the thought.

Some of the other uniformed figures look very young – they had been called up for National Service at 18, but were doing a short course before going into a specialist unit. And actually, most of the ex-service men were not now in uniform, but were visibly older than us schoolboys, and the occasional trim moustache gave them away. When the winter came they got out their very warm service greatcoats, and then you could tell where they had served. Naval duffel coats became a fashion item. And if you look very closely at David Udy's face, what looks like a streak of light across the bridge of his nose leads up to the gash in his forehead caused by a near-mortal wound. (Before the war he had thought he would be a monk, and

went off to a monastery. When it came, he thought, no, he would be a commando, and went off to the war. The injury made it hard for him to do exams, but he was a very good actor.)

But in October 1945, less than six months after the end of the war, the release of ex-servicemen had just started, and more came up in 1946. They were not all undergraduates: the dons had been in the services too, and I remember Robbie Jennings briefly in uniform, and Vivian Fisher limping from a leg wound.

It was a remarkable generation: I was only 17, too young to be called up, and allowed to do my degree first. But those men were well on in their twenties, some of them; and the mere age difference was as nothing to the difference in experience. Of course, we had all been through the war, and as a child in a seaport I had been regularly bombed and heard ships being mined and sunk in the bay. Boys a year to two ahead of me in school had been called up and killed. But these men had really been through it, and were unimaginably older. And while some found it difficult to settle down to a life of study, others drank it up; their maturity showed in what they said and wrote.

We ex-schoolboys accepted quite naturally the very firm – I might say quasimonastic – discipline inherited from the old pre-war days: gowns worn after dark and

Freshmen, October 1945.

Proctors roaming the streets to see that you did; back in College at 10 p.m. when the gate closed; allowed in after knocking at the door up to midnight; serious trouble after midnight. Hence the legends – indeed whole books – about climbing in over the impediments. Gowns had to be worn also to supervisions, lectures and examinations and in Hall. Dinner in Hall six nights a week: Mr Austin, the Head Porter, in formal gear of frock coat and striped trousers, looked round pricking our names on the College list, and keeping the record. Tutors had to be seen each term, and were the source of *absits* and *exeats*. Those who had been to boarding schools would find that they actually had a bit more freedom now; the rest of us just accepted all this as the way things were.

The College was acting *in loco parentis*, and a pretty old-fashioned parent it was. It could be thought that our virginity, certainly our virtue in the old sense, was being preserved. Having a relationship with a member of staff meant that she was sacked and you were sent down – I saw it happen. For this reason bedders (bed-makers) had to be as unattractive as possible. Mine had an irremovable old black hat and only one eye, but was nice and motherly. On the sole occasion when I got drunk and vomited she cleaned up uncomplainingly, so I felt ashamed as well as horribly hung-over.

My impression is that it was realised that ex-servicemen might very well feel that all this regulation was a bit childish. I think those who lived in lodgings – and most did – were not too strictly supervised. But keepers of lodgings were expected to see that the proper houses were kept by others. Some married ex-servicemen actually lodged outside town.

Given the strictness of food rationing, eating in Hall simply solved the problem of getting enough. Your ration book came up to Cambridge with you and was handed in at the College Office. In the passage-way to the Cloister was the Buttery Office, where you could get part of your butter and tea ration, and bread, so that you could make tea and toast in your room. It was possible to go into town, to a restaurant, and contemplate a tiny wizened steak, or a dubious sausage and chips, but it was very expensive. No question of buying things at Sainsbury's and taking them back to warm up in College: supermarkets didn't exist, or ways of heating up convenience food, which also didn't exist.

In the bitter winter of 1947 there were fuel shortages and power failures, and those of us who depended on coal fires had only two scuttles of coal a week. So we spent the evenings with whoever had a fire that night.

Evening entertainment was limited: the cinema – especially the old Cosmopolitan, renamed the Arts Cinema and now a restaurant, in Market Passage, where you could see foreign films, including a lot of classics; the Arts

Theatre if you felt like giving yourself a real treat; or – mostly – a quiet evening with a friend or two in one of the more pleasant pubs, where you could talk over a pint. We didn't have much money and, relatively, all these things were expensive. But of course we smoked, for cigarettes and pipe tobacco were cheap. Today an evening in Cambridge is immensely more lively – and noisy.

If dinner in Hall was required, given all the circumstances it was a pleasant social occasion. Hall meals were adequate but boring: one got a lot of sprouts in winter. English institutional cooking was appalling then, and the shortages made it worse. But the formality was pleasant and sociable: one tended to have a fixed place, with friends around. Scholars and exhibitioners had to read the long Latin grace, and I enjoyed the moment of attention.

We were also expected to read the lessons in Chapel. I escaped this by sending a solemn letter to the Dean in which I explained that my conscience wouldn't let me pretend to a faith I had lost (something like that). I had a dry letter back excusing me from attendance. 'Sorry to hear about your conscience,' he said. Dons: my memories

Post-war austerity: The Buttery Shop by Kenneth Lindsay (1941) – there is not much on the shelves!

Chanticlere, May Term 1946

THE BUTTERY SHOP   by K.T.L.

are mostly warm. My supervisor in English was A.P. Rossiter, a legendary figure: more of him below. One who went to some trouble to be socially available was Laurence Picken, exceptionally wide-ranging mind: the cliché is 'Renaissance man' – except that I think he left the Renaissance way behind. He was a biologist, and had worked in many countries – especially in Asia – and became interested in ethnic music, especially Chinese music of the Tang Dynasty. Much later, I found myself publishing his books on it. He was small, and had a very gentle voice. It seemed right that in his room he would play, to anyone who wanted to come in and listen, a clavichord, also small and gentle voiced – one leaned forward to hear him and it. (In his contribution below, Roger Scruton beautifully captures all this.) Laurence once memorably produced *Comus* in Cloister Court, with David Udy as Comus.

My musical education was also forwarded by W.H. Thorpe, another biologist. He had in his room a gramophone from the custom manufacturers in Soho, with huge superb upward-flaring horn and fine wooden body – still a wind-up affair. So a devoted undergraduate would wind it up, and another would sharpen the bamboo stylus which reduced wear on the old shellac 70 rpm discs. I learned to love German *Lieder*. It was all part of my education – at some point I acquired a tiny portable radio (wireless, we called it) and could listen to the BBC's new Third Programme in its glorious first days. Freddy Brittain once sent a porter across the court to tell me to turn it down – I had the window open. Rossiter, known as A.P., came up in 1945 like me – indeed he told me he remembered my Higher papers, which he had marked that summer. Tillyard had now become Master, and had stopped College teaching, though he went on lecturing. A.P., like Laurence Picken, had taught in Asia – five years in Japan as an instructor in the Imperial Navy. He had read Natural Sciences and English at Cambridge, and had collaborated in the development of Ogden's and Richards's basic English; he wrote a book, *The Growth of Science*, in Basic and it became a Pelican. Basic had a vocabulary of 850 words, but the technical terms went well over the limit.

He was an extraordinary man, very athletic. I remember him with a length of rope (for climbing) round the waist of his trench-coat instead of a belt. He rode a motorbike, which killed him in the end – his second accident – and one was left thinking he didn't want to grow old like other people. He was very handsome in an unconventional way: shining black wavy hair, very dark penetrating deep-set eyes, big nose, firm closed mouth (page 204). He too had a quiet voice, but somehow *intense*. He was a star lecturer, especially with the women students. It was said that he once used the word 'knickers' and they almost fainted – probably a legend, but it tells you something.

I don't know what he actually taught me. I think it may just have been how to read, think, and get out in words what I was trying to say. Almost everything, you could say. I would spend a week doing an essay for him, and the next week pondering the comments in his tiny writing in the margins and at the end. He produced a succession of brilliant students who went into university English teaching.

An abiding memory is of sitting in his room in supervisions, looking up at the superb paintings which I now know to have been by Martin Block – one of the artists expelled from Germany in the 1930s and received with blank incomprehension by the English, who thought that the only good art came from France. Looking at them week after week was all one needed to be convinced – but it's a lot to ask of most people. A.P. married Bloch's daughter Barbara, whom I had glimpsed as a beautiful young woman occasionally about the place. She had been his student at Durham. (Her daughter Charlotte Grant, by her second marriage, later became a Fellow, which seemed a neat succession.)

Those were great days in the English Faculty. The other originators – Forbes, Richards, Empson – had died or left, but Leavis had entered his major phase, and was making all the running. But the Faculty was riven, and predominantly against him. A.P. took no part in this, I think; certainly he said nothing to indicate antagonism. So I could speak and write freely. My headmaster had put a copy of *Revaluation* in the school library, and it had helped me through the Higher course by giving me words to use – Leavis's, of course, but that is how you make your way into intellectual life. I think A.P. recognised the condition.

I was naïve about all that, and it got me into trouble. I won an essay prize in my first year, and thought I would try again. I can't remember what the subject was, or what I said, or how he got to know about it, but I was sent for one evening by Tillyard in the Master's Lodge. He had read the essay and gave me an almighty row; pink, and trembling with rage, he told me that if I went on like that I would come to no good. White, and trembling with shock, I went into Hall and ate my meal in silence. Looking up I could see, above the High Table, in gold capitals *Ecce quam bonum et quam iucundum fratres habitare in unum.*

Tillyard must have thought one of his bright young men was going wrong and needed to be brought back into the fold. It was a silly way to do it. Years later, he met my boss at the University Press, Dick David, in the street. By this time I probably looked like one of his bright young men again. He asked Dick how I was getting on and told him he had once given me that almighty row, but that I bore him no ill-will. He was wrong about that, I told Dick.

It was a little sign of the animosity which existed, and how intellectual disputes can degenerate into personal feuds. Leavis gave as good as he got – rather better, in fact. It gave me satisfaction later to supervise the reprinting of *Scrutiny*, and actually to get to know him. But my immediate reaction was to change to Modern Languages, which I found to be in a pre-Richards-Empson-and-Leavis sleep, a sort of innocence. After National Service I came back and finally took Part II English. I was careful to look up the names of the examiners – something which would not have occurred to me earlier. I got my first.

Getting the Spirit of the Place

GERALD STUDDERT-KENNEDY (1954)

Kennedy, you have been at this place two years and you haven't got the spirit of the place yet!

Eric Tyndale-Biscoe (T.-B.) was an overpoweringly tall headmaster. A small boy could legitimately avoid meeting his eye. I hung my head in submission, confused, since I had, after all, enjoyed his Sheikh Bagh School, where I learnt to swim, though perhaps too casual about the basic life-saving skills so important to him. I was embarrassed now on account of my father, the least assertive of Anglican clergymen, who was standing beside me, holding a receipt. Having travelled from Simla to Srinagar, in Kashmir, he was concluding his career as a government chaplain. Sheikh Bagh had been founded to school the offspring of expatriates stranded by war. Now 'We' were hustling the Germans out of Italy, and civilians could join convoys 'Home', via Suez. I was to enrol at a very different establishment in Oxford, where my aquatic competence was valued, my spiritual failure unknown, and my parents could worry about my execrable Latin, French and maths – and my slim chance of admission to the 'right' public school. My father never referred to T.-B.'s cruel adieu, and I made no reference to it when I met Eric years later, sensing that it had neither been forgotten nor regretted. Eric was a Jesuan.

So was his father, the famous CMS missionary Canon Tyndale-Biscoe, who lived near our school, in retirement from the network of CMS establishments he had created. The Canon, incidentally, had no interest in formally converting Kashmiris or anyone else. We loved it when he stood in for Eric at evening prayers! Vesper pieties brushed aside, we hung on to every detail of his life-long subversion of the devil and all his works in the poisoned Eden of Kashmir. We seemed almost to participate in the ingenious exposure of some corrupt official, bullying money-lender or abuser of helpless women and animals. We thrilled at the raised stick which routed a rabble of

mendicant 'holy men', and basked in the glory of Kashmiri pupils who had saved lives from fire, water and pestilence, and had cleaned the city's filthy alleys.

We understood that Kashmir in some sense belonged to the 'Maharajah', but that the Canon had got the measure of him. Empire, we knew for certain, was Ours, thanks to the Canon's friend Lord Roberts of Kandahar and, indeed, to the industry and integrity of one's parents, who sustained its beneficent purposes. How appalling that I might even have betrayed the expectations of this delightful man, having humiliated my father, who knew him well.

It was at my public school that I glimpsed the possibility of expiation, and wrote a letter, not to T.-B. (now a headmaster in New Zealand), but to the Canon himself,

Canon Cecil Tyndale-Biscoe (1881), Honorary Fellow and father of Eric (1919).

Bronze bust by Clara Quien, *c.*1940

who had returned 'Home' to Rhodesia to die. Might he not be pleased to learn that I would shortly be rowing, at number 6 in the School VIII at Henley, for the Princess Elizabeth Cup? The Canon had coxed the Cambridge boat to victory in 1884, and the Jesus College winner of the Grand Challenge Cup at Henley in 1886. He had introduced oarsmanship to Kashmir, forcing his Brahmin pupils to ignore their caste distance from the occupation of common watermen by manning the long racing shikaras which he himself, I suspect, had paid for. These were moored for weekly regattas on the Dal Lake, across which T.-B. made us swim. We raced the shikaras against the Mission School boys, who beat us.

To my delight, the Canon responded to my letter. I would give a good deal to find his long-since-lost message. Following a friendly line of greeting, it simply contained a striking trope, or asseveration, which the Canon had shared with the famous Steve Fairbairn. The Canon, at a mere 8 stone, had won the College Pairs with Fairbairn. Their message to me, indeed to everyone, was brief enough:

As you meet your stretcher, so you will meet your God.
(Obituary, *The Times*, 30 June 1932)

Its gnomic obscurity seems to underwrite a pretty ultimate challenge.

Alas, however a literary-critical reader might unpack their message, I already had a problem with it. Having failed T.-B., I was going to fail the Canon for sure. That year at Henley, Winchester dead-heated with St Paul's in the first round. We were required to re-row, with little time to recover, only to be beaten by a few feet.

'Eights' on Dal Lake,
Srinagar, Kashmir, *c.*1930.

Somewhere in the agonising minutes of that re-row I realised that I would never voluntarily expose myself to such punishment again. A merely decorative National Service would give me plenty of time to contemplate the alternative opportunities of undergraduate life. Little did I know, however, that those choices would expose me to suspicions more severe even than that crushing annihilation at the feet of T.-B.

See me, then, one floor up, on staircase P, Second Court, tinkering with a set of my mother's old curtains. A peremptory bang on the door, and I am confronting an angry young man whom I do not know.

Angry Young Man: *Studdert-Kennedy, I see you have not put down your name for the Boat Club. I take it this is an over-sight?*
S.-K.: *Well, no.*
Stunned silence, then:
Captain of Boats: *What are you going to do?*
S.-K.: *Work? Perhaps?*
Captain of Boats: *Good GOD!*

I can still hear the crash and echo of my door as he departed. Ian Ball was to be a very distinguished Captain of Boats.

I came to know very few rowing men, regarded by those aware of my existence, quite reasonably as I have come to realise, as a Jesuan in defiant breach of contract. My anxious Winchester house master had, of course, puffed school boy performance on the river, and these glad tidings had been passed on, I suppose with my tacit consent.

But I received as a freshman, I should also confess, a bleaker reminder of the contingency of my membership of the College. I only once met the Dean, the Revd Percival Gardner-Smith, who was entering my name on the College roll at the time. As he did so, he murmured quite distinctly: 'I hope, Studdert-Kennedy, that you will not waste your time here, as your cousin did.'

It is the case that my cousin Michael's Tutor, A.P. Rossiter (my unforgettable supervisor, until his appalling accidental death) (page 204), more than once saved Michael from being sent down, to the chagrin of Captain Austin, Head Porter. A delighted bed-maker informed me that 'They never caught him climbing in, not even with the cotton and fishhooks!' But A.P. had been right. After an extraordinary sequence of false starts, Michael eventually retired as a sometime president of Haskins Laboratories, New Haven, having been a professor at the City University, New York and at Yale. I would one day hear him in a head-to-head at Harvard, challenging Noam Chomsky's understanding of the evolution of language. He was among the first to attempt to bring language within the neo-Darwinian framework of modern evolutionary theory.

My own, maturing sense of 'the spirit of the place' at Jesus I associate rather precisely with a College feast in my final year, to which, as a Scholar, I was for this occasion invited. Dinner followed a service in Chapel, for the annual Commemoration of Benefactors, to two of whom, Rustat and Roumieu, I had been nominally indebted. I seem to recall the tables clearing as individuals broke away from their immediate company and joined others. Moses Finley, the great revisionist of modern classical scholarship, whom I never met but wish I had, was leaning on a chair and laughing. Laurence Picken, musicologist extraordinary and generous host to the Literary Society, slipped away. Was the brilliant Bob Dart there? He had given me time for advice about Renaissance music and its instruments, when I should have sensed that he was unwell. Perhaps I am retrospectively installing him and others in the subdued lighting of Hall. For my thoughts that evening were constantly circling round the delicious fact that Ben Nicholson intended to find room in his *Burlington Magazine* for my first original contribution to scholarship, a paper on the implications of musical imagery in Titian's intriguing painting of *Venus with a Lute Player and Instruments*, at the Fitzwilliam Museum. A.P. had secured for me a long vacation grant to work on it, and had written a sly letter to the University Librarian to ease my access to material relating to Titian's scandalous buddy Aretino. My paper would one day find itself absorbed into the voracious scholarship of Irwin Panofsky's *Problems in Titian: Mainly Iconographic*, though that would never have happened but for an unbelievably generous response from Ernst Gombrich to a clumsy early draft. Gombrich was to become a visiting professor and an Honorary Fellow of the College, one in the community of scholars, which I, even I, might join.

What a snort, though, the Canon would have released over my Titian 'scholarship'!

Of course, two or three papers do not turn one into an art historian, and I never became one. By looping stages, I came to concern myself with British imperialism in South Asia, with a particular interest in the distinctive complex of Christian 'religious' beliefs that had seemed to many to sustain and justify the Raj. I found myself writing some biographical essays for *The Oxford Dictionary of National Biography* – among them, to my unqualified delight, that of the Canon, an opportunity to celebrate a great and good man who had almost succeeded in giving British imperialism a good name. I have scanned the record for indications that his enthusiastically received 'special' sessions with the oarsmen, when on furlough and visiting the College, might have tempted some individuals into the mission field. I found none, though the steady recruitment of Rustat Exhibitioners and Scholars into the Church continued as of old. But the Canon's was a particularly tough act to follow, as bishops and proconsular generations humbly acknowledged.

In any event, the Commemoration is over, and Hall is now clearing, except for a figure I seem not to have noticed edging towards me, and now sitting opposite, a long, minatory forefinger repeatedly thrust toward me, as if to pin me beyond release to the panelling behind. What is the question with which he threatens to stun me?

Ian Ball, for it is indeed he: *WHY DIDN'T YOU ROW?*

I do not recall my response. But we were to meet again within a few weeks, for what I recall as a pleasant occasion, at the hospitable table of Alan Pars (who else?). What did we talk of? Titian? Perhaps. The Canon? I hope so.

A Mathematician's Tale

JOHN HUDSON (1955)

AIMING FOR JESUS

I first heard of Jesus College, Cambridge, in 1954 when the headmaster of my school announced that it was time to put in our applications for admission to Cambridge. I was about to take my A-levels and the critical question, as always, was which college to apply to. The list was a bit smaller than now – Churchill, Robinson and New Hall had not been invented and Girton and Newnham were restricted to persons of the female gender – but it was long enough. I was called in for an interview with the Old Man and, with the appearance of giving the matter some weighty thought, he suggested Jesus or St John's as good colleges for a mathematician. In the end he came down to Jesus first and St John's second choice, as he thought I would be better off at a smaller college. When I came up I found that the school had an Old Boy teaching Mathematics at Jesus, which was probably the real reason for picking the College.

I was deeply impressed by the application forms when they turned up; they exuded an air of certainty and superiority, beautifully printed on high-quality white paper reminiscent of the old £5 note. I remember writing the address on the envelope and having a panic over the spelling of the word 'College'. I was certain they wouldn't take me if I spelled it wrong.

In the summer, after A-levels, the parents of a school friend of mine, Mike Davis, took us both up to Cambridge to show us what we had applied for. Mrs Davis bought me a post-card of Jesus – the usual shot of the Chimney and front gate, which has hardly changed in the fifty years I have known it. Even the well-worn steps which lead down through the gate from the public street don't seem to have become any more worn down than they were when I first saw them. There was a line of railings with revolving spikes on top across the open ends of First Court and Pump Court, and North Court did not exist; instead there was an old Tutor's house, like East House,

Pump Court and Small Hall (without ivy), *c.*1960. Compare Celia Murray's engraving (page 34). In 1962 the Small Hall was demolished and the 'Dark Entry' under the Main Hall's oriel window leading to Cow Lane and the Cloister reopened.

converted to student rooms – it was Q staircase. At the open end of Chapel Court there was another line of railings with revolving spikes and all the outside ground floor windows had bars on them. This made the College inaccessible at night, except to the very agile, unless entered by the main gate in First Court, all other gates being locked. The passage (Cow Lane) from Cloister Court to Pump Court was closed at the Pump Court end – and that is why, I was told, the cow got stuck in it. Mr Seeley kept the Buttery Shop in Cow Lane, just opposite G staircase, where he sold bread, milk, and other edible stuff. The stairs up to Hall were from just inside Pump Court. At the top you turned left for Small Hall and right for Hall. The whole structure, including Small Hall, is long gone. Two Fellows' sets occupied the space where Upper Hall is now. The horse wasn't there, nor was Daedalus, and the Quincentenary Library and the rest of Library Court did not exist. There were no daffodils round the tree opposite Angel Gate in Chapel Court, and the other lawn, which faces the gates, was surrounded by pleached limes (trees which had been trimmed back to look like many-armed Hindu gods with arthritis).

I spent the autumn in the third-year sixth form, working towards the scholarship exam in December. And then, after the end of Cambridge Full Term, we came up on the train to stay in undergraduate rooms in the College of our first choice, to take the papers and attend a couple of interviews. Basil Jervis was with me at Jesus. He had been Captain of School, Football, Cricket and maybe one or two other things. He was given a place by the College, postponed for two years, so he had then to do his National Service. I was deeply apprehensive at the thought of joining the army or air force (the navy didn't take national servicemen) and avoided it by staying in full-time education. By the time I finished, National Service had been abolished. The College interviews were pleasant affairs. One was with the Senior Tutor, Robbie Jennings, and the other with the Mathematics Fellow, Leopold Alexander Pars – the aforementioned Old Boy of my school. Pars always invited the candidates from the school to tea before the interview and was, as always, a charming host. After tea he handed round a cigarette box. 'Do you smoke?' he asked. At that time I regarded a free smoke as the height of luxury and immediately took one. 'Filthy habit, filthy habit,' boomed Pars, which rather took the edge off the pleasure.

The exams were, I think, in the small examination hall on the New Museums Site, or some similarly gloomy venue. We were directed by an invigilator – a short man in a gown standing on the stage – and at the end we were supposed to take our scripts up to the front. I forgot and was wandering out when I heard the cry, 'That gentleman there!' I had never been referred to as a gentleman in my whole life and knew that the invigilator wasn't referring

to me. Eventually his penetrating voice got through to my thick skull and I realised that I was a gentleman and that I was also an idiot. This was my introduction to the Cambridge use of the word 'gentleman', which simply meant 'undergraduate' with no implied respect. It was a term used fairly generally even though there were young women about. But the male to female ratio was 10:1 and it was only nine years since women were finally allowed to take a Cambridge degree. One of the papers in the exam was a translation paper. There were two passages, one easy and one not so easy, in each of several languages. I translated the two French passages as planned and found I had half an hour left. So I thought I would show off and do the easy passage in Latin. To get in to Cambridge, you had to have an O-level (or equivalent) in either Latin or Greek and, about eighteen months before, I had got a distinction in Latin. However, I discovered I couldn't

Cow Lane

Stipple engraving by E. Joyce
Shillington Scales, 1918

"Cow Lane"

E. Joyce Shillington Scales
Dec. 1918

even get started on the Latin passage. I must have forgotten Latin faster than any other single thing in my life.

Soon after Christmas 1954 I received a letter from Jesus College saying that I had been awarded a minor scholarship of £60 in Mathematics and Physics, and that I was expected to take up residence in the following October. Later on I discovered that there was a typical Cambridge code based on that word 'and' which I had completely failed to decrypt. If it had been Mathematics with Physics, it would have meant that the award was for the Mathematics and the Physics result was OK. As it was, I discovered much later that it was my physics paper that had dragged me up into the scholarship class, and I was rather peeved at this. In the sixth-form culture of my school, pure mathematicians looked down on applied mathematicians who, in turn, looked down on physicists, and I wanted to be a mathematician, preferably pure.

The scholarship didn't make me any richer as an equal amount was deducted from my State Scholarship, but it meant that I would be expected to read the lesson on occasion in Chapel, and the Grace in Hall before dinner. Now I had nine months to occupy myself before I went to Jesus.

COMING TO JESUS

In the words of a poem, published in *Chanticlere*, 'The band played "Come to Jesus" and so I came.'

I was driven up to Cambridge in October by my Uncle Phil, who had married my mother's sister. I think my mother had asked him to do this as he was the only member of our family who had gone to public school, and we didn't have a car. He had left that school at 16 with minimal academic qualifications and so probably didn't know a lot about Cambridge. But he looked and sounded the part – he wore a toothbrush moustache and a monocle. One of the porters helped us lug my trunk up the stairs to my rooms, O5, and Uncle Phil gave me half a crown (2s 6d – 12.5p) to tip the porter. On later occasions when I went up to Cambridge or came back home, I used the train, or the coach (which was cheaper). My belongings followed in a large trunk which was carried by British Rail or British Road Services.

The staircase did not have a door on it, nor was there any heating on the stairs. My rooms consisted of a bedroom facing the Close and a keeping room facing Pump Court. Both rooms had their own doors and there was an outer door, called an 'oak'. If you were out, had gone to bed, or were working and didn't want to be disturbed, you would shut this door (known as 'sporting your oak') and you would be left alone. As far as I know, only drunks broke this rule and banged on someone's closed oak. The

bedroom had no heating, but I was used to that as, like most people, we didn't have central heating at home. But the windows fitted so badly that, when it came on to snow in the winter, I shut them tight and still woke to find unmelted snow on my bed. I went to the Porters' Lodge to complain and was told – in tones suitable for a child – that if the carpenter were to make my windows fit now, they would swell up in the spring and stick. I walked away feeling somewhat frustrated.

My keeping room had the one source of heat – a gas fire. This made the best toast ever. The way to do it was to turn the fire up to maximum and, when the elements glowed red hot, get a slice of bread on the longest fork you had and press the bread against the bars. After a few seconds the bread would start to crackle and smoke and then you turned it over to do the other side. The toast was brown and crispy on the outside and soggy in the centre. Outside my room, on the landing, was a small gyp room with a single gas ring and a sink with a cold water tap. There was no hot water anywhere. Each morning my bed-maker would come into my keeping room while I was still in bed and tidy and clean. Then she would boil a kettle of water and bring it in the bedroom for a wash and shave, which I carried out in a large china bowl on a washstand, aided by cold water in a ewer. When I left, she would make the bed and clean and tidy the room. Bed-makers would wash up, but were likely to baulk at the remains of a large party. However, the facilities for entertaining were so limited that such events were rare. One of my friends had a bed-maker who would always finish off any left-over beer which even students had rejected as being 'off'. Bed-makers were also a good source of informal information about the College and the town. In my first Michaelmas term I complained to my bedder that it was jolly cold. 'Ah,' she said, 'wait until next term – it will get a lot worse.' And it did.

The toilet was one floor down. Baths were across the court in the ugly building in the corner of Pump Court that is now occupied by the College Bar. The baths there were huge and I could submerge the whole of my 5 feet and 11 inches with just my eyes, nose and forehead out of the water. That was just as well as the place was unheated and water used to condense on the ceiling and drip onto the bathers. I don't remember the College having any showers at all. In those days you could believe the widely circulating story that the Fellows of Trinity (or any college the teller wished to denigrate) opposed the provision of baths for the undergraduates on the grounds that they were only up in Cambridge for eight weeks at a time. When I came up, the English generally had one bath a week. This made it difficult for students from India, for instance, who were used to bathing every day. If they were in digs, their landladies were unlikely to allow it.

One major feature of the staircase was that the electricity was reduced to 50 volts, presumably because of the poor state of the wiring. I had been warned about this and had borrowed a heavy transformer from a friend. You could buy 50-volt light bulbs at Woolworths, but I needed the transformer for my radio, record-player and an iron; when I used the iron, all the lights on the staircase went dim. With the transformer inside, my trunk became extremely heavy, so my mother felt obliged to pay a handsome tip when the man staggered down our path with it.

One of the perks of having a scholarship, which I managed to retain for all three years, was that I got a room in College each year. Another perk, which I discovered when I became a research student, was that I could have a College room free during the long vacation term. This was a period of about six weeks in July and August which was used by Medics to get in some of their dissection practice and by Engineers for similar practical exercises. Undergraduates who were at risk of being thrown out for a poor academic performance were also often required to attend to catch up on their studies and to take an exam at the end of it, which would determine whether they were to come back next term or not. As for my duties, I quite enjoyed reading in Chapel, but the main thing to aim for with the Grace was to get it over as quickly as possible, so it was important to concentrate on speed. You knew you had done well if you were called in for a ticking-off from the Senior Tutor.

When I was a post-doc, some time in the '60s, a message appeared in chalk above the exit gate in the courtyard of the Department of Applied Mathematics, reading 'Caution, you are now entering Reality'. A similar message appeared where it could be read on leaving the Cavendish Laboratory; this one recommended 'Caution, you are now entering Noddyland'. It now seems to me, looking back fifty years, that 'Noddyland' is a pretty good description of my student days. I think that, at the time, we all understood that the University was a unique place with its own strange rules and customs, and we implicitly agreed to play the game. We were locked in at 10 every night, and porters patrolled the College walls with their revolving spikes and broken glass on top, even though about half of us had done National Service, some in Cyprus and Malaya. One student I knew had actually been shot (admittedly from behind by one of his own men who had tripped over his rifle). The National Service men, having been trained for two years in discipline and soldierly behaviour, usually reacted to any order by doing the opposite, on principle. In the fifth Fairbairn boat of 1955, the stern four were ex-National Service and bow four were straight out of school. When the coach left us towards the end of an outing in the hands of our rather bumptious cox, who tried to put us through 'tiger-tens' and practice starts, stern four mutinied and shipped their oars, leaving us in the bow section to haul them back to the boat-house.

The first thing that citizens of Noddyland ('the young gentlemen') had to do on arrival was to buy a gown of the appropriate College design. I went to Bodgers on Sidney Street, and I must have bought the cheapest second-hand gown. The material had lost its nap and it was beginning to get that greenish tinge that adorned most of the gowns of the senior dons. Since one had to wear a gown for almost everything, and had to wear it over all other clothing, it naturally took on a weathered look after a while. Gowns had to be worn outside the College premises at all times after dusk. One of the Proctors – dressed in gown, tabs and square – patrolled the streets with two 'bulldogs', University (not police) constables. We were told that there was no point in running away from them as they were very fast and possessed enormous stamina. In fact, encounters with the bulldogs were generally very gentlemanly, and most people complied when asked to have a word with the Proctor and were truthful in answering his questions. I remember one bulldog, whose day-job was on the front desk of the University Library. He was in his forties, stood about 6 feet high, looked pretty fit and had a broken nose. He also had a fairly aggressive manner. I don't think I would have argued with him. The standard fine for doing something naughty was a mark – two thirds of £1 (13s 4d). When a friend of mine was caught for not wearing a gown, the fine was reduced by half on the grounds of chivalry – it was a cold night and his girlfriend was wearing it. One of

Dr L.A. (Leo/Alan) Pars (1915), Fellow 1921–85 and benefactor.

Pencil drawing by Claude Rogers, 1962

the reasons why the Proctors could carry out their duties so easily was that male undergraduates could be identified by their clothes. Almost all of us wore grey flannels or brown cavalry twill trousers and a sports jacket, and usually a tie. The town boys, when they were out for the evening, wore dark suits with narrow trousers and 'creeper' shoes (with thick crepe soles). Later on, they wore 'teddy boy' outfits with winklepicker shoes. Their haircuts were d-a's (ask your granddad) and ours were short back and sides. There was a real cultural divide (well portrayed in the 1974 film *That'll be the Day*). Popular undergraduate music was traditional jazz – we had never heard of rock 'n' roll. And, apart from Friday and Saturday nights, the town was very quiet in the evenings. There were no discos or clubs and most undergraduate activities took place in the colleges. Even at the weekend, the place went dead about half an hour after chucking-out time at the pubs. I once talked to someone who had moved to Cambridge from Norwich to take a job. He said that the street lights outside his digs off Hills Road were switched off at 9 p.m.

An odd thing about Cambridge in those days was that, although people were extremely honest about most things, it was open season on gowns and bikes. If you were pressed for time to get to a lecture across town, it was regarded as OK to pinch the nearest bike. Similarly, at any gathering outside College, those who left early took the better gowns. Whoever left last might be left with a couple of armholes tied loosely together with string – or nothing. The authorities seemed to be remarkably tolerant of gowns in the last stages of disrepair. Of course, all our lecturers, supervisors and tutors wore their gowns and many of these were not in great condition and often sloppily worn. Senior members' gowns had less gravy on but more chalk. One of our lecturers smeared his writing with his gown as he passed along the board, leaving us to make of it what we could.

Gowns were worn not only for lectures, but for supervisions, using the University Library and when meeting your Tutor – in fact on all official academic occasions. It was also useful for blocking the draught under the door of your room. We were required to eat dinner every evening in Hall (with gowns on), with the option of signing off two days in any week. The Head Porter ticked us off on a list, pricking through our names on a piece of paper pinned to a frame with hessian stretched across. One College myth was that the porters knew every one of us by sight. I suppose it just might have been true. The waiters serving us in Hall were mostly young lads who were paying off the hire purchase on their motor-bikes, and they wanted to get it all done as soon as possible. So the gowns were useful in keeping the gravy off our jack-

ets. I never heard of anyone actually having their gown cleaned and I had an idea that, if I became really strapped, I could boil up my gown to make a thin but nourishing soup. Breakfast was cafeteria style and was the full English – cereal, bacon and eggs or something similar, and endless leathery toast, made acceptable by loads of butter and marmalade. The coffee appeared to have been brewing all night; it was black, thick and strong. It contrasted strangely with the coffee served at College feasts, which was thin and feeble.

Hall had an etiquette all of its own. The tables were all pushed together so that, to get politely to the seats against the wall, you could only slide in from either the top or bottom end. Most people walked across the table – trying not to trample on the cutlery, of course. There was no 'After you, Cecil' about the tureens of vegetables. I have seen students with healthy appetites help themselves to the whole contents of a dish of potatoes. (Mind you, I have also seen a senior Fellow on High Table take almost all a dish of asparagus in spite of the protestations of the waiter.) It was important to get to the roast potatoes quickly as the replacements were always the boiled variety. We tended to follow the waiters' example and eat up and get out. The 'tradition' that the remaining undergraduates in Hall clap the last Fellow as he bows and retires was invented in a more recent (and leisurely) time. Out of Full Term, when most of the undergraduates had gone down, dinner improved quite a lot. The soup became thicker, and the beef was cut from the bone, rather than cooled, sliced and heated up again.

SPORT AT JESUS

In the first few days in Cambridge, I had interviews with my Director of Studies, my Tutor and the Dean. The Dean asked me what sport I did. I was pretty bad at sport, so I said I didn't do anything. 'You should row,' he said. He was widely believed to have once told a freshman – who eventually rowed for the first boat and got a blue – to row, and to be now trying to repeat this earlier success. So I rowed all that year and got as far as the fourth May boat. But I grew a beard over the summer vacation and this seemed to unsettle the Boat Club, who were very strict about appearance. So I went off to play football instead. But I certainly enjoyed my year of rowing. The Boat Club created an atmosphere of togetherness and teamwork, based on being different and always being right. In that way they were very similar to the Christian Union, which I also joined in my first year. In the boathouse, a picture of Steve Fairbairn, the most successful of coaches, looked benignly down on his disciples from his cloud. Steve's chief apostle was the boatman Percy

Bullock, who had known him personally, and encouraged that sense of superiority that Steve had clearly instilled into all his boats. A new motto from Steve's book was pinned up on the boat-house board every day. Steve was always right. Lady Margaret Boat Club, dressed appropriately in scarlet, was the Antichrist. It was all rather comforting. However, the pressure to win was so great that I used to have the needle for a whole week when the Lents and Mays were on. Percy was an upright, generous and kindly man who was very strict with the oarsmen, particularly with regard to the handling of his boats. Once, as we were rowing back from an outing, an oar caught on the projecting concrete of a drain. About 6 inches of the blade came away, and we all thought that the oar was ruined, so we just rowed back to the boat-house. After giving him a piece of his mind, Percy sent the cox back in a scull to fetch the missing piece and, when he had got it, he glued it back on. I was amazed that this could be done.

The Boat Club did have one or two strange rituals; one of these was cold baths in the morning in the run-up to racing. It went like this – someone would run a bath in one of the cubicles below Chapel Court full of cold water and we queued up at the door. You stepped in the bath, sat down, lay down, jumped up and out of the bath, all in the space of about ten seconds. Water went everywhere, over the floor and up the walls. There was one rowing hearty who just lay in the bath and enjoyed it. I put it down as one of the less attractive effects of a public school education. The showers in the boat-house produced what seemed to be a solid vertical cylinder of cold water from a very large shower head. They certainly cooled a person down. A pint of shandy in the garden of the Fort St George was, to me, a much better prospect. Another feature of pre-race preparation was that the Boat Club took over Small Hall where everyone was served with extra portions of meat at dinner. In the Fairbairns we (the fifth boat) were coached by a rather dissolute character from the second boat. After the race, as we rowed the boat slowly back up to the boat-house, he coached us in the etiquette of the Fairbairn dinner – to take on as much liquid refreshment as possible and 'if there are sprouts or rolls on the menu, I want to see them moving about'.

In the middle of the Lent term, the election of the secretary of the JCR took place. The officers of the Boat Club picked on a second-year lawyer to stand for the post and told all of us to get out and vote for him. He got in. Then there was the practice of burning the boat if the College came Head of the Lents or Mays. This took place around one of the penalty areas of the soccer pitch. When I took to playing football, I regarded this as an act of pointless vandalism. It was also accompanied by a certain amount of violence. If someone appeared on the scene wearing the blazer of another boat club, it generally got taken off him, shredded and burnt along with his trousers. It was wise, also, to be sure that your bike was nowhere in the region of the fire as, otherwise, it would very likely go on it. In fact, anything moveable would be considered. Another event on the Boat Club calendar was the annual rugby match against the Rugby Club. To give the boaties a bit of help, the rugby team put their backs in the scrum and their forwards played as half-backs and three-quarters. This meant that there was considerable power in the tackles outside the scrum. I had never played rugby before and received enough damage to make me regret taking part.

Football at Jesus had an ethos about as far away from that of the Boat Club as you could get. We played football because we enjoyed it and, if we lost, it was no big deal. The team was in the second division, which was just as well; if it had been a first division side, I probably wouldn't have got in. The second eleven seemed to be made up mostly of converted rugby players, one of whom was famous for having introduced the 'up and under' to the round ball game. A few years later, some good footballers came up to Jesus, including Deryck Murray the West Indian wicketkeeper, and I went to play for Cambridge Wanderers in the Cambridge Thursday League (Thursday used to be early closing day in Cambridge), having been introduced to the team by the son of one of the porters. That way I got to play at the Abbey Stadium, home of Cambridge United, in the final of some cup competition.

Our first team had a regular away fixture against Jesus, Oxford. After the game we had dinner in the college hall and later we were entertained by our opponents – they laid on a barrel of beer and we sat round it – or we would have done if most of our team hadn't belonged to the Christian Union. So we mooched off to some Bible study or other, leaving the captain and one or two of the less scripturally minded to tackle the beer. Another away fixture was against a team from the Cambridge Mission to Bermondsey and took place on Peckham Rye. Our opponents were generally on the small and weedy side, but they always beat us – even though they were still smoking their half-time cigarettes when the kick-off for the second half took place. After a bit of tea, we were offered the chance of an evening tour of Bermondsey with the lads as guides. Bermondsey then had the reputation of being a place where even the police did not stroll about on their own. I hopped on a bus to see my folks in Teddington and I think most of the others did something similar.

As a junior Fellow, I was introduced to High Table cricket. The team was recruited and captained by Derek Taunt, my former Director of Studies. The players varied from the very enthusiastic and moderately skilful, like Derek, to those who, like me, had proved at school that they were hopeless at the game. But Derek's dedication carried us through. I used to field on the boundary, where I could do least damage. The most important game was the one against the College staff. One of the groundsmen, Fred Wisbey, was reputed to have played for Cambridgeshire, and the staff were extremely hard to beat. We took tea with wives and children in the Pavilion. It still seems to me that this is the way that cricket should be played, where you know many of the players and there is a sprinkling of non-playing friends about. Everyone does their best to win, but the result is of no importance.

DIFFERENCES

Two things stand out for me as being different about the College in those days. One was the formal occasions, which brought its members, senior and junior, together. We were expected to eat together in Hall most days of the week, and we had to keep going to see our Tutors for a variety of reasons: for permission to leave Cambridge, come back to Cambridge, stay out late, and so forth. The other was the quiet – no discos, no College bar, no stereos and no televisions. In the vacations it was wonderfully peaceful in College – no undergraduates and practically no tourists. My memories of a long vac term spent in College are of a period of great tranquillity in warm sunny weather. It was not a great time for doing serious work, though.

The town was different, too. It was a market town, not a tourist trap. There was a great variety of shops, butchers, fishmongers, grocers, hardware stores, tailors and so on, owned by local people. There were hairdressers for women and barbers for men. I patronised one Przjborsky (the spelling is close, if not entirely correct) who claimed to have been the hairdresser to the Austrian court. His shop was at the divide between Round Church Street, which was much narrower then, and an alley off to the side. Mr Przjborsky used hand-operated clippers which he always warmed on a small gas jet, and he charged 1s 9d (8.75p) for the haircut, the cheapest in town. The bookshops were mainly academic in style. Heffers was in Petty Cury, which was a street with buses travelling down it. Bowes & Bowes was on the corner of Trinity and Market streets and Deighton & Bell was further up Trinity Street, on the corner of Green Street. The best shops for mathematics and science were Heffers and Galloway & Porter (still in Sidney Street). Galloways had a very helpful assistant called Dudley Davenport who had wide knowledge of science and maths books although, as far as I know, he knew nothing about those subjects.

There were some good cheap places to eat – so long as you were not too picky about your food: a café in King Street that provided a pretty decent two-course Sunday lunch for 2/9 (13.75p); the Waffle, on a first floor in Petty Cury; and the Civic Restaurant, opposite Lloyds Bank. The Horse & Groom (now the King Street Run) served meals, but generally you were lucky to get more than a packet of crisps and maybe a pork pie in a pub. There wasn't much in the way of foreign cuisine, although there were a few Indian restaurants (actually Pakistani – now Bangladeshi, I believe): for instance, the Koh-i-Noor in St John's Street and the Taj Mahal opposite Downing. In the late '50s the Corner House, run by Greek Cypriots, opened on the corner of King Street and Malcolm Street, They served risotto and chips for 2s 3d (11.25p) which kept me going while I was a research student. Undergraduates were banned by the Proctors from patronising the Athens Restaurant on St Andrew's Street. They were also forbidden to run up debts at any shop in town, and if it happened the shop was put out of bounds. I can't remember what happened to the undergraduate who had run up a slate at the Athens. In these ways the University still dominated the town.

Undergraduate Life in the Late 1950s

JOHN RIMINGTON (1956)

I first saw Cambridge on a misty morning in the late spring of 1951. Two years before, also on a sixth-form school trip, the playwright Alan Bennett had thought it the most beautiful place he had ever seen. I was struck by its antiquity and peace, perhaps the same impression. Such little traffic as there was travelled unimpeded up King's Parade and Trinity Street, and men were lazily playing chess at tables set by King's gate. The colleges did not seem as they now do, shuttered oases in a choking modern city. Simply, they were the place, serenely dominant. Seven years later, after the traffic had quadrupled, Cambridge was still enough of a country town for me to have the fright of my life when, turning on my bicycle from the market place into Sidney Street ahead of the lights, I stared into the wild faces of two runaway horses, abreast, tearing towards me at 15 yards' distance. I ended up, heaven knows how, on the bonnet of a parked car.

Two years after that first visit I came up for the scholarship examination. In those days the 11 o'clock train from Nottingham stopped at Kettering, and there one had one's lunch, attended by a porter, in a small dining room awaiting the slow train to Cambridge, arriving at Jesus College in a December dusk. The medal had reversed. The feeling, assisted by foreboding of the task in hand, was of fog and gloom. The College, its patina unscathed by modern restorative fluids, was cold and a little dirty. The post-war gas fires burned low, and R.Y. Jennings, then Senior Tutor, interviewed me in his room in the Waterhouse building in semi-darkness lit by a single standard lamp, his kindly face emerging from the shadows like a moon. The College Hall with its high chocolate panelling, then approached via an external stone staircase from Pump Court – itself dubiously ornamented with an unkempt seventeenth-century formal garden – seemed to be lit only by the chatter of young men far cleverer than me.

My call next day on Freddy Brittain, arranged by a thoughtful school tutor, was scarcely less sinister. As I mounted to his rooms in First Court, a distraught youth emerged from his door and charged wildly past me down the stair. I entered apprehensively to find Freddy, whom I had been taught to look upon as God, standing impassively on his hearthrug. With no word of introduction, he said with austerity: 'Do you know that feller? He calls Marsales "Marsoyle"! Why, they'll be callin' wittles "victuals" next!' My predecessor had unluckily bruised Freddy's principal King Charles's head, his intense dislike of an overeducated replacement of traditional spelling and pronunciation. I was to get to know Freddy better later on. He was never intentionally unkind, and to me he was most courteous that day.

I got the open scholarship I was after, but it was nearly three years before I saw the College again. We freshmen

Dr F. (Freddy) Brittain's rooms on C staircase, 1955.

assembled by the gate to be led through the courts by the Head Porter, Captain Austin. Most of us had just emerged from military service, and to be shuffled in a pack and redealt was common form. Austin, a Royal Marines veteran of two wars, now uniformed in a silk top hat and morning suit, fitted the occasion perfectly. As we sauntered uneasily along in column of three, he released at various stopping-points information about washing arrangements, times of attendance in Hall, the opening hour for the Manciple's stores and so on, fetching up eventually on the gravel before the Waterhouse building in Pump Court, the scene of his *pièce de resistance*. Explaining that he was about to demonstrate survival in case of fire, he stepped smartly into the staircase by the Waterhouse tower and twenty-five seconds later emerged backwards from an upper window clutching a rubber pipe with which he abseiled, or rather marched, down the wall at an angle of about 60-degrees, his top hat still firmly clamped to his skull. The subsequent freshmen's photograph was something of an anti-climax. It must have been the last such exhibition, for Austin was shortly afterwards succeeded by another ex-marine, Mr West, always known

as such. There was no nonsense about abseiling. Mr West was to Captain Austin as sirloin is to brisket, and it is doubtful that the apparatus would have stood the strain of his descent.

About halfway through nearly every century of English history, there has occurred a turmoil after which a new era has emerged without the old one having arranged its obsequies or the new one declared its form. Post-war England was such an era, and Cambridge is a fair test of the thesis. Many old habits and assumptions, now dead, still held good or could be traced in contemporary life. The inhabitants even of the College's grander parts were still mainly undergraduates rather than dons or researchers. Many of the undergraduate rooms were still sets, the keeping room warmed by a small gas fire, the bedroom abandoned to the elements. Dinner in Hall, attended by droves of balding black-clad servants, was compulsory and the menu was very likely to be venison repellent to human teeth and crème brulée – said to have been invented by the college chef fifty years previously when an assistant in the Savoy kitchen. This dish, consisting of an impenetrable slab of caramelised sugar

1/70

The Chimney

Screen print by Julian Trevelyan, *c.*1950

topping a generous quantity of hot thick custard, posed considerable dangers to sitters-by.

Above all, the tone in College was strongly masculine and women were – at least in principle – excluded after a certain hour. From 11 o'clock at night onwards, fortress conditions prevailed, the heavy gates closed, the College walls topped by ferocious spikes and the courts patrolled by porters. The spikes were thought a fair test for the nightowler – my friend and contemporary Mark Tully bears scars to this day, though there were in fact more convenient means of clandestine entry, via certain loose bricks and a hospitable window at the back of the Carpenter building. The real – by no means infrequent – test came when Jesus was Head of the River. On such nights Goths from first and third Trinity and LMBC would loudly besiege the walls, the porters would patrol with staves, and many of the rest of us with walking sticks.

It was still, to an extent, an age of bachelor dons. The College boasted a fair number. In First Court lived Laurence Picken, a world authority on fish and ancient music, weird instruments hanging from his walls; and also Thurston Dart, the harpsichord virtuoso, his music tinkling across the grass on summer mornings. David Shackleton Bailey, the Latinist, lived in or by the Waterhouse tower with his cat and his incomparable collection of Wagner records, allegedly best enjoyed by sitting in the sink at the foot of the tower with an ear to the water-pipes. He was attended by a minute Tibetan lady, presumably his pupil, for he was also the University Lecturer in Tibetan. She could be seen three times a week trotting through First Court at about 11 in the morning under her parasol, rain or shine. He eventually abandoned Jesus for Caius, the cat-flap his only memorial within our walls.

However, by general consent, the grand seigneurs among the College bachelors were Freddy Brittain, who had not yet discovered his allegiance to Muriel; and Leo Pars, an eminent mathematician whose elaborate pretence of senility deceived no one. Both men were closely concerned with clubs that still exist, to both of which I have belonged. That founded by Leo Pars was known simply as The Club. Its constitution provided for a membership of twenty, six fellows and fourteen undergraduates, and it was in practice an extension of Leo's hospitable mission to bring together different species of the College fauna. It consisted in my time of some of the better-connected undergraduates and some of the more intellectually or artistically inclined, and its habit was distinctly genteel.

There were certain rites of passage into The Club, consisting of invited attendances at tea and muffins before Leo's fire, culminating in a weekend theatre trip with him to London. Our functions consisted mainly of *conver-*

sazione either in Leo's rooms or in the rooms or houses of the other senior members – who included Derek Taunt, Alan Sharpe and, less frequently, Vivian Fisher, the *beau ideal* of a don, a leonine figure though with a limp from war service, and possessed of wonderful humility and accuracy tempered with kindness. These affairs took place generally in Park Terrace overlooking Parker's Piece, and there was also an annual dinner of some splendour. It was on one such occasion that Derek Taunt told me that he had had only eight and a half seconds of mathematical inspiration in his life, distributed as to eight seconds at a single occasion before his shaving mirror and the half-second elsewhere. I was mad enough to ask him whether the benefits from the first immersion had been sixteen times that from the second, when I was privileged to see the archetypical Cambridge don rigorously considering whether a point at issue merited the full Cambridge treatment, or whether levity was intended. Eventually, he hitched up an eyebrow and, gazing sternly, replied, 'I congratulate you on your arithmetic.'

Freddy's club, the Roosters, was a very different affair, its familiars – also a mix of dons and undergraduates – of

**D.J.V. Fisher, Fellow 1945–93,
Senior Tutor 1955–64.**

Dona Haycroft, *c.*1970

a very different type. In his autobiography *A Don's Life*, Freddy describes the Roosters as a blending of a social club, a light-hearted debating society and a light dramatic society, and indeed it was all those things. Its goings-on could be sublimely funny, but could also sink to asininity, making it a controversial and sometimes rowdy element in College life, disapproved of by some. Based on the

The Roosters process through First Court (bounded by chevaux de frise) to their Breakfast-at-Lunchtime, February 1951.

College Founder's symbol, a rooster perched on an orb, the Roosters represented themselves as a Chaucerian Parliament of Fowls, with a gallinaceous language, spelling and pronunciation all their own. Thus the Chief Rooster, or 'Old Cock', sits on a 'grainsack', debates are 'crowed' rather than 'spoken', the word 'order' is pronounced 'odour', and the highest honour is elevation to the Order of the Red Herring. A debate on, for example, whether the College is an educational institution would be quite likely to delve into questions such as whether the moon had risen in the correct piscal fashion, or if it was high tide at Jesus Lock.

The Rooster caricature of human aspiration is not without its point, and the *Codex Gallorum* (laws of the cockerels) is a notable document, an exploration, more or less deliberate, of those features of the human universe that render our transactions vain and our rational impulse nugatory – an obsession with precedency, a facility for irrelevance and an inclination towards the mob: in sum, a sort of Netherlandish painting brought to a kind of life.

My own acquaintance with the Roosters proved costly. Having attended one meeting and being declared an 'Egg', I amused myself with other things until one day, I found, pinned to the Hall door, a notice briefly stating that Egg Rimington had been declared addled. Many years later, having thought nothing further of the Roosters, I mentioned this misadventure to a colleague on a diplo-

matic assignment who had himself been 'Old Cock'. Correspondence ensued, leading to an invitation to propose a procedure whereby I might be instated in the dignified office of Doctor of Rooster Lore. I forthwith proposed bribery in lieu of examination, and having forwarded six bottles of excellent port, delivered a dissertation in praise of corruption at a Rooster dinner at which Sir Alan Cottrell, then the Master, was present. The Upper Perch retired to consider my appointment, eventually reappearing to pronounce the bribe sufficient only to crow me in as a Bachelor of Rooster Lore. Not until I had paid danegeld in the shape of six bottles of Sauternes was I granted the red silk wattles of a Doctor.

There were, of course, and no doubt still are, many other clubs in the College, some social, some learned and some evanescent. I cannot speak of The Natives, since I was never a member, but I will give the instance of a club which I co-founded and which flourished for some years. A neighbour in College had not been well favoured by nature, having roughly the form of a tree trunk to which were appended bandy legs and a squint. A prominent member of the College's second row, he one day received a thrust which broke his nose and occasioned reflection as he awaited the ambulance. The next morning, his head swathed in bandages and his eyes black as well as crossed, he favoured me with the proposal that we should together found an 'Ugly Man's Club'. Notwithstanding the resignation of several of our friends before they had been invited to join, we went ahead, our first rule being not to conjugate with ugly ladies; and our second, always to pass the marmalade anti-clockwise at our breakfasts, to be eaten in pyjamas. No invitations were more prominently displayed on mantelpieces in the women's colleges than those of the Ugly Man's Club, though in those severer days pyjama-clad breakfasts with ladies were not on the agenda. No doubt such undergraduate clubs still exist; I hope so.

In all these ways and in others, the undergraduates of those times went on much as undergraduates always had, but the shape of the new age was becoming apparent before the '50s ended. The modern idea that a university is exclusively an academic institution rather than primarily a civilising one would probably have occurred to few of us, but we were nevertheless a more serious bunch than the pre-war toffs who had confronted toryism with a sly communist idealism, or than the unruly existentialists of the immediate post-war period. Our generation had grown up with austerity and had done military service. Those of us without means or connections worked earnestly to gain our tickets-of-entry to the career boxes provided in a newly socialised Britain. We were no iconoclasts, and we looked upon authority as fundamentally good, provided it was exercised with style and restraint.

Within the University as a whole, the prevailing intellectual climate in matters of politics and religion was a presumptuous and rather arrogant liberalism, which paved the way to many permanent changes in college life and organisation now taken for granted. It is hard to forget the shock when a journalist, Lord Altrincham, proposed the admission of women to the ancient colleges, or when King's College suddenly removed its nocturnal defences, declaring them unsightly and uncivilised. It would have been more conformable to sentiment in Jesus College to have charged the spikes with ineffectiveness and to have omitted reference to the obvious. As it turned out, the College was one of the last to replace its spikes and railings, which gave place in First Court to the low rather unmannerly wall we now see.

Throughout the '50s the College remained true to its rather quirky conservative tradition. In religion the College's official churchmen – the Dean, Barry Till, afterwards Dean of Hong Kong Cathedral, and the Chaplain, Simon Burrows, afterwards Bishop of Buckingham – sedulously guarded the forms of worship descended from the College's patriarch, Cranmer, though the Dean's stated

view that gin was the finest drink of all, with claret a tolerable second, trod the outer bounds of orthodoxy. In politics the College could almost claim to have been the cradle of the revanche, since our tutor in political thought, Maurice Cowling, afterwards at Peterhouse, is now acknowledged the modern prophet of the British, perhaps also the American, right. Himself one of the bachelor dons though at that time non-resident, he cycled regularly up from London, the first sign of his arrival a peremptory request through a porter to read one's essay to him in the Prioress's Room at, say, 2 or 3 a.m. There he would be found in front of a log fire with three or four bottles of claret warming in the hearth, his eyes arching absurdly at any departure from sense and his lips ever poised to form the sardonic comment 'You are far too clever for me.'

And there perhaps one should leave the College of those days – a happy place where the brands of scholarship burned brightly in the hands of such men as Moses Finley, Cowling, Charles Wilson, David Daiches, Shackleton Bailey and R.Y. Jennings and, among the scientists, Laurence Picken, W.H. Thorpe and others – a place of youth and age where a level-headed devotion to the good and charitable things in life was maintained, eccentricity was tolerated, no one sought to measure the unmeasurable, and beauty abounded in the open spaces with which the College is so generously endowed. It abounds still, for each new generation.

An Indian's Excursion

SUMANTRA NAG (1967)

It was a wonderful rediscovery of the College for me when I was able to visit Jesus with my wife Sujata in June 2005, spending three glorious sunny days there, staying in the guest rooms in Cloister Court, and dining at High Table and lunching with alumni in the Fellows' Garden. Sujata, a reader in English literature in Delhi University, discovered the link with Thomas Cranmer during a visit to the College Chapel, and was delighted to find herself in the College where Sterne and Coleridge had also been students.

So I am happily writing this account of an Indian student at Jesus College, though fully aware of my lack of specific distinction in any field – whether among the larger population of British students in the College, or even among the Indian students in my time, who distinguished themselves quietly, in the academic field in particular. All I can claim for myself is my affinity to a variety of activities in Cambridge and in College in particular, and for an informal social involvement with others through which I enjoyed absorbing conversation, humour, fellowship and some lasting friendships.

I went up in 1967 as an Affiliated Student and took my Tripos in two years in 1969. I started with Physics, my subject at Delhi University, but was happy to be able to make the change (with the kindly help of my Tutor, Dr Cameron Wilson) to History and Philosophy of Science for my second and final year. Despite the fact that the study of my new subject was somewhat rushed because it had to be completed within a year, I acquired an interest in history in general, while in later years I found myself immersed in philosophy, which also came about indirectly through my introduction to the philosophy of science. My interest in literature, which had grown strongly while I was in Delhi University, had inclined me towards the humanities while I was still reading Physics.

On my first Sunday morning in College, in October 1967, I heard the familiar opening chorus from *La Traviata* (the 'drinking song') being played in a neighbour's room in North Court. This was a piece my father was fond of playing on Sunday mornings at home in Delhi! (He had seen the opera performed in Paris when he was a student at the London School of Economics in the 1930s, and was deeply moved by it.) I soon discovered a widespread familiarity with European classical music among the friends I made in College, and the record library provided a ready store of music, along with a room with high-quality equipment for playing it. The College also had a separate music room with a piano, and a friend would sometimes oblige me by playing pieces by Chopin or Liszt, with which I had just become familiar. I had always been fond of piano music and Chopin was a major discovery for me, thanks to my friends who introduced me to his music. Some students also had pianos in their rooms, so I was sometimes treated to music there as well, and was able to meet talented musicians including the Organ Scholar. I became a member of the Cambridge Union mainly to listen to the debates, but often used the large music room there, with speakers placed in concrete columns, where I played Chopin's first piano concerto to enormous advantage, the romantic melody and the piano chords just filling the whole space around me. In fact, this piece has now become associated in my mind with my days in Cambridge!

Twenty years after I was at Jesus, my sister Deepa came to Cambridge in 1989 for post-doctoral research and was given rooms in Newnham College. One day she heard her neighbour actually singing lines from the opening chorus from *La Traviata*. She later introduced herself, and told her neighbour about our personal history of what she was singing, recounting my own experience as a newcomer at Jesus in 1967. She found that her neighbour was rehearsing for a performance of the opera and was very warmly given an invitation to the performance.

After gaining admission to Jesus in 1967, but before leaving for England, I happened to meet a young officer in the British High Commission in Delhi who had been an undergraduate in the College. I had heard from him about the Literary Society and sought it out on my arrival. Some of my most memorable evenings in College, and indeed in Cambridge, were spent at its meetings, which were always held in Dr Laurence Picken's rooms in First Court. The first meeting, held to read and discuss poems submitted anonymously for the occasion, was well attended by some of the College's brightest literary minds. My own poem, sent in for the occasion, received what I presumed to be a just critical appraisal, but seeing the steady quality of poetry submitted for this comparatively private gathering, I realised that I would have to temper my earlier hopes as a would-be poet! The Literary Society also held readings from Dickens just before Christmas, when Dr Picken served his famous milk punch. I later extended my interest in writing in a small way by reporting for the University newspaper *Varsity* during two terms of my second year, and I received much encouragement from the undergraduates who were editing the paper, more than one of them from Jesus.

Dr Picken's rooms were the venue for another society of interest to me, the Asian Music Circle. The walls of the main room were adorned with a host of Asian musical instruments collected from the far eastern to the western ends of Asia, and there was also a baby Steinway grand piano (of 1894 vintage, to the best of my recollection) and a harpsichord. One memorable evening, there was a performance by Rajeshwari Dutta, the noted singer of Rabindrasangeet (the poet Rabindranath Tagore's Bengali songs). As an accompaniment to her singing, she was playing the *tanpura*, a long four-stringed instrument tuned to the requisite scale, on which the musician plucks the strings in turn, to create an accompanying drone in the background. Soon after the performance began, one of the strings of the instrument broke. Dr Picken stepped across to one of the walls of the room, simply lifted a *tanpura* which was displayed there, and bending down before the singer, graciously handed it to her as a substitute! But after trying out the *tanpura* which had so magically appeared before her, Rajeshwari Dutta mildly announced that the instrument was designed and tuned specifically for the male voice. So she proceeded, like any other accomplished musician, to restring her own and continued with her performance.

I was very keen on sharing the pleasures of Rabindrasangeet with my English friends. So, in my second year, I suggested to the secretary of the Literary Society that we should have a meeting where I could provide a brief introduction to Tagore and some (amateurish) English translations of his songs while they were played on a record player. This was done, but even here Dr Picken's trained hearing was able to discern some departures from the traditional mode of singing in the recorded version of Rabindrasangeet then being played.

Common interests in music and literature brought me close to people I met, and I made other friends in College who were helpful and friendly and whose company I cherished throughout my stay. In my first year in North Court, I shared common facilities with three immediate neighbours, whom I vividly remember – along with others on my staircase – for their cheerful and friendly presence. And with some of these friends I have been able to maintain contact through the intervening years. I was generously invited home during the vacations, to stay with their families in the country, or dine with them in London. Their families looked after me with an unforgettable warmth and attention.

The extensive playing fields and the grass tennis courts within the precincts of Jesus are unique, I think, even for Cambridge, with its large, varied sporting facilities. I was no sportsman, but in a 'rowing college' like Jesus I should have had a go at rowing, at least as a gesture to my father, who had captained the LSE rowing club. But he came from Kolkata, where people rowed on the lakes, whereas in Delhi, where I was brought up, there was no tradition of rowing. But I played tennis, and in my second year even played for the second team in Jesus, although I know for certain that many other who played infrequently could have done better than I did, if only they had bothered to join the teams and play in the matches!

My two years at Cambridge also exposed me to the widely held social concerns of undergraduates at that time, and my later reading therefore broadened out to include books relating to social and economic issues in the developing world, and to those of India in particular. In College, I heard the economist Joan Robinson speak at a meeting organised by the William Frend Society, in a room in First Court which may have been once occupied by Coleridge. This growing interest in social and economic issues was important, because while being interviewed by ICI in India I expressed a strong preference for working in those product streams of the company which dealt most closely with the overall industrial development of the country. I was recruited into its industrial explosives division, in the department dealing with the supply of inputs for production – which came from different corners of the country – and posted to ICI's explosives factory in the mineral-rich state of Bihar, where I spent some of the most fulfilling years of my working career. Here I joined my colleagues in schemes for developing the small neighbouring villages, which lacked many basic facilities.

While Cambridge indirectly but strongly influenced my fields of interest as an industrial executive, and directed them towards the spheres of basic development in

Leaf Figure

Bronze sculpture by Henry Moore

India, I never expected that History and Philosophy of Science as a subject would bear any direct relevance to my future professional work. But here I was surprised at the turn of events, which later led me into a research-oriented career combining precisely the discipline of this subject with my active industrial experience. After about twelve years in industry, I joined a government research institute in Delhi in 1982, which was devoted to interdisciplinary studies on science, technology and society. It was my academic exposure to the discipline of HPS at Cambridge which, together with my working experience in industry, led to my recruitment to this institute in a city which by now was a home of many years' standing. Continuing my interest in issues relating to economic development in specific areas, I worked on a field-based project, where I studied the development and growth of ancillary and small-scale industries in the vicinity of the

Looking towards the beech trees in the Orchard from Pump Court, 2006.

large steel plants, which had arisen in the remote areas of India. In discussions on the social aspects of science and scientific research, I found myself encountering the philosophies of Kuhn and Popper, which had formed part of my syllabus at Cambridge. Although *The Logic of Scientific Discovery*, prescribed in Cambridge in my days, defined Popper's philosophy of science, I now discovered him as a social philosopher in *The Open Society and its Enemies*. This entry into research led to a new career of market research and corporate planning in the steel

industry that lasted for nearly two decades. In due course my personal interest in western philosophy increased and I found myself reading habitually in the subject. Now, in my current profession of part-time management teaching, I find concepts from the philosophy of science, and particularly those from Kuhn and Popper, being invoked in management theory, and philosophy being increasingly brought to bear in management studies.

Reading western philosophy has now become a part of my modest intellectual diet – a sporadic pastime on the fringe of my professional work. I remember reading somewhere recently, in a communication emanating from Cambridge, a rather stern warning to prospective students against building their expectations of Cambridge on *Brideshead Revisited*! I was astonished that such a warning should be necessary in meritocratic Britain in the twenty-first century. Even in 1967, when I went up to Cambridge, any excessively idyllic images of Oxbridge conjured up from their depiction in books or conversations – particularly those harking back to the 1920s or 1930s – were rudely shaken by the stern demands of academic work. Cambridge then seemed to reveal itself as a valuable precursor to professional life where people were grimly conscious of impending responsibilities in a competitive world. Against the beauty of the architecture and landscape and the variety of activities in Cambridge, I can admit to a period of stress prompted mainly by academic pressures; but this prepared me for many demands and even upheavals in the future, apart from instilling habits of intellectual discipline, which led to the pleasures of continual learning, however modest their scale.

When we visited Jesus in June 2005, the leaves of the copper beeches were in full splendour before North Court, as they had been nearly forty years ago. Witnessing what Sujata referred to as the 'midsummer madness' of the May bumps, or seeing the new sculpture on the lawns and remembering the names of Henry Moore and Barbara Hepworth – who were already represented in the JCR art collection and the works that were on display on the Jesus lawns in 1967, I couldn't help marvelling at what had still been preserved! And if Jesus, exemplifying Cambridge, should stimulate the creation of beauty and grace in living, while it demands more effort in a world which also demands more in mundane terms, then that may well be the creative balance to be bestowed by the College on coming generations.

Dons: A Group Portrait 1950–75

In the third quarter of the twentieth century – the 'fifties, 'sixties and 'seventies – Jesus was, for the first time in its history, home to a large body of scholars and scientists who were, or who were soon to become, internationally renowned figures. The two Masters – Eustace Tillyard (1945–59) and Sir Denys Page (1959–73) – were acknowledged leaders in their fields: Tillyard's was Shakespeare's plays and Milton's poetry, Page's the poetry and drama of Homeric and post-Homeric Greece. Page became President of the British Academy on his retirement from the mastership. Gathered around them was this remarkable group of Fellows, not all of whom had much direct contact with the College's students. As in many other colleges, the Fellowship is more than the dons who are directly involved in guiding its students' studies, and anyone seeking to understand why colleges command such strong loyalties and display such fiercely self-protective instincts (and sometimes provoke such extreme antipathies) will need to examine this dimension of these complex communities. So this chapter, with its pen-portraits of just eight of the most notable Fellows of Jesus of that quarter-century – two ancient historians, an architect, a cultural critic, a Latinist, two lawyers and a philologist – attempts to give some impression of a generation of dons on which we can look back with particular pride. There are accounts on pages 264, 151 and 146 of three more – Laurence Picken, who did notable work in the biological sciences before abandoning his laboratory to become a path-breaking Asian musicologist; Philip Anderson, Nobel Laureate in Physics; and Martin Rees, a research Fellow who was to become Astronomer Royal and (as Lord Rees of Ludlow) Master of Trinity College and President of the Royal Society. And there were another half-dozen who might also claim a place here:

William Thorpe (1932–86) who, with Tinbergen, was one of the two founders of the science of animal behaviour; Charles Wilson (1938– 91), the pioneer historian first of Anglo–Dutch relations and then of modern international business; Trevor Jones (1955–84), who set out to compile, and single-handedly nearly completed, a multivolume German–English dictionary; Lloyd Austin (1955–6; 1961–94), editor of eleven volumes of the correspondence of Mallarmé; Gwilym Jones (1962–95), who, after a career as a district officer in Nigeria, came to Cambridge in middle age to teach anthropology, curate its museum, and be commissioned to report to Parliament on ritual murders in Basutoland; and Frederick Raby (1948–54), who while Chief Inspector of Ancient Monuments had edited four large volumes of early Christian and medieval Latin verse, becoming a Fellow on retiring from the Civil Service. And among the younger Fellows who were beginning their scientific and scholarly careers which would come to maturity a little later (and who must await another volume) were Sir Denys Wilkinson (1944–59), who was elected a fellow of the Royal Society at the age of 34, and was to be professor of nuclear physics at Oxford and vice-chancellor of Sussex University; Sir Hugh Lloyd-Jones (1948–54), the leading Greek scholar of his generation, any one of whose many books would have secured his reputation, who became regius professor of Greek at Oxford aged 38 in 1960; and K.L. Johnson (1954– ; page 216), the doyen of the world's tribologists and the recipient of a string of medals, including (like Wilkinson) the Royal Society's highest award, the Royal Medal. There was a formidable body of talent to be found in the Combination Room at Jesus in those years.

The Ancient Historians

PETER GARNSEY

Two ancient historians of genius resided in Cambridge during the period 1951–86: A.H.M. ('Hugo') Jones (1904–70) and Moses I Finley (1912–86). There could hardly have been a greater contrast of models between the two: profound familiarity with the ancient sources in all their variety (Jones), opposed to sheer intellectual brilliance (Finley); the one, the best of British, the other, European and cosmopolitan. Jesus was fortunate to have had them both.

> A slight, wiry man, dogged by ill health throughout his Cambridge career, he was a tireless walker (the only recreation he listed in *Who's Who*), and talker, especially a talker of shop. He had a phenomenal memory and a shrewd wit, and behind the façade of austere scholarship, a kindly humanity that revealed itself not only in his warm relations with his students, but also in books he wrote for them and for the educated public generally.

So wrote an obituarist on A.H.M. Jones. My own acquaintance with Jones was limited to three encounters with him, all brief, and each in its own way, for a raw graduate student, intimidating and unforgettable. They are revealing less of Jones's 'kindly humanity' than of his interest in the primary sources for history. Once he appeared in my rooms at University College, Oxford, unannounced, just after breakfast. He went straight to the point: 'I am Jones. I want to talk about your article.' I had, with the rashness of youth, questioned one of his doctrines concerning the nature of the Roman judicial system. He challenged me to name my source. I stammered out a reference to Tacitus, *Annals*. He reached into his pocket, pulled out a match-box, and wrote the reference down on the back of it. The rest of the conversation has vanished in the mists of time.

Jones must have been a remote figure to the students of the College, where he came as Professor of Ancient History in 1951, with the exception of those who were graduate students in ancient history. Many of the latter had come from overseas to study with him, for his fame as a historian was worldwide. His graduate seminars were legendary. They were held in his splendid study in Fen Ditton Hall, which could easily incorporate the twenty or so graduates in ancient history. His wife Frieda would first serve a choice of Indian or China tea, poured from silver pots. Her withdrawal signalled the beginning of the session, which invariably took the form of a PhD student reading a more or less painfully detailed account of their research. The detail was not discouraged; quite the contrary, for Jones himself had an unrivalled capacity to recall passages and testimonies from classical authors (and other ancient sources), which he evidently knew by heart. He is credited, for example, with 'total recall' of the works of Cicero. But the student who appeared to have misconstrued or misunderstood any particular text was unlikely to escape unscathed.

One derives a rather different impression of Jones from those students who wrote their doctorates under his supervision, as distinct from merely participating in his seminars. It seems that he gave them freely of his time and attention. I spoke to two such, who were entirely different in temperament and interests: each was convinced that he was particularly favoured by the Professor. In retrospect it seems to me that his relationship to his successor, Moses I Finley, bears witness to the same capacity to identify and promote excellence wherever he saw it. They could not have been more unlike in background, training and character, yet it was Jones who captured Finley for Cambridge, and for Jesus.

As a lecturer to undergraduates Jones did not flourish. One former student, Richard Gordon, a Jesuan, reports:

Professor Sir Moses Finley,
Fellow 1957–76, Honorary
Fellow 1976–86.

As the Part II Special Subject lecturer, he was a very considerable disappointment: his presentation consisted in reading out, in his very poor voice, the proofs of his little book on Sparta. He never discussed anything, and was too shy to stay and talk. What was incredible, however, and immensely impressive to us even then, was the fact that he had written the entire book while in Alexandria, from memory, having no books to hand. He simply knew all the sources.

No doubt he could have repeated this feat for other areas of ancient history. And his coverage of the ancient world was extraordinary. No other historian of his lifetime could match his range of familiarity with the evidence for ancient history from early archaic Greece to the end of the Roman Empire.

Emphasis on the primary sources was an Oxford trait. Jones was a splendid specimen of Oxford scholarship. He did not however pursue an orthodox Oxford career. His prize fellowship at All Souls' College (from 1926) was interrupted by a period (1929–34) spent as reader of ancient history at the Egyptian University of Cairo, and his lectureship at Wadham College (from 1939) by service in the Ministry of Labour during the war years. He resumed his academic career by taking up the chair of ancient history at University College London in 1946, a post which in 1951 he left for the Cambridge chair.

Already a prolific author, whose expertise extended to more than a millennium in the history of Greece and Rome, he had in his sights the work that was to dominate his oeuvre, a study of the society, economy and administration of the later Roman Empire (AD 284–602), eventually published in three volumes in 1964. The book is written almost entirely (or so it would appear) from the primary sources; hardly any scholarly literature is cited. This raised some eyebrows. But one can see Jones's point (and he faces the issue candidly in the preface to his work). The sources for late imperial Roman history are so voluminous that he could not make time to read them all, and his fluency in the classical languages (and, one might imagine, his work-rate) was unequalled. Be that as it may, this massive work has been described as 'the greatest contribution in English to Roman imperial history since Gibbon'. It is not surpassed by any work of ancient history produced in the twentieth century.

Finley came to Cambridge as a political refugee. Born in New York as Moses Finkelstein (he changed his name in 1946) of immigrant parents, he was descended from one of the great rabbinic dynasties of central Europe on his mother's side, while his grandfather had been chief rabbi of St Petersburg. A child prodigy, excelling in particular at mathematics, he majored in psychology at Syracuse University and graduated BA *magna cum laude* at the age of 15. He took an MA in law at Columbia, and worked as a legal clerk and then as research assistant to the distinguished Roman lawyer A.A. Schiller. He began to study ancient history under W.L. Westermann, inheriting his teacher's special interest in slavery. Also in the 1930s he became associated as editor and translator with the Institute for Social Research, known as the Frankfurt School, which had abandoned Germany in 1934. A later intellectual influence, from 1952, was the Hungarian exile Karl Polanyi, economic historian and anthropologist. In the meantime Finley learned Latin and Greek and secured a PhD at Columbia (1950) with a thesis entitled 'Studies in Land and Credit in Ancient Athens'. When published as a book in 1952 it was hailed as a landmark study in ancient Greek economic and legal history. He taught, first at the City College of New York (1934–42) and subsequently as lecturer, then assistant professor, at Rutgers University (1948–52). His left-wing views led him into activity on behalf of the republicans in the Spanish Civil War, the launching among university teachers of the American Committee for Democracy and Intellectual Freedom (in 1939), fund-raising for Russian war relief during the Second World War – and an appointment with the Internal Security Subcommittee of the US Senate (under Senator McCarran of Nevada) in 1952. He pleaded the Fifth Amendment, and was deprived of his post by Rutgers. He left for Britain in 1954, returning to his native land for the first time in 1972 to give the Sather Lectures at Berkeley and the Mason Welch Gross Lectures at Rutgers. He had in the meantime become Lecturer, Reader and Professor of Ancient History at Cambridge (succeeding Jones in 1970), and a Fellow of Jesus (from 1957). He was Master of Darwin College from 1976 to 1982. He became a British citizen in 1962, and was knighted in 1979.

It is worth contemplating his early career in order to appreciate the singularity of Finley within the setting of Cambridge and Jesus College. He stood out, even among the group of distinguished exiles who decorated our universities in the middle decades of the twentieth century and beyond. His background in history, law and the social sciences was unique amongst classicists in the UK, and this fed through into his voluminous publications, which greatly extended the subject matter of ancient history and transformed its image, winning it an enhanced reputation and a greatly expanded audience in academic circles and among educated laymen.

In Cambridge, the teaching of ancient history took off on a new route. Before Finley the course structures, the methodologies and the typical products of the system were not very different from those of Oxford. Under Finley's influence (and there was no deliberately planned programme of reform, let alone revolution), syllabuses were loosened up, flexibility and variation were introduced. Lecturers were encouraged to invent new courses and to introduce broader and more adventurous bibliographies, with a comparative historical and interdisciplinary element.

For the young, the presence of Finley in Cambridge was something of a miracle. For Richard Gordon: 'He always had the air of an Exot[ic], blown to Cambridge by a fortunate and implausible wind. He seemed to know about everything, Marx, Weber, Mauss, Bloch, ancient Mesopotamian land-tenure systems, the late Roman colonate, medieval kingship, etc., and to keep up friendships with the most distinguished of the other Fellows, for example, Ilya Gershevitch and Raymond Williams (both of whom he invited to talk at his graduate seminar later).'

For the more talented and responsive students he was an inspiration, raising their sights and extending their mental horizons beyond the mere addressing of particular, traditional historical problems. One may wonder how far he was interested in the run of undergraduates, but his impact on graduates and young scholars was enormous. They came in numbers to study with him and engage with him, and found him accessible, generous and inspiring. Doctoral students from Mexico, Israel, and the USA

who to came to Cambridge to work on Greek history told me that their eyes were opened by *The World of Odysseus* (1954). This was the book which, according to another eminent ancient historian and exile (Arnaldo Momigliano), established Finley as 'the best living historian of Greece and the one most prepared to face the methodological problems which social history implies'. Other students, from the mid-1970s, developed a sudden penchant for ancient economic history, caught in the currents stirred up by the book of the Sather Lectures, *The Ancient Economy* (1973), Finley's 'most read', most translated and most controversial book.

Finley loved an argument, and in *The Ancient Economy* he cast down some sacred idols. In influential circles today there remains resentment against Finley, and periodic attempts are made to stir life into what is now an old and rather stale controversy, and to swing the pendulum back in the direction of a modernistic interpretation of ancient economic history. Finley had argued, here as elsewhere, for the singularity of the ancient world, and the impossibility of finding any meaningful parallels between the economies of ancient Greece and Rome and those of Europe before and after the Industrial Revolution. One way or another, Finley was the most influential ancient historian of his generation, and probably of his century.

The Architect

NICHOLAS RAY

For much of the second half of the twentieth century no British architect commanded so much international respect as Sir Leslie Martin (1908–2000). He had a profound effect on architecture in Britain, as a designer, as a patron of other architects, as an educator and as a theoretician.

Martin's most famous work remains the Royal Festival Hall, probably Britain's most popular post-war building. He had become deputy chief architect at the London County Council under Robert Matthew in 1948 (succeeding him in 1953 as head of the largest public office in the world) and was given responsibility for the centrepiece of the Festival of Britain. But he was also in charge of an enormous school and house-building programme. Roehampton West was immediately hailed by Nikolaus Pevsner and others as a brilliant and particularly English interpretation of Le Corbusier's *Unité* concept: a series of slabs deployed in echelon in the park. In later private practice, he and his associates were responsible for university buildings at Hull, Leicester, Oxford and

Cambridge, where the sculptural Harvey Court, designed with Colin St John Wilson and Patrick Hodgkinson, after publication in European journals became a place of pilgrimage for architects and sprouted imitations immediately in the United States as well as Europe. In the 1970s Martin built in the Middle East, Portugal (the Gulbenkian Gallery) and Glasgow (the Concert Hall and Academy of Music and Drama). His *Buildings and Ideas 1933–83* illustrates the remarkable consistency of his oeuvre.

Martin always worked in collaboration with others and gave them full credit for their contribution. His own house and studio at Shelford was designed with his wife Sadie Speight. Often he initiated large-scale projects and then enabled his collaborators to start their own practices: Patrick Hodgkinson at the Brunswick Centre in Bloomsbury, Trevor Dannatt at Leicester. On other occasions major commissions were granted on his advice – the University of East Anglia to Denys Lasdun, for example – though he failed to persuade his friend Alvar Aalto, the great Finnish architect, to allow his name to go forward for the new Cripps building for St John's at Cambridge, where Powell and Moya were later appointed. He was one of the small panel of assessors who plucked out the project by a little-known Danish architect, Jørn Utzon, as the prize-winning scheme for the Sydney Opera House competition. He also ceaselessly promoted younger talented architects, such as James Stirling, Colquhoun and Miller, and Bill Howell.

Leslie Martin had become the head of the architecture school at Hull in 1934 aged only 26, attracting Jacob Bronowski, Lazlo Moholy Nagy, Marcel Breuer, Herbert Read and others to lecture to his students. In 1956 he became a Fellow of Jesus, on accepting the chair in architecture at Cambridge, where he set about not only refashioning the course (which had previously had no post-graduates), but also transforming architectural education nationally: he was the guiding spirit behind the 1958 Oxford Conference which established the pattern that broadly remains today.

If architecture was to take its place in a university it needed to engage in research, embracing all aspects of the subject. The early work of the Centre for Land Use and Built Form Studies (subsequently named, appropriately, the Martin Centre) which he founded at Cambridge arose directly from his own practical concerns, and in turn fed its results back into practice. Engaged at the time in ambitious plans for the redevelopment of Whitehall, he made these the springboard for examinations at all scales into the geometrical configuration of buildings using the mathematics of Fresnal. Martin had a firmly Popperian view of the nature of science, and unlike Richard Llewelyn Davies at the Bartlett, did not believe that architectural research could be undertaken without practical ends in mind: these hypotheses he entitled 'speculations' in *Urban Space and Structures*, which he edited with Lionel March in 1972. His introductory essay shows that, while he appreciated the romance of cities and the mixture of uses they encouraged, he regarded it as the architects' duty to test their propositions rigorously against agreed criteria. His own formal preferences were fashioned in the 1930s, when he made friends with Henry Moore, and with Ben Nicholson and Naum Gabo – with whom he edited *Circle* in 1937. *Circle*'s contributors included the American architect Richard Neutra and the historian Lewis Mumford, the painter Piet Mondrian, the choreographer Leonide Massine and the scientist J.D. Bernal. The contents of *Circle* revealed Leslie not only as a man who bridged the two cultures but also, at a time when Britain was decidedly insular, as a true European.

Leslie's own architecture was generally modest. Very often, as at the University of Leicester, his work provided the calm background against which the more flamboyant architecture of Lasdun or Stirling could be played. And as a person Leslie was always polite and diffident. In the College he supported and advised the students in building up their art collection (page 274) that contains pictures by Ivon Hitchens and sculpture by Barbara Hepworth; his own room was furnished sparsely, but included a spectacular lampshade by Aalto. At his home and studio in Shelford, where he and Sadie used to entertain students, there was a collection of paintings by Ben Nicholson to rival that at Kettle's Yard, the house and gallery that Leslie had designed for Jim Ede.

If there was one quality that Leslie Martin sought all his life, it was clarity – a virtue that he did not believe to be incompatible with richness. His best work illustrates this: the conceptual clarity of the Royal Festival Hall, the

Professor Sir Leslie Martin, Fellow 1956–2000.

masterful organisation of complex circulation in the Oxford libraries. He would reassure his clients that his solution to their brief would make everything 'perfectly clear'. At the same time he was always at pains to preserve the wider picture; just as each building was seen as an example of a generic type, his invariably gentle criticism of student work was not directed at the particular individual, but at what contribution their project might make to a more general debate. Martin outgrew an age of optimism and certainty, and in the 1980s and 1990s was attacked for what were considered his totalitarian urban prescriptions, but it is certain that his work will continue to be studied when that of many currently fashionable names is forgotten.

The Cultural Critic

STEPHEN HEATH

Raymond Williams was born in 1921 in Pandy on the Welsh border, in the shadow of the Black Mountains, where his father was a railway signalman. The close-knit community in which he spent his childhood gave him the values and concerns that were to inform his life and work; when he came up to Trinity to read English in 1939, he came with the strength of the world he had left and was 'not oppressed by Cambridge, not cast down by old buildings, for I had come from a country with twenty centuries of history written visibly into the earth'. He edited the student newspaper, ran the Union and took Part I of the Tripos before service as an officer in the 21st Anti-Tank Regiment of the Guards Armoured Division, participating in the Normandy landings and the Allied advance into Germany and the liberation of the infamous Sandbostel POW camp. Demobilised in 1945, he took Part II of the Tripos the following year.

After Cambridge, he became a tutor in literature in the Oxford Extra-Mural Delegacy, teaching for the Workers Educational Association. The experience on the periphery of the educational establishment was crucial for the development of his work, and in the first instance for

the task he set himself of analysing the idea of culture as it had been developed by a line of writers from Coleridge through to the Cambridge critic F.R. Leavis and used in arguments against democracy and socialism – Leavis was a strident defender of 'minority culture versus mass civilisation'. This analysis became the enormously influential *Culture and Society* (1958) and was subsequently extended through a series of studies of cultural production that sought to understand the history of industrial capitalism in connection with the new forms of communication integral to it. *The Long Revolution* (1961) brought these studies together and signalled Williams's insistence on the importance of struggles for the public ownership of means of communications (he was later to do major work on television). Culture is a material production of meanings and is not to be taken as secondary, determined – the conventional Marxist view – by the economic base. 'The long revolution' was a process involving politics, art, communications, economics and family organisation in which none of these was to be accorded some abstract priority. Moreover, 'culture is ordinary', not limited to some sphere of 'high culture', but to be understood in terms of the meanings and values that make up a society's way of life. Given this, the study of aspects of culture became vital for understanding society and social change, and Williams was the significant influence in the emergence of 'cultural studies', though its eventual detachment from any political sense and its academic trivialisation moved far from his concerns.

Within the ordinary culture, the arts are special processes of discovery, giving the experience of new meanings, creatively testing values. Literature in particular engages the living sense of a culture and Williams's critical books – *The English Novel from Dickens to Lawrence* (1970), for example – demonstrate this, neither reducing texts to mere reflection of their society nor treating them as unattached aesthetic objects but offering an analysis attentive to forms and conventions, to the histories and connections of words, to the experiences and values expressed. The concern to understand the complexity of social process in human terms led him to write too in specifically literary genres, notably that of the novel. Typically, his novels run across generations and involve characters who, having moved away from their Welsh roots, are drawn back in circumstances in which personal, social and political commitments intertwine. *Border Country* (1960), the first, is perhaps the best introduction to Williams and his work: a carefully realised account of community centred around a young lecturer's return to

Raymond Williams, Fellow 1961–88.

Dona Haycraft *c.*1970

the border village of his childhood where his railway-signalman father is dying. The most remarkable of the novels is *People of the Black Mountains* (1989–90), published posthumously (intended as a trilogy, only two parts were completed). It covers the history of the people of his native border country from 23000 BC to the present (unfinished, it reaches AD 1415). That the vast amount of research involved was successfully worked into the form of a novel, that the reconstructions of landscapes and events are powerfully done as literature, is testimony to his ability as a novelist and the sheer strength of his imaginative response to Wales.

Williams's commitment to socialism was early and strong. Throughout his life, he was politically active, concerned both to respond to particular situations and to contribute to socialist cultural and political theory. He became a significant left intellectual with an important influence on European Marxism; in Britain he played a key role in the development of the New Left and maintained a sustained critique of the failings of Labour governments, without ever losing faith in the socialist project or ceasing to reflect on the conditions and strategies for its achievement. Increasingly he described himself as a 'Welsh European': the sense of the necessary European – and international – movement towards socialism going along with the equally necessary rootedness in local identities and struggles.

Williams's written and spoken voice alone, with its measured strength and dignity, can give the full sense of his commitment, the power of his example. 'You're a Marxist, aren't you?', he was often asked, and he would reply:

I believe in the necessary economic struggle of the organised working class. I believe that this is still the most creative activity in our society, as I indicated years ago in calling the great working-class institutions creative cultural achievements, as well as the indispensable first means of political struggle. I believe that it is not necessary to abandon a parliamentary perspective as a matter of principle, but as a matter of practice I am quite sure that we have to begin to look beyond it … I believe that the system of meanings and values, which a capitalist society has generated, has to be defeated in general and in detail by the most sustained kinds of intellectual and educational work … we have to learn and to teach each other the connections between a political and economic formation, a cultural and educational formation, and, perhaps hardest of all, the formations of feeling and relationship which are our immediate resources in any struggle. Contemporary Marxism, extending its scope to this wider area, learning again the real meanings of totality, is, then, a movement to which I find myself belonging and to which I am glad to belong.

The Latinist

JAMES CLACKSON

D.R. Shackleton Bailey was the finest Latinist of his time, indeed one of the finest ever. During his time as Fellow at Jesus (1955–64) he held a University post not in classics, but in oriental studies, as University Lecturer in Tibetan. Although there are stories of his hiding in his rooms while the Dalai Lama visited Cambridge, his early work on Sanskrit Buddhist texts and their Tibetan translations is impressive, and may have helped in his election as a Fellow of the British Academy at the comparatively early age of 40 in 1958. When he told potential undergraduate students in Tibetan to come back once they had learnt Sanskrit, it was not only a means of ensuring that he avoided teaching the language, but also a reflection of his own training, since he had taken Sanskrit for his Cambridge Part II after achieving a first in Classics in Part I.

By the time Shackleton Bailey was elected as a Fellow at Jesus to direct studies in classics, he had moved away from research on Buddhist texts, and he was to publish his first book on a Latin author, *Propertiana*, in 1956. He was later to write of the attractions of working in a tradition with a larger accumulated weight of scholarship – dictionaries, grammars and treatises on all aspects of ancient life and history. In attempting to restore the texts of ancient writers to their original state, and remove errors which had crept in through the long process of copying and recopying over centuries, Shackleton Bailey was able to build on a long chain of predecessors, stretching back to antiquity. This did not mean that he found nothing fresh to contribute, but that his techniques were 'more sophisticated and controlled, as those of a surgeon in an operating theatre'. The medical simile is telling, and it recurs elsewhere. Just as modern surgery rebuilds and restructures the sick body, and uses the knife more sparingly than the sawbones of earlier ages, so Shackleton Bailey attempted to restore the works of ancient authors through careful elucidation of the meaning, and by adding a couple of letters here or inserting an extra word there he made formerly ailing texts better. Like the very best doctors, he was an excellent diagnostician, and he used his unrivalled knowledge of Latin texts to detect when something was amiss. In these days when it is possible to search all Latin literature at the click of the mouse, the learning of men like Shackleton Bailey is almost impossible to conceive. If he claimed that the word *rogitare* occurred twenty times in Livy, fourteen in Tacitus, six in Juvencus, twice in Vergil and once in Caesar, Sallust, Seneca the Younger *et al.*, this knowledge was only gained by reading through these authors and remembering the occurrences. Twelve years before his death, Shackleton Bailey estimated that he had made 'perhaps two or three thousand' conjectures, that is suggestions for improving the health of a Latin text. Other scholars have made more, but very few have made so many good ones.

While at Jesus, Shackleton Bailey began what was to be a 26-year research project on the work for which he is now best known, the ten-volume edition, with commentary, of Cicero's correspondence. This proved to be a worthy challenge for Shackleton Bailey and a lasting contribution to scholarship. The letters are full of allusions to contemporary figures and events, and to earlier Greek and Latin literature and philosophy; many of them are written in a condensed idiomatic Latin, peppered with switches into Greek. They provide a mass of information about the social and political history of the late Roman Republic, and a unique insight into the psychology of one of the ancients. In Shackleton Bailey's words, 'Nothing comparable survives from the classical world … In Cicero's letters we see a Roman Consular, on any reasonable estimate one of the most remarkable men of his eventful age, without his toga.'

Shackleton Bailey saw himself as part of an academic tradition, in a constant dialogue with past scholarship and past scholars, who were perhaps more real for him than many of his contemporaries. One in particular acted as a mentor, almost a rival even, the poet and former Kennedy Professor of Latin at Cambridge, A.E. Housman. As a first-year undergraduate in 1936 he had been advised by his Director of Studies to attend a lecture by Housman. Arriving late after some trouble in finding the lecture room in Trinity, he was rewarded with 'a brief glance of tired hostility from the spare figure at the desk'. Housman died two weeks later; this was his last lecture, and the only physical meeting between the two. Yet

Shackleton Bailey dedicated *Propertiana* to the shade of Housman, who had also worked on Propertius as a young man, and he described reading Housman's edition of the Latin poet Manilius as 'the most memorable intellectual experience of my life'. In challenging some of Housman's verdicts on Manilius, he defended himself on the grounds that 'Housman wrote for readers who will occasionally call him wrong – at their peril, and on their knees'. He emulated Housman in his clear, crisp English style, with frequent dashes of humour, and in his intolerance of incompetents and charlatans. His defence of some of Housman's more ferocious personal attacks is worth repeating: 'Housman … was hardly ever wrong when he denounced. Robinson Ellis *had*, among scholars, the intellect of an idiot child, Francken *was* a born blunderer, marked cross from the womb and perverse, van Wageningen's commentary *does* most resemble a magpie's nest.'

Yet Shackleton Bailey departed from Housman's example in a surprising way. He was dedicated to making classical works more accessible. He championed the translation, which many of the traditional classicists of his and later generations saw as beneath the dignity of a scholar. After all, clever boys (and they were always boys) could learn Latin and Greek at school, and there was little point on wasting energy on writing for those who hadn't done so. Cambridge University Press, which published Shackleton Bailey's edition of Cicero's letters, did not, and still does not, usually include an English translation with published classical texts and commentaries. They made an exception for the early Cicero volumes, but after 1970 a concern for economy meant that the translation was dropped (it was published separately as a Penguin Classic). In the last two decades of his life Shackleton Bailey continued to provide readable, lively and unexpurgated English versions of Latin texts, translating Cicero's letters, Martial, Statius, Valerius Maximus and Quintilian's declamations (eighteen volumes in all) for the Loeb Classical Library, and helping to transform the reputation of the Loeb series from the last resort of the desperate undergraduate to a respected scholarly resource.

By all accounts Shackleton Bailey was not an easy man to get on with, introverted and impatient with undergraduates and teaching, preferring cats to people. But the dictum of Hazlitt, which he cited in reference to Housman, also applies to him: 'If a man leaves behind him any work which is a model in its kind, we have no right to ask whether he could do anything else.'

The Lawyers

JOHN HOPKINS and PETER GLAZEBROOK

The two lawyer Fellows, Robert Jennings and Glanville Williams, had both taught at the London School of Economics and both shared a deep love of the English countryside, but in almost everything else offered striking contrasts. One was a rather conservative Yorkshireman, for whom cricket was more than a game, and by nature a mediator; the other a Celt, though one with little sympathy for Welsh nationalism or the Welsh language, who was a radical and razor-sharp critic of English law and its institutions. One accepted the proffered knighthood, as is only usual; the other declined it: he had been a conscientious objector, and (as one obituarist said) 'thought it incongruous that a man who had refused to wield a bayonet should theoretically bear a sword'. Jennings, who devoted himself for close on sixty years to the study and practice of international law, had not hurried to publish, gaining fame and becoming most influential only after he had retired (at the customary age of 67) from his Cambridge chair. Williams, the common lawyer, had displayed a dazzling precocity in his prolific writings in several legal disciplines and many areas of the law – most notably criminal law, where he set the academic agenda for most of the next fifty years – and had become a household name among English-speaking lawyers, holding two chairs at the University of London (including its most senior one) before, aged 44, he became a Fellow of Jesus. When Jennings was appointed the University's Professor of International Law in 1955, the College had, at his prompting, asked Williams to advise it in choosing a new Director of Studies in law. The Fellows, who were unable to reach agreement among themselves on any of the short-listed candidates, were much relieved when they learnt that Williams himself would be happy to accept election. The candidates (whom he had interviewed) were astonished.

It was almost despite himself that Jennings became one of the world's most influential international lawyers. From 1982 to 1995 he was a judge, and then president, of the International Court of Justice at The Hague, and when, while still at the height of his powers, he stepped down from that Court he continued to act as an adjudicator of international disputes which the parties could not, or did not wish to, take there. Composed of fifteen judges elected, in the first instance, by the General Assembly and Security Council of the United Nations, the Court is in many ways a pretty odd tribunal: first, because it has jurisdiction only over states and has it only when the state parties to a given dispute voluntarily consent to its exercising jurisdiction, and second, because the

law it applies is a pretty odd system of law. International law has few central law-making processes, and there are no obvious means of enforcing its rules against sovereign states. And so, perhaps unsurprisingly, there have been occasions, including in the late 1970s and early 1980s, when it has, as it were, wanted for business. It is a measure of his greatness and achievement that when Jennings retired from the Court in 1995 (he had been elected its president by his fellow judges in 1991), its standing and repute had never stood higher and the number and importance of the cases being referred to it had never been larger or greater.

The Court has its own distinctive procedures. After lengthy written submissions by the states involved, oral submissions and arguments ensue; on their conclusion, discussion amongst the judges follows and then, crucially, a small committee of them drafts a judgment which is then put into revised shape and final form by all the judges. Jennings's drafting skills and his accuracy, clarity and felicity of expression ensured that he was almost always a member of that committee, his influence being apparent in many a judgment of the Court. A judge may enter a separate or dissenting opinion, but Jennings seldom did so. He sat in twenty-six cases and gave but three

Professor Sir Robert Jennings, Fellow 1939–2004, Senior Tutor 1949–55.

Peter Edwards, 1993

separate and four dissenting opinions – most famously in the *Nicaragua – United States Case* (1986) where his superb – and superbly clear and concise – dissent is in sharp contrast to the lengthy majority and other judgments. It is still frequently cited. After retiring from the Court he was appointed, aged 83, president of the arbitral tribunal established to resolve bitter territorial disputes between Yemen and Eritrea; it concluded its business in 1999, still under his presidency, by which time he was 86. He returned to the International Court as judge *ad hoc* in the *Lockerbie Case* between the United Kingdom and Libya. And as if all this was not enough, he wrote a series of brilliant opinions concerning investment disputes between Canadian companies and the United States.

His literary achievements, though slow at first in appearing, were ultimately also enormous. A slim volume of lectures on *The Acquisition of Territory in International Law* (1963) became a classic which is still frequently cited by jurists and before international tribunals. It inevitably fuelled demands for his services as an advocate, enabling him to put to good use the great expertise in interpreting maps, charts and aerial photographs that he had acquired while serving in the Intelligence Corps during the Second World War. He was counsel for Argentina in its arbitrations with Chile involving, first, the Rio Encuentro and then the Beagle Channel, a dispute which had taken the two countries to the brink of war. He represented the United Kingdom in its arbitration with France concerning the boundary of the continental shelf in the English Channel, and he appeared in the Sharjah/Dubai and Tunisia/Libya cases as well. A steady and, as the years

Professor Glanville Williams,
Fellow 1956–97.

Dona Haycraft, *c.*1970

went by, increasing stream of highly influential articles followed. And then, in 1992, jointly with Sir Arthur Watts, a former legal adviser at the Foreign and Commonwealth Office, he published what professed to be the ninth edition of *Oppenheim's International Law*, but was in truth virtually a new book, two massive volumes that were at once acclaimed as the most authoritative work of scholarship and reference on international law in the English language.

But this was only the half of it. Throughout a long working life that continued to within days of his death at the age of 90, Robbie Jennings remained the quintessential Cambridge don. He was quietly proud of his Yorkshire roots (he was the first pupil of Belle Vue Secondary School, Bradford, to come to Cambridge; his father managed a small factory manufacturing paper tubes; his mother had worked in the local mill; his maternal grandfather was illiterate); deeply valuing, as he movingly affirmed (in words quoted on page 2), his membership of three colleges – Downing (where he was an undergraduate), Jesus and Trinity (by virtue of his professorship) and loyally devoted to them. He readily shouldered administrative as well as teaching responsibilities; remembered by many Jesuans as Senior Tutor from 1948 to 1955, he also served on both University and City councils. An engaging lecturer, he was, as Whewell Professor of International Law, a gentle and kindly guide to generations of graduate and research students who had come to Cambridge from all over the world, not always confident in their use of the English language, but all sure that it was *the* place to study international law, and many returning to serve in the foreign offices of their own countries. So it was not altogether surprising that his nomination to be a judge of the International Court received the largest ever number of affirmative votes in the UN's General Assembly. 'Few judges carried their knowledge and wisdom, that rich harvest of a lifetime, so lightly and with such comfort and ease', was the verdict of the International Court's librarian, someone especially well placed to give it.

Until the publication in 1953 of Glanville Williams's *Criminal Law: The General Part*, followed within two years by *The Proof of Guilt*, the critical study of English criminal law – the structure and extent of its prohibitions, its methods of trial and its rules for the gathering and use of evidence – still stood pretty much where the great Victorian judge and jurist Sir James Fitzjames Stephen had left it at his death in 1894. Little money was to be made in the criminal courts and little thought had been given to the law they applied. *The General Part* stands high on the list of great books written about English law in the twentieth century, transforming scholarly and (rather more slowly) judicial and professional attitudes to its subject. The mapping of the territory was so comprehensive, the analysis so penetrating, the critique so trenchant, and the prose – enriched with echoes of the Bible and the English classics – so lucid and so elegant. In *The Proof of Guilt* (1955) the English rules on the powers of the police, trial procedures and what may and may not be used in court as evidence were subjected to similar critical scrutiny, two sacred cows, trial by jury and the right to silence, receiving a beating. And two years later *The Sanctity of Life and the Criminal Law* (1957) delivered a sustained attack on the law governing the beginning and the ending of human life. It was, for law faculties in England and North America, the first dawn of the now flourishing study of medical law and ethics.

Much of Williams's subsequent writing (which continued for nearly four decades) developed, elaborated and defended the principles propounded in these books, to which he adhered with remarkable consistency and, in almost all instances, well-warranted tenacity. His unswerving devotion to legal scholarship was inseparable from his unswerving commitment to law reform: the many letters to *The Times* that emerged from his typewriter were a higher art form. Serving for more than thirty years on government committees and Law Commission working parties, he frequently wrote the papers on which their discussions centred and their reports were founded, thereafter constantly dispatching memoranda to MPs, ministers and parliamentary committees in defence of their recommendations. He took a leading part in the Abortion Law Reform Association's long campaign culminating, during his presidency, in the 1967 Act; his satisfaction at its success in almost entirely eliminating back-street abortions was mixed with sadness that the medical profession betrayed the trust placed in it by Parliament. And with one spectacular article he persuaded the House of Lords

to reverse a decision it had reached less than a year before. More fortunate than Stephen, Williams lived to see several of the reforms for which he had been the first to campaign implemented by Parliament or, with the aid of the Human Rights Act, the courts.

Lying behind the missionary zeal evident in all his writing about English criminal justice was his belief that, being entangled with the 'mystical' concept of retribution, it was quite unnecessarily punitive, far too often causing more avoidable human suffering than it prevented. He sought a criminal law that would operate less heavy-handedly and less discriminatorily, and be less susceptible to the gales of vindictive passion and emotion. There was truth, as well as mischief, in a colleague's comment that he was 'Jeremy Bentham's only legitimate descendant'.

Glanville Williams was not only a zealous law reformer, he was also an innovative and crusading law teacher (though no great lecturer). His *Learning the Law*, written in less than a month in 1944 to meet the needs of students, many of whom were soon to return to their books after the interruptions of war, was for sixty years and for almost all English lawyers their introduction to their profession. It combined penetrating insights, astringent comments on legal institutions, astute awareness of what bemuses the student and what they need to know first, with a bevy of practical tips on how to set about the whole business, conveyed with a sense of enthusiasm and a slightly conspiratorial air – the author was most definitely on the students' side – in language of marvellous lucidity. Among books on English law only Blackstone's *Commentaries* has sold more copies. Many of his Jesuan pupils forgot the law he taught them, but none his concern for them – or the banana fritters he cooked for his after-dinner parties in his gyp-room on D staircase.

The Philologist

JAMES CLACKSON

Said Ahura Mazdah to Zarathustra the Spitamid:
'When I created grass-land magnate Mithra, O Spitamid, I made him such in worthiness to be worshipped and prayed to as myself, Ahura Mazdah.
The knave who is false to the treaty, O Spitamid, wrecks the whole country, hitting as he does the Truth-owners as hard as would a hundred obscurantists.'

So begins Ilya Gershevitch's English version of the fifth-century BC Zoroastrian song of praise to the god Mithra, translated from the ancient Iranian language known as

Avestan. The translation appeared in Gershevitch's second book, *The Avestan Hymn to Mithra* (1959), published shortly before he joined Jesus as a Fellow in 1962. The translation immediately conjures up the exoticism of the field, but the strange names and the delightful English style, jumping between archaism and invention, only hint at the extraordinary range of learning which went into writing it. Some idea of the scope of Gershevitch's knowledge can be gained from the fact that the word index includes material not just from over twenty other Iranian languages and dialects, but also from as many non-Iranian tongues, including Armenian, Hebrew, Gothic and Middle Irish, as well as Latin, Greek and Sanskrit. The linguistic mastery served a larger purpose, the elucidation of the text and meaning of the Avestan hymn and the reconstruction of the cultural and religious beliefs of its composers. To do this required not only the command of related languages, in order to unearth the significance of obscure words or grammatical constructions in the original, but also an extensive knowledge of everything that had been written by and about the early inhabitants of Iran and its neighbouring lands, and about the Mithraic religion which spread as far as Britain during the Roman Empire. The commentary on the nine lines translated above covers six pages, during which Gershevitch discusses the meanings or connections of individual words at length: the Iranian word rendered as 'Truth-owners' is set in its full religious context; and the epithet 'grass-land magnate' (a 'somewhat uncouth translation chosen for its comparative brevity') is revealed to survive as the name of one of Mithra's attendants in Latin inscriptions, Cautes. Gershevitch wanted to elicit as much truth as possible from all of the diverse sources at his command, and land a counter-blow to the obscurantists (among whom he numbered some other Iranianists). *The Avestan Hymn to Mithra* is still widely recognised as a model in Iranian studies: a work which gives a full and accurate commentary for one part of the Avestan scriptures, and to a standard that matches the best work done on better-known texts such as Homer, Vergil or Shakespeare, which have received a great deal more scholarly attention, leaving less spade-work for the individual. The difficulty, perhaps one should say impossibility, of living up to Gershevitch's model can be most easily seen by the fact that in the half-century following the publication of the work no scholar has achieved, or even attempted, anything comparable. Gershevitch himself did not attempt any further book-length commentaries on Avestan texts; instead he devoted himself to further work across the whole field of Iranian studies and beyond.

In his first book, *A Grammar of Manichean Sogdian* (1954), he had demonstrated his control of the detailed linguistic material of the subject, and the Iranian languages remained at the heart of his work. Naturally adept at solving problems and extracting good sense where others could only see nonsense, he used his expertise in the various and difficult Iranian languages to its best advantage in a number of articles written on a wide array of subjects (a selection of these were reprinted in the volume *Philologica Iranica* in 1985). He also did immense service to the subject in his work as editor of Volume II of the *Cambridge History of Iran*, for which he marshalled twenty-one articles by eighteen different contributors from all around the world (including classicists, Egyptologists, numismatists and art historians) to create a coherent and enduring synthesis of Iranian history from the sixth to third centuries BC.

Gershevitch had such a wide diversity of interests that any attempt at summary is bound to fail. Instead, snapshots of two of his research interests in the same year, 1990, give a flavour of his inventiveness and wit, and they also testify to the importance of Jesus to his work, since both arose through collaboration with other Fellows of the College. (For more than twenty years he was also the College's Praelector: generations of Jesuans remember the elegance – admired throughout the University – with which he presented them to the Vice-Chancellor in the Senate House and, too, the lunches he gave in his rooms in the immediately preceding terms.)

First, Robin Donkin's encyclopaedic knowledge of pearls and the pearl trade, to bear fruit in his later book *Beyond Price: Pearls and Pearl-fishing*, led Gershevitch to consider the origin of the Greek word for pearl (from which in turn English 'margarite' and the name Margaret are derived). He delivered a paper in Cambridge on the subject to an audience of classicists, linguists and geographers. With a combination of daring ingenuity and obscure learning that is familiar to anyone who knows his work, Gershevitch derived the Greek term from the Iranian word meaning 'bird', citing a similarity in shape between pearl mussels and birds and supporting his argument by reference to, among other things, the Ethiopic translation of the Greek author Arrian, which defined a pearl as 'a bird from the sea'. Even the most sceptical members of the audience found themselves gradually won round by the gradual accumulation of evidence in favour of this theory; most striking of all was the reproduction of a picture of a bivalve looking exactly like a pigeon.

The second collaboration was of a different kind. In September 1990 he visited south Ossetia, in the newly independent republic of Georgia, having flown there in Michael Waring's plane, with Michael as pilot. Gershevitch was undertaking research on Ossetic dialects, and he revealed a grammatical form which had been overlooked previously by western scholars: the ending *-æt* used as a third plural imperative, current in the everyday speech of his Ossetic hosts. Gershevitch's own published account of his discovery reminds us of his gift for infecting others with his enthusiasm, his delight in new knowledge, and his warm enjoyment in meeting new people: 'my new friends were greatly amused at learning that Iranologists at large knew nothing of it [the third plural imperative ending *-æt*], and would be bound to consider it of unusual interest'.

Laurence Picken

ROGER SCRUTON

Coming from our local grammar to a college dominated by self-confident boys from Eton and Harrow, bearing a scholarship in a subject that I abhorred, and finding myself in a suite of chill, bare Victorian rooms at the start of the coldest winter on record, my first instinct was to run away. It was an instinct that I could not act upon since there was nowhere to run to, I having already run away from home nine months before in one of those definitive adolescent gestures which I was planning at some stage to revoke – though in fact I never got round to it. There was nothing for it but to go to this old geezer who had been appointed *in loco parentis* and to tell him that I was not going to read Natural Sciences, that the thought of crystallography, biochemistry and microbiology filled me with disgust, that there must surely be some other subject – Chinese, for instance – that would answer to my bohemian yearnings without damaging my brain, and that in any case if he didn't come up with something better I was leaving the College that night, so there.

My agitated knock was greeted with silence. I listened carefully. I discerned a faint, mouse-like scraping somewhere behind the door. After a while I realised that the sound was music – though music played so softly that it was like music remembered, rather than music heard. I knocked again and, after a short pause, was greeted with a quiet 'come in'. Bursting through the door like the proverbial bull, I found myself in a china shop, surrounded by precious vases, delicate musical instruments and a hundred polished and fragile things, among which none appeared more fragile or more polished than the loco himself – a large porcelain head which turned faint blue eyes in my direction from behind a clavichord, on the keys of which his beautiful ivory hands were resting. 'You are my tutor,' I blurted out, overcome with confusion.

He looked at me anxiously. 'I feared as much,' he said at last.

'I need to talk to you.'

He got up from the clavichord and quietly closed the lid. With slow studied gestures, like a bomb-disposal expert, he turned and tip-toed to his desk, from where he gestured me towards an armchair. I stood by it, not sitting, and delivered my prepared speech. He winced every now and then at some particularly coarse turn of phrase, but otherwise remained seated, motionless behind a neat array of pens, papers and green jade dragons. When I had finished and after a moment's silence during which he studied me apprehensively, he quietly addressed the problem, as though speaking to himself and in a voice so soft that I had to strain to hear him.

'I cannot recommend Chinese,' he said. 'It is a language I happen to know, collection of languages I should say, and requires an immense amount of work and dedication. We can rule out English since obviously you will read those books in any case, and that really leaves no choice save history or moral sciences. Not that I approve of either.'

'What,' I asked, 'are moral sciences?'

'Well may you ask. It is the traditional Cambridge name for philosophy.'

' Moral sciences, then,' I instantly decided.

Dr Picken sighed reproachfully. 'We admit you young men to read the Natural Sciences, which are, you know, the greatest legacy of this University, and you can never stay the course.'

'Would *you*?' I asked, looking around at the books and instruments, the scrolls and vases, and assuming myself to be in the presence of a distinguished orientalist.

'I did,' he replied.

'You mean you are a scientist?' I asked incredulously.

He nodded. 'I branched out a bit,' he added. 'But I stayed the course.'

I eagerly accepted the glass of sherry which he poured from a decanter. He told me about his work in cytology, concerning which he had written a large book. I asked to see it, and turning over the pages I saw that the last chapter was entitled 'Envoi', a word that I knew from Ezra Pound's Cavalcanti translations. I looked across at Dr Picken with renewed interest. This old geezer was clearly not *loco* at all, nor was he so very old. I asked him what he thought of Ezra Pound. He responded with a shy but authoritative lecture on the Confucian Odes. Pound's inaccuracies in the translation, he told me, were offset by some real felicities in the feeling. He went on to talk about the Noh plays, indicating without stating it that he knew Japanese as well. And when at last I was convinced that this man was quite the most learned person I had ever met and that I ought to take his advice, he got up slowly, and said, 'Moral sciences it is then. I will send you to Dr Ewing.'

His manner was somehow precarious, and it became clear to me that I was intruding, that I had been intruding all along, that only a carefully nurtured veneer of politeness had enabled him to carry on a conversation with me, and that his interrupted session at the clavichord had probably been going on in his mind throughout our talk. I left with a note for Dr Ewing, and so began my career as a philosopher.

Dr Picken, I discovered, was a conscientious Tutor who refused quite categorically to make favourites of his pupils, and who invited us all to dinner, five at a time, once a year. I know that I was a trouble to him, often visiting him at unauthorised hours for an emergency *exeat*, which he would grant while looking at me from distant and fearful eyes, as though not sure whether I was tricking him into complicity in some crime about which he would rather not know. He retreated from emotion, and would not allow me to express it. And sometimes, passing his room in the evenings, and seeing him seated at the clavichord, or at the lovely old chamber organ on which he played the chorale preludes of Bach, I would have the sense of a creature so fragile that merely to touch him would cause him to fall in fragments to the floor. And yet, when I was reported to him as a candidate for rustication – a collection of woman's clothes having been discovered in my wardrobe, along with empty gin bottles and other signs of dissipation which, in those days, were sufficient to jeopardise an undergraduate's career – he entered quietly and doggedly into my defence, upheld with the faintest of smiles my story that I had transvestite leanings, and successfully protected me from punishment.

We became friends, and sometimes we would play together on the two grand pianos in the College music room, working through the Mozart piano concerti, one of us as soloist, the other as orchestra. He said very little but played with a kind of vulnerability that suggested depths of feeling, depths of suffering too, that he could

admit to in no other way. Once I put in some Mozartian ornaments, and he spoke out approvingly across the room. Seldom has praise been so precious to me.

If Dr Picken spoke about any topic, it was because he knew everything about it. Yet he spoke always with exemplary respect towards his listener, and with a complete modesty of demeanour. His learning astonished me. He seemed to know every European language, the Slavonic tongues included, and was an ethnomusicologist of the first rank, who had gone over the ground first opened up by Bartók, Kodaly and Janáček. Although you could be forgiven for thinking that he had never left his College rooms, he had in fact pursued his scientific career all over the world, beginning before the war with four years' work on freshwater *Ciliata* in the Balkans, where he had learned Serbo-Croat and written down the folk songs, moving thereafter to the École de Chimie in Geneva, and so beginning adventures that took him back and forth across Europe, picking up languages and melodies wherever he went.

He had researched not only folk music but also the instruments that accompanied it, most of which he could play. He was the world expert on Turkish folk instruments, which he collected and catalogued at a time when they were fast disappearing from popular use. He was fluent in Turkish and of course could read it in the Arabic script that the Turks themselves have now forgotten. Oriental languages were another love, along with the lit-

erature and music that had traditionally accompanied them, and he was an expert on Japanese Gagaku, as well as the old folk orchestras of China and the gamalan of Bali. He had researched Bach deeply, and I was told that he had even discovered a previously unknown Bach fugue.

Dr Picken was also quietly knowledgeable about wine, and I can still remember the conversation with which he launched me on another of my professional careers. He had cheered me up with some burgundy left over from one of his dinners and we were standing in his little kitchen, as neat and clean as every other part of his museum-like rooms, as he carefully washed up – it being intolerable to him to see a dirty glass polluting the chair-side table.

'I should tell you,' he said, 'that the burgundy you have just drunk was not very good. In fact commercialisation has more or less destroyed the region, and people of your generation will probably never know burgundy as we knew it. With one exception. There is a small domaine in Vosne-Romanée called Domaine de la Romanée-Conti. If you ever come across it you should give it a try. It has the perfect balance of stalk and fruit, and the soil speaks through it too. Nobody else now knows how to make wine like that.'

That advice was given to me in 1964. Shortly afterwards Romanée-Conti was discovered by the trade, and today it is probably the most expensive wine you could buy. But I remembered Dr Picken's little speech, and was able to repeat it at all kinds of gatherings where knowledge about good wine was rewarded with a glass of it.

Dr Picken was, for me, the very image of the bachelor don, who had retreated from life in order to immerse himself in learning. He typified the osmotic process whereby a cultural and intellectual inheritance was transmitted within college walls. You could pick up from him any amount of knowledge on any number of subjects – from the wave structure of the benzene ring to the translation of Dante, from Frazer's theory of magic to the chronology of the Upanishads – and the very irrelevance to the surrounding world of everything he knew made the learning of it all the more rewarding. He justified, in my eyes, the rigorous monasticism that had been nurtured by the Cambridge colleges, living as he did in permanent retreat from ephemera. His attitude to learning was the very opposite of that which has come to dominate the schools and universities today. He did not believe that the purpose of knowledge was to help the student. On the contrary. For Dr Picken, the purpose of the student was to help knowledge. He was throughout his life the willing and self-sacrificing trustee of an intellectual inheritance. Young people mattered to him because they had the brains into which his reservoir of learning could

be poured. He looked at us students sceptically, but always with that underlying hope that, in this or that undisciplined young face, there was yet the outward sign of a brain large enough and dispassionate enough to capture some of the accumulated knowledge of mankind, and which could carry that knowledge through life without spilling it, until finding another brain into which it might be discharged.

As a graduate student I again became friendly with Laurence, as I now called him, and discovered the warmth and humanity which he had conscientiously withheld when I was *in statu pupillari* and he *in loco parentis*. Sometimes he referred to his experiences – including his extensive travels in China, which he had first visited in 1944 when he joined Dr Joseph Needham in the Sino–British Scientific Co-operation Office, the Chinese being keen to hear about the blood transfusion techniques on which Laurence had been working in Cambridge. Needham was beginning to collect the materials for his great *Science and Civilisation in China*, and both men were experiencing the impact of a culture which was equally an object of scientific curiosity and a mirror to the soul. By the time I came to know him, Laurence, unlike Needham, had become disillusioned with communism, and welcomed my budding scepticism concerning the revolutionary nonsense that I was witnessing during my vacation in France. He had devoted his time in China to studying the great culture that the diabolical Mao Tse Tung was beginning to wreck. He had learned to play the old instruments, to read the Chinese entablatures, and of course to read and write the characters and to speak some of the languages. And he was already working on recreating from later Japanese materials the imperial court music which had been entirely lost in China, but which was to be heard there again, after a silence of six centuries, when it was played, under Laurence's direction, in Shanghai in 1998.

Laurence's reminiscences had an extraordinary tone of tenderness. He had handled Chinese culture just as he handled the fragile instruments and ornaments in his rooms in College: it was something infinitely precious to him, which he had to internalise in order to preserve it. And that was, it seems to me, his attitude to everything – to translate what he loved into something inner, inviolable because no longer made of breakable stuff, and to watch over it until he could pass it on to a mind that vibrated to his own. I doubt that he ever found that mind: he was too private a person, in the end, to do himself and his learning full justice. But he remains in my thinking as one of the intellectual peaks of Cambridge, an ascetic who purchased through his solitude the right to call himself a sage.

High Table, Porters' Lodge, Gardens and Bursary: Personalities

JOHN HUDSON

HIGH TABLE

My Director of Studies throughout my undergraduate career in the Mathematics Tripos – I came up in 1955 – was Derek Taunt. He was a charming, rather formal and meticulous man who couldn't pronounce his r's properly. Words like 'heuristic' and 'empirical', which he used quite regularly, remain in my memory exactly as he pronounced them. He wrote solutions to the problems he had set, using an old-fashioned pen with a steel nib which he regularly dipped into an ink pot. He used the backs of the printed lists giving the entries for the various University examinations, which were sent from the Old Schools to tutors in all the colleges, on sheets of paper varying in size according to the length of the list. He was a pure mathematician, an algebraist and, although his manner was rather dry, he managed to get the beauty of the best mathematics and his love of the subject across to his students. When he surveyed my ham-fisted, two-page efforts at a solution, he sighed and you could feel the pain. His pen would then, in a few lines, scratch out a solution which was both elegant and satisfying. The problems set for supervisions were almost entirely taken from old Tripos papers. This scheme worked very well since the content of the Mathematical Tripos had not changed in a long while. College fellows formed themselves into groups in which each member contributed model solutions to the problems set in the previous year's exams. This way they all had a complete set of solutions to all the problems in all the papers going back many years. In the '60s, by which time I was teaching too, the Tripos began to change. One year the College had a pair of very bright students, John Stewart and Roger Salmon, who made it clear to Derek and me that supervisions would also have to change. I realised, in supervising these two, that I could no longer teach across the whole of applied mathematics in Part II (because, in some areas,

they knew more than I did), and John told me that he had informed Derek that he should no longer supervise applied mathematics in Part I. John Stewart went on to become a member of the Mathematics Faculty and a Fellow of King's, while Roger went off to be a merchant banker and was later reincarnated as Bursar of King's.

Derek was a true gentleman. He had been a keen oarsman and was now official timer for the Fairbairn races, which have always been run by the College. He recruited me to help, which involved starting a stopwatch at the start of the first boat at the Fort St George bridge, and cycling hard to reach the finish, up near Baits Bite lock, ideally before the first boat also arrived. The road isn't as straight as the river and it wasn't easy. Once, while we

Dr Derek Taunt (1936), Fellow 1947–2004, Bursar 1964–79.

Pencil drawing by Richard Sell, 1989

were clocking the arriving boats, a rather extrovert chaplain of another college said, within our hearing and apparently in reply to a question, 'Who's going to win? The red and black of course – they run it and they win it.' Derek said nothing. The implication was ludicrous. Later, when he gave up mathematics to become Bursar, many changes were taking place in the colleges. He, in common with most of the older Fellows, loved Jesus just the way it was. It was clear that he regretted some of the decisions taken by the Fellowship and Council but nevertheless he carried them out faithfully. During the Second World War, he like Denys Page (the Master) and Trevor Jones (the Fellow in German) had worked at Bletchley Park: Derek with the team that had cracked the Enigma code. I had no idea about this until a book came out in the '80s describing the work in detail and naming names. As far as I know, Derek never spoke about his part in this heroic endeavour until then.

The other mathematical Fellow was Leopold Alexander Pars, known in the Fellowship as Alan, and among students as Leo. (The use of personal names changed a lot from the '30s on. Derek Taunt told me that, when he was a junior Fellow in the '40s, he greeted an older Fellow by his title, Dr Thorpe, and the latter replied, 'My dear fellow, please call me Thorpe.' In my day he was called Bill.) Pars was a typical Cambridge don, a bachelor who lived in College and stayed with his sister in Acton during the vacations. He idolised his old nurse and his mother, of whom he had a large portrait in his keeping room. He entertained quite a lot and occasionally took undergraduates to the theatre. On the whole the students liked him, but he had the embarrassing habit of putting his arm round their shoulders and giving them a hug. I assume that this was acceptable behaviour when he was young – the early years of the twentieth century. I never heard of any scandal associated with him. He had a rather hearty manner, played the piano, kept up with the latest offerings at the theatre, and ran a society called The Club, which existed to bring together selected Fellows and undergraduates for talks and discussions. I was invited to dine with him in his rooms when I was a junior Fellow, and fortunately realised that he would automatically expect his guests to wear black tie. However, he was not put out in the slightest by those who failed to observe this code. A student friend of mine who also dined with others with Pars said that he led the way into the dining room with 'Well now, children, it's just a snack.' Lifting the lid of the first dish, he exclaimed, 'What have we here? Ah! Lobster.' He gave good and clear supervisions, although he always seemed more concerned with rewriting our solutions than solving the problems we couldn't solve. Once he went through the principles of the Joukowski aerofoil, which showed how the lift force on

The Revd Percival Gardner–Smith (1906), Fellow 1923–85, Dean 1922–1956.

Dona Haycraft, *c.*1970

an aeroplane wing is generated. 'There,' he said, 'and if that didn't happen, those bloody aeroplanes wouldn't fly.'

During the Second World War, when much of the College was occupied by servicemen and women of one sort or another, Pars had been given an electric razor by the commander of a nearby US Air Force base who had been invited to High Table. An electric razor was a great novelty and he was very proud of his present. He plugged in the socket and immediately burnt it out – it was, of course, built for American voltage. Pars confessed this sad story to the officer when they next met and he kindly provided a replacement. So Pars, with the help of a transformer, shaved with it from then on. At lunch one day, he sat next to Percy Gardner-Smith, who commented, without naming names, that it was interesting to note that people who shaved with electric razors came to resemble hedgehogs. (It is possible that envy played a part here.) They didn't speak to each other much after that. Like many of the older Fellows (and probably a large section of the population), Pars looked back on the period before the Second World War as a golden age. He once spoke of the time when the University had its own Members of Parliament. 'They were always Independent of course,' he said, 'but the right kind of Independent.'

I met him one day when he was coming out of the Chimney into Jesus Lane on his way to the Senate House to vote on the proposal that undergraduates should no longer be required to wear gowns after dusk. Votes had then to be given in person and it was necessary to wear a gown. 'Are you coming to vote?' he asked me. I said I would but I needed to go back to fetch my gown. 'Borrow mine!' he replied and we set off to the Senate House together. He went in and voted and then I did. When I came out he said, 'I hope you voted the right way.' I assured him that I had, but I am sure that I had just cancelled out his vote. I expect he knew that as well.

Freddy Brittain was probably the Fellow best known among the undergraduates, mainly because he ran the Roosters, the other society for selected Fellows and undergraduates, whose activities were based essentially on puns on the name of Bishop Alcock. (Freddy had a huge collection of statues of cockerels, including one made of anthracite.) He came from South Mimms and had retained his Hertfordshire – really north London – accent. At Jesus he taught French which he spoke, according to my informants, with much the same accent. Freddy loved the College – so much so that he was said to be married to it (in fact, he said so himself) – and a number of the College's traditions were invented by him. He was, like Pars, a typical bachelor don – or he was until he married Muriel. Freddy added a lot to the atmosphere of the College and Muriel supported him in everything. There was always a welcome for Old Members in his rooms. When he was ill, Muriel became the first woman to have permission to reside in College. After his death she carried on the good work.

Percy Gardner-Smith was Dean (of Chapel) when I came up. He had a deep gravelly voice and a black and very dry sense of humour. In Chapel his sung responses were extraordinary as he incorporated a slow vibrato three or four semitones wide. But his sermons, short and pithy, were treasured by many. I remember he summed up the Cold War with the words 'The trouble with the Russians is that they are not gentlemen.' Another time he described the excellent work of certain missionary schools in India where the boys were introduced to 'manly sports'. Apparently masters with whips were stationed around the pitch 'to encourage the cowardly boys'. As Eustace Tillyard, the Master, was not keen on giving speeches, Percy spoke to our year just before graduation. He promised that the College would keep in touch with us through 'the little red book' (the report of the Jesus College Cambridge Society) 'with news of our obituaries'.

Percy was a great supporter of the Boat Club. A photograph taken at the end of a Fairbairn dinner shows the first boat members, grinning hugely, on High Table and a wall of swaying, well-oiled undergraduates rising up behind them. At the centre of High Table sat Percy, as grave and imperturbable as ever. He lived with his wife in Fen Ditton and invited the Boat Club to a garden party there each summer after the May races. I guess I went to the last of these. Afterwards, Percy gave a number of us a lift back to College. He drove a large old Humber tourer with an open top. There were four of us in the back seat, the rest sat on the folded roof behind them. We would certainly have been arrested these days.

A feature of Hall dinners was the pronunciation of the Latin of the Grace. All of us undergraduates had had to pass Latin or Greek at O-level and generally used the pronunciation approved by the Classics Teachers Union, but Percy learnt his Latin in far-off times and, in his

Malcolm Street: once mainly lodging houses, now entirely 'external staircases' and flats for graduate students.

unique bass voice and – as usual, without appearing to move his lips – pronounced his v's as w's, and I think his c's were always k's and j's always i's. Denys Page was Professor of Greek, and therefore would have known more than a little about Latin as well. His accent was a sort of Plain English in which *ego* was pronounced 'eggo' and *hujus* as 'hugeous'. You could imagine you understood it even if you knew no Latin. The most pleasing performance was by Ilya Gershevitch, who originated in Russia, attended school in Switzerland and university in Rome. Finally, to our great benefit, he came to Jesus College. Ilya was a kindly, scholarly and gentle man and read Grace in an Italian accent, slowly and with meaning.

Vivian Fisher, who became Senior Tutor shortly after I came up, was also Tutor for the mathematicians, including me. He was a historian, and a wound sustained in Athens towards the end of the Second World War had given him a pronounced limp. Unfortunately, his eyes didn't work together, which was rather disconcerting to a nervous freshman. However, I found him to be very fair and kind. He used to come in to Hall dinner slightly late and looking rather harassed, and would sit down with a huge sigh. After that, the cares of a Senior Tutor's life seemed to roll off him and he joined cheerfully in the conversation. When a new government edict came out demanding that Cambridge, and therefore the colleges, should take more students, he claimed that the quality of most of the applicants the College rejected was such that they would not be able to cope with the Tripos. So he said he would go to Wales and get a rugby team. ('They might as well do something useful while they are here.') Fortunately, it never seems to have come to that. When I became a Fellow, the President, who at that time was Alan Pars, briefed me on what should be worn at High Table – dark suit, tie, gown, etc. – and he added that he would like to say black shoes, but as the Senior Tutor always appeared in brown suedes, he couldn't insist on it.

Moses Finley, whose stature as an ancient historian is described by Peter Garnsey elsewhere (page 254), was an American whose middle name was I. Named simply Moses, he apparently had felt the need for a middle initial and had just inserted the letter I. As a result he carried on a light-hearted correspondence with the University's officers who insisted on putting a full stop after the I. He argued that, since it was not an abbreviation, no full stop was needed. He added greatly to the social and intellectual atmosphere of High Table. My main memory is of his contribution to the debate on the proposal to allow women to dine there. The discussion should have been recorded for posterity. It was surreal even then and today it would seem hilarious. To have left such a decision to the 1970s is extraordinary enough, but the objections raised against it were equally so. The gen-

eral concern appeared to be that women would lower the intellectual content of the conversation by talking about babies and knitting. So it was proposed that only academic women should be allowed to dine. Moses wanted to know how many O-levels would qualify as 'academic'; was his wife academic seeing that she constructed the indexes for his books? Another proposal was that women could be allowed in but not if undergraduates were present, which raised the question as to what sort of women we were talking about. In the end the pass was surrendered almost without a shot. The Senior Tutor said that he had been concerned that, whereas male supervisors from outside the College were rewarded with a meal at High Table, the female supervisors simply got a letter of thanks. So, to avoid this discourtesy, women were finally allowed to eat there.

PORTERS – AND LANDLADIES

The Butler, Mr Fuller-Rowell, had acted as Head Porter during the war and no doubt had a pretty difficult time. When the air-raid siren sounded, the Master used to lead the Fellows down into the shelters, which are those lumps in the Orchard looking rather like tumuli. When the Fellows thought it might be safe to emerge, they used to send out Mr Fuller-Rowell to report on the situation above ground, much as Noah sent out the dove. He carried out the job of Butler with imperturbable calm. In those days Fellows were served lunch by the waiters in much the same way as at dinner. Once, there were just two of us students eating lunch on the lower tables while the Chaplain, Simon Burrows, was the only occupant of High Table. Simon decided to be sociable and join us, and walked the length of Hall to where we were sitting. Mr Fuller-Rowell clearly didn't approve of this but set his face and brought the Fellows' plates and cutlery for the Chaplain and served him lunch in the proper way. It was all a bit odd. When out in the city, Mr Fuller-Rowell wore a long black coat over his suit and tie, and a black homburg hat. He was, undoubtedly, much smarter than any of the Fellows.

The Head Porter when I came up was Captain Austin (page 224). The College's custom had been to choose its porters from the Marines; in 1940 the Lodge was almost denuded – four of the five porters were Marines' reservists. Captain Austin (NCO in the First World War, commissioned in the Second) was a spare upright man who did not appear to have much of a sense of humour. It was said that at night he waited in the shadows near the favourite entry points of students wishing to evade the penal consequences of returning after hours. As they touched down after a tricky climb over revolving spikes or something equally dangerous, Captain Austin would feel their collar. John Rimington has described (page 246) his demonstration of the use of the Davey fire escape apparatus: it was pure pantomime.

Captain Austin's deputy, Mr Ayres (who had also been commissioned during the war) became Head Porter for one year after he retired and then Mr West, another ex-Marine, an RSM this time, was appointed. He was a real change from Austin both in shape and character. Mr West was rotund and had a round face which was inclined to smile a lot. At the annual cricket match, the Master would be behind the stumps for the High Table team and Westy kept wicket for the staff. In his top hat and morning coat, he had considerable presence. Once, when the College was electing a new Master and almost all the Fellows were in attendance, it was decided to take a group photograph. The banks of seats were set up and the photographer was waiting for the Fellows to sort themselves out. After a lot of ineffectual milling about, it was clear that the Fellows weren't going to make it, so Mr West took command. 'You Sir – there. And you Sir – here.' Within moments we were all in place.

Jim West, like Sir Denys Page, had to cope with the '60s. In the old days, if Captain Austin booked you, you were booked. Mr West increasingly found that his bookings were unbooked when they got to the Tutor, as the College rules were revised. The revolving spikes around the courts were taken down and a more lenient view was taken of the presence in College of persons of the opposite sex. Apart from the difficulty of keeping up with changes which Mr West clearly found unbelievable, some of the fun had gone out of a Head Porter's life. No more lurking in the shadows for the late night climbers and no more pouncing on the undergraduate who had accommodated his girlfriend in College overnight.

Walter Langford had what I think was the ideal temperament for a porter. He was relaxed and good natured but was perfectly capable of saying 'no'. He knew just how far he had to go in his job and wouldn't go further if he didn't want to. Although the porters, along with the rest of the College staff, were referred to as College servants, they knew (as did all the staff) how to get their own way. It didn't really pay to be on the wrong side of them. If you were late for Hall and had forgotten your gown, you might pop into the Porters' Lodge to see if they had a spare gown you could borrow. But if you were in their black book, the porters would have just lent their last gown. Mr Langford told a lot of stories about the College in pre-war days – mostly involving violence of some kind, but always funny. One day, he asked me if I would be prepared to give his 'old boy' some coaching in A-level mathematics. I said I would, although I wasn't sure who his 'old boy' might be. It turned out to be his son, Anthony,

and not his father as I had imagined. I very much enjoyed the lessons with Anthony, who was a bright and entertaining lad who later won a scholarship in Natural Sciences at Clare, and in due course took a PhD.

Mr Buxton had been a comedian on the music hall circuit. He was small, wrinkled and lively and he wore his bowler hat at the angle you would expect from an old comedian. One day the Head Porter said something to him to the effect that he should be grateful to get a regular wage as opposed to the precariousness of his earlier profession. So Mr Buxton fetched out his payslip for a week playing dame in a pantomime. Mr West didn't raise the subject again. Mr Buxton's stage name was Gene Durham, Durham being his home town, and his wife had been in the chorus. When he heard that I was playing the piano for an old-time music hall that a local youth club was putting on, he offered me a choice of costume from his hampers of stage clothes. He had some wonderful dame costumes in there, including bloomers with the Union Jack on the seat. He lent me a plus-fours suit in a loud orange check. It fitted me fine even though I was a good 6 inches taller than him. He said that he saw the suit in the window of a tailor's shop and had gone in to buy it. The shop assistant objected, saying that it was too big for him. 'If you wear that, people will laugh at you,' he said. 'Fine,' said Gene. I also borrowed his bowler hat, although I had to wear it at an even jauntier angle than he did as it was too small. Finally he offered me some jokes, which I declined on the grounds that I didn't have a speaking part.

Landladies acted as bed-makers in their lodgings but they also had to keep an eye on their lodgers and report them if they got up to mischief. Some landladies had become so fed up with difficult lodgers that their houses were full of notices requiring lodgers to wipe their feet, keep the noise down and so forth. Others were very kind and treated their lodgers like their own children. It was a real pleasure to have tea with a friend who lodged in Abbey Road – his landlady provided ham sandwiches and buns and other delights. On the whole, though, landladies were thought of as dragons. They were supposed to wait up if one of their lodgers was late coming in, whether he had permission or not. They had, in particular, to report the time of arrival to the porters. One friend of mine had a landlady who drank to while away the time so that, if he was late, he was met by a person of very uncertain temper. Often lodging houses were taken by College staff – the wife ran the lodgings and the husband worked as a porter or in the office. Myrtle West, wife of the Head Porter, ran 49 Jesus Lane and Mr Buxton's wife ran Little Trinity. As it happened, I married into another husband-and-wife pair. Phyllis Pettit, my auntie-in-law, ran a lodging house in Malcolm Street while her husband, Den, was butler at Sidney Sussex. Even Phyllis's family thought she was a dragon, but I always found her very amiable, and one of my students liked the lodgings so much he booked in for a further year. When I first came up, if you wanted quiet College was the place to live. Later, as College became noisier, certain lodgings were the quietest places to be.

THE GARDENS

Bill Howard was a slight, nervous man with a strong Cambridge accent, whose chrysanthemums won all the prizes at flower shows. He kept the College gardens beautiful, and ruled his staff with a rod of iron. If Mr Howard wanted to point out the error of his ways to an under-gardener, there were few people in College who didn't hear it. I once was across Chapel Court from him when he was explaining to a couple of bemused tourists that they shouldn't be walking on the grass. 'Can't you read?' etc. The volume was turned up so high on his local accent that I don't think they understood what he was on about. He was equally vociferous about undergraduates who stepped on his bedding plants. Denys Page said that one of the duties of a Master of Jesus was to talk to Bill Howard from time to time, let him unburden his soul, and convince him that the world was not against him and that the College was really pleased with the gardens. I had been walking out with a girl who lived in Maid's Causeway and went to Sturton Street Methodist Chapel on Sundays. Bill Howard lived near Sturton Street and came up to me one day, and said, 'Didn't I see you, Sir, walking down Sturton Street the other day?' I said that he probably had, and he replied, 'I thought so – I said to myself "There's Dr Hudson, out of bounds."' Clearly he thought that Fellows shouldn't be seen anywhere in the environs of Mill Road. Just over the railway bridge, it enters Romsey Town, which was known as Little Russia – presumably because the inhabitants, who were largely railway workers, had vaguely socialist leanings.

THE BURSARY AND COLLEGE OFFICE

Mr Robinson started in the kitchen office as a young lad but, when I arrived at Jesus, he was the Bursar's Agent which meant, I think, that he did everything in the Bursary that the Bursar didn't do. He was a squarely built man with a firm, and occasionally jolly, manner. The College at one time had used outside agents to collect the farm rents, but had decided to do the job in-house. So Mr Robinson was dispatched to the tenant farmers to try to part them from some of their money. Farmers were not

doing too well at the time and, at one farm, Robbo was met by a determined-looking gent carrying a shotgun who told him to go away. It was not long before Robbo gained the confidence of the tenants. He went out for a drink with them and had a few good laughs and, at Christmas, there were gifts of dead game. The College used to entertain the farmers at a yearly tenants' lunch, a most enjoyable occasion, when Robbo was in his element. There were quite a few such occasions: he took great pleasure in telling people how many silver spoons went missing after a lunch for incumbents of College livings. Like most College staff, Robbo had a way of protecting his patch and of restricting his workload to manageable proportions. At the tea for the College's landladies he would move among them with great bonhomie while they told him about their rickety stairs and the leak in the cistern. 'I'm afraid I have forgotten to bring my notebook with me,' he would say, and would promise to try to remember to call in some time. There was an ongoing dispute between Mr Robinson and the Head Porter. I don't know how it began but, when the back gardens of the Jesus Lane houses were shortened to provide space for the Malcolm Place flats, the tenants were given garages elsewhere. The arrangements were in Robbo's hands, so the Wests' garage was a day's march away from their house. He was a considerable figure in the world of allotments' associations, and in September huge marquees for the display of their produce appeared in the Close.

The College Clerk was in charge of all the academic bureaucracy of the day. Mr Lenoir ran his office with smooth and silent efficiency. He was a slight, pale man without much personality that one could see, but he was completely trustworthy and a pillar of the local closed Plymouth Brethren. The College relied on him totally to get the Tutors' returns back to the Examinations Syndicate and so forth. The whole system was documented inside Mr Lenoir's head. When he retired, David Newman took over and found himself entirely without guidance as to times and dates. There were no notes and Mr Lenoir had taken his head with him.

One of Mr Lenoir's young assistants was Mary Rayner. Mary was good hearted, cheerful and generous. She was meticulous in her work, typed the Master's letters when a (carbon) copy needed to be kept, and never had the heart to turn down any request to do some task or other. Never married, she led a full life, being a regular spectator at Fenners, a fervent supporter of Cambridge United and a carer for her ageing parents. Sadly, the advent of computers into her world defeated her and she retired early. Her upbeat view of life is occasionally still seen in letters to the local press.

Jesuan Moments: Contemporary Art and College Finance

ROBERT HELLER (1952)

Memory is a fickle friend, but among my myriad memories of the College from 1952 to 1955, one which stands out is the formation of the Jesus College Art Fund in February of the latter year (a date I would never have recalled unaided). The College had and has umpteen clubs and activities, some still strange to me, like the Roosters, but outsiders in the early '50s wrongly thought Jesus a rather beefy place, associated with oars rather than art, still less contemporary art. People now know better.

Much, much later, I was invited to join in another voluntary venture that changed the face of Jesus. The subject was money – never far from the surface when art

is discussed, but this time purely in the context of the College's finances. Since graduation, those invited to join the Finance Committee had all found fame and fortune, in varying degrees, through their post-Jesus connection with what's loosely known as the City. Now the Master and the Bursar wanted to consult this collective brainpower on the highly important matter of the College investments.

Investment in art was not a runner in these discussions, although contemporary art and the City relate more to each other now than they did in 1955 when, in Britain as a whole, artistic taste was backward by the standards of other nations. The Cubist works of Picasso – incontestably the century's greatest living artist – were commonly cited as examples of modern work that the citer couldn't stand, or understand. It did little good to point out that this 'modern' work dated back to before the First World War. But despite the doubters, an art revolution was under way – and Cambridge, while not in the forefront, was plainly a participant.

Leading the local way was Kettle's Yard, an easy stroll from Jesus Lane, where the brilliant collection formed by H.S. 'Jim' Ede presented, as it still does, an elegant and comprehensive guide to what Modernism truly means. The Yard celebrated its fiftieth anniversary in 2006. Especially strong in sculpture, with stunning pieces by Gaudier-Brzeska, Brancusi, Moore and Hepworth, Ede's collection showed what could be achieved with limited means. But the undergraduate art-lovers at Jesus were far more limited still, and had neither the resources nor the facilities to emulate the Yard.

Not that the founding fathers of the Jesus Fund had grand ambitions, anyway. They did, however, hope that their initiative would lead on to the acquisition of a substantial array of work, mostly financed by undergraduate subscriptions, that would help to open more eyes to what was happening on the British art scene – and to demon-

Woman's Head

Silkscreen by Fernand Léger

strate the enjoyment and value of living with art. Both aims were to be fully realised.

The precise circumstances that led to forming a committee to initiate the Jesus College Art Fund are lost to memory (my memory, anyway). The idea was simple. The ultimate aim was that 'every member of the College, who so wishes, should be able to borrow an original work of art to hang in his rooms' (no 'her' then, of course). That sentence dates from 1958–9, by which time the first years of the fund had achieved 'an impressive selection of some 40 works'. Many of the purchased artists were indeed impressive: Henry Moore, Fernand Léger, John Piper, L.S. Lowry, Michael Ayrton, William Roberts and Josef Herman.

These were all blue-chip names, men of the '30s whose reputations had soared in the '40s. They are still big names today – several decades later I found myself writing a monograph on Herman, the last of the old and grand school of European expressionists. Equally impressive was the response of the undergraduates, 150 of whom promised to cough up a guinea apiece to fund the purchases. This wasn't the first such scheme in Cambridge, but it had begun vigorously and sensibly ('the purchases are likely to be mainly of contemporary English work').

But who, if anybody, was the prime mover? The College's 2005 *Annual Report* declared that 'Michael Zander (1953) and M.R. Cornwall-Jones (1953) are the surviving members of the original committee of five.' At the moment of writing, I seem to be surviving; maybe I wasn't on the committee, but that's not my recollection. It's also hard to believe that Michael Podro, later a distinguished art academic, and a staunch supporter of Frank Auerbach's work, wasn't involved. (Michael Zander's sister Angelica, incidentally, became a deeply respected historian and curator of modern art, based in the US; Cornwall-Jones, when a distinguished City figure, did not record art among his recreations).

I think we bought three works to set the ball rolling – and, interestingly enough, one was a Ben Nicholson. Since nobody else put in a bid, I enjoyed the company of this marvellous drawing of St Ives until I went down. Nicholson, unusually for him, had added small patches of colour to this black-and-white piece, but there's no mention of him in the fund's lists of purchased artists that I've seen. I did, however, spot a suspiciously similar drawing in the Redfern Gallery's Summer Exhibition many years later. In any event, Nicholson's work may well mark the watershed in British contemporary art: world-class abstraction created by a genius whose reputation originally loomed larger abroad, but then came to blossom fully at home. Little did I know it at the time, but one of the Fellows, the late Derek Taunt, was a link to Nicholson: his wife, Angela, was a very valuable aide to

the artist, and has an impressive collection of the great man's work.

The 245 works in the fund's possession in 2006 included several of the younger generations who, starting with the BritPop explosion of the '60s, brought a new vitality and different language to British art: John Bellany, Barry Flanagan, Dame Elisabeth Frink, Sir Eduardo

(Above) Petworth Park Gates
Lithograph by John Piper

(Left) Town Scene
Lithograph by L.S. Lowry

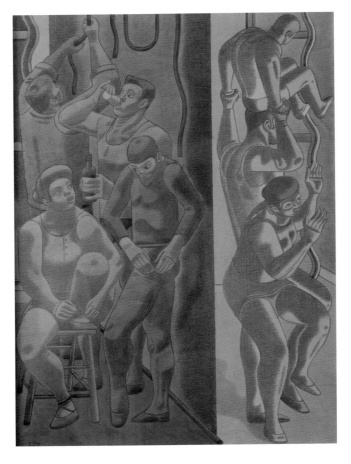

Back Cloth

Watercolour by William Roberts

Paolozzi, Richard Long. Following that early purchase of a Léger, there have been other exceptions to the Buy British preference: very notably the great Spanish abstractionist Joan Miró. The choice of a new work has continued to be in the hands of an undergraduate curator and committee; they call on the advice of the senior treasurer and a Cambridge gallerist. Gifts are made from time to time. Fellows rent the pictures of their choice, but undergraduates pay only a deposit.

The College's links with important artists, moreover, have strengthened remarkably since the '80s, when Colin Renfrew brought his collection and artistic enthusiasms to the Master's Lodge. The passion of an archaeologist for avant-garde art may be a piquant combination, but it worked wonders. Before Lord Renfrew's advent, four prized items from the fund (a Moore, a Piper and two by Paul Nash) had been put on permanent display in the Marshall Room, and succeeding years have seen several other contemporary works added to the College walls and lawns, many of them as a consequence of the hugely successful biennial exhibitions of 'Sculpture in the Close', of which Rod Mengham has written (page 50). Some sixteen works now adorn public rooms and the courts: some of the artists (who include Albert Irvin, Antony Gormley, Richard Long, Barry Flanagan, William Turnbull and Eduardo Paolozzi) became close friends of the College. The presence of a powerfully primitive bronze head

by Turnbull in Cloister Court, close to the hallowed architectural beauty of Chapter House and Chapel, is a reminder that art is timeless, and that all artistic leaders, including so strongly contemporary a figure as Turnbull, stand on the shoulders of their great predecessors.

The 'Sculpture in the Close' exhibitions make the same point with equal force. Where the Art Fund is an internal (though outward-looking) activity, the sculpture show is an important – and delightful – event for the British art world as a whole. The College grounds might have seemed an unlikely place for an uncompromisingly contemporary display of some of the best work by living British sculptors. But Colin Renfrew's 1986 inspiration has brought total success. Each exhibition has represented another advance in the importance of this cleverly and seductively planned and placed show. The summer openings have attracted a star-studded array of artists and art-world makers and shakers, and have given the College undoubted distinction as an art entrepreneur.

Many famed artists have lent their work, while sponsorship and financial contributions have come from corporate friends of the College. In 2001 Jesus scored a hat trick by getting Anish Kapoor, Julian Opie and Richard Wentworth – all three international stars – to join the exhibitors. Subsequent shows brought in other big names: Rachel Whiteread, Philip King and Alison Wilding in 2003; Sam Taylor-Wood, Cornelia Parker and John Gibbons in 2005 (the last-named being the first selection from the Angela Flowers stable, with which I have long been associated).

The 1996 show, the fifth, inspired a thoughtful essay on contemporary sculpture (which can be found on the College website). Its divisions give a strongly articulated idea of the preoccupations of today's artists: Illusion and Figuration, Organic and Beyond, Constructs and Concepts, Image and Imagination. Each of these themes presents the artist, and thus the viewer, with a different set of tactile and visual challenges. The essay admirably expresses this process:

> The relationship between subject and meaning, between
> form and content, between concept and realisation is
> always a complex one. Over the past two decades we have
> come to realise that more clearly. The present exhibition,
> in its diversity, exemplifies that complexity. And it offers us
> the opportunity to explore these things at leisure, first with
> our eyes, then with our hands – for sculpture entails
> material reality – then with our minds.

That passage gives a clear idea of where Jesus stands in the current art scene. What might be called 'the Saatchi connection' stands on the other side of the hill. The most recent splendid breakthrough of British con-

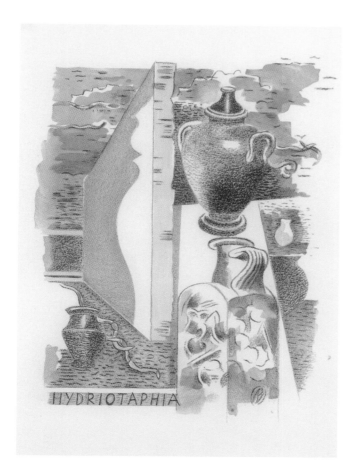

HYDRIOTAPHIA

Renfrew's), which provided the economic background to the deliberations of the dons and the outside members.

The moment for our initiation – 1978 – was propitious. The College was a conservative investor, relying heavily, as I recall (and Stephen Barton confirms on page 78), on government bonds and on investment trusts with a British bias (less admirable in this context than in that of the art collection). The investment world was moving towards global strategies, while individual equities were poised for a series of booms that offered greater opportunities than the investment trust sector. The outsiders were unanimous in recommending that the portfolio be restructured accordingly, and that view found general favour – with quite spectacular results.

There was only one catch. The profitable restructuring was once-for-all, and could not easily be repeated. As memory serves, there were no further bulls'-eyes of the same enriching size. But the Masters, Bursars and economics-minded dons seemed to enjoy the discussions, which were lively backgrounds to the tender loving care of the portfolio. The talks came first, in the early evening. We then adjourned to another room for sherry, before continuing our conversations over dinner. These meals were suitably grand, with one odd exception: the wine (always excellent) was served in glasses roughly the size of large egg-cups. As a guest, I politely never raised this odd matter, but I was agreeably surprised on another, much later visit, to find the claret in appropriate glassware. Maybe that was an incidental result of our investment advice, which continued until, after twenty years, the College allowed the committee to fall into abeyance – not before time, I would say – reviving it with a new generation of members in 2006,

(Top left) Hydriotaphia

Lithograph by Paul Nash

(Below) Harvesting in
Burgundy

Oil on board by Josef Herman

temporaries, initially engineered by the scale and extravagance of Charles Saatchi's purchasing of 'New British Artists', has been powered by the shock of the new. Novelty, however, is not achieved only by the shocking, nor is it the only virtue or value in art. The College's art history since 1955 emphasises that vital truth.

The paths of Jesus College, sculpture entrepreneur and host, and Jesus College, City investor, never crossed directly although, like everything else, the art activities must have benefited from the improved financial base that followed formation of the Finance Committee. It was an inspired idea of the Master and Bursar (Sir Alan Cottrell and John Killen) to bring in advice like that of Sir John Craven, one of the City's most innovative and successful figures (who became chairman of Deutsche Morgan Grenfell). Other active professional investors like Charles Rawlinson made weighty contributions, while the non-resident guru was Sir Sam Brittan, brother of Leon and economics editor of the *Financial Times*.

Sam and I had been exact contemporaries at Jesus, but only learnt after the event that we had both applied to the *FT* and been accepted. I later followed Sam over to the *Observer*, where my key roles included nursing Sam's weekly column on a sometimes jerky route from initial inspiration to eventual (and influential) publication. On the committee, he was deferentially requested to enlighten the members with a *tour d'horizon* (the term was Colin

after the thorough-going review and reorganisation of its investment management that had been undertaken during the preceding five years.

Our advice had been largely confined to stocks and shares, anyway, and the College had other, very considerable investment property in real estate – houses (steadily being sold off), commercial property and agricultural land. The division of the overall portfolio was within our remit, and the subject of some debate within the College. I was much amused when a friend, once an Oxford don, recalled a similar experience at his own college, which had to decide where to invest a windfall, and held a meeting to determine the issue. The younger dons were all for the stock market. But the estates bursar, not surprisingly, spoke for the older and more conservative members. For the last four hundred years, he argued, investment in land had served the College excellently well. From the back of the room, the senior history tutor cleared his throat. 'Yes, Bursar,' he said, 'but you have to understand that, historically speaking, the last four hundred years have been a very anomalous period.' This anecdote naturally came to mind when the Finance Committee debated whether to retain the splendid Park Terrace houses, 'the jewels in the College's crown', as the Bursar recognised. The issue, left in timeless abeyance, was in fact rapidly decided – in favour of sale – when a suitable offer appeared. As the tale

(Top right) Head

Pencil drawing by Dame Elisabeth Frink

(Below) Flux De L'Aimant

Lithograph by Joan Miró

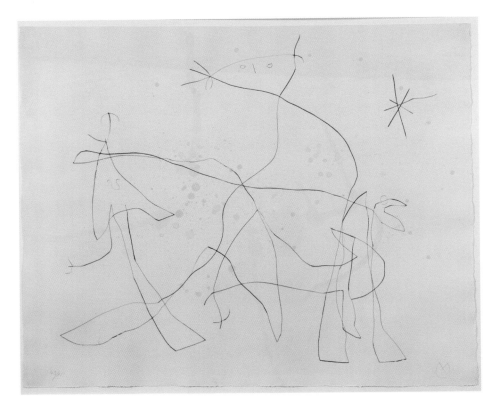

tells, the College's approach to managing its assets has been essentially pragmatic.

With the help of this realism and its professional advisers, the College has invested soundly and well. This hadn't always been the situation before the committee came into existence, and its 'lay' members can feel pleased with their part in the turnround. The sessions were certainly a learning experience for me. Never before had I entered the esoteric world of University and College finance, replete with such profound mysteries as 'internal taxation' (that is, of colleges by the University), and with all manner of unintelligible accounts. The mysteries remained mysterious to all except their keepers. But the College visibly and proudly demonstrated its financial soundness and sense by the exceptional improvements – new rooms, a new library, updated creature comforts and much else – which have progressively made Jesus a notably better place in which to live and work. The key word here is 'progressively'. The equally progressive developments on the art side have embellished and strengthened this steady advance into a world of unremitting change.

An American at Jesus

ANDREW SOLOMON (1985)

When I was 11, I was on a trip to England with my parents and we went to visit the son of some friends of theirs, who was studying at Balliol. He showed us around and introduced us to some of his fellow students, and I decided that day that I wanted to attend such a historic British university. The idea never faded. By the time I finished my studies at Yale, I had decided that Cambridge was a more elegant destination than Oxford, less obvious and less urban. But what to do about this mysterious array of colleges? It seemed best to avoid the ones that were famously overstocked with Americans, and the modern colleges didn't appeal, and I selected Jesus because a friend of the younger sister of a good friend of mine was at Newnham and had said that her best friends were at Jesus; while someone else I knew, who was at Oxford on a Rhodes Scholarship, said she had heard that Jesus was sympathetic to literary theory, which was my field of study. It seemed like kismet that the social and the academic recommendations had coincided. In 1985, I matriculated.

I came to Cambridge hoping to know another society, and arrived to find that I had been assigned to a ghetto of international students in Maid's Causeway, an arrangement that the College thought might be less alienating for foreign nationals than the tough route of mixing with the British. I had not come all the way to England to pass my days with other Americans. So I went to the Tutor for Rooms and asked to be moved into College, a request that was summarily dismissed. A few days later I had a bad cold and stopped in to see Sister George for a Paracetamol. She took down my details and noticed my sniffling and asked whether I might be allergic to the carpeting in Maid's Causeway, which had been treated with what she believed to be toxic chemicals. I said that it seemed like a sure bet, and she wrote a note to the Tutor for Rooms, who called me in, looked at me skeptically over his glasses, and with a long-suffering sigh assigned me a room in North Court. Thus began my stubborn engagement with the British.

I had put in four good years of being an undergraduate in America, and my Cambridge affiliated degree course provided me with the opportunity to do two more, in the form of a two-year Part II in the English Tripos. I was rather good at being an undergraduate by this time, and applied my expertise to squeezing pleasure from this pleasant extension of student life. I read and studied things that interested me. I wrote poetry and ate strawberries and drank much more than I ever had in America. I joined a philosophers' society and sat up late arguing about existentialism. I tried to learn the rules of cricket and rugby well enough at least to watch. I went to Third World First lunches, and volunteered to read aloud to elderly locals with compromised eyesight. I listened to different music (Elgar in particular) and read different books (Philip Larkin); I learned that the language the US and UK shared did not connote parallel tastes. I mastered Practical Criticism. I fell in and out of love slightly too frequently for my own good, and developed a true appreciation for tea, and for roses. I advanced my native sense of irony considerably, and laughed at new jokes that were funny for new reasons (the word 'vicar' seemed to come up often). I developed my skill at punting; I got thrown into the Cam. I went to the occasional evensong and saw a great deal of student theater. I spent weekends in the country. I wrote to friends that *Brideshead* was less a work of fantasy than I had supposed. I learned to enjoy privilege even as I learned to hate the English class system. The British reserve that I and other foreign students were supposed to find so alienating was readily undone by British drinking, and the undergraduates with whom I socialized were, like all undergraduates, in the game to make a lifetime's bonds. I opened my arms and made friends, with many of whom I am still in touch and to a few of whom I am close two decades later.

I have always liked the feeling of being on the inside track, and Jesus felt to me like that. It wasn't as obvious as Trinity or King's, but it was historical and splendid. It seemed you could own Jesus, feel that it was your place; it was less impersonal than those over-touristed colleges. The slight remove from the Backs meant that we were, architecturally and socially, our own world, exclusive to each other, intimate. I liked the quirkiness, the leaning topiaries and the blustery porters and the local homeless man who was forever wandering into the College and who knew at least half of us by name; and I also joined The Natives and felt terribly grand. I was fond of the headed note paper you could get at Heffer's, and the little antique stores in King Street, with their random teapots, and, once, a Regency silver-plate muffin basket for £9 (I have it still). I liked the red and the black of Jesus, and the cockerel, and the long chute of the Chimney, and thrilled to the feeling of permanence that seemed strongest in Cloister Court. Though I did not end up spending a great deal of time with the vaunted friends of my American friend's sister's friend, I liked the other students, and also liked my Director of Studies, Stephen Heath, and was deeply engaged by his focus on post-structuralism. Jesus was a place where you could stretch your intellect, but it wasn't academic in any desiccated sort of way. It was thrilling to enter so long a parade of tradition; but Jesus was also a place where there was room for radicalism and for leaps of the imagination.

Of course, like all Americans arriving there, I had my catalogue of discontents. Though the scale of the rooms was glorious and the buildings magnificent, which was exciting to me after Yale's more diminutive campus, the plumbing was appalling; after I'd taken my first properly British shower, I understood why the habit has never properly caught on in the UK. I could not fathom why basins didn't have mixer taps. There were only three telephones in College, all in rather filthy booths in basements. Never had I seen so much rain, and that rain conspired cruelly with the trans-Siberian wind that blows straight across East Anglia. What truly astonished me was that the damp cold was allowed to seep inside; I ran several illegal electric heaters in my room all winter, and it was the only warm room in Cambridgeshire so far as I could tell. The plentitude of cyclists seemed like some strange thing out of communist China, and I had an unfortunate habit of wandering in front of them when hurrying off to lectures, forever befuddled about which direction traffic was going. The concept of formal Hall bespoke a cloistered majesty, but any resemblance between the vegetables that were served and living, growing things had been obscured beyond oblivion; Cambridge also boasted innumerable restaurants where people paid in hard cash for similarly grim grub. Thanks

be to God for the culinary aftermath of the Raj; I lived on curries. What else? I couldn't understand why the plugs were so big or why electrical goods were sold without them. I couldn't understand why stores all closed so early. I couldn't understand why anyone had allowed anything as ugly as the Grafton Centre to be built. But I loved being there nonetheless.

At a more academic level, British and American education complemented each other nicely. My experience of American universities was that they tended to be focused on the utility of intellect. It might be that what we were learning would be applied in no more pragmatic arena than the academy itself, but there was nonetheless an awareness of how what we said would go down with the pros, of what doors it pushed open or swung shut. In Britain, university education felt in many ways like a luxury. It was available to less of the population and was predicated on pursuing knowledge because the pursuit of knowledge was rich and pleasant rather than simply because it was useful. The fact that marks came of finals rather than of continual assessment allowed students more leeway to ramble down unlikely paths, and the fact that most students were not paying fees made the purposefulness of education less urgent. It is unfortunate that some of that ease of the British university system is under siege; the introduction of fees constitutes a grievous loss.

I am often asked whether I preferred Yale or Cambridge, as though the American and British systems were locked in a conflict that could be resolved with a resounding judgment from one student. I loved both, and I loved them in sequence. Cambridge gave me perspective on Yale, and England gave me perspective on America, and Yale and America gave me perspective on Cambridge and England. I grew to love Britain passionately, but for none of the reasons inherent in the anglophilia that brought me there. After two years at Jesus, it was too late to return to the monocultural prejudices with which I had arrived; I was to see everything in dialectical terms for the rest of my life. In time, I would become a dual citizen, serve as godfather to seven children in England, and divide my time between New York and London, never again content with only one world.

In 2002, a year after the publication of my third book, I received an invitation to lecture at Jesus. I was touched and delighted. Walking down the Chimney once again, I caught myself looking at what had been the windows of my closest friends to see if their lights were on. I succumbed to a passing melancholy because I was no longer a Jesus undergraduate, and could see in the faces of the actual students who walked by me that my interior flush of post-adolescence was sadly out of keeping with my 37-year-old physical self. I gave my lecture in Upper Hall, and in the evening went to dinner at the Master's

Lodge. I loved listening to the way people threw academic arguments at one another, the engaged and often mischievous banter around ideas. That mixture of earnestness and playfulness that had been so much in evidence when I studied at Cambridge subtended this repartee, and it made me very nostalgic for this environment. Talking with Stephen Heath, I alluded to a fantasy of getting a PhD.

To my surprise, he took me seriously, and said that it could well be done on the new part-time PhD scheme. Unfortunately, the English Faculty did not allow part-time PhDs, but Social and Political Sciences did, and since the book about which I had been lecturing dealt with depression, it seemed like an easy call. I wrote to

Juliet Mitchell, one of the SPS Fellows at Jesus, and she agreed to take me on, so I find myself back at Cambridge, a student again. When I go from New York to Cambridge (in my part-time way), I stay in the College guest rooms, and in the afternoons I sit with my supervisor in her sunny rooms in Chapel Court, and the late sun streaks in through her windows, when there is sun, and I have the feeling once again that education is a luxury, that the mind is elastic, that living between cultures is richer than living in only one. Jesus College has a great deal more history than I do, but a good bit of my history is bound up with Jesus, and its colors are among my own. For me, it remains a place of happy revelation.

A Jesuan dreams of America

Cocks of the Roost: LXXXII. – Alistair Cooke

The 20th of November was a day of ill omen to many. Sir Charles Hawtrey saw a black crow on the left, Debussy was observed to walk under a ladder, Max Beerbohm was thirteenth at a dinner party, the Mistress of Girton dreamed of a black fox attacking her chickens, and the Cambridge gutters ran with blood outside the A.D.C. For on this day, in Manchester, was Alfred Alistair born.

Having spent his early babyhood on a horizontal bar, he migrated in 1917 to Blackpool. Here he entered the school which was to have such a profound effect on his life, the co-educational Blackpool School, his parents having apparently disregarded the advice of Sister Annie (a Wesleyan nurse) who, seeing his green eyes, had warned them to keep him away from the girls. While still in the second form, he began taking the fifth and other Upper School forms in gymnastics; and before he left he was vice-captain of cricket, a rugger colour, editor of the school magazine, head of his house, and senior prefect. Nor was this all. Alfred's first play was produced during his first year at school; his first personal appearance on the stage was as Valentine in *You never can tell*. At midnight at the annual school dance his arrangement of "It ain't gonna rain no more" as a Beethoven symphony was performed by the school orchestra.

In 1927 he came up to Cambridge, which refused to use his first name and hailed him Alistair. He jumped at Fenners with "Ghost" Williams for the College, but soon found that other interests prevented the continuation of his athletic career. His caricature of "Q" gained him prompt admission to the pages of the *Granta*. In 1928 he plotted in secret with Mr Bedford Shope of Queens', and founded the C.U. Mummers.

1929 was a big year in Alistair's life. A permanent position on the *Granta* staff, the part of Lord Grizzle in Fielding's *Tom Thumb the Great* at the Mummers' first performance, and a first class in the first part of his English Trip. Later on

in the year, his heart somehow got carried away across the Atlantic, though his body, alas, remained behind, as a "super" in Matheson Lang's *Jew Suss*. From this event dates his career as a dramatic critic, and he can claim to have been the discoverer, in his first review for the *Manchester Guardian* of *Jew Suss*, of the real talent of Miss Peggy Ashcroft, whom it was his duty to throw every night on to the stage. He wrote regularly, for the *Nation* and the *Atheneum*, as well as the *Guardian*, reviews of the Festival; and the Manchester paper still sells out every Friday in Cambridge.

1930 found him sighing for new Theatre Worlds to conquer. More parts in the Mummers, and an appearance on the variety stage with Mr Erik Chitty left him still unsatisfied; so he packed himself with twenty other enthusiastic Mummers over the waters to Jersey, and as President and Producer acted General Botcher in *Press Cuttings* and Dermott in *At Mrs Beams'*.

Having by now contrived to forget all about America, he crossed over to Normandy, with one comrade and a tent little bigger than an umbrella, returning after three weeks' idyll in which the name of one Mlle. Pot mysteriously figures.

And here for the present we must leave him; when he is not talking, playing squash, making new friends, writing poetry, composing music, fretting before the footlights, sitting in stalls not payed for, charming Lancashire lasses with his touch on the piano, writing theses, drawing caricatures, reading Katherine Mansfield, furnishing other men's rooms, entertaining, studying sexology, or writing essays on cider in the College Kitchen suggestion-book, you will find him wasting somebody's time – probably your own.

Pet abominations: Punctuality, spirits, and the English gentleman.

Chanticlere, *Michaelmas Term 1930*.

The Film Society

CLIVE BROWN (1967)

The late 1960s saw an extraordinary upsurge of interest in film, with a dawning realisation that cinema had a past as well as a present. The silent film was rediscovered, helped by Kevin Brownlow's masterly portrait of the early days of Hollywood in *The Parade's Gone By* ..., which was published in 1967. A number of cinemas began showing classic films, and an increasing number of 16mm film libraries fed the popularity of film societies.

Cambridge was not left behind by this renaissance. Cinemas such as the Rex and the Kinema had revivals of classic films, the Arts Cinema had a varied and interesting programme, there was a University Film Society, and an array of college film societies as well. The Jesus Film Society, formed in the Lent term of 1968, led the way. In retrospect, this is not surprising. The founders included Jeffrey Richards, Richard Taylor and Tony Rayns, the first two of whom have become pre-eminent as film historians, and the last-named as a critic. Even at the time, they had diverse interests and knowledge of the cinema:

British and American (Richards); Russian, French and German (Taylor); and Japanese and underground cinema (Rayns). The result was a rich and varied fare. A fourth protagonist was Trevor Page, who was the technician in the group, although he clearly also had a hand in the choice of films – as is evident from the programme notes.

Films were shown on a 16mm projector bought with a loan from the College. The shows were usually held in Upper Hall, which was almost always full to capacity. There was a magic about being part of an audience at those shows. Crammed together in a darkened room, with the whirr of the projector in the background, we were in thrall. There was always, of course, the possibility that something would go wrong. To be fair, screenings in the College usually ran smoothly, but the result could be spectacular when things went awry. I shall not forget a screening of *Conquest* (not in the College) when Charles Boyer's head burst grotesquely into flame as the film stuck in the gate of the projector.

While the expressed aim was to show films that were not to be seen elsewhere, the programme was a clever mix of the popular with the more adventurous and off-beat. The first film shown was *The African Queen*, a relatively safe choice, but films shown later in the year included Eisenstein's epic *Ivan the Terrible*, Rudolph Valentino in *Son of the Sheik*, Roger Corman's *Masque of the Red Death*, Renoir's *La Grande Illusion* and John Ford's *Stagecoach* and *The Lost Patrol*. By popular demand, there were regular showings of Marx Brothers comedies. Jeffrey Richards remembers that these always guaranteed full houses.

The Film Society committee was clearly determined to educate its audiences, and detailed programme notes were produced, the first of which was written by Richard Taylor for *Ivan the Terrible* in April 1968. After that, programme notes were a regular feature and were always well researched and informative. It was nonetheless not an easy path. The account in the College *Annual Report*

'Darkness and Light – Jesus College'

Derek Langley, *c*.2000

for 1968–9 concludes, rather pompously, by saying: 'To break down prejudice and ignorance about the cinema is a hard and often thankless task. If the JFS has been able to do something towards this, its work will not have been in vain.'

In the second year of its existence the society showed some thirty-five films. The Marx Brothers again featured by popular demand, and other films included the delightful *Swingtime* with Fred Astaire and Ginger Rogers, and D.W. Griffiths's controversial masterpiece *Birth of a Nation*. There was a double bill of horror films, *The Hounds of Zaroff* and *White Zombie*. Screenings included films by directors as diverse as Renoir, Eisenstein, Zoltan Korda and Victor Sjostrom.

The most controversial event, however, was a proposal by Tony Rayns to show films by the underground film-maker Kenneth Anger. This divided the committee as the films were uncertificated and there were fears of a police raid. A rumour spread through the College that they contained obscene subliminal images. In the event, the problem was solved by the Master, Sir Denys Page, allowing a private showing of the films in the Master's Lodge. (Kenneth Anger is now largely forgotten, and Leslie Halliwell dismisses his films as 'mainly short, inscrutable and Freudian'.)

The Film Society also caused a College revolution of a different kind. It was the only society in the College to make large sums of money, and because of this, as Richard Taylor recollects, the JCR wanted the society under its wing. At the time the JCR was dominated by the Boat Club, which commanded half the votes on the JCR. The Film Society only agreed to join if the JCR changed its constitution so that each member society had equal representation. This radical constitutional change went to a vote and was overwhelmingly supported.

Looking back after nearly forty years, the choice of films does not seem as unusual as it did then. Many are now the common currency of television film programmes, and widely available on video or DVD. The availability of our film heritage to a mass audience is in large part due to the pioneer film historians who located and showed films they thought worthy of preserving, helped to distinguish the good from the bad, and taught the place of films in the social history of their time. The College Film Society played its small part in this, and for its faithful core audience, of which I was one, provided a crash education in cinema from early silent film to *film noir*, and from America's Capra and Ford to the cinema of Europe, Russia and Japan.

Not all the films shown were worth reviving, however. My wife and I were married in Cambridge in June 1969, and a wedding present from the Film Society was a late-night showing of *Land Without Music*, a vehicle for Richard Tauber. While it is a curiosity, the film has rightly been reconsigned to oblivion. It is, however, a mark of the dedication of the committee that they (and we) thought this a wholly appropriate way for us to spend part of our wedding night.

There are reports of the Film Society in the College *Annual Report* as late as 1985–6, after which it disappears from view. I suspect that wide availability of video contributed to its demise. Sadly, also, video (and now DVD) has changed the way most people watch films. In these days of modern technology it is often a solitary exercise. It is no longer necessary to crowd into the intimacy of Upper Hall. The 16mm projector has become obsolete. But films were made to be shown on a large screen to a mass audience, and the magic of those days, with its comradeship and shared enjoyment, has been irretrievably lost.

A College within the College: The Graduate Students

MICHAEL MINDEN

What we now a little confusingly call 'graduates' were originally people who for one reason or another undertook further study after their first degree, but were not, or not yet, fellows of a college. Since the beginning of the eighteenth century the College has received benefactions to fund post-BA study, such as that from Dr Lionel Gatford (*c*.1642–1715) 'sometime scholar here, and afterwards Archdeacon of St Albans and Treasurer of St Paul's, London [who] gave a yearly pension of twenty pounds for two Clergymen's Orphans from the Degree of Batchelors till they commenced Masters in Arts'. In 1890 Dr French's son-in-law, Sir Edwin Kay, a Lord Justice of Appeal, endowed three scholarships for graduates from any college who wished to read Theology at Jesus.

In 1895 a University regulation allowed graduates of other universities to be admitted to Cambridge as 'Research Students'. Before then, they simply followed the courses and sat the examinations for the BA degree like everybody else (so, in 1859, William Everitt, having already spent three years at and graduated from Harvard, came and spent the further ten terms then required, reading first Mathematics and then Classics). From 1897 research students were known as 'Advanced Students' and if the work they submitted 'was of distinction, as a record of original research' it earned a Certificate of Research by means of which they could proceed to an existing degree, such as the BA, LLB or MA. Not all such students had College attachments. Jesus did not entertain many of them (most were found at Caius, Christ's, Emmanuel, St John's and Trinity), but two are recorded. Our earliest advanced student seems to have been Charles McNeil (1886–1959), who came after obtaining honours at Glasgow University, but had to abandon the Mechanical Sciences Tripos owing to eye trouble and so took a BA by research instead, which he was awarded in 1910. In May 1920 the degree of PhD was introduced. This was a way

of making Cambridge more attractive to outstanding young researchers, especially in the sciences, from parts of the world like Germany and the United States where such doctorates already existed (as indeed they did in other parts of the UK – not for the first or last time, Cambridge was catching up). Three years' residence was required for it.

In 1949 the College had fifteen research students and twenty-seven other post-graduates, but these figures probably reflected careers interrupted by war, for in 1952 there were only six research students and twelve post-graduates. Expansion here, as elsewhere in the university world, occurred only in the 1960s. By the 1980s the College had 140 graduate students, of whom 96 were working for the PhD (the graduate community continued and continues to be heterogeneous in its make-up, since the category also includes medics and vets after their first degrees, lawyers taking the LLM, those training to be teachers, and some others). Of that 140, 103 were men and 37 women (women graduates having been first admitted in 1978). In 2006 the College had 243 graduate students (counting those in their fourth year of PhD work), of whom 150 were men and 93 women, and the bias towards PhDs in natural sciences and engineering noted in the 1980s had become even more marked. But the most important change was in the structure of the graduate community. No longer is this predominantly a community of PhD students augmented by small groups of vocational specialists, but that of a substantial and rapidly growing cohort of post-graduates taking one of the many MPhil courses (both taught and by research) introduced since the 1980s. These have been created for much the same reasons as the PhD in 1919: to formalise a point of transition between levels of scholarly activity, and to attract outstanding students from beyond Cambridge and beyond the UK to come and study here, providing, too, the training in research skills which had been conspicuously lacking under the old system. In 2006 the College had 35 candidates for the degree of MPhil (about one third of the total graduate intake for that year) and, of the 150-odd PhD students, at least 17 had started their post-graduate studies with a Cambridge MPhil and many others with similar post-graduate qualifications from another institution. The remainder of the graduate community was made up, as ever, of medics, vets, LLMs and educationalists, although by then a further vocational specialism had been added: those studying for the MBA.

Ken Johnson, talking elsewhere (page 225) about why the job of Graduate Tutor in Jesus was first created, says that the colleges had to do something to justify the fee they charged graduates. That was in 1962, and the topic is still, or again, a hot one. The position of research students and MPhil students in relation to their college is a little anomalous since they are neither admitted to the University by the colleges (in most cases this is done by the faculties, operating through the Board of Graduate Studies), nor taught by or in them. What, then, do the colleges offer their graduates (all of whom are required to be members of a college, and pay college fees), whether they have metamorphosed from the familiar undergraduate state or arrived from nearly every conceivable place on earth to pursue post-graduate study at Cambridge and, in our case, in Jesus?

The first contribution, perhaps the most abstract – though no less important for that – that colleges make or should make to the experience of being a graduate student is the possibility of an identity within a community. That is not simply the community of the College as experienced (in different ways) by undergraduates and Fellows, but a community 'in between' these, made up of a really quite extraordinary range of nationalities and disciplinary affiliations. The most concrete way that Jesus, more successfully than the other colleges, creates the condition for the members of this heterogeneous group to become identified with each other and the College itself, is by providing them with accommodation (it now has 182 units of graduate accommodation, housing the great majority of graduates who are required to be in residence and wish it).

Stretching from the Lower Park Street gate, there is a virtually unbroken line of graduate houses describing the boundary of the College. A terrace of about thirty cottages, opening directly onto the College grounds at the rear, in each of which two or three tenants live, sharing a kitchen and bathroom, is followed in Park Street by a series of ten town houses converted to accommodate between five and eight residents each. At the elbow of the two streets there is a vacant plot upon which every Graduate Tutor dreams of one day erecting a building

Lower Park Street: cottages built for College servants in the nineteenth century were turned back to front to become rooms for graduate students, 1970–2000.

purpose-designed for graduates with families. At the corner of Park Street and Jesus Lane stands Little Trinity, a splendid eighteenth-century house which is home to over a dozen graduates (and where the John Eliot Scholar, nominated each year by Harvard, has his or her own dedicated room), and further along Jesus Lane there is a large house, recently refurbished, with rooms for sixteen students, and another adapted to make four relatively inexpensive units of partner accommodation. Just beyond the Four Lamps roundabout a large house of indeterminate original purpose, 24 Maid's Causeway – for a long time something of an outpost of graduate life – has recently been brought up to the required standard and integrated into the graduate housing stock. That leaves the austere terraces of Malcolm Street, in which undergraduates and graduates face each other on either side of the road. This is where our most spacious flats are located as well as a fair stock of single rooms.

The accommodation ranges from attic hideaways to suites of rooms with their own bathrooms; the entire stock was refurbished between 2001 and 2005, all are wired for direct access to the internet, and all lie close to the ancient core of the College. It is this unique concentration of accommodation that gives our graduate community its vibrancy and coherence, making it quite natural for most of our graduate students to use the College as a base for leisure, sport and socialising.

The existence of a dedicated Tutor for graduates notwithstanding, a great deal of credit for maintaining the sense of community among the graduates must go to the annually elected Graduate Society Committee. There

is unflagging willingness amongst our graduates to stand for the various offices (which now include that of a president), and this is particularly – although certainly not exclusively – true of incomers to Cambridge, from amongst whom most of the recent presidents have been drawn. These elected members, together with the Graduate Tutor or Tutors of the day, look after business and pleasure. Long, serious and extremely fair rent negotiations have resulted in a rent structure that strikes the balance between the College's need for the cash flow required to maintain its housing stock at current levels of repair, and the graduates' often severely limited spending capacity. On the social side, the committee promotes a whole series of events (only the induction day and the November Fellows and graduates' dinner are run by the College) such as black-tie dinners for Burns' Night (a special favourite nowadays, with tremendous speeches and toasts from Scots of many nationalities), Hallowe'en, Christmas and so on. The committee is particularly active at the beginning of the academic year, making newcomers – some of whom will necessarily be prey to sometimes quite severe culture shock – feel welcome.

The focus of graduate communal life is the weekly Graduate Hall: informal come-as-you-are occasions, but spread over a leisurely and medium-sumptuous four courses, affording time to talk, meet others and entertain guests. These dinners are hugely popular, although – with a large and active constituency now involved in examinations and frequent deadlines, rather than just ongoing private study and laboratory work – there is some seasonal fluctuation. There have been many splendid national cuisines featured in themed 'international' evenings, reflecting the cosmopolitan nature of our community, as well as the expertise and willing support of the catering department: Chinese, Finnish, Greek, Italian, Irish, Japanese, Korean, US, for instance, and – regularly and noisily – Australian.

Many national groupings contribute to the College's graduate community, forming distinct groups within it. One thinks again of the annual cohort of Australians (mainly, but not just, lawyers, often encouraged to apply here by a scholarship long funded by the Foreign and Commonwealth Office in conjunction with the College and the Cambridge Commonwealth Trust to commemorate Australia's bicentennial celebrations, and now to be continued thanks to the generosity of an Old Member), or the growing number of Chinese students, many of whom come to study under a Fellow, Peter Nolan, at the Judge Business School. (The first of them to come, soon after the ending of the Cultural Revolution, during which he had worked in a bicycle factory, was X.-H. Zhang, who later won one of the College's research fellowships.) The Chinese students,

The cottages now face into the Close.

Cambridge's Chileans

The Chilean community has been an active one in Cambridge. Jesus College, and probably Churchill as well, has hosted most Chileans coming to study to Cambridge. Most Chileans have come to carry out PhD studies, primarily in Economics or related subjects (at one point in 2001 there were more than eight Chilean PhD students in Economics). There are also two well-known Chilean lecturers who probably attract Chilean students, Gabriel Palma in the Faculty of Economics and Marcial Echeñique in Architecture.

The Chilean community at Jesus has been very active in College life. When myself and my husband arrived in Cambridge in 2001, there were three Chilean couples living in Malcolm St, and as we learned that year, in the previous years there have been a similar number of Chileans living in that street; Malcolm Street has become a bit of a 'little Chile'. Apart from being numerous, Chileans at Jesus have 'made noise' in Jesus College life. Frequent attendants of the Grad. Halls and College parties, Chileans have also been an important part of the 'work force' in the evening invigilation of the Quincentenary Library. But the classic example of how 'noisy' Chileans have been at Jesus is the annual celebration of the National Chilean Day, held in the College in September. This is a big BBQ which has been carried out for years (at least seven) and that gathers the Chilean community not only from Cambridge, but from all over the UK, including the Chilean Ambassador, the Consul, etc. Around one hundred people, mainly coming from London, Oxford, Birmingham, Brighton and other cities in the UK participate in this celebration enjoying Chilean music (the 'cueca') and the traditional Chilean BBQ with meat, wines and 'pisco', coming from South America.

Chileans have also made their name known outside Jesus. Partners of students started some time ago a network of informal childcare for children of Chileans and other Latin American families, called 'Semillitas', which has become very well known among the Latin American community in Cambridge.

– Macarena Ibarra

like the Australians, are encouraged to come to the College by the generosity of an alumnus, in this case Raymond Kwok, who with his wife Helen has fully funded a PhD student from the People's Republic of China each year since 2002.

Chilean Jesuans have also stood out, as the testimony of one of them, Macarena Ibarra, who received her PhD in Economics in 2005, evidences (above).

One Tutor for Graduates would like to bear personal witness to the excellence of the hospitality (and especially of the beef) at the barbecues, as well as to the family feeling brought to our graduate world by the Chileans (as by several other graduate couples). The population of Chile has increased by at least four as a result of unions in Jesus. The presence of married graduates, often with children (by the time they leave if not when they arrive), has had a significant impact on the community: it is a pity we cannot, as things stand, do more for graduate families. Working in the Quincentenary Library – the twenty-first century's version of being a sizar in the seventeenth – brings, as Macarena notes, many graduates into the life of the College, not just Chileans (and adds to their income).

There is all this, then, that we can say that the graduates get in return for their fee. But the feeling at the moment is very much that we should try to do more for them, and this especially in one particular direction. While the mix of nationalities makes for unique international communities in the heart of the East Anglian Fens – from which networks might, we hope, develop across the globe to the ultimate good of all – the unique mix of academic disciplines likewise frames a situation of enormous poten-

tial. 'Interdisciplinarity' and 'knowledge transfer' are the current watchwords in higher education thinking and policy, and it is hard to identify any existing academic communities better placed naturally to foster such co-operation across the various divisions of scholarship and science than those that already exist in Cambridge and Oxford colleges.

The challenge now facing the College is to realise this potential, and make a difference to the academic and scholarly experience of its graduates, as it already does to

Pump Court: St Radegund's Garden, 1996.

St.Radegund's Garden
Given by the Graduate Society
in 1996 to commemorate the
Priory of St.Mary and St.Radegund
dissolved for the foundation of the College.
Its planting derives from that of
the Saint's garden in Poitiers
in the sixth century

other aspects of their lives. Ways of increasing the integration of the graduates with the Fellows, not just in the social context (graduates are invited to dine at High Table regularly), but in the academic one also, are being actively sought. Lectures and seminars are being organised and introductions effected; ways of entertaining supervisors of research students, where those supervisors are not themselves already Fellows are being explored; and research students are being encouraged to learn how to present their work to interested and intelligent outsiders.

The feasibility of classes or workshops on aspects of graduate work which can be of use across the disciplines has to be investigated, while thought might be given to resurrecting the annual meetings at which graduates offered advice to undergraduates contemplating post-graduate study.

The graduate sector in the College, as in the University, is in a state of rapid change. While a basic continuity and atmosphere of earnest endeavour is provided, as ever, by our research students, they have been joined by a large cohort of bright and committed students from all over the world who stay for only one year and want the maximum intensity of work and play from their time at Cambridge – for which they have frequently had to find the funding themselves, and this often only with difficulty and at the cost of some considerable sacrifice by them and their sponsors. The College will continue to be equal to these demands, but it will need as well to think about new ways of supporting graduate work, especially in the form of stipends or bursaries for those excellent candidates who, for one reason or another, simply cannot find the finance required to undertake post-graduate work. This applies to UK students (applications from whom went down by 30 per cent between 1995 and 2005) as well as to outstanding students from abroad, for whom we have to compete with North American universities, able to offer full funding packages. Jesus College has so much to offer post-graduates, and they have so much to offer in return!

The Admission of Women

MARY LAVEN

In June 1964, when the government of Britain's last aristocrat Prime Minister, Sir Alec Douglas-Home, was drawing to a close, and when 'You're My World' by Cilla Black was riding high in the charts, a visionary possibility opened up at a meeting of the College's Council. According to the minutes, 'Notice was given of a proposal "that the Council be asked to investigate and report on how the College could be made a mixed Society of men and women".' But, as one tactful commentator has put it, 'the climate was not yet right'. The Council in its wisdom elected to do nothing, and the enlightened Fellow who had made the proposal soon left Cambridge to take up a chair at King's College, London.

Thus Jesus missed a precious opportunity to lead the way in offering equal opportunities to men and women. In the following year the University repealed the statute that prohibited mixed colleges. The graduate colleges – Darwin, Clare Hall and University (now called Wolfson) – immediately opened their doors to women. And in 1972, more threateningly, the first female students matriculated at Clare, King's and Churchill. Not until 1979 would the first women undergraduates enter Jesus.

Perhaps it was unsurprising that Jesus was not in the vanguard of men's colleges seeking to admit women. After all, this was the College that had waited until 1882 – twenty-two years after the repeal of the 1570 statute enjoining celibacy on fellows of colleges – before it had permitted its own Fellows to take wives. The Cambridge of the late nineteenth century was, it seems, a testosterone-fuelled place, 'ruled' (a historian tells us) 'by arrogant, public school, rowing undergraduates, philistine in outlook and behaviour'. He has placed Jesus in the centre of that picture (page 156), drawing attention to a Dean who was ready to sacrifice everything for the credit of the boats. And yet even in this fiercely homosocial environment, the rights of women to participate in College life was already a subject capable of generating debate. In the 1889 Easter term issue of *Chanticlere* one writer engaged in an exercise of prescient fantasy:

> We may imagine, say in AD 2070, a paper being read by a female Fellow of the College to the Coleridge Society on the College during the dark ages, with a learned disquisition of an eight oar in the nineteenth century, and a description of the incredible brutality of football as played in a time when ladies (such was the bigotry of man)

Granta, 29 February 1896.

A Dream of the Future

were not allowed to be members of male colleges. In that time, great indeed will be the honour paid to the gallant Cooper Patton [the society's Honorary Secretary] for his support of the claims of the sex.

This flippant but revealing piece of student journalism registers, perhaps for the first time, that the exclusion of 'ladies' was fundamentally a matter of 'bigotry'.

Such bigotry was still alive and kicking in the 1960s and 1970s when the debate over women was renewed, this time in earnest. In the *Jesus College Cambridge Society Report* for 1969, amid a list of members' 'achievements', we find the following:

> Mr Frank Bown, a freshman, expounded the aims of his League for the Preservation of Gentlemen's Colleges on the radio programme *Today* in April this year. The League seeks to 'discourage or prevent the introduction of co-educational colleges at Cambridge and Oxford and to promote the establishment of another ladies' college at Cambridge'.

Among the Fellows, the retired Dean, Percy Gardner-Smith, urged the College to exercise profound caution and to observe closely 'the result of a feminine invasion in other colleges which have taken the plunge' before acting. As for the argument that the admission of women would lead to an improvement in academic standards, he insisted that the College should be seen as much more than a machine for churning out graduates. 'There is no

A woman mistreated? Upper Hall roof boss, *c.*1510.

denying the character of the College would be changed.' Moreover, he suggested (and this was, he might have assumed, his trump card) that those Old Members who had given so generously to the College in the past 'might lose their enthusiasm for a co-educational establishment'.

Gardner-Smith's views shed some light on a College that, in 1964, still found the idea of incorporating women as students and Fellows hard to stomach. Critically, the Master, Denys Page, was an opponent of the admission of women, though his views are less well documented. However, although no polls were taken, it seems that this tough rump of opposition was a fast-dwindling minority. As the recollections of Alan Sharpe and Ken Johnson (page 216) confirm, it was more the desire for institutional tranquillity than entrenched opposition that delayed the changing of the College statutes to permit the advent – or more accurately the return – of women to the Jesus Close. (The College had of course been built around the suppressed nunnery of St Radegund – a saint who was the embodiment of sixth-century girl power.)

By 1974, ten years after the idea had first been mooted in the College Council, the 'climate' was apparently now 'right' to reconsider the question of women: Sir Denys Page had retired in 1973. In a paper entitled 'Admissions for 1974', the Senior Tutor, Bruce Sparks, voiced his concern regarding the decline in the number of applications for undergraduate places. He noted that while Jesus *had* attracted one more application than in the previous year (little cause for celebration), the ratio of applicants to places of 1.75 to 1 was unsatisfactory. The cause of the problem and its potential solution were evident: 'it seems likely from present experience that mixed colleges will be popular and likely to have a larger share in better quality applicants'. To avoid the accusation of 'egalitarianism' – evidently a dirty word among the Fellows of Jesus College at the time – Sparks, who is remembered as the epitome of low-key diplomacy, insisted that 'these arguments concern only the intellectual standards of the College'.

For Sparks, going mixed was primarily (or overtly) about attracting the best male applicants. By contrast, John Adkins (Fellow and Director of Studies in Physics) was explicit in outlining the advantages that would derive from the presence of women members. In a paper submitted to the Fellowship, he made the claim (obvious and yet controversial in the context of a four-centuries-old men's college) that a mixed society would be a more stable, enjoyable and stimulating community. Secondly, he argued that Cambridge, by accepting only 17 per cent of its female applicants (to the women's colleges and the colleges that had already gone mixed), must be rejecting women of a higher calibre than some of the men admitted. King's College, he noted, was now awarding 45 per cent of its places to women applicants 'on purely academic grounds'. Thirdly, Adkins predicted that any college 'which drags its feet over this issue' would gain a reputation that could cause harm for many years to come, not least through its effect upon the quality of the Fellowship. In the event, it was to be the women's colleges and some of those that had already become mixed that – for their own and differing reasons – sought (albeit unsuccessfully) to slow the pace of change.

For the student body – the generation that had grown up with Cilla Black – the argument hinged not on academic standards, but on 'equality'. True, the JCR Executive's statement that 'support for co-residence within the undergraduate body is known to be great' somehow lacked the ring of radical protest. Nevertheless, the Executive made its case forcefully in a submission to the Fellows regarding amendments to the College Statutes (10 June 1974). It took the view that education should be open to all those capable of gaining from it, regardless of sex as of other social and financial factors. This would require an overhaul of the Cambridge admissions system, of which an end to the exclusion of women was merely a starting-point. The submission contended that the 8,000 students of the University were united in wishing to see an end to discrimination on the grounds of sex. In one respect, however, the Jesus JCR Executive diverged from the party line of the Cambridge University Student Union. Whereas the latter favoured 'positive discrimination' which would promote women in subjects where it could be argued that they had been disadvantaged at school, Jesus students stayed true to the principle of 'free academic competition', whereby places would be offered to the best applicants irrespective of sex.

Just three days after the JCR made its submission, the Fellows decided that it was 'desirable that the College should have the power to admit women as members'. This power could only be obtained by repealing or amending the 1926 College statute I.6, which stated: 'No woman shall be elected or admitted as Pensioner, Scholar, Officer, Fellow, or Master of the College.' Asked by the Fellows to prepare a statement of conditions that should govern the admission of women, the Senior Tutor reported that the questions regarding quotas, admissions procedures, domestic segregation and the timing of the entry of women were 'all perfectly soluble if there is the slightest will to resolve them'. As for the election of women to the Fellowship, Sparks was in favour, but he saw no reason for rushing them into post. After all, he was sure that many of the male fellows would be quite as well equipped to advise female undergraduates as any 'middle-aged spinster in a women's college'. Indeed, the only special arrangement that might be necessary was the provision of 'an odd loo or two with appropriate pictorial symbols in

this non-literate age'. Women were, it seemed, so little trouble it was a wonder that they had not been admitted centuries before.

But, in one respect, Percy Gardner-Smith was nearer the mark: there was no denying that the character of the College *did* change. On an autumn evening in 1976, beneath the Chapel's tower, Jesus's first female Fellow was about to be admitted. For a Renaissance scholar, immersed in neo-Latin texts, the prospect of reciting the cumbersome Fellows' oath was no doubt less daunting than it has been to many others. The thirty or so men who encircled her – her colleagues for the next ten years – were perhaps more anxious, since Lisa Jardine, newly elected English Fellow, and vastly pregnant, looked for all the world as though her waters might break.

The admission of women certainly shook an institution which, in many respects, was still rooted in its nineteenth-century past. Only the year before Jardine's admission, the College's *Annual Report* included a simpering notice:

> Lady guests, including wives, may now be introduced as guests at High Table on most ordinary nights and at the four Lesser Exceedings (All Saints', St Radegund, the day of the late June Council meeting, and the Name of Jesus).

Professor Lisa Jardine, the College's first woman Fellow (1976–89); Honorary Fellow 2006.

Dona Haycraft, *c.*1977

Fellows will also be permitted to bring lady guests to the Audit and the Rustat Feasts from the start of the Michaelmas Term 1975.

This utterly patronising concession would make no sense in an institution where, at last, men and women stood on an equal footing – where 'ladies' might be 'hosts', not 'guests'. Lisa Jardine was soon joined by three women research Fellows: Vivien Law (1977), and Suzanne Kappeler and Kathleen Wheeler (1978). In the last of these years five women graduate students entered the College, to be followed in 1979 by thirty-one under-graduates, one of whom (Helen Warburton) was to be President of the JCR in 1981–2. In less than a decade there was the first christening in the Chapel of a baby both of whose parents (Camilla, née Davis, and Brett Robinson, both 1979) were members of the College, and in 2005 the first undergraduate to be similarly qualified, Richard Stuart, matriculated. The number of women has risen steadily since 1976, more rapidly, of course, among the student populations – with their relatively quick turnover – than among the Fellowship. Today (2006–7) the undergraduate population is made up of 212 women to 268 men; there are 108 female graduate students com-pared with 165 men; and 18 women Fellows to 65 men (the latter figure swollen by 21 Emeritus Fellows).

The presence of women in the old men's colleges has not guaranteed equality for women and men throughout the University. Those who are familiar with recent debates about the relative success of male and female stu-dents in the Tripos, or the respective pay of male and female academics, or the career opportunities and pros-pects for women in the sciences will realise that. Others may ask if the time has not come for Newnham, New Hall and Lucy Cavendish to readdress the question of whether they are justified in refusing applications from men; they are evidently guilty of their own brand of sex discrimina-tion. But the admission of women was never merely an issue of gender equality. It signalled the start of a process of modernisation, and the sweeping away of a culture.

1977–2006: Reflections of Six Fellows who were Students in the College

JULIAN DOWDESWELL (1977)

I may have first visited Jesus College as a boy, in about 1970, when my parents drove us over from Oxford, my home town. Maybe, but maybe not – Jesus is a little like that for the casual tourist. It's not on the Backs and is just a minute or two's walk from Sidney Street. This, of course, is part of the College's character. It is quiet, at least outside term-time, and is certainly free of the crowds that beset many of the central colleges. So, I can only say with any certainty that I did come to the College for interview in the late autumn of 1976. I remember being impressed with the surroundings in a general way, but the specific picture I have is of waiting, for what seemed an age, outside Robin Donkin's room, which was then on the ground floor of K staircase. The interview itself passed in a blur, followed by days of waiting for the letter postmarked 'Cambridge'.

The following October, I came up to read Geography. I was taught by Robin Donkin and Bruce Sparks – Sparks was also the Senior Tutor, and was widely regarded as rather formidable. Both Robin and Bruce were exacting as supervisors and Robin took great care of us as Director of Studies. The supervision system did its work, and I think I learned more from Robin than from anyone before or since about how to analyse and dissect an academic problem, and then how to set the problem out in a well-argued yet concise way on paper. I still have the image of him in C1 First Court, sitting in an armchair under a lamp and, after offering us sherry, asking just why I had made a particular assertion in an essay. Both he and Bruce, although the latter retired relatively early, were very supportive during my subsequent academic career.

The College still had an all-male undergraduate cohort, and this may have been why many spent less time in Jesus than the mixed group of undergraduates forming the more balanced community that exists now – women were first admitted during my time as an undergraduate. However, just as today, Jesus had better provision of accommodation for undergraduates than most other colleges, and a gyp room entered from any one of four study bedrooms in North Court was a good way to meet other new students at the beginning of the first year. The hockey pitch, where I was always one of the weakest two or three in the first XI, was just across the grass. One league match ended for me with a visit to Addenbrooke's for stitches and a penicillin injection, followed by not altogether clear recollections of an evening of readings by John le Carré at the Cambridge Union.

A glimpse of First Court from near C staircase.

I was to live out in the second year, and to have a set of rooms in Jesus Lane, with Mrs Collins as landlady, in my final year. No alarm clock was needed, because the first bus along Jesus Lane each morning rattled the single-glazed windows as a wake-up call. Now the landladies are all gone, and the bulk of houses on Jesus Lane and Malcolm Street have been very well refurbished to provide popular 'external staircases' for second- and third-year undergraduates.

The setting of the College, in the extensive grounds of the old nunnery, gives it a unique feel among the central colleges of Cambridge. The walk down the Chimney forms a clear separation from the road, and the three-sided courts suggest openness and space. Certain memories are strong: drinks and photographs in the Orchard after Evelyn and I were married in the Chapel on a fiercely hot day in the summer of 1983; croquet on the lawn of Chapel Court after the exams were over (a tradition that seems to have lapsed recently); graduation drinks in Chapel Court. Cricket teas on the veranda of the thatched pavilion during an occasional outing for the second XI also remain more notable than the matches themselves.

It was a great pleasure and privilege to be invited back to Jesus as a Fellow when I returned to Cambridge as Director of the Scott Polar Research Institute and Professor of Physical Geography in 2001. When I was first approached concerning the chair, I was clear that Jesus was the College that I wanted to come back to if the opportunity arose, largely because it held so many positive associations with my earlier life and career. I was

admitted to the Fellowship in 2002, after speaking a long Latin oath to the Master and circle of Fellows under the tower of the Chapel. The simple admission ceremony, in that setting, gave a strong sense of continuity and also of community. My clear impression over the subsequent five years is that the College community is thriving. At the end of Arctic and Antarctic field research programmes on the British icebreaker, it is traditional for the chief scientist to speak at the end-of-cruise dinner. I usually end by concluding that we have worked hard as a team to complete the science, and, importantly, that we have enjoyed ourselves doing it. This, I think, also sums up the College today.

This sense of community is shared not only among our undergraduates, but also by the 250-strong Graduate Society. This group is truly international, as it was when I was a doctoral student at the Scott Polar Research Institute in the early 1980s. Both Evelyn and I remember dinners in Upper Hall, with Peter Glazebrook, the Tutor for Graduates, providing ready conversation and a warm welcome to the new students. Now, I attend those dinners with my own graduate students. We often bring in guest speakers after seminars in glaciology or high-latitude environmental change at the Institute, retiring to the bar afterwards by way of a sometimes-noisy contrast.

I was reminded recently of the passing of time when asking a group of Jesus supervisees whether they were going to the May Ball. The answer was 'Of course', and the question that followed was 'And have you ever been to one?' I recounted the Jesus May Ball of 1978, with the amusing and tongue-in-cheek Glam-Rocker Alvin Stardust as the lead act. I could see the students doing the calculation – 'We weren't even born then.'

What has changed in the thirty years since I came up to Cambridge? North Court, where I spent my first year, has been completely modernised and I assume that the heating may now work. There is a splendid new library, whose architecture, many feel, will stand the test of time. Sculptures are scattered liberally around the College grounds. My own favourites are what I interpret as wooden sea-shells on a wall in the Fellows' Garden, and the thin metallic birds in the very pleasant little court that has been formed between the Chapel and the Quincentenary Library. And I still don't think the rather aggressive Paolozzi looks quite right next to the Chapel. The Chapel, of course, remains a serene reminder of pre-University Cambridge, the new uplighting behind the altar picking out the details of the ancient columns – the columns are repeated in Cloister Court, this time rooted about a metre below its present level, suggesting history through stratigraphy. In other ways, rather little is different. The crocuses produce their annual spring carpet of yellow and mauve under the great trees and sweet-scented

... and another from North Court.

Julian Dowdeswell, 1978

wisteria blooms in First Court. But perhaps most of all, the Jesus undergraduates are still as bright, as interested and as courteous as ever they were, and they are still young. It's simply I who have grown a few years older.

IAN WHITE (1977)

Until sixth form at school, it had not crossed my mind that I might leave Northern Ireland for an English university. Although parts of my family had travelled far and wide, and the troubles were in full flow, the benefits of an English higher education had not registered. Although students from my school had applied and entered Oxbridge, their number had been few, partly because they had had to remain in school to make seventh-term applications. Just prior to my reaching sixth form however, some Cambridge colleges had started to make A-level offers to candidates, and as a result my school encouraged more to consider applying. My parents, believing that I would come to no good taking a year out of full-time education, encouraged me to consider applying for immediate admission, and the choice of college was settled when a long-standing family friend, Norman Fleck (now head of the Mechanics Materials and Design Division in the University's Engineering Department), went up to Jesus College on this basis.

I applied the following year, finding the interview process an education in itself. There was the anticipation, the preparation (I recall buying a special jacket for £6.50), the journey to London and then to Royston where at the time the electric line finished, and a second train ferried us to Cambridge. I stayed overnight with other candidates, some of whom were to become long-term friends. The most challenging part of the process for me was the interview with the Senior Tutor, Mr Sparks, who was bemused as to why I should enter the College without taking a year out, not least because I was still 16 at the time. Nonetheless, he took pity on me, and the following year I became a fresher.

I continued to benefit from the advice of Norman Fleck, and preparations for coming up were soon developed in detail. I was directed to requesting rooms in L staircase, then reputed to be the cheapest in Cambridge (£45 a term). L had four sets of rooms so each student had three rooms: a living area, bedroom and small gyp room. There was no running water and the staircase had no bathroom facilities, unlike other staircases at the time. L staircase also had a most formidable but caring bedder. My first meeting with her was very early one morning, when she came into my room with me still asleep in bed to greet me, and open the bedroom curtains and window to help me awake. This was to continue for the rest of the year no matter what the weather. It was clearly part of the

job. I never fully understood her, evidenced by my surprise at being fined at the end of the year for having left rubbish in my room, when my intent had been not to throw away food that I felt she might enjoy. Through my early days I came to recognise that the senior members of College were keen to take an interest in undergraduates, including the Master, Sir Alan Cottrell. The Head Porter, Mr West, whilst also formidable, was a fount of knowledge that really mattered, and was much valued.

Socially, I was to learn a lot, and differences would turn up in unexpected areas. For example, the prevailing views on the relative merits of smoking and drinking at Cambridge were not far from being the reverse of those from my home circle (interestingly, not completely without parallel to the differences that some Cambridge and MIT exchange students have observed more recently). In the early days, I found my accent needed attention. I had to work at making myself understood (I remember in the early days trying to buy a 'towel' only to be repeatedly directed to 'tiles'), but also as others were to point out to me later, it had benefits as my accent was, to my English friends at least, classless.

I had joined a College where friendliness and kindness seemed at the heart of its traditions, and this meant a great deal. I came to understand a much wider range of attitudes than I had been used to, but somehow these never were considered more important than the unity of College life. I had good friends involved actively both on the right and left wings of politics, but even at a time when the country was moving from Callaghan to Thatcher, differences never spilled into tension. The same for me was true of religious views. I became committed to the Christian Union in College and the CICCU, and much appreciated large events such as the Billy Graham mission. At the time, where inter-collegiate University activities were perhaps more prominent than now, the College still had allegiance.

I was one of those who enjoyed his work at Cambridge. I found the dons exceptionally helpful. My year was the first for which Dr Stan Evans was Director of Studies, and I was very grateful for the close support, advice and guidance he provided: his great concern was for us as individuals, rather than simply how we did. Our supervisions by Stan and Professor Ken Johnson were very important to me, particularly at the start of the Tripos. My biggest surprise was the choice of my laboratory and supervision partner. To have come to Cambridge, an Ulster Protestant, to be paired with a southern Irish Catholic, albeit one with a perfect English accent, struck me (as it did him) unusually coincidental. Needless to say, we became close friends.

The College itself was in something of a transition during my undergraduate years, as in my third year women came up as freshers. I was especially aware of the gender imbalance in Cambridge, my recollection being that there were six women engineers in my year out of three hundred in total, and that the numbers of women in lectures on one or two Saturday mornings increased considerably, with girlfriends up in Cambridge on visit coming in to see what they were like. I am delighted that the number of women studying engineering is now in excess of 30 per cent. Within College, as far as I was aware at the time, there was nothing but support for the change, but little was said to students, the first real indication for me being the refurbishment of 1CC and 2CC staircases with improved facilities. On a personal level, the change opened the door for both my wife-to-be and my sister to come up.

My final year in Electrical Sciences allowed me to carry out intensive practical studies over a wide range of topics. The course developed by Sir Charles Oatley, the inventor of the scanning electron microscope, had numerous alumni including Ray Dolby and Lord Broers. Twice weekly laboratory sessions, governed by a wonderful ex-army chief technician, encouraged us to tackle difficult problems, on occasion without relevant prior lectures, and to develop our own research skills. The course convinced me that I should seek to study for a PhD degree, and I rapidly decided I wanted to remain in Cambridge for it. The Department was a hive of activity at the time. As undergraduates we were very aware of the overall contributions of Sir William Hawthorne and Professor William Mair (the current Master's father). The research activities of Haroon Ahmed, Frank Fallside and John Carroll all seemed to hold much promise and impressed me greatly (and indeed have since grown strongly, forming the foundation of work by others now in the Department). I was particularly attracted by the field of optical communications, which appeared to offer great opportunity (although at the time the internet which resulted from it was a far-off vision). So I applied to work under John Carroll, was lucky in gaining a PhD grant from the Department of Education in Northern Ireland, and started a working relationship that still continues. The initial phase of my research concerned the cause and nature of 'kinks' in the light current characteristics of laser diodes (now the dominant laser in communications and consumer applications such as in CD and DVD players). As it happened, my father's PhD had begun studying the 'kinks' in thermionic diodes. Although the dynamics were very different, a few years later different phenomena were discovered where the dynamics were indeed very similar; *plus ça change*.

My PhD days were also to introduce me to the 'other side of the fence' in supervisions. I enjoyed these, learning much from the undergraduates with whom I worked. I never failed to be fascinated by their breadth of interests and depth of understanding. Only once, I believe, did I find myself completely unable to teach: when both my (male) supervisees were very friendly with the same New Hall undergraduate. One, aware of the other's diligence, decided to be with her when his colleague was in supervision with me, arriving approximately thirty minutes late, the remainder of the supervision being taken up with determining the cause of lateness and a forceful expression of views.

The aim of my research had been to use the phenomena to develop simple optical switches, and when this was achieved it was suggested that I apply for a college research fellowship. I applied to a large number of colleges, aware that success was unlikely, particularly at that time for engineers, and I was very touched indeed to be made an offer by my own College. The application process involved submitting a short article, followed by a thesis or combination of papers, and then a panel interview. The last greatly impressed me as it was chaired by the Master, Sir Alan Cottrell, who, despite being in a very different field, showed great insight into my own – though when proposing the healths of the new Fellows after our admission, he focused on the research achievements of the others, but commented on my having 'done the hoops' in the College bar. (Technically I may not in fact have achieved this feat, since I was sober at the time.) Being part of the Fellowship meant a great deal. The support that one receives and the stimulation of debate at High Table is a real strength of the Cambridge system. Interdisciplinary research has made major contributions over the years to Cambridge's research successes.

My roles within the University changed greatly during this time. I began to lecture, my first lecture being particularly memorable because of the two hundred or so imitations after I mentioned the word 'mirror' for the first time, and the undergraduate who, at its end, informed me that it was the worst lecture that he had ever attended. This poor start with him did however improve rapidly and we became friends.

During the 1980s, as a Fellow, not only did I teach within the College, but I served as Tutor for Rooms, opening for me a new view of College life. Although I had been in lodgings during my second year as an undergraduate, I was now able to build up a much fuller picture of the then major role of the College's landladies and their families, consulting (and mediating) with them as occasion demanded. The College had begun introducing external staircases, and so the Tutor for Rooms became directly involved in the rooms' ballot and was made aware of the conflicting wishes and needs of undergraduates. Fortunately, in general – not least because of an extremely able secretary, Brenda Welch – conflicts were few. Indeed I was frequently impressed by the confidence of our students, the best example being the fresher who when asked on his rooms' form whether he had any special preferences for his first-year accommodation simply answered 'a sea view'.

Before I left to become professor of physics at the University of Bath, the College also gave me the opportunity to be senior treasurer of the JCR and the Tutor to Graduates. My move to Bath crystallised how much had occurred in my time at Cambridge, and how much I had changed and yet had not changed. I remember saying at my farewell dinner how I felt that I had been changed greatly by Cambridge, and yet the first question that I was asked in Bath when I had joined the staff there was exactly the same as had been asked in Cambridge when I first arrived: 'What year are you in?'

When, in 2001, I was very fortunate to be offered the opportunity to return to Cambridge as Van Eck Professor of Engineering, I was especially grateful to be offered a fellowship again – along with Julian Dowdeswell, who had been also in my undergraduate year and was returning as Director of the Scott Polar Research Institute. As one might expect, I have noted changes. The College is run on a more professional footing, and there has been a substantial investment in the fabric both in the College and its student houses. The career structure of academic staff has changed more than in many other universities that I know of, in part reflecting the substantial growth in research that has occurred in the University in the past fifteen years. Although some are concerned about the changing balance of activity in the University between research and teaching, and for that matter undergraduate and post-graduate study, I am not. Just as external studies over the university sector have demonstrated that strong research-active universities tend to be strong teaching universities, so it is noticeable that the priority within the College of ensuring maximum quality of teaching has not changed; indeed there appears to me to be more college-based teaching now than when I was an undergraduate.

And the core values have not changed. The friendliness that I first became aware of under Sir Alan has continued under Lord Renfrew, Professor Crighton and Professor Mair. Key features of College life – its sports, music, societies and Chapel – are healthy. I have been able to appreciate anew the privilege of being with such able students and their wide interests. For that I am most grateful.

IAN WILSON (1985)

First impressions are important, they say, and my first impression of Jesus College, Cambridge, was one of *déjà vu*: walking down the Chimney path in my interview suit

on a dark, foggy December evening towards the only light streaming from the wicket gate still reminds me of the posters advertising Peter Sellers' last film, *Being There*. How was I to know that I would still be there over twenty years later, albeit with a couple of periods living in places almost as far away as one could get, Vancouver and Auckland? Not one iota, of course, and therein for me lies the wonder of Cambridge and the College which I now see year on year as one of the dons: a place full of able and bright people, mainly young, coming together for a period which will launch them on their adventure in life through training, experiences, opportunities and connections that are rarely available in such a concentrated form anywhere else.

An adventure it was, too, on so many levels. I had spent a gap year in England before starting at Jesus, but voluntary work in south Yorkshire during the miners' strike was as different from Cambridge as Belfast, and my memories of the first term are simply a blaze of events,

The Queen with the Master (Lord Renfrew) on the day of the College's Quincentenary celebrations, 8 March 1996.

meeting people, and trying to figure out where you were supposed to be. Studying Natural Sciences did not help; as Director of Studies in the same subject fifteen years later I found myself looking after perfectly able students simply seeking to survive the first year. My strongest memory of that first year is of the kindness of others, particularly to one with such a confused accent. The other dominant memory is talking late into the night … about what, I do not recall, except that we stretched our minds, our imaginations, our worldviews, our core beliefs and our bodies' ability to function on little sleep.

Friendships started then remain to this day, with other students, Fellows and the porters. The Fellows were in the main a mystery to me, with the exception of my Directors of Studies and Tutors. The main connection to the administration was therefore through the Porters' Lodge; someone else is bound to mention the role that the porters at Jesus play in the fabric of the College, and I don't think that their contribution can be overstated. I'm truly glad to see the pattern of caring, good-natured yet strong individuals manning the Lodge continues – even if Peter Stretten did go back through the discipline records to see if he could unearth any skeletons when I became responsible, as Dean of College, for discipline. I organise conferences in the College periodically and we have to advise our visitors that the porters are not luggage handlers; lately we have come to describe them as 'guardians', which I find encapsulates their role rather well. They certainly differentiate Jesus from other colleges that I am familiar with.

In subsequent years I spent increasing fractions of my time outside the College, partly as a result of being the only student in my subject in my year at Jesus and mostly due to playing University hockey. By the fourth and

final year I was living off Mill Road and being steadily weaned off life in College, rather than confronted by the sudden separation at graduation. I was ready and happy to move on, never imagining that I would return to Cambridge and the College five years later. That final year helped me to see some of the differences between student life at Cambridge and other universities, and to appreciate the enormous benefits of the College system for study, proximity and resources. It also makes me wonder if there is a better way to prepare students for life beyond the high-intensity cauldron of relationships that marks undergraduate existence.

The intervening years have witnessed enormous change, particularly in the fabric and environment. I returned from Canada to find the city of Cambridge no longer an academic island with poor transport links, but a busy technology-fired centre awash with tourists and shoppers. Flying back to Belfast from Stansted brings back memories of long journeys on coaches and ferries (for about the same price in real terms), but this is nothing compared to the digital revolution. The computer, the web and the mobile phone have changed student life irrevocably, and not just for studies: no longer do you have to cycle over to a porters' lodge and leave a message or wait on a doorstep for someone. How, I wonder, does this affect social interactions and the training in human nature that those visits imparted? As a member of the 'DOS generation' – who had to understand how the computer worked in order to get it to do anything – I now marvel at what can be achieved *in silico*, and conversely am alarmed by how much students will believe their black/white/silver box. On the positive side, students can now wander via the internet through a virtual Jesus College to get an idea of the place before selecting it, rather than approaching a long list of colleges with a set of haphazard criteria. I still remember selecting Jesus on the basis of a good reputation for food and facilities. Sadly, we academics also have to wonder if the immaculate essay or project report before us is our supervisee's own work. In almost all areas technology has turned full circle and people are the factors limiting the rate of progress, reinforcing the need for training the individual to think and develop his or her own ideas as the collegiate system aims to do.

There are noticeable changes in culture, many originating from within. The College's student body has expanded enormously in terms of geographical and ethnic background, preparing students for, as well as responding to, the mixed society that is twenty-first century Britain. It now grates when politicians, basing themselves on their experience of decades past, refer to Oxford and Cambridge as nurseries of the establishment. The fabric of the College, too, has changed enormously and I think that

Prince Edward (1983) with the staff of the Porters' Lodge (Mr Peter Bacon, Head Porter 1984–2002 on his left), 1986.

endowments to underwrite the enterprise – but I do wonder how the collegiate system will evolve to meet the very real challenges posed by, among others, targets on undergraduate background, reduction in government funding for education in real terms, the demands of conducting research in the digital age, and the recruitment of new staff when a successful company in Silicon Fen can offer much higher salaries. Universities are adopting more business-like models and the College, which I believe has always placed high priority on each student as a valued individual and on education as a broad palette of training and experience, needs to negotiate some tricky ice in order to maintain its course.

MARY LAVEN (1989)

Cazimir, the Polish café on King's Street, is seldom without a Jesus College presence. I'm a mid-morning frequenter. I go there partly because I can't make it through to lunch without feeling the need for a snack, and partly because I crave neutral territory in which to think. There are clearly others like me, who would rather sit on wooden stools, their notebooks and computers endangered by tall glass mugs of milky coffee, than enjoy the quiet of a library or their College rooms. I keep my head down, but am dimly aware of familiar faces. Students from Malcolm Street drop by for a caffeine fix. Some college sportsmen tackle the healthy salads with surprising alacrity. Another Fellow dashes in for a take-out. Not that the place is dominated by academics.

There was no Cazimir in 1989, the year I came up, though the still-thriving Clowns on the opposite side of the street was already purveying pasta and cheesecakes with ineffable Sicilian charm. Living for two years at the roundabout end of Jesus Lane, my friends and I viewed King Street as the centre of our existence. We shopped (when we were desperate) at Every Occasion, where you could buy a carton of orange juice, a sliced loaf and a piece of plastic Edam: all that was necessary to subsist. We used the launderette in the scruffy run of shops owned by Christ's. (We were the sort of women who preferred to give our money to Clene Machine rather than to come into direct contact with the underpants of identifiable rugby players in the College laundry.) We had our hair cut by Stefano (now to be found halfway up Maid's Causeway). And of course we drank in the legendary pubs. There's no doubt that the street has gone up in the world. Few can regret the day that Efes, the Turkish restaurant, took over from Mr Chips, or when Yippee – a noodle-bar much frequented by staff, students and Fellows of the College – replaced the repulsive Corner Shop. And I'm sure that no one truly lamented the

Mr Grahame Appleby, Head Porter 2002– .

this reflects an important change in attitude towards its own task and place. Almost everything in brick and mortar seems to have been refurbished, while the gardens continue to provide the most wonderful scents through the spring and summer. The Quincentenary Library is a remarkable success, and the students appear to have taken advantage of this as well as the sports facilities, as tripos and cuppers performances appear to indicate.

The unseen fabric, however, is where I perceive the greatest challenges to lie. As a student I never really considered what sort of body or organisation the College was: it seemed to belong somewhere between a school and a charity. Nowadays I see that the College is also a higher education centre with a multimillion pound turnover and more than fifty full- and part-time staff meeting the needs of over eighty dons and seven hundred and fifty students, which must operate within a regulated and ever-evolving framework. Facilities have to be provided for students who, in a competitive market for that education, will expect high levels of both facilities and comfort. Sustainability is a key issue: providing a place of 'education, learning, religion and research' for generations to come requires the College to manage its resources responsibly and with a vision for the future. It is often remarked that no one nowadays would establish a university along the lines of Oxford and Cambridge – partly, no doubt, due to the difficulty of securing the demise of 'Every Ock'. As for the launderette, that and its neighbours are long gone, replaced by an enormous and intimidatingly stylish designer clothes outlet. But the College's environment has not been fundamentally changed. I'm struck by how many of my own mundane student experiences could be almost exactly replicated today. Coming back from Little Sainsbury's, laden with shopping bags. A toasted sandwich at the Maypole. Or walking down a wisteria-scented Orchard Street on a May evening to the Free Press.

Within the precincts of the College, the rhythms of student life continue much as I remember, despite some profound physical changes. Millions of pounds have been spent on restoring North Court, bringing our students decisively into the en-suite era. There is a shiny new accommodation block (not to mention a new library) in something called Library Court. In Pump Court there is a bar of which we are no longer ashamed. But for those who seek it, shabbiness may yet be found. It's still possible to see people running barefoot in bathrobes from the few showerless staircases in Chapel Court. Those fake pine wardrobes, with a tendency to lean to one side, remain in operation. And modernisation turns out to have its drawbacks: it is an amazing fact that the spacious kitchens in the refurbished North Court do not provide any cooking facilities. This subtle piece of social control, doubtless justified on the grounds of 'Health and Safety', is designed in conjunction with the ever-rising Kitchen Fixed Charge to make eating in Hall mandatory. Will the new generation of students – male and female – never learn how to cook 5,001 dishes out of a tin of tuna?

It is the student's financial relationship with the College and the University that has altered most drastically over the past decade and a half. Debt was common but lamentable when I was a student, but now it is built into educational policy in the form of student loans, financing maintenance and tuition fees that look set to rise and rise. Within the College, students' rents have been steeply increased. Subsidising students across the board, regardless of their personal and familial economic circumstances, is judged to be a bad use of money; better to charge realistic rents, and to help out those who really need it. The argument makes sense, but there was something attractive and egalitarian about uniform largesse.

Despite, or perhaps because of, these developments, students today seem much less political than their forebears. The first communication I received from Jesus, after my letter of admission, was a notification from the JCR President that the students were about to embark on a rent strike, and that we should accordingly make our cheques out to the JCR, not to the College. In 1990 I went with various other JCR executive members to the anti-poll-tax protests in London. Back then, carrying a

rape alarm took on a feminist significance that would bewilder current undergraduates. Perhaps the quiescence of the younger generation is an illusion – there is now a Lesbigay representative on the Student Union, and for all I know plenty of Jesus students marched against war in Iraq. Yet it's hard to rid oneself of the sense that something in the mindset has changed.

With depoliticisation (if it exists) comes efficiency. More students work harder, and they get better results. There is less studied indolence. Even a Director of Studies for History would no longer say, as mine did when we turned up in 1989, that there was little point in going to lectures, and that if one got the urge one might as well gatecrash those in another faculty. Students are more focused on their work and on their play, during which they process the endless information that streams into their mobiles and their email inboxes. Less productively, some spend many hours dallying with something called 'Facebook', an online gossip-network and dating-agency, which displays student images and profiles, enabling you to 'poke' those whom you find attractive. In addition to the well-established procrastination strategy of checking one's email, students go online to see if they have been poked.

Though it inevitably changes more slowly, the staff and Fellowship have also been transformed since my undergraduate days. Some much-loved figures have retired; and defining members of the College community (such as Mike Jackson and Charlie Moore, Ilya Gershevitch and Robin Donkin) have died. College lecturers and chaplains, who remain on five-year contracts despite the advent of new employment laws, have been forced to move on. Less controversially, the mastership is a ten-year appointment – a term that usually coincides with the last decade of an eminent career. It is only because of the tragic death of David Crighton in post that I have witnessed three Masters in eighteen years. And then there is the brain drain, which has bitten particularly hard in my own subject. Keith Wrightson and Richard Tuck were my guiding lights as a student. They both came from Tyneside, though from contrasting backgrounds (Keith from a mining village, Richard the son of an eminent educationalist). They are both historians of the seventeenth century, but utterly unlike in their demeanour: Keith a social historian, balding with a sandy-grey beard; Richard a historian of ideas, clean-shaven with a lustrous dark-brown mop of hair. Inevitably, these two gems were snapped up by Ivy League universities: Richard by Harvard, Keith by Yale.

As for the College's ethos, that remains largely unchanged, for better and worse. A disproportionate number of students come from independent schools, and matriculation photos suggest more sameness than diversity. Rowing and rugby still figure very prominently, and the drinking clubs continue to flourish. Formal Hall looks much as I remember it, although the colour of the Hall has changed. But the College is now associated with modern art as well as with rowing. There are contemporary sculptures all over the grounds, an Antony Gormley in the library and an Andy Goldsworthy in Upper Hall. And student music recitals can be heard in Chapel every week during term. Crucially, the proportion of female undergraduates has grown from roughly a third to roughly a half (the Fellowship lags far behind in this respect). Back in 1989 it was a relief to discover that Cambridge wasn't entirely dominated by young men in striped blazers carrying teddy-bears, though there was disappointment on the part of some that there were precious few Jeremy Ironses walking through the cloisters of Jesus. Brideshead it wasn't and isn't, but Jesus College has a way to go before it can claim to reflect the society of which it is a part.

SHAILAJA FENNELL (1990)

My journey to Jesus College in 1990 had roots that stretched as far back as 1984 when as a lowly undergraduate sitting in St Stephen's College Library in Delhi I was transfixed by a piece written by Dr Peter Nolan, Fellow of Jesus, which gave a powerful account of the differences between Russian and Chinese communism. I must have re-read that article in the *Economic and Political Weekly* many times during the course of my undergraduate degree, and it was this encounter with a Jesuan in a college that was set up by the Cambridge Mission to India in 1881 that sowed a tiny seed that was to become a full-grown ambition to study at Jesus College, Cambridge.

In 1990 I was an Indian who came to Cambridge with little knowledge of the University beyond the fact that the Faculty of Economics and Politics was the home of the Cambridge tradition, but shored up by the encouragement given by leading Indian economists, foremost among them Professor Sukhamoy Chakravarty, deputy chairman of the Indian Planning Commission and a leading macroeconomist, who had spent time at Cambridge and spoke highly of the intellectual environment. My unerring intention was to seek out Nolan at the earliest opportunity with a view to requesting that he might consider taking me on as a doctoral student. In those early weeks and months at Cambridge I visited Jesus on numerous occasions, sometimes to dine at one of the lower tables in Hall – where I noticed that the height of the step between high and low tables was identical to that at St Stephen's College, Delhi – and more regularly to attend the weekly seminars organised by Peter Nolan that introduced me

to the stalwarts as well as to new emerging scholars in the field of Chinese political economy. The seminars were held in his room on G staircase, from where I could see across Chapel Court to Midsummer Common and beyond.

In that first year I had little idea of the long-standing connections between the College, the making of modern India; and my chosen topic of research on long-term agricultural trends in India and China that the dusty volumes of the Malthus collection – kept under lock and key in the Old Library – would reveal. I remained a complete stranger to the Old Library until I made the transformation from graduate student to Fellow in the summer of 1994. In the preceding three years I had become fully acquainted with the War Memorial Library, housed on the second floor of A staircase, both as a graduate student supervising undergraduates, but more eagerly as a voracious reader of its excellent collection of classic economics texts. This enjoyable exercise also brought to my attention the fact that I was following in the illustrious footsteps of Dr Amiya Kumar Bagchi, the first Indian to be a teaching Fellow of the College and the author of the definitive text on the political economy of industrialisation in independent India. During this period I worked away on the statistical records of agricultural production in modern India and China at libraries in Delhi, Beijing and Cambridge, but did not know of the academic riches that lay behind the heavy door that stood at the top of the staircase leading to Upper Hall.

It was in the winter of 1994 that I found myself clutching the key to the Old Library and entered the cold and silent rooms behind that heavy door to discover the many volumes that make up the Malthus collection. The hundreds of books there proved a source of continued delight to me for the next five years. I became a regular fixture in the inner room, pouring over the twenty-four pocket volumes of Jesuit accounts of travel across China that had been thumbed by Robert Malthus, reading through Malthus Senior's copies of Ricardo's early works, and scribbling down every reference that I could find to improvements in agricultural production. The intellectual pleasure that I gained from trawling through a treasure trove of books from the eighteenth and nineteenth centuries, relating to land and agriculture ranging from geographies of the British Isles, through the Mediterranean, to the distant eastern countries of India and China, nourished my doctoral work and provided the inspiration for organising a Malthus workshop in the College in 1998 to mark the bi-centennial of the publication of *An Essay on the Principle of Population*. The knowledge that Malthus had been an inveterate seeker of statistical knowledge on population and was still making enquiries about access to sources in the East and writing for this purpose to one of his students, who was resident in

Nepal, a year prior to his death in 1834, gave me the courage to persist with my comparative research on agricultural trends in modern India and China.

The revelation that the research that I had embarked upon had a strange symmetry with that of another Fellow of Jesus, some two centuries before, inexorably changed the way in which I regarded my own relationship to the College. The notion that I was a Fellow from afar who was navigating between two countries, cultures and traditions was unequivocally replaced by a sense of sharing a similar quest with other Fellows, past and present, of the College. It is a quest which, like my journey, was begun in wonderful libraries, and it is one that I hope I shall be able to continue to pursue at Jesus for many decades.

ANDREW JOHNSTON (1990)

It is not easy to compare my experiences as a student at Jesus – I came up to study Law in 1990 – with those I have been having during a hectic and enjoyable first year as a Fellow. The nature of the place is that change is incremental and is measured in decades rather than years or months. And many of my experiences have mirrored those I had as a student, so this piece is a tale less of simple change and more of change of perspective.

Interviewing admissions candidates was the job that I had anticipated the most keenly; it would be – and obviously was – strange to be sitting on the other side of the interview, and far less nerve-racking, but no less of an intense experience, I being acutely conscious of the importance of the decisions we would make. The inter-

**The Chimney: wall 1608;
bicycles 2004.**

view process has changed little, although law students now have to sit a national (and not just the College's own) law aptitude test that is still in the early stages of its development, the aim being to help in sifting through the huge numbers of students who want to study the Law – for the beauty of the Law in itself rather than as a means to an end, of course!

In October the new freshers had appeared nervous at first and were caught up in the whirl of freshers' week, which seems to have changed remarkably little. The second-year students wasted no time in sharing the wisdom of their year's accumulated experience and were very welcoming generally. Freshers' cocktails for lawyers are exactly the same as they were fifteen years ago, although there was no repeat of an occasion I remember well where – due to some kind of oversight – only sherry was served. Cocktails remains a misnomer as there is only wine! A number of our new law students are living in the recently refurbished North Court and are very happy with the changes to the accommodation – kitchens are now in the basement and bathrooms are attached to each of the bedrooms – if none too happy about room rents, heating costs and the kitchen fixed charge. *Plus ça change*!

Formal Hall appears to remain a focal point of College social life, and it is striking that most students dress up for it; fifteen years ago, as I recall, most people simply put on a gown over whatever they were wearing. Interestingly, there is now a formal limit on how much wine each diner can take in. The end of dinner tradition (dating, I am told, from the 1980s) of applauding the last Fellow continues; now I am making the exit from High Table, but have yet to manoeuvre sufficiently adroitly to receive the applause.

On the educational side, pressures of time weigh as heavily as they ever did. Study, sports, socialising and numerous other activities besides are crammed into ridiculously short terms. Most students work extremely diligently – perhaps more so than fifteen years ago – although that could just be my perception from the other side, and with a lot of water under the bridge. The benefits of small-group teaching in supervisions are obviously still appreciated by both sides, most of the time. Repeated interactions allow the Fellows to get to know the students both intellectually and on a more social basis in a way that is simply not possible where groups are much larger. Classes can be tailored to the students' needs and demands far more effectively. From my point of view, this remains one of the major strengths of the Cambridge system – and one that I regret that more people do not get to experience while in higher education.

Stress levels still rise palpably around the College during Easter term as exams loom large. While I was, of course, conscious of this as an undergraduate, I can now

*1977–2006: Reflections
of Six Fellows who were
Students in the College*

303

The College bar has moved downstairs in its Pump Court location, although since becoming a Fellow I have learned that once it occupied what is now the Marshall Room, with its student pigeonholes. It seems that students still check their pigeonholes as often as I did – although many of them never seem to check their emails. I felt rather sad that the slightly down-at-heel, dingy but familiar feel of the 1990s bar has been replaced by something rather closer to a 1980s-style neon-lit cocktail bar with ceiling speakers that destroy any chance of conversation, yet without producing any audible music! Smokers have been ejected and are forced to gather – like hordes of office workers up and down the country – just outside the entrance. Table football is there, and – I am happy to report – the standard still seems high, so work pressures are obviously not telling too hard. As everywhere, security measures have increased, and most access points to College require the use of a magnetic key to enter. Moving beyond the College walls – which I did so rarely as a student – other local attractions have been lost. Parrot Records in King Street, which had already moved from its old premises into a new and strikingly bland development, fell victim to commercial pressures and the internet, like so many independent record retailers. Garon Records similarly disappeared from King Street. What a sad loss to a street which used to offer the prospect of a pub crawl followed by spending all one's remaining money on records and CDs. For those whose memories go further back – and mine certainly doesn't – I am reliably informed that King Street has lost five pubs to a modern housing development, turning the King Street run into a more leisurely amble, even more so now that opening hours have been lengthened. Sadly, the Grafton Centre remains.

Quincentenary Library: indications of an 'essay crisis'?

observe it from a slightly greater distance, although for us Fellows, of course, the exam period heralds a wave of anxious questions by email followed by a pressurised period of exam marking. Still, there is the happy prospect of May week and diaries are starting to fill up.

I am conscious that this appears to be a tale of continuity, so I should point to a few things that have changed.

Tailpiece: May Balls

Why should not an attempt be made to give a College ball next May term? It would probably be feasible if only some energetic members of the College set to work early this term to get promises for a sustentation [*sic*] fund. If for example enough guarantors could be found for the sale of 150 tickets at a guinea each the thing would be as good as done.

So *Chanticlere*'s editorial for the Lent term 1896. The guarantors were found, the ball was held – with the practical assistance of Messrs J. Lyons & Co. (its outside catering business predated its teashops) – and another College tradition was born. It may perhaps be said that the 1896 ball – which 'ended as an unqualified success' after beginning 'with every appearance of a fiasco' – was not the first ever Jesus May Ball, but it was the first to be held inside the College. A decade earlier, in 1886, the first year of H.A. Morgan's Mastership, a ball 'of unparalleled splendour … universally spoken of as the best Ball ever given in Cambridge', with five hundred guests, among them the Duke of Clarence (the Prince of Wales's eldest son), had been held to mark the ten successive years (1896 proved to be the eleventh) in which Jesus rowed Head of the River. It had, however, taken place in the Guildhall and the Corn Exchange ('almost smothered in flowers and plants'), and the University Boat Club, the organiser of the May (and the Lent) races was also involved: 'the Varsity oars', as well as eleven years' worth of Jesus ones, decorated the Guildhall.

Initially triennial events, Jesus May Balls became biennial in the 1960s, and in the 1990s began to be held annually. They are now, 110 years on, much larger, more sophisticated – with 'themes' such as 'The Sinking of the Titanic' or 'Through the Looking Glass' – more costly (though less so than in the 1980s), and demand from the Ball Committee markedly greater business and administrative skills as well as more elaborate precautions against gate-crashers than the 1896 ball did. In 2007 a total of 1,300

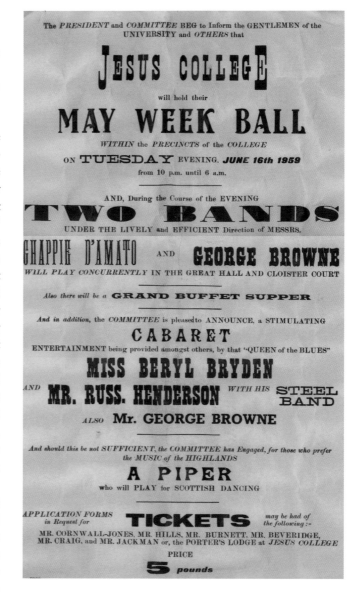

The PRESIDENT and COMMITTEE BEG to Inform the GENTLEMEN of the UNIVERSITY and OTHERS that

JESUS COLLEGE

will hold their

MAY WEEK BALL

WITHIN the PRECINCTS of the COLLEGE

ON **TUESDAY** EVENING. **JUNE 16th 1959**

from 10 p.m. until 6 a.m.

AND, During the Course of the EVENING

TWO BANDS

UNDER THE LIVELY and EFFICIENT Direction of MESSRS,

CHAPPIE D'AMATO AND **GEORGE BROWNE**

WILL PLAY CONCURRENTLY IN THE GREAT HALL AND CLOISTER COURT

Also there will be a **GRAND BUFFET SUPPER**

And in addition, the COMMITTEE is pleased to ANNOUNCE, a STIMULATING

CABARET

ENTERTAINMENT being provided amongst others, by that "QUEEN of the BLUES"

MISS BERYL BRYDEN

AND **MR. RUSS. HENDERSON** WITH HIS **STEEL BAND**

ALSO **Mr. GEORGE BROWNE**

And should this be not SUFFICIENT, the COMMITTEE has Engaged, for those who prefer
the MUSIC of the HIGHLANDS

A PIPER

who will PLAY for SCOTTISH DANCING

APPLICATION FORMS in Request for **TICKETS** may be had of the following :-

MR. CORNWALL-JONES, MR. HILLS, MR. BURNETT, MR. BEVERIDGE,
MR. CRAIG, and MR. JACKMAN or, the PORTER'S LODGE at JESUS COLLEGE

PRICE

5 pounds

tickets 'competitively priced' at £95 (without dinner) were sold – as late as 1956 tickets were still only 4 guineas (£72 in 2007 money); there were several bands – in 1947 the

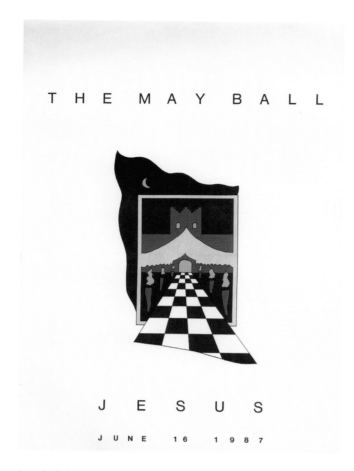

band of the Royal Marines sufficed – and a variety of 'entertainments' and amenities, including fairground dodgems, with awnings and marquees stretching from Library Court to the hockey pitch. But most features of the 1896 ball remain. Dinner is served in Hall as 'supper' was then; and a survivors' photo is still taken (at 6 a.m. rather than 4.30 a.m.). But the dance floor which was, and continued into the 1930s, to be in a covered-over Cloister Court had in 2007 moved to First Court – though the Cloister walks, lit by lanterns, were still used for sitting out.

It has, of course, never been possible to rely on the weather. In 1899 'the evening was exceedingly chilly and the grounds could not be much used'; in 1902, after four days of constant downpour, the rain stopped just in time: 'everything was dripping wet', and it was 'very cold', but there were 'some large baskets full of charming white shawls for the ladies' and their chaperones. In 1985, with no chaperones to be considered, 'the only disappointing factors were the rain and chilly wind. The presence of the group MUD summed up conditions underfoot, but otherwise the ball was a thoroughly enjoyable success.'

Similar fortitude was called for six years later:

Despite the cold and rain the May Ball on Tuesday 18 June 1991 was highly enjoyable. *Pinkerton's Parade* and the *Criterion Discotheque* were hugely popular in Cloister Court, while *Microgroove* with Funk, *Galliano* with Acid Jazz and *Fat and Frantic* with Acoustic Pop were some of the attractions in the main bands marquee. The Prioress's Room was turned into a casino and all sorts of Jazz were played in First Court.

It is, no doubt, inevitable that May Balls should contribute to those misleading media images of Cambridge that the College and the University would prefer to be without. Yet who would be greatly surprised if told that for many Jesuans it was the May Ball rather than Degree Day that conjured up the more poignant memories of the closing days of their life in the College, any more than that there have been those who have reported (as one did in 1947) that 'I enjoyed myself so much that I remember singularly little'?

Contributors

JOHN ADKINS read Natural Sciences at Christ's, was elected to a research Fellowship at Jesus in 1957, and from 1960 until his retirement in 1999 taught Physics in the College and the University, being Head of the Low Temperature Physics Research Group at the Cavendish Laboratory for seventeen years. President of the College Music Society since 1972, he plays the oboe.

ANTHONY BAGSHAW came up in 2005 from Bootham School, York, and is reading History.

STEPHEN BARTON came up from Birkenhead School in 1965 to read Law, and worked as a solicitor and partner in the City firm of Herbert Smith from 1969 to 1997, specialising in corporate banking and insolvency law. Returning to the College, initially as a Fellow Commoner to teach Law, he was Senior Bursar from 1999 to 2007.

MICHAEL BLACK, having read English and Medieval and Modern Languages at Jesus, and served in the Intelligence Corps during his National Service, worked for the Cambridge University Press for thirty-six years, the last eight of them as University Publisher, and wrote its history. A Fellow of Clare Hall since 1982, and an Honorary D.Litt. of the University of Birmingham, he is also the author of six books of literary criticism.

ANTHONY BOWEN read Classics at St John's, and taught at Bradfield College and Shrewsbury School (where he was Head of Classics) before returning to Cambridge in 1990 to direct the University's courses in Greek for undergraduates from Greek-less schools. Elected a Fellow Commoner in 1990 and a Fellow in 1995, he was University Orator 1993–2007 and is the College's Praelector.

FREDERICK BRITTAIN had been at Queen Elizabeth's Grammar School, Barnet, but it was only when 25, and after service as a nursing auxiliary in the RAMC, that he came in 1919 with an ex-serviceman's gratuity to read Modern Languages. Appointed a College Lecturer in 1930, a Fellow in 1937, and University Lecturer in Medieval Latin in 1946, Freddy (as he was always known) was until his death in 1969 the very personification of the College for successive generations of Jesuans.

CLIVE BROWN came to the College from the University of Stellenbosch in 1967 to read for the LL.B., thereafter becoming a solicitor and partner in the London firm of Cameron McKenna, where he specialised in aviation law. A keen sailor and narrow boatman, and a Cambridge resident, he is a Conservator of the River Cam.

JAMES CLACKSON has been a Fellow and Director of Studies in Classics since 1999, and is a University Senior Lecturer. A Trinity man, and a philologist, his most recent books are *Indo-European Linguistics* (2007) and (as joint author) *The Blackwell History of the Latin Language* (2007).

JONATHAN COLLIS read Theology at Selwyn and worked in the Archbishop of Canterbury's Faculty Office and for the Ecumenical Patriarch in Istanbul, before training for ordination at Westcott House. He served as a curate in St Neots before becoming the College's Chaplain in 2002.

JONATHAN COOK came up in 2005 from Queen Elizabeth High School, Hexham, and is reading History.

JOHN CORNWELL read English in Oxford, coming to the College in 1989 as a professional Fellow Commoner, when he was Managing Editor of the *Observer*. A research Fellow from 1990 to 1996, he is again a Fellow Commoner, organising symposia to discuss the ethical implications of scientific research. He is the author of studies of Coleridge, mysterious deaths in Devon and the Vatican, of papal diplomacy, and the American pharmaceutical industry, as well as of several novels and an autobiographical memoir, *Seminary Boy* (2006).

RICHARD DENNIS read Economics at Queen Mary College, London, and served as a regular army officer before, as a Lieutenant-Colonel, retiring to work in charities' fund-raising, first for the Hospital of St John in Jerusalem and then for Pembroke College, Cambridge. He became Jesus's Development Director in 2000 and a Fellow in 2007.

JULIAN DOWDESWELL was an undergraduate reading Geography and then a research student at Jesus, working on glaciology at the Scott Polar Research Institute. He subsequently taught at University College, Aberystwyth, and was Professor of Physical Geography at the University of Bristol, before returning to Cambridge in 2002 as Professor and Director of the Scott Polar Research Institute, and to the College as a Fellow.

SHAILAJA FENNELL read Economics at the University of Delhi, came to the College in 1991 as a research student and became a Fellow in 1994. She is a University Lecturer in Land Economy, and was the College's Admissions Tutor (Arts) 2002–2007.

PETER GARNSEY was an undergraduate at the University of Sydney before going as a Rhodes Scholar to Oxford, where he became a research Fellow of University College. He taught for six years at the University of California, Berkeley, coming to Cambridge in 1974 as University Lecturer in Ancient History and a Fellow. Author of many books on the social, legal and economic history of the ancient world, and a Fellow of the British Academy, he was Professor of Classical Antiquity 1997–2006.

PETER GLAZEBROOK read Law at Oxford and taught there and at the University of Exeter before coming to Cambridge in 1967 as the College's Director of Studies in Law and a Fellow, and as a University Lecturer, with a special interest in criminal law. At Jesus he has been a Tutor, Tutor to the Graduates, Keeper of the Old Library, President and Vice-Master.

ARTHUR GRAY entered Jesus as a pensioner in 1870 and, save for three years spent as a schoolmaster, resided every term until his death, aged 87, in 1940, having been Master for twenty-eight years – the first layman to be elected. A Fellow from 1874, he became College Lecturer in Classics in 1877, and was subsequently a Tutor and then, from 1895 to 1912, Senior Tutor, and also, as H.A. Morgan's health declined (1907–1912), Vice-Master. He wrote extensively on the history of Cambridge – town, University and the College. His *History of Jesus*, first published in 1902, still repays reading.

GEOFF HARCOURT read Economics at the University of Melbourne and has been a Fellow of Jesus since 1982. A research student at King's and then (1964–1966) a University Lecturer, he returned to the University of Adelaide where he had taught first between 1958 and 1963, and where in 1967 he became Professor of Economics. The author or editor of more than two dozen books and two hundred papers, he was Reader in the History of Economic Theory 1990–1998. He is an officer of the Order of Australia.

STEPHEN HEATH came from Enfield Grammar School in 1964 to read English, and was a Fellow of Downing from 1967 to 1972 before returning to Jesus as a teaching Fellow. He has served as President and Vice-Master, has written extensively about literary theory and film, and is now Professor of English and French Literature and Culture.

ROBERT HELLER worked for the *Financial Times* and the *Observer* after reading History at Jesus and before spending twenty-five years as Editorial Director of Haymarket Publishing, and writing a series of books on business management from *The Naked Manager* (1971) to *The Essential Business Manager's Manual* (1999). He now works as an art dealer and publisher, running his own firm.

STEPHEN HLADKY graduated from Dartmouth College, New Hampshire, came to Cambridge for his Ph.D., and has been a Fellow of Jesus and Director of Studies in Medicine since 1976. He is now Reader in Membrane Pharmacology.

JOHN HOPKINS was an undergraduate and then (1965–2005) a Fellow and Director of Studies in Law at Downing College, and a University Lecturer, teaching international, constitutional and property law and frequently supervising Jesuans. He is a Bencher of the Middle Temple.

JOHN HUDSON came from Loughborough Grammar School (with which the College has had close connections since the seventeenth century) and after the Mathematics Tripos remained as a research student before becoming a Fellow in 1962, directing studies, and being Tutor for Graduate Students. He has been Reader in Electrodynamics, a Vice-President of the Royal Astronomical Society, and editor of *Geophysical Journal International*.

DANIEL HYDE became a Fellow of the Royal College of Organists aged 16, and then read Music at King's, where he was Organ Scholar 2000–2003. He has been Director of Chapel Music at Jesus since March 2004, is co-director of the University Chamber Choir, Music Director of the Harlow Chorus, and made his debut at the BBC Proms in 2006. He has undertaken concert and recital tours in Europe, America and Australia, as well as regular recording work for CD, television and radio. His recording of Christmas Music on the organ of King's College Chapel was released in 2007.

KEN JOHNSON has been a member of the College since 1954, when he came to Cambridge from the University of Manchester as a University Lecturer in Engineering, and a Fellow since 1957, serving as Director of Studies in Engineering, Tutor to Graduate Students and President. He was Professor of Engineering 1977–1992, and is a Fellow of the Royal Society, receiving its highest award, the Royal Medal, and many others including the Gold Medal of the Tribology Trust and the Timischenko Medal of the American Society of Mechanical Engineers.

ANDREW JOHNSTON came from Liverpool College to read Law. He worked as a solicitor in the City and in the Government Legal Service, before going to the European Institute in Florence, where he obtained his doctorate. He returned to the College as a Fellow in 2005, after teaching at the Universities of Warsaw and Sheffield.

MARY LAVEN came from Simon Langton School for Girls, Canterbury, to read History. She was a research student at the Warburg Institute and the University of Leicester before becoming a research Fellow of St John's. She returned to Jesus as a Fellow in 1998, and is Director of Studies in History, a University Senior Lecturer, and author of *Virgins of Venice* (2004), a study of Venetian convent life from the sixteenth to the eighteenth centuries.

CHRISTOPHER McDOUALL came up in 1956, read Engineering and rowed. He has since coached countless Jesus boats and is a trustee of the College Boat Club Trust. A Fellow of the British Institute of Management, he runs his own consultancy, McDouall Associates.

MARGARET MAIR read Law at Oxford, qualified as a barrister, and worked in the Government Legal Service (most recently in the Department of Health and the Cabinet Office). She and Robert Mair married in 1981 and have a son and a daughter.

ROBERT MAIR was elected thirty-ninth Master of Jesus in 2001. Professor of Geotechnical Engineering since 1998 and a Fellow of the Royal Society, he went to the Leys School and was an undergraduate and research student at Clare, subsequently establishing his own firm of geotechnical engineering consultants and acquiring an international practice advising on the construction (and collapse) of tunnels.

J.A. MANGAN is Emeritus Professor of the University of Strathclyde and Founding Editor of the *International Journal of the History of Sport*. He read Social Anthropology at the University of Durham and Education at (the then) Loughborough College. His *Athleticism in the Victorian and Edwardian Public School* (1981; 2nd (expanded) ed. 2000) has been acclaimed as 'a milestone book' and 'a classic work'.

ROD MENGHAM, who has been a Fellow since 1989 and is Reader in Modern English Literature, was an undergraduate at Jesus, did his doctoral research in Edinburgh, and taught in Poland, where he was Reader in English at the University of Lodz, before returning to the College. He is a Director of Studies in English and Curator of the Works of Art.

MICHAEL MINDEN, a Fellow since 1978, is University Senior Lecturer in German (with special interests in twentieth-century literature), and was Tutor for Graduate Students 1996–2006. An undergraduate at St Catharine's, he was for three years a lecturer at the University of Reading.

JULIET MITCHELL read English at Oxford and then lectured at the University of Reading, thereafter practising as a psychoanalyst for twenty years before returning to academic life. She has been a Fellow since 1996, and is now Professor of Psychoanalysis and Gender Studies. Her first book was *Women's Estate* (1972), her most recent is *Asking again: What does a Woman Want?* (2007).

COLIN MUMFORD read Medicine at the University of Nottingham, was a Research Registrar in Neurology at Addenbrooke's and is now a Consultant Neurologist in Edinburgh. He was a Fellow Commoner in 1992.

ANN MURRAY came up in 2005 from Parmiter's School, London, and is reading History.

SUMANTRA NAG came in 1967 as an affiliated student from the University of Delhi to read Natural Sciences. He returned to India to work first for ICI and, since 1982, for the Indian Institute of Planning and Management, an official governmental body.

MICHAEL O'BRIEN, who read History at Trinity Hall, joined the College as a Fellow Commoner in 1993. He taught for twenty-two years at American universities, and was Shiver Professor of History at the University of Miami 1987–2002. Elected a Fellow in 2002, he is now Professor of American Intellectual History. His *Conjectures of Order: Intellectuals and the American South 1810–1860* (2004) won five prizes, (including the Bancroft Prize), and was nominated (a runner-up) for the Pulitzer Prize in History.

GEOFF PARKS read Engineering and did his doctoral research at Trinity Hall, coming to the College as a teaching Fellow in 1988. A University Lecturer, he has a special interest in nuclear energy, has been Director of Education in the Engineering Department and Jesus's Admissions Tutor (Sciences) (1997–2007), and is Director of Admissions for the Cambridge Colleges. He also captains the High Table Cricket XI.

NICHOLAS RAY went to Trinity from Felsted School to read Architecture, and then to University College, London, for the Diploma course. A Fellow and Director of Studies since 1979, he was Reader in Architecture. His own architectural practice, Nicholas Ray Associates, has been responsible for many buildings in Cambridge, including ones for King's, Magdalene (Quay Side), Clare Hall, and Jesus. He is the author of *Cambridge Architecture: A Concise Guide* (1994) and, most recently, a study of *Alvar Aalto* (2006).

LIAM RICHARDSON came up in 2005 from Barton Peveril Sixth Form College, Eastleigh, and is reading History.

JOHN RIMINGTON came from Nottingham High School to read History, joined the Civil Service, working in the Board of Trade, the Treasury, the Department of Employment and the Diplomatic Service, and was Director General of the Health and Safety Executive (with the rank of Permanent Secretary) 1983–1995. He is Vice-Chairman of the Consumers' Association.

WILLIAM SASLAW was an undergraduate at Princeton, became a research Fellow of Jesus in 1967, and has been Professor of Astrophysics at the University of Virginia since 1970. With special interests in the gravitational physics of stars and galaxies, he spends part of each year in Cambridge and continues as a Fellow.

S.S. SAXENA was born in India, received his secondary education in seven countries in three continents, graduated simultaneously in History and Physics at the University of New Orleans, and obtained his Ph.D. in Physics in Cambridge, to which he came on a Cambridge Commonwealth Trust – Trinity College Scholarship. He was a research Fellow of Girton 2000–2002, and a Fellow and Director of Studies in Physics at Jesus 2002–2006. He works in the Quantum Matter Group at the Cavendish Laboratory, and is a consultant to UNESCO for education in Afghanistan, Central Asia and the Middle East.

ROGER SCRUTON came from the Royal Grammar School, High Wycombe, in 1967, read Moral Sciences, was a research student in Philosophy, and was elected a research Fellow of Peterhouse in 1969. He taught at Birkbeck College, London, 1971–1992, where for the last eight years he was Professor of Aesthetics. The author of more than a score of books (not all of them on philosophical subjects), he now divides his time between England and the United States.

ALAN SHARPE came from the City School, Lincoln in 1940 as an exhibitioner, to read Natural Sciences, returning in 1945 after three years in the Chemical Inspectorate of the Ministry of Supply to complete his degree and begin research in inorganic chemistry. Elected a research Fellow in 1948, and a teaching Fellow a year later, he was Senior Tutor 1964–1970 and again in 1984–1985, after having served as the first Senior Tutor of the newly founded Robinson College (1979–1983).

ANDREW SOLOMON came from Yale University in 1985 to read English. A writer for the *New York Times Magazine*, he is the author of (among other books) *A Stone Boat* (1999) and *The Noonday Demon: An Anatomy of Melancholy* (2001), and a director of several charitable foundations, including the World Monuments Fund, The Shakespeare Project and the CEC International Partnership.

MARIE LOUISE STIG SØRENSEN read Archaeology in Denmark at the University of Aarhus, and came to Cambridge for her doctoral research. A Fellow of Clare Hall 1985–1987, she then became a Fellow and Director of Studies at Jesus, and is now a University Senior Lecturer. Her special interest is gender archaeology.

PAUL STEARN, who is Cambridge born and bred, and first worked in the gardens at Jesus 1983–1986, was, when appointed Head Gardener in 1989, the youngest person to occupy such a post in any college in the University. He holds the Advanced Certificate of the Royal Horticultural Society.

GERALD STUDDERT-KENNEDY came from Winchester College to read English. He has taught at the universities of California (Berkeley), York and Birmingham where he is now Emeritus Professor. He has written extensively on the relationship between Christianity and British imperialism.

STEPHEN TAYLOR read History at Peterhouse, was a research Fellow at Jesus 1986–1988, and since then has taught at the University of Reading, where he is now Professor of History and Director of the Graduate School in Arts and Humanities. He is also General Editor of the Church of England Record Society.

ADAM TOOZE, who has been a Fellow since 1996 and is the son of a Jesuan, went from Highgate School to King's to read History. He obtained his Ph.D. at the LSE and is now Reader in Twentieth Century History. His most recent book, *The Wages of Destruction* (2006), won the Wolfson History Prize.

MICHAEL WARING went from the Friends' School, Lancaster, to Downing to read Natural Sciences. He has been a teaching Fellow of Jesus since 1965, serving as Director of Studies in Biological Sciences, Librarian and Fellows' Steward. He is now Emeritus Professor of Chemotherapy.

IAN WHITE came from Belfast Royal Academy to read Electrical Sciences and was an undergraduate, research student and, from 1983, a research Fellow at Jesus, before becoming a teaching Fellow and Tutor for Graduates. He was Professor of Physics at the University of Bath and Professor of Optical Communications at the University of Bristol, before returning to Cambridge (and the College) as Van Eck Professor of Engineering in 2001.

TIM WILKINSON read Engineering at the University of Canterbury (New Zealand), did his doctoral research at Magdalene, was a research Fellow of Pembroke 1996–1999, and has been a teaching Fellow at Jesus since then. He is Keeper of the Plate. A University Senior Lecturer, his special interests are optical engineering and liquid crystals.

FRANCES WILLMOTH read History at the University of Birmingham, did her doctoral research (on a seventeenth-century practical mathematician) at Emmanuel, qualified as an archivist at the Bodleian Library, was editor of the three-volume edition of John Flamsteed's correspondence, and has been College Archivist for ten years. She is a Fellow Commoner.

IAN WILSON came from Sullivan Upper School, Holywood, to read Chemical Engineering and obtained a Hockey Blue. His doctoral research was undertaken at the University of British Columbia. He returned to Cambridge in 1994, was elected a teaching Fellow the following year, and is now Reader in Chemical Engineering.

DAVID WOOTTON came from Bradford Grammar School in 1969 and read Classics and then Law, and was Captain of the Boat Club. He has worked for Allen & Overy, the City law firm, where he is a partner, since 1973. A trustee of the Boat Club Trust, he is also a member of the Society of St Radegund.

RACHEL WROTH read Physics at Oxford and Computer Science at New Hall, and worked in the computing group in the Engineering Department for twenty-three years, for ten of which she was a Fellow, Director of Studies in Engineering and a Tutor at St Catharine's. She began her research into nineteenth-century Cambridge college servants as a retirement project.

ACKNOWLEDGEMENTS

The College Council, which commissioned this volume, is immensely grateful to all who have helped in its making: a band that extends far beyond the authors of its forty-five chapters. Special thanks are due to Janet Nurse (Fellows' Secretary), to Alison Rolfe (Web and Information Officer), to Frances Willmoth (Archivist), and, for their photographs, to John Henwood (1954) and Salima Virji (Development Officer). At the publishers, Jo'e Coleby (Managing Editor), Debbie Wayment (Production Manager), Peter Dolton (Book Designer) and Colin Walsh (Managing Director) have been genial midwives bringing the book to birth.

Some Further Reading

General

GRAY, Arthur and BRITTAIN, Frederick, *A History of Jesus College Cambridge* (1960).

VICTORIA HISTORY OF THE COUNTIES OF ENGLAND, *Cambridgeshire*, vol. III (1959).

'INGELPHUS', *Tedious Brief Tales of Granta and Gramarye* (1919) [reprinted as GRAY, Arthur, *The Everlasting Club and other Tales of Jesus College* (1996)].

St Radegund's Nunnery

GRAY, Arthur, *The Priory of St Radegund, Cambridge* (1898).

VAN HOUTTS, Elizabeth, 'Nuns and goldsmiths: the foundation and early benefactors of St Radegund's priory at Cambridge' in ABULAFIA, D. (ed.) *Church and City 1000-1500* (1992).

The College's Founders

GRAY, Arthur (ed.), *The Earliest Statutes of Jesus College Cambridge ... A.D. 1514-1515* (1935).

GRAY, Sir John, 'Jesus College Grammar School' *Proc. Camb. Antiq. Soc.* vol. LX (1967).

Buildings

ROYAL COMMISSION ON HISTORICAL MONUMENTS (ENGLAND), *The City of Cambridge*, Part I (1959).

WILLIS, Robert, and CLARK, John Willis, *Architectural History of the University of Cambridge*, vol. 2 (1886).

Gardens and Close

McKIE, Duncan and MILLS, John, 'The Gardens and Close of Jesus College', *The Cambridge Magazine* (1988); *ibid.*, *The Magazine of the Cambridge Society* (1998).

Libraries and Archives

WARNER, Lynden, Fellows, 'Students and their Gifts to Jesus College Library 1496-1610'. *Trans. Cambridge Bibliographical Soc.* vol. XI (1996).

JAMES, Montague Rhodes, *A Descriptive Catalogue of the Manuscripts in the Library of Jesus College, Cambridge* (1895).

HARRISON, John et al., *The Malthus Library Catalogue* (1983).

Heraldry

GRAY, Arthur, 'College Heraldry: True and False', *Chanticlere*, May Term 1929.

The Chapel

MORGAN, Iris and Gerda, *The Stones and Story of Jesus Chapel Cambridge* (1914).

Chapel Music

DAVIDSON, C.H., *Sir John Sutton: A study in true principles* (1992).

THISLETHWAITE, N., 'The Organs of Jesus College, Cambridge', *The Organ*, vol. 54 (1975).

The Boat Club

BRITTAIN, Frederick, PLAYFORD, Humphrey B., et al., *The Jesus College Cambridge Boat Club 1827-1994* (3 vols) (1928, 1962, 1995).

Jesuan lives

BRITTAIN, Frederick, *Bernard Lord Manning – A Memoir* (1942).

BRITTAIN, Frederick, *Arthur Quiller-Couch* (1948).

BRITTAIN, Frederick, *It's a Don's Life* (1972).

BRITTAIN, Muriel (ed.), *Fifty Years at Jesus* (2001).

EDGAR, Katherine Frances, *Edward Daniel Clarke (1769-1822) and the Collecting of Classical Antiquities* (Ph.D. thesis, University of Cambridge 2001).

FAIRBAIRN, Steve, *Fairbairn of Jesus, being the Personal Reminiscences of ...* (1931).

HARE, David, 'Cycles of Hope: A Memoir of Raymond Williams' in *Writing Left-Handed* (1991).

HAYMAN, Ronald (ed.) *My Cambridge* [Raymond Williams contrib.] (1977).

HEILBRONER, Robert, *The Worldly Philosophers*, 6th ed. (1986) [Malthus].

HOLROYD, M., (ed.), *Memorials of the Life of George Elwes Corrie, D.D.* (1890).

KEYNES, J.M., *Essays in Biography* (1933) [Malthus].

KNIGHT, Frida, *University Rebel – The Life of William Freud* (1971).

MORGAN, Iris L. Osborne, *Memoirs of Henry Arthur Morgan* (1927).

OTTER, William, *The Life and Remains of Edward Daniel Clarke* (1824).

TYNDALE-BISCOE [Cecil] of KASHMIR, *An Autobiography* (n.d.) [1951].

WINSLOW, Ola Elizabeth, *John Eliot "Apostle to the Indians"* (1968).

Index of Names

Finis: May Ball Survivors, 1990.

JESUS COLLE

The College of the blessed Virgin Mary, Saint John the Evangelist and the glorious Virgin Saint Radegund, known as JESUS COLLEGE, was established in 1496 by *John Alco*
Chapel, the Master's Lodge and the Prioress's room - have their origins in the 12th century, as does Pump Court. The present Gatehouse and the two brick walls
which was completed in 1869. *Carpenter* and *Ingelow* designed the first of Chapel Court's buildings (the Carpenter building) in 1884, to which *Morley Horde*
middle of the Fellows' Garden is an oriental plane, planted and grown from one of several seeds brought back from Thermopylae by the Fellow and traveller *Edward Dar*